THE ROUTLEDGE HANDBOOK OF DIGITAL WRITING AND RHETORIC

This handbook brings together scholars from around the globe who here contribute to our understanding of how digital rhetoric is changing the landscape of writing. Increasingly, all of us must navigate networks of information, compose not just with computers but an array of mobile devices, increase our technological literacy, and understand the changing dynamics of authoring, writing, reading, and publishing in a world of rich and complex texts. Given such changes, and given the diverse ways in which younger generations of college students are writing, communicating, and designing texts in multimediated, electronic environments, we need to consider how the very act of *writing* itself is undergoing potentially fundamental changes. These changes are being addressed increasingly by the emerging field of digital rhetoric, a field that attempts to understand the rhetorical possibilities and affordances of writing, broadly defined, in a wide array of digital environments.

Of interest to both researchers and students, this volume provides insights about the fields of rhetoric, writing, composition, digital media, literature, and multimodal studies.

Jonathan Alexander is Chancellor's Professor of English and Informatics at the University of California, Irvine, where he is also the founding director of the Center for Excellence in Writing and Communication. The author, co-author, or editor of thirteen books, he writes frequently about multimedia, transmedia, digital literacies, pop culture, and sexuality. With Jacqueline Rhodes, he is the co-author or co-editor of the award-winning texts *On Multimodality: New Media in Composition Studies* (2014), *Techne: Queer Meditations on Writing the Self* (2015), and *Sexual Rhetorics: Methods, Identities, Publics* (2015).

Jacqueline Rhodes is professor of Writing, Rhetoric, and American Cultures at Michigan State University. She is the author, co-author, or co-editor of a number of books and articles that explore the intersections of materiality and technology, including *Radical Feminism, Writing, and Critical Agency* (2005), *On Multimodality: New Media in Composition Studies* (2014), and *Sexual Rhetorics: Methods, Identities, Publics* (2015).

THE ROUTLEDGE HANDBOOK OF DIGITAL WRITING AND RHETORIC

Edited by
Jonathan Alexander and Jacqueline Rhodes

Taylor & Francis Group

NEW YORK AND LONDON

First published 2018
by Routledge
52 Vanderbilt Avenue, New York, NY 10017

and by Routledge
2 Park Square, Milton Park, Abingdon, Oxon OX14 4RN

First issued in paperback 2020

Routledge is an imprint of the Taylor & Francis Group, an informa business

© 2018 Taylor & Francis

Library of Congress Cataloging-in-Publication Data
A catalog record for this book has been requested

ISBN 13: 978−0−367−58074−2 (pbk)
ISBN 13: 978−1−138−67136−2 (hbk)

Typeset in Bembo and Minion Pro
by Florence Production Ltd, Stoodleigh, Devon, UK

CONTENTS

Contents

Contents

FIGURES

CONTRIBUTORS

About the Editors

Jonathan Alexander is Chancellor's Professor of English and Informatics at the University of California, Irvine, where he is also the founding director of the Center for Excellence in Writing and Communication. The author, co-author, or editor of thirteen books, he writes frequently about multimedia, transmedia, digital literacies, pop culture, and sexuality. With Jacqueline Rhodes, he is the co-author of the award-winning texts *On Multimodality: New Media in Composition Studies* and *Techne: Queer Meditations on Writing the Self*.

Jacqueline Rhodes is professor of Writing, Rhetoric, and American Cultures at Michigan State University. She is the author, co-author, or co-editor of a number of books and articles that explore the intersections of materiality and technology, including *Radical Feminism, Writing, and Critical Agency* (2005), *On Multimodality: New Media in Composition Studies* (2014), the born-digital *Techne: Queer Meditations on Writing the Self* (2015), and *Sexual Rhetorics: Methods, Identities, Publics* (2015).

About the Contributors

Mel Alexenberg was professor at Columbia University, head of Pratt Institute art department, dean at New World School of the Arts, and research fellow at MIT Center for Advanced Visual Studies. In Israel, he was professor at Bar-Ilan and Ariel universities and Emunah College. His artworks exploring digital technologies and global systems are in the collections of forty museums worldwide. He is author of *Photograph God: Creating a Spiritual Blog of Your Life, The Future of Art in a Digital Age: From Hellenistic to Hebraic Consciousness*, and *Educating Artists for the Future: Learning at the Intersections of Art, Science, Technology, and Culture.*

Mark Amerika's artwork has been exhibited at the Whitney Biennial of American Art, the Denver Art Museum, the Institute of Contemporary Arts in London, and the National Museum of Contemporary in Athens. He is the author of many books including *remixthecontext* (Routledge, 2017), *remixthebook* (University of Minnesota Press, 2011), and *META/DATA: A Digital Poetics* (The MIT Press, 2007). He was recently appointed Professor of Distinction at the University of Colorado. At UC-Boulder, he is the Founding Director of the Doctoral Program in Intermedia Art, Writing and Performance and a Professor of Art and Art History.

Kristin L. Arola is an associate professor in the Writing, Rhetoric, and American Cultures Department at Michigan State University. Her work brings together American Indian rhetorics, multimodal composition, and digital rhetoric so as to make visible and disrupt colonial practices within theoretical frameworks and pedagogical practice. She is mixed Anishinaabe and Finnish from the Upper Peninsula of Michigan, and she spends her free time trying to reason with a stubborn toddler and an old dog.

William P. Banks is director of the University Writing Program and the Tar River Writing Project, and is professor of Rhetoric and Writing at East Carolina University, where he teaches courses in writing, research, pedagogy, and young adult literature. His essays on digital rhetorics, queer rhetorics, pedagogy, and writing program administration have appeared in several recent books, as well as in *College Composition and Communication*, *College English*, and *Computers and Composition*. His books include *Reclaiming Accountability: Improving Writing Programs through Accreditation* and *Large-Scale Assessments and Re/Orienting Writing Studies: Queer Methods, Queer Projects*.

Lemi Baruh (Ph.D. University of Pennsylvania, Annenberg School for Communication) is associate professor at the Department of Media and Visual Arts at Koç University in Turkey. Lemi Baruh's research interests include new media technologies, particularly focusing on social media usage patterns, identity, surveillance, privacy attitudes, and culture of voyeurism. He is an associate editor of *International Journal of Interactive Communication Systems and Technologies*.

Estee Beck holds an assistant professor of professional and technical writing/digital humanities position in the Department of English at The University of Texas at Arlington.

Kristine L. Blair is professor of English and Dean of the College of Liberal Arts and Social Sciences at Youngstown State University. In addition to her publications on gender and technology, graduate education, and online learning, Blair currently serves as editor of both *Computers and Composition* and its separate companion journal *Computers and Composition Online*. Among her numerous awards are the Conference on College Composition and Communication's Technology Innovator Award and the Computers and Composition Charles Moran Award for Distinguished Contributions to the Field. In 2017, she received a Distinguished Woman Scholar Award from her doctoral alma mater, Purdue University.

Casey Boyle is an assistant professor of Rhetoric and Writing and the Director of the Digital Writing and Research Lab at the University of Texas, Austin. He teaches and researches in the areas of rhetorical theory and media studies. His research has appeared in *College English*, *Technical Communication Quarterly*, and *Computers and Composition* as well as edited collections and various other venues. Finally, he is the author of *Rhetoric as a Posthuman Practice* (The Ohio State University Press), a book that examines the role of practice and/as ethics in digital rhetoric.

Carol Burke, professor in English, combines her ethnographic skills as a folklorist with her interest in literary journalism. Publications include *Camp All-American, Hanoi Jane, and the High-and-Tight*, a study of military culture; *Women's Visions*, which explores accounts of the supernatural and the uncanny exchanged by women in prison; *The Creative Process* (coauthored with Molly Tinsley), a creative writing text; *Plain Talk and Back in Those Days*, collections of family folklore—the latter coauthored with Martin Light; and *Close Quarters*, a collection of poems. Articles have appeared in magazines such as *The Nation* and *The New Republic* as well as scholarly journals and collections. Before joining the faculty at UCI in 2004, Professor Burke taught courses in literary journalism at Vanderbilt and Johns Hopkins universities.

Jordan Canzonetta is currently a doctoral candidate studying Composition and Cultural Rhetoric at Syracuse University. Her work has appeared in *Journal of Writing Assessment*. Her expertise includes areas related to plagiarism, rhetoric and technology, assessment, and professional writing. She holds a Master's degree in Rhetoric and Professional Writing from Northern Illinois University. She is currently writing her dissertation on automated writing assessment technologies and their relation to labor practices in higher education.

Dànielle Nicole DeVoss is a professor of Professional Writing at Michigan State University; her research interests include digital-visual rhetorics; social and cultural entrepreneurship; innovation and creativity; and intellectual property issues in digital space. DeVoss's most recent books include *Cultures of Copyright* (with Martine Courant Rife; 2014, Peter Lang) and *Making Space: Writing Instruction, Infrastructure, and Multiliteracies* (with Jim Purdy; 2017, University of Michigan Press/Sweetland Digital Rhetoric Collaborative. DeVoss has two other projects in production: *Type Matters: The Rhetoricity of Letterforms* (with C. S. Wyatt) and *Explanation Points!: Publishing in Rhetoric and Composition* (with John Gallagher).

Regina Duthely is an assistant professor of Writing, New Media, and Digital Literacies in the Department of English at the University of Puget Sound in Tacoma, Washington. She is interested in digital writing and rhetoric, Black feminism and popular culture. Her work looks at popular culture, blogs, and social media to examine new forms of protest, the digital public, and the ways that race, gender, sexuality and resistance manifest themselves in these spaces.

Julie Faulkner is a senior lecturer in the Faculty of Education at Monash University, Melbourne. She writes on matters of literacy, popular culture, identity, and digital reading and writing practices. Her research supervision includes areas of curriculum design, intercultural communication pedagogies, critical reading practices, and digital games as powerful learning environments. She has edited *Disrupting Pedagogies in the Knowledge Society: Countering Conservative Norms with Creative Approaches* (IGI Global), and has jointly edited *Learning to Teach: New Time, New Practices* (Oxford University Press), currently in second edition.

Laura J. Gurak is professor and founding chair of the Department of Writing Studies at the University of Minnesota. She holds an M.S. in technical communication and a Ph.D. in communication and rhetoric from Rensselaer Polytechnic Institute. Her research investigates how language both shapes and reflects our uses and perceptions of digital technologies, with an emphasis on issues of ethos and trust. She is author of *Cyberliteracy* (Yale UP, 2001) and *Persuasion and Privacy in Cyberspace* (Yale UP, 1997); co-author of several leading technical communication textbooks; author or co-author of numerous journal articles.

Angela M. Haas currently serves as Graduate Program Director for the Department of English and is an associate professor of rhetoric, technical communication, ethnic, and women's and gender studies at Illinois State University (ISU). Her research and teaching interests include technical communication, American Indian rhetorics, cultural rhetorics, decolonial theory and methodology, digital and visual rhetorics, indigenous feminisms, and technofeminisms—and this work has been recognized by honors such as the Conference on College Composition and Communication Technology Innovator Award, the Computers and Composition Ellen Nold

Best Article Award, and ISU's College of Arts and Sciences Outstanding Teacher in the Humanities.

Bump Halbritter is associate professor of Rhetoric and Writing and Director of the First-Year Writing Program at Michigan State University. His research and teaching involve the integration of video-based, audio-visual writing into scenes of college writing and scholarly research. Bump's 2013 article, "Time, Lives, and Videotape: Operationalizing Discovery in Scenes of Literacy Sponsorship," co-authored with Julie Lindquist, received The Richard Ohmann Award for Outstanding Article in *College English*. Bump's book, *Mics, Cameras, Symbolic Action: Audio-Visual Rhetoric for Writing Teachers* received the Computers and Composition Distinguished Book Award for 2013. Bump serves on the CCCC Executive Committee (2017–20).

Steven Hammer is an assistant professor of Communication and Digital Media at Saint Joseph's University in Philadelphia, PA. His art, teaching, and scholarship investigate the roles and politics of emergent technologies on composition methods, the affordances of glitches and other "dirty new media" art practices, and accessible design practices.

William Hart-Davidson is a senior researcher in the Writing in Digital Environments Research (WIDE) center and Associate Dean of Graduate Education in the College of Arts and Letters at Michigan State University. He has published over fifty articles and book chapters and is co-inventor of *Eli Review*, a software service that supports writing instruction.

Byron Hawk is an associate professor of English at the University of South Carolina. His research interests are histories and theories of composition, rhetorical theory and technology, sonic rhetorics, and rhetorics of popular music. He is the author of *A Counter-History of Composition: Toward Methodologies of Complexity* (University of Pittsburgh Press, 2007), which won JAC's W. Ross Winterowd Award in 2007 and received honorable mention for MLA's Mina Shaughnessy Prize in 2008. His forthcoming book is titled *Resounding the Rhetorical: Composition as a Quasi-Object*.

Allison H. Hitt is assistant professor of Writing at the University of Central Arkansas where she teaches professional and first-year writing classes. Her work on disability, rhetorics of universal design, and multimodal composition has appeared in *Business and Professional Communication Quarterly*, *Composition Forum*, *Rhetoric Review*, *The Oxford Guide for Writing Tutors: Practice and Research*, and *Praxis: A Writing Center Journal*. Her research and teaching in all courses attends to rhetorical issues of accessibility and social justice.

Mary E. Hocks is an associate professor of English at Georgia State University in downtown Atlanta, where she teaches undergraduate and graduate courses in composition theory and practice, digital rhetoric and multimodal composition. She currently serves as the Director of the GSU Writing Studio. Dr. Hocks has published articles in *College Composition and Communication*, *Rhetoric Review*, *Writing Program Administration*, and *Computers and Composition*, as well as book chapters in *Virtual Publics*, *Feminist Cyberscapes*, and *Webbing Cyberfeminist Practice*. Her co-edited collection, *Eloquent Images: Word and Image in the Age of New Media*, was published by The MIT Press in 2003 and she co-authored the *Handbook of Technical Communication from Pearson Educational Press* (2009). Her most recent project is a book about sonic rhetorics.

Les Hutchinson is a PhD candidate of Digital Rhetoric and Professional Writing in the Writing, Rhetoric, and American Cultures department at Michigan State University. Her work focuses on the intersections of privacy, surveillance, copyright, and intellectual property. She will have co-authored articles soon appearing in *Communication Design Quarterly* and *Computers and Composition*, and is coediting an essay collection titled *Writing in a Digital Age: Surveillance, Privacy, and Writing Infrastructures*. Her dissertation, *Privacy, Property, and Sovereignty*, looks into the cultural practices of local Chicanx and Indigenous people within social media platforms.

Kylie Jarrett is Senior Lecturer in the Department of Media Studies at Maynooth University, Ireland. She has extensively researched the commercial Web, having published studies of eBay, Facebook, and YouTube. She is author of *Feminism, Labour and Digital Media: The Digital Housewife* (Routledge) which analyses digital labor from a Marxist feminist perspective. With Ken Hillis and Michael Petit, she is also co-author of *Google and the Culture of Search* (Routledge) and has also co-authored *Not Safe for Work: Sex, Humor, and Risk in Social Media* with Susanna Paasonen and Ben Light (forthcoming from MIT Press).

Athina Karatzogianni is an associate professor in Media and Communication at the University of Leicester. She contributes to work theorizing cyberconflict, and exploring the potential of ICTs and network forms of organization for social movements, resistance and open knowledge production. Prof. Karatzogianni's work includes *Firebrand Waves of Digital Activism* (2015), *The Politics of Cyberconflict* (2006), *Power, Conflict and Resistance: Social Movements, Networks and Hierarchies with Andrew Robinson* (2010), and, as editor, *Cyber Conflict and Global Politics* (2009), *Violence and War in Culture and the Media* (2012), and *Digital Cultures and the Politics of Emotion*, co-edited with Adi Kuntsman (2012).

Amy C. Kimme Hea is currently Chair of Consortium of Doctoral Programs in Rhetoric and Composition, and is Associate Dean for Academic Affairs and Student Success in the College of Social and Behavioral Sciences at the University of Arizona. Dr. Kimme Hea has published research in composition studies, computers and composition, and professional and technical communication on new media, hypertext theory, spatial rhetoric, assessment, and service learning. Recognized for her edited collection *Going Wireless: A Critical Exploration of Wireless and Mobile Technologies for Composition Teachers and Researchers* and a special issue of *Technical Communication Quarterly* on social media, Dr. Kimme Hea has published numerous essays in peer-reviewed journals and edited collections.

Bri Lafond earned her M.A. in Composition from California State University, San Bernardino in 2014. She has worked since then as a lecturer at both the community college and university level. Her research interests include innovative composition pedagogy—including multimodality and digital media—and queer theory. She is currently working on her Ph.D. at the University of Illinois at Urbana-Champaign with the Center for Writing Studies.

Adela C. Licona is associate professor of English, Director of the University of Arizona's Institute for LGBT Studies, Vice Chair of the Graduate Minor in Social, Cultural, and Critical Theory, and is affiliated faculty in Gender and Women's Studies, Institute of the Environment, and Mexican American Studies. Her research/teaching interests include cultural, ethnic, gender, and sexuality studies, race, critical rhetorics, community literacies, action-oriented research, borderlands studies, space/visual culture, social justice media, environmental justice, and feminist pedagogy. She has published in such journals as *Antipode*, *Transformations*, *Latino-Latin American Studies*, *Sexuality Research and Social Policy*, *Annals of the Association of American Geographers*, and *Critical Studies in Media Communication*.

Julie Lindquist is professor of Rhetoric and Writing at MSU, where she teaches courses in writing, rhetoric, literacy and composition studies, and research methodologies. She is author of *A Place to Stand: Politics and Persuasion in a Working Class Bar* (Oxford) and, with David Seitz, *Elements of Literacy* (Pearson). Her writings on rhetoric, class, literacy, and writing pedagogy have appeared in *College Composition and Communication, College English, JAC*, and *Pedagogy*, as well as in several edited collections. Her article "Time, Lives, and Videotape: Operationalizing Discovery in Scenes of Literacy Sponsorship," co-authored with Bump Halbritter, was awarded The Richard Ohmann Award for Outstanding Article in *College English* in 2013.

Elizabeth Losh is an associate professor of English and American Studies at William and Mary with a specialization in New Media Ecologies. Before coming to William and Mary, she directed the Culture, Art, and Technology Program at the University of California, San Diego. She is a core member and former co-facilitator of the feminist technology collective FemTechNet, which offers a Distributed Open Collaborative Course, blogger for Digital Media and Learning Central, and part of the international organizing team of The Selfie Course. She is the author of *Virtualpolitik: An Electronic History of Government Media-Making in a Time of War, Scandal, Disaster, Miscommunication, and Mistakes* (MIT Press, 2009) and The War on Learning: Gaining Ground in the Digital University (MIT Press, 2014). She is the co-author of the comic book textbook *Understanding Rhetoric: A Graphic Guide to Writing* (Bedford/St. Martin's, 2013; second edition, 2017) with Jonathan Alexander and editor of the forthcoming edited collection MOOCs and *Their Afterlives: Experiments in Scale and Access in Higher Education* (University of Chicago, 2017).

Ben McCorkle is an associate professor of English at The Ohio State University. He teaches courses in composition, rhetoric, and digital media studies, primarily on OSU's Marion campus. He is the author of the book *Rhetorical Delivery as Technological Discourse: A Cross-Historical Study*, as well as several articles in publications including *Computers and Composition Online, Rhetoric Society Quarterly*, and *Composition Studies*. Currently, he serves as the co-director of the Digital Archive of Literacy Narratives (daln.osu.edu).

Kristen Macias is a lecturer at California State University, San Bernardino where she earned her M.A. in English Composition and Teaching English as a Second Language in 2014. She has also taught first-year composition at the University of La Verne and CSUSB's Palm Desert campus. Kristen has presented at various English studies conferences since 2012 with projects that range from developing the role of tutors in writing center sessions to exploring multimodality through popular comics in composition studies to bringing video gaming into the first-year composition classroom.

Heidi A. McKee is an associate professor in the Department of English and an affiliate faculty member of the Armstrong Institute for Interactive Media Studies at Miami University. She is author, co-author, or co-editor of five scholarly books in digital writing and rhetoric, including (with James Porter) *Professional Communication and Network Interaction: A Rhetorical and Ethical Approach* (Routledge, 2017).

Aimee C. Mapes is assistant professor of English and Associate Director of the Writing Program at the University of Arizona. She has published research on composition studies, literacy studies, identity, teacher education, and instructional design. With a Ph.D. in Literacy, Language, and Culture from The University of Iowa, her work explores literacy and identity in institutional settings and has appeared in *AHEAD, CCC, Journal of Adolescent and Adult Literacy*, and

Reflections. This chapter shares findings from a longitudinal study of student writing funded in part by 2014 CCCC Research Initiative Grant and the Council for Writing Program Administrators.

Jason Markins is a doctoral candidate in Composition and Cultural Rhetoric at Syracuse University. He is interested in DIY, multimodal, and critical making practices in the composition classroom, and his research looks at the rhetoric of the nineteenth-century arts and crafts movement alongside the contemporary maker movement. He earned a Master's degree in Literature from West Virginia University and a Bachelor's degree in English from Hanover College.

Zarah C. Moeggenberg is currently a Ph.D. candidate at Washington State University. She holds an MFA in Poetry from Northern Michigan University. Her research focuses on queering approaches to composition and queer identity online. Her book, *To Waltz on a Pin*, was released in 2015 with Little Presque Books.

Stuart Moulthrop is professor of English at the University of Wisconsin-Milwaukee. He is the author of several notable projects in digital art and literature, including *Victory Garden* (1991) and "Deep Surface" and "Under Language," which in 2007 won Ciutat de Vinarós Prizes for narrative and poetry. He has also published numerous essays on media and cultural theory and served as co-editor of the online journal *Postmodern Culture*. With Dene Grigar, Moulthrop launched the NEH-funded Pathfinders project to preserve early digital writing. In 2017 Moulthrop and Grigar published *Traversals: The Use of Preservation for Early Electronic Writing*, with MIT Press.

Marcel O'Gorman is professor and University Research Chair in the Department of English at the University of Waterloo. He is also founding Director of the Critical Media Lab, which provides a context for his research and artwork. O'Gorman's most recent book, *Necromedia* (Uiversity of Minnesota Press Posthumanities Series) explores the relationship between death and technology by moving between philosophical arguments and explorations of O'Gorman's own critical art interventions.

Jason Palmeri is associate professor of English at Miami University in Oxford, Ohio. Palmeri is the author of *Remixing Composition: A History Of Multimodal Writing Pedagogy* (SIUP 2012) as well as numerous articles and chapters about the history, theory, and practice of teaching writing with diverse technologies.

Mihaela Popescu (Ph.D. University of Pennsylvania, Annenberg School for Communication) is associate professor in the Department of Communication Studies and Faculty Associate with Academic Technologies and Innovation at California State University, San Bernardino, USA. Her research interests address the relationship between digital media policies and social inequality in the areas of privacy, digital literacy, and digital media use.

James E. Porter is a professor of rhetoric and professional communication at Miami University, with a joint appointment in the Armstrong Institute for Interactive Media Studies and the Department of English. He is the author or co-author of five scholarly books in rhetoric, including, most recently, a co-authored book (with Heidi McKee) titled *Professional Communication and Network Interaction: A Rhetorical and Ethical Approach* (Routledge, 2017).

Ana Milena Ribero is assistant professor of rhetoric and composition at Oregon State University, where she researches and teaches about migrant rhetorics, critical literacies, digital composition, and feminist critique. She is also affiliated with OSU's Center for Latin @ Studies and Engagement. Her current book project complicates citizenship in undocumented Latinx youth activism. Her work can be found in *Present Tense: A Journal of Rhetoric in Society* and *Decolonizing Rhetoric and Composition Studies*.

Jeff Rice is a Martha B. Reynolds professor of Writing, Rhetoric, and Digital Studies and Chair of the Department of Writing, Rhetoric, and Digital Studies at the University of Kentucky. He is the author of numerous books, articles, and chapters.

Ingrid Richardson is associate professor in Communication and Media Studies at Murdoch University, Western Australia. She has published on a broad range of topics including virtual and augmented reality, wearable technologies, games and mobile media, digital ethnography, remix culture, and Web-based content creation and distribution. She is contributing co-editor of *Studying Mobile Media: Cultural Technologies, Mobile Communication and the iPhone* (with Larissa Hjorth and Jean Burgess, Routledge, 2012) and co-author of *Gaming in Social, Locative and Mobile Media* (with Larissa Hjorth, Palgrave, 2014).

Michael Schandorf is a lecturer in the Writing, Rhetoric, and Profession Communication Program in the Department of Comparative Media Studies at the Massachusetts Institute of Technology.

Chad Seader is a doctoral candidate in Composition and Cultural Rhetoric at Syracuse University where he teaches service-learning courses in Technical Communication. Chad's research inquires into how programmatic assessment practices could be adapted to develop and strengthen relationships between institutions of higher education and community-based organizations. He earned his Master's in Writing, Rhetoric, and Discourse from DePaul University and his Bachelor's in Philosophy from Northeastern Illinois University.

Greg Stuart is a percussionist whose work draws upon a mixture of music from the experimental tradition, Wandelweiser, improvisation, and electronics. An active performer, he has appeared at numerous festivals and notable venues presenting experimental music including MaerzMusik (Berlin), Café Oto (London), Cha'ak'ab Paaxil (Mérida), Issue Project Room (New York), REDCAT (Los Angeles), and Non-Event (Boston) among many others. Stuart has recorded for Edition Wandelweiser, Gravity Wave, Erstwhile, and New World. He is currently an Assistant Professor at the University of South Carolina School of Music where he runs the Experimental Music Workshop.

Pamela Takayoshi is professor of English at Kent State University. Her work includes several edited collections (the most recent one co-edited with Patrick Thomas: *Literacy in Practice: Writing in Public, Private, and Working Lives*) and articles that have appeared in *College Composition and Communication*, *Computers and Composition*, *Research in the Teaching of English*, and numerous edited collections.

Derek Van Ittersum is associate professor of English and Coordinator of Digital Composition at Kent State University. His work has appeared in *Composition Studies*, *Computers and Composition*, *Kairos*, and *Technical Communication Quarterly*.

Stephanie Vie is chair of the Department of Writing and Rhetoric at the University of Central Florida in Orlando. Her work centers on the construction of digital identities in social media spaces as well as critical approaches to composing technologies such as plagiarism detection services. Her research has appeared in journals such as *First Monday, Computers and Composition,* and *Kairos,* as well as multiple edited collections. Her textbook *E-Dentity* (Fountainhead Press, 2011) examines social media and twenty-first century literacies, and her forthcoming co-edited collection *Social Media/Social Writing* (the WAC Clearinghouse) showcases current social media scholarship around publics, presentation, and pedagogies.

Carl Whithaus is a professor of Writing and Rhetoric and the Director of the University Writing Program (UWP) at the University of California, Davis. He studies digital rhetorics, writing in the disciplines (particularly communication in the sciences and engineering), and writing assessment. His books include *Multimodal Literacies and Emerging* Genres (University of Pittsburgh Press, 2013), *Writing Across Distances and Disciplines: Research and Pedagogy in Distributed Learning* (Routledge, 2008), and *Teaching and Evaluating Writing in the Age of Computers and High-Stakes Testing* (Erlbaum, 2005). He is the co-editor for the *Journal of Writing Assessment.*

Kathleen Blake Yancey, Kellogg Hunt Professor of English and Distinguished Research Professor at Florida State University, has served in several leadership roles, including as President of NCTE and Chair of CCCC. Currently, she leads "The Writing Passport Project," an eight-site research project focused on the transfer of writing knowledge and practice. Author/co-author of over 100 articles and book chapters, she has also authored/edited/co-edited 14 scholarly books—most recently *Writing Across Contexts: Transfer, Composition, and Sites of Writing* (2014); *A Rhetoric of Reflection* (2016); and *Assembling Composition* (2017). She has received several awards, including two CWPA Best Book Awards; CCCC's Research Impact Award; and Florida State's Graduate Teaching Award, which she has won twice.

ACKNOWLEDGMENTS

We thank our numerous contributors for their diligent and thoughtful work on their chapters, as well as our editors at Routledge, Felisa Salvago-Keyes and Christina Kowalski, who shepherded the process with grace and support. Special thanks to Jens Lloyd and Jasmine Lee for much-needed assistance when managing the dizzying array of items at play in putting together such a collection.

INTRODUCTION

What Do We Talk about When We Talk about Digital Writing and Rhetoric?

Jonathan Alexander and Jacqueline Rhodes

As we write the introduction to this collection, separated physically by nearly two thousand miles—Alexander in southern California and Rhodes in central Michigan—we pause to reflect that, as part of our composing process, we have been texting ideas back and forth. Those texts have steadily become parts of email chains, which in turn have become shared Google documents augmented and revised over time through further conversations conducted in bits and pieces through other texts, emails, Skype, and phone. Only once in the last year did we actually sit face-to-face and talk about this book, and then only with our computers in front of us, exchanging files and making notes on a shared document.

Is this *digital writing*? As we consider changes to our own composing processes, the extent to which most of the actual composing of this project has been conducted via digital platforms is striking. Such is an experience very likely shared by many working across a variety of fields and professions, as well as communicating with others socially and as citizens. Indeed, what we understood as once relatively stable concepts—author, writer, text, even communication—have become productively troubled as much communicative action has moved from print to screen. But have the processes and experiences of writing and of being rhetorical actually been *changed* or *transformed* sufficiently to warrant consideration of a new thing called "digital writing"—something qualitatively different from the "writing" we have traditionally known and practiced?

Our experiences as writers suggest yes, they have. Alexander remembers writing his dissertation in longhand twenty-five years ago, taking each roughly completed chapter to the university's new Mac lab to type it in. Most of the "writing" was already done, and the Macintosh LCII served primarily as an advanced typewriter to record and store his dissertation, as well as provide some nicer formatting than Alexander could muster on his old Brother electric typewriter. For Rhodes, composing before 1994 meant first manual typewriters, then IBM Selectrics, then an Apple IIe and a dot-matrix printer, then a really expensive (at the time) Mac Performa 575 with a whopping 1 MB of RAM and a 14.4 modem. After 1994, with her first Internet connection and the World Wide Web at her fingertips, composing meant chat rooms and bulletin boards, MOOs, HTML, and an overwhelming sense of the connected world watching, reading, and composing alongside her. By 1996, both Alexander and Rhodes were working with students on designing websites as composing projects, and they joined the worlds of computer and online gaming, writing about them and other digitally enabled forms of composing in their book, *On Multimodality: New Media in Composition Studies* (2014) and the born-digital *Techne: Queer Meditations on Writing the Self* (2015).

While our *experiences* of writing and being rhetorical seem to have changed, we still pause to ask, as scholars, what do such changes mean for writing and rhetoric more generally, if anything? And, if writing is indeed changing, *how* is it changing in response to the digital platforms that currently enable many contemporary composing practices and through which many people, at least in the global north, communicate, seek and build information ecologies, and navigate a variety of personal, social, cultural, and political relationships? Put bluntly, what do we really mean when we say "digital writing" or "digital rhetoric?"

In approaching such questions, some scholars have pointed out the generational dimensions of contemporary composing, much as we gestured to our own experiences in the opening paragraphs above by articulating a "before" and "after" focused on the emerging availability of networked computing in the 1990s. In *Writing and the Digital Generation: Essays on New Media Rhetoric*, Heather Urbanski writes with enthusiasm about "the recent explosion of participatory digital media, [by which] rhetorical reality is quickly catching up with rhetorical theory. The idea of audience participation in texts is at least as old as Aristotle; now that theory is made manifest by digital media" (3). Urbanski notes the importance of thinking about the many ways in which the *participatory* dimensions enabled by digital platforms can potentially enliven our sense of the rhetorical, of actually communicating with audiences and publics in new ways. She understands this rhetoricality as particularly significant for those now growing up, at least in the global north, with access from birth to such platforms. As she puts it,

> Within the Humanities, we have long accepted a rhetorical view of reading as transaction in which we re-create, or even re-write, a text each time we read it, but today's "Digital Generation" seems to take that theory to an entirely new level, often literally creating the narratives as they experience them. (3)

Others, though, have cautioned against seeing generational divides and rather try to deepen our sense of the technological means of production and dissemination as having always already been an integral (if sometimes unremarked) dimension of writing and rhetorical practice. Stuart A. Selber, for instance, in *Rhetoric and Technologies: New Directions in Writing and Communication*, puts the case this way:

> In both theoretical and practical terms, technology does not really function as a separate category or subcategory of consequence. It tends to infuse each and every area of the discipline, even under fairly narrow circumstances. In fact, it is difficult to imagine a rhetorical activity untouched by ongoing developments in writing and communication technologies. Their increasingly widespread integration into all facets of culture has encouraged scholars and teachers to reinterpret (yet again) the traditional canons of rhetoric. Invention strategies, for instance, now address powerful search capabilities and the ways in which database structures shape access to an intellectual landscape. Rhetorical education on arrangement no longer assumes a linear organizational pattern—or a patient reader, for that matter. More than occasionally, writers and communicators today anticipate reader control with modular hypertexts that can support multiple interpretive pathways and that can invite textual transformations and revisions. (2)

Considering the *long* history of technological dimensions of composing practices is an activity perhaps sparked by the rapidity of changes we are currently experiencing, and Selber's work models a useful approach to thinking writing, rhetoric, and technologies simultaneously—not as separate or even separable "fields" but as deeply intertwined practices that must be theorized together.

Still others rightly worry over who gets to write such histories and interpret such intertwinings. As only one example of many, we could cite Adam J. Banks's *Digital Griots: African American Rhetoric in a Multimedia Age*, in which Banks pointedly asks, "how can African American rhetorical traditions and practices inform composition's current endeavors to define, theorize and practice multimedia writing?" (2). Banks is concerned that alternative, non-dominant, and marginalized rhetorical traditions—traditions whose participants are often actively engaged in their own rich online and digital composing practices—might be ignored, elided, or even derided when considering how we as scholars, thinkers, intellectuals, teachers, and activists might theorize which digital writing and rhetoric are.

These scholars all come from the broad and capacious field of "rhetoric and composition," which itself pulls together numerous methods, epistemologies, and approaches in taking "writing" and "rhetoric" as primary objects of study. Scholarly activity in this field around digital writing and rhetoric has been considerable in the past decade. Our own *On Multimodality: New Media in Composition Studies* challenges the field to evolve as it embraces new media technologies of composing, while Bump Halbritter's *Mics, Cameras, Symbolic Action: Audio-visual Rhetoric for Writing Teachers* presents theories of multimodal pedagogy and scaffolded teaching exercises to prompt such evolution. Carl Whithaus and Tracey Bowen's edited collection *Multimodal Literacies and Emerging Genres* focuses primarily on the challenge of new media texts to the discipline's understanding of genre. Bedford/St. Martin's *Multimodal Composition: A Critical Sourcebook*, edited by Claire Lutkewitte, brings together "classic" essays from nearly two decades of scholarship on teaching writing with computers to trace the evolution of thinking about multimodal writing in the field. And more broadly still, Doug Eyman's *Digital Rhetoric: Theory, Method, Practice* looks at a range of disciplinary ways of thinking about digitality and rhetoric, asking how we might better understand the challenges and possibilities for rhetorical action in a "digital age." Even Routledge, publisher of this current collection, has put out several books that set the stage for a book such as ours. Julia Gillen's *Digital Literacies* looks at the intersections of language and the digital turn, but focuses primarily on issues in linguistics, and Carolyn Handa's *Multimediated Rhetoric of the Internet: Digital Fusion* lays out a rhetoric of the Web and argues for a digital "fusion" of analytic skills. Where our book might differ is that we assume that that acceptance of digital fusion has already happened in the field—and in writing and rhetoric—and ask instead how can we understand the transformations to writing and rhetoric already under way.

Our brief gloss here in no way pretends to be comprehensive. Indeed, we have long passed the moment when scholarly and critical reflection on "digital writing and rhetoric" could be neatly or cogently summarized. Numerous fields—ranging from the relatively newly formed and still evolving digital humanities to more established disciplines such as sociology, anthropology, education, English studies, composition, and rhetoric—have entered the fray to debate and continue to discover what we mean when we say "digital writing and rhetoric."

We can take this very volume as a case in point. While all of the contributors understand that a great deal of composing and rhetorical action is currently enabled by digital platforms, none of us assume that the terms "digital writing" and "digital rhetoric" refer to fixed or even obvious practices. In fact, one of the dimensions that enlivens chapters throughout this collection is the extent to which various scholars keep the definitions of digital writing and rhetoric relatively open and capacious. As such, contributors tackle the definition of digital writing and rhetoric— as well as their challenges, limits, and possibilities—from a variety of standpoints, experiences, and theories.

So, with that in mind, what does this volume attempt to do? Well, we respect the many diverse views and approaches to digital writing and rhetoric by *refraining* from defining practices and processes that are themselves still evolving—perhaps necessarily and inevitably so as platforms for communication continue to change, develop, and transform. With that said, we recognize with Urbanski, Selber, and Banks above that writing and rhetorical practice in the contemporary world (1) have been affected by changes in technological platforms, (2) should best be understood as developing and evolving over time and through history, and (3) are enriched by the experiences and traditions of many diverse people and communities. With that said, we don't assume a technological determinism; that is, chapters collectively attempt to situate shifts and changes in what "writing" is in the longer histories of composing and mediation, as opposed to assuming that *now*, after the 1990s for instance, writing is fundamentally different or changed. Instead, grounding inquiry in composition and rhetoric while simultaneously recognizing the broader multi-, trans-, and interdisciplinary engagements with digital writing and rhetoric, our collection attempts to tackle the broader implications of digital forms of communication for how we conceptualize and understand writing and rhetoric. We have solicited essays from writers who reflect specifically on the changing definitions of "writing" and the "rhetorical" in an age of increasing digital composing, and the collection as a whole is ultimately less concerned with the changing disciplinarity of the field of composition and rhetoric and more with the ways we as writing studies scholars more broadly conceptualize writing and rhetoric themselves as ever-evolving complex practices.

To reflect a diversity of approaches to these practices, we have organized chapters around broad themes. In many ways, this organization not only mirrors the concerns of scholars currently working on digital writing and rhetoric; it's also an attempt to help *construct* the parameters of the conversation as they are taking shape within the field and in disciplines adjacent to and contributing to it. Those conversational parameters include (1) inquiries into cultural and historical contexts of writing, (2) theories that consider contemporary practices "beyond writing," or what we normally understand as writing, (3) explicit investigations of what it means to be rhetorical through the digital, (4) an ongoing concern with issues of selves and subjectivities *vis-à-vis* digital writing and rhetoric, (5) attempts to regulate and control the proliferation of various forms of digitally enabled composing, (6) the development of multimediated, transmediated, and participatory cultures in relation to digital composing, and (7) a look at the politics and economics of digital writing and rhetorical practice.

What are some of the significant highlights in the conversations as we have curated them here?

Our first section, "Cultural and Historical Contexts," focuses on broad histories and contexts of contemporary digital writing and rhetoric, looking in particular at questions of how, historically, the emergence of new communications technologies challenge our understanding of writing and the rhetorical. Leading us off is Dànielle Nicole DeVoss, who offers us techno-pedagogies for the different contexts of digital writing. The piece is followed by a historical look at tablets, from wax to Newtons to Galaxies (Ben McCorkle); a critical examination of multimodality "before and beyond" the digital (Jason Palmeri); and a look at soundwork as embodied practice (Byron Hawk and Greg Stuart). The section ends with a meditation on making/paying attention to technology by Marcel O'Gorman.

The next section, titled "Beyond Writing," explores what it means to write in digital spaces, offering broader theoretical pieces as well as essays focused on specific contexts for writing and composing with particular platforms. Beginning with Kathleen Blake Yancey writing on the notion of textual assemblage, the section moves through pieces on mobile writing, mobile literacies, and desire (Aimee C. Mapes and Amy C. Kimme Hea), and intersections of materiality and writing technologies (Pamela Takayoshi and Derek Van Ittersum). Mary E. Hocks writes on sonic composition as an activist practice that develops empathy, and Julie Faulkner ends the section by offering brief, cogent studies of students curating digital identities.

"Being Rhetorical and Digital" contains chapters that analyze the expansion of our sense of the specifically rhetorical possibilities enabled by digital writing. The chapters focus, for instance, on how public spheres are changing in relation to the circulation of digital forms of composing. Stephanie Vie writes about social media and networked relationships, while Laura J. Gurak explores the implications of trust and "post-truth" for scientific and technical discourse. Next, Elizabeth Losh writes about the politics of Pokemon and "phoneurs" in the context of smart cities. The following two pieces focus on specific sites of rhetorical/political action: Standing Rock (Michael Schandorf and Athina Karatzogianni) and QTPOC digital environments (Ana Milena Ribero and Adela C. Licona). Mark Amerika's multivocal dialogue/performance on remix, rhetoric, magic, and heuretics offers a playful way of thinking through digital rhetoricality, and the section ends with Allison H. Hitt's call to make space for non-normative rhetoricity, in this case the "betweenity" of "mad composing."

The next section, "Selves and Subjectivities," looks at the particular constructive capabilities within digital spaces for considering the "self," as well as collectivity based on shared subjectivities. Issues of gender, race, ethnicity, class, and sexuality form and transform as they are scripted and rescripted across multiple digital platforms. Casey Boyle leads off with an exploration of posthumanism as postscript, followed by Kristin L. Arola's foregrounding of a land-based digital design rhetoric that draws on indigenous epistemologies. Next, Kristine L. Blair calls for technofeminist activism to reshape cultural narratives of women and technology; Zarah C. Moeggenberg explores how three queer people use online spaces to challenge the "flattening" of user experience; and Carol Burke and Jonathan Alexander provide a case study of Elliot Rodger, the deeply troubled, tech-savvy murderer of six people in 2014 near UC Santa Barbara. William Hart-Davidson ends this section by telling us that "robots write." But can they do rhetoric?

"Regulation and Control" is the fifth section of the book, and chapters within it inquire about the cultural forces behind the shaping, regulation, and control of digital spaces. For instance, contributors consider the challenges of plagiarism and textual/content ownership (James E. Porter); new conceptions of authorship (Chad Seader, Jason Markins, and Jordan Canzonetta); recommender systems (Mihaela Popescu and Lemi Baruh); algorithms (Estee Beck); doxing and online privacy/safety (Les Hutchinson); assessment (Bump Halbritter and Julie Lindquist); and, finally, testing and educational politics (Carl Whithaus). How do these issues impact our understanding of what writing and the rhetorical are?

Moving beyond considering changes to writing and rhetoric in relation to specific platforms, "Multimodality, Transmediation, and Participatory Cultures" asks how composing is changing as it occurs across multiple platforms at once. As more and more reporting, storytelling, and narration are *transmediated*, how is our understanding of what composing means further challenged, and what affordances for being rhetorical are opened up (or elided)? William P. Banks offers us a queer/trans* lens on transmediation, while Regina Duthely explores the connections between hip-hop rhetoric and multimodality; Mel Alexenberg dives deep into relationships between digital and Hebraic writing; Bri Lafond and Kristen Macias look at generative and pragmatic intersections of multimodality and adaptation theory; and Jeff Rice uses Bikram yoga to explore virtuality. Ingrid Richardson ends the section with an in-depth consideration of paratextuality and play.

Our final section—"The Politics and Economics of Digital Writing and Rhetoric"—returns us to a core aim of this collection: emphasizing the importance of a *critical* approach to digital writing and rhetoric. This section examines the implications of swift technological/cultural changes for the future(s) of digital writing and rhetoric, with an eye toward such topics as increasing corporate control of digital spaces for composing, the impact of creative economies of our understanding of digital writing, and the use of digital writing and rhetoric for acts of resistance and socio-political re-imagination. Heidi A. McKee and James E. Porter provide an overview of ethics and rhetoric in digital contexts to lead off the section. After that, Angela M. Haas moves us toward a digital cultural rhetoric that works "in excess to digital writing," while Kylie Jarrett looks at digital labor and consumption and Steven Hammer explores the politics of the disciplining function of soundwriting interfaces. In the final chapter of this section—and the collection as a whole—Stuart Moulthrop asks us to consider the futures of digital writing and rhetoric, the possibilities of "traversal functions, operations that turn potentialities into expression."

Our section categories are necessarily broad, and contributors inevitably treat their subjects in ways that cross those large categories both insightfully and productively. Our hope has been to provide through this volume a rich and conceptually engaging way to approach the complexities of digital writing and rhetoric. Ultimately, we hope the book will be of use to scholars in the field and, more important, to graduate students and newcomers to rhetoric and writing studies, communication studies, media studies, and other fields that look at digital scholarship. There are many conversations yet to be had about digital rhetoric and writing. We hope we have at least given a bit of shape and direction to what some of those interesting conversations might be.

Works Cited

Alexander, Jonathan, and Jacqueline Rhodes. *On Multimodality: New Media in Composition Studies*. NCTE, 2015.

Banks, Adam J. *Digital Griots: African American Rhetoric in a Multimedia Age*. Southern Illinois UP, 2011.

Eyman, Doug. *Digital Rhetoric: Theory, Method, Practice*. U of Michigan P, 2015.

Gillen, Julia. *Digital Literacies*. Routledge, 2014.

Halbritter, Bump. *Mics, Cameras, Symbolic Action: Audio-visual Rhetoric for Writing Teachers*. Parlor, 2012.

Handa, Carolyn. *Multimediated Rhetoric of the Internet: Digital Fusion*. Routledge, 2014.

Lutkewitte, Claire, Ed. *Multimodal Composition: A Critical Sourcebook*. Bedford/St. Martin's, 2014.

Selber, Stuart A., Ed. *Rhetoric and Technologies: New Directions in Writing and Communication*. U of South Carolina P, 2010.

Urbanski, Heather. *Writing and the Digital Generation: Essays on New Media Rhetoric*. McFarland & Company, 2010.

Whithaus, Carl, and Tracey Bowen (Eds.). *Multimodal Literacies and Emerging Genres*. U of Pittsburgh P, 2013.

PART I

Cultural and Historical Contexts

1

DIGITAL WRITING MATTERS

Dànielle Nicole DeVoss

The Call to Write on the National Day of Writing website (now http://whyiwrite.us/) reads, in part:

> Whether we call it texting, IMing, jotting a note, writing a letter, posting an email, blogging, making a video, building an electronic presentation, composing a memo, keeping a diary, or just pulling together a report, Americans are writing like never before.
>
> Recent research suggests that writing, in its many forms, has become a daily practice for millions of Americans. It may be the quintessential 21st century skill . . .

The National Council of Teachers of English statement on twenty-first century literacies argues for an expansive and culturally linked notion of literacy, and articulates the roles of digital technologies. The statement describes the skills necessary for twenty-first century readers and writers to cultivate, including:

- managing, analyzing, and synthesizing multiple streams of simultaneous information; and
- creating, critiquing, analyzing, and evaluating multimedia texts.

This chapter is a response to this call to write and recognition of the ways in which writing happens in today's context, and also hearty support for the NCTE statement. The title of this chapter works two ways: first, as an argument: digital writing *matters*. Then, second, as a promise: matters of digital writing. My departure point for this chapter is *Because Digital Writing Matters*, a National Writing Project book that Troy Hicks, Elyse Eidman-Aadahl, and I published in 2010. In that book, we discussed the ways in which writing changes shape in and across digital spaces, and oriented toward providing teachers, K–12 administrators, and policy-makers information about how we can best navigate these shifts. And, frankly, these shifts aren't particularly new or surprising; the ways in which we understand writing, and, indeed, literacy itself, are complex, multifaceted, rhizomatic, and organic. Writing grows. Writing shifts. Writing becomes. Writing changes shape. Although the shifts aren't particularly new and although writing has evolved for as long as we've engaged it as a species, what is new are the digital spaces and places where writing happens.

In this chapter, I'll hone in specifically on three ways in which digital writing matters, and three matters of digital writing: the networked context, collaborative composing spaces and practices, and the ways in which digital writing is policed. The technology in and of itself is hardly a revolution. As scholars including Jim Porter have noted, rather, it is the networked connectivity and its potentials that are perhaps the most revolutionary aspects of digital spaces. Further, digital spaces nurture, facilitate, and often require robust practices of collaboration. And digital writing practices are policed, specifically and especially when considering issues of copyright and multimodal composing. I'll explore each of these matters, and then share a technopedagogical stance toward these matters in the writing classroom.

Digital Writing in/and the Networked Context

The Networked Context

In the late 1960s, engineers working primarily in governmental and university contexts connected a handful of computers and equipped them to communicate with one another. During the 1970s, the Internet grew and became multifaceted and global. In the 1980s, computers became more widespread; more and more, companies relied on computers across their systems and services. Computer access in colleges and universities spread, and more and more K–12 institutions had a computer in some of the classrooms. For instance, in the school I attended in the mid-1980s, we had one computer in just one classroom shared by sixth, seventh, and eighth grades, that sat in the back of the room, unused the majority of the time. Because we had a Commodore 64 in the home, I knew the basics of using a computer, and figured out how to boot up and play the one game that came with the school's computer. As far as I remember, that was the only use the computer got in 1984.

In the early 1990s, when the Internet was still text-only and exclusively hierarchical-menu-based, Tim Berners-Lee wrote a proposal for what would eventually become HTML and create an expansion to the Internet; this expansion was the Web (Hafner; Isaacson). By the mid-1990s, Web writers could hyperlink across pages and spaces, and embed images onto the pages they created. URLs became more commonplace than Internet protocols, and Web traffic sped past the activity of the Internet. In the early 2000s, "Web 2.0" emerged, anchored by more social, collaborative, networked approaches to content development and sharing.

To hone in on the networked aspects of digital writing and one particular Web 2.0 space, in July 2009, "Tom" had 264,987,947 friends on MySpace. In October, he had 268,880,678 friends. Tom made almost 4 million friends in less than three months. On MySpace, millions of people embraced the networked capabilities of the Web—posting updates, sharing experiences, adding photos, showing identity affiliations (by connecting with bands, actors, etc.), and more. By January 2012, however, Tom had 11,806,655 friends on MySpace. Tom had lost more than 257 million friends in just over three years; three years of Internet time happens at light speed. During this time, new spaces emerged and invited participation. New digital places were developed and allowed for different kinds of networked experiences. Facebook, during this time, transitioned from a school-specific (Harvard) site, to a national student-oriented site, to an open and public space. In late 2017, Facebook is home to more than 2 *billion* active users.

Another digital networked space is WordPress, which hosts more than 1.5 million new posts daily. Writers use this space to read, write, post, comment, upload, search, embed video, connect to other media spaces (such as Flickr, Twitter, and Instagram) and more. The first tweet was sent on March 21, 2006. In late 2016, more than 10,000 tweets were sent *every second*. In an interesting moment of digital–analog convergence, the Library of Congress (LoC) began archiving all public tweets in April 2010. In a white paper released almost three years into the project, the LoC eloquently noted:

> As society turns to social media as a primary method of communication and creative expression, social media is supplementing and in some cases supplanting letters, journals, serial publications and other sources routinely collected by research libraries . . . Archiving and preserving outlets such as Twitter will enable future researchers' access to a fuller picture of today's cultural norms, dialogue, trends and events to inform scholarship, the legislative process, new works of authorship, education and other purposes. (Allen; Library of Congress)

As of late 2016, however, the project was still stalled. Andrew McGill, in an August 2016 article in *The Atlantic*, asked, "Can Twitter Fit Inside the Library of Congress?" The issue isn't with storing what's happening across networked, digital spaces. The issue relates to making the cultural ephemera—expressed in more than 500 million public tweets per day—usable, accessible, and understandable. McGill further pointed out that when the LoC began archiving public tweets, only 5 million or so were sent per day, and those were text-only. Twitter today supports the embedding of images and video, and hashtags themselves have emerged as a unique language. Preservation becomes a bigger issue than storing tweets on a server; making this big data accessible requires anchors to cultural norms, historic trends, and complex ways of parsing the data tweets contain.

Another networked space that has truly transformed the media landscape is YouTube, which launched in 2005. Traditionally, with conventional media, users are viewers. The majority of people who watch movies, watch television, and listen to radio do so in a fairly passive, consumerist role. With networked, digital media, however, users engage their roles in broad ways—consuming, producing, remixing, sharing, revising, and more (Dubisar and Palmeri; Fulwiler and Middleton; Halbritter; Morain and Swarts; Verzosa Hurley and Kimme Hea). On YouTube, users upload 24 hours of video *every minute*.

Digital is networked, and this network connectivity can, potentially, have a big impact on our classrooms. Jeff Grabill—a rhetoric and writing studies scholar, business owner, digital writing innovator, and software developer—has argued: "I just happen to be a writing teacher interested in the digital at the greatest moment in human history to be interested in both writing and the digital." Grabill notes that the "dramatic and revolutionary transformation in our lives is the network. It's the combination of computing and networking that allow us to write in radically new ways."

Techno-pedagogy for the Networked Context

Networks and certainly social networks span analog and digital spaces, the seemingly ephemeral and the material, the personal and the professional, and other boundaries. Networks are contextual, and "local" in whatever ways we might identify and orient toward locality across spaces. In an upper-level writing course offered in our Professional Writing program at Michigan State University, we invite students to deeply engage and robustly analyze networks. Recently, for instance, one student pursued a project framed by her research question: How are nonprofits in the Lansing area networked? And what do those networks *mean*? She engaged in mapping activities, starting by mapping organizational websites and then interviewing organizational leaders, focusing on twelve area nonprofits. Her maps of both the digital and physical networks revealed a common thread: the organizations most linked to others and in the middle of the network maps were those that seemed to have the most reach in the area, and the most impact on their communities. Although her results aren't necessarily solid quantitatively, the project itself was a fascinating one, and models for us approaches through which we might invite students to analyze how networks function, and, more importantly, what networks do.

Digital Writing and Collaboration

The Collaborative Context

These three matters of digital writing are certainly not discrete; rather, they are entwined in complex ways. Part of the networked nature of digital writing discussed above is certainly the ways in which digital writing fosters—and often demands—collaboration. For instance, on the cheezburger network, thousands of users, on a daily basis, share, caption, tag, and comment on photos of cats. To maintain a feline focus, hundreds of users collaboratively drafted, crafted, edited, and published a complete translation of the King James Bible in "lolcat," or Kitty Pidgin English. Genesis 1, verses 1 through 3 read:

1   Oh hai. In teh beginnin Ceiling Cat maded teh skiez An da Urfs, but he did not eated dem.
2   Da Urfs no had shapez An haded dark face, An Ceiling Cat rode invisible bike over teh waterz.
3   At start, no has lyte. An Ceiling Cat sayz, i can haz lite? An lite wuz. An Ceiling Cat sawed teh lite, to seez stuffs, An splitted teh lite from dark but taht wuz ok cuz kittehs can see in teh dark An not tripz over nethin. An Ceiling Cat sayed light Day An dark no Day. It were FURST!!!1 ("LOLCat Bible Translation Project")

Apparently few things can leverage and mobilize the networked, collaborative aspects of digital space like cats can.

To turn toward a topic closer to home for rhetoric and writing studies scholars, on fanction.net, just one of *thousands* of fan fiction communities, writers remix, revise, reread, reinterpret, and collaboratively create, edit, and generate fan fiction—work that takes characters, themes, and chunks from existing literature and reshapes it. *Pride and Prejudice*, for instance, has more than 4,000 available riffs on fanfiction.net. However, the most popular body of literature to rethink and revise is that of Harry Potter. More than 763,000 original fanfiction works have been shared on fanfiction.net as of April 2017, which is an increase of more than 11,000 writings since October 2016. This community of writers is inspired by the site's tagline: "unleash your imagination," and collaboration is a key composing convention in this particular community. Pieces are commented on in-process; drafts are shared online—under and across the site; editorial feedback gives shape to revisions; pieces are co-created by multiple writers.

An argument that colleagues and I made awhile back is that collaboration—in the many different ways of sharing—is perhaps the most significant impact of computer technologies on the contexts and practices of writing (WIDE Research Center Collective). Computers themselves are just machines. They're just tools. When we connect them, and when we create and use the interfaces to make meaning together and share ideas across distances—that's the computer revolution.

Techno-pedagogy for the Collaborative Context

Shared content creation in collaborative, synchronous spaces is a context in which our students will create, share, revise, and produce text. In 2013, I polled students in an introductory Professional Writing course regarding their familiarity with Google Docs. Many of the students hadn't used Google Docs, or hadn't used it extensively. I created a Google Doc before class and connected students to it, and in class we filled in a grid with three columns together. The columns were: your name, a reason to use Google Docs, a reason not to use Google Docs. There were a handful of surprised murmurs as we each watched and contributed to the development of the doc. Together, we generated a smart set of approaches for when to leverage the networked, collaborative power of Google Docs, but also when such a tool may not be an appropriate composing route.

More recently, I observed a colleague, Casey McArdle, teach our introduction to Web authoring course. I arrived at the room early and noticed students were on Google Drive, with a doc open, reading and taking notes. When Casey arrived, he opened the doc on the instructor screen and pointed out a set of prompts he had posted. Casey and the students spent the first 20 minutes or so of class responding to the prompts, adding to the document, and then talking about their observations. In this way, the class not only started with a rich, robust discussion of the day's readings, and the connections Casey wanted students to draw from the readings, but they also collaboratively contributed to a living document and resource. I observed Casey's class seven weeks into the semester, and the ongoing class reading notes, examples, and resources doc was more than fifty single-spaced pages, and open and accessible to everyone in the course.

Our institutional course-management system is an excellent tool for delivering content to students and storing class materials. It is not, however, an ideal space to engage in a collaborative, networked way. This semester, in a document design course I'm teaching, I'm using Google Drive and Google Classroom extensively. Early in the semester, we read pieces on rhetorical approaches and document design (Dobrin, Keller, and Weisser; Ehses and Lupton; Markel; Schriver). Given the 2016 presidential election, I chose the campaign logos for Donald Trump, Hillary Clinton, and, although he was no longer active in the race, Bernie Sanders. I included the logos in a Google Doc and asked students to identify the context in which these images might be seen and explore the purposes they serve. I then asked students to identify one document design element and read that one element for the logos-, pathos-, or ethos-based approach it engaged. On another day this semester, students read chapters on rhetorical effectiveness and slideshow design (specifically, chapters from Duarte; Reynolds; Williams) and then created a slide and added it to a slidedeck I built in Google Presentations. I asked them, on their slide, to include *and* illuminate a key point from the reading. These networked, collaborative resources will live on Google Drive long after the course ends, and have been a space for students to brainstorm and build together.

The Policing of Digital Writing

The Legal Context

We well know that in academic contexts, if you copy and paste passages from *Pride and Prejudice* without appropriately attributing that material to Jane Austen, you are guilty of plagiarism. Elsewhere, however, if you copy and paste passages from *Pride and Prejudice* without appropriately attributing that material to Jane Austen, you are guilty of nothing. Indeed, you may choose to invoke and include "Jane Austen" in your work to align yourself with a writer with high authorial cultural value, but you may *choose* to do so; there's no scholarly or professional requirement that you *must* do so because *Pride and Prejudice* is in the public domain. Its copyright has expired and it is owned by all—to remix, revise, rethink, reshape, etc. Seth Grahame-Smith (2009) took full advantage of this opportunity when he created *Pride and Prejudice and Zombies*; he even gave authorial credit to himself and to Jane Austen.

In academic contexts, if you copy and paste passages from *Gone with the Wind*, include those passages in quotation marks or block quotes, and appropriately cite Margaret Mitchell, you are a good, ethical scholar and user of source material. Elsewhere, however, if you adapt characters from *Gone with the Wind* and rewrite the novel from a plantation slave's perspective, you will get sued by the estate of the original author and her publishing company, because *Gone with the Wind* is still under copyright, and will be until 2031 (death of the author plus 95 years, per US Copyright law). This copyright is jointly held by Margaret Mitchell and a trust that manages international copyright protection for the book (which entered Australian public domain in 1999). In this case, Alice Randall's 2002 *The Wind Done Gone*, a cultural critique and fiction response to the original novel, won in court, with Randall and her publishing company allowed to continue distributing copies of her book. Each copy produced, however, must be accompanied by a "THE UNAUTHORIZED PARODY" declaration.

In 2007, Steve Vander Ark, who ran a fan-/crowd-sourced based website, The Harry Potter Lexicon, was sued by J. K. Rowling and Warner Bros. for the production of a book-version of the resource (*Warner Bros. Entertainment Inc. et al. v. RDR Books et al.*). Vander Ark's lawyers attempted to argue that the lexicon worked like a Cliffs Notes book or "resource" text, which are primarily made up of summaries, snippets, and compilations of other work. The court decided against Vander Ark, stating that he drew too heavily from the characters, plots, and more of the Harry Potter series, and demanded he make revisions to the book adding much more "original" content; a revised *Harry Potter Lexicon* was published in 2009 with the subtitle "an unauthorized guide." If we turn back to digital space, however, in 2015, KfaceTV released "Dark Lord Funk" on YouTube; as of late 2017, the video has had more than 14 million views. In it, actors dressed as Harry Potter characters sing a revision of Mark Ronson and Bruno Mars' song "Uptown Funk." "Uptown Funk" opens with

> This hit, that ice cold
> Michelle Pfeiffer, that white gold
> This one for them hood girls
> Them good girls straight masterpieces
> Stylin', whilen, livin' it up in the city
> Got Chucks on with Saint Laurent
> Got kiss myself, I'm so pretty

"Dark Lord Funk" opens with

> This wiz, I'm ice cold
> I'm Voldemort, that white cold
> This one for that HP, says he hates me
> But what can he do?

The "Dark Lord Funk" song and video draws upon at least three copyright-protected circulating works: "Uptown Funk," the Harry Potter character and themes, and the original score from Harry Potter, which is sampled through the song. The song and video, however, have been left intact in digital space to circulate, in large part because they function as a derivative work that is labeled parody. Parody, news reporting, cultural critique and commentary, and other acts fall under the Fair Use provision of US copyright law.

These examples show us how deeply and importantly matters of authorship and copyright happen in and beyond academic contexts, especially where digital writing is concerned. Students, today, can relatively easily take, capture, download, and rip, and then make, mix, mash, and put back into circulation derivations of the work of others (Edwards; Ray; Stedman). It's not reasonable for us to ask students, when producing multimodal compositions, to write and score their own music, then perform and produce it. It's not reasonable for us to ask students to become professional photographers, setting shoots, taking shots, and editing photographic work for their multimodal compositions. It's also not reasonable for us to demand that they do so; cultural work *exists* that students can draw from, remix, and integrate to make for their rhetorical purposes. The digital context invites students to work within and connect across networked spaces to robustly collaborate on different types of texts—texts that may require them to draw or sample from other existing copyright-protected texts. Indeed, both Siva Vaidhyanathan and Lawrence Lessig argue that this "remix culture" is *the* contemporary composing paradigm.

Techno-pedagogy for the Legal Context

To best address the ways in which authorship and ownership shift across spaces (e.g., analog and digital; academic and professional), we should talk frankly with students about rhetorical context and about the legality that frames the writing people do. Students need to know about Fair Use and what Fair Use allows them to do for the purposes of research, parody, cultural commentary/critique, and more. They also need to know how those affordances change shape once they leave an academic context. They can't bring these educationally cultivated scholarly practices into, for instance, a job or internship context. They *can* bring the rhetorical moves they've learned, the technical skills they've honed, and the writerly approaches they've developed, but the copyright-protected media pieces themselves have to stay behind in the classroom.

Students are often captivated by discussions of copyright, which isn't surprising given the murkiness of intellectual property in digital space *and* given that students are rarely, if ever, situated as producers. They're warned not to torrent. Not to take. Not to download. Not to rip. They're always already consumers. And potential thieves. In the context of an upper-level digital rhetoric course I taught, students and I spent a chunk of time talking about copyright and digital contexts. I asked students to tell me what their authorial, compositional, writerly values were, and to defend those values rhetorically. This conversation was so rich it evolved into a critical, networked, collaborative, multimodal, remix webtext, where students and I presented a manifesto about copyright. Students presented remix work they produced and also presented arguments including:

- All knowledge and its manifestations—through art, music, digital media projects, etc.—is cumulative. We build on the past and require open cultural and artistic commons to do so. Our current laws hamper the healthy building of a cultural and artistic ecosystem.
- Information is meant for dissemination. What this means is that old work is—and should remain—accessible, distributable, downloadable, and usable by the next generations of digital workers, writers, and artists. (Digirhet)

Along with engaging students about discussions of how they see and situate authorship and writerly practices, activities that ask students to wrestle with copyright enhance their understandings of digital spaces as policed. For instance, in my document design class, I've provided students with a hypothetical non-profit client who needs a brochure created. I ask students to identify what materials they would need to create the brochure, and then to identify *where* those materials would come from. Among other topics, our discussion includes taking original photographs and addressing issues of photo releases and consent, discussions of public domain archives and when they're a good resource, and conversations about stock photography and other for-pay archives as a professional resource.

Conclusions

These three matters of digital writing—that digital is networked, collaborative, and policed—are certainly not the *only* matters of digital writing, nor are they the *only* ways in which digital writing matters. Digital writing is multimodal. Digital writing is remixed. Digital writing is, in some ways, fixed; in other ways, it circulates. However, these three produce a particular technological and philosophical platform from which we can better understand the affordances and possibilities of the larger digital writing landscape, and from which we can craft teacherly approaches that invite students into critical conversations about both analysis and production in/with/across digital spaces. And digital *is* the context in which our students work and play—where they articulate their identities as readers, researchers, citizens, writers, and more. In today's composing contexts, and in today's writing classrooms, we have to equip learners with a deep, expansive skillset oriented around transferrable skills—skills they can experiment with and hone in the classroom, skills they can apply in their internships or in their co-curricular experiences, and skills they can take and adapt in a workplace that is constantly and rapidly evolving.

Our best practices as writing instructors are an anchor across these skills and across these contexts. Supporting students in composing in rhetorically effective ways trumps any particular technology. Helping students to be the most effective communicators and the best writers they can be is what we do. Supporting students in exploring different tools and enhancing their writing practices and processes is what we do. Equipping students to engage critical and rhetorical strategies for negotiating different audiences, purposes, and contexts is what we do.

Works Cited

Allen, Erin. *Update on the Twitter Archive at the Library of Congress*. 4 Feb. 2013, blogs.loc.gov/loc/2013/01/update-on-the-twitter-archive-at-the-library-of-congress/. Accessed 4 Oct. 2016.

Austen, Jane, and Seth Grahame-Smith. *Pride and Prejudice and Zombies: The Classic Regency Romance—Now with Ultraviolent Zombie Mayhem!* Quirk, 2009.

DeVoss, Dànielle Nicole, Elyse Eidman-Aadahl, Troy Hicks, and The National Writing Project. *Because Digital Writing Matters*. Jossey-Bass, 2010.

Digirhet. "Old + Old + Old = New: A Copyright Manifesto for the Digital World." *Kairos: A Journal of Rhetoric, Technology, and Pedagogy*, vol. 12, 2005, technorhetoric.net/12.3/topoi/digirhet/. Accessed 10 Oct. 2016.

Dobrin, Sidney I., Christopher J. Keller, and Christian R. Weisser. *Technical Communication in the Twenty-first Century*. 2nd ed., Pearson, 2009.

Duarte, Nancy. *Resonate: Present Visual Stories that Transform Audiences*. John Wiley & Sons, 2010.

Dubisar, Abby M., and Jason Palmeri. "Palin/Pathos/Peter Griffin: Political Video Remix and Composition Pedagogy." *Computers and Composition*, vol. 27, 2010, pp. 77–93.

Edwards, Dustin W. "Framing Remix Rhetorically: Toward a Typology of Transformative Work." *Computers and Composition*, vol. 39, 2016, pp. 41–54.

Ehses, Hanno, and Ellen Lupton. *Design Papers: Rhetorical Handbook*. Halifax, Nova Scotia College of Art and Design, 1988.

Fulwiler, Mega, and Kim Middleton. "After Digital Storytelling: Video Composing in the New Media Age." *Computers and Composition*, vol. 29, 2012, pp. 39–50.

Grabill, Jeffrey T. "Robots are coming: Technologies are changing the teaching of writing." Keynote address at the Zeeland Education and Teacher's Academy (ZETA), Zeeland, MI. *YouTube*, 13 Aug. 2015, www.youtube.com/watch?v=6B8LtNRN6kw.

Hafner, Katie. *Where Wizards Stay Up Late: The Origins of the Internet*. Simon & Schuster, 1998.

Halbritter, Bump. *Mics, Cameras, Symbolic Action: Audio-visual Rhetoric for Writing Teachers*. Parlor, 2012.

Isaacson, Walter. *The innovators: How a Group of Hackers, Geniuses, and Geeks Created the Digital Revolution*. Simon & Schuster, 2014.

Lessig, Lawrence. "Remix Culture." Conference on College Composition and Communication, March 2005, San Francisco, CA. Conference presentation.

——. *Remix: Making Art and Commerce Thrive in the Hybrid Economy*. Penguin, 2008.

Library of Congress. "Update on the Twitter Archive." Jan. 2013, www.loc.gov/today/pr/2013/files/twitter_report_2013jan.pdf. Accessed 15 Oct. 2016.

"LOLCat Bible Translation Project." www.lolcatbible.com/index.php?title=Main_Page. Accessed 30 Aug. 2016.

McGill, Andrew. "Can Twitter Fit Inside the Library of Congress?" *The Atlantic*, 4 Aug. 2016, www.theatlantic.com/technology/archive/2016/08/can-twitter-fit-inside-the-library-of-congress/494339/. Accessed 10 Aug. 2016.

Markel, Mike. *Technical Communication*. 11th ed. Bedford/St. Martin's, 2014.

Mitchell, Margaret. *Gone with the Wind*. 1936. Reissue edition. Scribner, 2011.

Morain, Matt, and Jason Swarts. "YouTutorial: A Framework for Assessing Instructional Online Video." *Technical Communication Quarterly*, 21, 2011, 6–24.

National Council of Teachers of English. "NCTE Framework for 21st Century Curriculum and Assessment," Feb. 2013, www.ncte.org/governance/21stcenturyframework. Accessed 1 Oct. 2016.

Porter, Jim. "Why Technology Matters to Writing: A Cyberwriter's tale." *Computers and Composition*, vol. 20, 2002, pp. 375–94.

Randall, Alice. *The Wind Done Gone*. Mariner, 2002.

Ray, Brian. "More Than Just Remixing: Uptake and New Media Composition." *Computers and Composition*, vol. 30, 2013, pp. 183–96.

Reynolds, Garr. *Presentationzen: Simple Ideas on Presentation Design and Delivery*. New Riders, 2008.

——. *Presentationzen Design: Simple Design Principles and Techniques to Enhance Your Presentations*. New Riders, 2010.

Schriver, Karen. *Dynamics in Document Design*. John Wiley & Sons, 1997.

Stedman, Kyle D. "Remix Literacy and Fan Compositions." *Computers and Composition*, vol. 29, 2010, pp. 107–23.

Vaidhyanathan, Siva. *Copyrights and Copywrongs: The Rise of Intellectual Property and How It Threatens Creativity*. New York UP, 2003.

Vander Ark, Steve. *The Lexicon: An Unauthorized Guide to Harry Potter Fiction and Related Materials*. RDR, 2009.

Verzosa Hurley, Elise, and Amy C. Kimme Hea. "The Rhetoric of Reach: Preparing Students for Technical Communication in the Age of Social Media." *Technical Communication Quarterly*, vol. 23, 2014, pp. 55–68.

Warner Bros. Entertainment Inc. et al v. RDR Books et al, No. 1:2007cv09667—Document 92 (S.D.N.Y. 2008), law.justia.com/cases/federal/district-courts/new-york/nysdce/1:2007cv09667/315790/92/. Accessed 10 Aug. 2016.

WIDE Research Center Collective. "Why Teach Digital Writing?" *Kairos: A Journal of Rhetoric, Technology, and Pedagogy*, vol. 10, 2005, kairos.technorhetoric.net/10.1/coverweb/wide/. Accessed 10 Oct. 2016.

Williams, Robin. *The Non-Designer's Presentation Book: Principles for Effective Design*. Peachpit, 2010.

2

A TALE OF TWO TABLETS

Tracing Intersections of Materiality, the Body, and Practices of Communication

Ben McCorkle

Our world is enriched when coders and marketers dazzle us with smartphones and tablets, but, by themselves, they are just slabs. It is the music, essays, entertainment and provocations that they access, spawned by the humanities, that animate them— and us.

(Nicholas Kristof)

Machines, once made, make men.

(Ralph Waldo Emerson)

If your particular brand of geek cred, like mine, combines a fascination with obsolete technologies and a love for *The Simpsons*, then you likely remember a scene in the 1995 episode "Lisa on Ice" (S6E8) that depicts what very well may be the first autocorrect fail in popular culture. Annoyed by the nebbish student Martin during a school assembly, resident bully Kearney instructs his henchman Dolph to take a note on his Apple Newton MessagePad, an early-90s digital tablet that predates the era of the Personal Digital Assistant by several years. The handwriting recognition software mis-translates "Beat up Martin" to "Eat up Martha," causing Kearney to simply throw the device at Martin out of frustration, beaning him in the head for a cheap bit of physical humor at the Newton's expense.

Setting aside what Newton enthusiasts have long claimed to be an unfair slight (as an owner of one myself, I can attest that later models of the MessagePad actually had quite reliable handwriting recognition), this scene illustrates an important, if inauspicious, moment in popular culture: our coming-to-terms with the emergence of a new digital technology of communication. Having become habituated to decades of clacking away at keyboards while hunched over our office desks and kitchen tables, we suddenly found ourselves introduced to a new category of digital device with a somewhat new user interface: decidedly more portable, more tactile, and potentially more intuitive by engaging what for most of us is our earliest method of alphabetic text production, writing by hand. As far as the computing devices of the early 90s were concerned, the Newton MessagePad was simultaneously exotic and familiar, a combination of increasingly faster and smaller processors combined with capacitive touch screens and packaged in a shape that reaches back thousands of years.

18

As a writing technology, the form factor we generally categorize as the tablet has had remarkable durability during the roughly 2.5 millennia that the Western world has been a literate civilization. Developed during Antiquity, the Greek δέλτος (*deltos*) or Roman *tabellae* (also referred to as *cerae* or *pugillares*) were erasable wax tablets written on with styli, commonly used by orators, scholars, merchants, and other literate professionals throughout the middle ages and well into the modern era. They were used for teaching students how to write, for drafting orations, for keeping records of inventory, and for transcribing speech in formal situations such as court testimony, among other uses. The longevity of this original wax tablet speaks well of the device's versatility, reusability, portability, and durability.

Today, our communications ecosystem is becoming increasingly populated by a tablet of a different sort: the modern-day tablet computer, exemplified by devices such as Microsoft's Surface, Apple's iPad, and Samsung Galaxy TabPro S, to name but three. These consumer-grade pieces of technology encourage a wide range of expression from their users, from the casual (the random tweet, a FaceTime chat with a geographically distant friend) to the more structured or formal (composing reports in a word processing app, or navigating through a slideshow presentation accompanying a class lecture, for instance). The digital tablet enjoys many of the same affordances of its ancestral forebear—compared to traditional computing devices, for example, they are much more portable and tactile—but also they serve as conduits or windows through which we glimpse the communal knowledge and cultural output of the entire World Wide Web, even allowing us to contribute to that self-same output.

This chapter proposes that we can engage productively in a comparative analysis of these two iterations of the tablet—taken together, they bookend a fascinating history of how communication, the body, and the materiality of our writing-based technologies have always been bound up with one another. Briefly put, I seek to make the argument that *deltos* largely served to support more writerly forms of communication, and that this particular technology was highly instrumental in helping to usher in the initial phase of literacy in Western society. Even in the context of oratorical performance, tablets acclimated users to adapt to an increasing writing-centric approach to the entire rhetorical process, from invention, style, and organization (the "compositional" canons), even down the pipeline to memory and delivery (the "performative" canons). Digital tablets, on the other hand, mark something of a return for us: they reintroduce real-time embodied and spoken components into our communicative practices that, for centuries, have largely privileged written over oral expression. Recognition of this return has implications for how we give shape and contour to newly emerging genres and forms of communication using these types of devices, as well as how we teach students to communicate more effectively when using them.

We can trace the beginnings of the wax tablet to at least the Homeric period of antiquity—an inexact origin point, but anywhere from eighth to twelfth century BCE—as Homer makes among the earliest mentions of the device in the *Iliad* (Smith 1091). In fact, among the artifacts recovered from a salvage operation of a fourteenth-century BCE shipwreck off the coast of Turkey were fragments from a framed wax tablet with a partial hinge, lending credence to the notion that the device was in common use during that era (Payton 99). *Deltos* were believed to be integral tools for the production of writing well before the disciplinary beginnings of rhetoric in Athenian culture around the fifth century BCE.

It should be noted that the history of the wax tablet recounted here leans in a decidedly Western direction, especially as Eastern cultures had developed and widely adopted the technology of paper much earlier than the Western world (circa third century BCE), and before that used materials including sculpted bone and scrolls made from bamboo (Tsien 40). The wax tablet as it was known in ancient Greece, Rome, and medieval Europe, though, grows out of earlier form factors and materials for the tablet that circulated throughout North Africa, the Near East, and the Mediterranean (Giuseppe). There were older variants of the wax tablet popularized in ancient Greece and Rome that were the result of these influences, notably the clay tablets used by the scribes in Ancient Egypt, Sumeria, and Babylonia. Clay tablets were slightly different from wax tablets, in that they were typically fire-hardened once completed, and they were used for purposes such as accounting ledgers, agricultural records, and recipes, among other uses. From this impliable clay ancestor, though, the comparatively flexible wax tablet would eventually develop.

From their earliest introduction, wax tablets were used in a variety of contexts, among them legal documentation, historical records, and accounting. Over the centuries, and owing to this variety of use scenarios, the tablet took many form factors: typically written on with a stylus (although the finger was sometimes employed), *cerae* or *tabellae* through the classical Roman and medieval eras consisted of either single rectangular wooden trays commonly filled with pliable wax (usually beeswax), and sometimes several such tablets conjoined by thread or cording into diptychs, triptychs, or even multiple-panel configurations (Smith 1091; Montague 144).

The wax tablet was an integral part of the composing process for a variety of scholastic and oratorical purposes, and the historical record offers us a variety of pictorial and written mentions of how tablets were used, as well as the conceptual space they occupied in the composing process. As historians Richard Rouse and Mary Rouse document, medieval writers conceived of writing as involving both mental and material factors—in medieval illustrations and paintings, figures were often depicted with wax diptychs to signify their status as authors (180). As they explain:

> This process of drafting takes place jointly in the mind and on a writing surface. It is readily apparent from the literary and pictorial evidence that adult writers from antiquity to early modern times composed on tablets. The wax tablet was the drafting medium of prior ages, just as the yellow pad, typewriter, or computer is to us. There are a number of instances in which an author describes the process of composition in these terms, and in which the process is depicted in manuscripts of his works. (177)

In fact, in at least one extant medieval text on the Seven Liberal Arts, Rhetoric is symbolized as a wax tablet, signifying the technology's integral position within the tradition of oratorical practice and performance (176).

In his introduction to Cicero's letters, Andrew Montague explains how wax tablets were commonly used to compose and disseminate correspondence among Roman citizens, offering us this detailed physical description in the process:

> But in far more general use [compared to paper and ink] were waxen tablets (*tabulae* or *tabellae*, sometimes *cerae*), thin pieces of wood of oblong shape covered with wax; and the *stilus*, an iron instrument, in shape like a pencil, sharpened at one end for scratching upon the wax, and flat and circular at the other end, which was used to render the wax smooth again, and thus to obliterate, when it was necessary, what had been written. Only the inner sides of the tablets were covered with wax, the outer sides consisting merely of wood. [. . .] "To prevent the wax of one tablet from rubbing against that of the other, there was a raised margin around each."—*Dict. Antiq.* When a letter was finished, the tablets were bound together with a packthread, the knot of which was sealed with wax and stamped with the signet ring (*signum*), which, in the case of a letter dictated to a secretary, was the only signature or evidence of authorship. Few Romans wrote their letters. They dictated to amanuenses (*librarii ab epistolu*). Cicero,

however, wrote many of his letters with his own hand (Ad Quint Fr II 16) and he sometimes wrote so rapidly that his writing became almost illegible (Ad Quint Fr II 15). (12–13)

Within the rhetorical tradition, Quintilian was the one who paid the most attention to this particular writing technology. Rouse and Rouse recount Quintilian's reliance on the unique physical properties of the wax tablet as a composing aid, preferring it over dictation or writing on "friendlier" surfaces because it was erasable, thus making it easy to edit and revise; moreover, the physical act of writing was *productively* slow so as to promote deliberate reflection upon diction, syntax, and thought in general (177–9).

As Bernhard Bischoff notes, the wax tablet was still in use in the Western world well into the nineteenth century—in very much the same form as its ancient counterpart—aiding the calculations of ship merchants and accountants (14). Among the latest accounts of their use, as recounted by French historian Elisabeth Lalou, was as an accounting tool used regularly in the fish market of Rouen up until 1860 (280). Were we to conduct a postmortem of the wax tablet's longevity, we would conclude that the durability and utility of this particular writing apparatus, coupled with strong traditions of cultural entrenchment and bodily habituation, contributed to a lifespan that stretched well over two millennia—seen alongside the entire constellation of writing technologies, it enjoyed a remarkably good run.

As we turn our attention to more recent times and the digital tablet computer, it is fascinating to note that although these two tablets might feel as if they existed ages apart, their respective timelines very nearly overlap: in 1888, a US patent was filed for an invention known as the telautograph, an electro-mechanical stylus that a user used on regular paper, whereupon the input was transmitted to a paired device over telegraph wires and the sender's handwriting would be replicated (Huurdeman 151–2). Although that particular technological mutation never quite gained a foothold, the origins of the more familiar contemporary iteration of the tablet can be traced back to the 1950s and early 1960s, when The RAND Corporation produced a rudimentary tablet with pen input and handwriting recognition (Lux). In 1972, computer scientist Alan Kay proposed a device called a Dynabook, aimed at children, which would help enhance their literacy skills. Before the launch of Apple's Newton in 1993, several companies in the 1980s and early 1990s launched modestly successful versions of the digital tablet: Atari, GRiD Systems, Wang, and Microsoft, along with a host of other also-rans that were not nearly as successful.

Although many of these products were intended to be marketed to a diffuse user base, they gained traction in specialized areas such as warehouse logistics, finance, education, or the medical field. The tablet's existence as a mass market, general consumer product has been rather recent, with the advent of Apple's iPad in 2010 (and similar devices close behind, including Samsung's Galaxy tablets, the Amazon Kindle Fire, and Barnes and Noble's Nook tablet, among others). Unlike prior devices that used resistive touchscreens and specialized styli for input, this recent generation of devices typically use capacitive touchscreens, which accept input directly from fingers, oftentimes allowing for intuitive gestural interface cues–pinching to zoom, swiping to scroll down a page, and the like.

In *Writing Space*, Jay David Bolter describes the wax tablet as a "secondary" writing technology, akin to "chalk boards, typewriters, stenographs, dictaphones, and so on—each fulfilling needs that could not be easily met by the dominant technology" (22). As of this writing, we might say the same of the digital tablet; for example, although I took preliminary notes on my iPad Mini (a combination of voice notes and text typed on the device's virtual keyboard), I am currently composing this chapter on my laptop and desktop computers because they afford easier production of alphabetic text. As time goes on, however, and we see increasing degree of multimodal production such that the ratio of alphabetic text to the various modes diminishes, the digital tablet might ascend to a more prominent position in the communication hierarchy. The likelihood of this ascension, however, is threatened by forces such as market saturation and device fragmentation—in other words, the overabundance of different size/specs of products ranging from full-sized tablets to hybrid phablets—and in recent economic quarters, the tablet market as a whole has been experiencing a noticeable decline in overall earnings and raw sales (Perez).

Considering the original *deltos* alongside the digital tablet invites a useful opportunity for comparison, and raises inevitable questions about the roles that materiality and agency play when our bodies interact with technologies in the communicative act. One way we can consider these two implements is in terms of how they have each contributed to changes in their respective communication environments, more specifically the relationship between body, technology, social space, and rhetorical performance. As a tool for writing and writing instruction, the wax tablet not only served directly as a technology for the production of alphabetic text, it also fit within a larger ecosystem that supported an increasingly *writerly* culture of rhetorical practice, instruction, and theorization. In other words, the tablet is one instrument among several—some material, some instructional, some conceptual—that together created a trajectory that fostered greater production of, and hence greater habituation to, the written word. Classical rhetoric historian George A. Kennedy termed this cultural shift from an emphasis on oral to literate modes of communication *letteraturizzazione*. For Kennedy, the phenomenon of *letteraturizzazione* describes what he sees as an historical pattern where the rhetorical arts transition from an emphasis on spoken to written production, and with that transition corresponding changes to the genres and social occasions associated with rhetorical performance. He explains:

> It has been a persistent characteristic of classical rhetoric in almost every stage of its history to move from primary to secondary forms, occasionally then reversing the pattern. For this phenomenon the Italian term *letteraturizzazione* has been coined. *Letteraturizzazione* is the tendency of rhetoric to shift focus from persuasion to narration, from civic to personal contexts, and from speech to literature, including poetry. (5)

A central reason for this shift, Kennedy concludes, is the formalization of rhetorical instruction, especially for younger pupils. A corresponding factor that Kennedy identifies is the decline in opportunities and occasions for civic engagement; as he argues, *letteraturizzazione* is inward facing, helping shape an individual's sense of self and the creative expression of that self. It is precisely within such a setting that the wax tablet thrived.

In the context of classical oratorical performance, the increasing adoption of *deltos* in ancient Greece helped usher in a decidedly writerly approach to a rhetorical tradition that had once placed verbal and physical components at the forefront. In one respect, this influence is obvious: the tablet was used to explore ideas in the preliminary stages (invention), to arrange the proper order of proofs and appeals (arrangement), and to refine figurative turns of phrase (style). But more than assisting with the work of those particular canons, the tablet also served as a physical repository for offloading the rhetor's memory (recall Socrates' recounting of Thamus' harangue against writing in *The Phaedrus*). And taken collectively, a culture that once placed such a premium on delivery and in-the-moment performance as the *sine qua non* of the entire rhetorical process, over time, comes to elevate the principles associated with logocentrism (McCorkle 43–4). Derrida's notion of "archi-writing," put forth in *Plato's Pharmacy*, gets at this shift: writing comes to precede speech in the Western tradition, becoming a kind of origin point where language, regardless of its ultimate form or medium, is subject to the rule of "fixedness" found in the written word.

The rhetorical body itself serves as an agent of *letteraturizzazione* in the sense that it employs its voice and gesture, its sense of social space and context, to perform what has predominantly become *textualized* discourse—the body is in a real sense supported by text, and the technologies required to produce that text, throughout the process. Beyond the boundary line of the rhetorical body lies the array of technologies called forth during the service of such actions and implicated in the writing process as well; in a similar vein, James Brown and Nathaniel Rivers contend that the QWERTY keyboard functions as a kind of externalized cognitive agent that reflects, manifests, and abets our own thoughts about what it means to communicate (223). Such technologies are amalgamations of concepts that beget designs that beget mechanisms that beget feature sets that beget habits of use that beget genres and conventions and on and on. . . . There are remarkable degrees of freedom within such circumscribed systems, but systems they remain.

For example, the medium of the wax tablet literally gave shape to the letter forms it contained, because etching wax with a stylus constrained the writer's hand so as to produce angular, wedge-like lettering (Rouse and Rouse 184). As nineteenth-century historian William Fox writes, "The style of writing on wax was about mid way between that on papyrus and that on lead; that is to say, it is marked by only an average number of curves and up-strokes" (51). Beyond that specific restriction, though, like traditional writing media of all types, the wax tablet fixes those letters in space and time; with digital tablets, however, this isn't necessarily the case, as traditional writing becomes more fluid, moves around, is able to be seen developing in real time in geographically disparate locations. Whereas Quintilian's tablet was limited by its absolute physical dimensions and slowness of the wax medium—he made rhetorical lemonade out of those constraints, suggesting that they aided in focusing the composer's thinking—the tablet computer affords its user a much greater degree of immediacy and responsiveness that reaches beyond the individual writer's physical sphere to aid in the composing process: the ability to cut and paste text; features such as autocorrect, autocomplete, or dictation-to-text applications; the ability to locate quotations residing on Internet-connected servers on an entirely different continent; or ever-increasing amounts of internal or cloud-based memory for storing large amounts of data.

The implications behind these differences are hardly matters of only speed, reach, connectivity, and convenience—through our interactions with such devices, they limit or delimit compositional possibilities at the level of conceptualization and physical interaction. Rouse and Rouse remind us of how both interdependent tool and maker end up becoming imbricated in such a relationship, the tablet serving as a stalwart accessory hanging always from the scribe's belt like an additional appendage and making its way into the very thoughts and language of its user in the process:

> Tablets are kept constantly at hand by emperors, chancellors, authors, students, to jot down what occurred to them lest it be forgotten. Wax and stylus become metaphors for giving "shape" (words) to one's thoughts, and a writer's stylus becomes his "style." The wax tablet affected letter form, affected literary forms, provided instantly recognized metaphors, participated intimately in the process of education and composition. (188)

The tablet as it exists today constitutes a quasi-return to the rhetorical dynamics we associate with the early classical sophistic era: because of the multimodal facility of this new device, it has the capacity to reintroduce embodied verbal and physical components (often in real time) back into our communicative practices. Because of its expanded reach and connectivity, the digital tablet has, comparatively speaking, greater potential to facilitate public, civic-oriented communication. As Kennedy acknowledges, we occasionally reverse what he classifies as an historical pattern of *letteraturizzazione*. But to suggest this return brings us back to some sort of pristine original state of rhetorical embodiment is something of a fiction, especially given that these embodied components have now become augmented by the very technologies that once alienated our bodies—as Thomas Wolfe cautioned us, you can't go home again (nor should we necessarily even want to). In some cases, this augmentation affords interesting new dimensions that reconfigure classical rhetorical practice, as Kalin and Frith have argued:

> Whereas the classical art of memory relies upon a more figurative sense of movement wherein the rhetor imagines herself walking through her memory palace, applications like Foursquare, Facebook, and Instagram help to make this movement literal: Users find their way into places and memories while on the move through city space. And importantly, the mobile applications help turn these spatial and mnemonic activities into a digital archive, but one that acts more like a hybrid memory palace, combining digital and physical memories, digital and physical places. This hybrid memory palace combines both memory and access to memory. (232)

Although we might well be tempted to view this not-quite-return enthusiastically and positively in the sense that newer digital technologies offer us a value-add to extend more of our bodies (and the long-standing rhetorical traditions shaping those bodies) back into the communications sphere anew, it can also reinscribe—perhaps even more subtly so—traditional practices of silencing and marginalization onto those bodies.

The body figures into writing in ways that we don't always recognize or acknowledge; in fact, we often work deliberately to forget it, striving instead to frame our writing selves as brains in jars, Enlightenment-era ascetics dead set on denying the realities of the flesh. And yet writing is the result of embodied human endeavor at every turn: the inception of ideas generated during a walk in a neighborhood park; the act of putting pencil to paper to jot down rough notes; opening Google Docs to flesh out those notes with deliberate finger movements; the graphic designers and printer operators who bring the thing to life by throwing their wrists, backs, and shoulders into their labors. The French feminist philosophers who launched *l'écriture féminine* movement decades ago argued for a body-centered conceptualization of women's writing, one that is characterized by fluidity, openness, connection. In fact, Hélène Cixous's manifesto "Laugh of the Medusa" in some ways anticipates the multivocal, networked, embodied nature of writing that the digital tablet portends:

> Her writing can only keep going, without ever inscribing or discerning contours. [. . .] She lets the other language speak—the language of 1,000 tongues which knows neither enclosure nor death. [. . .] Her language does not contain, it carries; it does not hold back, it makes possible. (358)

Of course, lofty a sentiment as it is, Cixous's vision of a radically open and inclusive philosophy of writing risks becoming little more than marketing hyperbole so long as we continue to adopt composing practices that favor deeply entrenched logocentric ways of thinking and producing.

If I were pressed to generate a forecast, I don't think the digital tablet will have anywhere near the staying power of its waxen forebear; it will, I believe, serve as a transitional device of sorts, one that signals an increasing awareness of the whole body's reemerging role in the communicative act. We are already beginning to see the green shoots of technologies that lie beyond the tablet's form factor, devices of various shapes and sizes that enlist a far greater range of embodied input from their user.

Our next-generation technologies, if you believe the futurists and forecasters of the tech sector, will comprise a personal area network of interrelated wearable devices—early examples include the Apple Watch, the HTC Vive virtual reality display, or the ill-fated Google Glass—that incorporate what User Experience developers refer to as Natural User Interfaces, or NUI. The interface logic of NUI, which seeks to incorporate "intuitive" gestural, vocal, and other physical inputs into its feature set, works to render an entire array of technologies invisible for the end user. And even though there seems to be great potential for NUI-based environments to promote a rich, robust culture of body-centric rhetorical production, this culture must be actively encouraged, at least in part, through properly engaged pedagogy and scholarship so as not to perpetuate consumer-driven passivity.

The state of technology as of this writing makes the tablet and its near-relatives better suited for producing conversational, ephemeral content such as tweets or video clips on Instagram than for more substantive (and potentially more meaningful) production tasks. Promoting an active culture of production—and beyond that, a critically reflective, rhetorically aware culture of production—is an essential key to achieving this goal: from a pedagogical standpoint, this means assigning innovative multimodal composing projects, encouraging hacks to the tools at hand, producing similar work ourselves. Taking into account how the body uses—and is used by—these new devices, genres of communication, and interface paradigms is a crucial component of empowering students as active users of their technologies. A recognition of this return to embodied (albeit digitally supported) rhetorical practice has implications for how we develop newly emerging genres and forms of communication using these types of devices, as well as how we teach students to utilize these new technologies in rhetorically effective ways.

Works Cited

Bischoff, Bernhard. *Latin Palaeography: Antiquity and the Middle Ages*. Cambridge UP, 1990.

Bolter, Jay David. *Writing Space: Computers, Hypertext, and the Remediation of Print*. 2nd ed., Lawrence Erlbaum, 2001.

Brown, James J., Jr., and Nathaniel A. Rivers. "Encomium of QWERTY." *Rhetoric, Through Everyday Things*, edited by Casey Boyle and Scot Barnett. U of Alabama P, 2016, pp. 212–25.

Cixous, Hélène. "Laugh of the Medusa." *Feminisms: An Anthology of Literary Theory and Criticism*, edited by Robyn R. Warhol and Diane Price Herndl. Rutgers UP, 1997, pp. 347–62.

Derrida, Jacques. "Plato's Pharmacy." *Dissemination*, translated by Barbara Johnson, Chicago UP, 1981, pp. 61–172.

Fox, William Sherwood. *The Johns Hopkins Tabellae Defixionum*. The Johns Hopkins UP, 1912.

Giuseppe, Robert Anthony. "Ancient Sumeria." *International World History Project*. 2003, http://history-world.org/sumeria.htm. Accessed 25 April 2017.

Huurdeman, Anton A. *The Worldwide History of Telecommunications*. John Wiley & Sons. 2003.

Kalin, Jason, and Jordan Frith. "Wearing the City: Memory P(a)laces, Smartphones, and the Rhetorical Invention of Embodied Space." *Rhetoric Society Quarterly*, vol. 46, no. 3, 2016, pp. 222–35.

Kay, Alan C. "A Personal Computer for Children of All Ages." *Vision and Reality of Hypertext and Graphical User Interfaces*, mprove.de/diplom/gui/kay72.html. Accessed 20 April 2017.

Kennedy, George. *Classical Rhetoric and Its Christian and Secular Tradition from Ancient to Modern Times*. 2nd ed., U of North Carolina P, 1999.

Lalou E. "Inventaire des Tablettes Médiévales et Présentation Genérale." *Les Tablettes à écrire de l'Antiquité à l'Epoque Moderne*, 1992, pp. 233–88.

Lux, Alan. "Yesterday's Tomorrow: The Origins of the Tablet." *Computer History Museum*, 17 December 2014, computerhistory.org/atchm/yesterdays-tomorrows-the-origins-of-the-tablet/. Accessed 19 Nov. 2016.

McCorkle, Ben. *Rhetorical Delivery as Technological Discourse: A Cross-Historical Study*. Southern Illinois UP, 2012.

Montague, Andrew Philip, Ed. *Selected Letters of M. Tullius Cicero*. Eldredge & Brother, 1890.

Payton, Robert. "The Ulu Burun Writing-Board Set." *Anatolian Studies*, vol. 41, 1991, pp. 99–106.

Perez, Sarah. "Overall Tablet Market Declined By As Much As 10 Percent In 2015." *TechCrunch*, 1 Feb. 2016, techcrunch.com/2016/02/01/overall-tablet-market-declined-by-as-much-as-10-percent-in-2015/. Accessed 19 Nov. 2016.

Rouse, R.H., and Rouse, M.A. "Wax Tablets." *Language and Communication*, vol. 9, no. 2/3, 1989, pp. 175–91.

Smith, William. "Tabulae." *A Dictionary of Greek and Roman Antiquities*. London, 1875, pp. 1091–1092.

Tsien, Tsuen-Hsuin. *Paper and Printing, Science and Civilisation in China*, edited by Joseph Needham, vol. 5, part 1. Cambridge UP, 1985.

3

MULTIMODALITY BEFORE AND BEYOND THE COMPUTER

Jason Palmeri

In many ways, digital writing and rhetoric has been a field oriented to the present—a field focused first and foremost on engaging *current* technological changes arising from developments in computing technologies. Yet, when we build our pedagogies and theories primarily in response to the latest technological tools embraced by a patriarchal, racist, capitalist system, we risk exaggerating the potential positive effects of new technologies while at the same time excluding the voices (past and present) of those who compose via other means (Baca; Banks; Haas; Shipka, *Toward a Composition Made Whole*). To develop and enact transformational digital writing pedagogies, then, it's necessary that we look *before* and *beyond* the computer to historicize our work. To this end, this chapter reviews and synthesizes the diverse ways digital writing scholars have recovered past multimodal pedagogies and composing practices to reimagine digital writing pedagogy in the present. In addition to making a case for how historical scholarship can enable us to rethink how we study, teach, and practice multimodal composing, I also point to directions for future work—arguing especially for the need for the field to embrace digital, multimodal methods of historiography.

The Emergence of "Multimodality" as a Keyword in Digital Writing Studies

Before articulating how multimodality has functioned as a theoretical framework for historical inquiry in digital writing studies, I first pause to historicize the *kairotic* moment of the early twenty-first century in which digital writing scholars first employed the terminology of "multimodality" to analyze how digital texts make use of diverse semiotic modes of meaning-making—linguistic, audio, visual, spatial (Ball; Kress; George; New London Group; Selfe). In articulating the value of multimodality as a theoretical frame for teaching writing in the digital age, digital writing scholars drew upon the work of the New London Group and one of its most prominent members, Gunther Kress. Although the New London Group explicitly pointed to the proliferation of digital writing technologies as an exigence for literacy teachers to pay more attention to semiotic modes beyond the linguistic, they also importantly asserted that "all meaning making is Multimodal. All written text is also a process of Visual Design" (New London Group 29); in other words, all forms of writing—whether by hand, by typewriter, or by computer—involve a combination of alphabetic and visual modes of communication. Extending this point, Kress argues that all meaning-making is multimodal because the human body itself has "a wide range of means of engagement with the visual world. These we call our 'senses'. . . . That, from the beginning guarantees the multimodality of our semiotic world" (184). In this sense, multimodality is as old as human communication itself, and Western culture's tendency to privilege alphabetic text over other forms of meaning is a relatively new and limited vision of how communication works. In this way, Kress and the New London Group's capacious understanding of multimodality as a fundamental aspect of embodied human communication opens up space for digital writing scholars to explore how our approaches to contemporary digital writing might be informed by the much longer history of multimodal composing practices.

As we revisit the historical legacy of the New London Group in the field, we should also remember that the New London Group's work emerged from the collaborative dialogue of a group of international scholars primarily concerned with how K-12 literacy education needed to be reimagined in response to cultural, ideological, and technological shifts in an era of globalization. Given the global view of the New London Group members, their articulation of the value of multiple semiotic modes of meaning-making was deeply connected to their assertion of the value of multilingual approaches to English pedagogy that resist the hegemony of "Standard English" and indeed the hegemony of any form of English as a communication medium.[1] In this way, the theoretical framework of multimodality ultimately asks digital writing scholars to actively resist institutional hierarchies that privilege (standardized) English over other languages, alphabetic text over other semiotic modes, new media over old media, college instruction over K-12 education. In other words, the New London Group call us to imagine and enact an inclusive literacy pedagogy (K-College) that enables students and teachers to draw on a wide range of semiotic modalities, languages, and technologies in their work.

Recovering Multimodal Writing Pedagogies (K-College)

As multimodality came to prominence in the field of digital writing and rhetoric, scholars worked increasingly to historicize how past writing teachers had engaged and/or ignored non-alphabetic forms of composing in their classrooms. In one of the first articles in writing studies to reference the New London Group's work as a rationale for teaching visual composing in the writing classroom, Diana George offers a compelling history of the often limiting ways that English teachers have engaged visual images primarily as objects for analysis or prompts to spur alphabetic writing. George demonstrates resonances between how 1960s English teachers responded to television and how contemporary teachers respond to digital multimedia texts. She also recovers the many ways in which past composition textbooks—from the current-traditional *Writing with Purpose* to the cultural studies *Ways with Reading*—have included activities in writing *about* images. Although George finds merit in these past approaches to teaching visual analysis, she argues that this narrow focus on *reading* images has unnecessarily constrained our ability to engage students in composing compelling visual arguments—arguing powerfully that "our students have a much richer imagination for what we might accomplish with the visual than our journals have yet to address" (12).

While George's history of multimodal pedagogy focused primarily on the visual, Cynthia Selfe's article, "The Movement of Air, the Breath of Meaning," recovers the history of aural forms of composing in the field. In her work, Selfe tells a complex historical narrative that emphasizes how rhetorical instruction in US colleges focused primarily on speaking until the later nineteenth century when rhetorical oratory courses were replaced with first year "composition" courses that focused nearly exclusively on alphabetic writing instruction. As Selfe reviews the history of twentieth-century writing instruction, she notes that considerations of aurality have largely been limited to theorizing "voice" as a metaphor for alphabetic writing, to engaging audio texts as objects of analysis, or to employing audio recording as a method for providing feedback on student writing. Like George, Selfe concludes that compositionists have too narrow a vision of the role of multimodality in the writing class and she points to contemporary students' experiments with digital audio production as inspiration for how we as a field might expand our purview to value multiple modalities of communication.

Writing in a moment when "multimodality" was still a relatively new term in the field, Selfe and George's histories understandably focused on critiquing the often limited ways that past writing scholars and teachers had engaged non-alphabetic forms of composing—laying the groundwork for arguments that positioned the "multimodal turn" as a novel approach unique to the contemporary moment. Yet, in seeking to establish the innovativeness of multimodality as a theoretical construct, early advocates of the multimodal turn (George; Selfe; Yancey) tended to reinforce the common assumption that the interrelated fields of English and Writing Studies have traditionally been focused on alphabetic writing—an assumption that has led many to question whether writing scholars have the disciplinary expertise needed to engage students in composing robustly multimodal texts.

Countering this tendency to position multimodal composing as a new, largely digital phenomenon within the field, Shipka's *Toward a Composition Made Whole* grounds contemporary multimodal pedagogy in relation to the "communications approach" to writing instruction that flourished briefly in the 1940s and 1950s in the early days of the *Conference on College Composition and Communication*. Drawing on primary sources as well as the work of other composition historians (George and Trimbur; Heyda), Shipka articulates how the "communications approach" (integrating instruction in writing, speaking, and multimedia) offers an alternative path that we might build upon to develop "a discipline dedicated to examining the communicative process *as a dynamic whole*" by engaging the "complex relationship between writing and other modes of representation" (28). In recovering the history of multimodal communication pedagogy before the digital era, Shipka seeks to remind scholars that the multimodal and the digital are *not* synonymous—that limiting students to composing multimodal texts only with digital tools risks "missing or undervaluing the meaning-making and learning potentials . . . of still other representation systems and technologies" (11).

Although Shipka usefully recovers the 1940s multimodal communications approach to teaching writing, she positions the 1960s and 1970s process era in Writing Studies as a moment in which the field problematically re-narrowed its emphasis to alphabetic writing. In contrast, my own *Remixing Composition* looks to this period to recover ways in which multimodality has always already been a central foundation of writing research, theory, and pedagogy. Offering a revisionist reading of canonical and lesser-known theorists of process-based and rhetorical approaches to writing instruction, I demonstrate that composition scholars have long studied and taught writing as an embodied, multimodal process that shares affinities with visual and performing arts. Challenging the notion that multimodal composing must necessarily represent a departure from traditional writing instruction, I draw on the archive of process-era composition scholarship to demonstrate how multimodal composing activities can enhance students' invention and revision of more traditional alphabetic texts. At the same time, I also recover the more radical work of composition scholars in this period who employed "new media" (Super 8 cameras, Xerox machines, tape recorders) to challenge the field's tendency to privilege linear alphabetic text over other forms of knowledge making. Finally, I articulate and practice a remix methodology of historiography that resists rigid periodization and categorization in favor of creative sampling and juxtaposition of past and present pedagogies and technologies—arguing that a remix methodology can better enable us to draw useful pedagogical inspiration from our disciplinary past.

While *Remixing Composition* emphasizes productive ways that contemporary digital writing teachers can build on past multimodal pedagogies in the field, Kelly Ritter's *Reframing the Subject* sounds an important cautionary note about how our field's multimodal past continues to influence the present. In her work, Ritter recovers how 1940s and 1950s writing teachers employed instructional films in service of current-traditional pedagogies that reinforced classist, sexist hierarchies. Ritter carefully articulates the complex network of governmental and corporate power that enabled the rise of the current-traditional instructional film, and then she powerfully demonstrates how a similar nexus of power is encouraging many contemporary designers of massively open online courses (MOOCs) to employ digital video in similarly problematic ways. Ultimately, Ritter's work compellingly reveals how historical scholarship can help us develop a critical perspective on contemporary multimodal pedagogies.

Thus far, most histories of multimodal pedagogy have tended to rely on case study methodologies that emphasize close reading of a relatively limited number of texts in a relatively narrow period of time. Although such case study methodologies can reveal important critical insights, they can also make it difficult to grasp how multimodal pedagogies have evolved over time. To counter this limitation, Ben McCorkle and I have recently published a brief "distant reading" (Moretti) of nearly 800 articles about multimodal and "new media" pedagogies in 100 years of *English Journal*, the longest running pedagogy journal in the field. Complicating Ritter's narrative about the conservative uses of instructional film in the post-Second World War period, our study points to the 1930s as a radically innovative period in which numerous English instructors sought to engage students in *producing* both films and radio broadcasts (sometimes using professional tools, sometimes using makeshift approximations). Our quantitative coding and data visualization demonstrates that multimodal production pedagogies tend to flourish when media are new and then wane when media become more established; for example, the initial burst of interest in student film and radio production in the 1930s ultimately declined in the post-Second World War period as teachers increasingly positioned radio programs and films solely as texts to be analyzed; yet, interest in student film production picked up again somewhat in the late 1960s and early 1970s when more inexpensive consumer cameras, such as the Super 8, came on the scene. In this way, we suggest that moments when media are new present opportunities for multimodal pedagogical innovation, but we must carefully guard against a disciplinary tendency to revert to conservative models of textual analysis once a medium becomes more established.

In addition to coding trends in media production pedagogies, we also track the evolution of ideological assumptions about multimodal pedagogy over time. On the one hand, we note that the argument that multimodal media are "engaging for students" because they "expand audiences beyond the teacher" is both ubiquitous and persistent across the twentieth century—a finding that can urge us all to be more humble when we make these kinds of claims about contemporary multimodal pedagogies (McCorkle and Palmeri 20). At the same time, we note a persistent commonplace that multimodal activities are most valuable for enhancing the teaching of traditional alphabetic reading and writing—a commonplace that has tended to constrain our imagination about how new media might radically transform our pedagogical practices.[2]

When we zoom out on the history of multimodal pedagogy before the computer era, we can understand that the discipline of English (from which Writing Studies arises, at least in part) has a long history of engaging students in both producing and analyzing multimodal texts—a history that we can draw upon as we design pedagogies in response to contemporary digital writing technologies. At the same time, the discipline of English also has a long history of constraining new media by seeking to use them to reinforce traditional and often oppressive pedagogical practices—a history that we must remain vigilant to avoid replicating.

Multimodal Composing Histories Beyond the Classroom

Although histories of multimodal writing instruction in formal educational settings can be useful for helping us rethink contemporary pedagogical practices, we must remember that formal schooling (as Ritter compellingly argues) is often a deeply conservative enterprise. If we seek to develop multimodal writing pedagogies that disrupt dominant power relations, it's necessary that we look beyond the classroom and beyond our mostly alphabetic archives to find inspiration for pedagogical practices that challenge "business as usual" in the university. To this end, numerous digital writing scholars have turned to exploring how diverse multimodal art traditions and cultural practices can offer theoretical perspectives on writing pedagogies that disrupt many of the ideological assumptions of traditional academic writing instruction.

In *English Composition as a Happening*, Geoffery Sirc works to excavate the implicit theories of composition and writing in the work of canonical avant-garde and punk artists associated (directly or implicitly) with the happenings movement, including Kaprow, Duchamp, Pollock, and the Sex Pistols. Sirc draws on the avant-garde tradition to foreground not the finished product on the page, but rather the embodied process of "composition—as a record of tracings, of gestures, of a body moving through life" (111). Sirc's work demonstrates how the history of avant-garde art and punk music can inspire teachers to design pedagogies that engage students in composing with diverse materials (visual, alphabetic, audio, gestural) to create experimental texts that radically challenge academic genre conventions. While Sirc's work powerfully emphasizes the role of the body in multimodal composing, he focuses his attention almost wholly on the embodied processes of white, male artists. On the one hand, Sirc's work is radical in its challenge to the privileging of "coherent" print texts in the field, yet it is also deeply conservative in its reification of white male "genius."

Extending Sirc's work recovering avant-garde writing pedagogies, Jeff Rice's *Rhetoric of Cool* offers an alternative genealogy of the field of composition studies that seeks to "reimagine ourselves and our field entirely" (157), asking how the field would look different if it had paid more attention to various "cool" forms of art practice proliferating in the year 1963. Challenging the ways in which the 1963 revival of rhetorical approaches to writing pedagogy focused narrowly on linear, persuasive argument in print forms, Rice recovers the work of a range of experimental artists, writers, and theorists including Burroughs, Baraka, Anger, and McLuhan (among others). From this archive, Rice develops a vision of digital multimodal writing pedagogy that emphasizes nonlinear juxtaposition of found materials—the cut-up, the montage, the collage, the remix. Ultimately, Rice draws on avant-garde traditions to argue that students should be challenged to compose associative multimodal texts that resist closure—texts that seek less to persuade and more to invite audience participation in the meaning-making process. Although Rice usefully moves beyond the Eurocentric art canon to engage meaningfully with the work of Amiri Baraka, he still problematically enacts a "great man" school of historiography that situates Baraka's work almost exclusively in relation to other canonical white male artists and theorists.

In contrast, Carmen Kynard's *Vernacular Insurrections* offers a vision of multimodal writing pedagogy grounded in the collective work of the Black Arts Movement in which Baraka played a key (but also limited) role. Looking at the activist artistic practice of visual artists, writers, and performers associated with the Black Arts Movement (or BAM), Kynard articulates how BAM offered a vision of multimodal pedagogy that "redefined art to be functional and relevant to the lives of black people" (123). While Kynard discusses some prominent BAM artists and writers, she focuses less on individual stars in the movement and more on the collective activist work members did to challenge racist art institutions and establish alternative art spaces (122). Here we see a vision of avant-garde writing pedagogy that engages students not in pursuing an individual aesthetic vision, but instead in working collectively to compose multimodal texts that challenge racist power structures.

Importantly, Kynard also recovers how the art practice of the Black Arts Movement influenced the work of Geneva Smitherman and other members of CCCC Black Caucus who were instrumental in advocating for the organization's 1974 "Students' Right to Their Own Language" resolution. Kynard demonstrates powerfully that

> Smitherman's work unfolded how BAM could propel new writing and composing possibilities not just for artists and activists, but for students in English classrooms, thus launching an attack on the field's prior definition of what counted as writing and who counted as writers. (123)

Although Smitherman's work is most known for transforming how we engage with linguistic diversity in the writing classroom, it's important to note that she also powerfully critiqued the limitations of alphabetic ways of knowing and argued in favor of a critical multimodal pedagogy that integrated speaking, writing, and visual composing (Palmeri 72–9). In many ways, Kynard's work offers an important corrective to my own discussion of Smitherman in *Remixing Composition* in which I problematically positioned her work in conversation mostly with other well-known white scholars—failing to account for the ways in which Smitherman's multimodal pedagogy must necessarily also be historicized in relation to the collective resistance and art practice of Black people both within and beyond the academy.

Further demonstrating the importance of situating multimodal writing pedagogies within particular cultural, historical, and ideological contexts, Adam Banks's *Digital Griots* offers an important challenge to the tendency of many white scholars (myself included) to deploy "remix" and "sampling" as a theoretical lens for understanding multimodal composing histories and practices without engaging or acknowledging how the idea of remix arises in many ways from African American hip-hop and storytelling traditions. For Banks, to speak of remix without engaging the historical work of African American DJs is to position one's scholarship in "the long line of those who have 'taken our blues and gone' as Langston Hughes would call it" (13). In contrast, Banks' work historicizes contemporary practices of digital remix in relation to a long history of sampling in African American culture among DJs, mixtape makers, storytellers, and preachers who used diverse technological tools to repurpose existing materials to move audiences and challenge racist structures. In insisting on historicizing how contemporary theories of remix arise out of historic and ongoing African American rhetorical practices, Banks ultimately works to "build theories, pedagogies, and practices of multimedia writing that honor the traditions and thus the people who are still too often not present in our classrooms, on our faculties, in our scholarship" (14). By theorizing digital pedagogy through a recovery of African American traditions of technological storytelling, Banks outlines a multimodal pedagogy of community engagement that moves beyond the university classroom to engage diverse community members in composing multimodal texts that both build upon and extend their own cultural traditions of meaning making.

In another powerful argument for the value of centering the voices of the marginalized in conversations about multimodal writing pedagogy, Damian Baca's *Mestiz@ Scripts, Digital Migration, and the Territories of Writing* reclaims pre-colonial Aztec codices as a powerful multi-modal inscription system whose influence persists in contemporary Mestiz@ cultural production. Drawing on the work of Anzaldúa and Mignolo (among others), Baca demonstrates that the imposition of alphabetic literacy in the Americas constituted an act of colonial violence and he argues for a re-imagination of histories of composition and writing that starts with indigenous pictograph rather than the alphabetic letter—a vision that refuses to position alphabetic literacy as privileged over other forms of knowledge-making and that also radically challenges the notion that multimodal writing practices are "new." In this way, Baca's work argues that our teaching of multimodal composing risks reinforcing settler colonialist hierarchies unless we center the histories and ongoing composing practices of indigenous composers who have long resisted disembodied, alphabetic-centric hierarchies of knowledge.

Further demonstrating the relevance of indigenous traditions of making for contemporary digital pedagogy, Angela Haas has articulated how the historic and ongoing tradition of American Indian wampum belts can be recognized as an alternative genealogy of hypermedia composing—a genealogy that challenges white, patriarchal narratives of the development of multimedia hypertext. In her work, Haas importantly critiques the conflation of the digital with the computer, arguing that " 'digital' refers to our fingers, our digits, one of the primary ways (along with our ears and eyes) through which we make sense of the world and with which we write into the world. All writing is digital" (84). By centering digital writing scholarship on embodied cultural practices of making rather than on particular computer-based tools, Haas's work calls on digital writing teachers to resist reinforcing technological progress narratives and instead engage students in diverse forms of associative, multimodal composing grounded within particular cultural traditions.

Haas' evocation of the digital as referring to the work of the human hand solidifies one of the key insights that runs across all the histories I review here: we can gain a more capacious and inclusive understanding of digital writing pedagogy if we center our attention on the embodied act of composing with diverse materials rather than on dominant narratives of computer technologies. While it can be transformative to highlight embodied processes of composing in our work, we must also be careful not to position the embodied act of making as a kind of individualist artistic genius—always remembering that "what any body is and is able to do . . . cannot be disentangled from the media we use or from the times and cultures in and technologies with which we consume and produce texts" (Wysocki 8). When we come to recognize multimodal composing as both deeply embodied and culturally situated, we can work to resist narrow, digital-centric visions of multimodal pedagogy in favor of a broader, historicized view that enables students and teachers to bring all their diverse culturally situated, semiotic resources to the table.

Digital, Multimodal Methods of Historiography

Despite calling for embodied, multimodal re-imaginings of how we theorize and teach writing, the scholarship I've discussed so far largely takes conventional print form in which alphabetic text is privileged over other forms of meaning making. In recent years, however, digital writing historians have sought to compose scholarship that enacts the very kinds of embodied multimodal composing that they advocate. For example, while Alexander and Rhodes's recent book, *On Multimodality*, takes print form, it prominently features numerous digital image collages that enact their vision of a "*historicized* and *poeticized* understanding of new media" (69) that can open up our conceptions of the kinds of multimodal texts writing scholars and teachers might compose. Challenging the common tendency to ask students to remediate traditional print genres with new media tools, Alexander and Rhodes recover the work of Guy Debord and the Situationist movement as a possible inspiration for a more disruptive praxis of multimodal writing pedagogy. Offering a queer reimagining of the situationist practice of *detournement*, Alexander and Rhodes demonstrate how teachers and students can tactically manipulate photos in ways that disrupt normative visions of gender and sexuality—importantly "showing not telling" (Ball) about queer multimodal disruption by presenting a variety of manipulated images that demonstrate the embodied queer "excess" of their own collaborative writing partnership.

In Rhodes and Alexander's recent born-digital book, *Techne: Queer Meditations on the Writing Self*, they more fully demonstrate what a multimodal queer practice of historiography might look like. Placing the collaborative queer art practice of Jean Cocteau in dialogue with Sara Ahmed's articulation of queer phenomenology, Rhodes and Alexander argue that Cocteau's work offers a vision that can enable "our composing, our multimodal poeticizing, to be disruptive, even to disorient—perhaps, in a word, to *queer*." Importantly, Rhodes and Alexander don't just call for a queer practice of *disorientation*, but they radically enact *disorientation* in a robustly multimodal webtext that blends words, images, and sounds in associative, nonlinear ways—offering complex, multilayered stories of their own queer life histories that resist simplistic models of identity and narrative closure.

In another example of historical scholarship that not only analyzes but also enacts avant-garde art practice, Susan Delagrange's interactive webtext, "*Wunderkammer*, Cornell, and the Visual Canon of Arrangement," presents a multimodal argument for a digital pedagogy that emphasizes composing as a deeply embodied process of juxtaposing and rearranging found materials. Not only does Delagrange draw theoretical inspiration from sixteenth *wunderkammer* and twentieth century assemblage art, she presents her historical argument as a digital "cabinet of wonders" in which images and words are juxtaposed in complex and ambiguous ways that open up diverse interpretations. Furthermore, Delagrange followed up her initial work with a reflective webtext, "When Revision is Redesign," in which she details the complex, iterative process of composing historical scholarship that enacts imagistic juxtaposition as a method of knowledge making. Pointing to the limitations of composing multimodal histories in alphabetic print media, Delagrange suggests that we might best understand how avant-garde art traditions can inform digital pedagogy if we ourselves work to compose born-digital historical scholarship that challenges alphabetic print conventions.

Further showing how digital multimodal composing can help us re-see histories of writing, a recent born-digital collection, *Reconstructing the Archive*, features a variety of digital video engagements with archival writing practices. Jody Shipka's video chapter, "On Estate Sales, Archives, and the Matter of Making Things," offers a complexly layered reimaging of a series of mid-century scrapbooks composed by an everyday woman otherwise forgotten by official history. Shipka's video highlights her own embodied process of engaging with the multimodal scrapbook archive, and makes an important call for multimodal writing historians to move past official archives to explore everyday archives of multimodal composing found in unlikely places (such as estate sales). Shipka's video also documents a collective project in which she invites diverse scholars to create multimodal reconstructions or reimaginings of texts found in her scrapbook archive. Challenging the common tendency of historians to attempt to stabilize the meaning of archives by writing about them in solo-authored alphabetic text, Shipka repositions the archive as a site for collaborative multimodal art practice—suggesting that historical scholars might best understand multimodal archives if we compose our own diverse multimodal texts in response to them.

In another contribution to *Reconstructing the Archives*, Trisha Campbell creates a video remix of the life and work of Josephine Miles—a compositionist and poetry scholar who developed a deeply embodied, materialist vision of both composition pedagogy and quantitative textual analysis. Refusing the position of a distant, "objective" historian, Miles performs a creative monologue based on her archival research into Miles' life and work—carefully layering archival images over her own embodied performance. In this way, Campbell seeks to highlight the "resonant entanglement between . . . [her] voice and Miles's voice, between the digital and the body." Not only does Campbell make a powerful argument for the value of reclaiming Miles's deeply embodied approach to composition and textual research, but she also demonstrates how historians can employ digital video to better highlight the ways in which their own embodied experiences influence how they locate and make sense of archival materials. In this way, Campbell shows the potential of born-digital, multimodal scholarship to radically challenge common assumptions about historiographical methods.

In addition to re-seeing history through creative multimodal art practice, we also should work to make greater use digital methods of textual analysis—text mining, topic modeling, digital mapping—that can enable us to visualize trends in larger historical archives over time (McCorkle and Palmeri; Miller; Moretti; Mueller). By quantitatively coding large historical data sets (with a mix of human and machine reading), we can potentially add more complexity to our understanding of multimodal pedagogical histories. While distant reading may enable to ask new questions of larger swathes of archival data, we must remember too that it—like all ways of knowing—is deeply embodied and culturally situated. Large digitized archives tend to privilege the knowledge of the powerful; furthermore, any quantitative coding scheme or machine reading technology that scholars develop will be deeply influenced by their own embodied experiences. The point of embracing digital, multimodal methods of historiography is most certainly not to arrive at a definitive history, but rather to open up more complex, multivalent and (perhaps even) contradictory stories we might tell about our multimodal writing pedagogies past and present.

Looking Back, Looking Forward

In this chapter, I've demonstrated that historical scholarship about multimodality has played an invaluable role in helping the field of digital writing and rhetoric develop more capacious, inclusive visions of digital writing pedagogy; yet, I've also suggested that historical scholarship can lead us to be wary of how multimodality can be employed for conservative, repressive ends. In many ways, to study the history of multimodal writing pedagogies is to revisit a litany of calls for radical disruption in academy that have gone largely unheeded. I suggest one reason this has been the case is that much scholarship in in English and Writing Studies has continued to be governed by alphabetic, print conventions. The fact that I'm writing this chapter about multimodality in a traditional print volume is a case in point. Yet, when I review the born-digital multimodal work of scholars such as Rhodes, Alexander, Shipka, Delagrange, and Campbell (and others) that radically foregrounds embodied forms of knowledge-making, when I find myself working on a collaborative historical book project that simply cannot be contained in alphabetic print, when I see more and more scholarly venues opening up where such robustly multimodal work can be published, I'm given hope that *this time* the "multimodal turn" might really have the momentum to resist those ever-present, conservative disciplinary forces that have for too long constrained our work.

Notes

1. For a useful discussion and visual timeline of how multimodal, multilingual, translingual, and transmodal pedagogical approaches intersect in the field, see Horner, Selfe, and Lockridge.
2. At this point, McCorkle and I have only published a brief snapshot of our findings in *English Journal*; we are currently at work on numerous multimodal webtexts and a born-digital book that more fully represent the complexities of our archive.

Works Cited

Alexander, Jonathan, and Jacqueline Rhodes. *On Multimodality: New Media and Composition Studies.* NCTE, 2014.

Baca, Damian. *Mestiz@ Scripts, Digital Migrations, and the Territories of Writing.* Palgrave Macmillan, 2008.

Ball, Cheryl E. "Show Not Tell: The Value of New Media Scholarship." *Computers and Composition,* vol. 21, no. 4, 2004, pp. 403–25.

Banks, Adam J. *Digital Griots: African American Rhetoric in a Multimedia Age.* Southern Illinois UP, 2011.

Campbell, Trisha. "I Am Josephine Miles: A Digital Reprocessing." *Provocations: Reconstructing the Archive,* edited by Patrick W. Berry, Gail E. Hawisher, and Cynthia L. Selfe. Computers and Composition Digital Press/Utah State UP, 2016, ccdigitalpress.org/reconstructingthearchive/campbell.html. Accessed 2 July 2017.

Delagrange, Susan H. "When Revision is Redesign: Key Questions for Digital Scholarship." *Kairos: A Journal of Rhetoric, Technology, and Pedagogy,* vol. 14, no. 1, 2009, kairos.technorhetoric.net/14.1/inventio/delagrange/. Accessed 2 July 2017.

———. "*Wunderkammer,* Cornell, and the Visual Canon of Arrangement." *Kairos: A Journal of Rhetoric, Technology, and Pedagogy,* vol. 13, no. 2, 2009, technorhetoric.net/13.2/topoi/delagrange/. Accessed 2 July 2017.

George, Diana. "From Analysis to Design: Visual Communication in the Teaching of Writing." *College Composition and Communication,* vol. 54, no. 1, 2002, pp. 11–39.

George, Diana, and John Trimbur. "The 'Communication Battle,' or Whatever Happened to the 4th C?" *College Composition and Communication,* vol. 50, no. 4, 1999, pp. 682–98.

Haas, Angela M. "Wampum as Hypertext: An American Indian Intellectual Tradition of Multimedia Theory and Practice." *Studies in American Indian Literatures,* vol. 19, no. 4, 2007, pp. 77–100.

Heyda, John. "Fighting Over Freshman English: CCCC's Early Years and the Turf Wars of the 1950s." *College Composition and Communication,* vol. 50, no. 4, 1999, pp. 663–81.

Horner, Bruce, Selfe, Cynthia and Tim Lockridge. *Translinguality, Transmodality, and Difference: Exploring Dispositions and Change in Language and Learning.* Enculturation/Intermezzo. 2015. intermezzo.enculturation.net/01/ttd-horner-selfe-lockridge/index.htm. Accessed 2 July 2017.

Kress, Gunther. "Multimodality." *Multiliteracies: Literacy Learning and the Design of Social Futures,* edited by Bill Cope, and Mary Kalantzis. Routledge, 1999, pp. 179–200.

Kynard, Carmen. *Vernacular Insurrections: Race, Black Protest, and the New Century in Composition-Literacies Studies.* SUNY, 2013.

McCorkle, Ben and Jason Palmeri. "Lessons from History: Teaching with Technology in 100 Years of *English Journal.*" *English Journal,* vol. 105, no. 6, 2016, pp. 18–24.

Miller, Benjamin. "Mapping the Methods of Composition/Rhetoric Dissertations: A Landscape 'plotted and pieced.'" *College Composition and Communication,* vol. 66, no. 1, 2014, pp. 145–76.

Moretti, Franco. *Distant Reading.* Verso, 2013.

Mueller, Derek. "Views from a Distance: A Nephrological Model of the CCCC Chairs' Addresses, 1977–2011." *Kairos: A Journal of Rhetoric, Technology, and Pedagogy,* vol. 16, no. 2, 2012, kairos.technorhetoric.net/16.2/topoi/mueller/. Accessed 2 July 2017.

New London Group. "A Pedagogy of Multiliteracies: Designing Social Futures." *Multiliteracies: Literacy Learning and the Design of Social Futures,* edited by Bill Cope and Mary Kalantzis. Routledge, 1999, pp. 9–38.

Palmeri, Jason. *Remixing Composition: A History of Multimodal Writing Pedagogy.* Southern Illinois UP, 2012.

Rhodes, Jacqueline, and Jonathan Alexander. *Techne: Queer Meditations on Writing the Self.* Computers and Composition Digital Press/Utah State UP, 2015, ccdigitalpress.org/techne. Accessed 3 July 2017.

Rice, Jeff. *The Rhetoric of Cool: Composition Studies and New Media.* Southern Illinois UP, 2007.

Ritter, Kelly. *Reframing the Subject: Postwar Instructional Film and Class-Conscious Literacies.* U of Pittsburgh P, 2015.

Selfe, Cynthia L. "The Movement of Air, the Breath of Meaning: Aurality and Multimodal Composing." *College Composition and Communication,* vol. 60, no. 4, 2009, pp. 616–63.

Shipka, Jody. "On Estate Sales, Archives, and the Matter of Making Things." *Provocations: Reconstructing the Archive,* edited by Patrick W. Berry, Gail E. Hawisher, and Cynthia L. Selfe. Computers and Composition Digital Press/Utah State UP, 2016, ccdigitalpress.org/reconstructingthearchive/shipka.html. Accessed 2 July 2017.

———. *Toward a Composition Made Whole.* U of Pittsburgh P, 2011.

Sirc, Geoffrey. *English Composition as a Happening.* Utah State UP, 2002.

Wysocki, Anne Frances. "Introduction: Into Between—On Composition in Mediation." *Composing (Media)=Composing(Embodiment): Bodies, Technologies, Writing, the Teaching of Writing*, edited by Kristin Arola and Anne Frances Wysocki. Utah State UP, 2012, pp. 1–22.

Yancey, Kathleen Blake. "Made Not Only in Words: Composition in a New Key." *College Composition and Communication*, vol. 56, no. 2, 2004, pp. 297–328.

4

ENGLISH COMPOSITION AS A SONIC PRACTICE

Byron Hawk and Greg Stuart

In *English Composition as a Happening*, Geoffrey Sirc wrote a counter-history of composition that entangled written composition with modern art. Duchamp and Pollock provided him with models of creative practice that countered both current-traditional formalism and composition's emphasis on critical interpretation. Importantly, John Cage also figures prominently in Sirc's conception of "composition-in-general." Cage, he argues, valued life over art and experimentation over formalisms, locating composition not in theory or institutions but in lived places and practices. This lived practice is what Sirc desires for his composition classrooms—the creation of an environment "where anything can happen," where an experimental practice can be deployed through a curriculum. Jody Shipka has taken up this kind of experimental practice in her composition pedagogies in relation to found objects, as she shows in *Toward a Composition Made Whole*, but also in relation to chance. Instead of summarizing and discussing readings, for example, she puts students into presentation groups and asks them to "enact, challenge, extend, update" key concepts, arguments, or approaches in the readings by creating an activity for the class. In one session,

> the presenting group created six differently themed activity stations around the classroom. Upon entering the classroom, students were put into groups based on a learning style survey the presenting group had assigned earlier in the semester. Groups each rolled one die to determine which of the six activity stations they would work at for the first seven minutes of class. Once everyone was in place at their first station, the presenting group offered a constraint to the group. This constraint determined how the activity would be undertaken by the group. . . . Every seven minutes the group called time and a die was rolled again to determine where students would go next. At this time, a new constraint was offered to the group. . . . The roll of the die determined who, if anybody, and/or how many people might be working at the same station. ("Happening")

This kind of experimental practice echoes Cage's approach to music, and encourages a more hands-on approach to learning through doing, an approach that emphasizes putting invention in the students' hands along with the chance of the dice throw in the context of productive constraints.

The emphasis on practice has been gaining steam recently in composition. Casey Boyle's "Writing and Rhetoric and/as a Posthuman Practice" takes the emphasis on habit and practice in the Framework for Success in Postsecondary Writing—a 2011 document collaboratively written by members of NCTE, the National Writing Project, and the Council of Writing Program Administrators—and turns it more explicitly toward embodied, aleatory activities. The Framework is grounded in eight habits of practice that should be fostered for writing success: curiosity, openness, engagement, creativity, persistence, responsibility, flexibility, and meta-cognition. All of these quite clearly would support practices such as Shipka's, but Boyle warns that an overreliance on metacognition could work against some of the other habits. Traditional approaches to metacognition could pull students away from embodied activities that promote curiosity, openness, engagement, and creativity. If reflective exercises rely on critical distance from the world, they can separate the practitioner from the material conditions and activities that co-produce the other habits. But reflective practices that happen through continual embodied activity both emerge from and fold back into a flow of embodied practice to enable new relationships and an ongoing habit of engagement. For Boyle, "This habit/habitat is an ecology whose inventiveness is accelerated when its tendencies are exercised" (551). So when Shipka asks her students to respond to texts by inventing activities rather than limiting response to reading and writing, she is working to activate forms of reflection that emerge from and produce habits of curiosity, openness, engagement, creativity, and flexibility.

Recently, composition and rhetoric scholars have been turning to sound artists for these kinds of embodied practices and rhetorical experiences. In "Glenn Gould and the Rhetorics of Sound," for example, Jonathan Alexander turns to Gould's work with multiple voices and splicing techniques in his musical and audio compositions. Gould's radio documentaries on living in the extreme environment of the arctic north put the listener in the midst of a more environmental experience. He splices interviewee voices together to complicate their multiple perspectives and mixes them with ambient sounds of trains heading north, arctic winds, bits of music, and dense sound effects. For Alexander this approach is less about traditional reflective argumentation and more about creating a complex experience where multiple overlapping voices and sonic elements "resonate with and at times contradict one another" (83). More soundscape than discursive statement, Gould's work puts the audience in a space of active listening and co-participation in the ecology. Similarly, in Michelle Comstock and Mary Hocks's "The Sounds of Climate Change," they examine the work of sound artists Susan Philipsz and Bernie Krause as alternatives to visual accounts of environmental change such as photographs or data charts. Their sound installations reveal the surface time of sounds emerging and decaying in an environment and the deep time of species coming and going from the earth. When species die out, the sonic environment is changed, and juxtaposing past and present soundscapes does more than document the environment; it makes these larger temporalities perceptible and reshapes the listeners' "very sense of time, place, and self as environment" (166). For them, this co-productive aspect of sound helps listeners imagine and experience the world more actively and changes the material conditions for reflecting on the issue.

We extend Sirc's composition-in-general through a more explicit encounter with experimental music as such a sonic practice. Stuart's seminar on John Cage combines Cage's post-1952 music with the process-oriented philosophy of Gilles Deleuze to enact a pedagogical intervention into the music history classroom. A traditional musicology course focuses on students learning *about* musical styles, repertoires, and chronologies. But Stuart reimagines the class as a dynamic site where students learn *from* the material through performance and concept creation. In his experimental pedagogy, musical scores are no longer the privileged objects of technical, historical, and/or critical analysis, but rather constitute the ground for the production and enactment of the new. Through regular in-class performances, a recording project that culminates in a new version of Cage's *Musicircus* (1967), and a large-scale concert and recording session with Swiss composer Jürg Frey, students explore, construct, and are confronted with the "unthought" in sound. Stuart's performance-centric classroom has clear implications for digital composition by extending digital texts into larger material practices of composition in general and reducing the goal of professionalization in teaching technologies.

Experimental Music

With roots and influences in a variety of early twentieth-century modernisms and the avant-garde, "experimental music" emerged as a distinct musical practice after World War II. Influential studies of experimental music, such as Michael Nyman's *Experimental Music: Cage and Beyond* (1974), center the practice on the wide-ranging influence of the American composer John Cage (1912–1992). Nyman locates in the work of Cage and others in the New York School an emphasis on "process" but distinguishes the process-oriented pieces of Cage from other experimental composers of the post-war European avant-garde (i.e., Boulez, Stockhausen, Xenakis, Berio, etc.) (Nyman 1). A score by Boulez, for example, might specify with a high degree of detail musical elements such as pitch, rhythm, dynamics, timbre, and articulation, but an experimental piece by Cage would engage various levels of "indeterminacy" by purposefully leaving such information out so those elements would be productively open to the contingencies of musical performance. While Nyman's distinction is useful, George Lewis has written persuasively about how Cage's hostility towards jazz (and improvisation in general) has consistently served to write the work of African American musicians, such as those in the Association for the Advancement of Creative Musicians (or AACM), out of the history of experimental music (Lewis 101–102). Through a parallel reading of Charlie Parker and John Cage, Lewis argues for the importance of improvisation (or "real-time music making") to both the jazz and experimental traditions and sets the stage for an expanded definition of experimental music that includes improvisation and communal authorship as functions of experimental performance.

This expanded sense of experimentation informs more recent efforts to theorize experimental music. Jennie Gottschalk, for example, sees a seemingly unlimited potential for what it might be:

> Experimental music is challenging to pin down because it is not a school or a trend or even an aesthetic. It is, instead, a position—of openness, of inquiry, of uncertainty, of discovery. Facts or circumstances or materials are explored for their potential sonic outcomes through activities including composition, performance, improvisation, installation, recording, and listening. These explorations are oriented toward that which is unknown, whether it is remote, complex, opaque, or falsely familiar. (Gottschalk 1)

While Gottschalk does include familiar touchstones such as Cage in her post-1970, post-Nyman world, it is this sense of experimental music as a "position of openness" rather than a single unified genre or style that allows her to explore a wide range of musics—everything from Toshimaru Nakamura's improvisations using "no-input" mixing boards to Elaine Radigue's recent acoustic music.[1] Following Gottschalk, we can begin to see experimental music arising in potentially any situation where musicians attempt to traverse and/or otherwise rethink the relationship between "music and sound" (Gottschalk 8); to think this relationship between sounds in the world and their continual reorganizations into music is a gesture of radical inclusion and constitutes a basis for the development of any experimental practice.

The fact that scholars such as Gottschalk are rethinking contemporary experimental music practices opens up a space to also reconsider Cage. In *The Process That Is The World: Cage/ Deleuze/Events/Performances*, Joe Panzner reads Cage's music alongside the philosophy of Gilles Deleuze. With Deleuze, Panzner finds a philosophy and ontology capable of extraordinary resonance with the aesthetic-compositional world of Cage's musical practice. He argues that despite the limited number of interactions/references between Cage and Deleuze during their lifetimes, their respective projects exhibit an almost uncanny similarity. Whereas most of Cage's own philosophical supports for his music (as well as by those writing about his work) come from the East (i.e., Zen, Indian Philosophy, the I-Ching, etc.), Panzner highlights a kind of "minor" line in Cage's thinking, and indeed those of the New York School as well, that openly embraces several of Deleuze's predecessors, specifically those interested in "becoming and open-ended futures" (Panzner 5). Thus alongside Cage's ever present Zen are references to Nietzsche, with his "insistence on the aleatoric 'throw of the dice' underpinning the eternal return" as well Henri Bergson's "world of ceaseless invention and variation" (Panzner 5). Expanding on these concerns, Panzner concludes that we might think of Cage as:

> the music-world equivalent of a traumatic figure such as Charles Darwin, whose theory of evolution revealed a world in revolt against stable categories, continually driven by a productive motor of chance. In place of stable types and essences, the apparent stability of species (or musical works) was merely a product of the restriction of this variation— and that even the most stable of structures would eventually submit to the flow of chance. With Cage, the ongoing demotion of the intentional self and humanism enters into the realm of musical composition and performance. (Panzner 5)

It is with this sense of a "world in revolt against stable categories" that Panzner sets Cage directly in dialogue with Deleuze, finding both concerned with a similar set of problems: "difference versus repetition, the conditions required for the emergence of the new, becoming versus being, the tenuous linkage between cause and effect, and the habit constriction of the organism versus the dynamism of open-ended systems" (Panzner 9).

Cage's experience in the anechoic chamber at Harvard University in 1951, for example, transforms his practice along these lines. Since the room was designed to isolate it from exterior sound waves and absorb any interior sound, Cage expected to hear pure silence. But instead he hears two sounds: a lower sound of his blood pumping through his veins and a higher pitched sound of his nervous system in operation. This experience moves him decisively towards the creation of *4'33"* in 1952, which relies on foregrounding aleatory, ambient sounds in the background environment for the performance. Standard accounts of Cage's encounter with the anechoic chamber, such as James Pritchett's in *The Music of John Cage*, place the experience firmly within Cage's then increasing acceptance of Zen's "interpenetrating and non-dualistic reality" (i.e., that silence does not exist, there are *only* sounds) (Pritchett 75). But Panzner argues that this is not the only way to view this central story. By placing Cage in dialogue with Deleuze, he can see that instead of teaching Cage that there "is no such thing as silence" it became a "parable about performance as *creation* rather than *reproduction*" (Panzner 3). The anechoic chamber is a kind of performance situation as "event," one that:

> de-centers the familiar image of agency (human intentions) and affirms something altogether stranger: the impersonal activity of *things coming together*, acting together with a will greater than any single individual can contain . . . [a] story of chance encounters, unthought actors, and unconscious creativity. (Panzner 4)

If performance is fundamentally about this kind of creation rather than the reproduction of a traditional score, how does this manifest itself in practice? Cage's expansive electronic work *Roaratorio* (1979) suggests some answers. Composed in response to a request from Klaus Schöning and West German Radio, Cage devised a compositional procedure to assemble recorded sound clips and instrumental performance around James Joyce's *Finnegan's Wake*. Using the mesostic "JAMES JOYCE," Cage was able to create a text (the *Second Writing Through Finnegan's Wake*) that would be vocalized by Cage in performance. Along with this text would be a collage of sounds related directly to lines of the original text of *Finnegan's Wake*. Cage asks for both sounds coming from specific locations in the book as well as the inclusion of sounds mentioned in the book (i.e., dogs barking, people laughing, etc.). Alongside Cage's vocal performance and the sound collage is a "circus" of traditional Irish music that comes and goes throughout the work. While there is a concrete recorded version of Cage's reworking of *Finnegan's Wake* into sound, Cage also made a score for the process called ____, ____ ____ *circus on* ____, which details how one would go about turning any book into a piece of recorded music.[2] This kind of score is more of a collection of "tendencies" than a blueprint. In fact, two different versions of the piece using the same book as source material could be wholly unrecognizable as being related. In other words, Cage's scores draw upon the deep wellspring of the Deleuzian "virtual"—the active circulation of energies that drive the creation of new thoughts, practices, or worlds when tapped into through an encounter. Things that emerge form a performance, in other words, inevitably repeat the score with a difference. Panzner writes:

> As opposed to . . . "copies of copies," . . . they are copies without a model, actualizations that overturn the very validity of the model-copy distinction. Each actualization relates difference to difference without the mediation of a model that could be used to determine a fixed, timeless identity. (Panzner 57–58)

Panzner urges us not to return to the anechoic chamber as a kind of "model" for performance, but rather to extend its process of creativity into new situations.

Experimental Pedagogy

This idea of "copies without a model" drives Stuart's pedagogy. While all of Stuart's training and professional activity is in performance (as a percussionist specializing in experimental music), he teaches in the academic unit of Music History. Accordingly, he brings an entirely different set of assumptions and experiences into the classroom than a musicologist. Traditional music history classrooms typically consist of lectures, tests, research papers, and surveys of periods, composers, and works. In her essay "Cage and the Chaotic Classroom: Pedagogy for the Avant-garde," Jessie Fillerup notes that when teaching Cage's music in the music history classroom, her students "would be quick to note the disjunction between provocative course content and conventional classroom procedures" (Fillerup 178). So Stuart knew that his graduate-level music history seminar on John Cage wasn't going to be "about" Cage in any traditional sense. As a performer, his preferred teaching approach is to get students making music, while at the same time providing them with the necessary historical and conceptual framing for doing so. After a brief introductory period, the class would alternate between days of open, non-hierarchical group discussion and student-led performance.[3] The goal is not to have the students know a lot about Cage, though that might happen, but to affect them as musicians and listeners in some way, to somehow alter their musical practices. The precise nature of this change in the students wouldn't be, couldn't be, predetermined. Like Cage's own definition of experimental music, the class would be "an experimental *action* . . . the *outcome* of which is not foreseen" (Cage, "Experimental Music").[4] It would enact pedagogy as experimental action, a series of new copies rather than attempts to accurately model Cage.

In Stuart's class, the students come primarily from the Western classical performance tradition, which for many students can be extremely stressful, both physically and emotionally.[5] In the disciplinary space of the music school, "bodies and acts are measured by their resemblance to a standard that stands outside any concrete case" (Panzner 11). In a pedagogy based on this kind of pure imitation, the performer is "sent away to a practice room, [disciplining] herself and the materials she comes in contact with, eliminating the tics and interferences of dumb matter in an effort to sound a performance of worthy correspondence to its heavenly counterpart" (Panzner 72). What "speaks" in the classical model is not the student (nor the world) but the score as transcendent object, for which the student is under moral obligation to reproduce as faithfully as possible. Altering Spinoza's formula of "we don't know what a body can do," the classical performance tradition says "this is what [fill in the instrument] can do"—and should do. Stuart's Cage seminar would not necessarily displace these deeply ingrained habits (although for some, it might) but would aim to open up new spaces that would not be subject to the moral judgment of the "proper" tone. Cage's post-1952 music, with its use of chance operations, indeterminacy, and silence, is in many ways ideal material to question students' conceptions of overarching, transcendent standards in musical production. With a performance-based pedagogy functioning in the place of "content delivery from the lectern," the students would simply be unable to avoid the more radical nature of the material because they would have to engage with it directly through performance on a regular basis.

The decision to have over half of the course consist of performance-activities, as opposed to traditional classroom work, was informed by Stuart's sense of a fundamental disconnect among his graduate students between their perception of experimental music from reading about it and what they could experience in performance. Several years prior to the Cage class, Stuart taught a traditional classroom-based graduate course on twentieth-century music. During a unit focusing on early minimalist music in the United States (i.e., Young, Riley, Reich, Glass, etc.), Stuart showed the class the score to LaMonte Young's *Composition 1960 #7*. The score simply consists of a treble clef containing a perfect fifth (B and F#) and the instruction "to be held for a long time." The students audibly laughed at seeing the score. "How could this thing with two notes possibly be a piece of music?" their jeering seemed to indicate. In an improvisational pedagogical act, Stuart cancelled the activities for the following class session on the spot, and announced that the next class period would consist of the entire class (around twenty students) doing an hour-long version of the piece. After an hour of doing the very thing they had openly derided in the class before, they were caught up in the performance. There was indeed something—a lot, even—that Young's terse score could simply not communicate in a traditional classroom pedagogy. Experience was necessary to open up a "world of psycho-acoustic events behind a simple acoustic phenomenon," such as "combination tones . . . and the possibility of hearing the balance of partials within each note of the interval quite differently in different parts of the room" (Potter 52). The students needed to become active participants rather than passive observers. They needed to find themselves inside a complex field of vibration—both enmeshed in it and responsible for it—in order for the piece to make sense. They did not necessarily need to know about Young, they needed to do Young, and through this doing they produced a new copy of Young and a knowing that corresponded to it.[6]

In the Cage class, Stuart would continue this pedagogical strategy, but instead of having the students perform once during the course of a semester filled with traditional classroom activities, performance would be primary and occur on an ongoing basis. At the beginning of the course, students were incredibly insistent on receiving Stuart's "authorization" for their performances. In the case of Cage's *Variations II* (a piece worked on early in the class), the students regularly asked questions such as "Is this how I should be playing this piece?" "Is it OK if I do this?" and "How should this sound?" among others. *Variations II* is written for "any number of players and any sound producing means." And while it provides performers with a toolkit-like set of materials for making determinations about things such as frequency, amplitude, timbre, and duration, it doesn't provide any universal metric for how those things might be measured. So Stuart explicitly refrained from answering these types of "should I" questions—doing so would undermine the very processes *Variations II* attempts to engage. However, over the course of the semester (and in the absence of explicit instruction) it started to occur to the students that they could take ownership of their decisions for constructing performances. That is, scores ceased to be singular sources of musical knowledge to be *reproduced*, and instead became material-vectors in more complex assemblages or ecologies of *production*. This new, de-centered environment included not only the performer as material agent, but also, and more importantly, the contingencies of the entire performance situation.

In addition to performances during class, Stuart had students perform individually and collectively outside of class. For final projects, each student had to perform and record a CD-length set of pieces from Cage's post-1952 music, and the entire class had to collaborate on a recording project with Stuart's undergraduate South Carolina Honors College Experimental Music Workshop, the Swiss composer Jürg Frey, and the American violinist Erik Carlson. The individual Cage recording project was initially intimidating to students. For the typical music major, recording functions as the ultimate test of the model-copy ontology. Recording is a space of judgment demanding filial resemblance, not one of enacting the new. But after weeks of in-class performances, recording became a space to make new sounds, try unknown techniques on their instruments, take risks, and surprise themselves.[7] The students had, in Panzner's Deleuzian/Spinozist influenced terminology, moved from morality to ethics. Rather than following pre-established models faithfully, each student had to make rhetorical and situational choices to produce new versions of Cage's works. This turn was critical to the collaborative recording project that had the graduate students work with a major post-Cagean composer, a professional violinist in contemporary and experimental music, Stuart as a percussionist, and fifteen undergraduate non-music majors, some who had never played an instrument before.[8] The side-by-side placement of professional, amateur, and novice performers continued the de-centering of singular sites of musical knowledge and meant the students had to let go of fidelity and embrace experiment. The student playing a plastic cup and a bag full of leaves was no less important than a "professional" on violin or clarinet. The displacement of the standard music history classroom into performance creates a transformative series of activities for students. The experience of being a performer, composer, and listener produces a focus on knowledge production that traditional pedagogies are challenged to emulate.

Digital Writing and Rhetoric

Stuart's experimental pedagogies show that the digital always operates within wider ecologies of practice, extending digital texts into larger material practices of composition in general. In "Toward a Resonant Material Vocality for Digital Composition," Erin Anderson argues that digital writing and rhetoric hasn't fully embraced sonic practice, focusing predominantly on voice in multimedia and more recently podcasting rather than the materiality of sound. Anderson calls for a return to invention through "experimental compositional practices," which "remain largely unexplored" in order to collaborate with sound through a shared, ecological sense of rhetorical agency. Stuart's work in many ways responds to this call with a concrete set of sonic practices. In the Cage class, Stuart had students perform a version of Cage's *Song Books* (1970). *Song Books* is a large collection of four types of pieces (songs, songs with electronics, directions for theatrical performance, and directions for theatrical performance with electronics) that employ a range of texts, mostly from the journals of Henry David Thoreau, but also from Erik Satie, Marcel Duchamp, and Norman O. Brown, among others. In the in-class performance, students simultaneously used typewriters, played their instruments, chopped vegetables, sung, moved throughout the space, and projected video, among numerous other activities, which placed the electronics in an entirely new classroom ecology. Similarly, Stuart's work with Cage's *Musicircus* (1967), entangled material performance and digital technologies. *Musicircus* essentially asks performers to make music in the same space together as "an invitation rather than a directive: musicians of whatever persuasion are invited to occupy a certain space (or spaces) for a certain time. This brings about neither ensemble nor counterpoint, but rather simple coexistence" (Brooks 221). In the final pedagogical act of the course, Stuart took all of the students' individual CD-length Cage recordings and mixed them together into a single piece, producing a new version of *Musicircus*. Stuart simply laid the nine individual student recordings on top of one another using the digital audio workstation Cubase, creating a dense ecology of instrumental, electronic, electro-acoustic, and environmental sound enacted through the digital.

The distribution of sonic and digital practices through a wider ecology heightens the need for different kinds of listening practices to go along with digital pedagogies. In "Tuning the Sonic Playing Field," Katy Fargo Ahern suggests that we see such pedagogical practices as forms of attunement. "Tuning," she writes, "is a literal, material practice that takes place when large groups (or even small groups for that matter) choose to play together" (82). It is a negotiated assemblage of bodies through practices of listening. A large part of what the metaphor of tuning does for Ahern's class is modify their listening practices, shifting them away from "a standard of being right" toward an agreed upon similarity (83). It moves authority away from the teacher, the material, and individual student choice and instead aims for the group's co-responsibility in that moment of listening to create a "shared notion of appropriate sound" (83). Ahern is mostly concerned with centering collective attention on "different practices and experiences of listening" (85). But Stuart shows what this attention could do if it were coupled with production and performance. The remixed *Musicircus* recording, for example, further de-centered the students' sense of being "intentional" actors in musical performance. When listening to the recording, the students got a sense of "the impersonal activity of *things coming together*, acting together with a will greater than any single individual can contain," a sense of "unthought actors, and unconscious creativity" (Panzner 4). At times what they had played individually could not be heard, or would be radically reconfigured by other performances or the chance layering of Stuart's digital mix. Conversely, there were moments when individual parts came through with extreme clarity. During the final listening session to the *Musicircus* recording, the students began to hear something as music that they would have previously cast off as mere noise or cacophony. But for Stuart it was critical that they took a material part in the construction of the recording. Simply presenting the concept to them *fait acompli* (i.e., listening to some other version of *Musicircus*, or just telling them about it) would not have been effective or affective. They needed a pedagogy in which they were, so to speak, *in* the mix, co-producers as well as listeners of experimental action.

Another implication of Stuart's ecological sonic practice is that digital writing and rhetoric doesn't need to focus on "professionalization" of technology use but instead on a democratization of practice. Many in the field already embrace versions of a do-it-yourself ethic, but Stuart's pedagogy seems to call for more shared and collaborative work across non-majors and majors, amateurs and professionals, students and professors. His Experimental Music Workshop, for example, is composed of fifteen undergraduate students who come from a variety of musical backgrounds as well as courses of study. The one thing that most of the students share in common is that they have never been involved in any kind of experimental music making situation, not unlike a typical digital writing class. Because the students are coming to experimental music for the first time (that is, they don't have the disciplinary habits of music majors), they tend to come to class open to interesting ways of playing and composing. These students have neither a cynical "it's all been done before" attitude nor a kind of hypercritical self-awareness that prevents anything interesting from *happening*. Pedagogy in this case functions not as a kind of breaking down of a "performance tradition" but instead opens up an entirely different educational space than the standardized testing model that produced most of their educational habits. In an educational system that is often only about facts and increasingly asks them for the "right answer," it provides them with a space of creativity and allows them to have an aesthetic experience in a curriculum. Perhaps more of our digital assignments, then, could look like LaMonte Young's *Composition 1960* #7 with a score that only has two notes and one simple instruction. Such an approach to digital pedagogy would establish an open, exploratory space for creativity and reflection. The extent to which digital writing and rhetoric pedagogies can tap into these practices, they can better instill the kinds of habits that the Framework calls for. Rather than see Sirc's work as an outlier or as one strand of work in the field, the larger implication of Stuart's pedagogies is that such experimental, digital practices could be far more central to the goals of the Framework than we've yet to acknowledge.

Notes

1. For more examples see Novak's "Playing Off Site," and Casey's "The Composing Body."
2. For a recent version of Cage's *circus on*, see Holter's album *Cookbook*.
3. Course readings were drawn primarily from Panzner's *The Process That is the World* (the central text of the course), Haskin's compact Cage biography, and a few associated journal articles and essays. There were also texts that bridged the gap between reading and performance taken from Cage's *Silence*, such as *45' for a Speaker* (1954), and *Lecture on Nothing* (1959), which the students performed aloud in-class. Performance materials consisted of post-1952 Cage pieces that are playable by either individuals or small groups such as *Variations I* (1958), *Variations II* (1961), *Song Books* (1970), *Hymnkus* (1986), and the *Number Pieces* (1987–1992).
4. As Deleuze notes: "For nothing can be said in advance, one cannot prejudge the outcome of research. . . . For a doctrine in general, there is nothing regrettable in this uncertainty about the outcome of research" (180–181).
5. See Stephenson and Quarrier's "Anxiety Sensitivity and Performance Anxiety in College Music Students" (119).
6. Composer Michael Pisaro elaborates on the centrality of performance in experimental music when he says: "In a sense, within experimental music, the notion that the writing of the score is inseparable from the music is so pervasive, it may seem that there is nothing really important to say. There is some value to this idea: where this music really lives is in the doing of it, not the talking about it. Someone who has worked her way through the pieces, preparing performing versions of the scores, will know much more than if she has only read about what has been done." (28)
7. As Panzner notes, "A mistake is beside the point" (68).
8. The group recorded over an hour of Frey's music, which was released in 2017 on CD as *Ephemeral Constructions* by Edition Wandelweiser Records, a highly regarded label in contemporary experimental music.

Works Cited

Ahern, Katherine Fargo. "Tuning the Sonic Playing Field: Teaching Ways of Knowing Sound in First Year Writing." *Computers and Composition*, vol. 30, no. 2, 2013, pp. 75–86.

Alexander, Jonathan. "Glenn Gould and the Rhetorics of Sound." *Computers and Composition*, vol. 37, 2015, pp. 73–89.

Anderson, Erin. "Toward a Resonant Material Vocality for Digital Composition." *Enculturation*, vol. 18, 2014, enculturation.net/materialvocality. Accessed 12 May 2017.

Boyle, Casey. "Writing and Rhetoric and/as a Posthuman Practice." *College English*, vol. 78, no. 6, 2016, pp. 532–54.

Brooks, William. "Music and Society." *The Cambridge Companion to John Cage*, edited by David Nicholls. Cambridge UP, 2002, pp. 214–26.

Cage, John. "Experimental Music." *Silence*. Wesleyan UP, 1961, pp. 7–12.

———. *Hymnkus*. Edition Peters, 1986.

———. *Number Pieces*. Edition Peters, 1987–1992.

———. *Musicircus*. 1967.

———. *Roaratorio*. Mode Records, 1992.

———. *Silence: Lectures and Writings*. Wesleyan UP, 1961.

———. *Song Books*. Edition Peters, 1970.

———. *Variations I*. Edition Peters, 1958.

———. *Variations II*. Edition Peters, 1961.

Casey, Rob. "The Composing Body: Naldjorlak and the Nature of Musical Meaning." *Musicology Review*, vol. 8, 2013, pp. 130–57.

Comstock, Michelle and Mary E. Hocks. "The Sounds of Climate Change: Sonic Rhetoric in the Anthropocene, the Age of Human Impact." *Rhetoric Review*, vol. 35, no. 2, 2016, pp. 165–75.

Deleuze, Gilles. *Difference and Repetition*. Continuum, 2004.

Fillerup, Jessie. "Cage and the Chaotic Classroom: Pedagogy for the Avant-garde." *Vitalizing Music History*, edited by James R. Briscoe. Pendragon, 2010, pp. 177–88.

Frey, Jürg. *Ephemeral Constructions*. Edition Wandelweiser Records, 2017.

Gottschalk, Jennie. *Experimental Music Since 1970*. Bloomsbury, 2016.

Haskin, Rob. *John Cage (Critical Lives)*. Reaktion, 2012.

Holter, Julia. *Cookbook*. Sleepy Mammal Sound, 2008.

Lewis, George E. "Improvised Music After 1950: Afrological and Eurological Perspectives." *Black Music Research Journal*, vol. 16, no. 1, 1996, pp. 91–122.

Novak, David. "Playing Off Site: The Untranslation of Onkyô." *Asian Music*, vol. 41, no. 1, 2010, pp. 36–59.

Nyman, Michael. *Experimental Music: Cage and Beyond*. Cambridge UP, 1999.

Panzner, Joe. *The Process That Is The World: Cage/Deleuze/Events/Performances*. Bloomsbury, 2015.

Pisaro, Michael. "Writing, Music." *Ashgate Research Companion to Experimental Music*, edited by James Saunders. Routledge, 2009, pp. 27–76.

Potter, Keith. *Four Musical Minimalists: La Monte Young, Terry Riley, Phillip Glass*. Cambridge UP, 2000.

Pritchett, James. *The Music of John Cage*. Cambridge UP, 1996.

Shipka, Jody. "Happening Day in the Texts and Contexts Class." Facebook. 1 Dec. 2016.

———. *Toward a Composition Made Whole*. U of Pittsburgh P, 2011.

Sirc, Geoffrey. *English Composition as a Happening*. SIUP, 2002.

Stephenson, Hugh and Nicholas F. Quarrier. "Anxiety Sensitivity and Performance Anxiety in College Music Students." *Medical Problems of Performing Artists*, vol. 20, no. 3, 2005, pp. 119–25.

Young, LaMonte. *Composition 1960 #7*, 1960.

5

WRITING WITH A SOLDERING IRON

On the Art of Making Attention

Marcel O'Gorman

> I can't imagine that students today would learn only to read and write using the twenty-six letters of the alphabet.
>
> *(Friedrich A. Kittler)*

In a famous scene from Jean-Luc Godard's film, *Two or Three Things I Know About Her*, Robert Jeanson (Roger Montsoret) sits in a café stirring a cup of espresso with a small spoon. His wife Juliette, the star of the film, sits nearby, strangely distant from him. As Robert stirs the coffee, the camera closes in on its whirling black, frothy cosmos. Enter the whispering, omniscient voice of the narrator, God-ard himself:

> Maybe an object is what serves as a link between subjects, allowing us to live in a society, to be together. But since social relations are always ambiguous, since my thoughts divide as much as unite, and my words unite by what they express and isolate by what they omit, since a wide gulf separates my subjective certainty of myself from the objective truth others have of me, since I constantly end up guilty, even though I feel innocent, since every event changes my daily life, since I always fail to communicate, to understand, to love and be loved, and every failure deepens my solitude, since . . .

After this monologue, the spoon sends the cosmos whirring once again, and we cut to Juliette, who glances stoically at Robert. She plays with her wine glass, Robert takes a pull from his cigarette, a suspicious barman in cool shades reaches for the tap and pours a beer. Close-up on the hands. Then back to a super close-up of the coffee-as-cosmos.

> Since . . . since I cannot escape the objectivity crushing me nor the objectivity expelling me, since I cannot rise to a state of being nor collapse into nothingness . . .
> I have to listen more than ever I have to look around me at the world, my fellow creature, my brother.

I have taken a risk here by trying to convey in words, in an essay on writing even, what can only be conveyed in film. To borrow from Foucault, "the space where [written words] achieve their splendor is not that deployed by our eyes but that defined by the sequential elements of syntax" (9). If I have failed to communicate the visual complexity of the Godard clip, I hope to at least recover it as an object-to-think-with. This scene, like this essay, is about contemplative objects, thinking hands, and paying attention (*faire attention*).

Contemplative Objects

I was introduced to the Godard scene while enrolled in a course with Robert Ray at the University of Florida. For Ray, this scene demonstrates how filmmakers use objects to direct the viewer's attention and open a space for poetic contemplation. In this case, as Ray suggests in *The Avant-Garde Finds Andy Hardy*, "the camera's near-exclusive attention on an ordinary object (a cup of coffee) releases a lyrical meditation about subjectivity's place in the modern world" (122). More interestingly, perhaps, Ray uses this scene to launch into a discussion of hypermedia, noting that the coffee cup is like a node in a network. Citing Marcos Novak, Ray writes, "Every image [is] an index. . . . Every node in a hypermedium is therefore an information space, a space of potential information" (Novak 231). In order to make the transition from film to hypermedia, Ray must turn this scene of contemplation, a scene that painstakingly embodies boredom, into a site of hyper-attention. Thanks to the rhetoric of hypermedia, the coffee cup is no longer a gateway onto contemplative existential thought, but a node in a vast network of associations connected by hyperlinks. Back in 1995, I was excited by this transformation of the coffee cup from a dark, profound cosmos into a frenetic portal onto digital culture. Today, I am less sanguine about this seemingly emancipatory move. What we need today, more than ever, are not clickable images, but opportunities for profound and sustained attention. I don't want to click Godard's coffee cup and consume it in an instant—I want to drink it slowly, think with it. And I want to make other objects to think with. For this, I have dedicated myself to learning the art of writing with a soldering iron.

In my book *E-Crit: Digital Media, Critical Theory and the Humanities*, I celebrated hypermedia (a word that rings with 1990s nostalgia) as a new mode of writing more suitable for a digital, image-oriented culture. Since then, I have come to understand that the humanities can engage with digital culture without turning toward the logic, rhetoric, and cognitive style of *hyper*. In fact, what the humanities, exclusively, has to offer digital culture is the opposite of *hyper*, whether we call it *linear, deep, slow,* or perhaps even *hypo*, as in *hypomnesis*, the technical externalization of memory identified by Plato in *Phaedrus*. The *hypomnesis* I invoke here, in opposition to *hypermedia*, is in the form of close reading and critical writing, which are relatively slow techniques for the externalization of memory.

But already I have gotten ahead of myself, and now I am guilty of binaristic thinking. First, it would be more accurate to say that the opposite of *hypo* is not *hyper* but *ana*, as in *anamnesis*: recollection from within, remembrance that has not been externalized. Hypermnesis is merely an exaggerated form of hypomnesis; it is a multiplication of external memory that finds its apotheosis today, perhaps, in the Google search engine. Second, by setting up a value-laden binary between hypermnesis and hypomnesis (or between hypomnesis and anamnesis for that matter), I am engaging in the sort of dualistic thinking that led Socrates to reject the technology of writing in *Phaedrus*. King Thamus's indictment of the discovery of writing has been told too many times, but I dare to repeat it again here: "The specific (*pharmakon*) which you have discovered is an aid not to memory, but to reminiscence (*hypomneseos*), and you give your disciples not truth, but only the semblance of truth" (Plato). What Thamus failed to see, perhaps, is that the distinction between inside (*ana*) and outside (*hypo*) is not clear-cut. As Derrida observed, anamnesis (internal memory) is always-already infected with hypomnesis (externalized memory), and the two can hardly be separated.[1] What's more, and this is my main point, the acts of reading and writing themselves are conspicuously embodied acts of decoding and encoding that demand long circuits of cognitive processing. What the humanities have to offer digital culture then, is a mode of resistance—in the form of deep reading and slow writing—to a hyper-externalizing social apparatus that has delegated reading and writing to efficient machines.[2]

In *Proust and the Squid*, an investigation of literacy and cognition, Maryanne Wolf suggests that reading, above all, has given the human species "the gift of time" (229). As an advanced technical skill, reading gives us time to make inferences, think analytically and critically. The reading brain engages in a slow and "profound generativity" that is difficult to achieve in more hyper, networked reading environments that promote just-in-time information access over careful rumination (Wolf 23). The same might be said for writing. Even rote transcription, word by word, which I require my students to do as a mnemomic form of note-taking, provides time for contemplation and generativity.[3] My own effort to transcribe the scene from Godard offers the same rare opportunity to spend time generatively. By attempting to transcribe the film—to create an object "that serves as a link between subjects" (Godard)—I have engaged in what Bernard Stiegler calls a "literal [e.g., alphabetic] synthesis," ("Anamnesis") knowing that both the reader and I share a technical capacity to read and write, and that we are both committed to taking the time for decoding and encoding, successfully or not, the object of transmission. What matters is not whether my transcription of Godard is truthful, but that I have made the attempt to convey it, and the reader has taken the time to assess my attempt, as part of a a literal exchange of subjectivity. This entire process of sharing and connecting might be described, in a term often wielded by Stiegler, as *transindividuation*,[4] which he describes as a *long circuit* that allows humans to individuate themselves. Digital service industries can potentially short-circuit[5] this process and rob individuals of opportunities for world-building. Taking time to read and write, carefully, deeply, even slowly, is a radical intellectual and cognitive act in our ever-accelerating technocultural milieu. Why then, would one want to complicate things further by writing with a soldering iron?

Thinking Hands

My invocation of "taking care" is a nod to Stiegler's book *Taking Care of Youth and the Generations*. While this book might be described as an indictment of technoculture's cognitive assault on youth by means of psychotechnological marketing technics, Stiegler surprisingly finds in digital technics both an ailment and a cure. As I have noted elsewhere,[6] Stiegler's description of technology as a *pharmakon*, following Plato, indicates its double-edged nature. But rather than promoting a Luddistic form of resistance to psychotechnologies of marketing, Stiegler calls for technological "first-aid kits" that will resist the "merchants of the time of brain-time divested of consciousness" (*Taking Care* 85). He makes a similar suggestion in the essay "Anamnesis and Hypermnesis," noting that "Cooperative digital technologies can be placed in the service of individuation, providing industrial politics of hypomneses are implemented in the service of *a new age of anamnesis*" ("Anamnesis," emphasis in original). Beyond the technics of reading and writing that I have already invoked, what forms of hypomnesis—digital hypomnesis—can be mobilized in the service of a new age of anamnesis? The notion of service here is crucial, and I will return to it later in a discussion of *caretaking*. First, it is time to consider what it could mean to write with a soldering iron.

Writing with a soldering iron might first of all call up thoughts of pyrography, the technic of decorating wood or other materials by burning them with a heated object. This is an ancient practice that was common in Ancient Egypt, and as pyrographer Robert Boyer suggests, it was likely one of the first ways that early humans expressed themselves symbolically, using ashes from their fires. All of this conjures a certain Promethean context for understanding the act of writing with a soldering iron. Above all, I want to avoid this Promethean trap, sidestep the notion of the soldering iron as a phallic icon of technical progress, the soldering iron as the enlightening torch of STEM. I want to figure the soldering iron not as an instrument for the external marking of surfaces, but instead as an instrument for internal conjuration, and for making ideas concrete or solid[7] in a cyclical process of anamnesis and hypomnesis. I want to reclaim the soldering iron then, as a non-phallic and non-Promethean enducement to contemplation. To get to this point, it is useful to consider soldering within the history of technics.

I nearly entitled this essay "Soldering Iron for the Hand, Critical Essay for the Face," in reference to French anthropologist André Leroi-Gourhan's instructive aphorism, "Tools for the Hand, Language for the Face" (19–20). This simple, two-part phrase encapsulates Leroi-Gourhan's complex understanding of how humans co-evolved with technics; put simply, tool use by early humans provoked brain development necessary for the development of language. Ultimately, this co-evolutionary process between humans and technics (language itself being one such technic) engenders the verticality of the early human, a verticality that supports a cranium poised for additional brain growth and a jaw liberated from its primary grasping function so that it can be opened for face-to-face communication. Of course, erect posture also liberates the hands, which makes it possible for speech to be exteriorized in written symbols. In fact, this entire process, according to Leroi-Gourhan, might be described in a single world: *exteriorization*.[8] Indeed, all technics are a form of exteriorization, and in Leroi-Gourhan's formulation, we must conclude that the human is a technical animal. In Stiegler's words, "the human invents himself in the technical by inventing the tool—by becoming exteriorized technologically" (*Technics and Time* 141). The question I am asking here is whether we can be more selective about how and when to engage in technical, specifically digital, forms of exteriorization. Can we be more careful about how we invent ourselves in the technical?

Leroi-Gourhan's strikingly concise evolutionary vignette calls to mind those ubiquitous cartoon charts of the hunched monkey, discretely transformed in four or five steps into an upright human with an idealized physique. Or more relevantly in this case, is the equally ubiquitous chart of the monkey transforming itself—in a few more steps—into a human hunched in front of a computer or bent over a handheld device. I don't want to give into such temptations here, by suggesting that technology ultimately leads to some form of human devolution. Instead, I will dispel this myth by re-invoking the notion of the *technopharmakon*. That said, I will ask the following questions: What kind of cognitive developments are we stimulating with our hands today? What is the relationship today between hands, speech, writing, and soldering? Where is the poison in our various technical exteriorisations, where is the tonic, and who gets to decide which is which? This final question brings up once again the problem of binaristic thinking. Ultimately, my goal is not to suggest that the sort of cortical activity provoked by hypermedia, for example, is the poison, and that close reading and slow writing are therefore the tonic. Instead, my suggestion is that given the spectrum of possible cognitive activities, digital service industries have created an imbalance, favouring hyper modes of cognition over those that are more calm, focused, and linear. Following what Katherine Hayles has suggested, but without invoking the binary of "Hyper and Deep," we might regain balance by concocting a careful tincture of cognitive modes.[9] The real question then, is this: How might we put Leroi-Gourhan's evolutionary formula in the service of inventing a mode of digital writing that regains the cognitive balance discussed here? One answer would be to splice soldering and writing together for the sake of building long circuits of transindividuation.

I have taken a somewhat circuitous route to arrive at the point where I can summon, anti-climactically and almost bathetically, the stupidly cute term, *thinkering*. In his book-length study of craftsmanship, Richard Sennett suggests that "Western civilization has had a deep-rooted trouble in making connections between head and hand, in recognizing and encouraging the impulse of craftsmanship" (9).[10] *Thinkering*, a term coined by Michael Ondaatje in *The English Patient*, gets to the heart of this problem by spooning together the notions of thinking and tinkering into a single word. I want to expand the conception of thinkering in digital writing so that it moves beyond the screen and keyboard to embrace other digital materialities. On several occasions in my career, I have quoted the following mythical anecdote from German media theorist Friedrich Kittler: "at night after I had finished writing, I used to pick up the soldering iron and build circuits" (Griffin 731). But rather than viewing this anecdote as a STEM legitimation of Kittler's theoretical work (Kittler prided himself on being an engineer), we might understand it instead as a formula for thinking—one in which soldering and writing are picked up together, and inextractibly spliced into an engaged modality for action.

Paying Attention (*Faire Attention*)

In a small but powerful book entitled *In Catastrophic Times: Resisting the Coming Barbarism*, Isabelle Stengers provides a cutting and urgent indictment of a technocratic form of politics driven blindly by global economic competition. She dedicates the book to those who are attempting to "learn concretely to reinvent modes of production and of cooperation that escape from the evidences of economic growth and competition" (24). As one concrete solution to the problem of "irresponsible, even criminal" growth—for this is a book that offers solutions and not just indictments—Stengers suggests that we have to reclaim the "art of paying attention" (21, 62):

> What we have been ordered to forget is not the capacity to pay attention, but the art of paying attention. If there is an art, and not just a capacity, this is because it is a matter of learning and cultivating, that is to say, making ourselves pay attention. (62)

Much like Stiegler's suggestion that we should make technological "first-aid kits" designed to resist hyperindustrial "attention control via cultural and cognitive technologies," Stengers's version of "paying attention" involves concrete action (22). But this is almost lost in translation. In French, *faire attention* has a different connotation than paying attention. *Faire attention* can be literally translated as *making attention*. As opposed to *paying attention*, which implies a financial transaction that reflects our current attention economy, *making attention* describes a more deliberate and productive act. Stengers' translator has tried to capture this in the phrase "making ourselves pay attention" (22) but I would suggest that the phrase *making attention* is more productive. *Making attention*[11] belongs to the same species as *thinkering*, an art of attention that allows us to resist the "merchants of the time of brain-time divested of consciousness" (Stiegler, *Taking Care* 85).

Another way of understanding the art of paying attention I am trying to develop here is to bring it under the umbrella of "critical making." This term has been used by instructors at the Rhode Island School of Design (RISD) to define a common practice of speculative design[12] as a form of critical engagement.[13] Matt Ratto at the University of Toronto has championed this term, noting that it provides a label for "various distinctive practices that link traditional scholarship in the humanities and social sciences to material engagement" (86). Put more succinctly, critical making is a form of "material technoscientific critique" (86). My own contribution to this discourse comes in the form of what I have called Applied Media Theory (AMT) (O'Gorman,

"Broken Tools," *Necromedia*). AMT, which is the guiding practice of the Critical Media Lab, fosters a feedback loop between reading, writing, and making that defines a nexus of activity suitable for attentively responding and contributing to technological developments. With AMT, media theory and the philosophy of technology are put to service in the creation of objects-to-think-with that intervene directly in the production of technoculture. In this way, AMT engenders modes of technocultural production that "escape from the evidences of economic growth and competition," while critically directing attention to the relationship between technology and the human condition (Stengers 24). To demonstrate this modality of attention formation in action, I will describe two projects that my students have allowed me to share in this essay. These projects, created in the Critical Media Lab for a graduate seminar on "Digital Abstinence,"[14] are not meant to serve as ideal models or perfect exemplars, but rather, they help flesh out the technics involved in Applied Media Theory, demonstrating less abstractly what it could mean to write with a soldering iron.

Project 1: *Basket Case*

Basket Case is a sensor-equipped, hand-woven basket created by Caitlin Woodcock, a Master's student in the Experimental Digital Media (XDM) program at the University of Waterloo. This project responded to the assignment of creating an object-to-think-with that focuses attention on "digital abstinence." As an avid maker, Caitlin decided first of all to tinker with pottery making and basketweaving as a way of occupying her hands,[15] so that her mind would have time to focus on the assignment. Caitlin wanted to use this project as a way of contesting the value of speed in contemporary technoculture, an idea fuelled by her reading of Jacques Ellul's *The Technological Society*, Bratich and Brush's "Fabricating Activism: Craft-Work, Popular Culture, Gender," and other texts. She ultimately chose to pursue a basketweaving project, based on her research into Amish and aboriginal domestic practices. In the essay portion of the assignment Caitlin writes, "I wanted to focus on domestic aspects because they provide the opportunity to engage with the idea of technological control through *female-knowing*" (2). She quotes Tassoula Hadjiyanni and Kristin Helle's observation that "craft making and its connective abilities strengthen ... and reclaim cultural and gender identities as women craft makers reestablish their role as safekeepers of tradition" (77, qtd. in Woodcock 2). Of course, there is a soldering component to this project; the basket contains a Force Sensitivity Resistor (FSR) at its base and a small LCD screen woven into its rim, both of which are soldered to an Arduino Nano microcontroller.[16] The end result is a basket designed to hold a handheld device, freeing the hands of the user for other activities besides texting, surfing, and gaming. When the user retrieves the device, the LCD screen displays what percentage of the basket the user could have woven during the time their hands were liberated from the device.

The project aims to recapture some of the domestic practices of the Amish, without activating the gender hierarchy that seems to be embedded in these practices. For this, Caitlin turns to the Amish concept of *Gelassenheit*, which might be described roughly as "calmness, acceptance, and yieldedness" (Kraybill, Johnson-Wiener, and Nolt 98). She writes,

> Like the Amish values associated with *Gelassenheit*, crafting finds itself incompatible with the present reality of a technological society and, in order to preserve it, alternative ways of interacting with technology need to be determined. Slowness does not have to remain associated with the idea of wasted time or missed opportunities. It can, instead, become a powerful vehicle for being and doing in ways contrary to the norm. (Woodcock 7)

The term *Gelassenheit* was also used by Martin Heidegger in his "Discourse on Thinking" to describe the practice of worlding. In Heidegger's terms, *Gelassenheit* does not focus instrumentally on objects, but rather, it "begins with an awareness of the field within which these objects are, an awareness of the horizon rather than of the objects of ordinary understanding" (24). *Basket Case* harnesses the connective and contemplative potentials of craftmaking, drawing specific attention to how we might spend our time more attentively in a culture obsessed with speed and efficiency.

Project 2: *Mindflux*

Mindflux is a prototype for an Arduino-based bracelet designed by Megan Honsberger, another M.A. student in the XDM program who took my course on "Digital Abstinence." The project is inspired by Buddhist prayer beads or *malas*, which can be used to count breaths or to keep track of the recitation of mantras during meditation. Buddhist rituals, which are rooted in mindfulness, can provide productive technics for relearning the art of paying attention. Aware that the term *mindfulness* is "a trending buzzword in Silicon Valley" (Honsberger 8), Megan focused the project on Buddhist traditions. In her project essay, she included the following quote from an introductory book on Buddhism, revealing that mindfulness is not just about self-betterment, but about bettering the world through acts of attention: "the clarity of mindfulness provides the mental awareness of self and world needed for skillfully changing oneself for the better and skillfully contributing to bettering the world in which one lives" (57, qtd. in Honsberger 5–6). Unlike a traditional mala bead bracelet (an object that unsurprisingly has been co-opted by fashion accessory companies such as Lokai and stripped of its sacredness), Megan's wearable is designed to facilitate a feedback loop of mindfulness between humans and their digital prostheses. As Megan describes it, whenever the user of *Mindflux* responds to a digital distraction,

> they must first touch the bracelet (via touch sensor) to make a digital LED "bead" light up. As the day progresses, the user has a visual representation of how often they have performed the activity they are trying to curb. (9)

The bracelet thus has the potential to serve as a sort of digital "scarlet letter," calling attention to the user's distracting digital rituals (11). The religious connotations of this object-to-think-with are not lost on its creator, who suggests further that unbounded progress "fuels the fervency of faith in digital technology as an infallible tool to divine a supreme existence. And it is this devout, though unconscious, belief which in turn creates vice-like, unconscious, and . . . mindless use of digital media" (2).

The title of Megan's project is actually a splicing together of the words *mindful* and *UX* (User Experience). This brings to mind Megan's awareness of the fact that her project is imbricated in a rationalist discourse on digital production in which UX is code for *digital rhetoric*, or the art of persuasion by means of digital technology. While *Mindflux* co-opts the tools and techniques of that world, it is not beholden to it. Put otherwise, the project is in that technocapitalist world, but not of it. To this end, Megan's work is inspired by the self-proclaimed "cyborg-Luddite" Steve Mann, whose wearable inventions are designed to short-circuit technocapitalism:

> The Wearable Computer can then be understood as a crucial beginning to a new phase of technological development that not only extends human senses, but, more importantly, allows us, the (post) human beings, the cyborg Luddites, to reassert our

autonomy over technology wherever and whenever we choose. (Mann 34, qtd. in Honsberger 8–9)

The reference to posthumanism here calls attention to where Honsberger's project differs from Mann's *Wearcomp* apparatus. In his attempt to develop "existential technology," Mann ultimately celebrates the autonomous, neoliberal humanistic subject (*Cyborg* 57). The posthumanism Honsberger's project brings to mind is one that focuses instead on what comes after humanism; it decenters the human in a humbling act that connects thing to thing, self to world, and reveals the destructive side of technological progress.

Conclusion

Projects such as Caitlin and Megan's respond productively to Debbie Chachra's criticism of maker culture as a male-dominated movement that renders invisible other forms of labour, mainly caregiving. Citing Gloria Steinem to make her point, Chachra notes that

> "We've begun to raise daughters more like sons . . . but few have the courage to raise our sons more like our daughters." Maker culture, with its goal to get everyone access to the traditionally male domain of making, has focused on the first [i.e., raising daughters like sons]. But its success means that it further devalues the traditionally female domain of caregiving, by continuing to enforce the idea that only making things is valuable.

While I can imagine how Chachra's immersion in the STEM world might lead to the blanket statements made in her essay, the relationship between caregiving and making is more complex than the gender binary she has assigned to it. Here, it is useful to revisit the translation of "paying attention" once again, simply to note that in French, *"faire attention!"* can also mean, "be careful."[17]

Caitlin's project, for example, recuperates traditionally female and domestic practices of making, at once valorizing them and asserting them productively within contemporary practices of digital production. To borrow the words of Daniela K. Rosner and Sarah E. Fox, Caitlin offers a "counter-narrative of hacking grounded in legacies of craftwork that disrupt conventional ontologies of hacking," and this sort of work can lead to questions about "who counts as innovative" (560). Megan's project, on the other hand, asks us to reconsider the definition of "caregiver" not just as one who performs a service for others, but one who is attentively open to a world-making beyond the worlds offered to us by the digital service industries. It is not an exaggeration to draw such philosophical conclusions from the two projects described here because they are not just the product of soldering, but of writing. The process of making these projects involved carving out space, with the hands, for contemplative and generative consideration of technological being. As a result of this careful consideration, these students have not just made objects-to-think-with, they have also crafted philosophical essays. This, at last, should explain what it means to write with a soldering iron.

Notes

1. Derrida suggests that Plato is not offering a general condemnation of the externalization of memory; rather, he is targeting sophisitics. For a more detailed discussion of this point and its relationship to digital media, see my essay in *CTheory*, "Taking Care of Digital Dementia."
2. In a manifesto entitled "Anamnesis and Hypomnesis," Bernard Stiegler suggests that industrial society is founded on the production of hypomnesic objects that, in their efficiency, reduce the necessity for humans to retain specific forms of knowledge.

3. I explore this idea more carefully with Stiegler in the interview "Bernard Stiegler's Pharmacy: A Conversation."
4. The term *transindividuation* comes from French anthropologist Gilbert Simondon, specifically as described in his book *L'individuation psychique et collective*.
5. This short-circuiting is described rather lucidly in Stiegler's article, "Teleologics of the Snail: The Errant Self Wired to a WiMax Network."
6. See *Necromedia*, specifically Chapter 1: "Necromedia Theory and Posthumanism."
7. Note that the word soldering has roots in the Latin term *solidus*. From the Online Etymology Dictionary: "early 14c., *soudur*, from Old French *soldure*, *soudeure*, from *souder*, originally *solder*, 'to consolidate, close, fasten together, join with solder' (13c.), from Latin *solidare* 'to make solid,' from *solidus* 'solid.' "
8. Tim Ingold describes exteriorization as "a displacement or decentration of the source of operational behaviour from the physiological locus of human being" (433). This is a foundational concept for technology-based conceptions of posthumanism. See Cary Wolfe, *What Is Posthumanism?*, specifically Chapter 2: "Language, Representation and Sepcies: Cognitive Science versus Deconstruction."
9. In "Hyper and Deep Attention: The Generational Divide in Cognitive Modes," Hayles imagines a form of pedagogic experiment that "might try enhancing the capacity for deep attention by starting with hyper attention and moving toward more traditional objects of study" (196).
10. Sennett begins his argument with a discussion of his mentor Hannah Arendt's distinction between *Homo Faber* and *Homo Laborans*. His ultimate goal is to challenge Arendt's (supposed) assumption that "the mind starts working once labor is done" (7).
11. The problem with building an argument on the value of *making* is that it risks replicating the political problems and emancipatory rhetoric associated with "Maker Culture." For more on this topic, see my chapter "The Making of a Digital Humanities Neo-Luddite" in *Making Things and Drawing Boundaries*, edited by Jentery Sayers.
12. On the specific topic of speculative design, see Dunne and Raby, *Speculative Everything*.
13. See *The Art of Critical Making: Rhode Island School of Design on Creative Practice*. Of special interesting in this context is the chapter by John Dunningan on *thingking*.
14 For more information on this course, see criticalmedia.uwaterloo.ca/crimelab/?page_id=9.
15. The conspicuous focus on hands in this chapter opens the possibility for a critique of the ableism that seems prevalent in the *handy* co-evolutionary theories of Leroi-Gourhan, Stiegler, and others. With this mind, I will note that the term *basket case* itself, which is contemporary slang for a disturbed and agitated person, originated during the First World War as a way to describe quadriplegics who had to be carried in a basket. My point is not only that we must pay attention to such matters, but that a critical discourse on technics should not fetishize the hands. Rather, it should focus more capaciously on the ways in which we might become "hypnotized by the amputation and extension of [our] own being in a new technical form" (McLuhan 15).
16. An Arduino microcontroller is a small open-source computer, seemingly ubiquitous in digital DIY projects, that can be programmed to allow analog objects, like hand-woven baskets, to connect interactively with digital objects, like LCD screens. For a more formal definition, see arduino.cc.
17. Andrew Goffey makes this observation in a footnote of his translation of Stenger's book. For a more developed discussion of care and making, see my book *Necromedia*, especially Chapter 9, "Digital Care, Curation, and Curriculum: On Applied Media Theory."

Works Cited

Arendt, Hannah. *The Human Condition*. Chicago UP, 1958.
Bratich, J. Z., and Brush, H. M. "Fabricating Activism: Craft-Work, Popular Culture, Gender." *Utopian Studies*, vol. 22, no. 2, 2011, pp. 233–60.
Chachra, Debbie. "Why I Am Not a Maker." *The Atlantic*, 23 Jan. 2015, www.theatlantic.com/technology/archive/2015/01/why-i-am-not-a-maker/384767/. Accessed 6 July 2017.
Derrida, Jacques. *Dissemination*. U of Chicago P, 1981.
Dunne, Anthony, and Fiona Raby. *Speculative Everything: Design, Fiction, and Social Dreaming*. The MIT Press, 2013.
Ellul, Jacques. *The Technological Society*. Vintage, 1967.
Foucault, Michel. *The Order of Things: An Archaeology of the Human Sciences*. New York: Vintage, 1970.
Godard, Jean-Luc, director. *Two or Three Things I Know About Her*. Performances by Marina Vlady, Anny Duperey, Roger Montsoret. Argos, 1967.

Griffin, Matthew, Susanne Herrmann, and Friedrich A. Kittler. "Technologies of Writing: Interview with Friedrich A. Kittler." *New Literary History*, vol. 27, no.4, 1996, pp. 731–42.

Hadjiyanni, Tasoulla, and Kristin Helle. "(IM)Materiality and Practice: Craft Making as a Medium for Reconstructing Ojibwe Identity in Domestic Spaces." *The Journal of Architecture, Design and Domestic Space*, vol. 7 no. 1, 2010, pp. 57–84.

Hayles, N. Katherine. "Hyper and Deep Attention: The Generational Divide in Cognitive Modes." *Profession*, 2007, pp. 187–99.

Heidegger, Martin. *Discourse on Thinking*. Trans. John M. Anderson and E. Hans Freund. Harper & Row, 1968.

Honsberger, Megan. "*Mindflux*: From Use to Non-User Or, Application of Micro Digital Abstinence." Term paper, University of Waterloo, Ontario, Canada, 2016.

Ingold, Timothy. *Making: Anthropology, Archaeology, Art and Architecture*. Routledge, 2013.

Kraybill, Donald B, Karen M. Johnson-Weiner and Steven M. Nolt. *The Amish*. Johns Hopkins UP, 2013.

Leroi-Gourhan, André. *Gesture and Speech* [1964]. Trans. A. Bostock Berger. The MIT Press, 1993.

McLuhan, Marshall. *Understanding Media: The Extensions of Man*. New American Library, 1964.

Mann, Steve, and Hal Niedzviecki. *Cyborg: Digital Destiny and Human Possibility in the Age of the Wearable Computer*. Doubleday Canada, 2001.

Mitchell, Donald William. *Buddhism: Introducing the Buddhist Experience*. Oxford UP, 2008.

Novak, Marcos. "Liquid Architectures in Cyberspace." *Cyberspace: First Steps*, edited by Michael Benedikt. The MIT Press, 1992, pp. 225–54.

O'Gorman, Marcel. "The Making of A Digital Humanities Neo-Luddite." *Making Things and Drawing Boundaries: Experiments in the Digital Humanities*, edited by Jentery Sayers. U of Minnesota P, 2018. Manuscript in press.

——. "Broken Tools and Misfit Toys: Adventures in Applied Media Theory." *Canadian Journal of Communication*, vol. 37. no. 1, 2012, www.cjc-online.ca/index.php/journal/article/view/2519.

——. *E-Crit: Digital Media, Critical Theory, and the Humanities*. U of Toronto P, 2006.

——. *Necromedia*. U of Minnesota P. 2015.

——. "Taking Care of Digital Dementia." *CTheory*, Feb. 2015, journals.uvic.ca/index.php/ctheory/article/view/15128/6105. Accessed 6 July 2017.

O'Gorman, Marcel, and Bernard Stiegler. "Bernard Stiegler's Pharmacy: A Conversation." *Configurations*, vol. 18, no. 3, 2010, pp. 459–76.

Ondaatje, Michael. *The English Patient*. Vintage Canada, 1993.

Plato. *Phaedrus*. Trans. Benjamin Jowett. *The Internet Classics Archive*. http://classics.mit.edu/Plato/phaedrus.html. Accessed 2 July 2017.

Ratto, Matt, Sara Ann Wylie, and Kirk Jalbert. "Introduction to the Special Forum on Critical Making as Research Program." *The Information Society*, vol. 30, 2014, pp. 85–95.

Ray, Robert B. *The Avant-Garde Finds Andy Hardy*. Harvard UP, 2002.

Rosner, Daniela K., and Sarah E. Fox. "Legacies of Craft and the Centrality of Failure in a Mother-Operated Hackerspace." *New Media and Society*, vol. 18, no. 4, 2016, pp. 558–80.

Sennett, Richard. *The Craftsman*. Yale UP, 2009.

Simondon, Gilbert. *L'individuation psychique et collective*. Aubier, 1989.

Stengers, Isabelle. *In Catastrophic Times: Resisting the Coming Barbarism*. Trans. Richard Goffey. Open Humanities Press, 2015.

Stiegler, Bernard. *Taking Care of Youth and the Generations*. Trans. Richard Beardsworth and George Collins. Stanford UP, 2010.

——. "Anamnesis and Hypomnesis: Plato as the First Thinker of the Proletarianisation." *Ars Industrialis*. http://arsindustrialis.org/anamnesis-and-hypomnesis. Accessed 2 July 2017.

——. "Teleologics of the Snail: The Errant Self Wired to a WiMax Network." *Theory, Culture and Society*, vol. 26, nos. 2–3, 2009, pp. 33–45.

——. *Technics and Time 1: The Fault of Epimetheus*. Trans. Richard Beardsworth. Stanford UP, 1998.

Wolf, Maryanne. *Proust and the Squid: The Story and Science of the Reading Brain*. Harper Perennial, 2008.

Wolfe, Cary. *What is Posthumanism?* U of Minnesota P, 2010.

Woodcock, Caitlin. "Becoming a Basket Case: Resisting Technology to Preserve Craft-Skill." Term paper, University of Waterloo, Ontario, Canada, 2016.

PART II

Beyond Writing

6

"WITH FRESH EYES"

Notes toward the Impact of New Technologies on Composing

Kathleen Blake Yancey

The advent of electronic textuality presents us with an unparalleled opportunity to re-formulate fundamental ideas about texts and, in the process, to see print as well as electronic texts with fresh eyes.

(N. Katherine Hayles)

Last spring, I gave a talk to a group of undergraduates majoring in Editing, Writing, and Media, a media-rich program we launched in 2009. Having read my 2004 article "Looking for Sources of Coherence in a Fragmented World: Notes toward a New Assessment Design," they asked how that article might read were I to revise it, a question I have more thoughtfully considered since that time. Entailed in that question are three issues surrounding current print and digital models of composing that I detail in this chapter. The first issue is the multimodality of composing, with research showing scholarly enthusiasm for multimodality, but a less energetic curricular adoption of multimodality, at least programmatically. The second issue is the way we theorize composing, by means of attention to materiality, to curation as a theory of composing, and to assemblage for a language and theory explaining both composing and texts. The third issue is the set of developing reading practices responsive to new texts and instructive regarding what we value in new composing practices and texts. In addition, I close by briefly considering how we define writing, given automation not only in writing assessment, but also as writing itself. Collectively, these issues show us the relationship of newer composing practices and texts to older ones; demonstrate that new conceptual frameworks to describe and theorize composing are being developed; and point us toward challenges we have yet to fully articulate or address.

Multimodality

Multimodality, which conceptualizes texts and the processes composers use to create them through the concept of modes, has helped scholars theorize writing in new, often provocative ways. Some see multimodality as a kind of synonym for digitality, including in its definition the circulation of texts; others conceptualize multimodality as an inherent feature of all composing. As important, both early and current research on multimodality in pedagogical contexts suggests that while many in the field advocate for and endorse it, most schools do not yet require students to practice it intentionally.

In 2004, Jim Porter published his award-winning "Why Technology Matters to Writing: A Cyberwriter's Tale," which narrativizes his writing development as he theorizes writing more generally, referring to Dennis Baron's argument in *A Better Pencil* that technology doesn't change writing. In opposing this view and arguing that technology is by definition fundamental to writing, Porter identifies as a pivotal moment the teaching of his first desktop publishing class in the late 1980s. "Teaching that course," Porter says, "pushed me to consider visual design, page layout, and graphics as integral to rhetoric and writing" (381). The word "integral" categorizing features such as visual design signals that such features are neither decoration nor afterthought, but rather central to meaning-making. Of course, these features—visual design, page layout, and graphics—are just a few of what Gunther Kress calls modes for communication, his view that all communication is multimodal, a view Lester Faigley shares and historicizes:

> Images and words have long coexisted on the printed page and in manuscripts, but relatively few people possessed the resources to exploit the rhetorical potential of images combined with words. My argument is that literacy has *always* been a material, multi-media construct but we only now are becoming aware of this multidimensionality and materiality because computer technologies have made it possible for many people to produce and publish multimedia presentations. (175)

Likewise, as Jason Palmeri demonstrates, our writing curricula, even in pre-digital times, have been oriented to multimodality.

At the same time, there isn't consensus in the field on the terminology referring to such texts, those in print benefiting from features such as visual design and physical materiality and those in digital environments employing modes such as animation and sound. As Claire Lauer has demonstrated, multimodality and multimedia compete as descriptors. Still, most in the field recognize multimodality as the most common term referring to a more capacious composing drawing on all the available resources—whether composed in print, in digital environments, and/or made with physical materials (Shipka). Our engagements with these modes, however, has been uneven, with words and images garnering the most attention and with others often neglected. Until fairly recently, sound was largely ignored, but considerable scholarship is now addressing that gap (e.g., Ahern, Ceraso, Selfe). Similarly, the tactile continues to be under-theorized, although Shipka has attended to it, especially in the context of objects and pedagogy; Yancey and Davis, comparing vintage scrapbooks and electronic portfolios, have traced something of its genealogy as well as students' nostalgia for the feel and experience of print.[1]

Multimodal Curricula, or Not

Composing curricula also seem to lag behind the field's enthusiasm, except in writing in the disciplines contexts where writing is intentionally, explicitly multimodal—though conceptualized through other lenses, for instance, in the language of Tufte's visual display of information.[2] Likewise, recent writing studies' research on transfer has investigated how multimodal transfer occurs, some of it finding that when students compose multimodal texts, they often draw on out-of-class literacies (DePalma; Zawilski). Still, despite interest and activity in multimodal scholarship and pedagogy, there is much less on-the-ground practice, a point made by Jonathan Alexander and Jacqueline Rhodes, and especially at the program level, as confirmed empirically in two studies, one on the major by Rory Lee and one on FYC by Logan Bearden.

The context for both studies is an early large study of individual and institutional adoption of multimodal curricula, funded by a CCCC research grant (Anderson et al.) and intended to learn "more about what Composition teachers were doing with multimodal composing, what technologies they used in support of composing multimodal texts, and how faculty and administrators perceived efforts to introduce multimodal composition into departmental curricula and professional development" (63). Taking up this task, they designed a 141-question survey completed by 45 respondents, including 29 tenure-track faculty, five graduate students, and one non-tenure-track faculty member. A large majority of the respondents (84 percent) identified the unit of multimodal activity as class-based rather than course- or programmatically based; common class activities included analysis as much as or more than production; challenges to teaching multimodality included lack of technological infrastructure and other support (e.g., pedagogical professional development) and a dearth of ways to assess multimodal texts. Pedagogically, multimodality seemed in a nascent stage.

More recent research speaks to progress that, depending on the study, seems either steady or incremental. Rory Lee, in his 2013 dissertation "Now with More Modes? The Curricular Design and Implementation of Multimodality in Undergraduate Major Programs in Writing/Rhetoric," examined the adoption of multimodality in the major, surveying nineteen programs in the major, in part to determine if multimodality is a specific feature of the programs, and if so, how it has been incorporated. The survey targeted four areas of interest: the teaching of multimodality; the assessment of multimodality; support for multimodality; and information about the major. Some change, according to the survey respondents, has occurred. Specifically, as Lee reports, "there is now more programmatic attention devoted to multimodality, . . . there are more committee-designed assessments for evaluating multimodal texts, . . . there are more laptop-ready classrooms, and . . . there is more technology available for students composing multimodal texts" (92), with 18 of the 19 reporting undergraduate major programs in writing/rhetoric "requir[ing] a set of courses to offer multimodal instruction and/or emphasize multimodality as a defining feature of the major." In sum, this research suggests a shift from the instructor as the agent-of-change, as reported in the earlier survey, to the curriculum-as-agent. Respondents to the Lee survey, however, also expressed frustration with several elements of programmatic implementation, including teaching resources, assessment, and guidelines for scholarship and promotion.

It may be that programs in the major are particularly responsive to incorporating multimodality, especially when compared to first-year composition programs: such an inference could be drawn when putting the Lee study into dialogue with Logan Bearden's study "Favorable Outcomes: The Role of Outcomes Statements in Multimodal Curricular Transformation." Like Lee's study, Bearden's drew on a national survey, in his case of forty-eight WPAs speaking to the role of outcomes in shaping their programs and also to the ways that multimodality is represented. Here, both conceptualization and implementation were slow. As Bearden observes, "1)[first-year] composition programs at the national level still focus overwhelmingly on print, proving that multimodal curricular transformation has not yet taken place; [and] 2) there is little consensus on what a multimodal composition curriculum looks like or includes" (2).

In sum, while multimodality is being theorized in increasingly sophisticated ways, its practice in composition programs has yet to be fully implemented.

Theorizing Composing: Materiality

Since the height of writing process, several theories of composing have emerged, perhaps most instructive among them, in addition to multimodality, those oriented to materiality, curation, and assemblage. Each of these theories highlights a feature of composing characteristic of new composing practices and helps us understand composing's complexity more fully, with materiality pointing to the multiple surfaces, implements, and environments we compose on, with, and in; curation to the multi-textual nature of writing; and assemblage to the re-purposing central to composing practices and texts.

In early studies of composing, the writer wrote alone and a-materially (see, for example, Flower and Hayes); now materiality is at the heart of composing, as Bret Zawilski's 2015 snapshot description of two students' composing processes demonstrates.

> Mary scribbles on a small pad of paper next to the keyboard, quickly jotting down ideas for the project while scanning through the prompt on the screen of the computer in front of her. She draws boxes and columns on paper, thinking across 3 possible iterations of the text she hopes to construct, a YouTube video chronicling the genre of flash fiction. When the rough concept becomes more detailed, she shifts to the keyboard, opening a Word document and refining the lists from the scratch paper as she begins the process of storyboarding. Adam, another student in the same class, props a tablet next to his laptop computer, pulling up his original print project—a newsletter defining visual rhetoric and simultaneously exploring the complexity and influences of modern electronic dance music. On the tablet, he navigates to an online magazine, considering how he might frame his text in a similar way. His hands move back and forth between the two devices, browsing through texts and gathering raw materials. While the tablet continues to display model texts, Adam shuffles through windows on the desktop of his computer, opening documents in Word and InDesign while searching through his personal photography both on his computer and on the digital photography platform Flickr. (2)

What's interesting here, of course, is the multiply diverse materials the students intermingle in composing—paper and pen, laptop and tablet, social media sites and conventional software—using them seamlessly to complete a task. What's also interesting is how these miniature portraits show us what recursiveness looks like; while historically, recursive composing has been contextualized relative to time, here it's spatial at least as much as temporal.[3]

Looking at materiality through a much larger lens and collaborating with seven institutions in 2010, Michigan State University's WIDE center sought to identify the kinds of texts college students currently compose, a study particularly sensitive to materiality in the context of technologies. Reporting on a survey of 1366 first-year composition students at very different kinds of institutions, among them private and public four-year schools as well as community colleges (Elon University, Indiana University-Purdue University at Fort Wayne, Lansing Community College, Leeward Community College, Michigan State University, the University of North Carolina at Pembroke, and the University of Texas at El Paso), the study highlighted the genres, purposes, and platforms locating students' writing:

- SMS texts (i.e., texts using short message services on mobile devices), emails, and lecture notes are three of the most frequently written genres . . . of writing
- SMS texts and academic writing are the most frequently valued genres
- Some electronic genres written frequently by participants, such as writing in social networking environments, are not valued highly
- Students write for personal fulfillment nearly as often as for school assignments
- Institution type is related in a meaningful way to the writing experiences of participants, particularly what they write and the technologies used
- Digital writing platforms—cellphones, Facebook, email—are frequently associated with writing done most often [and]

- Students mostly write alone, and writing alone is valued over writing collaboratively. (Grabill et al., "Writing")

Here the materiality of composing is informed by technologies, with students valuing some materialities more than others, as the study suggests in reference to Facebook:

> Our results show that Facebook is used frequently among first-year college students, and they use it to write a broad range of genres. The reasons why students do not report valuing this writing as highly are unclear, but it likely means that when faced with a list of types of writing, they still attach a lot of value to traditional print forms such as research papers and academic writing vs. shorter, born-digital forms such as status messages and instant messages. (Grabill et al., "Writing")

At the same time, as a later WIDE report on the same project observed, these students are not dichotomous in their use of technologies for writing, consistently preferring one technology to others, but rather, as Zawilski's portraits suggest, flexible, often using one technology inside another: "students report using word-processing programs for e-mail (8 percent of word-processing program use) and text messages (5 percent of word-processing program use). Perhaps they draft these genres using word-processing programs" (Grabill et al., "Revisualizing" 9). As important, as the later study suggests, there are still many questions related to materiality for which we do not have answers, among them,

> *what precisely* are students writing when they use specific technologies to write in specific genres? *How* are they using these technologies to write these genres? Do they *use* these technologies differently when they write for different audiences? . . . Do students continue to use pencils for some tasks because, in the context where they most often write the corresponding genre, they are not allowed to use or do not have access to digital composing technologies? ("Revisualizing" 11)

Composing as Curatorial Practice

Another theory of writing, contextualized by prior practices, understands new composing and texts in the language and practices of the old. Carolyn Miller and Dawn Shepherd exemplify this approach in linking blogs to the antecedent genre of a ship or airplane log:

> a detailed chronological record, updated periodically, with its origins in marine navigation (and its etymology based in the measurement of sailing speed with a log thrown overboard). Logs are required for the voyage of a ship, the flight of an airplane, the duty of a lighthouse keeper, so use of the log as a record of either server or individual web surfer activity is consistent with the imagery of navigation as applied to the internet. The marked chronology and regularity of updating, mandatory features of the log, are bequeathed to the blog, along with the implication that the genre is the record of a journey whose details may be significant to others. The blog has been called a "log of our times" (Whatis.com, 2003). (11–12)

Blogs thus carry forward characteristics of their antecedents, chief among them the *marked chronology* and *regularity of updating*.

More generally, however, when assigning students online writing tasks, what we are doing, according to Krista Kennedy, is asking them to *curate*, especially as creators of encyclopedias do. In renaming writing as curation, Kennedy argues that students need to learn what she identifies as the labor of curating, including "the basics of project management, information gathering and filtering, strategic linking, metadata management, and basic site architecture" (177). Such composing includes three essential processes—arranging, interconnecting, and recomposing— and several stages, among them "filtration, recomposition, and [the design of] structures for findability and navigation" (177). Key to such writing, Kennedy says, is

> closer attention to the canon of arrangement. Successful curation requires a broader conceptualization of textual organization that moves outside of individual texts, such as the individual encyclopedia articles I examine in this piece, and into the ecologies they exist within (Brooke, 2009), both in their original state and in the new ecology they form through recomposition. (177)

Such composing does seem to be under way, again, if like multimodality, somewhat slowly. Yancey (2004b), for instance, points to arrangement in electronic portfolios as a source of invention, and has also pointed (2016) to the curation practices that successful ePortfolios require. Similarly, both undergraduate and graduate students at Florida State University (FSU) are literally curating exhibits for two online museums, the award-winning FSU Digital Postcard Archive and the Museum of Everyday Writing. Likewise, scholarly organizations are beginning to engage scholars in parallel efforts: the Modern Language Association, for example, has commissioned a digital archive of fifty key terms helpful for teaching developed through curation and published as *Digital Pedagogy in the Humanities*, as the editors explain.

> Each keyword . . . is curated by an experienced practitioner of digital pedagogy, who . . . contextualizes a pedagogical concept and then provides ten supporting artifacts, such as syllabi, prompts, exercises, lesson plans, and student work drawn from course, classrooms, and projects across the humanities. These artifacts are annotated and accompanied by lists of related materials for further reading. The collection is published under a Creative Commons BY-NC license to encourage circulation, editing, and repurposing by other practitioners.

In sum, curation as a concept and set of practices is useful for theorizing composing, emphasizing especially the shifting responsibilities of a composer and a new role for arrangement and helping us see the new, particularly as it is anchored in the prior.

Assemblage

A third conceptual lens for theorizing composing is that of assemblage: as texts "built primarily and explicitly from existing texts to solve a writing or communication problem in a new context" (Johnson-Eilola and Selber 381). Explored and developed in both art and critical theory (Yancey and McElroy 4), assemblage theory makes no ontological distinction between primary and re-used texts, and indeed celebrates and tags as normal such repurposing, which is often employed to call into question, or to account, the canonical (Schwitters). Likewise, as Yancey and McElroy explain in the introduction to their edited *Assembling Composition*, scholars and pedagogues in the composition community are drawing on assemblage theory both for theorizing composing and for teaching it:

In his 2016 *Assembling Arguments: Multimodal Rhetoric and Scientific Discourse*, Jonathan Buehl has recast assemblage as "rhetorical assembly," which he defines as a fundamental composing practice for multimodal writing in the sciences. Focusing on what he calls the transformative quality of assemblage, Dustin Edwards, in a 2016 *Computers and Composition* article, sees in its transformative nature both an extension and an adaptation of classical imitation. And . . . in her 2015 *College Composition and Communication* article Jacqueline Preston understands assemblage as the centerpiece of a new radical pedagogy, one in which previously transgressive textual practices are the norm. (3–4)

Within *Assembling Composition*, other scholars re-imagine composing more dramatically. Alex Reid speaks to the role that the non-human in any media ecology plays in composing; Stephen McElroy demonstrates how a given assemblage informs a multimodal trifecta—the postcards of everyday writing, Bruce Springsteen's music, and New Jersey's politics; and Jim Kalmbach theorizes the rhetorical engagements of assemblage:

> Creating an assemblaged text is not a simple linear process; for digital composers, it is better thought of as a coalition of *engagements* (technology engagements, architectural engagements, interface engagements, media engagements, textual engagements, code engagements, template engagements, . . .), as well as *negotiations* of the *embedded expertise* in those engagements. Learning to create assemblaged texts . . . [involves] a process of managing these coalitions of engagements and negotiating among the expertise that is embedded in them. (60)

Collectively, such theories of assemblage, as Yancey and McElroy assert, are especially useful for composing theory and practice given their ability to (1) articulate current "digital and material composing practices," (2) help students understand and approach writing as a living practice, (3) assist students to "trace earlier composing practices in the world as variants of assemblage," and (4) define assemblage as an ethical practice (17).

In sum, theories of composing located in three conceptual frames—materiality, curatorial practice, and assemblage—speak to what's new about such new composing; help historicize new practices relative to their antecedents; and foster a new language for describing composing.

Reading the New Compositions: What It Helps Us Understand about Writing

How we *read* texts rich in multimodality and materiality, curatorial in process, and assemblaged in texture isn't entirely clear, although, as aforementioned, such texts are available. In addition, some theory has sought to articulate the reading practices and challenges these texts prompt, in part to assist readers, of course, and in part to help us understand composing and compositions.

Scholars have begun theorizing both practices and challenges, especially in reviews. Such was the case of Kaitlin Clinnin, who reviewed the born-digital *The New Work of Composing* for *Computers and Composition Online*:

> The experience of reading *The New Work of Composing* is more aptly described as exploring. Just as born-digital, multimodal projects require the writer to rethink the composing process, the reader is also asked to rethink how texts are consumed. The editors and many of the authors play with the possibility of non-linearity both in the compilation of the collection as a whole and within the individual productions.

For some readers, this lack of linearity in terms of traditional claim-support based argumentation may be frustrating and make the collection seem inaccessible. However, the open organization of *The New Work of Composing* encourages multiple readings and new connections . . . among the projects. The option to structure the collection according to a traditional table of contents is present, but the scattered table of contents encourages a productive juxtaposition. When seemingly unrelated articles are explored in this scattered formation, the pieces . . . 'talk back' to one another in ways that a traditionally bound book is unable to, and the reader is able to take a more active role in the construction of the text and its meaning.

Here the reader, according to the review, might need to tolerate some potential frustration, but in doing so could exercise more agency and could invent both interaction and juxtaposition among chapters for a richer reading experience, a claim echoing that of hypertext theorists in the 1990s (e.g., Landow). At the same, such reading processes raise other questions, chief among them about the relationship of (1) form, (2) the arrangement of material a reader makes within a composition, and (3) a text: put succinctly, does it matter that different readers construct different texts?[4]

An approach to the same issue located in taxonomy was taken up by Jim Sosnoski in the 1990s. In conceptualizing reading electronic texts, Sosnoski identified the practice as hyper-reading; categorically, he defined it as distinctive both from reading in print and from reading exploratory hypertexts and articulated eight kinds of reading moves available to the reader:

1. filtering: a higher degree of selectivity in reading [and therefore]
2. skimming: less text actually read
3. pecking: a less linear sequencing of passages read
4. imposing: less contexualization derived from the text and more from readerly intention
5. filming: the ". . . but I saw the film" response which implies that significant meaning is derived more from graphical elements as from verbal elements of the text
6. trespassing: loosening of textual boundaries
7. de-authorizing: lessening sense of authorship and authorly intention [and]
8. fragmenting: breaking texts into notes rather than regarding them as essays, articles, or books. (163)

The list seems intuitively descriptive: filtering and skimming are likely activities that Facebook users employ daily, for example. At the same time, no study to date has inquired into or traced how well these descriptors account for our reading practices, nor have the implications of such practices for composing been theorized.

Another approach, twofold, to conceptualizing reading practices is located in genre and in an empirical methodology: in the genre of the electronic portfolio and methodologically in a documented sustained engagement with an instantiation of that genre. As part of a project intended to describe a screen-based eportfolio-specific reading process, Yancey, McElroy, and Powers "read" a single electronic portfolio. In doing so, they found three eportfolio reading practices they called viewing/reading:

First, there's the viewing/reading of each individual text—which itself involves different reading practices for different kinds of texts—print, static screen, animated multi-media (animated video files, academic "papers," etc.). Second, there's the reading of the portfolio on the screen, where basically one toggles from the reading of the screens and print files and animated files to the reading of the portfolio as a composition, and where in this toggling one constructs the portfolio one is viewing/ reading. And third, there's a spatial reading, which helps us understand in practical, embodied, and theoretical ways the portfolio as a composition. (np)

What these researchers traced is a set of reading and viewing practices operating concurrently and at different levels of scale—the individual texts constituting the portfolio; the portfolio itself via the screen; and the portfolio itself via a material representation of its contents.

As this scholarship illustrates, one of the issues at the heart of reading digital texts, and digital texts interspersing with print texts, is the vocabulary describing how we are reading and what we are valuing. In part, that's the task both Sosnoski and Yancey, McElroy, and Powers took up, Sosnoski attuned to Web reading generally, the ePortfolio readers to an empirical reading of a specific genre including texts in different media. Crystal Van Kooten offers a third approach, hers pedagogical, generating another set of terms designed to help students invent and compose electronic texts, divided into "rhetorical features" and "mulifaceted logic." The first category, *rhetorical features*, combines Bitzerian-like characteristics with Kressian modes identified as "technical features," for instance purpose, audience, fonts, animation and movement, and circulation and attribution. The second, *multifacted logic*, refers to metaphor, juxtaposition or collage, musical rhetoric, appropriation, counterarguments, and citation. What's interesting in this model is its distribution of rhetorical features across both categories; what's also interesting is its incorporation of vocabulary newer to composition—juxtaposition or collage[5] and appropriation, for instance—with more established vocabulary like purpose. This strategy resembles Yancey, McElroy, and Powers', which combines the familiar reading with the newer viewing; it may be that such a strategy, combining terms speaking to the new with relevant prior terms, will provide a remixed vocabulary sufficiently capacious for reading, writing, and assessing that is also sufficiently particular in its specification of the features we value in electronic texts.

Coda

While the composition community has theorized composition, and the reading of it, newly, insightfully, and sometimes provocatively, we have attended less to a relatively new phenomenon: machinically composed texts. We have, of course, studied other machinic-oriented composing-related activity, researching and critiquing machine assessment of writing, often called Automated Essay Scoring (AES); documenting its effects; advocating for human readers; and authoring position statements in print and on the Web (see, e.g., http://humanreaders.org/petition/). But while we have engaged on the issue of AES, we seem to have ignored the larger elephant in the room, the writing that is composed *by* machines that many of us read on a regular basis— even if, perhaps especially if, we do not recognize it as such.

Such machine-created prose, sounding remarkably human, includes texts ranging from sports stories to corporate reports for companies such as Credit Suisse and Deloitte. Consider, for example, an Associated Press story reporting on a minor league baseball game between the Brooklyn Cyclones and the State College Spikes, confirming the State College win: "Dylan Tice was hit by a pitch with the bases loaded with one out in the 11th inning, giving the State College Spikes a 9–8 victory over the Brooklyn Cyclones on Wednesday." And yet, the game wasn't a total loss for Brooklyn, as the story reports: "Despite the loss, six players for Brooklyn picked up at least a pair of hits. Brosher homered and singled twice, driving home four runs and scoring a couple. The Cyclones also recorded a season-high 14 base hits." This story: a machine-written text produced and circulated by the Associated Press.[6]

What *this* composing means—for our composing, for that of our students, for the field, for the country: that has yet to be determined. At the least, however, it is fair to say that such machine writing is a phenomenon calling into question what writing is, what human contributions to writing might be, and what such questions might mean for a political system calling itself a democracy.

Notes

1. As other research is documenting, many students express a nostalgia for print; see, for instance, Craig.
2. See University of Minnesota's Writing Enriched Curriculum (WEC) program for detailed writing plans expressing various disciplinarily inflected versions of multimodality.
3. Materiality is a part of composing for many writers of imaginative texts. Eudora Welty, for example, used paper, scissors, and pins in a Matisse-like assemblaged writing process, pinning her revisions like a writing seamstress: "I revise with scissors and pins . . . With pins you can move things from anywhere to anywhere, and that's what I really love doing—things in their best and proper place, revealing things at the time when they matter most."
4. For a more complete account of such differences in reading and their potential implications, see Yancey, "Print, Digital, and the Liminal Counterpart (in-between): The Lessons of *Hill's Manual of Social and Business Forms* for Rhetorical Delivery."
5. Some of these terms also fit with theories of composing, as described above: collage and appropriation with assemblage, for instance. Likewise, certain terms, like juxtaposition, are articulated by several scholars theorizing new writing, reading, and assessing practices (e.g., Shipka, Yancey 2004a).
6. Clearly, this area merits much more attention. It may be that such writing is a variant of the big data assemblage writing defined by Reid; alternatively, it may be that such machine writing could serve as a replacement for human writing, as Shelley Podolny has argued in the *New York Times*. Of equal concern is the rhetoric contextualizing machine writing, which, at least in the advertisements for it, centers on relieving writers of the burden of writing, which parallels rhetoric rationalizing the value of e-rating: to relieve teachers of the burden of grading.

Works Cited

Ahern, Kati Fargo. "Tuning the Sonic Playing Field: Teaching Ways of Knowing Sound in First Year Writing." *Computers and Composition*, vol. 30, no. 2, June 2013, pp. 75–86.

Alexander, Jonathan, and Jacqueline Rhodes. *On Multimodality: New Media in Composition Studies*. NCTE (CCCC SWR Series), 2014.

Anderson, Daniel, Anthony Atkins, Cheryl Ball, Krista Homicz Millar, Cynthia Selfe, and Richard Selfe. "Integrating Multimodality into Composition Curricula." *Composition Studies*, vol. 34, no. 2, 2006, pp. 59–84.

Baron, Dennis. *A Better Pencil: Readers, Writers, and the Digital Revolution*. Oxford UP, 2009.

Bearden, Logan. "Favorable Outcomes: The Role of Outcomes Statements in Multimodal Curricular Transformation." Dissertation, Florida State U, 2016.

Buehl, Jonathan. *Assembling Arguments: Multimodal Rhetoric and Scientific Discourse*. U of South Carolina P, 2015.

Ceraso, Steph. "(Re)Educating the Senses: Multimodal Listening, Bodily Learning, and the Composition of Sonic Experiences." *College English* vol. 77, no. 2, November 2016, pp. 102–23.

Clinnin, Kaitlin. "Review of *The New Work of Composing*." *Computers and Composition Online*, cconlinejournal.org/reviews/Clinnin/NWCHome.html, Spring 2013. Accessed 25 May 2017.

Craig, Jacob. *The Past is Awake: Situating Composers' Mobile Practices within their Composing Histories*. Dissertation, Florida State U, 2016.

DePalma, Michael-John. "Tracing Transfer across Media: Investigating Writers' Perceptions of Cross-contextual and Rhetorical Reshaping in Processes of Remediation." *College Composition and Communication*, vol. 66, no. 4, Sept. 2015, pp. 615–42.

Faigley, Lester. "Material Literacy and Visual Design." *Rhetorical Bodies: Toward a Material Rhetoric*, edited by Jack Selzer and Sharon Crowley. U of Wisconsin P, 1999, pp. 171–201.

Flower, Linda and John Hayes. "A Cognitive Process Theory of Writing." *College Composition and Communication*, vol. 32, no. 4, Dec. 1981, pp. 365–87.

Grabill, Jeff, Stacey Pigg, William Hart-Davidson, Paul Curran, Mike McLeod, Jessie Moore, Paula Rosinski, Tim Peeples, Suzanne Rumsey, Martine Courant Rife, Robyn Tasaka, Dundee Lackey, Beth Brunk-Chavez. "The Writing Lives of College Students Revisualizing Composition Study Group." *Writing in Digital Environments Research Center*. 7 September 2010, http://compositionawebb.pbworks.com/f/whitepaper.pdf. Accessed 3 July 2017.

———. "Revisualizing Composition: How First-Year Writers Use Composing Technologies." *Computers and Composition*, vol. 39, March 2016, pp. 1–13.

Johnson-Eilola, Johndan, and Stuart A. Selber. "Plagiarism, Originality, Assemblage." *Computers and Composition*, vol. 24, no.4, Dec. 2007, pp. 375–403.

Kalmbach, James. "Beyond the Object to the Making of the Object: Understanding the Process of Multimodal Composition as Assemblage." *Assembling Composition*, edited by Kathleen Blake Yancey and Stephen McElroy. NCTE (CCCC SWR Series), 2017, pp. 60–77.

Kennedy, Krista. "Textual Curation." *Computers and Composition*, vol. 40, June 2016, pp. 175–89.

Kress, Gunther. *Multimodality: A Social Semiotic Approach to Contemporary Communication*. Routledge, 2009.

Landow, George. *Hypertext: The Convergence of Contemporary Critical Theory and Technology (Parallax: Re-visions of Culture and Society)*. Johns Hopkins UP, 1991.

Lauer, Claire. "Contending with Terms: Multimodal and Multimedia in the Academic and Public Sphere." *Computers and Composition*, vol. 26, no. 4, December 2009, pp. 225–239.

Lee, Rory. "Now with More Modes?: The Curricular Design and Implementation of Multimodality in Undergraduate Majors in Writing/Rhetoric." Dissertation, Florida State U, 2014.

Miller, Carolyn R. and Dawn Shepherd. "Blogging as Social Action: A Genre Analysis of the Weblog," *Into the Blogosphere: Rhetoric, Community, and Culture of Weblogs*, edited by Laura Gurak, Smiljana Antonijevic, Laurie Johnson, Clancy Ratliff, and Jessica Reyman. U of Minnesota P, 2004. Accessed 25 May 2017.

Palmeri, Jason. *Remixing Composition: A History of Multimodal Writing Pedagogy*. Southern Illinois UP, 2012.

Pigg, Stacey. "Emplacing Mobile Composing Habits: A Study of Academic Writing in Networked Social Spaces." *College Composition and Communication*, vol. 66, no. 2, Dec. 2014, pp. 250–76.

Podolny, Shelley. "If an Algorithm Wrote This, How Would You Even Know?" *New York Times*, www.nytimes.com/2015/03/08/opinion/sunday/if-an-algorithm-wrote-this-how-would-you-even-know.html?_r=0, 7 March 2015. Accessed 7 Dec. 2016.

Porter, Jim. "Why Technology Matters to Writing: A Cyberwriter's Tale." *Computers and Composition*, vol. 20, no.4, December 2003, pp 375–94.

Selfe, Cynthia L. "The Movement of Air, the Breath of Meaning: Aurality and Multimodal Composing." *College Composition and Communication*, vol. 60, no. 4, June 2009, pp. 616–63.

Schwitters, Kurt. "Mertz Painting." *I Is Style*, edited by Rudi Fuchs. Stedelijk Museum: Rotterdam: NAi, 2000, p. 91.

Shipka, Jody. *Toward a Composition Made Whole*. U of Pittsburgh P, 2007.

Sosnoski, James J. "Hyper-Readers and Their Reading-Engines." *Passions, Politics, and 21st Century Technologies*, edited by Gail E. Hawisher und Cynthia L. Selfe. Utah State UP and NCTE, 1999, pp. 161–77.

Van Kooten, Crystal. "Toward a Rhetorically Sensitive Assessment Model for New Media Composition." *Digital Writing Assessment and Evaluation*, edited by Dànielle DeVoss and Heidi McKee. Computers and Composition Digital Press/Utah State UP, 2013. Accessed 25 May 2017.

Welty, Eudora. *Conversation with Linda Kuehl, 1972*. Eudora Welty Museum, Jackson, MS.

Yancey, Kathleen Blake. "Looking for Sources of Coherence in a Fragmented World: Notes toward a New Assessment Design." *Computers and Composition*, vol. 21, no.1, March 2004, pp. 89–102.

———. "Postmodernism, Palimpsest, and Portfolios: Theoretical Issues in the Representation of Student Work." *College Composition and Communication*, vol. 55, no. 4, June 2004, pp. 738–62.

———. "What ePortfolios Have to Teach (all of) Us: Curricula, Curation, Cataloging." Association for Authentic, Experiential, and Evidenced-based Learning. July 2016. Conference presentation.

———. "Print, Digital, and the Liminal Counterpart (in-between): The Lessons of *Hill's Manual of Social and Business Forms* for Rhetorical Delivery." *Enculturation*, Fall 2016. Accessed 7 Dec. 2016.

Yancey, Kathleen Blake, Stephen McElroy, and Elizabeth Powers. "Composing, Networks, and Electronic Portfolios: Notes toward a Theory of Assessing ePortfolios." *Digital Writing Assessment and Evaluation*, edited by Dànielle DeVoss and Heidi McKee. Computers and Composition Digital Press/Utah State UP, 2013. Accessed 25 May 2017.

Yancey, Kathleen Blake, and Matt Davis. "Notes toward the Role of Materiality in Composing, Reviewing, and Assessing Multimodal Texts." *Computers and Composition*, vol. 31, Spring 2014, pp. 13–28.

Yancey, Kathleen Blake, and Stephen McElroy. "Assembling Composition: An Introduction." *Assembling Composition*, edited by Kathleen Blake Yancey and Stephen McElroy. NCTE (CCCC SWR Series), 2017, pp. 3–25.

Zawilski, Bret. *When All That is Old Becomes New: Transferring Writing Knowledge and Practice across Print, Screen, and Network Spaces*. 2015. Dissertation, Florida State U, 2015.

7

DEVICES AND DESIRES

A Complicated Narrative of Mobile Writing and Device-Driven Ecologies

Aimee C. Mapes and Amy C. Kimme Hea

Device. In its archaic sense, device signals an ultimate distrust. After all, devices are often associated with impulsive decisions, and those impulsive decisions might just be our undoing. As we covet new technologies and see them as the mediums by which we write, tweet, like, share, and thread, the devices themselves are manifestations and articulations of our desires. This dual articulation of devices as both being and becoming alludes to the conditions of ubiquity, suspicion, and celebration. As colleagues who study composing—and the ways it constructs and is constructed by cultural phenomenon of technology—we are tentative to assume that we can ever fully understand literate practices and issues of power, but we are committed, nonetheless, to advocating for a more complex exploration of mobility and writing in this time of the smartphone as the device *par excellence*. In this way, through our five-year longitudinal study of student writers at the University of Arizona and research on youth smartphone practices, we have come to understand students' relationships to their smartphones, not just as productive tools, but as material and metaphorical articulations of their relationships, identities, and literate praxes. In rhetoric and composition, we might be well-served as teachers and scholars to understand the smartphone both as a part of student device-driven ecologies that allow literate activities and as a device that stands for who they are, and who they are becoming, in the world. In this way, smartphones are not merely separate pieces of equipment, but rather appendages to the body and conduits for intensity and even transformation. Embodied and networked, mobile devices are about becomings within competing relations. Giles Deleuze and Félix Guattari frame desire as continuous flows that are always *becoming*, and, according to Michalinos Zymbulas, form a *productive desire* (336). For literacy, this means situating texts, mediums, devices within a broader ecology of "signs, objects, and bodies," a phenomenon Kevin Leander and Gail Boldt described as "literacy unbounded" (36). As *productive desire*, mobile literacies manifest capacious social practices that instigate pleasure and displeasure simultaneously.

In this chapter, we aim to discuss mobile writing first by examining dominant constructions of mobile devices and writing that happens in untethered spaces. We assert that smartphone users articulate strong relationships to the devices themselves and their everyday uses, and we find that for young adults, in particular, mobile devices are deeply embedded in their daily interactions. If we are to understand mobile writing, we must also examine the complex and often ambivalent articulation of mobile devices as literacy tools, and it is critical to understand emotional and desiring relationships that are part of smartphone use. After situating smartphones as strongly connected with emotions and technologies that form student data-driven ecologies, we review relevant literatures in our field and instructional design that examine student and teacher roles in mobile learning and mobile writing, specifically. Situated within these current conversations, we describe the context of our five-year longitudinal study of student writers at the University of Arizona and the participants' descriptions of their own mobile writing lives, including their smartphone use. For our participants, mobile devices conjure both the pleasures and promises of evolving identities. Mobile devices become mediums of desire, mediums for connecting to people, communities, and ideas. Participants also describe their mobile devices, particularly their smartphones, with some ambivalence when alluding to their "dependence." We find that students demonstrate a privileging of mobility over mere connectivity and a seemingly conservative view of their smartphones as a medium for writing. Our argument plays on the material and metaphoric assumptions about mobile writing to think through both the mundane and profound identifications and applications of mobile writing provided by students participating in our study and through the dominant discourses surrounding mobile writing practices. In conceptualizing mobile devices as desiring machines, we consider the ways students resist certain constructions of mobile writing as academic, or even academic enough, and the ways in which smartphones amid mobile writing ecologies are often controlled or conditioned as antithetical to educational aims.

Dominance of Mobile Devices

To understand our dependence on mobile devices and their role in our lives, the Pew Research Institute has collected data on public technology practices since 1983. Most recently, its attention turned to the ubiquity of smartphones. In "U.S. Smartphone Use in 2015," Aaron Smith revealed that "young adults have deeply embedded mobile devices into the daily contours of their lives" (2). Several years ago, one of us asked a question in her first-year writing class that was keyed to Pew's earlier research on millennials, asking on the first day of class—as an ice breaker—"what is something that you simply could not live without?" This question produced two dominant responses of either "my family" or "my friends," but quite expectedly several students boldly said, "my phone." Notably, Smith found in Pew's study that

> [s]ome 49% of smartphone-dependent Americans say that their phone is "something they couldn't live without," nearly identical to the 46% of users with even more internet access options who say the same. Indeed, there are a notable lack of differences between smartphone-dependent users and other smartphone owners across all of these choice pairs. (4)

In other words, even when the smartphone is only one of the device options available in Pew's study, its significance in the ecology of devices is still strong, and the emotional relationship to the smartphone is one that Pew found most compelling among younger survey respondents: according to the report,

> Fully 73% of 18–29 year old smartphone owners indicated that their phone made them feel "distracted" during the study period, 11 percentage points higher than among those ages 30–49 and 41 percentage points higher than among those 50 and older. (Smith 40)

Also profound for this cohort was the range of emotional depth, which was more pronounced on every level, from anger to happiness:

> Younger users were also around three times as likely as those 50 and older to say that their phone made them angry at one point or another during this study (22% vs. 7%). At the same time, younger users are significantly more likely than those in other age groups to indicate that they experienced being happy or grateful as a result of their phone. (Smith 40)

The range of uses, emotions, and attachments to the smartphone for a younger generation may not seem particularly surprising to most of us who teach and study technology and composition in higher education. The relationship students have with their smartphones is connected to a complex of technologies, particularly their laptops, tablets, and other devices. Perhaps now more than ever, students are negotiating a range of mobile devices that come to form their literacy ecology.

Mobile Writing, Mobile Literacies, and Desire

In *Going Wireless: A Critical Exploration of Wireless and Mobile Technologies for Composition Teachers*, Kimme Hea and colleagues wrote about dominate practices and discourses of wireless and mobile technologies, and in her own chapter, Kimme Hea asserted that non-place assumptions about wireless technologies give way to deterministic narratives of mobility that construct the 24/7 teacher and student, calling for place-based pedagogical practices that accommodate differential experience rather than erase access and agency (217). Today, we still see the ways in which dominant narratives of devices produce and are produced by certain assumptions of what it means to be a mobile writer. Stacey Pigg's *in situ* study of writers in semi-public contexts, such as a coffee shop and campus technology commons, demonstrated a range of literate activities that were part of participants' composition practices (252). Although the device of her research was the laptop, Pigg argued, "researchers can benefit from increased attention to the agentive role physical environments play in interactions with bodies and virtual spaces" (255). Such an approach to mobile writing means looking for relations across time and space instigated by social, technological, and economic forces (254). While mobile writing is more of a commonplace for students and researchers, we also believe that mobile writing might be even more elusive as constructions of both "mobility" and "writing" are often touted as placeless or, worse, pointless. In other words, the field acknowledges, as well, the shifting uses of mobile devices as the town hall speakers at 2011 Computers and Writing Conference expressed regarding future directions in the field. Doug Eyman suggested that two important directions in writing pedagogies will be "mobile devices" and "virtual environments" (329), and in this same conversation, Bill Hart-Davidson, Mike McLeod, and Jeff Grabill, members of The WIDE Research Center, discussed the shifting sense that users of mobile devices and other technologies are not necessarily thinking of them as computational tools but as mediums by which we act to fulfill our needs and purposes (333).

It is the case that mobile technologies conduct action and produce effects, and despite their seeming ubiquity and invisibility, there also is a deep connection between smartphone users and the device itself. This connection seems askew from the ways in which we might have once considered the networked or personal computer, even though the phenomenon of openness to other users and to different spaces was certainly part of the promise. Missing in current discourse is an exploration of desire that frames mobile writing more complexly within networks of competing relations. We draw from a branch of youth literacy studies committed to researching mobile literacies as capacious, distributed, embodied, and agentive. One substantive difference seems to be an intimacy with smartphones as part of identity, status, and near hourly conduct that makes it an intriguing case in the complex of students' mobile ecologies. Indeed, research examines the way the smartphone is an extension of our bodies and nearly constant practices of connection with others. Jonathan Donner, Shikoh Gitau, and Gary Marsden, specifically, examined how youth access to smartphones leads to local ecologies and digital literacies. In everyday life, argued Donner, Shikoh, and Marsden, mobile literacies remain "appealing, disruptive, and ubiquitous" (575). In the same way, Gleason's study of teen Twitter writing defines new literacies flowing through portable devices as "embodied, relational, and networked" (33). For Gleason, mobile devices, as mediums, initiate equally relevant "sociotechnical affordances" (33) that engender membership and identities. Amid an increasingly networked space, mobile literacies, according to Glynda Hull and Amy Stornaiuolo, make prominent "the rhetorical stances and ethical commitments involved in communicating across difference—the cognitive, emotional, ethical, and aesthetic meaning-making capacities and practices of authors and audiences" (17). That is, mobile devices are a means of fulfilling needs and purposes. The portability of mobile device and its continuous connection across various fields epitomize intense, ongoing assemblages of processes and effects. Mobile-centric in nature, distributed, embodied and agentive, these are features of *a productive desire* defined by Deleuze and Guattari as assemblages of elements, of processes, of affects. These desires are exemplified for us in the ways that participants in our study relate to the fuller range of the technology biome that includes their phones, laptops, readers, desktops, and other devices as mediums to their literate lives.

UA Longitudinal Study of Student Writers

This chapter focuses primarily on data collected in a Fall 2016 survey of eighteen remaining participants of The University of Arizona (UA) Study of Student Writers (UA Study), but the study itself has been ongoing for five years. We began the UA Study to contribute to literature in Writing Studies (see, for instance, Beaufort; Carroll; Negretti; Roozen; Sternglass; Wardle; Yancey, Robertson, and Taczak) and to engage critically with public claims about a decline in the literacy skills of college students (Arum and Roksa; Bauerlein). With 158 consenting participants in our first year (2012–2013) of this planned attrition study, we quickly came to realize that any study about writing experiences illuminates precarious and agentive connections between identity and language learning, or what Roozen and Erickson "densely literate landscapes" (1.06). Of the 158 participants from year one, sixty-one participants in the second year consented to remain in the study and participated in qualitative interviews and submitted writing samples (2013–2014). In years three and four (2014–2015 and 2015–2016), twenty-eight students participated in multiple data collection tasks, including surveys, interviews, and video logs and video literacy narratives. Eighteen participants have remained in the project in the fifth and final year (2016–2017), sharing writing samples, completing surveys, and participating in spring semester interviews. And as we have moved toward deep data, or gathering rich portraits of student writers' lifeworlds, our study emphasizes relationships between what students write and their writing development across contexts.

Throughout our study, we have noticed how student definitions of writing are often constructed along relatively conservative lines as compared to us researchers. For UA Study students, the predominate constructions of writing and their writing lives was their academic writing, particularly essays, lab reports, and other typical assignments throughout their college careers.

Common during interviews when prompted to describe out-of-school writing, students struggled to define writing other than academic. One nursing student in year three explained, "Now that I'm in nursing school, all the writing I do is when I'm writing notes or writing papers, you know. It's all kinda for school now. There's no time for fun writing!" So, too, during fall 2014, 28 students completed a writing experience survey. One question in the survey offered a ten-point scale to rate the level at which they believed specific digital literacy practices constituted writing. On the scale, a rating of 1 meant "I do not consider this to be writing at all" and 10 was "I definitely consider this to be writing." Students rated blogging, Facebook status, online chatting, tweets, Instagram/Snapchat, instant messaging, texting, Web content, and online comments along this 10-point scale. Only blogging and Web content, on average, received ratings above 5; blogging averaged 7.6 and Web content 7.2. The practices rated lowest, on average, were online chatting (3) and Instagram/Snapchat (3.7). Students' conservative constructions of writing are not necessarily surprising, especially given that our research study prompted participants to share academic writing samples and reflect on their development through surveys and through interviews with members of the UA Writing Program. They are immersed daily in writing for the purposes of their academic coursework and their definitions of writing—despite questions about personal and other less academic genres—are still dominated by writing for school purposes.

Across five years, we have collected information about digital and mobile device use through survey questions, video log introductions, and participants' own literacy narratives. In fall 2016, we designed a voluntary survey focused on mobile devices. This brief 14-question survey was provided as part of their welcome message for the final year of our longitudinal study, and each participant was offered an additional nominal incentive for completing the survey. Here, we turn to trace the responses of eighteen participants (2016–2017) as they answered questions about their mobile writing practices. Student mobile device use was strikingly similar to reports from Pew, but as our questions were related to literacy practices and our own ongoing study to understand students' literacy, we also asked questions about mobile writing practices that distinguish our survey. We do see, however, that students in the UA Study use their smartphones as part of a larger ecology of devices, that they are ambivalent about their dependence on their phones, and that they do not often think of smartphones as composing devices as much as they are willing to use them for reading and reviewing for writing activities.

Access and Connectivity in Device-Driven Ecologies

In terms of available technologies, all eighteen respondents reported having either a limited or unlimited data plan and a smartphone as part of their ecology of devices, and they are using their phones more than any other device to stay connected to others and to data they rely on. In order to understand students' technological access to connectivity, we asked about their data coverage, devices (e.g., smartphone, reader, laptop, desktop, smart television), and their Internet connectivity at and away from home. All students reported having mobile data access, although potentially limited by their plan, and no student selected "none" as an option across the complex of devices and connections. That means 100 percent of our respondents have connectivity with their phones and each also had at least one other means of connecting. Fifty-nine percent[1] of respondents also reported that they check their smartphone every 30 minutes to 1 hour, 35 percent stated checking their phones every 2–7 hours, and only 6 percent noted use about once per day (see Figure 7.1). In short, all connected daily.

And, among all students with both limited or unlimited data plans, the next means of connecting was their laptop with a home connection. Our limited sample of participants skews higher than Pew's research of "[y]oung adults (85% of whom are smartphone owners)," but

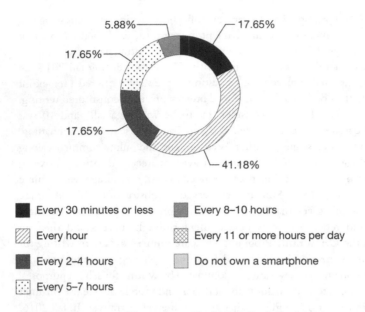

Figure 7.1 Frequency of Smartphone Use by UA Study Participants

our participants display similar commitments to using their smartphones for "a host of information seeking and transactional behaviors" (Smith 5). In fact, every student in our study relies heavily on their smartphones to stay connected to others and to information, but they also reported their laptops as a major part of their mobile data-driven ecology which, as we will discuss, comes to figure their academic writing experiences, dominant literacy practices, and social formations.

Student Relationships to Smartphones

Among the questions asked, we were most interested in the relationships that students have with their smartphones as part of their daily lives, and indeed, their identities and desires. To access those relationships, we provided a range of word pairs, asking the participants to select their top two pairs that best describe their relationship to their smartphone (unnecessary–indispensable; leash–freedom; distracting–connecting; bothersome–helpful; financial burden–worth the cost; work tool–entertainment source; hinders writing projects–helps with writing projects). Of these pairings "distracting–connecting" received 88 percent and "work tool–entertainment source" yielded 71 percent; the pairing about writing (e.g., hinders–helps with writing) was the only one to receive zero responses. As a follow up to these pairings, we asked an open-ended question where participants provided one word that best characterizes their relationship to their smartphone, and these responses were equally illuminating with terms such as "addicting," "addicted," and three times the term "dependent," all totaling 27 percent of our participants. Thought not generalizable, a pattern of emotion suggests the power of their smartphones as integral to their daily—if not hourly—existence. When we asked how many days our participants thought they could reasonably go without their phone, 41 percent suggested two days, but even when including those responses, 77 percent of all participants suggested no more than three days. We also found other study participants were less sanguine in their anticipated usage with 18 percent suggesting ten days or more, but even among those students, they also selected "distracting–connecting" or "unnecessary–indispensable" as at least one of their two dominant word pairs. These relationships are similarly found in Pew's more extensive study where emotional expressions of its participants highlighted not just the intimate relationship with smartphones among younger users but also the range of expressions and depth of these emotions with "[y]ounger smartphone owners tend[ing] to experience a wider range of these emotions compared with older users—they are more likely to report feeling positive emotions like 'happy' or 'grateful,' but also more likely to report negative emotions like 'distracted' and 'angry' " (Smith 10). Similarly, our study participants self report device usage as intense, multiple, and in flux.

Student Constructions of Literacy and Devices

Our participants' emotional responses and desired uses and purposes for their smartphones becomes even more interesting in the context of specific academic uses and literacy practices. Pew found that its cohort of 18–29-year-olds included "30% to take a class or get educational content" with their smartphone (Smith 20), but this project did not drill down into specific educational activities. For our part, we wanted to know how frequently UA Study participants were using a range of mobile and connected devices—smartphone, reader, tablet/laptop, desktop, or print journal or other paper option—to aid their writing activities of planning/brainstorming, researching, drafting, revising, and editing. Across all of these devices, students were to indicate frequently, occasionally, rarely, or never as common to the device and the writing practice. Without much surprise, we learned that laptops were coded as the dominant technology used to assist our participants in their writing activities, being listed across every category as either frequently (78 percent) or occasionally (76 percent) used to support their literacy work. With 28 percent of our participants owning a desktop, the lack of its use for most of these activities was unexpected, especially with "drafting" where even a journal or other paper option received higher rankings than the desktop. Thus, for our participants the mobility of device seems to eclipse the importance of mere connectivity.

While we know our participant pool is small, their privileging of mobility is one that we found strong in follow-up questions about using their smartphones for numerous writing practices: (a) to take notes or record assignment/project ideas; (b) conduct research for an assignment/project; (c) read online pdfs, books, or other materials for an assignment/project; (d) write part of an assignment/project; (e) review a draft of an assignment/project; (f) edit a draft of assignment/project; or (g) store an assignment/project. This question about practices and frequency (with the scale of frequently, occasionally, rarely, and never) yielded results with (c) reading at 68 percent and (b) researching at 34 percent as the greatest share with frequently and occasionally for our participants. This question was followed by one related to smartphone applications that the participants used for literacy activities and personal and professional connections. Among response options of compose collaboratively with other people; assign component of a project to other team members; store your work in the cloud; draft writing projects including written, visual, audio, and other elements of a project; create infographics or slideshows; maintain professional relationships; and maintain personal relationships, we noted that students in our study indicated using smartphones more to maintain professional and personal relationships than any of the activities suggested (see Figure 7.2).

As we followed the participants, we have noticed students' own ambivalence to connect some writing and literate activities typical of devices to their academic lives as writers. While they certainly have access to and participate in mobile writing, there remains a perceived divide between literate practices of their smartphone use in contrast to other devices, such as laptops. In the third

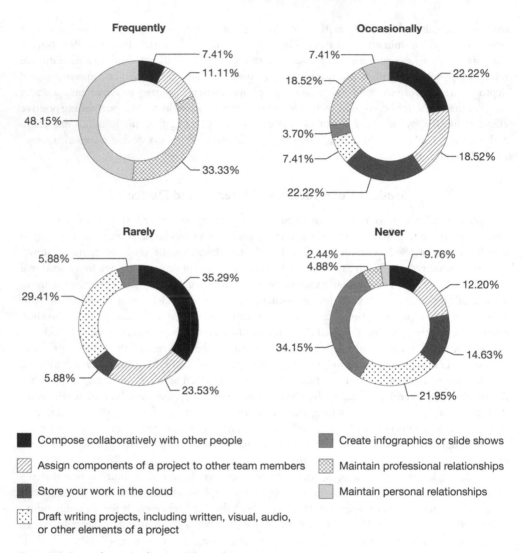

Figure 7.2 Smartphone Application Uses and Frequencies

year of our study, participants were asked to create video logs (vlogs) in the Fall 2014 as a means to introduce themselves to each other, and they were later asked to respond on video with their own literacy narratives. In both of these formats, participants often mentioned the joys of learning to read or being read to as the formative components of early literacy, and some participants also shared stories where other mobile technologies, not just print books (which are perhaps one of the earliest mobile literacy technologies we could identify) but also technologies such as "Leapfrog" were part of their literacy education. To see where students might construct that arc of a narrative now, we asked if any of them remembered using mobile technologies when learning to read or write, and six of the eighteen participants shared that they used either a Leapfrog or computer-based reading tool to facilitate their early learning. In other words, at least 25 percent of our participants have used digital, and often mobile, technologies as formative to their literacy learning, but many still seem to resist naming these devices as literacy tools. We understand that the ubiquity of such technologies can mask rather than illuminate their pivotal role in literacy experiences, but we also have come to see that students are reluctant to embrace certain technologies of personalization, play, and social force—whether early mobile devices such as the hand-held game or later devices such as the smartphone—as fully imbued literacy tools, or mobile writing devices, a point we will soon discuss as also intimately related to educational policy and forms of classroom control and surveillance.

Conclusions

Students' desires are articulated to their uses of devices, particularly mobile ones, from much earlier in their experiences than we might have imagined, and it seems, however, that their own personalization of devices such as the smartphone have a distinctive role in both their literate constructions and identity formations. In a white paper by Jeff Grabill and Stacey Pigg, et al., "The Writing Lives of College Students: Revisualizing Composition Study Group," which was an expansive study of student composing practices across a range of different institutions of higher education, their participants' frequency of writing tasks with smartphones (e.g., posting messages or updating social media sites) did not necessarily correlate with the value that those same students placed on the types of writing they participate in with that device. In fact, WIDE colleagues wrangled with students' seeming limited value of their more frequently composed writing with social media or texts with their increased value of writing academic genres such as research papers or argumentative essays by concluding that "when faced with a list of types of writing, they [students] still attach a lot of value to traditional print forms such as research papers and academic writing vs. shorter, born-digital forms such as status messages and instant messages" (9). We found a similar result with our participants not associating smartphones with more academic literacy practices. For instance, recall the nursing student who described not having time for "fun writing" during her junior year of college. When prompted further about social media writing during the same interview, she explained, "I make really cool Instagram captions. . . . I'm not super active on Facebook. It's more like when I share something, I'll write, like, my feelings about it." Fun writing and expression of feelings are linked to mobile composing, which does not seem to code for our participants as writing. We argue, it is not necessarily a result of students' misunderstandings or lack of sophistication, or even a purposefully narrow definition of literacy than our own as computer compositionists—while this may be part of it. Rather, certain culturally significant constructions of mobile devices might be reasonable rationales for students' constructions of mobile writing practices as still much more connected to laptops than smartphones while certain personal and affective desires might situate social texts amid a broader mobile literacy ecology that fulfill different needs for participants in contrast to their academic purposes.

To the former point, students in our study have been in K-16 settings where the presence of smartphones may not have been expected or necessarily exulted as a positive mobile learning device, and likely not one for composing. Consider that the mere presence of a smartphone in class has been maligned if not outright banned as part of their intellectual lives. The common policies of K-16 classrooms where smartphones are to be kept out of the space, or if found, confiscated to discipline students is part of the cultural landscape of the smartphone for participants in WIDE's study and the UA Study. For students, smartphones are defined as social spaces unwelcome in academic spaces. Their smartphones may well be deemed as in need of absolute restriction from use—as in the classroom—or of control as a means to surveil students' lives—outside of the classroom (Turkle). At our own home institution, University of Arizona, it is often the case that faculty prefer to restrict smartphone use in their courses rather than attempt to integrate it into lessons and academic practices. As recent as Fall 2013, the Code of

Conduct policy from UA Dean of Students included the following statement about the use of electronic devices: "This means no electronic devices in an ON position in class without permission of the instructor." These restrictive practices may be changing as more faculty across the spectrum of education practice BYOD—bring your own device—pedagogies, but the debate about benefits versus distraction[2] are still commonplace, leading often to the devices of social media, SMS, and other writing practices as holding seemingly less value as academic writing practices that are aligned with "real writing" in academe and beyond.

Across research studies on mobile literacies, students, youth, and other mobile device users are described as becoming, through a constellation of relations, "literacy unbound." Our study suggests students are situated locally and connected globally, allowing for desire as continuous flows that are always *becoming* and embodied (Zymbylas 336). In this way, student writers of the UA Study have helped us to understand the unboundness of mobile writing in terms of durable tensions of distraction and connection, constraint and affordance, irritation and pleasure. Students are keenly aware that their smartphones connect them to others, personally and professionally, and it is this very use that they have come to understand and enact. Thus, we might want to take seriously the ways smartphones are desiring machines for our students and ones that have become deeply intertwined with their social activities, identities, and intimacies of daily, nearly hourly, life. In fact, we began to see this relationship as one of the rationales as to why many participants in the UA Study consistently resisted labeling their interaction with these devices as a form of writing, yet we also want to further assert that this resistance is not unfounded. In their own experiences with "trying out" expressions, desires, and intensities, their smartphones have given them these opportunities, likely more so than classroom interactions. In coding these devices as "school" or "academic" devices—as we have yearned to do so ourselves—we also know that students would be seemingly giving up their own purposes in exchange for coding them as academic or as legitimate writing tools. In other words, as soon as their texts are academic, as soon as their devices are mobile writing tools, as soon as they can no longer engage in social media platforms without bumping into their teachers and parents, there is a re-coding of these devices from social and identity tools to ones of academe. While we know they can be both, we certainly know that the feelings expressed about smartphone use is still predominantly in the world of their lives outside of the classroom. If many young people, like our study participants, do not necessarily think of smartphones as purely composing tools, but as prominently mediums to engender memberships and to express different emotions, then it is important for us as teachers to be critical of educational narratives that prohibit such capacious desires. While we do not want to reinforce a binary between personal and professional or academic and social, we also understand that the affective and desiring relations of devices and identity are not easily discerned or sorted into "worthy" praxis for us as either teachers or researchers. It also does not mean that students are incapable of rearticulating their devices either. For our part, we can say that student writers of the UA Study have helped us to understand the unboundness of mobile device use. It is no wonder that their relationships to these conduits to personal, professional, and social experiences conjure mixed emotions—both fear and loathing—as students wrangle with the best and highest uses of their different devices that constitute their technological biome, and we teachers and researchers might want to interrogate our own desires for these devices as part of the future of the compositional landscape as well.

Notes

1. We round the percentages to whole numbers, but the percentages appear with decimals in figures.
2. The Boston Globe asked about BYOD and recoding student devices as academic ones: www. bostonglobe.com/lifestyle/style/2015/06/15/cellphones-school-teaching-tool-distraction/OzHjXy

L7VVIXV1AEkeYTiJ/story.html, and they discuss this UK study on such use: http://cep.lse.ac.uk/pubs/download/dp1350.pdf.

Works Cited

Arum, Richard, and Josipa Roksa. *Academically Adrift: Limited Learning on College Campuses*. U of Chicago P, 2011.

Bauerlein, Mark. *The Dumbest Generation: How the Digital Age Stupefies Young Americans and Jeopardizes Our Future*. Tarcher-Perigee, 2009.

Beaufort, Anne. *College Writing and Beyond: A New Framework for University Writing Instruction*. Utah State UP, 2007.

Carroll, Lee Ann. *Rehearsing New Roles: How College Students Develop As Writers*. Southern Illinois UP, 2002.

Deleuze, Giles, and Félix Guattari. *A Thousand Plateaus: Capitalism and Schizophrenia*. Trans. B. Massumi. U of Minnesota P, 1987.

Donner, Jonathan, Shikoh Gitau, and Gary Marsden. "Exploring Mobile-only Internet Use: Results of a Training Study in Urban South Africa." *International Journal of Communication*, vol. 5, 2011, pp. 574–97.

Gleason, Benjamin. "New Literacies Practices of Teenage *Twitter* Users." *Learning, Media and Technology*, vol. 41, no.1, 2015, pp. 31–54.

Grabill, Jeff, Stacey Pigg, William Hart-Davidson, Paul Curran, Mike McLeod, Jessie Moore, Paula Rosinski, Tim Peeples, Suzanne Rumsey, Martine Courant Rife, Robyn Tasaka, Dundee Lackey, Beth Brunk-Chavez. "The Writing Lives of College Students Revisualizing Composition Study Group." *Writing in Digital Environments Research Center*. 7 September 2010, http://compositionawebb.pbworks.com/f/whitepaper.pdf. Accessed 3 July 2017.

Hull, Glynda, and Amy Stornaiuolo. "Cosmopolitan Literacies, Social Networks, and 'Proper Distance': Striving to Understand in a Global World." *Curriculum Inquiry*, 44, 2014, pp. 15–44.

Kimme Hea, Amy. "Perpetual Contact: Re-articulating the Anywhere, Anytime Pedagogical Model of Mobile and Wireless Composing." *Going Wireless: A Critical Exploration of Wireless and Mobile Technologies for Composition Teachers and Researchers*, edited by Amy C. Kimme Hea. Hampton, 2009, pp. 199–221.

Leander, Kevin, and Gail Boldt. "Rereading 'A Pedagogy of Multiliteracies': Bodies, Texts, and Emergence." *Journal of Literacy Research*, vol. 45, no. 1, 2012, pp. 22–46.

Negretti, Raffaella. "Metacognition in Student Academic Writing: A Longitudinal Study of Metacognitive Awareness and Its Relation to Task Perception, Self-regulation, and Evaluation of Performance." *Written Communication*, vol. 29, no. 2, 2012, pp. 142–79.

Pigg, Stacey. "Emplacing Mobile Composing Habits: A Study of Academic Writing in Networked Social Spaces." *College Composition and Communication*, vol. 66, no. 2, 2014, pp. 250–75.

Roozen, Kevin. "Tracing Trajectories of Practice: Repurposing in One Student's Developing Disciplinary Writing Processes. *Written Communication*, vol. 27, no.3, 2010, pp. 318–54.

Roozen, Kevin, and Joe Erickson. *Expanding Literate Landscapes: Persons, Practices, and Sociohistoric Perspectives of Disciplinary Development*. Computers and Composition Digital P/Utah State UP, 2017, ccdigitalpress.org/expanding/. Accessed 3 July 2017.

Smith, Aaron. "U.S. Smartphone Use in 2015." *Pew Research Center*. April 2015, www.pewinternet.org/files/2015/03/PI_Smartphones_0401151.pdf. Accessed 3 July 2017.

Sternglass, Marilyn S. *Time To Know Them: A Longitudinal Study of Writing and Learning at the College Level*. Lawrence Erlbaum, 1997.

Turkle, Sherry. *Alone Together: Why We Expect More from Technology and Less from Each Other*. Basic, 2011.

Walker, Janice R., Kristine L. Blair, Douglas Eyman, Bill Hart-Davidson, and Mike McLeod. "Computers and Composition 20/20: A Conversation Piece, Or What Some Very Smart People Have to Say about the Future." *Computers and Composition*, vol. 28, 2011, pp. 327–46.

Wardle, Elizabeth. "Understanding 'Transfer' from FYC: Preliminary Results of a Longitudinal Study." *WPA: Writing Program Administration*, vol. 31, no. 1, 2007, pp. 65–85.

Yancey, Kathleen Blake, Liane Robertson, and Kara Taczak. *Writing Across Contexts: Transfer, Composition, and Sites of Writing*. Utah State UP, 2014.

Zymbylas, Michalinos. "Risks and Pleasures: A Deleuzo-Guattarian Pedagogy of Desire in Education." *British Educational Research Journal*, vol. 33, no. 3, 2007, pp. 331–47.

8

THE MATERIAL, EMBODIED PRACTICES OF COMPOSING WITH TECHNOLOGIES

Pamela Takayoshi and Derek Van Ittersum

Writing is always and always will be a material process of making, crafting, composing. It involves material tools (writing surface and stylus, computer, mobile phones) used by material bodies (intellectual and physical beings) to create a material product (print, digital, mono- or multimodal). Studies of composing technologies focus on the many uses and consequences of computers as composition and communication tools. Even when the word "material" is not used, studies of composing technologies, by centering the material technology through which composing is enacted, are studies of the materiality of writing. Studies of contemporary composing technologies are in this way connected to a longer trajectory of historical studies involving the materials through which writing is conducted, the ways the material possibilities of the tools shape the composing processes and products, and the ways technologies are a product and mediator of human communicative desires. Situated within the larger historical trajectory, composing technologies have revealed, while also pushing the bounds of, the always material, embodied nature of composing.

Writing studies' concern with how writing gets done and how the technologies shape contexts, writers, audiences, and texts suggests that the field has always been concerned with materiality. Thus, one way to examine the history of computers and writing is to explore the various ways scholars have engaged the materiality of technologies, especially in terms of people's embodied experiences of using these technologies.[1] First, scholars have studied the physical devices, infrastructures, and environments of digital composing. This is the sense of material that Haas defines as "having mass or matter and occupying physical space" (4). Second, scholars have focused on writers' material bodies in digital writing environments, exploring how the physical material self and one's identity connected to that material body's gender, race, class, sexual orientation, and able-bodiedness is a factor in composing and writing contexts. And third, scholars have begun focusing on mediation broadly, bringing together an interest in the physical infrastructures and tools that writers use and their cultural experiences of mediated embodiment.

In looking at the varying ways scholars have approached the materiality of writing and computers, we can not only see characteristics of writing that are true regardless of the mediating tool or the presence of the writer's physical bodies, but as Syverson suggests, understanding the ways writing is material, embodied, and mediated through bodies and tools allows us to better understand writing as a social, contextually situated act of meaning-making:

[C]omposing, like many other human cognitive processes, is irreducibly social and inextricably embedded in specific environments that are not merely supportive of but integral to the processes of thinking, writing, and reading. . . . our goals for improving or even understanding reading, writing, and thinking cannot be achieved without a careful consideration of the ecological systems within which these practices occur. (25–6)

In the following sections, we turn to a consideration of three aspects of the ecological system of writing.

Writing is Material

Writing is always mediated by the material world and tools, although it is easy to take for granted the presence of the tools we use to compose in part because when writers are working effectively, the tools they use are invisible (Bruce and Hogan). When new technologies enter into our practices, they often call attention to those practices in a new way and thus make us attentive again to the old. In this section, we describe two ways composing technologies have revealed writing's materiality: one, through attention to the design of effective learning spaces and the kinds of infrastructural support those learning spaces require, and two, through attention to how the specific technologies within those physical spaces shaped what writers actually do.[2]

One of the first spaces composing technologies threw into relief was the "traditional" or "proscenium" classroom. Accompanying the very first word processors to enter composition classes was a set of concerns about the physical materiality of learning and how teachers could scaffold and use the machines and how the physical classroom should be designed (LeBlanc; Skubikowski and Elder; Takayoshi and Huot; Taylor). Writing in 1987, Cynthia Selfe described the growth of "computer-supported writing labs" in the early 1980s as an effort by teachers to "shape a unique vision of technology's role in English Composition programs" ("Creating" 44). In addition to procuring funds for additional computers, faculty and students negotiated the physical environment of the classroom design by donating furniture, office supplies, and decorative elements (including "Sony Walkmen for students who disliked classical music" ("Creating" 55) which played on a classroom radio). Faculty were thus involved in decision making about the embodied uses of the space by writers and in an explicit recognition of materiality (of bodies, of computers, and of the arrangement of both in space). Gresham and Yancey argue that the architecture of a learning space is essentially rhetorical as it seeks to create something for a particular purpose for an audience or group of users, while Taylor points out that questions about the ways that technology can be used in writing instruction are often questions that can be answered by paying attention to classroom design. For these reasons, in a later piece, Selfe extols the field to "prepare English composition teachers to be architects of computer-supported learning spaces and virtual learning spaces" ("Preparing" 35). More recently, DeVoss, Cushman, and Grabill have focused on the "institutional infrastructures and cultural contexts necessary to support teaching students to compose with new media [because] these often invisible structures make possible and limit, shape and constrain, influence and penetrate all acts of composing new media in writing classes" (16). Further, they argue that attention to the materiality of composing new media ("the software, wires, and machines") is "absolutely necessary for writing teachers and their students to understand if we hope to enact the possibilities offered by new-media composing" (16).

Along with considerations about the physical layout and design of computer classrooms and labs, writing teachers also drew attention to the size of screens (Bernhardt; Hawisher, "Studies"), the labels on keyboards (Hughes), and increasingly zeroed in on specific technologies (pen and paper, word processors, computers) and how those tools shaped writers and their texts (Hawisher, "Research Update"). However, as Christina Haas showed, such concerns were not spreading to the wider research community: "despite the fact that the material tools and artifacts are inherently bound up in acts of writing, there has been scant explicit and detailed attention focused on this materiality in contemporary discussions of writing" (5). In her studies of writers' processes of composing with computers, Haas opened a space for considering material aspects of writing and provided a foundation for understanding writing as an embodied act:

> [T]he notion of *embodiment* can provide a necessary corrective to accounts of writing that emphasize the cultural at the expense of the cognitive, or that focus on writing as only an act of mind. Questions of technology always and inescapably return to the material, embodied reality of literate practice. (xv)

Later research has focused on specific materialities of writing, include personal digital assistants (Geisler), voice dictation (Honeycutt, Owens), and mobile devices (Swarts).

More recently, scholars have called for being critically and rhetorically attentive to the technologies we use in learning and teaching. Edbauer Rice and Selber both argue for the importance of paying attention to the technical mechanics of learning to use the tools. Selber asserts that focusing on what he calls a "functional approach to computer literacy" (32) is crucial to students acquiring successful/meaningful technological skills and Edbauer Rice argues that

> [l]earning the mechanical dynamics of textual creation not only diminishes the gap between producer and production, but it bridges the tensions between theory and practice that continue to pull us in different directions. Mechanics is where all texts— architectonic constructions that they are—must begin. (384–5)

Further, scholars have pointed out that the "mechanics" or materiality of writing processes involves both digital and nondigital writing materials. Wysocki defines "new media texts" as "those that have been made by composers who are aware of the range of materialities of texts and who then highlight the materiality" ("Opening" 15) while Chris Haas points to the influence of non-digital writing materials:

> Writing is situated in the material world in a number of ways. It always occurs in a material setting, employs material tools, and results in material artifacts. Writers sit in well-appointed desks in offices, or they slouch in less well-appointed ones in classrooms. Sometimes writers forego a desk altogether, preferring a kitchen table, or a lap, or the dashboard of a car. Writers use stubby pencils or felt-tip pens, cheap ball-points or lap-top computers; often writers use a number of these material implements in tandem. (4)

As these varied approaches to writing's materiality demonstrate, attention to the material tools we use within infrastructures to compose is crucial because even beyond computing, writing is clearly a material practice.

Writing is Embodied

The material tools involved in composing processes are, of course, engaged in meaning making through human bodies. In two ways, writing technologies have led scholars to think carefully about the role bodies play in communicative contexts. First, writing technologies created a new space for bringing together communicative networks of writers, audiences, and textual products both physically and virtually. Second, these new communicative configurations of writers, audiences, and texts drew attention to the subjectivities and embodiment of writers and audiences present in all communicative contexts.

Romantic depictions of writers as solitary figures putting their individual thoughts into words have long dominated the popular imagination. In the 1980s, composition scholars drew on social constructionist theory to counter these conventional depictions of writing and invention as individual acts. They sought to demonstrate the ways writing, and invention in particular, was social, dialogic, and collaborative. Such research paved the way for people to see computer technologies, especially networked computers, as reflecting the insights of social constructionism, dialogism, and postmodern theory (Barker and Kemp, Eldred, Handa). Susan Romano described how "[m]any of us who teach in networked classrooms have tried on the theoretical terminology of the past decade—collaborative learning, social construction of knowledge, decenteredness—and are pleased with the fit" (n.p.). Castner echoes that fit between theory and technology when she noted,

> Many compositionists who base their writing pedagogy on social epistemology began to teach in networked classrooms because computer networks allow an enormous increase in student conversations about, and in, writing. . . . [M]any factors these compositionists observed inhibiting student discussion in traditional classrooms (such as dominating students) could be factored out in networked classrooms. (259)

Early adopters of networked technologies even went so far as to be optimistic that "a level playing field" might be achieved through the dis-embodiment of online discussion forums:

> [M]any aspects of face-to-face communication are filtered out when the computer becomes the medium of exchange. These include body language, intimidating or distracting appearances, voice and intonation, aggressive or distracting speech mannerisms . . . and all the paraphernalia that allows physical context to intrude on and inhibit the pure exchange of ideas. (Barker and Kemp 21)

Likewise, Cooper and Selfe argued that online discussion groups create more egalitarian spaces for marginalized voices to be heard.

Feminists quickly problematized egalitarian narratives and the desire for filtering out writers' bodies through scholarship which reasserted the body as a political and ideological presence mediating and shaping written communication. Their qualitative research analyzed classroom transcripts and other electronic communication to demonstrate how such textual discussions are always shaped by embodied experiences (LeCourt; Romano; Takayoshi, "Building"; Webb). The prevalence of feminist approaches to technologies in early computers and composition scholarship is suggestive of the field's attentiveness to the troubled nature of body and technology, and those early feminist considerations contributed to a political and ideological awareness of the embodiment of writing with technologies. As scholars such as Cynthia Selfe encouraged us to understand:

> When technology, as an artifact of our culture, is employed by teachers who lack a critical understanding of its nature of a conscious plan for its use, and when these teachers must function within an educational system that is itself an artifact of the political, social,

economic forces shaping our culture, the natural tendency of instruction is to support the status quo. Technology is, in other words, inherently ideological; and all techno-logical decision in educational settings are, thus, inherently political. ("Preparing" 30)

Scholarship exploring the possibilities and constraints of the democratic potentials of technologies came to the conclusion that writing technologies were only as good as the theories informing their uses and, further that while in theory they allowed for a disembodied text, writing is never a disembodied act.

This initial recognition that writing is an embodied practice led to further descriptive and empirically grounded attention to the embodied, lived experience of writers occupying a number of social identity categories. Rather than assuming an unmarked body (which is of course marked by default as white, middle class, able-bodied, and male), scholars produced a robust body of intersecting scholarship examining composing technologies and gender (Blair and Takayoshi; Hawisher and Sullivan; Regan; Wahlstrom), race (Banks; Blackmon; Gruber; Romano), and sexual identity (Addison and Hilligoss; Alexander and Banks; Alexander "Out"; Comstock and Addison; DeWitt). This diverse body of work shares a focus on the cultural grounding of difference in people's bodies and an attendant resistance to erasure or inattention to material bodies. As Alexander and Banks argue, we need to "include paying attention to the sexed and sexualized bodies that sit in our classrooms and that use various technologies" and include LGBTQ experiences "to create not only spaces for alternative perspectives but to use queerness as a mode of critique and critical inquiry" (275). This body of scholarship focused on the embodiment of writing and counters the idea that online communication could separate bodies from texts they produce. Instead, this scholarship asserts, identity is fluid, moving through a "literacy of networks [that support the] negotiation of identification, belonging, and community" (Rhodes) and writing is always an embodied act of meaning making.

Writing is a Mediation of Bodies and Minds

Influenced by research exploring the embodied aspects of writing and the relationships between identity, physical bodies, and writing activity, current work on composing technologies has renewed attention to the material aspects of writing technologies and the ways they shape writing activity. This work has primarily been framed as a return to studying writing processes, although shaped by the insights gleaned from the social turn. Early studies of materiality were often focused on how specific technologies shaped the texts that writers produced; asking, for example, whether student writers could produce better texts with word processors or pen and paper, or whether students would revise texts more or more globally with word processors than with pen and paper. Contemporary studies of writing process have been less concerned with the texts themselves, attending more closely to the identities and relationships that can emerge from writing activities. As Shipka argues,

> In addition to treating the various materials and supports people employ while producing texts, our theoretical frameworks must help us trace the multiple spaces in which and times at which composing occurs, and attend as well to embodied activity, and co-practice. (39)

While the studies we review in this section draw strongly from the research trajectories identified in the previous sections, work in this area is a newer tracing of the material and embodied aspects of contemporary composing.

One way scholars have examined these traces is through a focus on mediation. Often, this focus mirrors that of earlier work on materiality, by examining "the various materials and supports (both human and nonhuman) people employ while composing texts" (Shipka 36). Contemporary scholarship considers how people employ these materials and supports in a world where technological actors are both social actors (they participate) and facilitative of more ubiquitous social activity (Alexander, *Digital Youth*; Buck; Haas and Takayoshi; Moore et al.; Takayoshi, "Short-Form"). As contemporary composing involves the mediating presence of multiple composing technologies (hardware) as well as multiple communication platforms (software) experienced in multimodal ways which draw in writers' physical bodies in new ways (Buck; Pigg, "Coordinating"), research has focused closely on mediation as a way we experience our physical and cultural embodiment. As Anne Wysocki argues, we are "always already embedded—embodied—in mediation" ("Introduction" 4) and "[m]ediation is not to be performed only *on* one; one is to be actively engaged with mediation, with attending productively to one's own felt experiences and with learning how to compose media out of those experiences, media for circulating and eliciting engagements with others" ("Introduction" 19). Likewise, Rhodes and Alexander insist that because it is imperative for contemporary scholarship to "not only theorize from the body but also deeply understand and feel our engagements with multimedia technologies as recursively embodied" (n.p.), in their work, they "attempt . . . to map out and to provoke visceral awareness of the interimbrication of bodies and technologies, orienting and reorienting one another" (n.p.). One important way composing technologies scholars have paid attention to and unpacked the interimbrication of bodies and technologies is through a disability studies lens.

With its complex attentiveness to the material body and its lived experiences both physical and virtual, Disabilities Studies scholars are developing "a more complex notion of telepresence—one that goes beyond imagining the normate body projected into various digital realms, and instead brings the disabled and re/mediated body together" (Price in Yergeau et al. n.p.). Price further suggests that without explicit attention to the material bodies of writers and the fact that disabilities exist, "non-normate bodies (bodies that are gendered, classed, raced, disabled in particular ways) . . . disappear" and "so those bodies quickly become absent materially as well as ontologically." (in Yergeau et al. n.p.). Disabilities scholars renew—and underscore—the earlier computers and composition work that insisted that material bodies matter and must be accounted for in theories of writing with technologies. Some of this work echoes earlier scholars' focus on the mechanics of composing technologies: Kerschbaum, for example, points to the embodied nature of "[m]ultimodal texts [which] use a variety of semiotic resources that aim to activate multiple senses (most often those of sight and hearing); multimodal environments entail multiple channels and interactional resources that, taken together, convey meaning" (in Yergeau et al. n.p.). But without attention to writing as an embodied act, she argues, "multimodal texts and environments can frustrate participants' ability to effectively engage within a variety of kairotic spaces. This situation results in what I call *multimodal inhospitality*" (Kerschbaum in Yergeau et al. n.p.). Bodies matter in the physical and virtual literate interactions of readers and writers. Broadly, this trajectory of research has led to research methodologies that attend closely to technologies, objects, and environments as agents, full-fledged mediators in literate activity. Motivated, in part, by theories of embodiment and developments in computing technology, including Web 2.0, mobile composing technologies, and writing software that breaks with the conventions of word processors, researchers have called for increased focus on writers' embodied practices with material objects and within material environments.

In their critique of postprocess theory, Brooke and Rickert argue for the importance of theories of writing that can acknowledge that "the world and its objects are essential to the ability to think, speak, write, make, and act" (168). They use the case of the social bookmarking website

Delicious to disrupt conventional images of individual writers drawing on static resources online to compose research texts. Instead, they frame Delicious as a "distributed environment" that far exceeds an individual's capacities and transforms people through their engagement with it. The "intelligence" that results from people's engagements with Delicious is neither solely biological nor digital, but instead represents an assemblage of human beings and computer and Internet technologies. They suggest that "[l]earning to function within such [smart] environments" (174) constitutes an important new research opportunity. Their call is echoed by Van Ittersum and Ching, who draw from Prior and Shipka's concept of "environment-selecting and-structuring practices" (181) to examine "the ways that people deliberately coordinate with mediational means [software] to shape and direct their activity and affective states" (n.p.). Their analysis of "distraction-free writing software" showcases not only the ways "particular visions of processes, meanings, and values of writing" (n.p.) are embedded in writing software, but the affective responses and motives people have for adopting and using them. As they show, some writers can become very invested "in actively shaping their writing processes through the selection and structuring of their [software] tools" (n.p.) via tinkering and experimentation. The writers described in their study showcase a few ways of functioning within smart environments, and these case studies demonstrate the rich potential of further inquiry into writers' design of their digital writing environments and practices.

However, "smart environments" need not only point to digital or virtual spaces. Stacey Pigg's observations and interviews of academic writers in two public spaces (a coffee shop and a university building called the "Technology Commons") reveal the important roles physical environments play in writers' movements through virtual spaces. Echoing Brooke and Rickert's call for research into how writers function within digital environments, Pigg extends this work by exploring "the agentive role physical environments play in interactions with bodies and virtual spaces" ("Emplacing" 255). Writers in Pigg's study used physical spaces to manage their affective states and ready themselves to write, to take themselves away from certain people or things, to work in close proximity with particular people, and to feel comfortable and safe. While most of their composing activity involves mobile computer technology, Pigg shows that such activity cannot simply take place anywhere, as advertisements might suggest—physical spaces matter for writing activity. Pigg asks compositionists to not only attend more closely to such practices and spaces, but to "become involved in the design of material literacy environments: both of on-screen interfaces and of campus and community social spaces" (270).

One key aspect of writers' physical and material environments that demands more attention from scholars is the extent to which they create or alleviate physical pain for writers. Owens and Van Ittersum describe the various pains writers have experienced and the ways these pains have been tied to their writing tools, from pens to keyboards. They draw on Mark Johnson's definition of embodiment as consisting of five dimensions to argue that too often in writing research cultural and social aspects of embodiment have overshadowed biological and phenomenological aspects. As they claim,

> The cultural practice of writing (or any artistic expression) as a means to relieve emotional pain is well known, but at the same time people who want to write their way out of emotional pain cannot do so if the physical practice of writing is too painful at a phenomenological or flesh-and-blood level because of carpal tunnel or similar afflictions. (90)

Owens and Van Ittersum recommend further research into somatic training that addresses the multiple dimensions of embodiment along with the infrastructures in which writers work.

As these studies show, the value of research into composing technologies is not only in more knowledge of word processors, or electronic discussions, or social media sites, but in an expanded understanding of the possibilities of mediated literate activity and the human experiences such activity affords. Further, these studies don't focus solely on the tools but use those tools as a way into understanding the more expansive ecologies of writing. As the tools of writing change over time, studies that reveal human communicative processes as material, embodied, and a mediation of bodies and tools become more than studies of the latest technology and instead offer a window into a complex ecology of human meaning making and the possibilities for human expression.

Conclusion

Throughout this chapter we have sought to demonstrate how the study of composing technologies has improved and expanded our understanding of writing activity writ large. New media technologies underscore the ways human experiences are mediated through technologies, but as we have shown, there are a multitude of tools, technologies, environments, and situations that participate in this mediation. For this reason, there remains significant value in continuing to study writing technologies and the complex and rich ways they shape and respond to writing activity and human experience more broadly. These new technologies will continue to take writing studies professionals out of our comfort zones, as they increase in technical sophistication and require additional literacies and expertise to use. Yet it is crucial that we continue to engage with them. As technologies for writing proliferate, as do the contexts within which they are employed, composing processes also expand, leading to new kinds of writing activities, new motives for writing, and new human relationships.

Therefore, along with this focus on material technologies and infrastructures, we need to continue to assert the value of caring about and being attentive to humans. The scholars discussed in this chapter remind us that human bodies matter—the ways our bodies interact with and use tools (with eyes, hands, ears) and the ways race, gender, sexual identity, (dis-)able bodiness, and class mark our bodies in culture. Technology is an extension of human culture in that new technologies arise from human contexts and desires for a future and are adopted into existing social and ideological contexts that they can change as well as adapt to. Writing studies' approach to composing technologies thus is not only about the mechanics of writing but about the technologies through which we write and are written and the essence of writing.

Notes

1. We would like to be clear here: we are offering this construct of the field as a heuristic for thinking about historical and contemporary studies of materiality in composing and technologies. Our discussion is necessarily partial (given the limitations of space) but we hope suggestive of a general trajectory in a large and robust body of scholarship. One of the difficulties in writing such a historical piece is the inability to discuss or even cite the many scholars who have contributed to this understanding.
2. Alexander and Banks suggest an interesting connection between writing as material and as embodied when they note that "work that has been done in technology and writing studies regarding the ways that various technologies disrupt traditional notions of writing and writing instruction, effectively queer spaces that were once dominated by pens, pencils, and loose-leaf paper" (274).

Works Cited

Addison, Joanne, and Susan Hilligoss. "Technological Fronts: Lesbian Lives 'On the Line.'" *Feminist Cyberscapes: Mapping Gendered Academic Spaces*, edited by Kristine Blair and Pamela Takayoshi. Ablex, 1999, pp. 21–40.

Alexander, Jonathan. *Digital Youth: Emerging Literacies on the World Wide Web.* Hampton Pr, 2005.

——. "Out of the Closet and into the Network: Sexual Orientation and the Computerized Classroom." *Computers and Composition,* vol. 14, no. 2, 1997, pp. 207–16.

Alexander, Jonathan, and William P. Banks. "Sexualities, Technologies, and the Teaching of Writing: A Critical Overview." *Computers and Composition,* vol. 21, no. 3, Sept. 2004, pp. 273–93.

Banks, Adam J. *Race, Rhetoric, and Technology: Searching for Higher Ground.* Routledge, 2006.

Barker, Thomas T., and Fred O. Kemp. "Network Theory: A Postmodern Pedagogy for the Writing Classroom." *Computers and Community: Teaching Composition in the Twenty-First Century,* edited by Carolyn Handa. Boynton/Cook, 1990, pp. 1–27.

Bernhardt, Stephen A. "Designing a Microcomputer Classroom for Teaching Composition." *Computers and Composition,* vol. 7, no. 1, Nov. 1989, pp. 93–110.

Blackmon, Samantha. " 'But I'm Just White' or How 'Other' Pedagogies Can Benefit All Students." *Teaching Writing with Computers: An Introduction,* edited by Pamela Takayoshi and Brian Huot. Houghton Mifflin, 2003, pp. 92–102.

Blair, Kristine, and Pamela Takayoshi, Eds. *Feminist Cyberscapes: Mapping Gendered Academic Spaces.* Ablex, 1999.

Brooke, Collin Gifford, and Thomas Rickert. "Being Delicious: Materialities of Research in a Web 2.0 Application." *Beyond Postprocess,* edited by Sidney I. Dobrin et al. Utah State UP, 2012, pp. 163–79.

Bruce, Bertram C., and Maureen P. Hogan. "The Disappearance of Technology: Toward an Ecological Model of Literacy." *Handbook of Literacy and Technology: Transformations in a Post-Typographic World,* edited by David Reinking et al. Lawrence Erlbaum, 1998, pp. 269–81.

Buck, Amber. "Physically Present and Digitally Active: Locating Ecologies of Writing on Social Networks." *Literacy in Practice: Writing in Private, Public, and Working Lives,* edited by Patrick Thomas and Pamela Takayoshi. Routledge, 2016, pp. 86–104.

Castner, Joanna A. "The Clash of Social Categories: What Egalitarianism in Networked Writing Classrooms?" *Computers and Composition,* vol. 14, no. 2, 1997, pp. 257–68.

Comstock, Michelle, and Joanne Addison. "Virtual Complexities: Exploring Literacy at the Intersections of Computer-Mediated Social Formations." *Computers and Composition,* vol. 14, no. 2, Jan. 1997, pp. 245–55.

Cooper, Marilyn M., and Cynthia L. Selfe. "Computer Conferences and Learning: Authority, Resistance, and Internally Persuasive Discourse." *College English,* vol. 52, no. 8, 1990, pp. 847–69.

DeVoss, Dánielle Nicole, Ellen Cushman, and Jeffrey T. Grabill. "Infrastructure and Composing: The When of New-Media Writing." *College Composition and Communication,* vol. 57, no. 1, 2005, pp. 14–44.

DeWitt, Scott Lloyd. "Out There on the Web: Pedagogy and Identity in Face of Opposition." *Computers and Composition,* vol. 14, no. 2, Jan. 1997, pp. 229–43.

Eldred, Janet M. "Computers, Composition Pedagogy, and the Social View." *Critical Perspectives on Computers and Composition Instruction,* edited by Gail E Hawisher and Cynthia L Selfe. 1989, pp. 201–18.

Geisler, Cheryl. "When Management Becomes Personal: An Activity-Theoretic Analysis of Palm Technologies." *Writing Selves/Writing Societies: Research from Activity Perspectives,* edited by Charles Bazerman and David Russell. The WAC Clearinghouse, 2002, pp. 125–58.

Gresham, Morgan, and Kathleen Blake Yancey. "New Studio Composition: New Sites for Writing, New Forms of Composition, New Cultures of Learning." *Writing Program Administration,* vol. 28, no. 1–2, 2004, pp. 9–28.

Gruber, Sibylle. " 'I, a Mestiza, Continually Walk Out of One Culture Into Another': A Virtual Reshaping of Feminist and Liberatory Pedagogies." *Feminist Cyberscapes: Mapping Gendered Academic Spaces,* edited by Kristine Blair and Pamela Takayoshi. Ablex, 1999, pp. 105–32.

Haas, Christina. *Writing Technology: Studies on the Materiality of Literacy.* Lawrence Erlbaum, 1996.

Haas, Christina, and Pamela Takayoshi. "Young People's Everyday Literacies: The Language Features of Instant Messaging." *Research in the Teaching of English,* vol. 45, no. 4, May 2011, pp. 378–404.

Handa, Carolyn. "Politics, Ideology, and the Strange, Slow Death of the Isolated Composer, or Why We Need Community in the Writing Classroom." *Computers and Community,* edited by Carolyn Handa. Boynton/Cook, 1990, pp. 160–84.

Hawisher, Gail E. "Research Update: Writing and Word Processing." *Computers and Composition,* vol. 5, no. 2, 1988, pp. 7–27.

——. "Studies in Word Processing." *Computers and Composition,* vol. 4, no. 1, 1986, pp. 6–31.

Hawisher, Gail E., and Patricia A. Sullivan. "Fleeting Images: Women Visually Writing the Web." *Passions, Pedagogies, and 21st Century Technologies,* edited by Gail E. Hawisher and Cynthia L. Selfe. Utah State UP, 1999, pp. 268–91.

Honeycutt, Lee. "Researching the Use of Voice Recognition Writing Software." *Computers and Composition*, vol. 20, no. 1, 2003, pp. 77–95.

Hughes, Bradley T. "Balancing Enthusiasm with Skepticism: Training Writing Teachers in Computer-Aided Instruction." *Computers and Composition*, vol. 7, no. 1, Nov. 1989, pp. 65–78.

Johnson, Mark. "What Makes a Body?" *The Journal of Speculative Philosophy*, vol. 22, no. 3, 2008, pp. 159–69.

LeBlanc, Paul. *Writing Teachers Writing Software: Creating Our Place in the Electronic Age*. National Council of Teachers of English, 1993.

LeCourt, Donna. "Writing (without) the Body: Gender and Power in Networked Discussion Groups." *Feminist Cyberscapes: Mapping Gendered Academic Spaces*, edited by Kristine Blair and Pamela Takayoshi. Ablex, 1999, pp. 153–75.

Moore, Jessie L., Paula Rosinski, Tim Peeples, Stacey Pigg, Martine Courant Rife, Beth Brunk-Chavez, Dundee Lackey, Suzanne Kesler Rumsey, Robyn Tasakai, Paul Curran, and Jeffrey T. Grabill. "Revisualizing Composition: How First-Year Writers Use Composing Technologies." *Computers and Composition*, vol. 39, Mar. 2016, pp. 1–13.

Owens, Kim Hensley. " 'Look Ma, No Hands!': Voice-Recognition Software, Writing, and Ancient Rhetoric." *Enculturation*, vol. 7, 2010, enculturation.gmu.edu/look-ma-no-hands. Accessed 3 July 2017.

Owens, Kim Hensley, and Derek Van Ittersum. "Writing With(out) Pain: Computing Injuries and the Role of the Body in Writing Activity." *Computers and Composition*, vol. 30, no. 2, June 2013, pp. 87–100.

Pigg, Stacey. "Coordinating Constant Invention: Social Media's Role in Distributed Work." *Technical Communication Quarterly*, vol. 23, no. 2, Apr. 2014, pp. 69–87.

———. "Emplacing Mobile Composing Habits: A Study of Academic Writing in Networked Social Spaces." *College Composition and Communication*, vol. 66, no. 2, 2014, p. 250.

———. "Ubiquitous Writing, Technologies, and the Social Practice of Literacies of Coordination." *Written Communication*, vol. 31, no. 1, Jan. 2014, pp. 91–117.

Prior, Paul, and Jody Shipka. "Chronotopic Lamination: Tracing the Contours of Literate Activity." *Writing Selves/Writing Societies*, edited by Charles Bazerman and David Russell. The WAC Clearinghouse and Mind, Culture, and Activity, 2003, pp. 180–238.

Regan, Alison. " 'Type Normal Like the Rest of Us': Writing, Power, and Homophobia in the Networked Composition Classroom." *Computers and Composition*, vol. 10, no. 4, 1993, computersandcomposition. candcblog.org/archives/v10/10_4_html/10_4_2_Regan.html. Accessed 3 July 2017.

Rhodes, Jacqueline. " 'Substantive and Feminist Girlie Action': Women Online." *College Composition and Communication*, vol. 54, no. 1, 2002, pp. 116–42.

Rhodes, Jacqueline, and Jonathan Alexander. *Techne: Queer Meditations on Writing the Self*. Computers and Composition Digital Press/Utah State UP, 2015, ccdigitalpress.org/techne. Accessed 3 July 2017.

Rice, Jenny Edbauer. "Rhetoric's Mechanics: Retooling the Equipment of Writing Production." *College Composition and Communication*, vol. 60, no. 2, 2008, pp. 366–87.

Romano, Susan. "The Egalitarianism Narrative: Whose Story? Which Yardstick?" *Computers and Composition*, vol. 10, no. 3, 1993. *ERIC*, computersandcomposition.candcblog.org/archives/v10/10_3_ html/10_3_1_Romano.html. Accessed 3 July 2017.

Selber, Stuart A. *Multiliteracies for a Digital Age*. Southern Illinois UP, 2004.

Selfe, Cynthia L. "Creating a Computer-Supported Writing Lab: Sharing Stories and Creating Vision." *Computers and Composition*, vol. 4, no. 2, Apr. 1987, pp. 44–65.

———. "Preparing English Teachers for the Virtual Age: The Case for Technology Critics." *Re-Imagining Computers and Composition: Teaching and Research in the Virtual Age*, edited by Gail E Hawisher and Paul LeBlanc. Boynton/Cook, 1992, pp. 24–42.

Shipka, Jody. *Toward a Composition Made Whole*. U of Pittsburgh P, 2011.

Skubikowski, Kathleen, and John Elder. "Computers and the Social Contexts of Writing." *Computers and Community: Teaching Composition in the Twenty-First Century*, edited by Carolyn Handa. Boynton/Cook, 1990, pp. 89–105.

Swarts, Jason. "Mobility and Composition: The Architecture of Coherence in Non-Places." *Technical Communication Quarterly*, vol. 16, no. 3, 2007, pp. 279–309.

Syverson, Margaret A. *The Wealth of Reality: An Ecology of Composition*. Southern Illinois UP, 1999.

Takayoshi, Pamela. "Building New Networks from the Old: Women's Experiences with Electronic Communications." *Computers and Composition*, vol. 11, no. 1, Jan. 1994, pp. 21–35.

——. "Short-Form Writing: Studying Process in the Context of Contemporary Composing Technologies." *Computers and Composition*, vol. 37, Sept. 2015, pp. 1–13.

Takayoshi, Pamela, and Brian Huot. "Composing in a Digital World: The Transition of a Writing Program and Its Faculty." *Writing Program Administration*, vol. 32, no. 3, 2009, pp. 89–119.

Taylor, Todd. "Design Delivery and Narcolepsy." *Delivering College Composition: The Fifth Canon*, edited by Kathleen Blake Yancey. Boynton/Cook, 2006, pp. 127–40.

Van Ittersum, Derek, and Kory Lawson Ching. "Composing Text/Shaping Process: How Digital Environments Mediate Writing Activity." *Computers and Composition Online*, no. Fall 2013, 2013, cconline journal.org/composing_text/webtext/. Accessed 3 July 2017.

Wahlstrom, Billie J. "Communication and Technology: Defining a Feminist Presence in Research and Practice." *Literacy and Computers: The Complications of Teaching and Learning with Technology*, edited by Cynthia Selfe and Susan Hilligoss. MLA, 1994, pp. 171–85.

Webb, Patricia R. "Narratives of Self in Networked Communications." *Computers and Composition*, vol. 14, no. 1, Jan. 1997, pp. 73–90.

Wysocki, Anne Frances. "Introduction: Into Between—On Composition in Mediation." *Composing(Media) =Composing(Embodiment): Bodies, Technologies, Writing, the Teaching of Writing*, edited by Kristin Arola and Anne Frances Wysocki. Utah State UP, 2012, pp. 1–24.

——. "Opening New Media to Writing: Openings and Justifications." *Writing New Media: Theory and Applications for Expanding the Teaching of Composition*, edited by Anne Frances Wysocki, Johndan Johnson-Eilola, Cynthia L. Selfe, and Geoffrey Sirc. Utah State UP, 2004, pp. 1–42.

Yergeau, Melanie, Elizabeth Brewer, Stephanie Kirschbaum, Sushil K. Oswal, Margaret Price, Michal J. Salvo, Cynthia L. Self, Franny Howes. "Multimodality in Motion: Disability and Kairotic Spaces." *Kairos: Rhetoric, Technology, Pedagogy*, vol. 18, no. 1, 2013, kairos.technorhetoric.net/18.1/coverweb/ yergeau-et-al/pages/access.html. Accessed 3 July 2017.

9

SONIC ECOLOGIES AS A PATH FOR ACTIVISM

Mary E. Hocks

When focusing on uses of sound as rhetorical material and as one of many compositional tools, writers and composition teachers can begin with Cynthia Selfe's generative calls to attention and to action in her two separate articles written and published in *College Composition and Communication* ten years apart. In 1999, as the Web was growing exponentially into a multi-directional "information superhighway," Selfe's "Technology and Literacy: A Story About the Perils of Not Paying Attention" galvanized the field of rhetoric and composition by insisting upon everyone's attention to educational technology and critical digital literacies. Ten years later, with writing and sharing media across social media platforms becoming the norm, Selfe's 2009, "The Movement of Air, the Breath of Meaning: Aurality and Multimodal Composing" gave voice to aurality as a critical rhetorical practice and a method for composition. Both articles are about the impact of digital technology on writing and yet they both reach beyond technology and into lived experience. As both articles demonstrate, cultural, phenomenological, and feminist theory have continued to offer complex and important tools for cultural critique that, I hope, can also result in new understandings and writing leading to change, even to progressive action.

Digital writing has amplified how the multimodal elements of a composition (e.g., aural, linguistic, visual), as first described by the New London Group in 1996, can work together to move student writers from simple analysis to the design and production of new knowledge. Rhetorical scholars and educators such as Selfe who embrace critical pedagogies want to help ensure that the most vulnerable members of a society are not just *represented* but *included* as the designers of social change. By illuminating the communicative affordances of every available means and modes of digital writing, teachers and researchers engaging with progressive rhetorical studies and digital writing pedagogies can look to embodied multimodality practices to find an expanded repertoire that helps writers communicate effectively and even create change in people's lives.

A sonic ecology that engages human interactions with soundscapes and other sonic experiences suggests that the immediacy of experiences with sound can actually help writers develop empathy, a capacity that can lead to activism. Sounds are vibrational and resonant in nature, and recognizing a sound's materiality opens opportunities for transformative experiences. Scholar and musician Steve Goodman identifies a sound's ontology with unique characteristics such as "vibrational surfaces, or oscillators" and specifically challenges "the linguistic imperialism that subordinates the sonic to semiotic registers" (101). How can experiences with sonic ecologies then become a path to progressive action? Feminist and environmental scholar Stacy Alaimo explains how materiality leads to activism:

> A recognition of how (post)humans are, on multiple scales, embedded within the material world, enables new forms of activism. . . . Explicitly or implicitly, matter and materiality have long been at the heart of many social justice concerns regarding sexuality, repro-duction, health, dis/ability, environmentalism and environmental justice, labor, economics, and colonialism. ("Introduction to Matter" 14–15)

Alaimo's concept of trans-corporeality, based in materialist feminist theory and post-human ontologies, illuminates critical human engagements with our environments to describe sonic ecologies and to achieve an environmental activist outcome. How might this dynamic work when applied to sound? Sensations of sounds attune us, through attention to our human communities and connections and a renewed access to the non-human environment and agents that surround us. Soundscape projects and sonic art that emphasize ecological goals also offer us their contingent ecologies of spaces, objects, active listeners and more (Comstock and Hocks, "The Sounds of Climate Change" 169–70). Rather than simply describing and gesturing toward activist ideas, writers, through their embodied experiences and actions with sound, can help create change and witness the results.

Sonic Composition

Interest in sound as rhetorical engagement and a compositional mode has emerged over the last two decades alongside interests in visual rhetoric and multimodal composition, but lagging somewhat behind; sound, especially digital sound, remained one of the more underdeveloped modalities in both media studies and digital rhetoric. In media studies, the lack of material on audio and "sonic literacy" were immediately apparent, for example, when Lev Manovich published his definitive and influential *The Language of New Media* in 2001, in which sound is merely mentioned as one of many modes, one of the multiple media that must be "computable" and "modular" in order to fit his ground-breaking definition of "new media" (44). The terms "sound" and "audio" appeared in his work and elsewhere as merely one in a list of media types or modes of expression.

In rhetoric and writing studies, sonic rhetorics, especially for digital composition, have seen increasing interest and attention. The most influential publications on sound in writing studies began in 1999 with the special issue of *Enculturation* on "Writing/Music/Culture" (Rickert), which demonstrated how music could help shape rhetorical choices and meanings for a writer when composing. The 2006 joint print and online issues of *Computers and Composition* on "Sound In/As Composition" (Ball and Hawk) captured the widening range and possibilities for sound-based compositions just as networked social media affordances took off. Emerging sonic rhetoric scholars at this time defined qualities of sound and the benefits of sonic projects for students composing in computer classrooms. Heidi McKee, for example, examines four elements of sound: "vocal delivery, music, special effects, and silence" in a number of works and she looks to film studies approaches to help evaluate these elements of sound (337). Bump Halbritter defines a "musical rhetoric" to describe how popular music uses rhetorical appeals and how student videos create arguments to "explore how the musical elements in integrated-media compositions ask audiences to interact with the rhetorical products they yield" (318). Michelle Comstock and Mary Hocks define sonic literacy as "the ability to identify, define, situate, construct, manipulate, and communicate our personal and cultural soundscapes" in relation to their work teaching students how to work with sound in video compositions ("Voice"). The special issue of *Currents in Electronic Literacy* on "Writing With Sound" (Davis), and the online journal *Harlot of the Arts* special issue on "Sonic Rhetorics" (Stone and Ceraso) catalyzed a number of critical and creative works, from sound maps and podcasts to remixed sound collages.

These scholarly works have prompted a proliferation of analytic and creative works in sound-based composing, but none more so than Selfe, who argues passionately that sound is an essential semiotic tool and then charges all teachers to "develop an increasingly thoughtful understanding" of aurality (618). As if in direct answer to this call, Halbritter explains in his award-winning 2012 book, *Mics, Camera, Symbolic Action: An Audio-Visual Rhetoric for Writing Teachers*, that a multi-track sound recording "represents unfinished writing" and such composing processes also inspire what he calls "*multidimensional rhetoric*; rhetoric that integrates a variety of modes, media, and genres" into audio-visual composition processes (26–7). These compositional approaches to multimodality have evolved into a rich and diverse collection of sonic practices and pedagogies.

Sound is an important rhetorical resource, but a critical approach to sonic rhetoric needs to include embodied, dynamic rhetorical engagements with sound itself (Comstock and Hocks). Here, the vibrational qualities of sounds and the experiential variations among particular bodies change how different people listen. In fact, sounds can offer unique relationships to features and elements of "the surround" in soundscapes that have culturally identifiable markers, as R. Murray Schafer explains in his definitive work, *The Soundscape*. Thomas Rickert examines soundscapes and the surround in order to argue that the ambient noises of our daily experience often go unnoticed yet strongly inform every rhetorical situation (*Ambient Rhetoric* 20). These approaches to sonic rhetoric all highlight an embodied sensibility and empathetic connection to the world and to sonic environments.

Tuning into Sound Studies

Writing studies scholars and rhetoricians have also turned to interdisciplinary sound studies, which draws together approaches from cultural studies, music, sound recording, and film to examine the everyday cultural effects of musical and other performances, of installations and events, of spaces and of noise. Using locations of sound as a method and an indicator for critically examining complex human spaces, objects and events, sound studies as a field offers multiple methodological approaches to analyzing sound in cultural context and within a dynamic ecology of affective sensory experience, or the sensorium. Pioneered by Schafer and developed by scholars such as Jonathan Sterne in edited collections and foundational works such as *The Audible Past*, sound studies offer theoretical frameworks for analyzing sound in specific cultural and historical moments. Sounds, as objects or events, can be experienced in and of themselves. However, other of the more influential and popular sonic studies include activist and environmental works by Bernie Krause, whose activist work and book *The Great Animal Orchestra: Finding the Origins of Music in the World's Wild Places* uses historical soundscape analysis to exert wide influence on ecological conversations. Brandon LaBelle, in *Acoustic Territories*, maps an urban cityscape from subways to the sky with sounds that explicate everyday life. These works are characterized by a sonic ecology emphasizing the effects of the surround and also expanding to include the non-human elements involved in sonic experiences.

Academic inquiries often require a new or appropriate taxonomy to describe the uses of sound. Film scholar Michel Chion, for example, uses a helpful listener-centered taxonomy to explain how perception and interpretation are constructed and inextricable from the listener's body and environment. Chion divides listening into three modes: *causal, semantic,* and *reduced.* In causal listening, the most common form, one listens for information about the source (sound is merely pointing at something else), while semantic listening interprets for a code or meaning. "Reduced listening," as defined by Chion, involves eliminating the first two modes and making the sound itself the object. Chion's model can help explicate sounds in and of themselves, which, in turn, help listeners to develop an embodied understanding of sound as a modality for expression. Sound studies scholarship provides helpful language to describe sounds. Like any medium or mode, sound requires a terminology that includes functions and uses, but goes beyond those elements to articulate the material characteristics of sounds.

Characteristics of Acoustic Sounds

- Temporal (experienced in time or sequence)
- Ephemeral (rises and decays)
- Vibrational (operates as waveforms)
- Experienced in relation to spaces, mediums, and surfaces (reflective, refractive, absorbed by materials)
- Indicative of cultural events, artifacts, humans and non-human agents
- Described by uniquely sonic qualities such as volume and pitch, timbre (character), sustain and decay, resonance and dissonance, rhythm and speed.

These fundamental characteristics are based in sound's object-ness and in how humans typically experience sounds, allowing deeper access to how sounds operate on humans and in the world. Offering a vocabulary establishes analytic tools to experience and understand sounds on their own terms and how these characteristics can be deployed (or digitally manipulated) to produce the desired effects upon an audience. Most importantly, using this vocabulary to describe the qualities and the experiences of sounds while embedding a sound's meanings in historical and cultural contexts can help writers to determine the best available means for deploying sound effectively and powerfully in practice.

Engagements with Sound Production

While insights from sounds studies have influenced our thinking about sound's characteristic affordances for digital writing composition processes, the field of rhetoric and composition's consistent emphasis on production—the composing of sound-based media and projects—has significantly pushed forward our best practices in digital composition. Early on, sound-based projects and assignments in composition classes emphasized alphabetic texts included in audio essays and podcasts. Forward-thinking scholars such as Jody Shipka (2006) argued for a more capacious kinds of multimodal composition, "made stronger still by attending to the use of sound. And perhaps a bit further down the road, it might be made stronger still by attending to the use of textures, and then scents, objects, embodied performances, and so on" (371). Others outlined new pedagogies and assignments, including the soundscapes analysis, spoken word soundstage performances, and human microphone amplification exercises as early attempts to move beyond the purely scripted linguistic or essayistic model for sonic compositions (Comstock and Hocks, "Voice").

Recent rhetorical studies have examined sound-only productions, installations and public artworks that disrupt or challenge our expectations to "disorient listeners" from their usual "auditory tactics" (Gauthier and Pasquier 427)—our unconscious ways of tuning in and tuning out sounds while sonically navigating our environments. Not only is sound an important rhetorical resource, but a critical sonic rhetoric should include embodied, dynamic rhetorical engagements with sound in itself (Comstock and Hocks, "Sounds of Climate Change"). Such engagements ought to be accessible to all, and as Steph Ceraso explains, "multimodal listening" is the best method "to expand how we think about and practice listening as a situated, full-bodied act" (103). Further, sounds can offer us unique access to features and elements of "the surround" that are culturally based, as Schafer posited. Rickert's many insights about a salient signal's dependence upon ambience results in changes to our sense of identity and embeds us into a fuller rhetorical field. Similarly, Comstock and Hocks argue that public artworks offer us ways of re-orienting ourselves as rhetorical subjects in the world and demonstrate how sound artists "themselves make explicit arguments for its materiality, its rhetoricity, and its capacity for artistic manipulation. Sculpting sound and interrupting the conventional auditory tactics of passersby, especially in outdoor public spaces, is a formidable task" (169). The examination of such auditory tactics within cultural soundscapes and the disruptions of conventional boundaries can help in both the teaching and producing of sonic rhetoric.

One of the challenges for writing studies and rhetorical scholars, then, has been to move away from reducing sound to an alphabetic text, and examining the work of sound artists has helped us to do so. Analyzing the works of Glenn Gould, the Canadian musician and multimedia artist who has produced experimental and ground-breaking new media works, Jonathan Alexander concludes:

> Attention to such work might help us consider what can be done with sound and voice in the production of multimedia texts where sound and voice act beyond the textual—not just as metaphors for textual meaning making, but as materialities with their own particular rhetorical and affective affordances and dimensions. (75)

A growing awareness of new materialities and the pedagogical possibilities has emerged, as Ceraso and Ahren explain, to work against "the assumption that sound will be used to create linear, narrative-driven texts like audio essays or musical soundtracks" (13). Experiences with sonic ecologies can offer these kinds of materialities and offer a means of creating new knowledge.

Affordances of Sound for Digital Composers

Writing teachers know that emphasizing any new mode of expression requires more time and attention, along with more tools to learn. Keeping up with the affordances of sound technologies can be daunting, as questions of audience, arrangement, and delivery constantly evolve within the available platforms and distribution models of current digital networks. Audio composition, unlike the sharing of raw media files, requires learning about basic editing and often, using multi-track audio mixers, complex editing techniques and file compression formats, along with operating microphones, audio recorders, and other hardware. Even basic recording techniques in locations for capturing a good recording and minimizing noise must be taught. Sound recording and editing equipment, audio capture, and playback on hand-held devices, still requires storage and movement of large audio files to a computer or an online platform for editing, mixing, and production. In most cases, then, work with sound first requires training and preparation. Examining sounds in day-to-day use and via current recording and distribution platforms also requires that writers make thoughtful decisions about the affordances of sound technologies for a particular composition at that moment.

As one example, Jentery Sayers offers an "audiography" assignment where students use a theme to create a playlist of sounds that represent their everyday soundscapes (www.jentery teaches.com). This challenge to communicate an overall theme to the audience requires the selection, the curation, and sequencing of music without a reliance on speech or writing. In his article for the Sound Studies Blog, Sayers notes the challenge of the playlist assignment "because it isn't rooted in any particular genre" so students may have to rely on highly technical directions for audio mixing to shape their playlist ("Scaffolding a Sequence of Assignments."). Similarly, Kyle Stedman describes his musical mix assignment

> to suggest new ways of thinking about sonic arrangement when composing musical mixes, whether the source material is on vinyl, cassette, CD, or mp3. When engaging in the *rhetoric* of making mixes . . . composing a curated collection of cuts is something like rhetorically composing an oration. (n.p.)

In fact, work in multimodal composition sometimes must occur without any immediate genres or models, and using less familiar compositional modes like sound; such work asks that writers imagine what does not yet exist, design it, and demonstrate its value to an audience without the benefit of genre-based social conventions.

Despite these newer forms of sonic composition, the more familiar linear audio essays and podcasts aren't disappearing anytime soon, given their continued popularity from radio venues to social media platforms. Using the radio-inspired conventions of a narrative voice persona, a signature soundscape that acts as introduction, edited sound-bytes from statements and interviews, along with the sound effect textures and musical themes, all signal rhetorical work by writers. This work uses the canons of rhetoric, including the creation of a style, the uses of transitions, and other arrangements for an effective delivery. As Jennifer Bowie explains in her webtext and podcast series on podcasting assignments for writing courses,

> I have found that students who podcast reconsider the five rhetorical canons and other rhetorical concepts in new ways and often end up not only creating rhetorically savvy podcasts, but also improving their writing skills in a variety of media. (Episode 6)

Bowie's work is particularly convincing in that it summarizes data based on students' self-reports and uses podcast episodes as her primary means of delivery. Also using student data as evidence, Crystal VanKooten has similarly demonstrated that development of rhetorical strategies for audio-visual delivery does transfer to other kinds of writing through students' "meta-awareness" from creating videos and other multimodal compositions. Understanding that sonic artworks, voice-overs, podcasts, videos, and multi-track mixes are not simply technical exercises or narrative devices, this body of research continues to outline critical sonic compositional practices as an important and expanded kind of writing.

When composing with sound, the digital technologies themselves and their visual representations within the software's interface can thus allow for both limited and increased possibilities. Every sonic representation builds upon the affordances of sound, but is also constrained by the interpretative interface being foregrounded. The waveforms and multi-track mixers used by audio composing software, for example, allow composers to shape the constituent features of a sound that can be displayed visually (e.g., pitch, volume, sustain), but training is necessary to recognize these kinds of qualities and distinctions. Multi-tracking audio mixing programs such as Audacity display sounds and their relative relationships in layers of individual sounds, requiring a nuanced understanding of how to hear a desired effect in "the mix" of sounds with their relative volumes and contrasts. The digital technologies writers use when composing with sound, while adding layers of complexity, and no small amount of audio editing time, may also be the best way to expand a writer's perceived sense of agency and impact through composition.

Activist Pedagogies and Sonic Rhetorics

Listener-centric activities and sound-based projects offer engaged and audience-driven learning for composition and rhetoric classrooms. Many assignments by numerous composition teachers have evolved to form this selection of best practices and help highlight the current moment of affordances for using sound in digital composition. By way of conclusion, then, these are specific learning and composing activities to begin teaching and learning with sound, followed by examples of what using sound rhetorically might afford us therein.

- *Reduced listening* uses Chion's model to foster more embodied, attuned, and nuanced listening practices.
- *Soundscape recording and analysis* helps writers to identify personal and cultural dimensions of soundscapes and events, to better identify meanings in the surround.
- *Voice(s)*, either delivered, recorded, or manipulated, helps writers to construct or call out to specific identities and communities.
- *Music*, as in film, can be used to establish mood and style, evoke emotion, build suspense, provide transitions, or help to recreate a historical moment.
- *Sound effects and sampling*, where composers sample and manipulate sonic characteristics, can add hyper-real or "natural" sounds to a composition to help tell a story or establish mood and style.
- *Scripts and storyboards* used to create audio essays, videos, narratives, and podcasts draw upon the radio-inspired or journalistic conventions and digital storytelling techniques of sequencing and voice-over narration.
- *Sound collages and remixes* can create juxtapositions, construct a cacophony, and in general defamilarize the typical conventions of arguments or narratives, along with the original texts/ performances.
- *Audio multi-track editing* allows composers to uncover, create, and/or mix layers of recorded sounds into the multiple dimensions of a sonic composition.

Learning any one of these techniques and using them in combination can afford digital writers that wider palate of multimodal composition, where they decide upon and deploy the best kind of media and technique for their purposes. A sonic vocabulary emphasizes the affordances of techniques available with sound and might empower those writers to better engage and persuade their audiences. Even simple musical recording—with no video—can train our students in "reduced listening," where they engage in experiential listening first, and can then lead to analytic responses rather than simple statements of musical taste. These reduced listening practices, when combined with focused attention on experiences and affective responses to sound, create opportunities for students to respond more deeply to music, or to focus more on recreating their immediate moment-to-moment experiences of a sound before moving into an analysis of those sounds. With an expanded definition that includes all embodied ways of *listening*—ways that register vibration, space, and affect, as well as meaning or source—such training will continue to make writers more sensitive to the human and nonhuman agents in their environments. The analytic and experiential approaches involved in multimodal listening help offer a *listener-centric* pedagogy that can prepare writers to use sound effectively as a compositional tool (Hocks and Comstock 136).

Questions remain about how much sonic composition experiences can transfer rhetorical strategies to other kinds of composition and to rhetorical development and persuasion more generally. Digital sonic projects often do not fit a particular set of writerly conventions or a familiar genre. Technologies and the various digital tools and interfaces mediate sounds and offer strategies for how to manipulate the characteristics and qualities of sound. When we continue to track everyday sonic practices, when a new technology, platform or application becomes available, the possibilities for interaction and rhetorical engagement expand. Communicative practices are continually re-evaluated and transformed. If the digital turn has changed what writing can accomplish, arguably because of unprecedented, immediate reach to public audiences and global interactions, then writers face more possibilities and also must take more ethical responsibility for their actions through writing in the world. Sonic ecologies, based in materiality and embodied experience, help amplify both empathy and ethics, offering writers a path to activism.

Works Cited

Alaimo, Stacy. *Bodily Natures: Science, Environment, and the Material Self*, Indiana UP, 2010.

——. "Introduction To Matter." In *Gender: Matter. The Macmillan Interdisciplinary Handbooks*, edited by Renée C. Hoogland, Nicole Fleetwood, and Iris van der Tuin. Macmillan, 2016, pp. xiii–xviii.

Alexander, Jonathan. "Glenn Gould and the Rhetorics of Sound." *Computers and Composition*, vol. 37, no. 3, 2015, pp. 73–89.

Ball, Cheryl, and Byron Hawk. *Sound in/as Compositional Space: A Next Step in Multiliteracies*, Joint Special Issue of *Computers and Composition*, vol. 23, no. 3, pp. 263–398, and *Computers and Composition Online*, Fall 2006, www2.bgsu.edu/departments/english/cconline/sound/. Accessed 9 Nov. 2017.

Bowie, Jennifer. "Podcasting in a Writing Class? Considering the Possibilities." *Kairos: A Journal of Rhetoric, Technology, and Pedagogy*, vol. 16, no. 2, 2012, kairos.technorhetoric.net/16.2/praxis/bowie/index.html. Accessed 3 July 2017.

Ceraso, Steph. "(Re)Educating the Senses: Multimodal Listening, Bodily Learning, and the Composition of Sonic Experiences." *College English*, vol. 77, no. 2, 2014, pp. 102–23.

Ceraso, Steph, and Kati Fargo Ahern. "Composing With Sound." *Composition Studies*, vol. 43, no. 2, 2015, pp. 13–18.

Chion, Michel. "The Three Listening Modes." *The Sound Studies Reader*, edited by Jonathan Sterne. Routledge, 2012, pp. 48–53.

Comstock, Michelle, and Mary E. Hocks. "The Sounds of Climate Change: Sonic Rhetoric in the Anthropocene, the Age of Human Impact." *Rhetoric Review*, vol. 35, no. 2, 2016, pp. 165–75.

——. "Voice in the Cultural Soundscape: Sonic Literacy in Composition Studies." *Computers and Composition Online*, Fall 2006, www.cconlinejournal.org/comstock_hocks/index.htm. Accessed 3 July 2017.

Davis, Diane, Ed. *Writing With Sound*, special issue of *Currents in Electronic Literacy*, 14, 2011, currents.dwrl.utexas.edu/2011. Accessed 3 July 2017.

Gauthier, Philippe-Aubert, and Philippe Pasquier. "Auditory Tactics: A Sound Installation in Public Space Using Beamforming Technology." *Leonardo Music Journal*, vol. 43, no. 5, 2010, pp. 426–33.

Goodman, Steve. *Sonic Warfare: Sound, Affect, and the Ecology of Fear*, MIT P, 2010.

Halbritter, Bump. *Mics, Cameras, Symbolic Action: Audio-Visual Rhetoric for Writing Teachers*, Parlor, 2012.

Hocks, Mary E., and Michelle Comstock. "Composing For Sound: Sonic Rhetoric as Resonance." *Computers and Composition*, vol. 43, no. 1, 2017, pp. 135–46.

Krause, Bernie. *The Great Animal Orchestra: Finding the Origins of Music in the World's Wild Places*, Little-Brown, 2012.

LaBelle, Brandon. *Acoustic Territories: Sound Culture and Everyday Life*, Continuum, 2010.

Manovich, Lev. *The Language of New Media*, MIT P, 2001.

McKee, Heidi. "Sound Matters: Notes Toward the Analysis and Design of Sound in Multimodal Webtexts." *Computers and Composition*, vol. 23, no. 3, 2006, pp. 335–354.

New London Group. "A Pedagogy of Multiliteracies: Designing Social Futures." *Harvard Educational Review*, vol. 66, no. 1, 1996, pp. 60–92.

Rickert, Thomas. *Ambient Rhetoric: The Attunements of Rhetorical Being.* U of Pittsburgh P, 2013.

——. Ed. *Writing/Music/Culture*, special issue of *Enculturation: A Journal of Rhetoric, Writing and Culture*, vol. 2, no. 2, 1999, www.enculturation.net/2_2/index.html. Accessed 3 July 2017.

Sayers, Jentery. "Audio Culture Series: Scaffolding a Sequence of Assignments." *Sounding Out!*, 3 Sept. 2012, https://soundstudiesblog.com/2012/09/03/sayers/. Accessed 3 July 2017.

——. "Audiography." 2010, www.jenteryteachers.com.

Schafer, R. Murray. *The Soundscape: The Tuning of the World*, McClelland and Stewart, 1977.

Selfe, Cynthia L. "Technology and Literacy: A Story About the Perils of Not Paying Attention." *College Composition and Communication*, vol. 50, no. 3, 1999, pp. 411–36.

——. "The Movement of Air, The Breath of Meaning: Aurality and Multimodal Composing." *College Composition and Communication*, vol. 60, no. 4, 2009, pp. 616–63.

Shipka, Jody. "Sound Engineering: Toward a Theory of Multimodal Soundness." *Computers and Composition*, vol. 23, no. 3, 2006, pp. 355–73.

Stedman, Kyle D. "Making Meaning in Musical Mixes." *Sonic Rhetorics*, special issue of *Harlot of the Arts*, no. 9, 2013, http://harlotofthearts.org/index.php/harlot/article/view/167/124.l. Accessed 3 July 2017.

Sterne, Jonathan. *The Audible Past: Cultural Origins of Sound Reproduction.* Duke UP, 2003.

Stone, Jonathan, and Steph Ceraso, Eds. *Sonic Rhetorics*, special issue of *Harlot of the Arts*, no. 9, 2013, harlotofthearts.org/index.php/harlot/issue/view/9. Accessed 3 July 2017.

VanKooten, Crystal. "Identifying Components of Meta-Awareness about Composition: Toward a Theory and Methodology for Writing Studies." *Composition Forum*, no. 33, 2016, compositionforum.com/issue/33/meta-awareness.php. Accessed 3 July 2017.

10

MAKING AND REMAKING THE SELF THROUGH DIGITAL WRITING

Julie Faulkner

In *Four Quartets*, T. S. Eliot described the venture of writing as "a new beginning, a raid on the inarticulate." If writing is about meaning-making in all its symbolic forms, authorial questions then remain about resources available to negotiate the "general mess of imprecision of feeling" (Eliot again). Writing in education has been constructed traditionally as a solitary activity, concerned with the use of print to persuade, inform, and motivate readers. Writers are asked to consider to whom they are writing, the context of their writing, and what kinds of written structures they are drawing on to effectively reach their audiences. These kinds of social understandings and rhetorical practices continue to ground technological processes (Verhulsdonck and Limbu), while the technologies themselves open expanded tools for making meaning. Moreover, we are now very conscious of the highly collaborative ways of working, playing, and socializing with and through the digital. We might then ask what these expanded possibilities in relation to writing might look like in a twenty-first-century writing environment. Further, how could the potential of digital technologies challenge inscribed approaches to learning and teaching writing?

Digital Resources and Meaning-Making

Elizabeth Losh argues that a conceptualization of "digital rhetoric" needs to move beyond any narrowly instrumental understandings and focus on design. Like Richard Lanham, who earlier argued that computers not only represent but also *alter* the textual experience, Losh contends that networked digital communication "may operate with some fundamentally different assumptions about systems of communication than do natural language models" (48). We are now more fully aware, for instance, of the procedural force of algorithms and their power to formalize human actions in rhetorical ways.

Returning to writing as a rhetorical practice, Bill Green argues that "techno-textuality" has been opened up in terms of what can now be authored ("English Teaching"). This occurs not only in terms of new kinds of content, but also of form. Multiliterate practices engage complex relationships among visuals, space, and text as well as interpreting a range of symbols in critically and culturally appropriate ways. As far back as 1993, Lanham identified the creative and pleasurable dimensions inherent in composing with digital technologies:

For Lanham (1993), what is intriguing about "composition" in the digital electronic age is its lack of seriousness, its wit. Here the playful or ludic aspect of postmodernism is made very clear, as is the range of reference and realisation across forms and modes of textuality. But it is always, at best, strategic: an attempt at unsettling the norms of textuality, and hence aimed at re-energising the protocols and practices of social production of meaning. This manifests itself as much in "theory" as it does in cultural practice. (Green 259–60)

In this chapter, I explore the ways that authors create self-representations purposefully, often through such playful and subversive interactions with digital technologies.

Digital spaces contain continuities with, and yet different affordances from those of the page. Jay David Bolter and Richard Grusin claim that cultural critics are in the thrall of the "new" when, in fact, new media is a refashioning, or "remediation" of older media. However, even pre-Internet, some writers saw rules and norms of cyberspace creating a distinctively new sense of spatial awareness, involving a "fracturing of space" (Lankshear and Bigum 457). We can now, they argue, shift back and forth between different modes of meaning, creating new design patterns. Space is no longer closed and purpose-specific, but "open, continuous and fluid" (Knobel and Lankshear 11).

Gunther Kress calls the ways that we can purposefully mobilize these resources *synaesthesia*, or the remaking of semiotic resources within (transformation) and across modes (transduction). Within each mode exist different systems, or organizing logics that affect the ways that the semiotic elements are integrated. W. J. T. Mitchell calls this process "braiding." While multimodality is not new, through rapidly changing technologies we can deploy innovative ways to overlay image, word, gesture, image, sound, and space. In this sense, the producer's relationship with the text has become something theoretically more generative and creative. The processes that drive this shifting meaning-making create qualitatively new forms from those that have previously existed, pre-Internet. Users of formerly-static systems can become remakers, or transformers, of representational resources. Three dimensional space opens prospects for cognitive reshaping of texts, which have become, Kress argues, digital affordances. In this sense, the producer's relationship with the text has in turn become something more generative and creative.

However, while the potential is there for new forms of meaning-making, research is limited in relation to writing and classroom practices. While Marc Prensky's conceptualization of young people as digital natives has been roundly critiqued (for example, Bennet and Maton; Kennedy et al.), I wanted to explore how a cohort of university students used digital spaces creatively to construct self-representations. Digital environments offer not only different time/space relationships but also a rich culture for play and identity performance. Play is now (re)acknowledged by educators as important to problem-solving, imaginative exploration, and identity formation (Bateson and Martin; Merchant). Online identities in video games have become a particular focus for identity play (Gee). Crucial to performance of identity, as well as situated literacy practice, are the notions of purpose and audience. These concepts framed my exploration, particularly in relation to what the students chose to communicate, and how they created such interpretations.

Identity

Asking young people to represent themselves in a shared, online space invited students to extend their everyday digital practices around self-representation. The popularity of Facebook, Instagram, Snapchat and so on reflect forms of self-curation writ large. Users build virtual profiles of themselves designed specifically to communicate with others in particular ways. Although forms of expression are constrained by site architecture, Web 2.0 has dramatically expanded opportunities for experimenting, composing, and networking personal profiles. Updating Prensky's images of "natives" and immigrants," David White calls young people who have only known post-Internet life "residents," while those over 30 are seen as "visitors" (White). Whatever labels we apply suggest the powerfully embedded ways that digital devices and Web 2.0 feature in young people's lives. However, teachers must consider the ease of alignment between embedded use of technology and formal learning. Further, is such use assumed to be characteristic across age/gender/cultural groups, or do we require more nuanced appreciation? And how might such an appreciation inform teaching now and into the future?

Underpinning these questions lie further questions in relation to young people, identity and self-representation: how do they construct versions of themselves for others to read? What counts for them in terms of impressions of how they would like their peers to view them?

Identity is a narrative we tell about ourselves, informed by the ways in which we are seen and described. The literature locates tensions between understandings of fixed selves and those that are subject to shifts over time; Guy Merchant's "anchored and transient" identities. In terms of the possibilities and limitations of the process, Barbara Kamler and Pat Thomson note that identities are continually being made and remade in and as action, formed from available discourses.

Rob Cover states that digital technologies provide potential for a range of representations of self. Drawing on Judith Butler, he conceptualizes identity (and, here, the *writing* of identity) as an ongoing process of becoming; a series of performative acts. We search to establish coherence across this "moving target" (Smith and Watson 71). "Coherence" requires "a matrix of identity categories, experiences, and labels" (Butler 40) that, through repetition, lend the illusion of an inner identity core (Butler 12). It is here that Potter's concept of curation becomes salient as a metaphor to capture the process of attempting to fix and communicate an identity.

If online (particularly Facebook) identities establish themselves as stable through such iteration and reiteration, the digital introductions in this study offered a similar, if single, opportunity to "play out" a self to others. Although there were task prompts provided to encourage student consideration of competing subjectivities, students could choose to position themselves in relatively static ways or as an articulation of "ongoing reflexive performance" (Cover 55). Such representational choices are not limited to digital spaces of course, but the remaking of semiotic resources allowed by new media, and alluded to by Kress earlier, presented an implicit challenge for the authors of the digital introductions. The challenge remained "implicit" because the students had no technical frontloading—in other words, while they were encouraged to work "at the edge of their digital expertise" (my communication to them), the programs they selected to use were of their own choosing. Students had to decide what aspects of themselves they would communicate to peers and how they would best effect this through available choices.

Curating Identities

If online spaces open new possibilities for authorship, how is agency then enacted within the structures (and constraints) of digital spaces? This question has continued to absorb researchers interested in what young people do with digital media (see, for instance, Merchant; Marsh; Ito et al.). Building on the metaphor of "curation," Potter identified the ways young people combine and recombine resources on the Web as creative practices. Potter described the levels that authors create within network technologies as a kind of meta-authorship (xvi):

In digital culture, curating is, in its most sophisticated form, about organizing how these different resources work *intertextually* [author's italics] to make meanings and that this is a new practice, resulting from human agency in the changed social arrangements, practices, and artifacts of the new media. (cf. Lievrouw and Livingstone 2)

This notion of intertextuality to create new meaning resonates with concepts referred to earlier—Kress's synaesthesia and Mitchell's (1994) braiding. In Potter's work, however, he directly links the processes of "collecting, distributing, assembling, disassembling" (xvi) to forms of digital self-representation. The extensive popularity of social media attests to the investment young people make in these "affinity spaces" (Gee). The question for me as a literacy educator working with young people is how we might take up these practices in classrooms, particularly those practices around curation, in ways that encourage and reflect rich learning.

Further questions thus emerged to guide my exploration:

* Do digital tools, as Potter, Kress, and Mitchell suggest, open generative spaces for new and/or disrupted (Green's "unsettling") forms of self-representation?

And as a corollary to this question:

* How do preservice teachers themselves mobilise available digital resources to create and communicate self-representations? What is the role of the teacher in this process?

The Study

In this project, I created a digital introduction task to complement a traditional written student introduction to preface an English preservice teaching method course. The study originally arose as a response to regulatory demands of a teacher education course: education graduates are expected to demonstrate content knowledge of ICT and how it can be used in the classroom, or TPACK, technological pedagogical and content knowledge (Mishra and Koehler). However, the preservice teacher responses quickly developed into something more complex and intriguing than I expected when I first designed the assessment task.

One aim of the task interaction was, on my part, to push students into a less comfortable space. This space was created through their need to learn new media skills, and critically reflect on the capacity of technology to shape their processes, as well as the choices they needed to make to characterize themselves for a particular audience. These "pedagogies of discomfort" (Boler) were, in turn, positioned by me as generative learning conditions in which students might be forced to reconsider and move beyond habituated practices often associated with learning and teaching. Whether users exploited expanded learning conditions remained for me, as a teacher researcher, to discover.

The study involved one graduate Education cohort, comprising twenty-three students. The university cohort drew from a culturally diverse mix of local applicants, most of whom were in their early twenties. The data collected included the students' written letters of introduction, their digital presentations to the class and their critical reflections. The data were highlighted, grouped, and regrouped to sift through different patterns of response, complicating and refining categories. Exploring links within written and digital introductions, including contradictions and assumptions in the writing, I investigated themes underpinning contributions, and connected these to ideas emerging from the literature in relation to digital writing, pedagogies of disruption and to emerging teacher identities.

Not all students from the cohort volunteered to contribute to the study, and particular findings are drawn from the fourteen who agreed to participate. While I consider all students' offerings broadly, specific data discussion emerging from this select group arguably skews the discussion. The students who volunteered to participate could be viewed as those most invested in the task.

The handwritten introduction was to be addressed to me, the lecturer, while the digital introduction was uploaded into a shared online space, to be viewed and commented on by peers. Hence, identities in play via the letters and digital texts were shaped further, not only by modalities but by audience awareness. Following the construction of the two introductions, and with a view to encouraging students' understanding of literacy dimensions of the writing, they were asked to critically reflect on the practices and technologies involved.

I viewed the activity as critically positioned in Green's sense, in its awareness of the socially constructed, selective nature of recreating a version of oneself. Gee, Hull, and Lankshear add to Green's conceptualization through providing the power to change and actively produce meanings. Moreover, I also saw it as potentially creative and critical in encouraging what Potter calls author curation of space. Self-representation involved "collecting, distributing, assembling, disassembling and moving [text] across different stages" (xvi). Multimodality has the power to play with what is possible, allowing new configurations of the self in digital contexts.

Thus, the study promoted exploration of how this kind of "meta-authorship" (Potter) might play out in an educational setting, realizing some of the potentials of new media while seeking to understand the complexities of the learning/teaching terrain. If the digital offers new forms of semiotic and discursive practices (Kress; Merchant), I aimed to investigate whether, and to what extent, students, and by implication teachers, could exploit such potential.

Findings

The written introductions to me covered student-perceived strengths and weaknesses in terms of literacy skills, reading histories, and so on. They varied in detail and control of written features: syntax, vocabulary range, tone, and register choices. Among those who considered the modal differences between the written and digital introductions were interesting "confessions." Handwriting had become a significant challenge to many students after years of digital writing, and a number admitted to struggling to recreate cursive script (despite the fact, as teachers of young children, they would have to teach handwriting as a skill). Some students acknowledged the necessity of using a digital device to compose; they wrote the draft of their letter first on a computer, then transposed the draft to paper. This suggests student comfort with digital technologies that reverses early practices with computers in classrooms used only as publishing tools. Here, the handwriting is the "publication" while the computer is the primary composing tool.

The digital introduction content ranged from limited, in terms of exploitation of form, to rich and boundary-pushing. Exploring the ways students drew on available resources to tell personal stories, I looked particularly at intersections between what was told and how it was told. Predictable content could be represented as digitally interesting while conceptually innovative material might be formatted in traditional ways. The most striking stories experimented with both content and form.

At the limited end, five presentations used the task as a kind of digital scrapbook, posting photos of friends, family, and pets, following a linear chronology from baby to university student, occasionally supported by a favorite music track. The visual and audio resources in these cases mimicked print resources of self-representation: they tended to be linear in structure, rely more strongly on written text, and draw upon known conventions such as photo albums. Others grouped aspects of their lives in Prezi frames, but explored none of the 3D potential of Prezi as a presentation tool. While it was possibly new software for many students, little had been made of online samples of Prezi being used effectively as an alternative to PowerPoint. Knowledge and use of visual grammar elements were limited. Although some had considered sequencing their narratives, transitions were often absent or clunky, with abrupt endings.

Other students, however, consciously wrestled with the "messiness" of ICT (Bigum), producing conceptually and visually compelling introductions. Their program range included iMovie, Prezi, Photostory 3, Movie Maker, PowerPoint, Google Earth, Animoto, YouTube, Flipagram, and websites, suggesting many students took on the teacher directive to extend their expertise. In most cases, music was added and acknowledged, reflecting the personal associations with the chosen song. A number of reflections detailed hours spent on learning new software, time willingly expended in pursuit of a program that would achieve narrative ends. Music, for example, was often problematic to add to images. Yet, reflections suggested that students read guides, searched blog and Youtube instructions and sought advice in their efforts to have their chosen digital platform achieve the effects they wanted for the intended audience.

Some students consciously mixed the analogue and digital. Ollie filmed himself sitting on his bed, looking deadpan at the camera while he flicked through piles of paper-printed photos reflecting aspects of his life. The lighting was (deliberately?) poor as he nonchalantly showed us travel and family photos and closed, wielding a neon Star Wars lightsaber.

James was filmed from waking to sleeping, engaging in a series of banal and self-deprecating events, such as learning to turn the Google sign around the right way on the computer screen. His travels, a much referred to event in students' lives, consisted of him flying a cut out paper plane over a print map of the world. Potter's curation includes juxtaposing and appropriating elements to create meaning, with the "meaning" here existing as a metatextual comment on digital representation itself.

In some cases, authors bent genre conventions as they played with identity constructions. This was done from a distanced perspective and often using knowing humor. While self-reflexive in intent, writers have achieved this with print, so the interest here lay in observing whether, and to what extent, use of the digital affordances value-added.

Some students played with the notion of self and how much to reveal or keep distant. Amy filmed people talking about her and talking *as* her—at no point did she ever either appear or disclose anything substantive about herself. Employing documentary and vox pop techniques, Tom edited clips of his family and friends discussing him posthumously, with one brother struggling to remember he had even existed (but could he now have his room). Another introduction engaged an animation program with computer generated, HAL-type voices (Xtranormal), to parody his decision to become a teacher education student. He chose a pre-provided Napoleonic war scenario to request safe passage to his outer suburb university.

In terms of "braiding" elements (Mitchell) to create new spaces for story, a number of students experimented successfully with technological possibilities. Koh from Singapore constructed an on-screen digital jigsaw puzzle with his name written in the centre section. Other digital pieces contained hyperlinked identity features (a Google map link to his street, satay recipes, a trailer to a favorite television series). Clicking and dragging the irregular pieces to the centre piece completed his jigsaw, which formed a map of his own country, with his name at the centre.

Liam filmed himself in profile, speaking intermittently. He then stood opposite his interactive screen profile and conducted a conversation with himself as postmodern subject—a playful, decentered expression of authorial voice.

Google Earth provided a platform for Matt to offer an annotated tour of the history of his relationship and work with a Japanese tent theatre company. He uploaded to Google Earth photographs and notes of events that took place in Tokyo and Melbourne linked to his ongoing collaboration, flying us to Tokyo and pasting theatre photos on relevant points of the map. The blending of literal and figurative modes extended his understanding of communication and representation. No two-dimensional form could replicate the geography space Matt wanted as a spatial layer to his photographic images.

The level of "orchestration" (Kress) in these examples was high, as students borrowed and experimented with combinations. While making no claims for such a small selection of introductions, the examples discussed here suggest that writers can take up the possibilities of new media in divergent and knowing ways.

However, perhaps less than one-third of the full cohort of students reflected in such depth and detail, or exploited the multimodal affordances of the technology. Some introductions made few connections beyond self-evident statements. David Buckingham (in Thomas) asserts, however, that "most of young people's use of digital technology is mundane rather than spectacular: it is characterized not by dramatic manifestations of innovation and creativity, but by relatively routine forms of communication and information retrieval" (x). Moreover, Goldstone, writing about picture books in ways that could apply to any text, describes characteristics that are seen as postmodern. These include nonlinearity, creating a self-referential or mocking tone and an anti-authoritarian stance. The challenge of contemporary authorship, therefore, is not limited only to multimodal opportunities, but also to moving beyond conventional, two-dimensional writing. Risk-taking at this level requires imagination, scaffolding and exposure to exemplars. Moreover, it asks learners to sit in a "discomforting" space, as Boler would see it, an ambiguous but open space.

To encourage new combinations and expression of students' local digital knowledge then, the role of the teacher becomes significant. However, as Green and Bigum argued, as long ago as 1993, it can be the teachers who are occupying uncomfortable positions, even more than the students. Teachers have to become learners as well, which does not necessarily connect with traditional conceptualizations.

Nor, as Selwyn reminds us, is creativity (highlighted here in Kress's synaesthetic affordances) inevitably implicated in digital technologies. The inventive play with time and space by students described in this study could have been mediated through other technologies. In this assignment design, there was a central focus on semiotic communication and representational interrelationships, highlighted by guided reflection questions. However, as the full range of introductions suggests, open-ended tasks per se guarantee no more "creativity" than more traditionally mediated invitations. Again, the role of the teacher in expanding and scaffolding authorial possibilities appears central here.

Conclusion

Effective teaching always comprises a complex negotiation of factors, heightened by the rapid technological shifts of the past four decades. The limited scale of this research does not attempt to make generalizations or broad claims about young people's digital use. However, it does affirm the importance of sound design principles lying at the heart of learning in relation to digital practice. Knobel and Lankshear argue that digital technologies open up a new ethos for participation, a Web 2.0 approach which emphasizes a significant shift in the ways students are now positioned as learners.

From this vantage point, Potter argues curatorship as an innovative literacy practice, noting that the act of digital curation "is now a metaphorical new literacy practice which incorporates the collection, production and exhibition of markers of identity through time in both digital production and social media" (123). Such a concept, he argues, describes the expanded practices new media allow young people to be creative and autonomous. These digital introductions attempted to value and extend the productive multimodal mindset of students while considering the impact of purpose and audience on text creation.

Many reflective comments, however, suggested that as learners, preservice teachers were working within their comfort zones and, when prompted, making limited connections between learning and teaching processes. The role of the teacher was thus significant in not only encouraging students to work at the edge of what they knew and push their own risk-taking in these environments. This needed to be kept in productive tension with a strengths focus through students taking control of their own narrative. To successfully create the self-representation, and then recognize the kinds of learning experienced to inform the implementation, preservice teachers needed to articulate a range of ways that learning occurred through working with the digital. They had to identify how they drew on peer knowledge, learning at the point of need and through trial and error—familiar strategies for digital learning, but perhaps not often articulated (Anstey and Bull; Gee).

Added to this was the impact of audience on autobiographical stories. Some students tried to protect their self-revelations through comments in the online forum (for example, "sorry guys, this is not very good"), while others controlled the relational aspects of their content through limiting exposure and personal information. Careful curation (Potter) was required as students made choices about what to share about themselves and their communities via their narratives. Vulnerability and distance at times played out against agency and the freedom to express oneself through digital formats.

The teacher's role in supporting student effort emerged as vital to the quality of the opportunity provided by the task. Task design can aim to maximize digital potentials but this study snapshot suggested that open-ended learning intentions and software choice are not enough. While researchers have pointed to new logics of using space differently to combine elements, innovation and creativity do not inhere in digital technology. To mobilize the possibilities of the rhetoric of twenty-first-century rhetorical practices, educators need to develop expanding understandings of the ways conventions can be pushed and challenged. Just as conceptualizations around new media content have changed, so then must pedagogies. The educator herself had to learn what was required beyond assessment task descriptors; that is, to identify and articulate strategies of experimentation, modeling, and critical reflection. Underpinning such strategies sits the knowledge that these learners are used to enhanced social autonomy in terms of the ways they approach learning. This shift must inform and shape our practice as we design curriculum for contemporary learning.

Works Cited

Anstey, Michèle, and Geoff Bull. *Teaching and Learning Multiliteracies: Changing Times, Changing Literacies.* International Reading Association, 2006.

Bateson, Patrick, and Paul Martin. *Play, Playfulness, Creativity and Innovation.* Cambridge UP, 2013.

Bigum, Chris. *Schools and the Internet. Reinventing the 1980s?* Incorporated Association of Registered Teachers of Victoria (IARTV) Seminar Series, no. 47, 1995.

Boler, Megan. *Feeling Power: Emotions and Education.* Routledge, 1999.

Bolter, Jay David, and Richard Grusin. *Remediation: Understanding New Media.* MIT Press, 1999.

Bennett, Susan J., and Karl Maton. "Beyond the 'Digital Natives' Debate: Towards a More Nuanced Understanding of Students' Technology Experiences." *Journal of Computer Assisted Learning*, vol. 26, no. 5, 2010, pp. 321–31.

Buckingham, David. "Introduction." *Deconstructing the Digital Natives: Young People, Technology, and the New Literacies*, edited by Michael Thomas. Routledge, 2011, pp. i–xi.

Butler, Judith. *Gender Trouble: Feminism and the Subversion of Female Identity*. Routledge, 1990.

Cover, Rob. "Becoming and Belonging: Performativity, Subjectivity and the Cultural Purposes of Social Networking." *Identity Technologies: Constructing the Self Online*, edited by A. Poletti and J. Rak. U of Wisconsin P, 2014, pp. 55–69.

Eliot, T. S. *The Four Quartets*. Faber & Faber, 1999.

Gee, James Paul. *What Videogames Have to Teach Us about Learning and Literacy*. Palgrave, 2003.

Gee, James Paul, Glynda Hull, and Colin Lankshear. *The New Work Order: Behind the Language of the New Capitalism*. Allen & Unwin and Westview Press. 1996.

Goldstone, Bette. "The Postmodern Picture Book: A New Subgenre." *Language Arts*, vol. 81, no. 3, 2004, pp. 196–204.

Green, Bill. "English Teaching, 'Literacy' and the Post-Age." *P(ICT)ures of English: Teachers, Learners, and Technology*, edited by Cal Durrant and Catherine Beavis. AATE, 2001, pp. 249–71.

——. "Subject-Specific Literacy and School Learning: A Focus on Writing." *Australian Journal of Education*, vol. 32, no. 2, 1998, pp. 156–79.

Green, Bill, and Chris Bigum. (1993). "Aliens in the Classroom." *Australian Journal of Education*, vol. 33, no. 2, 1993, pp. 119–34.

Ito, Mizuko., Sonja Baumer, Matteo Bittanti, danah boyd, Rachel Cody, Becky Herr, Heather A. Horst, Patricia G. Lange, Dilan Mahendran, Katynka Martinez et al. *Hanging Out, Messing Around, Geeking Out: Kids Living and Learning with New Media*. Cambridge: MIT Press, 2013.

Kamler Barbara, and Pat Thomson. *Helping Doctoral Students Write*. Routledge, 2006.

Kennedy, G., Dalgarno, B., Bennett, S., Gray, K., Waycott, J., Judd, T., Bishop, A., Maton, K., Krause, K., and Chang, R. *Educating the Net Generation: A Handbook of Findings for Practice and Policy*. Australian Learning and Teaching Council, http://netgen.unimelb.edu.au/. Accessed 7 Nov. 2017.

Knobel, Michele, and Colin Lankshear. *A New Literacies Sampler*, everydayliteracies.net/files/NewLiteracies Sampler_2007.pdf. Accessed 7 July 2017.

Kress, Gunther. *Literacy in the New Media Age*. Routledge, 2003.

Lanham, Richard. "Digital Rhetoric: Theory, Practice, and Property." *Literacy Online: The Promise and Perils of Reading and Writing with Computers*, edited by Myron C. Tuman. Pittsburgh UP, 1992, pp. 221–43.

——. *The Electronic Word: Democracy, Technology and the Arts*. U of Chicago P, 1993.

Lankshear, Colin, and Chris Bigum. "Literacies and New Technologies in School Settings." *Pedagogy, Culture, and Society*, vol. 7, no. 3, 2006, pp. 445–65.

Lievrouw, Leah A., and Sonia Livingstone, Eds. *Handbook of New Media: Social Shaping and Social Consequences*. SAGE, 2006.

Losh, Elizabeth. *Defining Digital Rhetoric with 20–20 Hindsight*. Digital Rhetoric Collaborative, 25 June 2012, www.digitalrhetoriccollaborative.org/2012/06/25/defining-digital-rhetoric-with-20–20-hindsight/. Accessed 7 July 2017.

Marsh, Jackie. "'Unboxing' Videos: Co-construction of the Child as Cyberflâneur." *Discourse: Studies in the Cultural Politics of Education*. Published online ahead of print, 25 June 2015.

Merchant, Guy. *Identity, Social Networks and Online Communication*. ldm.sagepub.com/content/3/2/235. full.pdf+html. *E-Learning and Digital Media*, vol. 3, no. 2, 2006, pp. 235–44.

——. "Electric Involvement: Identity Performance in Children's Informal Digital Writing." *Discourse: Studies in the Cultural Politics of Education*, vol. 26, no. 3, 2005, pp. 301–14.

Mishra, Punya, and Matthew J. Koehler. "Technological Pedagogical Content Knowledge: A Framework for Teacher Knowledge." *Teachers College Record*, vol. 108, no. 6, 2006, pp. 1017–54.

Mitchell, W. J. T. *Picture Theory: Essays on Verbal and Visual Representation*. U of Chicago P, 1994.

Potter, John. *Digital Media and Learner Identity: The New Curatorship*. Palgrave Macmillan, 2012.

Prensky, Marc. "Digital Natives, Digital Immigrants." *On the Horizon*, vol. 9, no. 5, 2001, pp. 1–2. www. marcprensky.com/writing/Prensky%20-%20Digital%20Natives,%20Digital%20Immigrants%20-%20 Part1.pdf. Accessed 7 July 2017.

Smith, Sidonie, and Julia Watson. "Virtually Me: A Toolbox about Online Presentation." *Identity technologies: Constructing the self online*, edited by Anna Poletti and Julie Rak. 2014, pp. 55–69, U of Wisconsin P.

Verhulsdonck, Gustav, and Marohang Limbu. *Digital Rhetoric and Global Literacies: Communication Modes and Digital Practices in the Networked World*. IGI Global, 2014.

White, Dave. http://daveowhite.com/.

PART III

Being Rhetorical and Digital

11

SOCIAL MEDIA AS MULTIMODAL COMPOSING

Networked Rhetorics and Writing in a Digital Age

Stephanie Vie

Social media, once considered a niche technology that few people used, is now ubiquitous worldwide. Social networks in particular have become increasingly prominent in the past decade, with technologies such as Facebook (launched in 2004), Reddit (2005), and Twitter (2006) becoming an indispensable part of daily life for many in the intervening ten years.

Facebook, for example, began with fewer than twenty million members in 2004; in 2016, 1.18 billion daily active users visit the site on average (for September 2016) and approximately 84.9 percent of those daily active users are outside the US and Canada (Facebook, "Company Info").

Similarly, when Twitter was launched in 2006, a mere 20,000 tweets were sent per day. Ten years later, 313 million monthly users post over 500 million tweets per day (Sayce, "Tweets per Day"). The majority of those accounts are outside the US, with 79 percent of users outside the US and more than forty different languages supported by Twitter (Twitter, "Twitter Usage"). And Reddit, which bills itself as the "front page of the Internet," included 73.15 million submissions with 725.85 million comments made by 8.7 million total authors containing 19.36 billion words in 2015 (Reddit, "Reddit in 2015").

With this shift toward widespread and worldwide social networking, how we maintain networked relationships with others has changed. Today, our public and private lives overlap in social media spaces—where we maintain personal profiles often viewable by both strong and weak ties in our networks, and where we communicate with and are accessible to friends, family members, employers, teachers, and a host of others. Facebook may have popularized "friend" as a verb ("friend me on Facebook") but those with whom we connect in social media technologies are of course not always those we would call friends offline. As such, considering the rhetorical aspects of networking with others in social media technologies is crucial in the twenty-first century. This includes the choices users make when constructing social networking profiles; the ramifications of the publicly visible connections among users of social media technologies; and the implications of users' choices about privacy in social media, including their awareness and understanding of privacy settings and policies and terms of service.

The importance of the maintenance of networked relationships and of the written communication in which we engage in social networks was thrown into sharp relief by the US presidential elections in 2016. Eli Pariser has written about the concept of the "filter bubble," wherein sites such as Google and Facebook rely on algorithms to shape the information presented to users, resulting in users seeing more content personalized for them. However, as Pariser points out, users can be trapped in a bubble of content that aligns with their own pre-existing views, showing them only content that reinforces what they already know or feel and not confronting them with opposing viewpoints. Recent Pew Research Center data note that a majority of social media users "are worn out by the amount of political content they encounter, and more than half describe their online interactions with those they disagree with politically as stressful and frustrating" (Duggan and Smith). Many US social media users blocked or unfollowed friends who posted political content, particularly if this content differed from their own viewpoints, and post-election, users ramped up unfriending and unfollowing activities in their shock at the election results (Lindner). And Duggan and Smith found that 84 percent of social media users believed that social media encouraged people to post political statements that they would never say in person, illustrating how individuals see the communicative space of social media technologies as markedly different from other non-digital, non-socially networked spaces.

The centrality of social media and social networks specific to the 2016 US presidential election process (and its aftermath) showcases the complexity of the multimodal composing that happens daily in these technological spaces. It is their complexity that makes them so compelling for scholars of digital writing and rhetoric to study. Social media users and non-users alike frequently fail to see the actions undertaken in social media as *writing*; such users may not believe that constructing a personal profile, hashtagging a picture in Instagram, or posting on someone's Facebook newsfeed is really writing. However, I argue that these multimodal composing acts are in fact noteworthy moments of digital writing that we should be paying greater attention to when considering how writing is changing in an increasingly digitally mediated world.

To illustrate how writing is impacted by social media technologies, in this chapter I draw on data from over 750 survey respondents and face-to-face interviews with thirty-five survey participants to illustrate critical tensions surrounding networking rhetorics in social media technologies. These participants—faculty members from universities nationwide—discussed with me their feelings about using social media personally, professionally, and pedagogically, and their discussions will be used to paint a broader picture of the role of relationship-building and maintenance, of the ramifications of networking in these spaces with strong and weak ties, and of the need for continued teacher training around social media. In doing so, I illustrate how networking rhetorics in social media are multimodal composing acts with the potential for significant impacts in our online and offline lives.

Method

Since 2005, I have been studying the impact of social media on writing and rhetoric, conducting interviews with both undergraduate and graduate students as well as faculty members to ascertain some of the major compelling trends in the field related to social media use and how writing is affected. My considerations of how writing is affected include both the nature of the writing itself—the composing practices in which social media users engage and the kinds of things that they write—as well as how writing instruction has shifted and continues to shift as a result of increasing social media use within and beyond the composition classroom. Early on, social media use was viewed with suspicion by the majority of my faculty participants, while the students I spoke to were troubled by the possibilities of the newly broadened audiences they faced in sites such as Facebook and MySpace—where employers, family members, parents, and others had recently been given access and were potentially now able to view the students' social network profiles (Vie, "Engaging Others"; Vie, "Digital Divide 2.0"). At this point in time (early 2005–2006), many of the social media users I spoke with were extremely concerned about privacy, which made sense given the changes in sites such as Facebook that had shifted from allowing only students with an .edu email address to join the site to allowing anyone with an email address to join. Yet despite their concerns about privacy, most of these research participants were unaware of privacy settings that were available and chose not to restrict access to their profiles to a narrower audience (Vie, "Engaging Others").

In 2014 and 2015, I revisited my study of social media users in writing and rhetoric by surveying a total of 786 faculty members nationwide and conducting follow-up interviews with a selected group of thirty participants. Overall, for those I surveyed, I asked questions that attended to the benefits and the challenges of social media use in higher education writing classrooms, particularly inquiring into the choice of some faculty members to not rely on social media at all in their teaching (either as a topic of content for the classroom or as a composing tool for writing). The twenty-nine possible questions asked respondents for demographic information, attitudes toward social media use in the writing classroom (e.g., "Would you be interested in or willing to use social media in your teaching in the future?"), specific social media tools used in the writing classroom, and a discussion of benefits and challenges to using social media in their writing pedagogy. The survey was coded using grounded theory (Glaser and Strauss) and I looked for themes that emerged from the data, such as privacy, time, assessment, and relevance. All participants were offered the opportunity to be pseudonymous, and the research was approved by the Institutional Research Board at the University of Central Florida prior to data collection.

The thirty follow-up interviewees were selected because they had indicated a willingness to continue discussing this topic with me, but beyond that, they were also selected because their survey responses were compelling in some way. Some faculty selected, for instance, were chosen because they were adamant about never using social media in their teaching; several described their commitment to alphabetic writing and detailed how the multimodal composing processes highlighted in social media technologies were not really offering students opportunities to write, at least in their eyes. Other interviewees presented an opposing viewpoint; excited about social media and how it could be used in teaching, these participants enthusiastically shared with me specific assignments, teaching moments, and other artifacts from their classrooms that engaged with social media in substantial ways. These hour-long interviews offered me the chance to delve deeper into the participants' survey responses but also to hear more about the faculty members' everyday interactions with social media: in the writing classroom, in their daily lives, in conversations with friends and family members, and so on. In some cases, for participants who chose not to participate in social media, our conversations revolved around that particular choice and the implications of being a non-user of social media in a world heavily saturated by such technologies.

In the section that follows, I offer findings from my study that attempt to address the question, "How has writing and writing instruction changed as a result of the greater incorporation of social media and social networks into our lives?" In keeping with this book's section that interrogates how public spheres are changing in relation to the circulation of digital forms of composing, I describe the many challenging situations these individuals found themselves in as a result of their writing in social networks.

Findings

Tensions around Politics and Activism

Earlier I described how the US political arena, particularly in the 2016 presidential election, was both impacted by and impacted social media technologies. That is, the election itself was (rather relentlessly) covered by various news media outlets and commented on by users on social media platforms such as Reddit, Facebook, and Twitter, among others. Presidential candidate Donald Trump was frequently lambasted for his Twitter outbursts and campaign staffers even moved to restrict his social media access late in the campaign (Schultheis, "Report"). In the aftermath of the election, social media users made difficult decisions about which friends to keep and which to jettison, and many posted heartfelt discussions about not knowing what to say or write in the days after the election results were provided. Such tensions around politics, audience, and tenure coalesced for many of the participants I spoke to, illustrating a central theme about writing in socially networked environments such as Facebook and Twitter today: users are extremely aware of the broad audience their social media writing may reach. In the wake of high-profile academic controversies such as Steven Salaita's dismissal from the University of Illinois after his highly publicized tweets about the Israel–Palestine conflict, these participants were careful to choose their words and their friends in social media carefully.

One participant, for example, remarked to me that she saw conflicts between the personal and professional personas she was expected to uphold as an assistant professor and writing teacher. I inquired what particular events might have prompted her to think about keeping her personal and professional life more separate in social media, and she said:

> Well, especially now that we have the start of the primary presidential campaign and I have certain thoughts, but I think that it's important to keep some of those thoughts to myself not just for tenure purposes. But really, I don't want to give the impression that I don't respect diversity and opinion, especially diverse political opinions in my classroom because I am a writing instructor or at least had a lot more composition, FYC responsibilities. One thing I don't feel comfortable doing, I mean, I just got to [my institution] and I'm actually really, really enjoying it here, but I didn't feel comfortable at [my previous institution] and I don't think I'd feel comfortable here talking about institutional issues on Twitter.

As I pressed further, this participant specifically invoked Salaita and noted that "being vocal about institutional issues . . . I don't feel that I can do that yet. I wonder if I were to do that, the potential consequences I think for me as someone pre-tenure could be a lot higher, a lot more severe." Other participants took a similar tack, stating that the tensions around political discussions and other forms of politically motivated or activist writing in social media seemed particularly dangerous for them as academics on the tenure track or the job market:

> I feel like especially for a person going onto the market it's fairly dangerous to get too involved publicly in a lot of political issues right now. Especially on social media because things are so remixable. Things come out with no context and I don't know, we just hear so many horror stories about it and I frankly have been warned about it.

Besides being fraught with potential danger, participants worried about their positionality in relation to writing in social media about politics and activism. The same graduate student who had been warned about the dangers of getting involved in politics noted further that he felt uncomfortable inserting himself into many conversations in social media because of his race and gender:

> And, you know, there's a certain amount of my subjectivity. It's like a lot of the politics that come up in my feeds are things about women, about people of color, and I don't know that I necessarily need to say something there. I don't necessarily think they need some white guy's statement about things as much as I just read a lot, I read everything people post. I just don't tend to comment very much because I'm not really sure what I would add to the conversation. . . . Beyond just not knowing what I would say that would be useful but there is always that feeling of "let's not insert myself into something that will blow up in my face."

Choosing whether or not to write about politics, race, gender, and other related topics in social media has become a difficult decision for many users, particularly academics. At the same time that social networks provide increased opportunities for connecting with a diverse group of others, that same diverse network of strong and weak ties (see Granovetter) has allowed for greater tensions around political participation. Yet it is precisely that digital network that—in the case of today's major social media technologies—allows for far broader reach to wider audiences than just a decade ago. And as a result, composers in social media may benefit from the networking opportunities available to them. Making decisions about what to say and who to say it to is nothing new to social media; it is simply that these digital networks have upped the stakes because the writing that happens in them often has wider circulation, greater rhetorical velocity (Ridolfo and DeVoss), and greater longevity. Authors of all kinds—whether faculty members on or off the tenure track, students writing in social media for a class, professional writers, and so on—must make far more complex decisions about their composing practices in social media than they did even ten years ago.

Tensions Related to Social Media Writing Pedagogy

While the discussion above attends to social media writing fairly broadly, when considering social media writing in a classroom setting, my participants articulated different but just as important concerns. As more faculty members choose to bring social media into their writing classrooms in some way (see Vie, "What's Going On," for a discussion of recent trends in social media pedagogy in the composition classroom), those faculty members will need to address not only what social media tools to incorporate, but also why they should be incorporated, and in what ways. One participant described the struggle to determine what "appropriate" social media writing might look like within the confines of his class:

> I think one challenge is, my social media and literacy class is like, what the heck are we supposed to post? Oh, so we have to use Twitter, what counts as a tweet for class? Can I post a picture of what I had for lunch and use the class hashtag, does that count? And to me, you know, students, I want them to gain experiences and gain understanding of this site and what do people use Twitter for? Well, some people do post pictures of their lunch right? So why can't we count that?

Social media writing is sometimes mocked as inconsequential, frivolous, and non-academic, but as scholars in rhetoric and composition have argued, students are engaging in a great deal of extracurricular writing (including in social media) that is meaningful for their literacy development (Fishman et al.).

Some participants pushed back against the quotidian composing that may be the hallmark of microblogging technologies such as Twitter and asked students to write in ways that the tool allowed for, but that might not be as common. In an echo of the participant quoted above, who talked about students posting pictures of their lunch with the class hashtag, the interviewee below referenced the social media/food trope as a means of explaining how she prompts students to "engage in conversations . . . larger than their immediate life":

> I think part of it is I want them to see how the tool [Twitter] is used in ways other than just posting what they had for breakfast so I went to . . . I think it's an effective way of getting students to engage in conversations that are much larger than their immediate life and in a very immediate kind of way so the first time that I had students do it was teaching the advanced writing class and it was all focused on political rhetoric. It was during the 2012 presidential campaign and so that seemed like a perfect time to bring Twitter in because obviously it was all over the place during that election season. And you know, like I said, some students really responded to it and other students had more difficulty or had difficulty engaging with it but I guess mostly it's the idea of getting them to interact with people that are outside of the classroom but are interested in some of the things that we're talking about.

The touchstone of food—of posting pictures of one's breakfast or lunch, of writing restaurant reviews on Yelp, or of sharing recipes on Facebook and posting comments about them—is indicative of the possibilities afforded to social media composers through the networks available in these tools. Yes, writing about food in social media may at first seem trivial, but as we look more carefully at the different ways one can write about food and interact with others (around an item that no human can live without, no less), food writing in social media becomes more than just a simple debate about should-we-or-shouldn't-we-write-about-food; it illustrates that debates about what the content of composition classes should be extend to classes that focus on digital rhetoric and social media, too. And that in fact these courses, by virtue of introducing writing in what is for many faculty members a new or unfamiliar space for writing, may make current debates in the field about themed writing versus writing about writing versus writing in the disciplines (and so on) seem even more fraught because of the added dimension of the networked writing that will happen in social media. In other words, digital writing and rhetoric in social media was particularly challenging for many participants because writing studies has not yet fully embraced what writing in digital environments might look like or how it might be assessed, let alone how social media writing for a rhetoric and composition course might be approached.

Tensions Related to Teacher Training

Finally, participants repeatedly described how a lack of teacher training was problematic in supporting their desires to include social media writing in their pedagogy. Again, lack of teacher training for particular writing environments—especially digital writing environments— is not new. But many faculty members are either unfamiliar with a variety of social media tools and how they might be incorporated into a writing classroom or they find themselves as the only faculty member in their department who teaches digital writing of any kind, let alone with social media. The same participant who discussed using Twitter for more than just posting about breakfast described the lack of interest in teaching writing with social media at her institution thus:

> Institutionally it's not something that is really talked about. We talk a lot about flipping the classroom and all of those types of things but I haven't seen . . . you know, we have faculty development day where we have workshops all day every year and there hasn't been anything about using social media in the classroom in those kinds of situations so it does seem that if you do it, it's because you're interested in it and you could figure it out on your own, or you're going to try it out on your own without getting a lot of context or research behind it. So there's not a lot of support for it, I don't think.

Certain technologies or approaches (here, flipping the classroom) have gained enough traction broadly to be supported or, alternatively, they have become so familiar in the classroom that they are nearly invisible (e.g., laptops, word processing). Social media, however, remains "new" enough in the writing classroom despite its inclusion in daily life for over a decade. While more and more rhetoric and composition scholars position themselves as social media experts of some kind—including in the classroom—these scholars are still frequently seen as a very niche group and their scholarship or pedagogical approaches do not yet have broad appeal to all writing classrooms at an institution.

Some classroom and pedagogical support spaces are making headway at incorporating social media effectively, and their examples may offer a model for other faculty interested in social media writing in the future. For example, many writing centers are using social media in exciting and effective ways, perhaps in part because of the great numbers of undergraduate and graduate students who work in them (who tend to use social media repeatedly and daily as compared to faculty members). A participant in this set of interviews associated with a writing studio at a large university detailed how she had spearheaded the inclusion of social media in the studio over the past few years: Twitter, Facebook, Instagram, WordPress, and Blogger had all been incorporated to build community among writers both within that particular campus and externally. This studio held monthly writing contests on Twitter, developed an Instagram account, and held question-and-answer sessions using social media, all in the name of increasing engagement among the writing studio consultants, their customer base, and their external audiences. Despite this success, though, she noted that she thought it unlikely that the English department in general would follow suit any time soon:

> I think it's an analogy of e-readers and e-books that whereas several years ago, people were very freaked out by e-readers or e-books as supplanting hard copy versions of books as like a thing that would eventually happen. And, I think we've seen that that's not been the case at all, so I'm very happy about that. So, I don't think people care. I . . . want to say, "Yes, of course, people will start to incorporate this more in their classrooms since they see institutional spaces doing it as a way of building community that's successful, then I can do that in my classroom and it can be successful as well, and it's manageable and it has a positive effect."
>
> Theoretically and ideally, that's what would happen. But I think people are much more hardened to staying within the known and like, "Hey, classroom instruction has gone completely well and successful for however many centuries like the way it is, why

do I need to bring in these additional tools that just complicate or increase learning curves or . . ." I don't know.

However, like any initiatives to incorporate digital technologies into the writing classroom, the inclusion of and training for social media initiatives is locally contextual. At least one faculty participant spoke about her institution's support for social media in pedagogy, noting that

> about two years ago at our graduation, the president of our college stood in front of everybody and took a picture of the audience, and put it on the Facebook feed. So I think that we are encouraged. I think they're getting into offering us our own Twitter, our own Facebook accounts as professors and its departments. And, there is support.

She detailed how she had just returned from a two-week NEH Institute on Digital Humanities supported by her institution, and that the "communal outlook on social media [at my school] is so different." Thus it's important to remember that support for teacher training at each institution will vary, but until social media become just as ubiquitous in the writing classroom as they are in everyday communication situations, such teacher training and support from upper administration for social media pedagogy will be crucial (see Vie, "Training Online," for further discussions of the crucial role that teacher trainers will play to support the embedding of social media in classroom pedagogy, particularly in online classroom environments).

Conclusion

It is clear that social media has changed writing. The choices that multimodal composers may make have become more complex thanks to the broadened reach, greater rhetorical velocity, and wider and more varied audiences prevalent in social media. Writing is happening all the time in social media. Hashtag campaigns around #blacklivesmatter and #yesallwomen, among many others, have allowed for social media writing to make significant activist inroads. Instagram captions and Pinterest pins give writers opportunities to curate the artifacts that matter in their lives and catalogue the images that represent significant moments. Tumblr, Facebook, and Twitter serve as journals, as political platforms, as spaces for professional networking, and much more.

At the same time that social media has changed writing, it is (albeit more slowly) changing the nature of the writing classroom in higher education. While students may not necessarily expect to be writing with or in social media tools in a classroom environment, nearly all will understand the importance of considering rhetorical principles in social networks, or of creating and maintaining a professional presence online for eventual employment, or of exercising critical thinking skills when confronted with scientific data or political articles in their social networks. But to rise to the challenge of the changing nature of writing in a social media environment, we require faculty members willing to hone their expertise in digital rhetoric who can push for needed teacher training and support, continue to challenge artificial hierarchies between personal and professional personas in social media, and argue for the need for digital literacies that include social media in the writing classroom. Given the massive changes that have happened as a result of social media in only the past ten years, it seems quite possible that the next decade will be one in which social media will play a much larger part in the landscape of higher education. Though the tools themselves will ebb and flow (remember Friendster?), writing in a multimodal world means writing in social media. And that means writing and researching more *about* social media writing in the future.

Works Cited

Duggan, Maeve, and Aaron Smith. "The Political Environment on Social Media." *Pew Research Center*, 25 Oct. 2016, www.pewinternet.org/2016/10/25/the-political-environment-on-social-media/. Accessed 3 July 2017.

Facebook. "Company Info." 2016, newsroom.fb.com/company-info/. Accessed 3 July 2017.

Fishman, Jenn, Andrea Lunsford, Beth McGregor, and Mark Otuteye. "Performing Writing, Performing Literacy." *College Composition and Communication*, vol. 57, no. 2, 2005, pp. 224–52.

Glaser, Barney G., and Anselm L. Strauss. *The Discovery of Grounded Theory: Strategies for Qualitative Research*. Aldine Transaction, 1967.

Granovetter, Mark. "The Strength of Weak Ties." *American Journal of Sociology*, vol. 78, no. 6, 1973, pp. 1360–80.

Lindner, Matt. "Block. Mute. Unfriend. Tensions rise on Facebook after Election Results." *Chicago Tribune*, 9 Nov. 2016, www.chicagotribune.com/lifestyles/ct-facebook-election-reaction-family-1109-201611 09-story.html. Accessed 3 July 2017.

Pariser, Eli. *The Filter Bubble: How the New Personalized Web is Changing What We Read and How We Think*. Penguin, 2011.

Reddit. "Reddit in 2015." 31 Dec. 2015, redditblog.com/2015/12/31/reddit-in-2015/. Accessed 3 July 2017.

Ridolfo, Jim, and Dànielle Nicole DeVoss. "Composing for Recomposition: Rhetorical Velocity and Delivery." *Kairos: A Journal of Rhetoric, Technology, and Pedagogy*, vol. 13, no. 2, 2009, kairos.techno rhetoric.net/13.2/topoi/ridolfo_devoss/intro.html. Accessed 3 July 2017.

Sayce, David. "10 Billions [*sic*] Tweets . . . Number of Tweets per Day?" 2016, www.dsayce.com/social-media/10-billions-tweets/. Accessed 3 July 2017.

Schultheis, Emily. "Report: Donald Trump Aides Took Away Candidate's Twitter Access." *CBS News*, 6 Nov. 2016, www.cbsnews.com/news/report-donald-trump-aides-took-away-candidates-twitter-access/. Accessed 3 July 2017.

Twitter. "Twitter Usage." 2016, about.twitter.com/company. Accessed 3 July 2017.

Vie, Stephanie. "Digital Divide 2.0: 'Generation M' and Online Social Networking Sites in the Composition Classroom." *Computers and Composition*, vol. 25, no. 1, 2008, pp. 9–23.

——. "Engaging Others in Online Social Networking Sites: Rhetorical Practices in MySpace and Facebook." Dissertation, University of Arizona, 2007.

——. "Training Online Technical Communication Educators to Teach with Social Media: Best Practices and Professional Recommendations." *Technical Communication Quarterly*, vol. 26, no. 3, 2017, pp. 344–59.

——. "What's Going On? Challenges and Opportunities for Social Media Use in the Writing Classroom." *Journal of Faculty Development*, vol. 29, no. 5, 2015, pp. 33–44.

12

ETHOS, TRUST, AND THE RHETORIC OF DIGITAL WRITING IN SCIENTIFIC AND TECHNICAL DISCOURSE

Laura J. Gurak

To understand more fully the relationship of digital writing and rhetoric in scientific and technical discourse, we should begin by asking about the effect of the D on the W and the R. In other words, for all types of content (scientific, technical, or otherwise), how does "being digital" change what we already know about persuasive (rhetorical) written discourse? Elsewhere I have argued that speed and reach are two key concepts of digital writing and rhetoric that span different media types and different time periods but provide a critical explanatory frame from which to understand both the power and the problems of digital rhetorics (Gurak, *Cyberliteracy*). In the age of social media, with new platforms emerging almost weekly, digital rhetoric has an even more powerful and complicated effect, including but not limited to the following: the flattening of traditional information and knowledge hierarchies; the democratization of information; citizen access to specialized information; the mix of visual and textual discourse; "echo chambers" that reflect and reinforce similar viewpoints and the ability of anyone with a mobile device and a Twitter feed to create what appear to be equivalent truths.

While these features span all kinds of discourse, one of the most interesting and important contexts for these shifts in power and authority, *vis-à-vis* digital writing and rhetoric, are the discourses of science and technology. Scientific and technical information, once accessible only to trained specialists, is now available to everyone. Yet, lacking the proper training, everyday readers and writers often misinterpret ideas and information that take years of training and experience to comprehend, rendering complex data and conclusions into ideas that reinforce existing biases and/or are not interpreted correctly.

Of utmost importance to this discussion is the question of how the rhetorical appeal of *ethos* functions in digital settings and how credibility is created, established, and reified in increasingly anonymous, abstract, short-burst-of-idea spaces. Earlier work (e.g. Gurak, *Persuasion and Privacy*; Warnick; Zappen) has explored ethos in online settings and provides a basis for a more nuanced analysis, which in this chapter will focus on the relationship between ethos and trust in the rhetoric of digital writing in scientific and technical discourse.

Rhetorical theory, enhanced with discussions of trust from sociology (e.g., Luhmann; Sztompka; Uslaner), help us understand the relationship between trust and ethos and subsequently, the complex nature of scientific and technical discourse in digital environments. The first part of this chapter discusses ethos, trust, and digital rhetoric more generally. The second part of this chapter presents examples of scientific and technical discourse in digital settings, noting ways in which trust is established and maintained, often despite the lack of traditional peer review or expert input. These examples are illustrative in and of themselves, and they also offer us an opportunity to enhance our understanding of ethos in a digital age and, especially, in relation to digital writing and rhetoric.

Ethos, Trust, and the "Post-Truth" Information Ecology in Relation to Digital Rhetoric

In November 2016, the Oxford dictionaries declared the word of the year to be "post-truth." Based on fake news sites and the rampant, unbounded use of social media during that year's presidential election, this term underscores the dark side of information democratization and flattened discourse hierarchies in digital rhetoric and writing. The concept (which for this chapter will be called confirmation bias) provides an explanation for an important point in this regard: people tend to trust what they already believe in, and they are more likely to have high trust when information comes from a trusted source within their social network of like-minded individuals and institutions. Defined as a "preference for existing beliefs, where people seek out and interpret information that is consistent with their expectations" (Hernandez and Preston), confirmation bias is long-standing and well-documented in psychological, sociological, and other experimental as well as critical literature (see e.g. Lord et al.).

Confirmation bias leads to the existence of "echo chambers," where the same information is reinforced over and over again via social media, television, and radio. On social media in particular, people add their own opinions and thoughts, typically presenting their own opinions as factual, the latter being a concept called "my-side bias" (Felton et al.). Echo chambers are visible and extremely powerful in digital writing settings, because of speed and reach, as mentioned previously. Speed in particular plays a vital role, one that must be considered in relation to all digital discourses but especially scientific and technical content. The rapid-fire speed with which people read and process complex information in the form of a meme, a tweet, or a short email is a central contributing factor in confirmation bias and the trust people place in self-reinforcing information. Speed leads people to read quickly and to select only those ideas that reaffirm their existing beliefs.

More general proof of this assertion comes from many studies of how people read online (quickly, in short bursts, skimming the headlines, and so forth). Specifically, in the Hernandez study cited above, when people were presented with information that ran counter to their beliefs and was written purposely to make their reading process more complicated (using a lexicon not familiar for these readers, which the authors called "disfluency"), confirmation bias was reduced because the more difficult lexicon "[promoted] careful, analytic reasoning" (178). The researchers note that "[j]ust like speed bumps cause one to drive more slowly and carefully, the experience of difficulty associated with disfluency prompts a slower, more careful mindset when making judgments, even when one comes to the issue with existing biases" (181).

Yet for most digital writing spaces, with their tightly ascribed and self-reinforcing information boundaries, readers never encounter these speed bumps, because these readers are processing the information in a familiar lexicon and then pressing "share" or "send" as quickly as possible. In the rapid-fire environment of digital rhetoric and writing, confirmation bias is thus very real, in large part due to the speed with which people read. Speed also functions in a different way: once an item has been read, all it takes is a few keystrokes to rapidly disseminate the information to thousands (if not more) people. This rapid speed of delivery, combined with wide reach, make every single piece of digital rhetoric and writing a potential broadside to the world. In addition, the number of "likes" or "shares" (what Wuebben calls "popularity metrics") a tweet or post has may, for many, correlate with a sense of what is real and true. People trust what they already know and what they want to believe in, and trust is thus a key dynamic in the power and the problematics of digital rhetoric and writing.

In rhetorical theory, trust can be viewed as connected to the appeal of *ethos*, which focuses on the character and credibility of the speaker and message. Although it is widely understood that all three appeals (ethos, logos, pathos) work together, Aristotle himself observed that of these three appeals, ethos can be the most powerful because "we believe fair-minded people to a greater extent, and more quickly . . . on all subjects in general . . . and completely so in cases where there is no exact knowledge, but room for doubt" (1.2.4, Kennedy translation).

Yet, between the first and second Kennedy translations of Aristotle's rhetoric, an important change about the understanding of ethos should be noted. In the first edition, Kennedy states that "ethos means the character of the person, not the rhetorical presentation of that character" (8), but in his second edition, Kennedy indicates that Aristotle's ethos is to be understood as "the projection of the character of the speaker as trustworthy" (15). But which is it: the character and credibility of the speaker, authentically, or the character and credibility as portrayed? Since, in digital settings, one may never know the true nature of authorship, or what is authentic, this question is central. Ethos on digital settings can be difficult to impossible to attribute. Yet we know that character and credibility of speaker and message are related to the trust that is placed in the speaker/message.

But what, exactly, is trust? As Susan Miller notes, when it comes to rhetorical theory, our "trust in texts" from the traditional Greek rhetorical system leaves unanswered many important questions that might move to the foreground if we are able to view said questions from other perspectives. One such question that we might ask is about the relationship to traditional discussions of ethos to questions about trust. Texts and discussions from other disciplines, particularly sociology, enhance rhetorical theory in this way and help extend the discussion.

The sociologist Niklas Luhmann offers an important observation in this regard when he notes that "[t]rust, in the broadest sense of confidence in one's expectations, is a basic fact of social life. . . . a complete absence of trust would prevent [a person] from even getting up in the morning." Trust, in this regard, reduces complexity by allowing us to make decisions "as though the future were certain" (10). Yet at some point in any encounter, as Möllering has observed, the process still requires a certain suspension of belief, followed by a "leap of trust" "across the gorge of the unknowable from the land of interpretation into the land of expectation" (412). In other words, trust requires people to make a leap, trusting that the information and/or source of origin is credible and trustworthy.

In digital writing settings, this leap is similar to our understandings about the dynamics of rhetoric exigence in digital environments. As demonstrated in both the Lotus MarketPlace and Clipper chip online protests, exigencies form quickly and information travels widely with little critical thought on the part of readers and with more emphasis on personal interpretations and emotional responses than on a more critical, logical analysis of all sides of the debate (Gurak, *Persuasion*). Möllering's "leap of trust" happens with hardly any thought, in many cases, especially if the information confirms what readers already believe or want to believe and comes from trusted sources such as new outlets (real or not), friends, family, and so forth.

Scientific and Technical Discourse in Digital Settings

In relation to ethos and trust, of the many content areas addressed in digital settings, scientific and technical topics are perhaps the most interesting to consider. Until very recently in human history, scientific and technical content in its most complex forms was dealt with in a top-down manner, with a lot of gatekeeping involved. For example, scientific research would be conducted and peer reviewed by other scientists; source and primary data would not be readily available to average citizens; news outlets would carry a lay person's version of the study. Even with publications that have wider audiences, such as *Scientific American*, content is still subject to careful editorial scrutiny.

Today, anyone with any sort of Internet connection can easily access scientific and technical data sets in raw form, even though many readers will not have had the education or training to interpret this content. It is also very easy for people to access academic publications typically read only by those with appropriate training. With scientific facts in a digital age subject to interpretation, and with confirmation bias at the helm (especially for topics that evoke emotion), speed and reach allow misinformed and completely misinterpreted ideas to be spread easily and quickly, with readers then becoming reified in their beliefs. People often fail to exercise what Sperber et al. (2010) call *epistemic vigilance*, or what, in relation to digital media in particular, Gurak (*Cyberliteracy*) has called *cyberliteracy*: a critical approach to analyzing the content, its source, and other potential viewpoints and facts.

Medical information in particular is highly illustrative in this regard. In the recent past, most people placed high trust in their doctor and could not run to Google (because there was no such thing) to query every new prescription or recommended treatment. But in digital environments, readers are not just readers. They are active participants in the creation of content, adding their views and opinions via customer and patient review sites (such as Yelp), curating and editing information on wikis and blogs, and adding to an overall ethos of "user-centeredness," where "users"—people who not only read but use information, share information, create new knowledge—are the new readers. The resulting sourced information has high appeal because of both individual and community ethos.

Technical and Scientific Information Online

In a study titled "Health Online," the Pew Research Center reported in 2013 that 35 percent of Americans had gone online to diagnose themselves or others (Fox and Duggan). As with all digital discourse, there are pros and cons to this approach. As noted by Segal in 2009, the pros include additional information available to patients, including "accounts of patient experience" (352) and other support systems. But a clear downside is the "unfathomable amount of health information available" (352) as well as the lack on the part of most patients of requisite technical expertise and training to adequately sort through and interpret information, especially when trying to assess published research studies, which are now readily available via the Web. Few if any lay readers have the medical background or years of health care experience sufficient to make a diagnosis. Why, then, do people trust the character and credibility of a website or a patient forum or an online discussion versus trusting their own doctor?

Part of the explanation comes from examining the rhetorical strategies that are used in these digital domains versus, say, the bureaucratic structures and language used in today's complex, often inaccessible medical clinics and settings. Digital rhetoric and writing about medical topics in the non-hierarchical, rapid pace, open space of the Internet creates an opportunity for patients to feel involved, another key feature of the Internet, described as "interactivity" (Gurak,

Cyberliteracy). In their study of how parents and health professionals communicate about the measles, mumps, and rubella (MMR) vaccine, Brownlie and Howson use the Möllering "leap of trust" concept to analyze discourse between patients and health providers; Brownlie and Howson note that trust in these situations involves "a number of levels including the individual, interpersonal, institutional, and socio-political" (235). Online, these other levels correspond to the many news sites, patient forums, Facebook postings, Twitter feeds, and other digital writing spaces that often function in the role of community and social network.

Möllering's "leap of trust" is part of a broader process that first requires people to suspend disbelief[1] in order to make the leap. Since the Internet allows for and even encourages very tightly conscripted spaces (such as highly biased user forums that cite cherry-picked research or even research that has been discredited by the mainstream medical community), a community's beliefs are continually reified, and there may not be any opportunity for an encounter with new information and thus an opportunity to suspend their own beliefs and make a leap of trust into a new idea (despite the wealth of data, information, and new ideas available online). In digital writing settings, the confirmation bias may preclude whatever attempts are made on the part of the writer to encourage new ideas and engage readers in other perspectives.

From a different vantage point, however, one can observe increasing numbers of new attempts at using social media as a basis for patients and caregivers to share information but also encounter varying points of view, including scientific data and crowdsourced information. In her 2015 study, Bakke analyzed three different e-health sites, including one that is driven almost entirely by patients who share detailed written information about their experiences with medications and treatments. These sites offer varying degrees of editorial curation, illustrating that with some level of oversight, medical rhetoric in digital settings, under the right circumstances, may be able to help readers overcome confirmation bias by providing opportunities for people to encounter differing ideas in settings that have high trust correlations with these readers. Bakke learned that "trust operated in e-health sites in ways one might expect but also operates in newer ways that are based upon community and person experience, aligning with the broad shift to Web 2.0" (i). She concludes in part by recommending that e-health sites could benefit from recommender and reputation systems, which would allow readers to have more confidence in the information encountered (216). Such approaches would offer the potential to open up readers to information that might run counter to their belief systems but is "verified" and thus worthy of more consideration. Of course, it would always be possible for someone or a group with a particular agenda to set up a "false equivalencies" site that mimicked the verification system of the original site using both textual and visual rhetoric as well as its own algorithm; here, rhetoricians need to continually consider how we incorporate concepts such as confirmation bias and false equivalencies in our theories, our critical analyses, and our writing practices.

For digital rhetoric and writing, then, medical discourse presents examples of both the potential and the problems with scientific information in digital settings. Similar claims can be made about other forms of scientific and technical discourse. A cursory examination of the discourse around climate change, for example, reveals a powerful rhetoric of thought and analysis by people who might normally have no credibility in a scientific discussion but whose rhetorical strategies seem to suggest equal weight in a digital environment where the logical fallacy of false equivalence is easily outweighed by discourse that looks like/sounds like actual peer reviewed, credible scientific information. Because people trust ideas that are familiar to them, or that come from others within their inner circle (confirmation bias), especially online, ethos, trust, and the rhetoric of digital writing in scientific and technical discourse present an important area of study for our field.

Beyond Texts

In addition to traditional rhetorical strategies used in text, visual strategies also have powerful rhetorical effects in the digital spaces of scientific and technical discourse. Anyone with even the most modest computer savvy can create a credible-looking website that, on visual appeal alone, makes a highly effective mode of communicating technical and scientific information. As Armfiel and others have argued, the power of visual information in digital settings is unprecedented. Humans respond to visuals very differently from how they do texts, and the combination of visual information and short bursts of information may not be the best way of communicating scientific and technical content in digital settings.

Another rhetorical device, but one hardly discussed at all in regard to digital rhetoric, is the use of technical features to make a site seem one thing when it is another. Daniels describes the use of "cloaked" websites by opponents of abortion as a way to hide the site's true identity from readers. Although deception is not new, as Daniels argues, digital media provides the ability to deceive in a way that is both easier and less traceable than previous media. Similar to the look and feel of fake news sites, this feature creates new areas for research on how trust and credibility function in relation to digital scientific and technical information.

Conclusion

Uslaner has commented that

> [t]rust is the chicken soup of life. It brings all sorts of good things . . . [y]et, like chicken soup, it appears to work somewhat mysteriously. It might seem that we can only develop trust in people we know. Yet, trust's benefits come when we put our faith in strangers. (1)

His point reminds us that trust can be most beneficial when people are moved out of echo chambers and into spaces where differing viewpoints flourish. In relation to scientific and technical discourse, this process would necessarily need to include some educational content about how to read and understand the information, written for broad audiences, as well as objective fact-checking systems that would parse words and images to help readers understand and avoid confirmation bias as well as false equivalencies. As Bakke has suggested (noted earlier), recommender systems and related tools might help; efforts are being made along these lines. For example, Menczer, in his work at the Center for Complex Network and Systems Research at Indiana University, has taken on this charge, noting as the Center's motive the very real fact, rooted in being humans, that

> [w]e humans are vulnerable to manipulation by digital misinformation thanks to a complex set of social, cognitive, economic and algorithmic biases. Some of these have evolved for good reasons: Trusting signals from our social circles and rejecting information that contradicts our experience served us well when our species adapted to evade predators. But in today's shrinking online networks, a social network connection with a conspiracy theorist on the other side of the planet does not help inform my opinions.

Menczer ends his article by calling for an interdisciplinary approach to the problem: "We need all hands on deck: Computer scientists, social scientists, economists, journalists and industry partners must work together to stand firm against the spread of misinformation." Teachers and scholars of rhetoric, writing studies, composition, and technical communication, with their training in motivated, symbolic uses of language and images, will be needed to continue our understandings of ethos, trust, and the rhetoric of all forms of digital communication, but especially in the rhetoric and writing of scientific and technical discourse online.

Note

1. The actual Möllering formula involves "expectation, interpretation, and suspension," which then leads to the leap of trust. See Möllering 2001.

Works Cited

Aristotle. *On Rhetoric: A Theory of Civic Discourse*, translated by George A. Kennedy, 1st ed., Oxford UP, 1991.

———. *On Rhetoric: A Theory of Civic Discourse*, translated by George A. Kennedy, 2nd ed., Oxford UP, 2007.

Armfield, Dawn Maurie. "From Traditional to Digital: Understanding Remediation of the Postcard through the Case of PostSecret.com." Dissertation, U of Minnesota, 2013, U of Minnesota Digital Conservancy, hdl.handle.net/11299/157574.

Bakke, Abigail. "A Rhetorical Perspective on Trust in E-Health Websites." Dissertation, U of Minnesota, 2015, U of Minnesota Digital Conservancy, hdl.handle.net/11299/175438.

Brownlie, Julie, and Alexandra Howson. "'Leaps of Faith' and MMR: An Empirical Study of Trust." *Sociology*, vol. 39, no. 2, 2005, pp. 221–39.

Daniels, Jesse. "From Crisis Pregnancy Centers to TeenBreaks.com: Anti-Abortion Activism's Use of Cloaked Websites." *Cyberactivism on the Participatory Web*, edited by Martha McCaughey. Routledge, 2014, pp. 140–54.

Felton, Mark, Amanda Crowell, and Tina Liu. "Arguing to Agree Mitigating My-Side Bias through Consensus-Seeking Dialogue." *Written Communication*, vol. 32, no. 3, 2015, pp. 317–31.

Fox, Susannah, and Maeve Duggan. "Health Online 2013." *Pew Research Center: Internet and Technology*, 15 Jan. 2013, www.pewinternet.org/2013/01/15/health-online-2013-2/. Accessed 7 July 2017.

Gurak, Laura J. *Cyberliteracy: Navigating the Internet with Awareness*. Yale UP, 2001.

———. *Persuasion and Privacy in Cyberspace: The Online Protests over Lotus MarketPlace and the Clipper Chip*. Yale UP, 1997.

Hernandez, Ivan, and Jesse Lee Preston. "Disfluency Disrupts the Confirmation Bias." *Journal of Experimental Social Psychology*, vol. 49, no. 1, 2013, pp. 178–82.

Lord, Charles G., Lee Ross, and Mark R. Lepper. "Biased Assimilation and Attitude Polarization: The Effects of Prior Theories on Subsequently Considered Evidence." *Journal of Personality and Social Psychology*, vol. 37, no. 11, 1979, pp. 2098–109.

Luhmann, Niklas. *Trust and Power*. Wiley & Sons, 1982.

Menczer, Filippo. "Misinformation on Social Media: Can Technology Save Us?" *The Conversation*, 27 Nov. 2016, theconversation.com/misinformation-on-social-media-can-technology-save-us-69264. Accessed 7 July 2017.

Miller, Susan. *Trust in Texts: A Different History of Rhetoric*. Southern Illinois UP, 2007.

Möllering, Guido. "The Nature of Trust: From Georg Simmel to a Theory of Expectation, Interpretation and Suspension." *Sociology*, vol. 35, no. 2, 2001, pp. 403–20.

Segal, Judy Z. "Internet Health and the 21st-Century Patient: A Rhetorical View." *Written Communication*, vol. 26, no. 4, Oct. 2009, pp. 351–69.

Sperber, Dan, F. Clément, C. Heintz, and O. Mascaro. "Epistemic Vigilance." *Mind and Language*, vol. 25, no. 4, Sept. 2010, pp. 359–93.

Sztompka, Piotr. *Trust: A Sociological Theory*. Cambridge UP, 2000.

Uslaner, Eric M. *The Moral Foundations of Trust*. Cambridge UP, 2002.

Warnick, Barbara. *Critical Literacy in A Digital Era: Technology, Rhetoric, and the Public Interest*. 1st ed., Routledge, 2001.

Wuebben, Daniel. "Getting Likes, Going Viral, and the Intersections Between Popularity Metrics and Digital Composition." *Computers and Composition*, vol. 42, 2016, pp. 66–79.

Zappen, James P. "Digital Rhetoric: Toward an Integrated Theory." *Technical Communication Quarterly*, vol. 14, no. 3, 2005, pp. 319–25.

13

WHEN WALLS CAN TALK

Animate Cities and Digital Rhetoric

Elizabeth Losh

On July 6, 2016 *Pokémon Go*, a free location-based application for smartphones, was launched in the United States, Australia, and New Zealand. Building on a fan base nostalgic for a nineties franchise of collectible cards, animated cartoons, and Gameboy programs that originated in Japan, this augmented reality game soon drew at least fifty million players on continents across the globe and was installed on mobile devices at least a hundred million times. Using the interfaces of their personal mobile phone screens, participants could gather resources from Pokéstop landmarks with a horizontal swipe and attempt to catch various exotic creatures (Pokémon) by hurling virtual Poké Balls at their targets with a vertical swipe. Players could also battle other "trainers" in specialized "gyms." All of this interaction with a virtual world—scanning the landscape, gathering rare items, managing inventories, and earning status—could take place while walking through fantastical computer-generated versions of everyday streets and neighborhoods. Players could also acquire new Pokémon by evolving digital organisms from their existing stockpiles of specimens or by hatching eggs. Additionally, as a fitness tracker, the game could reward pedestrian exercise, since walking and running in real life could accelerate progress in the virtual environment. Monetary investment was incentivized as well, because purchasing assets with real currency in the online store could facilitate leveling up activities in the game.

As an aggregation of billions of individual interactions connecting practices, platforms, space, and time, *Pokémon Go* at the height of its popularity promulgated a model of the animate city in the digital age that was messier, less idealized, and more representative of user experience than the idealized vision of a symbiotic and homeostatic ecosystem that was often promoted by urban planners as the paradigm of a healthy organic metropolis. The digital rhetoric of *Pokémon Go* was often occluded in its playable system where many of the more site-specific rules of the game might have seemed illegible or invisible to its users before consulting forums, maps, or social network sites. In this way the game produced an algorithmic overlay with its own politics of design, and players assembled their own communities of practice to interpret their divergent digital experiences of embodied mobility and situated geography.

Pokémon Go soon became a cultural phenomenon as a shared hallucination in which one's smartphone seemed to serve as a viewing apparatus that displayed animated characters otherwise invisible to the naked eye. Because the game's design suggested that a menagerie of shape shifting inhabitants occupied the built environment on another level from everyday experience, the normal processes of orientation and navigation could also become vexed by competing claims for attention. Parks, cultural heritage locations, historical sites, and public squares were sometimes jammed with hundreds of players simultaneously scanning for the presence of hidden digital animals and swarming after players who had found success at a particular location that could be mapped in Cartesian space.

As is often the case with a new form of media technology, a moral panic soon ensued. Public health experts warned about threat blindness that might increase the number of childhood accidents among youth mesmerized by the distractions on their screens. News coverage expressed dismay about players finding bodies, being duped into committing crimes, and crashing their vehicles while engrossed in play (Bogost, "The Tragedy of Pokémon Go"). Participating in the game even came to signify withdrawal from the world of political and civic life. At a campaign stop in Virginia, Democratic presidential candidate Hillary Clinton punctuated a speech advocating science and technology education with a punch-line about getting participants to "Pokémon go to the polls."

Although the total number of players had rapidly declined by the end of 2016 (Barrett), hardcore users continued to devote time to the game regularly, and norms of cosmopolitan interaction around space and place remained occasionally disrupted by the algorithms of the game. Established practices for appropriately crossing streets, listening attentively during tours of historical sites, and keeping mobile devices out of sight continued to be violated. More important, the large-scale launch and mass acceptance of *Pokémon Go* demonstrated that such games could have an intergenerational appeal that expanded typical core bases of early adopters. Its user population extended far beyond the relatively narrow demographics of those who might be attracted to non-mainstream "big urban games," such as hipsters, cool hunters, and others predisposed to seek out nostalgic and countercultural "street games." Unlike the densely inter-linked subgroups likely to participate in festivals such as *Come Out and Play* (Dixon), *Pokémon Go* players reflected a diversity and populism to which earlier street games could only aspire.

Design Politics

Some of the success of Pokémon Go could be attributed to the simplicity of its interface design, game mechanics, and the conventionality of its modes of social interaction with strangers. The design of the game was intended to be user-friendly because it deployed a familiar form of wayfinding that had become standardized in smartphone applications. The play screen replicated the color-segregated geographical components of green-spaces, waterways, arteries for auto-mobile traffic, and building outlines derived from Google Maps. When attempting to catch cartoon character Pokémon against a backdrop of familiar scenes depicted realistically by the device's camera, players were encouraged to capture and share screenshots on social media, so knowledge practices could be rapidly disseminated.

In approaching major design decisions, the game's architects appeared to have benefited from lessons learned in playtesting an earlier game produced by Niantic. Unlike *Pokémon Go*, that game, *Ingress* relied on a game story founded on complex conspiratorial narratives, including the premise that "public sculpture found in our cities is based on design seeded in the human mind." It also depended on new age vocabulary about "energy fields" and "portals" (*Ingress—It's Time to Move*). Furthermore, *Ingress* encouraged more direct interaction with strangers and presented the "line between reality and a game" as being more "blurred" (*Playing Ingress*), which might be troubling to those conditioned to more conventional forms of politeness and the suspension of disbelief.

Of course, *Pokémon Go* had many other progenitors in the history of pervasive gaming. Broadly speaking, from hopscotch to handball, urban spaces have been gamified for centuries. Early game theorist Johan Huizinga argued that games established consensual zones of exception by drawing a "magic circle" around the scene of play. However, many major contemporary theorists of digital games assert that the boundaries of play are messier and more permeable than those Huizinga described. Because game currencies, game assets, game relationships, and game rules have value in many non-game settings, the concept of an arbitrary demarcation between in-game and non-game behavior doesn't seem defensible to such critics, many of whom have been immersed in practices of participant-observation.

In emphasizing the place of *Pokémon Go* in game history, Ian Bogost advocates for the importance of the previous generation of alternate reality games that dramatized more interesting and challenging scenarios structured around "fourth-wall-breaking paranoia" ("The Tragedy of Pokémon Go"). Rather than describe urban games as "augmented reality," de Souza e Silva and Hjorth prefer the term "hybrid reality," because this kind of play experience "aims to challenge the role of copresence in everyday life—forging questions around boundaries between digital and physical spaces" (618). Even if digital behavior on a mobile device isn't easily labeled as augmented reality, alternate reality, or hybrid reality, Kazys Varnelis and Anne Friedberg insist that access to the channel of digital networks that communicate with remote others enables users "to be present in physical and networked places simultaneously." Presence entails absence, however, because users engage "often at the expense of non-digital commitments."

Additionally, according to Jason Farman, mobile media experiences such as *Pokémon Go* function as "locative media" that inscribe "an intimate relationship between the production of space and the bodies inhabiting those spaces" (4). Farman notes that this new locative media paradigm often exploits data gathered either from digital mapping, such as geographic information systems (GIS), or virtual signposts that are embedded in the environment by deploying technologies such as machine readable Quick Response (QR) codes that can be deciphered by a smartphone camera. In this way the rhetoric of communicating, locating, networking, and play is shaped by locative media.

There is also a strong kinesthetic component to the game experience. Specifically, when Pokémon are present in the immediate environment, the player's portable apparatus vibrates. If the player exits and then reenters the zone of contact, the device vibrates again. As in the case of more traditional forms of bodily ritual associated with "sensory responses, motor control, and proprioception" (Hayles 204), the posthuman features of embodied cognition seem to assert themselves. In this way the characteristics of computational sensing could be as important as those of human sight.

In "Design as Politics, Politics as Design" Christo Sims has argued that the goals of design culture can assume three different forms: "prescribing," "publicizing," and "proposing." In advocating for the value of activities associated with the category of proposing and publicizing, Sims is very critical of prescriptive approaches, which he believes often engineer solutions without adequate discussion of problems and without respecting community members as stakeholders capable of imaging their own possible futures. In urban planning, Sims is enthusiastic about speculative design and user-centered prototyping as experimental community-based arts practices. As an example he cites the "United Micro Kingdoms" project in which four fanciful scenarios for a divided UK explore the extreme consequences of radically different ideologies of state organization.

As an algorithmic system that builds on a prescriptive architecture of movement tracking, status checking, and conspicuous consumption, *Pokémon Go* doesn't really allow users to design their own alternative cities. Nonetheless, during 2016—when the company allowed users to nominate particular public places as Pokéstops (Cipriani)—it did give players an ability to participate in publicizing co-design activities that would make particular landmarks and even forgotten sites of historical memory more visible.

Reverse Engineering

As Lev Manovich defines it, "transcoding" designates the blending of "traditional ways in which human culture modeled the world and the computer's own means of representing it" (46). Broadly speaking, transcoding describes how media, culture, and designed environments are being reshaped and transformed by the procedural rules that are encoded in computer software. The computerization of culture is a process of transcoding, as "cultural categories or concepts are substituted, on the level of meaning and/or language, by new ones that derive from the computers ontology, epistemology, and pragmatics" (47). In the case of *Pokémon Go*, one could argue that the architectural aesthetics and urban planning regimes of cities—which are much more likely to host useful game assets than suburban or rural areas—are being remapped by the encoded program elements of the game, because the city is both system and lifeworld. In other words, the speed at which players drive, the frequency of choosing a particular street, and the likelihood of being close to water, public art, or historically significant monuments can be influenced by the game's functions that establish privilege and power in an urban setting. Thus densely packed cities become more attractive to players.

Furthermore, the transcoding of the algorithms of digital games onto sites of shared public space that serve as symbols of political power do not necessarily confirm trite truisms about distraction and disengagement. For example, Nishant Shah has described how participants in the Taiwanese Sunflower Student Movement found themselves "gamifying" protest. He analyzes how members of the supposedly apathetic "Strawberry Generation" took over government buildings following scripts learned in the popular game *Minecraft* by transposing the activities of exploring hallways, finding empty rooms, and barricading themselves against opponents, which were learned online, to the real world of the built environment.

Here I would distinguish between "gamifying" and "gamification," because too often the latter term has become associated with incentive systems in which participants have little opportunity to subvert the basic rules. In this way gamification represents a strategic approach adopted by corporations, educational institutions, and government agencies, which Bogost has characterized as "exploitationware." In contrast, to gamify an existing situation is to appropriate its scenes of interaction, codes of conduct, or rules of engagement, sometimes for purposes other than those intended by designers, architects, and planners. Similarly, in differentiating between strategies and tactics, Michel de Certeau once asserted that "the generalization and expansion of technocratic rationality have created, between the links of the system, a fragmentation and explosive growth of these practices which were formally regulated by stable local units" (40). In contrast, Situationist theorist and game designer Guy Debord adopted a more pessimistic view that contemporary urbanism actually "safeguards class power" as it fosters the "preservation of the atomization of workers who had been dangerously brought together by urban conditions of production" with the invention of the "pseudo-community" (paragraph 172).

Queer Animacies

By drawing upon queer theory, affect theory, and linguistics, Mel Chen has claimed that cultural anxieties about supposedly improper animacies (such as microbes, toxins, or other disquietingly vital materials) reveal dominant assumptions about race, gender, sexuality, and ability in delineating what counts as living in the context of a given interaction. Similarly, *Pokémon Go* introduces disruptive animacies into a world in which certain forms of matter, such as stone, have been designated as inert since Aristotle. By making these cartoonish interlopers desirable agents to seek out the moment their presence is registered by the phone, the game could be said to subvert certain border policing expectations about purity and danger.

At the same time, clear species hierarchies are also enforced, although serendipity and indeterminacy may also reward players with valuable specimens from supposedly inferior life forms. For example, creeping insects can metamorphose into butterflies, goldfish can transform into dragons, and small blobs can turn into more imposing blobs. Nonetheless existing prejudices about non-human agents can also be reinforced experientially throughout game play. For example, the most common Pokémon in urban areas tend to be variants of rats and pigeons, which are generally seen in quotidian terms as vermin and scavengers. Transmuted versions of domesticated animals that might be more likely to be perceived of as familial companion species, such as cats and dogs, appear rarely in the game, if at all.

Sources aggregated in the collectively authored *Pokémon Go* syllabus indicate that the game's seemingly inclusive invitation to participate often obscures its fundamentally exclusionary logics. For example, players with disabilities cannot access areas that require climbing stairs, and players of color may be wary about neighborhoods where police practice racial profiling. Thus, while flight simulators and Google Earth facilitate an aerial vision of digital geography in which "movement is frictionless, borders are non-existent, and mobility is just about limitless" (Presner), interaction with the mixed reality environment on the plane of the pedestrian participant walking toward the horizon is frequently frustrated by obstacles. While advocates for "spatial justice" argue that urban territory is "currently functioning as one the most important resources for the expression of disapproval and outrage in this political moment," they also recognize in the same manifesto that claiming areas for "play" are also constitutive for resisting oppression (The Design Studio).

Within my own community inside of the living history museum of Colonial Williamsburg there is a regrettable monument to the slave-holding Confederacy that serves as a *Pokémon Go* gym. Because players seek out this site to train and do battle, the game's procedural rhetoric potentially also lures young people to discredited myths of sacrifice and loyalty to states' rights that obscure troubling aspects of American historical memory and systemic racism. The Williamsburg monument to the Confederate dead was at one time located much more centrally in the civic space of the town on a highly visible public green, but it was moved in the 1930s to a secluded spot in a shaded dell to avoid displeasing Yankee tourists. Thanks to *Pokémon Go* the Confederate obelisk attracts a new cohort of visitors.

At the same time the game is drawing players of color to other kinds of public spaces in my largely segregated residential district, which is in a historical preservation zone of colonial-era homes owned by a nonprofit foundation. Membership in the community as a resident is rigorously vetted by a board that reviews character references, but visitors can have access, at least temporarily. Without *Pokésmon Go* the landscape of Colonial Williamsburg would probably be populated by citizens who were much more white, much older, and probably more politically reactionary than the game-playing denizens drawn by the game. Thus a cost–benefit analysis of the game's impact on the lived experience of spatial justice is complicated.

The *Pokémon Go* syllabus observes that some of the most contentious discussions about the game involve overlaps with perceived sacred spaces, particularly those that memorialize the dead. This is understandable, because the game locates public landmarks that are designated as Pokéstops for replenishing resources based on a crowd sourcing process of privileging spots that the game's designers considered to be sites with historical or cultural significance, popular upload locations for photos to Google-controlled sites for digital sharing, and portal suggestions volunteered by *Ingress* players. This heterogeneity of tagging practices means that many somber photo opportunities become commonplaces for the game and that places that commemorate mortality are liable to become sites of unexpected animation. For example, the reflecting pool at the September 11th memorial in New York City commemorating the victims of the 2001 terrorist attacks can become part of the game world as a hunting ground for Staryu, Horsea, Magikarp, or Dratini. Responding to complaints from officials at the Holocaust Museum in Washington D.C. and the Hiroshima Memorial, Niantic developers removed Pokéstops that might encourage disrespectful play in their shrines to the large-scale losses of life associated with the Second World War. Of course, one could argue that having a Hamburg stumbling stone (*Stolperstein*) intended to remember a person murdered by the Nazi regime serve as a Pokéstop is disrespectful, or one could claim that making these sites more visible for attention could potentially further positive ends of greater awareness. The challenge is understanding that points of reference in locative media that harvest data from many sources index metadata without enforcing the context of individual personalization. This decontextualizing of data may have both positive and negative effects.

Navigating through Screens

Users of ubiquitous computing technologies may be increasingly likely to inhabit so-called "filter bubbles" that channel all their activities into directed forms of social participation and civic interaction so mediated by algorithmic technologies that they are entirely lacking in risk or even surprise. In "Outrun" digital artist Garnet Hertz has parodied the distorting aspects of navigating via screen in an urban environment rich with complex stimuli by designing a vehicle that reduces the landscape to 8-bit graphics and completely obscures the windshield by filling the space with a digital display.

Despite the presence of algorithmic interference in a supposedly authentic, natural, and organic experience of space and place, it could also be argued that mobile apps such as *Pokémon Go* can facilitate types of social mixing and urban experimentation that might challenge existing norms, particularly if participants are motivated by treasure hunting behavior that takes them into unfamiliar environments in search of rare items. Unlike recommendation engines that are narrowly focused on generating personalized results, the player's level in the game appears to be the only segregating function in the experience of game play, and the game specifically rewards variety in collecting practices, since the longstanding motto of the game is "Gotta Catch Em All."

In her work on understanding the city as a platform (TEDx Talks), Beth Coleman argues that planners and constituents should be wary of having too many "efficiencies" imported into the city so that interactions with urban environments are entirely "smooth" with "no striations," "no surprises," no "chance operations," and no "serendipitous opportunities." In observing the stance of her fellow city dwellers as permanently "head down," she warns that foot traffic soon will need to be sorted into different "data lanes" to keep pedestrians flowing normally along sidewalks and public transportation corridors. She argues that validating the public arena not only as a civic space but also as a poetic agora is necessary in order to recognize the claims being made by "explosive behaviors" in the "ferocious reoccupation of public space." She worries that too often managers of so-called "smart cities" can be influenced by the tendency of powerful stakeholders to use technology to foster command and control mechanisms and subsume functions that may be more adaptive, fault-tolerant, and selectively blind and forgetful. Coleman laments that she doesn't "want to live in a city that doesn't have secrets."

The success of *Pokémon Go* relies upon the sharing of public secrets. Rare knowledge about sightings and spawning grounds for valuable creatures in the game is shared on online forums with the same enthusiasm of other specimen fanciers exploiting the resources of the modern zoopolis, such as birders, urban foresters, and terrier owners hunting rats. Popular websites already in use by other niche communities of interest, including Reddit and Google Maps, have been extensively annotated by *Pokémon Go* players, as have more specialized DIY services that may be specific to the city, community of play, or play style, given that the game supports both player vs. environment and player vs. player interactions. Around sites such as Central Park or Battery Park in New York City, it was possible throughout the Fall of 2016 to observe a specific variety of *Pokémon Go* tourism in which newcomers gravitated to resource-rich urban territories as travel destinations.

In considering the trope of digital navigation through game play, Bogost argues that "the *flâneur*'s role is fundamentally a configurative one," because his passage "through the city constantly opens up new paths, new glances at passersby, new storefronts and sidewalks, just as it closes down others." In this way "*flânerie* is fundamentally a passage through a space," and

> it bears much similarity to the configurative structure of procedural texts constructed of individual unit operations, some of which he configures as he traverses the city, some of which configure themselves for him based on the emergent effect of actions taken by all the other individuals in the vicinity. (*Unit Operations* 75)

The contemporary "phoneur"—as opposed to the pre-digital flâneur that Bogost and Walter Benjamin described sauntering through the streets of Baudelaire's Paris—may operate somewhat differently. Robert Luke has argued that this kind of smartphone user is navigating the city bearing the equivalent of a "remote-controlled radio collar" that follows and leads a subscriber of mobile services. Luke warns that the main "marker of social distinction" is now measured by the quantity and quality of the mobile phone service that a person consumes. "Where once social difference was measured by the possession of a cellphone, the ubiquity of these devices now means that there is no distinction in having one."

However, access to a generous mobile service plan is not the only constraint when it comes to collecting desirable creatures in *Pokémon Go*, because game play is frequently interrupted by challenges to connectivity that are dictated by the complexity and messiness of the infrastructures of wireless telephony. As Adrian Mackenzie observes in his book *Wirelessness*, as the infrastructural features of material connectivity recede "an enveloping conjunction of relations coalescing around problems of spacing, departure, arrival, proximity, and being-with-others" takes precedence. However, one could argue that the attitude of the phoneur predates the smartphone, because "[a]utomobiles are, in a sense, transitional mobile devices, accustoming individuals to browsing while in motion and to the experience of mobility with access" (Tuters and Varnelis 21). Ironically *Pokémon Go* has designed a number of safeguards to prevent playing the game while behind the wheel that also inhibit passenger success in the game, although many players have devised workarounds that counter the game's privileging of travel by foot in the game space.

Despite the fact that *Pokémon Go* clearly rewards the density of urban environments, Graham and Marvin challenge the "tyranny of spatial scale" that reinforces "the assumption that the urban scale must, *necessarily*, be the dominant scale of action and organisation." They blame "urban disciplines trying to bolster their own legitimacy in profoundly uncertain times" contrary to the claims of "real democratization." "Spatial scales and geographical levels ('corporeal', 'local', 'urban', 'regional', 'national', 'international', 'global')," according to Graham and Marvin, "are in a sense being continuously 'telescoped' within the contemporary networked metropolis as premium networked spaces and new networks of the modern networked city" (411).

The urbanism of *Pokémon Go* is also strongly Eurocentric, although players throughout the developing world may strive to complete their collections, compete with other trainers to claim status in urban space, and level up to have more agency in the game world. Playing the game in Cuba, where Internet users access the Internet from public hotspots with scratch-off cards, was impossible. Iran blocked the game based on security concerns and demanded that the app's data centers be located inside the country's borders. Despite the widespread use of proxies and virtual private networks in anti-American countries that use filtering software and network management to control access to content, *Pokémon Go* did become unavailable in some regions.

Among Indian scholars of digital culture studying the intersections of urbanism and activism in the Global South, Ravi Sundaram has been extremely critical of the "information city" that is often lauded as a measure of international development by techno-solutionists and techno-missionaries praising Western personal computing and advanced infrastructure. Sundaram observes that invisibility was "once the preserve of the urban crowd," but the tactics of civic liberalism have "shouldered the task of rendering visible the informal city" (174). According to Sundaram, modernism assumed that "transparency would come through revealing techniques of a Masterplan and architectural inventions," but now "information culture remains the overarching cultural attractor of power in the public realm" (174).

The Intelligent Grid

As Sundaram observes, the rise of the so-called "smart city" equipped with sensors, smart objects, and ubiquitous computing changes how public spaces in the built environment serve as sites for digital rhetoric. In networked urban environments the opportunities for dataveillance are increasing with the installation of surveillance cameras with facial recognition technologies, consumer use of location-aware applications for cellphones, radio-frequency identification (RFID) on portable objects, biometric authentification, chipcards replacing lock and key mechanisms, digital currency and tap payments, autonomous vehicles, and other technological conveniences and efficiencies that depend on machine sensing and machine-to-machine communication rather than human perception and verbal and nonverbal interchanges.

In her classic work on the "ballet" of large cities, Jane Jacobs identified a repertoire of possible moves in the *polis*, in which the participating parties might enjoy both relative anonymity and the security of human "eyes on the street." In contrast, today's cities are increasingly likely to be regulated by very different means of algorithmic monitoring. Certainly *Pokémon Go* provides extremely rich streams of data to the puppetmasters of Niantic. Obviously, at every moment the player's location can be pinpointed geographically. A journal records each step of game play in minute detail. If the camera is turned on, each time a player catches a Pokémon it means that the immediate environment could be documented through its lens and captured as part of a digital file, regardless of whether the player is on a public street or in a private space such as a bedroom or bathroom. Its measurement of daily physical activity could be of interest to health insurance providers or public agencies as well, particularly in the era of the quantified self movement. Moreover, signing into the game requires a Google login, which means that all of this data can be cross-referenced with information harvested from search engines, social networks, email communication, and online shopping.

Yet—as an aggregation of non-human entities asserting their agency and non-human digital participation—the animate city of *Pokémon Go* might serve as a space for exuberant expression as well as authoritarian repression. For example, in considering how the street might serve as a platform—in the technological sense—to support an operating system, Dan Hill lauds the vibrancy of the animate city's multiplicity of interactions and the diversity of its occupying agents. According to Hill, how the street "feels may soon be defined by what cannot be seen with the naked eye." He argues that "the street is immersed in a twitching, pulsing cloud of data . . . over and above the well-established electromagnetic radiation, crackles of static, radio waves conveying radio and television broadcasts in digital and analogue forms, police voice traffic."

For Hill this represents "a new kind of data, collective and individual, aggregated and discrete, open and closed, constantly logging impossibly detailed patterns of behaviour."

Because the game ultimately depends on achieving a profit model, which will probably be determined by micropayments, targeting advertising, viral marketing, or other strategies in the digital economies of attention and membership, it is important not to romanticize what *Pokémon Go* means to players independent of the demands of the market. As part of a specific consumer franchise Bogost has argued that the game is fundamentally ambivalent as an expression of the *Zeitgeist* and as an intervening form of computational media that has now been inserted into urban life:

> We can have it both ways; we have to, even: Pokémon Go can be both a delightful new mechanism for urban and social discovery, and also a ghastly reminder that when it comes to culture, sequels rule. It's easy to look at Pokémon Go and wonder if the game's success might underwrite other, less trite or brazenly commercial examples of the genre. But that's what the creators of pervasive games have been thinking for years, and still almost all of them are advertisements. Reality is and always has been augmented, it turns out. But not with video feeds of twenty-year-old monsters in balls atop local landmarks. Rather, with swindlers shilling their wares to the everyfolk, whose ensuing dance of embrace and resistance is always as beautiful as it is ugly. (Bogost, "The Tragedy of Pokémon Go")

Although I would argue that the queer animacies, transcoding perversity, and mixed reality of the game points to certain liberatory potentials in mobile gaming, I agree that it is important to be critical of the mythos of democratization and creativity that some, such as Henry Jenkins, may have associated too prematurely with *Pokémon Go*.

Nonetheless, *Pokémon Go* may have an important metonymic relationship to the smart cities that users of ubiquitous computing are increasingly likely to inhabit. Because game play is destabilizing to existing norms of solemnity, productivity, and passive spectatorship in urban environments, engagement with the game from a critical stance can be productive, particularly if the game is examined in the larger context of rhetorical exigence and smart devices and as a form of cultural expression that can be considered alongside works of digital art or electronic literature composed for tablets or smartphones (Losh).

As Anthony Townsend points out in *Smart Cities*, "industry attempts to impose its vision of clean, computed, centrally managed order" while netizens and outsiders in the media ecology introduce a flourishing set of new practices devoted to "messy, decentralized, and democratic alternatives" (9). Although Niantic, as a software company licensing valuable intellectual property attempts to police hackers, modders, and countergamers, containment will always be impossible in the crowded and heterogeneous environment of the animate digital city. Whatever happens with the *Pokémon Go* player community, it will likely continue to be difficult to predict the outcomes of these complicated interactions between digital and traditional worlds.

Works Cited

Barrett, Brian. "Pokémon Go Has Lost Millions of Players, But It's Still Making Millions of Dollars." *WIRED* 18 Sept. 2015, www.wired.com/2016/09/pokemon-go-just-fine-without/. Accessed 11 Jan. 2017.

Bogost, Ian. "Persuasive Games: Exploitationware." 3 May 2011, www.gamasutra.com/view/feature/134735/persuasive_games_exploitationware.php. Accessed 14 Feb. 2017.

———. "The Tragedy of Pokémon Go." *The Atlantic*. 11 July 2016, www.theatlantic.com/technology/archive/2016/07/the-tragedy-of-pokemon-go/490793/. Accessed 15 Jan. 2017.

———. *Unit Operations: An Approach to Videogame Criticism*. MIT Press, 2008.

Certeau, Michel de, and Steven Rendall. *The Practice of Everyday Life*. U of California P, 1984.

Chen, Mel Y. *Animacies: Biopolitics, Racial Mattering, and Queer Affect*. Duke UP, 2012.

Cipriani, Jason. "How to Request New Pokestops and Gyms in Pokemon Go." *CNET*, 14 July 2016, www.cnet.com/how-to/how-to-request-new-pokestops-and-gyms-in-pokemon-go/. Accessed 28 May 2017.

Debord, Guy. *Society of the Spectacle*. Black & Red, 1983.

de Souza e Silva, Adriana, and Larissa Hjorth. "Playful Urban Spaces: A Historical Approach to Mobile Games." *Simulation and Gaming*, vol. 40, no. 5, 2009, pp. 602–25.

Dixon, Dan. "Big Games and Hipsters: Cool Capital in Pervasive Gaming Festivals," isea2011.sabanciuniv.edu/paper/big-games-and-hipsters-cool-capital-pervasive-gaming-festivals. Accessed 7 July 2017.

Farman, Jason. *Mobile Interface Theory: Embodied Space and Locative Media*. Routledge, 2012.

Graham, Stephen, and Simon Marvin. *Splintering Urbanism: Networked Infrastructures, Technological Mobilities and the Urban Condition*. Routledge, 2001.

Hayles, N. Katherine. *How We Became Posthuman: Virtual Bodies in Cybernetics, Literature, and Informatics*. U of Chicago P, 2010.

Hertz, G., J. W. Lee, and C. Guevara. "OutRun: Exploring Seamful Design in the Development of an Augmented Reality Art Project." *2010 IEEE International Symposium on Mixed and Augmented Reality—Arts, Media, and Humanities*, 2010, pp. 33–8.

Hill, Dan. "Essay: The Street as Platform." *cityofsound*. N.p., n.d., www.cityofsound.com/blog/2008/02/the-street-as-p.html. Accessed 14 Jan. 2017.

Huizinga, Johan. *Homo Ludens: A Study of the Play-Element in Culture*. Routledge, 1980.

Ingress. *Ingress—It's Time To Move*. N.p. Film.

———. *Playing Ingress*. N.p. Film.

Jacobs, Jane. *The Death and Life of Great American Cities*. Penguin, 1965.

Jenkins, Henry. "Transmedia Storytelling." *MIT Technology Review*, www.technologyreview.com/s/401760/transmedia-storytelling/. Accessed 15 Feb. 2017.

Losh, Elizabeth. "Sensing Exigence: A Rhetoric for Smart Objects: Computational Culture." *Computational Culture*, computationalculture.net/article/sensing-exigence-a-rhetoric-for-smart-objects. Accessed 14 Feb. 2017.

Luke, Robert. "The Phoneur: Mobile Commerce and the Digital Pedagogies of the Wireless Web." *Communities of Difference*, edited by Peter Pericles Trifonas. Palgrave Macmillan, 2005, pp. 185–204.

Manovich, Lev. *The Language of New Media*. MIT Press, 2010.

Mackenzie, Adrian. *Wirelessness: Radical Empiricism in Network Cultures*. MIT Press, 2011.

"Pokemon Go Syllabus," docs.google.com/document/d/1xYuozfkON-RVZQkr7d1qLPJrCRqN8TkzeDySM-3pzeA/edit?usp=embed_facebook. Accessed 14 Jan. 2017.

Presner, Todd. "Digital Geographies: Berlin in the Ages of New Media." *Spatial Turns*, vol. 75, 2010, pp. 447–69.

Sims, Christo. "Design as Politics, Politics as Design." *The Routledge Companion to Digital Ethnography*, edited by Larissa Hjorth et al. Routledge, 2017, pp. 439–47.

Sundaram, Ravi. *Pirate Modernity: Delhi's Media Urbanism*. Routledge, 2010.

TEDx Talks. *City as Platform: Beth Coleman at TEDxEast*, www.youtube.com/watch?v=bCQZJEvoUis. Accessed 15 June 2017.

The Design Studio for Social Intervention. "Spatial Justice," static1.squarespace.com/static/53c7166ee4b0e7db2be69480/t/540d0e6be4b0d0f54988ce42/1410141803393/SpatialJustice_ds4si.pdf. Accessed 15 June 2017.

Townsend, Anthony M. *Smart Cities: Big Data, Civic Hackers, and the Quest for a New Utopia*. Norton, 2013.

Tuters, Marc, and Kazys Varnelis. "Beyond Locative Media: Giving Shape to the Internet of Things." *Leonardo*, vol. 39, no. 4, 2006, pp. 357–63.

Varnelis, Kazys, and Anne Friedberg. "Place: The Networking of Public Space." *Networked Publics*, edited by Kazys Varnelis. MIT Press, 2008, pp. 15–42.

14

#NODAPL

Distributed Rhetorical Praxis at Standing Rock

Michael Schandorf and Athina Karatzogianni

> . . . when we put the call out to our people, it's like all the nations on Earth responded.
> *(Faith Spotted Eagle in Chariton, "Veterans Ask")*

> [W]e are all surrounded by great clouds of witnesses, and it is to our great disadvantage to ignore them and a prime example of hubris and ignorance to believe that they ultimately can be ignored.
>
> *(Ealy 40)*

In the autumn of 2016, one of the largest gatherings of indigenous people in US history coalesced in Standing Rock, North Dakota to protest the construction of an oil pipeline through a critical water basin in Native territories (Gunderson; Solnit). Despite a lack of coverage by corporate news media, by late summer millions of people were reposting and retweeting independent news and other reports from the scene of the protest. As heavily militarized police and corporate security forces confronted unarmed, peaceful, indigenous protesters with dogs, batons, pepper spray, tear gas, tasers, rubber bullets, water cannons, and LRAD sound cannons, millions of Facebook users around the world checked in at Standing Rock to express solidarity with the local activists. These social media check-ins were spread by sympathetic online observers with hopes of disrupting the local authorities' surveillance of protesters via social media. Representatives of the Sacred Stone Camp, however, quickly responded that such actions were unlikely to cause any meaningful disruption. Nevertheless, the millions of Facebook check-ins offered symbolic co-presence in solidarity, and finally drew some corporate media attention to the protests, despite being functionally ineffective.

Like other contemporary practices of digital activism, including the "Arab Spring" uprisings and anti-austerity movements and parties (e.g., Podemos, Occupy, Syriza), the digitally networked activist practices of the Standing Rock Water Protectors and their supporters are overtly and explicitly rhetorical practices, but in their fluidity and dynamism they can trouble traditional understandings and categorizations of rhetorical and textual analysis as much as they flout conventional notions of effective action in sociopolitical resistance. What is the genre of a tweet or a Facebook post? Is a network of Twitter followers a discourse community given the flimsy notion and unaccountability of a "follower?" Are the conventional concepts of materiality and multimodality, or even the conventional understanding of rhetoric as *techne*, up to the challenge of accounting for the extreme fluidity of production and consumption in digital writing practices and text? Not far removed from these questions are empirical concerns as to how big data phenomena, the "Internet of Things," refugee hackathons, and worker platform cooperatives, might affect our understanding of what language (as "symbolic action") *is*, as well as how different languages (including computer languages and other digital codes) interact and intermingle in globally distributed territories of meaning.

Scholarship on digital activism has included extensive work on surveillance and censorship (Bauman and Lyon; Fuchs et al.; Morozov); the impact of ICTs on the ideology, organization, and mobilization of new socio-political formations (McCaughey and Ayers; Van de Donk et al.); the role of digitally networked media in supporting social movements and protest groups (Castells; Dahlberg and Siapera); and the influence of non-state actors in the deliberation of issues of ethics and rights at all levels of governance that connect with issues surrounding migration, the environment, and the rights of cultural and other minorities (Gerbaudo; Karatzogianni et al.; Zuckerman).

In an attempt to propose an integrative theoretical framework encompassing social movement theory, digital media network theory, and international conflict analysis, Karatzogianni's *cyberconflict* accounts for conflict among groups, organizations, and collective actors in digital networks by tracing:

- the historical, socio-political, economic, and communication-technological context;
- the impact of ICTs on mobilizing national framing processes and political opportunity structures;
- the ethnoreligious and cultural elements produced and reproduced in digital networks;
- the control of information, surveillance, censorship, political discourse dominance, and digital effects on policy; and
- the levels of mobilization of dissent in a given country within particular ideological orders, set against
  - which socio-political code,
  - within which labor process, with
  - which type of agency and social logic (Karatzogianni and Schandorf, *Surfing*).

Despite the possibility of accounting for the social and political effects of digital media far more broadly than any one of these particular foci, however, even the *cyberconflict* framework falls short. While it can help us to partly trace and sketch the historical and theoretical development of digital activism in the last two decades (Karatzogianni), even such an integrative analysis does not explicitly address transformations that digital technologies bring to the rhetorical practices of a specific movement, organization, or protest, nor account for the evolution of digital activist rhetoric over time.

There are two primary reasons for this lack. The first is how digital activism literature developed primarily by focusing on either the medium, the movement, or the specific issue at hand while drawing from disciplinary perspectives and research methodologies including semiotics, discourse analysis, various digital ethnographies, social network analysis, and eventually big data and text mining. The focus on *in-depth* rhetorical analysis, however, has been rare in studies of digital activist rhetoric—the "digital" typically being privileged over the "rhetoric" or even the "activism." The second reason is the problem of digital writing and rhetoric and how scholars of rhetoric have similarly approached "the digital." One particular event during the Standing Rock occupation serves as an example of the limitations of focusing on movement, medium, or text, even as it would seem ripe for conventional analysis.

Mediated Apology as *Apologia*

On December 4, 2016 Wesley Clark, Jr., a writer, media presenter, activist, and US Army veteran led approximately 2,000 US military veterans to Standing Rock, North Dakota in support of the predominantly Native American "water protectors" led by the local Lakota Sioux. Beginning in the spring of 2016, protests against the construction of the Dakota Access Pipeline had drawn thousands of indigenous protesters and allies from across the Americas and beyond, including many from tribes that have historically been enemies. The protest was prompted by the flouting of tribal sovereignty by the petroleum industry in collusion with federal and state authorities, and the fact that the pipeline was to be placed six feet below the Missouri River, a critical water source for the region that continues past the Standing Rock Reservation for 1,000 miles through four states before merging with the Mississippi River in St. Louis, Missouri. Wesley Clark was moved to support the Standing Rock protesters as an environmental activist, but also because Native Americans have historically served in the US military in very high numbers, and because the flouting of tribal sovereignty and the clear violations of the protesters' civil rights by the heavily militarized police and private security forces blatantly replayed the US government's history of atrocities against Native Americans while echoing some of the most infamous moments of the US Civil Rights movement.

The veterans' arrival in Standing Rock was marked by a reconciliation ceremony in which Clark delivered an apology for the US military's historical mistreatment of Native Americans to the Lakota's Chief, tribal activist Leonard Crow Dog. The Chief sat in a wheelchair in front of the stage with tribal elders to his right and younger Lakota to his left and on the stage above and behind. An audience of several hundred that included both Water Protectors and veterans surrounded a wide, open space before the Chief; those in the first rows sat or knelt. The last of the day's several speakers, Faith Spotted Eagle, concluded by declaring a "safe space" for open dialogue, which cued the approach of Wesley Clark, wearing a nineteenth century uniform of the US 7th Cavalry, the Army unit with which Clark had served—a unit that shares with the Lakota Sioux a bloody history. Clark had been standing just outside the open space, directly across from the Chief, with a diverse group of veterans behind him. Faith Spotted Eagle handed Clark the microphone as he came forward and cued the approach of the dozen veterans to fall in behind him in rough formation. The audience applauded as they stepped into the open space, and Clark, turning to Chief Crow Dog, began his apology:

> We came here to be the conscience of the nation. And within that conscience we must first confess our sins to you because many of us, me particularly, are from the units that have hurt you over the many years. We came, we fought you, we took your land. We signed treaties that we broke. We stole minerals from your sacred hills. We blasted the faces of our presidents onto your sacred mountain. Then we took still more land, and then we took your children. And then we tried to take *your* language and we tried to eliminate *your* language that God gave *you*, and that the Creator gave *you*. We didn't respect you. We polluted your Earth. We've hurt you in so many ways. But we've come to say that we are sorry. We are at your service, and we beg for your forgiveness.

His voice cracking with emotion at the last word, Clark and the dozen vets knelt before Chief Crow Dog with heads bowed. The Chief placed his hand on the back of Clark's bowed head, and audience members ululated. After 30 seconds of silence, apart from the clicking of dozens of cameras, Clark was signalled to look up with a touch on the arm. Tribal Elder Ivan Looking Horse asked the audience to rise and began to sing to the accompaniment of a handheld drum with some in the audience joining in. The microphone was then passed to Chief Crow Dog. Clark, facing the Chief, remained kneeling with the rest of the veterans whose heads remained bowed. After a moment, the Chief responded:

> The ways of life. Today, the Seventh Cavalry. In the beginning of the world, at the beginning of the east star, let me say a few words. I will accept thee in forgiveness. World peace. World peace. We will take a step. We are Lakota Sovereign Nation. We were the nation, and we're still a nation. We have a language to speak. We have preserved the caretaker position. We do not own the land. The land owns us. Our land, we kept. We didn't do what they did [. . .]. But we'll take this step [. . .]. The United States [has its] supreme law. But we have a supreme law, too, and we're going to take it this way: to the United Nations—to the United Nations. One of these countries will have to tell the truth: that we are human beings. We are going to take it to the Foreign Relations Committee—that we must be honored. 1868 Treaty. 1851 Treaty. 1889 Treaty. June 24, 1924: that we are come to be citizens of the United States. That's where it happened. That's where they thieved. That's why they have to lie. They make us live the lie, [make us] accept something that was not our dream, our vision. [. . .] We are a nation. We are a nation. We are going to take some steps, legally. All you tax payers, [. . .] as long as you can honor the Lakota Nation, among all tribal nations, 564 tribes, honour them. If you don't honor them, we ain't gonna pay no taxes anymore!

Until the eruption of applause at the rousing end of Chief Crow Dog's speech, and apart from a positive response to his call for world peace, the audience had remained solemnly quiet, excepting the incessant clicking of cameras. Finishing, the Chief took the kneeling Clark's hand.

While this ceremony was explicitly a welcoming of the veterans and a reconciliation of US soldiers with the Lakota Nation, it was also a media event: an apology from US soldiers serving as *apologia* for the ongoing dissent. The crowd included several journalists, and many of the audience recorded the event with mobile devices. As we can assume was planned or expected, several versions of this event made their way online in the days following. Five prominent video versions of the ceremony posted to YouTube and Facebook received more than 22 million combined views in the two weeks following, in spite of what had been characterized by activists as a mainstream media blackout (abetted by the active obstruction of journalists by local authorities, which included arrests, confiscation of equipment, no-fly zones banning the use of civilian drones, and suspicion of active interference with local telecommunications; see Chariton, "BRAVE"; Eidelman; Lacambra).

Digital Activist Rhetoric and the Limitations of Movement or Mode, Medium or Message

A conventional rhetorical analysis of Clark's apology might contextualize the situation in terms of the genre of *apologia* and the historical relations among the Lakota Sioux and the US government and military, shaped by Native American tropes. Such an account would focus on the speeches themselves and the ceremony's intended rhetorical function. An analysis focusing on the technologies of camera and screen, including semiotic, cultural, or visual rhetorical analysis, would focus on particular media texts shaped by, e.g., point of view. One of the most popular versions of the event, for example, was posted by Salon and received 3.2 million views on Facebook in the two weeks following ("We Beg"). This video comprises footage shot from the stage, behind and above Chief Crow Dog, looking down upon Clark, the veterans, and the surrounding audience. From this angle the viewer does not get an especially good view of the proceedings, but is positioned as an authentic witness through the minimally composed view of a mobile phone camera accompanied by an amplified voice reverberating in a public space. While most viewers would have seen this video as "content" alongside professional news tagged, posted, and embedded on Facebook, the production value re-presents the authenticity of the witness and avoids the objective and external positioning of the news report.

This particular video evokes the atmosphere of a town hall and positions the viewer as receiver of the apology, and thus in empathic identification with the Native American Other. The focus is on Clark as protagonist. Protagonist/apologist and receiver/forgiver represent the White and the Other, respectively, who face each other theatrically (supplicant on bended knee) while witnessed by a larger audience. With this positioning, the tone and text of Clark's speech (e.g., short, direct phrasing: "We came, we stole, we took your land") can be read as a mimetic representation of the stereotypical speech or trope of the "noble savage." This lexical register, mobilised within the rhetorical genre of *apologia*, serves to generate and perform identification with the Other, and thus subsequently acceptance and reconciliation—effecting the affective rhetorical intentions of the event itself as both ceremony and spectacle.

But such a conventional rhetorical, cultural, or semiotic analysis faces several confounding factors. The focus on a specific text can elide implications of mediated symbolic action embedded necessarily in a broader political and cultural economy, including the corporate profit-making served by the gestural sharing of activist videos edited and (re-)branded by media outlets such as Salon or AJ+ (Al Jazeera's digital media unit; e.g., "We Came"). Similarly, the Standing Rock protests were initiated, mobilized, and largely led and managed by indigenous women, particularly young indigenous women—not by male chiefs, warriors, and soldiers (Lattimer). Given this broader space of action, is this specific event, let alone this particular, highly edited version of the event, capable of—does it carry the authority, the *ethos*, to—document the act or present its wider rhetorical aims? The transcriptions above were made by comparing several different versions varying in length from 1:13 to 8:03 (the *Salon* version is 1:51). Given that this particular mediated apologia has been recorded, posted, and reposted in several different versions, taken from different angles and/or variously edited, with varying qualities of sound and graphic enhancements, which of these "texts" is authoritative? The claim that any one of these constitutes "the text," in fact, misses the point of the ceremony as a mediated and distributed rhetorical spectacle.

The problem is not simply a matter of intertextuality because it is not a matter of "texts": an event, no less than a movement, is neither a text nor a collection of texts, despite the requirements of analysis. The Standing Rock action was not an advertising or publicity campaign, though particular events—orchestrated, dynamic, or spontaneous—can serve to coalesce active motivations and intentions. But such a coalescence is not merely a collection of "texts" any more than it is merely a collection of "individuals." The rhetoric of activism cannot be understood merely in terms of texts produced and consumed.

Accounting for Distributed Rhetorical Praxis

Contemporary forms of activist rhetoric reflect contemporary quotidian discursive practices and have significant implications for our understanding of immediacy or presence, transmedia story-telling, and the political economy of the "immaterial" and affective labor of social media sharing—and thus the production and consumption of digital rhetoric and writing. The advantage that activist practices present is, in fact, their explicitly rhetorical character. Where the minimal effort and fluttering affect of the "like" or retweet can dilute or veil the rhetorical and ideological implications of the mediated gesture, the explicitly rhetorical motivations of symbolic action coalesce in the promulgation of activist discourse. However, the adherence to disciplinary *topoi* of digital activism, Internet and digital media studies, or rhetorical studies alone is inadequate to understanding these practices, which encompass them all.

In response to the complexity, dynamicism, and variety of contemporary activist rhetorical practices, a superficial share/retweet fetishism has evolved that analytically reduces activist rhetoric to, say, Facebook posts (specific technology/platform) or hashtags (specific rhetorical form/ genre), that is of little independent value beyond the merely descriptive. The capture and analysis of "data" in the form of text strips the affective force from rhetorical practices, which is precisely from where the "action" of activism emanates: "Practices of audiencehood—quoting, favoriting, commenting, responding, sharing, and viewing—all leave traces, and therefore have effects on common culture" (Burgess and Green 57)—these actions perform *effects that affect*. There is more to digital activism than data, just as there is more to symbolic action than text. Nevertheless, digital media studies continues to be enthralled by the data available to be analyzed as text. So much of this data is being generated so quickly that richness of quantity can masquerade as richness of quality, and problems of validity (and, hence, *ethos*) can be treated as problems, for example, of access to the appropriate APIs or appropriately tweaking machine-learning algorithms. Such assumptions elide the tenuousness of the equation of "text" (as word, as mutable contextually fluid signifier) with "datum" (as precise point of determinate relational value) (Schandorf, *Gesture Theory*).

Digital media studies' reliance on a reductive equation of language as text with data as information derives directly from post/modernist literary studies' emphasis on the text as object (Mowitt). Nearly all who have investigated the relationships among technology and rhetoric have been limited by basic assumptions about the production and consumption of discrete texts as found in "hypertext." Originally formulated by Ted Nelson as "nonsequential writing," hypertext was posited explicitly as a form of production that more closely aligned with the mind's natural thought processes jumping haphazardly along a chain of allusions and metaphors. The real challenge of hypertext was, thus, a challenge to the authority of the unified text— which is precisely what aligned hypertext theory with postmodern literary and critical theory (Landow), where, following originary moves by Barthes, etc., "text" in the literary sense is conflated with—or, depending on your perspective, inflated to or reduced to—"text" in the semiotic sense. Hypertext theorists understood that the ability to directly link texts fundamentally changed the notion of what constituted a single, coherent text: "a text" became a conglomeration of "chunks" or "blocks" or "lexias."

However, in the freedom of nonlinearity, a mass of discrete blocks can quickly lose all semblance of coherence (Delany): the coherence of hypertext can only be understood as spatial. While such a two-dimensional "writing space" (Bolter) offered novel aesthetic possibilities, it had little to offer the investigation and understanding of communication more broadly, and did little for understanding the mediation of natural conversation or the production of knowledge (Burbules). The metaphor of text as space (and hypertext as information space) privileges the production of a two-dimensional territory through which a reader–writer moves rather than a four-dimensional social spacetime that persons enact, despite the promotion of the (inter)active reader. The blocks or chunks of text remain static—if they did not, both the purpose and the function of the link itself would be undermined. Pointing to potential counterexamples such as wikis simply reinforces the point: there is a reason we don't like our students citing Wikipedia.

The naive claims to "text liberation" were one consequence of the original formulation of hypertext as a form of production and only secondarily as a form of consumption (Haas; Landow; Snyder). On the one hand, hypertext represented a rejection of " 'logocentric' hierarchies of language, whose modes of operation are linear and deductive," and that "admit a plurality of meanings" (Moulthrop 259). On the other, the consumption of the text, the reading, the path taken through the hypertext space remains necessarily linear, and the texts ("lexias") themselves remain necessarily authoritative units of information or meaning—an assumption consistent with the reductive inheritance of the intermingling of information theory and semiotics that gives us the equation of text and data as information as *signs* (Schandorf, *Gesture Theory*).

The consumption and the interpretation of information, therefore, sit together very uneasily—as they always have—between the objectivity of "data," constituted and structured by a set of formalized relations, and the subjectivity of the situated and contextual significance of information that we call knowledge. The text is composed, and information is extracted through interpretation. But the composition (i.e., production or articulation) and the interpretation (i.e., consumption or reproduction) of texts (whether "authoritative," "suspect," or "hyper-") has little to offer the understanding of the contemporary conversational text of social media forms ("with their fluid exchanges of textual *praxis*," as Aarseth described interaction in early text-only, temporally synchronous, digital spaces; 51). Contemporary digital interaction often has more in common with living, face-to-face conversation, and far more in the way of paralinguistic components and phatic functions, than with traditional literary notions of text production (Schandorf, "Mediated Gesture").

The early recognition that digital, conversational text was replicating or remediating forms of embodied interaction bolstered claims that a "secondary orality" was expanding literate cultures in a manner analogous to the way literacy had expanded oral cultures (Ong; Welch). This construct may have been useful to critically foreground and contrast novel forms of discursive practice among new forms of analogue electronic and broadcast media and, in the early days, of digital interaction limited to text. However, the thorough embeddedness and "multimodality" of digital communications technologies in twenty-first century life makes such a distinction misleading if not irrelevant, as exemplified by predominantly "oral/aural cultures" of the developing world that now commonly trade in cellphone network minutes and SIM cards. Nevertheless, the investigation and theorization of digital rhetoric remains bound to the linear "exchange" of text production and consumption.

For example, Greg Ulmer's "electracy" is a more robust version of Ong's "secondary orality" that emphasizes the broad rhetorical, cultural, and cognitive implications of a digitally mediated world. In doing so, however, the theorization and practices of "electracy" continue to explicitly privilege the production of "texts," though often in "multimodal" forms:

> In electracy, critique moves from "what does it mean?" to "how does it work?" By asking how something works, we can never know (nor would we desire to know) for sure what something represents, or means for certain, but we will always experience its force, intensity, and production. (Arroyo 46)

The problem can be traced back to Derrida's theoretical equation of writing with communication, which Ulmer applies as *grammatology*, "understood not only in the special sense of textualist *écriture*, but also in the sense of a compositional practice . . . Writing is privileged" (Ulmer x). This is perfectly consistent with the ways our basic concepts of reading and writing have been disciplinarily reified and fetishized as a relation of consumption to production (e.g., of "text as discourse" in Eyman). But the disciplinary emphasis on (and restriction to) the production (or "writing") of "text" has made communication as active interaction difficult to "read." Media technologies, as *techne* of production, have been bound to forms of consumption (as machines for "information processing" and "information viewing," see e.g., Trimbur), making multimedia digestible only in terms of multiple "literacies."

The emphasis on literacies, however, challenges our ability to connect the production and consumption of information as text with the *act*ual embodied inter*act*ion of the rhetorical as the effecting of affect in globally distributed media ecologies. Digital rhetoric scholarship, nevertheless, does attempt to embrace the performative character of digital rhetorical practices. Arroyo further argues that "electrate reasoning is movement, or, more specifically, the performance of meaning through the touching of external relations that map space in movement" (71). However, this performance is articulated by the determined data points and network edges of linear textual "performance," broadly conceived as textual production—the legacy of hypertext. Similarly, digital media scholars, trapped in their infinite nutshells of information, mine the data of posts, tweets, and hashtags but must generally set images to the side for lack of tools with which to adequately analyze them. Those who focus on images, ignore text and ironically tend to repudiate meaning, e.g., Manovich, from whom work in digital media and rhetoric often draws. Digital rhetoric scholars, trapped in the constraints of "literacies" similarly confine themselves to specific forms of textual production and imagine this as a liberation of rhetorical practice from the situational confines of speech and the printed page. "Unfortunately," notes Collin Brooke, "literacy ultimately makes for a questionable choice if our commitment is to multiplicity, to media in general, or to fluidity" (Brooke 130). Multimedia, hypermedia, or multimodal production of "texts" has thus been confined to more or less expressivist forms of rhetorical invention that ignore, resist, or downplay the fact that people communicate—in whatever forms and combinations—for reasons that motivate a multitude of tangible purposes and actual social goals beyond "expression."

These approaches, of course, are typically embedded in disciplinary priorities of teaching production, even if that production is understood to require attention to consumption, which is typically addressed in terms of a critical stance: the production of effective rhetoric requires the conscious and critical consumption of rhetoric, as effective "writing" requires "reading." Rhetorics of embodiment have attempted to transcend these distinctions, but have typically remained trapped in the production/consumption binary, as well as in the visual biases that undermine attempts to conceive *act*ual inter*act*ion (Levin). The distinction between production and consumption (or reproduction) is embedded within a broader set of binaries opposing, for example, expression, exhibition, and performance to representation, documentation, and archiving. And yet, all such binaries break down when the mediated character of all forms of communication becomes inescapable, whether as "reading" a "text" "(re)produced" long ago or interacting with another(s) in a temporally immediate "collaborative performance." In social media everyone is writer, everyone is reader. This "prosumerism" makes the distinction between production and consumption, and reading and writing, radically unhelpful, particularly in cases such as the Standing Rock *apologia* where authorship and authority are as multiple and complex as the multimodalities of production and consumption.

Distributed Rhetoric

Practices of digital activism demonstrate why contemporary rhetorical studies, and studies of digital rhetoric in particular, must move beyond the text and intertextuality (as much as hypertextuality), as well as beyond the individual actor, to understand distributed rhetorical processes of symbolic (inter-/co-)action. Focusing on the rhetoric of an individual, a text, or the rhetorical affordances of a medium (built upon and intertwined with uncritical assumptions about the constitution of information) misses entirely the distributed character of rhetorical praxis—which has always already been the case but is inescapable in a hypermediated world. The investigation of rhetorical processes—of what people in and as assemblages of actors and agents are doing in communication and/as interaction across places and media, and within or against the algorithmic rhythms of a political economy of corporate manipulation and state regulation—cannot be confined to the limitations of textual production and consumption if we hope to generate actionable understanding of those processes. Structural, organizational, and situational factors directly effect and affect the intertwingling of modalities of production and consumption, just as they shape individual rhetorical motives.

The rhetoric of digital activism is emblematic of the complex movements and intricate interlacings of multimedia production and multimodal hermeneutics that present the twenty-first-century Heraclitus with a digital stream of social consciousness in which passive audience can shift to active witness with the swipe of a screen. While millions of Facebook check-ins can be derided as ineffective "slacktivism," those gestures of globally mediated co-presence and solidarity in which "it's like all the nations on earth responded" reveal "clouds of witnesses." As with the thousands of veterans who were drawn to Standing Rock by Wesley Clark through social media, with the rhetorical positioning of witnesses as ceremonial participants in the mediated *apologia* of Wesley Clark's supplication we see the mobilization of social consciousness promulgated in the sharing of information otherwise unavailable.

Though it was ultimately a short-lived (but unlikely coincidental) victory, the day after the veterans arrived at Standing Rock, the US Army Corps of Engineers formally denied the pipeline's owners, Energy Transfer Partners, the required permit to drill under the Missouri River (Wong). That decision was soon reversed by a new executive administration, and as of this writing, the pipeline has been completed. However, final approval for its operation will likely be legally contested for years to come. Nevertheless, the Standing Rock protests galvanized, consolidated, and invigorated a wide-ranging global indigenous movement that continues to draw from the American Indian Movement of the 1970s, the radical environmental movements of the 1980s and 1990s, as well as more recent transnational digital activisms, such as the Zapatistas, the Indignados, and the Occupy movement, while benefiting from the support of other alternative and independent media producers and networks. The lesson for scholars of digital activism and rhetoric bound by text and medium is that rhetorical studies forever fixated on downstream swirlings will always miss the action.

Acknowledgments

The authors would like to thank Dr. James Zborowski (University of Hull) and Dr. Matthew Winston (University of Leicester) for their time and insight.

Works Cited

Aarseth, Espen. "Nonlinearity and Literary Theory." *Hyper/Text/Theory*, edited by George Landow. Johns Hopkins UP, 1994, pp. 51–86.

Arroyo, Sarah. *Participatory Composition: Video Culture, Writing, and Electracy.* Southern Illinois UP, 2013.

Bauman, Zygmunt, and David Lyon. *Liquid Surveillance: A Conversation.* Polity, 2013.

Bolter, Jay David. "Topographic Writing: Hypertext and the Electronic Writing Space." *Hypermedia and Literary Studies*, edited by Paul Delany and George Landow. MIT Press, 1991, pp. 105–18.

Brooke, Colin. *Lingua Fracta: Towards a Rhetoric of New Media*, Hampton, 2009.

Burbules, Nicholas. "Rhetorics of the Web: Hyperreading and Critical Literacy. *Page to Screen: Taking Literacy into the Electronic Era*, edited by Ilana Synder. Routledge, 1998, pp. 102–22.

Burgess, Jean, and Joshua Green. *YouTube: Online Video and Participatory Culture.* Polity, 2009.

Castells, Manuel. *Networks of Outrage and Hope: Social Movements in the Internet Age.* Polity, 2012.

Chariton, Jordan. "BRAVE Environmental Lawyer Explains Standing Rock Legal Issues." *The Yong Turks*, 16 October 2016, youtube.com/watch?v=_oAY4OvAU18. Accessed 5 July 2017.

——. "Veterans Ask Native Americans for Forgiveness at Standing Rock." *The Young Turks*, 5 December 2016, youtube.com/watch?v=YtvZXvDN03w&ab_channel=TYTPolitics. Accessed 5 July 2017.

Dahlberg, Lincoln, and Eugenia Siapera, Eds. *Radical Democracy and the Internet*, Palgrave Macmillan, 2007.

Delany, Paul. "The Rhetoric of Hypermedia: Some Rules for Authors." *Hypermedia and Literary Studies*, edited by Paul Delany and George Landow. MIT Press, 1991, pp. 81–103.

Ealy, Steven. "Past and Present in Robert Penn Warren's *Chief Joseph of the Nez Perce.*" *Modern Age*, vol. 56, no. 2, Spring 2014, pp. 33–41.

Eidelman, Vera. "FAA Helps Police Suppress Reporting From Dakota Pipeline Protests." *ACLU.org*, 16 December 2016, aclu.org/blog/free-future/faa-helps-police-suppress-reporting-dakota-pipeline-protests. Accessed 5 July 2017.

Eyman, Douglas. *Digital Rhetoric: Theory, Method, Practice.* U of Michigan P, 2015.

Fuchs, Christian, Kees Boersma, Anders Albrechtslund, and Marisol Sandoval. *Internet and Surveillance: The Challenges of Web 2.0 and Social Media*, Routledge, 2012.

Gerbaudo, Paolo. "Constructing Public Space| Rousing the Facebook Crowd: Digital Enthusiasm and Emotional Contagion in the 2011 Protests in Egypt and Spain." *International Journal of Communication*, vol. 10, 2016, pp. 254–73.

Gunderson, Dan. "At Standing Rock, Protest Camps Becomes a Movement." *Minnesota Public Radio News*, 14 September 2016, mprnews.org/story/2016/09/14/standing-rock-protest-camp-becomes-movement. Accessed 5 July 2017.

Haas, Christina. *Writing Technology: Studies on the Materiality of Literacy.* Lawrence Erlbaum, 1996.

Karatzogianni, Athina. *Firebrand Waves of Digital Activism 1994–2014: The Rise and Spread of Hacktivism and Cyberconflict.* Palgrave MacMillan, 2015.

Karatzogianni, Athina, and Michael Schandorf. "Surfing the Revolutionary Wave 2010–12: A Social Theory of Agency, Resistance, and Orders of Dissent in Contemporary Social Movements." *Making Humans: Religious, Technological and Aesthetic Perspectives*, edited by Alexander Ornella. Inter-Disciplinary Press, 2015, pp. 43–74.

Karatzogianni, Athina, O. Morgunova, N. Kambouri, O. Lafazani, N. Trimikliniotis, and I. Grigoris. "Transnational Digital Networks, Migration and Gender: Intercultural Conflict and Dialogue." *MIG@NET*, 2013, mignetproject.eu/?p=563. Accessed 5 July 2017.

Lacambra, Stephanie. "Investigating Law Enforcement's Possible Use of Surveillance Technology at Standing Rock." *Electronic Frontier Foundation* 15 December 2016. eff.org/deeplinks/2016/12/investigating-law-enforcements-use-technology-surveil-and-disrupt-nodapl-water. Accessed 5 July 2017.

Landow, George, editor. *Hyper/Text/Theory.* Johns Hopkins UP, 1994.

Lattimer, Michelle, director. *Rise.* Vice Studios Canada, 2016.

Levin, David Michael, editor. *Modernity and the Hegemony of Vision.* U of California P, 1993.

McCaughey, Martha, and Michael Ayers, editors. *Cyberactivism: Online Activism in Theory and Practice.* Routledge, 2003.

Manovich, Lev. *The Language of New Media.* MIT Press, 2001.

Morozov, Evgeny. *The Net Delusion: How not to Liberate the World.* Allen Lane, 2011.

Moulthrop, Stuart. "Hypertext and 'the Hyperreal'." *Hypertext '89 Proceedings*, Association for Computing Machinery, November 1989, pp. 259–67.

Mowitt, John. *Text: The Genealogy of an Antidisciplinary Object.* Duke UP, 1992.

Nelson, Theodor. *Computer Lib: Dream Machines* (Vol. 1974).Tempus Books of Microsoft, 1987.

Ong, Walter. *Orality and Literacy: The Technologizing of the Word.* Routledge, 2002.

Schandorf, Michael. *A Gesture Theory of Communication.* Dissertation, University of Illinois-Chicago, 2016.

——. "Mediated Gesture: Paralinguistic Communication and Phatic Text." *Convergence*, vol. 19, no. 3, 2013, pp. 319–44.

Synder, Ilana. "Beyond the Hype: Reassessing Hypertext." *Page to Screen: Taking Literacy to into the Electronic Era*, edited by Ilana Synder. Routledge, 1998, pp. 125–43.

Solnit, Rebecca. "Standing Rock Protests: This is Only the Beginning." *Guardian*, 12 September 2016, theguardian.com/us-news/2016/sep/12/north-dakota-standing-rock-protests-civil-rights. Accessed 5 July 2017.

Trimbur, John. "Composition and the Circulation of Writing." *College Composition and Communication*, vol. 52, no. 2, 2000, pp. 188–219.

Ulmer, Gregory. *Applied Grammatology: Post(e)-Pedagogoy from Jacques Derrida to Joseph Beuys*. Johns Hopkins UP, 1985.

Van de Donk, Wim, Brian D. Loader, Paul G. Nixon, and Dieter Rucht, Eds. *Cyberprotest: NewMedia, Citizens and Social Movements*. Routledge, 2004.

"We Beg for Your Forgiveness. Veterans to Native Elders in Standing Rock Ceremony." *Salon*, 5 December 2016, youtube.com/watch?v=do441aJdY3g&ab. Accessed 5 July 2017.

"We Came. We Fought You." *AJ+*. 14 December 2016, facebook.com/Upworthy/videos/858695574271951/. Accessed 5 July 2017.

Welch, Kathleen. *Electric Rhetoric: Classical Rhetoric, Oralism, and a New Literacy*. MIT Press, 1999.

Wong, Julia. "Dakota Access Pipeline: US Denies Key Permit, a Win for Standing Rock Protesters." *Guardian*, 5 December 2016, theguardian.com/us-news/2016/dec/04/dakota-access-pipeline-permit-denied-standing-rock. Accessed 5 July 2017.

Zuckerman, Ethan. "Cute Cats to the Rescue? Participatory Media and Political Expression." *Youth, New Media and Political Participation*, edited by Danielle Allen and Jennifer Light. MIT Press. dspace.mit.edu/openaccess-disseminate/1721.1/78899. Accessed 5 July 2017.

15

DIGITAL ART + ACTIVISM

A Focus on QTPOC Digital Environments as Rhetorical Gestures of Coalition and Un/belonging

Ana Milena Ribero and Adela C. Licona

Digital Art as Action-Oriented Practice *and* Location

An image: A mother and child stare through a wreath of flowers. Faces stoic, clothes ragged, hair disheveled. The words *"resistencia"* and *"esperanza"* adorn the wreath. This is not a picture of defeat but, rather, it is a drawing that imagines both resistance and hope as possibilities; possible spaces and possible (coalitional) acts. The quote that accompanies the drawing is an excerpt from a letter written by the woman pictured in the drawing, Lilian Olivia, while she and her son were being held in a family detention center in Texas. It reads, "To the people that don't like immigrants I would tell them that we're only migrating to save our lives." Cuban-American punk rock musician and zinester/graphic novelist, Cristy C. Road describes Lilian as a *"madre y luchadora"* whose family has been "thrown back and forth between safety and the system, for reasons very much to do with patriarchy and very little to do with justice." Road's statement ends with the following message: "Hope and resistance is resilience under pressure." This evocative text is part of *Visions from the Inside (VFI)*, a Tumblr collection of multimodal and bilingual alphabetic texts and visual textualities inspired by letters from migrants in detention who are experiencing the perpetual threat of deportation. *VFI* is a collaborative digital gallery co-created and co-curated by Culture Str/ke together with migrant-rights organizations Familia Trans Queer Liberation Movement, End Family Detention, Families for Freedom, and NWDC Resistance, as well as with twelve artists from across the United States. Culture Str/ke is a vibrant network of artists and activists—artivists—with a substantial online and community presence that we turn our attention to here. We focus on its efforts not only to build conditions for coalition but also to use critical and creative digital cultural productions to raise awareness and to educate across communities about shared oppressions, state violences, and the im/possibilities for linked actions.

At a time of heightened nativism and nationalism when racist, xenophobic, and trans* and homophobic discourses are increasingly commonplace in mainstream media, popular culture, political discussions, and governmental policies, online digital spaces such as *VFI* provide a venue where artivists can respond creatively and critically to socio-political hostilities while encouraging community education and activism through shared awarenesses and the corresponding possibilities for coalition. The digital rhetorics that constitute *VFI* illustrate how queer and trans* people of color (QTPOC) arts-based online environments gesture toward and are themselves designed to cultivate a networked coalition of artivists, activists, and educators to refuse de-valuations secured through manufactured distortions and instead mobilize new visions, cultural narratives, and relational community literacies for systematic and structural change. In other words, these digital artists simultaneously labor in coalition with one another and with migrants while also explicitly cultivating the digital environments in which their action-oriented textual and visual images circulate as images meant to confront dominant imaginaries. These online digital locations are also sites where visitors can arrive in recognition of shared urgencies and in search of information for collective action and social change that resists detainment and deportation.

In this chapter, we focus on QTPOC arts-based online environments to better understand the force and function of multimodal compositions—writing and illustrating—in digital landscapes especially for vulnerable populations threatened in and by the related regimes of deportation and distortion. The regime of deportation, following Nicholas de Genova (2010), can be understood as a context within which deportation and the threat of deportation are powerful forces with material consequences for migrants (and those assumed to be migrants) as well as for those who profit from the detention and deportation industrial complex. Relatedly, the regime of distortion, as defined by Adela Licona, is a context within which prevailing social imaginaries are produced and circulate as precarious rhetorics that function as imag(in)ed distortions with consequential de/valuations. As Licona writes, "in the regime of distortion, practices of looking are constrained by the given to be seen that is itself disciplined by specular logics that are predicated on false and limiting binaries"[1] ("Non/Images" n.p). Such specular logics, related to what Wendy Hesford names panoptic logics, operate to produce differential valuations such that people can be *seen* as either eligible for personhood and thereby worthy of social life or ineligible and so worthy of social death (see also Cacho). The discourses and images that are produced by and that circulate in such a regime secure and sustain precarious conditions for migrants and those imag(in)ed to be migrants. As *VFI* illustrates, QTPOC digital cultural producers are hyper aware of the differential valuations that are manufactured and the redistributed vulnerabilities they provoke. Through creative digital production, these artivists create new visual and textual narratives as rhetorical in(ter)ventions that challenge oppressive discourses, inform, inspire coalitional possibilities, and redefine the im/possibilities of community artivism and education especially in contentious socio-political contexts.

We propose that understanding these digital sites and their multimodal productions as spaces of reciprocal and relational literacies (Licona and Chávez; Martin) can enable a politics of un/belonging (Ribero) in which people can move from making rights-based claims for individual inclusion to making collective liberatory and context-based claims based on broad understandings and imaginings of justice. Ana Milena Ribero has elsewhere proposed that while much mainstream migrant-rights activism relies on making claims for migrants' belonging in the nation-state, scholars and activists must also continue to imagine the productive possibilities of un/belonging in order to avoid reproducing the always-exclusionary underpinnings of belonging. She writes, "A politics of un/belonging not only rejects belonging as a privileged position, but also recognizes and highlights that belonging is always exclusionary and can never reach egalitarian societal aims" (149). In other words, appeals for belonging are always predicated on belonging for some and unbelonging for others. Seemingly legitimizing efforts to legally belong presuppose that when someone is allowed in (to the nation, to the community, to the family, etc.), someone else must always be kept out. Such efforts also disregard the powerful distortions that continue to haunt those who (are made to) appear not to belong.

For example, migrant-rights activists working under neoliberal constraints backed President Obama's regularization program Deferred Action for Childhood Arrivals (DACA),[2] which allows at least temporary relief from deportation for undocumented young people in the US as long as they fit certain stipulations of age, education, and conduct. The exceptionalist logic of this program, however, creates a system of binary valuations in which the heteronormative aspirational subject is allowed reprieve, while the queer "bad" migrant is produced as unacceptable. While Obama created DACA to help regularize those exceptional young people who fit the law's strict criteria and are able to navigate the enrollment process, he disregarded the dehumanization of non-normative queer migrants, as illustrated when he asked security to remove trans* woman Jennicet Gutiérrez from the White House's Gay Pride celebration when she asked him to release LGBTQ migrants from detention.[3] Gutiérrez is the queer, bad migrant who is de/valued in opposition to the exceptional DACA recipients.[4] A politics of un/belonging understands appeals to belonging as messy and imperfect and looks for ways to achieve justice for migrants that must be understood as contingent and without reinforcing existing structures of valuation that rely on notions of exceptionalism. Such radical reconceptualizations of un/belonging are urgent to migrant activism aware of the differential material consequences that accrue and accumulate for particularized migrant bodies.

Engaging in relational literacies through coalitional gesturing together with an understanding of un/belonging we describe here, the QTPOC artivists and other contributors to *VFI* create meanings that encourage intersectional action against deportations and distortions. In their article on "Relational Literacies and their Coalitional Possiblities" Adela C. Licona and Karma Chávez offer "relational literacies" as "a third-space concept related to borderlands rhetorics, coalitional gestures, relational knowledges and queer migration politics that can intervene into the de-legitimation of particular bodies/bodies-of-knowledge" (96). Licona and Chávez note that relational literacies signal the desire for shared understandings and meaning-makings through participatory multimodal practice, performance, and action. They write, "Understood as practices, relational literacies imply the labor of making meaning, of shared knowledges, or of producing and developing new knowledges together" (96). They argue that because of their interdependency, relational literacies "enable the space for new kinds of understanding, interaction, and politics" (97). We draw from these considerations on relational literacies to focus next on practices and productions of shared meaning-makings and calls to action through coalition.

Countering Oppressive Regimes Through Coalitional Interventions

As a gallery, *VFI* is created and curated to counter the regime of distortion's dominant portrayal of migrants as criminals. Importantly, however, artists' renditions on the site do not create and reproduce renderings of migrants according to an oppositional logic of good and bad. A black and white carving on linoleum by black queer artist Matice Moore exemplifies the ways relational literacies work in *VFI* to convey new and complex meanings about migrants in detention. Moore's text features a nude body rising out of a detention center; its grand size refusing to move from the distortion of always-criminal to demure. Moore's migrant creature is simultaneously godlike and monstrous. This deity has black hair that is long and wild, reminiscent of Medusa's serpentine locks and also of a symbol of ethnicity. Chaotic clouds surround the creature. The small quarters and barb-wired fence of the detention center are rendered tiny in opposition to this formidable figure. Moore's creature rips away at the dominant imaginary in which migrants are effectively silenced, erased, and otherwise invisibilized; made to go away. Instead, the godlike and powerful monster is of-color, beautiful, and strong, refusing to be contained or erased. This creation also refuses the politics of respectability that would call for a taming of the wild and self-confident nature implied through the imagery. While circulating in a sociohistorical moment in which migrants are always to be feared, detained, and deported, *VFI* provides a venue for resistance, coalition, and an understanding of un/belonging.

Moore's captivating image was inspired by a letter written by Christina, a trans* woman in a migrant detention center. The excerpt from her letter reads,

> My hope is that they close that place. That the people in charge of taking care of detained immigrants treat us like human beings . . . I hope to God that he also frees the many trans girls in here because they don't deserve this.

Conveying a politics of un/belonging, Christina's letter advocates for justice, not through the assimilation of the detained migrants into the US nation-state, but through just treatment and the closure of the detention center as a site of injustice for all. Neither the image nor Christina's letter make arguments for belonging, but instead both seek justice and liberty for migrants held in detention.

Importantly, Moore's statement and Christina's letter make a coalitional gesture with the trans* community and with the fight to end mistreatment of trans* people in detention—a cause that the organization Familia Trans Queer Liberation Movement explicitly represents. *VFI* facilitates this gesture by providing a virtual space in which a black queer artist such as Moore, a trans* woman such as Christina, and a trans* advocacy organization can come together in the pursuit of liberty and justice. The three stakeholders are present in one space, fighting for a shared cause. Their asynchronous efforts for trans* migrant liberation gain synchronicity within the digital space and become a collective voice and vision that seeks to fulfill the mission of the larger project: "to bring awareness and a better sense of the realities that people are experiencing inside of for-profit detention facilities, what led them to migrate in the first place and, most importantly, highlighting the resiliency of the migrant spirit" (*Visions*).

Moore's artist statement also positions this text within a politics of un/belonging in which the goal is not to regularize detained migrants into existing structures of the nation-state, but instead to topple such structures through an appeal for love and transcendence. Moore writes, "Christina's story inspired me to imagine a God born from despair and perseverance, a God who transcends gender, who listens and frees us all." Moore's monster, itself a kind of reclamation of the monstrous distortions that circulate in mainstream media with regard to trans* individuals, presents the possibility of freedom out of oppression for the audience, the ally, *and* the oppressor. Through the digital juxtaposition of image, letter excerpt, and artist statement, *VFI* pleads for the salvation of a society that cannot be free as long as it perpetuates the cruelty of caged detention including trans* migrant detention. In this way, this digital composition functions to suggest all forms of detention are cruel and unjust.

In addition to the curated texts, *VIF* demonstrates relational literacies by pursuing and exemplifying the coalitional possibilities it seeks to inspire. Conceived of as "a collaborative project between visual artists and immigrants facing the for-profit detention monster" (*Visions*), the website animates what it calls forth; namely coalition through visual and con/textual appeals. In addition to the powerful stories and visual interpretations/representations brought together on the site, visitors are also informed about the multiple and intersecting oppressions QTPOC, in particular, face in the structuring violences of an ever-expanding militarized system of border control. They are offered insights through testimonies of violences perpetuated against QTPOC migrants and of the need for intersectional approaches for justice. Work that is co-produced is based on the experiential knowledges and living literacies of those detained, to which the artists give visual dimension. As a site of community education, relational literacies, and action, visitors are invited to "learn more" about what they might do to join in efforts to combat the injustices of privatized detention and increased measures of border securitization especially for LGBTQ migrants and their familias. The multimodal mobilizing functions across social networking sites, such as Tumblr, Twitter, Facebook, and Instagram.

This kind of coalitional intervention is further illustrated in *VFI* through a sketch by Bay Area comic book artivist and self-described "petite chapinaca" Breena Nuñez that critiques the American Dream and national identity through a juxtaposition of comic-style images, patriotic tropes, and migrant reflections. The sketch features four black and white comic book panels that tell a story in one scene. In the first panel, a hand with a paintbrush draws a red stripe of the US flag. The flag is not yet finished. The second panel shows the face and body of the artist, a young woman with curly hair and a slight slouch. White type on a black background states, "Since I was a little girl I always viewed America as a country of liberty and justice," while a curled hand reaches into the frame. In the third panel, the artist grabs the painting of the US flag and contemplates it with a smile as the hand behind her gets closer and opens up, as if grabbing at the artist. These three panels build on the patriotic trope of the US flag and the idea of the land of liberty and justice to portray an innocent sort of patriotism reminiscent of Lauren Berlant's infantile citizen—a neoliberal idealized citizen who "can have faith in the nation, 'free' from the encumbrance of ambivalent knowledge" (Berlant 51).

The fourth panel stands in contrast to the first three. Taking up more than half the image, the panel features excerpts from a letter by Ms. Rodriguez—a migrant in detention in Hudson County Correctional Facility in New Jersey. As the artist holds the image of the US flag, the hand reaches further into the frame and we can read the words "land of freedom and self-fulfillment" on its sleeve. The hand has grabbed the artist's face from her head. The woman is now faceless. The last words on the frame are excerpts from Rodriguez's letter. They read, "Basically, now I don't have a face, no identity while I'm being detained and processed by ICE."

Nuñez's argument moves beyond a critique of migrant detention and immigration policies. Nuñez along with the excerpts from Rodriguez's letter critique foundational US discourses of freedom and equal opportunity. This example is illustrative of the coalitional gestures that arise from and contribute to the meaning of each particular text in *VFI*. The image itself presents a critique of US nationalism. The ominous hand that creeps behind the artist is co-opting her ability to construct the nation. In her artist statement, however, Nuñez claims she makes an argument that is much more localized. She states, "A hand with a cuff that reads as 'ICE' stretches to grab the woman's face to represent the anti-migrant sentiments and policies that remove a person's sense of belonging to the US." Thus, Nuñez's intended focus is primarily on immigration policies and anti-immigrant sentiments. However, juxtaposing excerpts from Rodriguez's letter, the argument becomes much more grand: it challenges the idea of the US as a place of freedom and opportunity for all. When the three pieces come together—the image, the artist statement, and the migrant letter—the text ruptures the contentious sociohistorical moment in which it is circulating. While unable to avoid the discourses that frame dominant portrayals and perceptions of undocumented migrants, *VFI* illustrates that a different imagining is possible.

The images and narratives on *VFI* refute the "given to be seen" (Licona) by providing a counter-image (distinct from an oppositional image) of the detained migrant. In *VFI*, the detained migrant is not imagined as criminal, but instead as strong, powerful, and even beautiful. Visual artist Robert Trujillo's piece in *VIF* illustrates how the online gallery troubles a "given to be seen" in which migrants are always already dangerous. Trujillo depicts Mr. Gutierrez, a migrant in detention who experiences a rough encounter with detention officers. The artist draws two horizontal panels: in the first Gutierrez is being handcuffed by a white Immigration and Customs Enforcement officer and in the second he is rubbing his sore wrists after the handcuffs have been removed. The excerpt from Gutierrez's letter reads as follows:

> I have a couple of witnesses that saw when deportation officer [sic] handcuffed me in the back and they saw when I went back to the unit with several scars and bruises and scratches in [sic] my wrists from the handcuffs.

Although his stoic posture divulges a sense of sadness, what is most evident in this drawing is Gutierrez's calm. In neither panel does Gutierrez evidence erratic movement or emotional facial expression. His face and body are calm, as if he refuses to be an actor in this oppressive transaction. Instead, Gutierrez is the recipient of state violence. Trujillo's subdued color palette supports the feeling of calm that Gutierrez's face and body language exude. Yellows, beiges, and greens bleed into each other, with the exception of Gutierrez who is the only brown face in the image and wears a baby blue t-shirt that clashes with the monochromatic background. In his artist statement, Trujillo reflects on the emotional toll that detained migrants face, which he wanted to portray in the image. By highlighting Gutierrez's emotional suffering, Trujillo counters the image of migrant as terrorist and terrorizing criminal.

Each of CultureStr/ke's organizational partners listed on their site practices a similar community education.[5] The Familia Trans Queer Liberation Movement, founded "by trans and queer immigrants, undocumented and allies, youth leaders and parents" names itself as "the only national organization that addresses, organizes, educates, and advocates for the issues most important to our lesbian, gay, bisexual, transgender, and queer (LGBTQ) and Latino communities" ("About"). Familia Trans Queer Liberation Movement refuses representation of Latinx families and communities as always and only trans*phobic and homophobic. It is designed to "organize, educate, and advocate" and highlights trans-generational coalition across the US. As a manifestation of its intent to inform, the homepage for "End Family Detention" has a text crawl that announces the latest news from communities experiencing detention and the threat of deportation. As with all digital sites identified on the CultureStr/ke website, this site, too, has a bilingual English/Spanish option. It, however, adds Pinterest and Google+ as additional ways to circulate information and to mobilize calls to action. As a further demonstration of the cross-pollination between organizations and of the urgencies before them, the sites post daily updates from *VFI*. There are tips and tools for collective organizing against increased border militarization and to confront or otherwise subvert practices of securitization and detention. Finally, the site also hosts a running list of educational and human rights organizations linked on their front page as well. Northwest Detention Center, NWDC Resistance, similarly, is a grassroots organization that works to end all detentions and deportations. It is an "undocumentedlead movement" that like the undocuqueer movement rejects divisions and movement dilutions that are based on exceptionalisms in order to in build a broad-based coalition and more robust movement ("About Us"). These organizations come together through *VFI* to participate in coalitional action toward shared goals that are not organized strictly around belonging but collectively around refusals of the injustices of detention.

We read *VFI* as a digital environment whose rhetorical reach and im/possibilities come from the coalitional practices it expresses, espouses, and risks. The juxtaposition of images, migrant letters, and artist statements in *VFI* create a multivocal digital-graphic rhetoric that not only depict the struggles of migrants in detention and threatened with deportation as experiential knowledge, but also updates and creatively informs digital visitors of the ongoing injustices of migrant detention, the development of the privatized detention and deportation industry, the prison and military industrial complex's treatment of queer and trans* detainees, and the oppressive ambivalence of US immigration law. These digital rhetorics function as sites of community and activist resources and relational literacies that can inform visitors while also calling them to a more critical awareness, informed consciousness, and the im/possibility of collective action.

The Im/Possibilites of the Multimediated Digital Cultural Productions

The images and texts in the *VFI* website circulate, in what Mary Bloodsworth-Lugo and Carmen Lugo-Lugo describe as the 9/11 Project—a socio-political and ideological construct in which "protection, security and containment of threats [and, we add, imagined threats] have combined with matters of gender, race, and citizenship to become ideological tools for Americans' understanding of themselves and those around them" (9). Simultaneously constrained by and resisting the 9/11 project, *VFI* seeks to counter the effective and affective power of the regime of distortion wherein practices of looking are disciplined and "constrained by the given to be seen," which in post 9/11 configurations is often immigrant as terrorist and so terrorizing criminal. The creative productions that circulate through *VFI* function as a multimodal politics of refusal that reject the conceptual closure producing a given to be seen as always only criminalized immigrants in a regime of distortion. As Eithne Luibhéid (2002) and others have argued, it is those bodies marked as borderlands beings or those who carry the mark of crossing that are criminalized and surveilled and through those processes punished with detention and threatened with deportation (see also Cacho; Le Espiritu).

Through coalitional gestures and relational literacies *VFI* becomes "a space of convening that points toward coalitional possibility" (Chávez 8), so that contributors, artivists, visitors, migrants, and community organizers can envision a political un/belonging contextually based on working collectively, without regard for the exceptional, and toward sometimes shared goals. Following Chávez, we treat coalitional gestures as imaginings of networked political belonging and the im/possibility of coalitional actions. A coalitional gesture thusly conceived is an imagined connection, whether long lasting or brief, whether physical or ideological, and without guarantee. Through the coalitional gesture, we can look at how artivists connect to one another through digital means and mediations. Or don't. This understanding of coalitional gesture creates a more capacious view of coalition that we contend is especially appropriate for digital spaces and the artivism that circulates and might even emanate from there. By virtually convening those most affected by the injustices of border controls and their technologies of securitization, surveillance, and containment, digital spaces can be understood as spaces of un/belonging where coalitional gestures are expressed and can, in turn, inspire and encourage coalitional action. *VFI* produces coalitional gestures through asynchronous multivocality—the ability for multiple voices to speak asynchronously yet be understood as a collective (call to) action. In coalitional gesturing, *VFI* is a digital environment that forgoes making rights-based claims and arguments for inclusion and assimilation and instead creates the conditions of possibility for informed mobilizations. Such mobilizations are not always grand gestures of citizenship rights and status but may also be mundane interventions and resistances.

In her article "Iconographic Tracking: A Digital Research Method for Visual Rhetoric and Circulation Studies," Laurie Gries proposes a new materialist approach to the study of visual rhetorics to account for how their rhetorical effects change as images "intra-act with human and other non-human beings" (335), a methodological imperative she contends is particularly generative in the era of viral circulation via the Internet. Gries proposes that visuals must be analyzed not only within the context of their production, but also once they are produced and while circulating—what she describes as their "*futurity*—the strands of time beyond the initial moment of production when consequences unfold as things circulate, enter into diverse kinds of relations, and transform across form, genre, and media" (337). The emphasis on circulation highlights rhetoric's productive power to create assemblages—ever-newer associations as the image encounters multiply-situated human and non-human agents through various media and social contexts. We, too, pay careful consideration to the rhetorical consequences of circulation of digital visuals as we examine the images and texts that compose *VFI* and reflect on the distinct rhetorical qualities of QTPOC digital spaces. Expanding on Gries's methodology, we put iconographic tracking in conversation with Licona's non/image and regime of distortion, the Bloodsworth-Lugo and Lugo-Lugo 9/11 project, and Ribero's un/belonging so that our analysis emphasizes the racialized, sexualized, and gendered dimensions and distortions as well as the im/possibilities of always-contextualized circulation. In our analysis of *VFI*, we queer the study of circulation as not only the movement of the text from one hand to the next, or from one medium to the next, but as also the socio-political, historical, and spatiotemporal conditions under which it is moving and being distorted.

Conclusion

The potential of digital art to create social change has garnered much attention from those who are interested in the power of visual rhetorics in digital contexts. Chela Sandoval and Guisela Latorre notably write about the social potential of digital art, using the term "artivism" to connote the "organic relationship between art and activism" (Sandoval and Latorre 82). They parallel the rhetorical force and function of artivism to Gloria Anzaldúa's "new mestiza consciousness," a "human-technology convergence" that engenders new possibilities for coalition toward social action. We build here on Sandoval and Latorre to advance that the human-technology convergence in QTPOC digital artivism like that in *VFI* represents a distinct form of digital creating by, from, and about minoritized populations in response to threats of deportation, distortions, and other oppressions. While we recognize possibility in these digital sites and the practices they inspire, we also seek to decenter the techno-optimistic that is characterized as always or even primarily emancipatory or always collectively advantageous (Jasanoff; Turkle). We mean to call attention here to the limitations of the digital and multimodal that are not inherently libratory as well as to the fact that the digital, while widely accessible especially through mobile technology, requires new literacies of informational understandings in terms of accessing, searching, and meaning-making.

It is this cautionary reminder that calls us to approach the production and pursuits of new and change-oriented knowledges, understandings, and actions in the digital con/texts we explore here as sites of multiplicity, im/possibility, and un/belonging. Acknowledging that the digital divide continues to determine uneven access to computer and broadband technologies while also recognizing the increased access mobile technologies can offer to diverse communities, our analyses are undertaken in consideration of multiply situated subjects working in and through digital spaces, where multiple texts are posted and linked to facilitate coalitional gesture often expressed as a simultaneous multiplicity of stories and resources. We are interested in reconceived relationships that privilege neither the digital nor the social nor the human but rather understand these as reciprocally related through digital imbrication. The digital hypertext lends itself to the possibility of engagement with and from multiple audiences that despite (and/or because of) their shared and intersecting experiences and oppressions relate through these digital environments.

Circulating within the 9/11 project and the regime of distortion, *VFI* provides a distinct possibility for QTPOC youth to create cultural productions that respond to oppression and imagine new discursive formations. The coalitions gestured through *VFI* engage the idea that intersectional response to oppression is the best way to move forward in moments of neoliberal constraints that give salience to individualism. *VFI* curators saturate the gallery with a pro-migrant digital imaginary through activist voices and visions, critics of the ideologies that rationalize migrant detention. Building meaning collaboratively, the gallery enables QTPOC calls to action that push beyond arguments for belonging and instead search for possibilities for justice.

Notes

1. For a discussion on specular logics, see Silverman.
2. As we write, President-elect Donald Trump has threatened to undo all of Obama's executive orders including DACA, which will produce renewed precarity for undocumented young people who registered with the government to receive DACA benefits.
3. The ACLU reports that LGBTQ migrants detained by the Department of Homeland Security face disproportionate levels of violence and sexual abuse while in custody, and that prolonged isolation for LGBTQ migrants in "protective custody" is common practice in migrant detention centers (*In Their Own Words*).
4. As we write in this pre-inauguration moment, DACA students across the US are organizing and calling for a shift in discourse to a less specific naming of undocumented students. As they argue, "belonging" through DACA-designation has actually increased migrant student vulnerability in this Trump-inspired historic moment of still increased deportations, and threats of deportations, migrants in the US are facing.
5. While our focus is on the explicitly identified network of organizations identified on the CultureStr/ke website, we would be remiss not to make note of other sites that for us are so clearly connected and likely in some form of conversation or even reciprocal awareness with CultureStr/ke, its digito-political connections, and its mission. For example, the Familia Trans Queer Liberation Movement, which recognizes itself as the only national organization that "addresses, organizes, educates, and advocates" for issues important to Latinx communities may be similarly inspiring. For more on digital art and activist work that, like these other digital sites, articulates migrant and LGBTQ justice movements and possibilities, see also Mariposas Sin Fronteras, MSF, a Tucson-based group that advocates for LGBTQ migrants in detention and in so doing promotes an understanding of detention and deportation as extensions of the Prison Industrial Complex. While not making an explicit reference to CultureStr/ke and also while relatively less developed as a digital space, the resemblances in design, tone, and textuality are immediately recognizable. Like CultureStr/ke, MSF is also designed as a bilingual multimodal site aiming to inform and to inspire action through DIY maker culture, art, testimony, collective campaigns, and news updates. As a practiced refusal of the erasure of the LGBTQ migrant from questions of migrant justice, MSF is primarily focused on LGBTQ-migrant justice.

Works Cited

"About." Familia Trans Queer Liberation Movement, familiatqlm.org/about/. Accessed 20 Dec. 2016.

"About Us." NWDC Resistance, www.nwdcresistance.org/about-us/. Accessed 20 Dec. 2016.

ACLU. *In Their Own Words: Enduring Abuse in Arizona Immigration Detention Centers.* ACLU, 2011.

Berlant, Lauren. *The Queen of America Goes to Washington City: Essays on Sex and Citizenship.* Duke UP, 1997.

Bloodsworth-Lugo, Mary K., and Carmen R. Lugo-Lugo. *Projecting 9/11: Race, Gender, and Citizenship in Recent Hollywood Films.* Rowman & Littlefield, 2015.

Cacho, Lisa Marie. *Social Death: Racialized Rightlessness and the Criminalization of the Unprotected.* New York UP, 2012.

Chávez, Karma R. *Queer Migration Politics: Activist Rhetoric and Coalitional Possibilities.* U of Illinois P, 2013.

De Genova, Nicholas, "The Production of Culprits: From Deportability to Detainability in the Aftermath of 'Homeland Security,'" *Citizenship Studies*, vol. 11, no.5, 2007, pp. 421–48.

Gries, Laurie E. "Iconographic Tracking: A Digital Research Method for Visual Rhetoric and Circulation Studies." *Computers and Composition*, vol. 30, no. 4, 2013, pp. 332–48.

Hesford, Wendy S. *Spectacular Rhetorics: Human Rights Visions, Recognitions, Feminisms*. Duke UP, 2011.

Jasanoff, Sheila. "Technologies of Humility: Citizen Participation in Governing Science." *Minerva*, vol. 41, no. 3, 2003, pp. 223–44.

Le Espiritu, Yen. *Home Bound: Filipino American Lives Across Cultures, Communities, and Countries*. U of California, 2003.

Licona, Adela C. "Non/Images and Wild Refractions in a Regime of Distortion: Towards a Queer Visuality." *Precarious Rhetorics*, edited by Wendy Hesford, Adela C. Licona and Christa Teston. The Ohio State University Press, under contract.

Licona, Adela C., and Karma R. Chávez. "Relational Literacies and their Coalitional Possibilities." *Peitho: Journal of the Coalition of Women Scholars in the History of Rhetoric and Composition*, vol. 18, no. 1, 2015, pp. 96–107.

Luibhéid, Eithne. *Entry Denied: Controlling Sexuality at the Border*. U of Minnesota P, 2002.

Martin, Londie. "The Spatiality of Queer Youth Activism: Sexuality and the Performance of Relational Literacies through Multimodal Play." Dissertation. University of Arizona, 2013.

Ribero, Ana Milena. "Citizenship and Undocumented Youth: An Analysis of The Rhetorics Of Migrant-Rights Activism in Neoliberal Contexts." Dissertation. University of Arizona, 2016.

Sandoval, Chela, and Guisela Latorre. "Chicana/o Artivism: Judy Baca's Digital Work with Youth of Color." *Learning Race and Ethnicity: Youth and Digital Media*, edited by Anna Everett. The MIT Press, 2007, pp. 81–108.

Silverman, Kaja. *The Threshold of the Visible World*. Routledge, 1995.

Turkle, Sherry. *Along Together: Why We Expect More from Our Technology and Less from Each Other*. Basic Books, 2011.

Visions from the Inside. CultureStr/ke, visionsfromtheinside.tumblr.com/. Accessed 18 Dec. 2016.

16

REMIXTHERHETORIC

Mark Amerika

. . . an assemblage of hypertexual fictioneers, conceptual poets, Flarf enthusiasts, Twitter bot artists, feminist video game scholars and old school literary bloggers are congregating at Innisfree Poetry Café where the barista on duty, a PhD candidate in Intermedia Art who is known locally as one of the most beloved lead vocalists for a band whose name keeps changing but was last listed in the club across the street as The Pleurisy is expertly pouring a snifter of Nitro Toddy made with a new batch of Rwanda Kigeyo beans roasted by the pros over at Conscious Coffee while engaging in an off-the-cuff dialogue with the next person in line who just happens to be another PhD candidate in a different yet interrelated program focused on Information Aesthetics—

—Are you going to take his course in digital writing and rhetoric?

—Yeah, we all are. [Points to the packed community table in the far southeast corner near the front window]

—Oh, you mean that posse over there is part of the yack-yack tribe?

—Yeah, we're all in it together. We have to take it.

—Have to? You mean it's re—

—required, yeah, or not really required, but it's really the only course that makes sense for us this semester so here we are.

—And here you go [she hands him his Nitro Toddy with its surprisingly Guinness-like head which he takes from her and then walks over to the community table]

—You really like her, don't you?

—Who?

—Our Barista of Retro-Futurist Psychedelic Punk.

—She's got the ultimate theory-brain and her networked data sculptures are amazing. Did you see that piece she exhibited in Denver over the summer?

—Oh yeah, I loved it.

—What were you talking about?

—Where? Up there, when I was getting my coffee? She asked me what class we were all taking and if it was required.

—And?

—I told her it's not required, it's just that we have to have one course outside of our PhD "digital collaboratories" and since Walt's track is more about writing *in and with* new media instead of reading *about* writing and new media, we really had no choice.

—That's how I feel about it anyway.

—Seriously, who wants to write papers anymore?

—So lame. So *not* twenty-first century PhD style.

—You told her all of that?

—No. But that's what I was thinking.

—Does thinking it make it real?

—You mean is thinking enough or do I have to go out of my way to manifest it in some mode of personal expression that's more conducive to measurable outcomes like peer-reviewed article writing?

—Yes, that's what I 'm asking.

—Thinking helps me process whatever source material I happen to be embodying as part of my auto-affective praxis so that when it comes time to perform it, to remix it live in front of an audience, it just pours out of me like it's the most natural thing in the world.

—How so?

—Well, it relates to my project on blurring the lines of distinction between narrative and rhetoric, practice and theory, memory and materialization, and art and life.

—Oh, right, your twenty-first century *Gesamtkunstwerk*.

—That's old school. What I'm creating is less about the Total Work per se and much more about the fluidity of transmission and involves a lot of different inputs that then lead to different, often unexpected, some might even say auto-generative, outputs. Cougar, how did you put it in class yesterday, something about the artist becoming systemic, like a psychic automaton?

—Yes, I actually crystalized it into a tweet last night and am remixing it into this new performance I'm developing about artistic systems.

—Right, you were talking about how artists are like systems—

—The way I see it, artists, like systems, use their own outputs as readymade inputs. It's like an ongoing process of meta-making where we postproduce that which postproduces us.

—Heavy.

—Well, I basically stole it.

—How so? Who did you steal it from?

—I don't even know anymore.

—You probably nicked it off the Web.

—That's a given. But what I can't figure out is, did I steal it from myself? It's possible since I often try and build on things I have already posted on the net as my primary source material and just remix it for different intellectual or artistic contexts.

—You've turned it into a cottage industry.

—I guess you could say that, but not like Walt.

—Well, that's a given too.

—What's *not* a given is how self-consciously aware we are when we deploy these unconscious information behaviors that enable us to scrape whatever data we find ourselves attracted to while combing through cyberspace.

—Surf, sample, manipulate.

—Seems that way to me. Writing has become this process of hyperimprovisation where I jam with the network as a live remix-writing instrument to transform myself into a psychic automaton.

—Right, that's what you were saying yesterday. This idea of the psychic automaton is really intriguing. It reminds me of the Surrealist approach to spontaneous or automatic writing, what they called psychic automatism, but somehow you're turning it into this Post–Internet information behavior.

—Something like that.

—If I get what you're suggesting, you're saying a writer, the literary artist of our time whose practice is digitally based, has to go undercover and become one with the machine, to disrupt the flow or intervene in the processes predetermined by the so-called apparatus that operates in ways that are not immediately known or shaped by its operators.

—Yes, except in this case the apparatus is a psychic automaton that taps into their personal agency by unconsciously performing these information behaviors as if they were the most natural thing in the world.

—Creepy.

—Sounds a little dystopian for my tastes.

—Makes sense to me, especially since Flusser thought we were all turning into robots anyway.

—How so?

—In *Toward a Philosophy of Photography* which, let's not forget, was written in the Seventies, he basically shares with us a pre-Internet investigation into the way we humans are turning to what he terms "ritual magic" in a post-historical context.

—Post-historical?

—Yeah, as in: is there any way to pursue freedom in a world designed by the regime of algorithms? According to Flusser, images are taking over the world and are controlled by apparatuses that challenge humans to remain human. He envisions a world where writing disappears and humans become more robotic as they unconsciously channel images as a rote information behavior. Over time, things start switching the other way around and the information behaviors are preprogrammed into the psychic operating system. Before you know it, the humans have unsuspectingly *become* robots.

—Robots straining to create.

—Right, the robots are there, part of the practice of everyday life, spawning yet more robots, and we're occasionally made aware of it, but it's a gradual takeover and basically we get used to it. It becomes part of the information landscape. But what's weird is that *we* are the ones responsible for creating them, this power hungry algorithmic regime, and in some ways everything becomes so naturalized it's as if we don't see them coming. Slowly but surely, things "progress." We humans continue to program these interactive environments that slowly train other humans to do things like use their phones to take pictures and upload them to their Instagram account. Over time, the humans forget what they're doing and start acting like the robots want them to. They get better and better at performing these programmed tasks without even thinking about it and in the process start becoming robotic themselves. It's already happening in not too subtle ways. Think of how easy it is to just unconsciously perform an information behavior without really thinking about it. And what will happen when you don't have to tap on a phone or tablet, you just have to think it and transmit it? Or if someone else creates a program that they can easily embed into your psyche so that it, the program, does your thinking *for* you? It's already happening, right? All of the bots already know what my likes and dislikes are, what my stylistic tendencies are, what I'm thinking and how I will most likely express it depending on who the receiver is. It's like I'm becoming automated without noticing it creep up on me.

—I think you're right, although I thought that that's what the Surrealists were investigating with their nascent form of psychic automatism. It's as if this automation were already pre-loaded into the operating system and all we have to do is *channel* it.

—Maybe, but that's not what's happening today. What's happening today is that we humans are starting to lose our innate need to do things both intuitively and intentionally, to customize our rhetorical filters so that we can avoid becoming "like-minded" robots ourselves.

—*Like*-minded is right. I mean, who cares what you like or what you think needs to be expressed as your favorite this or that? It's just feeding the apparatus all of this metadata the better to control you.

—We program that which programs us.

—Until we're optimally programmed to execute our behaviors according to The Program's ultimate needs.

—You really do love the dystopian, don't you?

—Apparently so, and let's not forget that Flusser considered his speculations a kind of anti-philosophy and privately referred to them as science fiction.

—Well, you know what I like to say: what theory is to the language poet, science fiction is to the digital rhetorician.

—And like all great sci-fi writers, Flusser uses the writing process to prophesize the future.

—I guess that's why he refers to his brand of writing as a kind of magic.

—And yet, he seems so mixed on the use of images and how the network will change the way we communicate.

—He anticipated our loss of privacy as well as our inability to compose ourselves without being complicit in the coming reign of The Social Network.

—Facebook Über Alles!

—As far as apparatuses go, he would have had a field day with all of this stuff. Think about Flusser writing about Instagram.

—Well, that's what I was saying. He basically *was* writing about Instagram.

—If you think about it, Instagram actually gives us a good snapshot of what's happening in the Flusserian universe of technical images.

—I can't help but wonder: what does Instagram want?

—That's very clever of you.

—I'll tell you what it wants: basically, it wants to just keep adding new filter sets and features in order to retain and broaden its user base. It doesn't matter whether you're an expert photographer or an uncreative writer looking for images to help sustain you through your personal writing crisis. To Instagram, none of this makes a difference. As far as the apparatus is concerned, the technical images that people keep capturing and posting mean nothing when compared to the power of the apparatus as it greedily consumes all of our user data that can later be monetized for potentially unsavory interventions into our shared headspace.

—Meanwhile, we pretend it doesn't matter, or cleverly give voice to the self-contradictory nature of our actions as we struggle to maintain social network presence in the reputation economy.

—Robots 'R' Us.

—All your meme momentum belong to us.

—You got that right.

—I think he nails it.

—Who?

—Flusser.

—He *does* nail it, but that's because he's a great remix artist. He has no issue taking ideas wherever he finds them and transforming them into his sci-fi media studies rhetoric.

—I think of him as a kind of reality hacker. In fact, he challenges all writers to hack the apparatus by working against it, forcing it to do things it was never meant to do, to crack it open and let whatever innate creative potential still resides in the system to spill out of its inner cortex.

—Dystopian optimism?

—When did you read Flusser?

—In his Remix Culture course.

—Whose, Walt's?

—Yes, Walt. I thought you took that course.

—No, but I plan on it, if he ever teaches it again.

—I hear it's awesome.

—I took it. What I liked about it was how he challenges the class to embrace the so-called *logic of invention*.

—Really? The logic of invention? What's that mean exactly?

—Yes, it's not what I expected, not your typical remix class at all. It's about *heuretics*—

—Heuretics, where have I heard that before?

—Probably Ulmer, Greg Ulmer, the guy who invented the concept *electracy*.

—Sounds familiar.

—From what I can tell, it's what this course we're taking this semester is all about.

—What?

—Electracy.

—He's on the reading list.

—Who?

—Ulmer!

—Oh, right. Well, he was his student.

—Who? Ulmer?

—No. Walt. He was Ulmer's student back when he, Ulmer, was writing *Applied Grammatology*.

—Isn't that book about Derrida and Joseph Beuys and a new kind of performance art pedagogy?

—Yeah, I think so. The idea was to take some of the deconstructive tendencies of the day and apply them to both critical-making and pedagogical practice.

—So what's the relationship between heuretics and remix?

—Funny you should ask that because that's what I think I want to write about this semester.

—But you can't write a paper. That's one of the conditions.

—Exactly, so when I say it's what I want to write about, what I'm really saying is that it's what I want to compose, using my iPhone, iPad, laptop, the lab equipment, and the social media networks I'm experimenting with.

—What are you thinking of doing?

—I call it transmedia theory. It will be my attempt to use the new media apparatus to rethink digital forms of writing and rhetoric, to do it in such a way that it becomes less academic and more practice-based research into the creative arts. It's more experiential in nature

—*In nature* . . .

—*As if* . . .

—Well, that's just it. I'll approach it like performance art, except I'll turn it into an interactive process document. My research question will be something like, "How can I turn the artwork into a transmedia theory on digital rhetoric that *does what it says it's doing* and, in the process, becomes a model for a new kind of writing beyond text per se?"

—Thus the return to Ulmer.

—I think so. For example, check this out: I have my beat up paperback copy of *Heuretics* with me, Johns Hopkins Press 1994, right? Here it is—the opening pages continue to trigger so many ideas I can't even begin to tell you. Listen to this: "As an 'experimental' humanities, heuretics appropriates the history of the avant-garde as a liberal arts mode of research and experimentation."

—I'm with you on that.

—He thinks that traditional hermeneutics needs to be supplemented or even replaced by a much more generative form of productivity, something that comes from the history of practices associated with vanguard artists who make experimental work *out* of theory.

—Like Tel Quel.

—Yes, among others. The idea is to create *models of prototypes*, as he refers to them, models of prototypes that function critically as well as aesthetically.

—For example?

—One example for my research would be the work of the postmodern novelist Ron Sukenick who, in his book *Narralogues*, writes about narrative fiction as a form of argumentation. Instead of writing out his arguments *about* rhetoric in the style of an academic report or traditional article on how the contemporary rhetorician can tease out whatever meaning is to be found in the stylistic tendencies of specific literary authors, he actually composes a hybrid novel-critique that addresses these issues in narrative form.

—I've read it. It's a persuasive argument. I especially like the way he deploys dialogue.

—Yes, it's almost all dialogue.

—Gaddis played with dialogue too.

—Exactly, and think of the argument he was making about the self-made capitalist man in *JR*.

—No doubt there's money in them thar rhetorical hills.

—For me it just captures the flow of data better. I learn so much more from what, for lack of better, I would call conversational poetics.

—I agree. I mean I love reading heady essays that play by the old rules, not so much because I want to mimic them, but because I want to sample from and remix them through my own theoretical and stylistic filters.

—The point is to avoid succumbing to a preset formulaic style of academic writing.

—In my worldview, it's *praxis*, not theory that will save the world from disaster.

—That's exactly what Sukenick wrote in *Narralogues*.

—What do you mean?

—Oh, you have to read it. Basically, his take was that Literature, capital L, should not try to mimic our experience but should intervene in it. And the best way to do that, or so he thought, was to innovate narrative writing as a form of rhetoric that would liberate us from our preconditioned understanding of what literature and rhetoric are, to have the categories collapse into each other and reset the parameters of what it means to use language to trigger action. Like Ulmer, it's more about deploying the logic of invention as a creative process that intervenes in a discourse network than a preformatted reading analysis of what a discourse network could possibly mean.

—Exactly, and let's not forget that Walt knew Sukenick too. I think he served as a kind of professional mentor who later became a close friend.

—They both have an ear for dialogue.

—Funny you should mention dialogue again, since I hear Walt's new book plays with a defamiliarized version of polyvocal consciousness as a literary and rhetorical device that takes on some of the affects he picked up on when reading fictional works like *JR*.

—Although *JR* was about much more than dialogue. Those transitional textual interludes that served as scene breaks were like watching underground films on acid.

The sky above the Boulder flatirons was the color of television tuned to a glitch channel . . .

—*I think he's on to something.*

—Who?

—Walt. He doesn't want to talk about the study of rhetoric but to look at how it permeates all aspects of contemporary life in the form of continuous composition. It's as if he's suggesting that by inventing ones own stylistic tendencies over time, one is essentially composing their rhetorical performance as an artwork always already in the making.

—So instead of critically analyzing new forms of digital writing and rhetoric, Walt proposes that we use new media technologies to compose alternative versions of what an electronic form of writing can be while operating under the networked condition.

—As far as I'm concerned, writing is still the ultimate information behavior. We're just recontextualizing it for mobile media culture.

—Ah, but Walt would love that! He'd say that's a new way of writing, of composing a social media poetics that expresses an opinion and, in expressing it, attempts to influence whoever happens to be part of your cultural milieu.

—Instagrammatological essaying.

—Either that or assaying oneself as a curator of data in the universe of technical images.

—Now you're talking Flusser again.

—Yep.

—So what exactly *is* this theory of his about the so-called technological universe of pictures?

—Do you mean his theory on the universe of technical images?

—Is that it?

—Well, that's the title of his book: *Into the Universe of Technical Images.*

—Right, it sounds like a work of conceptual art—

—And maybe it is—

—Maybe, but if I understand what he's saying, and I'm not sure I do, he's suggesting that this universe of technical images comes from the imagination, that that's where it originates, that it comes from what he phrases "a kind of intellect." I like that: a *kind* of intellect. Not intellect per se, not emotional intelligence either. Maybe he's suggesting a kind of creative or intuitive intelligence, one that could also be applied to proprioception, but the improviser's version of it, where you don't have to know where you're going to know where you're going.

—For me, it's simple. It's like you post something you capture, let's say an image, on Instagram, because you want to initiate a process of decipherment. The idea is to share in the communal act of abstract conjuring, or to at least gesture in that direction.

—Interesting. And I guess it was Flusser who suggested that writing is now becoming a gesture that signals a search for the Other?

—*So* ahead of his time . . .

—But this gesturing toward the other, as part of a communal act of abstract conjuring, as if searching for a string of adjacent possibilities to personally express oneself in . . .

—Basically, you become self-aware of your role as a kind of digital artist-cum-rhetorician, you proactively position yourself to simulate aesthetic intention.

—Why *simulate* aesthetic intention?

—Because it's becoming more about the *gesture* of posting and revealing a stylistic tendency than about what the picture actually *means.*

—So you simulate to stimulate.

—Right, to stimulate yourself, it's somewhere between digital narcissism and networked autoeroticism.

—It's like "I capture data, therefore I am auto-posting it to the world."

—We're all exhibitionists now.

—I think it connects to the logic of invention.

—Do tell.

—OK, so let's think about how I'm trying to articulate my current praxis: there's the Instagram posting, there's the Twitter feed, there's an elaborate theoretical fiction I'm composing as a transmedia narrative that I'm producing using state of the art video and sound recording technology, and then there's my writing, just plain old writing but on a laptop in an MS Word doc. OK?

—Go on.

—And the way I operate now, the way I perform what I might otherwise refer to as my unconsciously embedded information behaviors as part of the practice of everyday life, *this is all writing to me,* and the systemic approach that we were talking about before, where all of the outputs become inputs as part of an iterative process of meta-making where we postproduce that which postproduces us, you remember?

—Yes.

—Well, that's what I call Being Digital. So even in conversation now, I'm able to improvise and create on-the-fly digitally edited remixes of everything I've been imagining or imaging while networking in my cultural milieu. Like I say, it's natural, and I want what's natural to come out in the writing instead of making it feel forced as if I have to conform to some kind of imposed reality that wants me to adhere to a more uniform logic that works against my instincts to be more proactively *heuretic* in my attempts—there's that word again—to improvise my compositional energy, which in this case is through fiction, albeit a fiction that wears its theoretical nuance on its sleeve.

—The thing about fiction is that sometimes it can seem so random, especially if it comes across as too improvised without the benefit of a good copy editor.

—Yeah, this all sounds so digressive to me. Should we walk it back and impose some order on it all?

—But that's it exactly. I want to let the random in to my thinking. I want it to help me trigger digressions into areas that might not otherwise get uncovered because of the invisible voice of the censor that effectively says *you cannot go there.*

—So if I get what you're saying, you see life itself as full of random surprises, let's categorize these surprises The Unexpected, and you figure why not model a more improvisational writing practice that uses spontaneity and even a kind of sketching or narrative self-portraiture to let things in that would otherwise get edited out.

—Yeah, something like that. I don't want to respond to or comment on your latest tweet or Instagram post or even old school blog post by writing an article about it, I want to speed read it, to scan it, process it, and instantaneously render an auto-affective response of my own *to* it. However I respond should instantaneously reflect on what I imagine myself feeling as a result of having read you.

—I know what you mean, and in my case, sometimes I don't even comment at all, or I save the comment as a sample that I store in my own notes that I later turn to when I'm jamming with the Internet.

—You mean when you're just free-jamming with your Google search page open using the network as a kind of infinite library of source material to rip, mix and burn into your brain?

—Definitely. I can't write without the Internet on. If I don't have a connection, I'm catatonic.

—But how does this all compute with your future job as an academic whose field of expertise is rhetoric and that requires traditional scholarly outputs?

—This is what I'm going to make my dissertation focus. It's going to be practice-based.

—Meaning?

—Meaning I am going to convert my research into a kind of performance art output that could be composed in any hybrid media language I happen to be playing around with at the time and get it out into the network asap so that it can live in the field of distribution as more open source content to be sampled and remixed by others into the networked space of flows.

—Where have I heard that before?

—I mentioned it in class. Remember that free e-book I suggested everyone download by the artist Seth Price, the one called *Dispersions*? He opens with that quote from the conceptual artist Marcel Broodthaers where he says, "The definition of artistic activity occurs, first of all, in the field of distribution."

—Got it.

—What I like about improvisation, and this is something that Sukenick used to always remind Walt about, or so he tells me, is that improv forces us to relax the rules and eliminates the need to inhibit ourselves as we explore or experiment with our potential to invent new methodologies, something that seems to almost define heuretics and that even Flusser wrote about in an essay titled "Essay." Do you remember that?

—No, can't say that I do.

—Mark Amerika opens his *META/DATA: A Digital Poetics* book with this really pertinent quote. I just quoted it in full on my Tumblr site. Here, I'll bring it up.

—You're such a digital hipster.

—No, really, it's basically saying the same thing but in a different way. Here it is: "No one thinks academically. People just pretend they do. They force themselves to think like that. Academic style is a result of effort (or, if you prefer, of mental discipline), so it is therefore a result of a first thought. The academic is a second thought, because it is a translation of a first thought. It is not spontaneous, but deliberate. The choice between the academic style and my own is therefore a half-choice: I will speak spontaneously, or I will choose 'academicism'."

—I like how academicism is in quotes.

—And I like how he acknowledges in the essay *about* essay writing or let's call it the *essaying process*, how he attempts to invent a new logic of invention, one that leans in on improvisation as way to influence the discourse network.

—I also like how he was self-consciously playing against the apparatus, as he called it, and waxed poetic on how *it*, The Apparatus, attempted to simulate thought processes.

—Yes, that's what we were just talking about. These gestures, these operationalized information behaviors that have become the go-to digital forms of expression that we used to call writing, call into question the conventional approaches we have come to expect from academic writing, approaches that may have been useful for the nineteenth and twentieth century professoriate to deploy and teach as a way to keep linear or historical consciousness in order, but that feel a bit antiquated already as we try and invent conceptual tools that can be brought into the kind of intermedia collaboratories students like us need if we hope to become the rising twenty-first century professoriate.

—You're such a digital hipster.

—Stop saying that! I'm just being me.

—Speaking of digital hipsters, look who just walked in.

—Professor! Walt! We're over here! Over here!

—Hey, what have we got here? The Psychic Automatons?

—That sounds like the barista's new band name.

—I could think of worse.

—Cool. Does anybody need anything?

—No, I'm Ok.

—Me too.

—I'm fine.

—We're good.

—OK, I'll be back.

—Actually, we all have to leave for Professor Lazlo-Cohen's guest-lecture on Online Identities and the Gender Continuum, so you'll have to excuse us if we skip out soon.

—OK, don't go anywhere.

Quick and furtive glances down below the table checking out new messages on iPhones and Androids while the electronica soundtrack from an underground film that no one has ever seen plays in the background.

—You should ask him.

—What?

—You know, about the book sprint.

—Oh right. We all should ask him. Stop putting the pressure on me to do it all the time.

—Hey folks.

iPhones and Androids disappearing into pockets—

—*What do you call that thing again?*

—What? This drink? It's a Toddy-styled ice coffee.

—Oh, right, not the cold version of a hot toddy but Toddy as in the last name of the guy who invented the 24-hour cold brew method.

—Or his version of it anyway . . . so what are you guys talking about, the book sprint?

—Well, we just started talking about it.

—I guess my presence signals *book sprint* to you.

—Among other things.

—I won't ask.

—So we were wondering if, since this is a collaborative authoring performance where we're all essentially going to be sampling and remixing source material off of the Web in realtime, I mean just searching and selecting data and then manipulating it to suit our own rhetorical agendas while simultaneously team-building and designing the look and feel of the book as digital art object, should we—what's the end product going to look like?

—Do you mean what will you have to show for your work after you all co-write the book together?

—Yeah, is it an e-book or a print-on-demand book or—

—Well more than anything it's a performance: think of it as a form of time-based publishing or as an experiment in collaboratively generated mystorical poetics and whatever output emerges is more like a formal manifestation of the creative process.

—What's *mystorical* mean again?

—It's a riff on a term I borrow from Ulmer. He refers to *mystory* as a digital form of writing that functions differently than the traditional argumentative approaches to rhetoric that have been with us for centuries.

—How so?

—Let's assume, for the sake of argument, that argumentation has its own set of limitations in that it's linear, overly logical, and even predictable in terms of what it seeks to accomplish as its final outcome: making a persuasive case to convince someone that a form of Truth exists or at least is possible to obtain. Now let's take a different tact, one that is more mystorical in nature, one that views the Internet as the collective unconscious, something that resonates with Benjamin's dream world of international culture, and that this collective unconscious is where collaborative forms of expression auto-compose rhetorically charged collage art out of the Source Material Everywhere. This utopian reservoir of source material reveals an adjacent possibility, one that opens up an alternative illogic of sense or dream logic that connects more with Benjamin's *Arcades Project* or Situationist *dérive* or what I sometimes refer to as *cyberpsychogeography*, i.e. drifting through cyberspace as a mode of nomadic searching. The search process is part of a personal narrative to find meaning in one's life, in one's thinking, in one's movement through the networked space of flows. Now, whenever something becomes part of a personal narrative that doubles as a contemporary form of artistic expression, it automatically signals an impulse to invent or reinvent oneself anew. This is when the artist, conceived here as the writer–rhetorician, taps into their aesthetic potential, their *mediumistic being* as Duchamp called it, so that they can perform the creative act.

—The Creative Act . . . that was the name of the lecture Duchamp delivered in Houston in, what was it? 1957?

—Exactly. In fact, I was going to draw our attention to it in the next class. I have a quote right here, where he says: "To all appearances, the artist acts like a mediumistic being who, from the labyrinth beyond time and space, seeks his way out to a clearing. If we give the attributes of a medium to the artist, we must then deny him the state of consciousness on the esthetic plane about what he is doing or why he is doing it. All his decisions in the artistic execution of the work rest with pure intuition and cannot be translated into a self-analysis, spoken or written, or even thought out."

—So this is where we get into intuition and the role it plays in forming a counter-argumentative style or mystorical approach to rhetoric.

—Exactly, and Duchamp was aware of this more than most. For the book sprint you all will be collaboratively generating, the challenge will be to put into full force all of your skills not only as writers, thinkers, and designers, but as performers, especially since you'll be required to deliver your rhetoric in narrative form. This will mean you need to take on different characters or characterizations or even caricatures or, as I sometimes call them, concept-characters.

—I want to be the Mystorical character.

—How will you play it?

—Well, I think the first thing I'll do is playfully mesh the various discourses I'm interested in enacting: fiction, theory, rhetoric, dialogue, narrative, the works.

—What else?

—I want to position my performance on the side of "wanting to know," instead of reproducing the knowledge that already is.

—But maybe you won't be able to help yourself. Any other concept-characters out there?

—I want to be Heuretics.

—OK, what will your performance read like?

—Instead of asking what can be made of Duchamp's famous *Large Glass* aka *The Bride Stripped Bare By Her Bachelors, Even*, I would instead ask, "What can be *made from* Duchamp's *Large Glass*?"

—Perfect. There's no telling where it will go.

—I don't even want to know. I just want to traverse the discourse network, or surf the Web as the case may be, finding stray bits of data here and there, cutting and pasting whatever source material seems to be calling out to me straight into a fresh text document, and then manipulating that source material into a story that resonates with whatever version of my "self" I happen to be projecting at that particular moment in time.

—Although the cool thing about time-based publishing is that it's really embedded in spatial practice.

—Exactly, and that's why I want my concept-character to be The Practice of Everyday Life.

—OK, you can be The Practice of Everyday Life. What will your performance entail?

—I'll provide the recipes.

—Recipes!

—Yes, but hopefully it won't turn into a recipe for disaster.

—Funny.

—Actually, you should take everything I'm saying with a grain of salt.

—I do, I do.

—Having said that, if all goes well, I'll deploy the twin DJ tactics of repetition and looping to create a reading pattern that sets up a stylistic parameter for *the form* of the recipe to generate an explosive take on diacritical thought.

—The language poet's version of the Anarchist's Cookbook?

—Yes! What did the Futurists say, something about "words in freedom"?

—Yeah, but the futurists were fascists.

—Oh shit! We're already late for the lecture.

Six bodies simultaneously rise and disembark waving goodbye before speedily maneuvering their way across the street against the light. No one gets killed. For now . . .

17

MAKING SPACE FOR NON-NORMATIVE EXPRESSIONS OF RHETORICITY

Allison H. Hitt

Face masked in plastic, the body dances with each new song that's played. Body lies flat, jumps up then down, rocks back and forth on the ground. As the music grows heavier, the video glitches. The body sits in front of the camera, voice clear and video distorted, disclosing a history of depression and suicidal ideation. The glitching intensifies until voice and outline are indistinguishable—a mass of moving color and sounds.

Multimodal texts present an opportunity to construct arguments through multiple and sometimes unusual modes, to juxtapose media and embody the madness of composition—symbolically and literally. In the example above, a student in a first-year composition course created a video to illustrate the relationship between music and mental health. The video is a translation of an argumentative essay where the student employed secondary and primary research to construct an argument discussing music's impact on depression and suicidal ideation. Although the student's essay was a great example of a thoughtful argument that considers multiple perspectives, the video offers something that the essay cannot: a multimodal space for expressing non-normative rhetoricity. Arguably, the behavior in this video is abnormal: the body is irrational, mimics nervous breakdowns, and discusses suicide. Rather than reading behavior as abnormal, or insane, I want to suggest that this is an example of *mad composing*: an act of embodying madness through the production of multimodal texts. I want to suggest that multimodality can be a channel through which multiple non-normative expressions of rhetoricity are recognized and valued for their rhetorical potential. In this chapter, then, I address how we can create spaces for non-normative expressions of rhetoricity within our digital writing and rhetoric classes.

The potentials of digital and multimodal writing to engage and respect non-normative bodies and composing processes raise several questions about who and what we value in higher education and within the specific context of the writing classroom. For example, do (digital) writing pedagogies value non-normative processes and productions? How can foregrounding digital and multimodal writing practices make our pedagogical spaces more accessible to and respectful of a range of embodied differences and non-normative expressions of rhetoricity? What are the rhetorical gains and challenges of encouraging both disabled and nondisabled students to engage with and compose multimodal texts? To ground these questions, this chapter will focus on mental disability and madness as specific examples of non-normative expression.

To structure this argument, I first draw connections across disability theories of madness (Kafai; Price, "Writing," *Mad at School*) and embodied theories of multimodal and digital composition (Alexander and Rhodes; Arola and Wysocki; Ceraso; Dolmage, "Writing Against Normal"; Rhodes and Alexander; Shipka, *Composition*, "Including"; Yergeau et al.) to illustrate the state of betweenity (Brueggemann) of mad composing: toggling between madness/abnormality and sanity/normality, digital and print, personal and academic. Next, I analyze student examples from a writing class focused on disability discourses to draw two main conclusions about the benefits of multimodal and digital writing: first, incorporating digital media encourages students to engage with and disrupt familiar genres, to make thoughtful and rhetorical decisions about their arguments in a new medium, and to participate in social justice and advocacy work. Second, incorporating both multimodal and digital writing practices into our classrooms makes space for non-normative expressions of rhetoricity and, when done critically, can encourage students to embody non-normative thinking and composing processes.

Mental Disability, Multimodality, and the Composing Body

Narratives of mental disability in higher education are situated within medical models that position it either as something that does not belong in the classroom or as a deficit that students must overcome or at least keep separate from academic writing. Disability studies rhetoricians have argued against the notion that mental and psychiatric disabilities strip people of their rhetorical ability (Prendergast; Price, "Writing," *Mad at School*; Pryal; Yergeau). Indeed, the claim that students with non-normative thinking and composing processes lack rhetoricity is particularly concerning when students are assessed within normative frameworks.

As Katie Rose Guest Pryal explains, disclosures of mental illness are highly tenuous in higher education where we are "often still devoted to the mythos of the good man speaking well, the bastion of reason, the *cogito ergo sum*." After talking to a professor about mental illness stigma, Pryal reports, "Although this stigma is common everywhere, she told me, 'in academia, one's brain is supposed to be the most essential asset one has.'" In *Mad at School*, Margaret Price makes a similar claim, arguing that keeping silent on mental illness "perpetuates the conventional view of academe as an 'ivory tower'—an immaculate location humming with mental agility and energy, only occasionally threatened (from the outside) by the destructive force of insanity" (7). The mentally disabled are often stripped of rhetorical significance and denied personhood, dismissed as rhetorically unsound. Catherine Prendergast has famously argued, "To be disabled mentally is to be disabled rhetorically" (577). And Price writes, "To lack rhetoricity is to lack all basic freedoms and rights, including the freedom to express ourselves and the right to be listened to" (26–7). These discourses position students as not having the right minds for composing the right texts. Instead of imagining mental disability as something that disables the composing process, I want to imagine mental disability as something that crips composition and that can lead to the valuing of non-normative expressions of rhetoricity.

Multimodality can be a channel through which non-normative expressions of rhetoricity are encouraged and valued. Our field has taken up multimodality in different ways, but a common theme echoes the principles of Universal Design for Learning with an emphasis on multiplicity in teaching, learning, and composing practices. Multimodal pedagogies present content in a range of forms and formats, which provides students with different modes of communication and engagement to compose and produce knowledge. Multimodal pedagogies are increasingly important in the writing classroom as we expand our definitions of literacy and textual production:

> Composition classrooms can provide a context not only for *talking about* different literacies, but also for *practicing* different literacies, learning to create texts that combine

a range of modalities as communicative resources: exploring their affordances, the special capabilities they offer to authors; identifying what audiences expect of text that deploy different modalities and how they respond to such texts. (Selfe 643)

As the field pays more attention to multimodality and the many ways in which media and composing are interconnected, we are presented with opportunities not just to discuss multimodality but also to incorporate it critically within our curricula.

Although the terminology may be new, many have argued that composition has roots in the multimodal. For example, in his history of multimodal writing pedagogy, Jason Palmeri argues that the "past compositionists in the 1960s, 1970s, and 1980s studied and taught alphabetic writing as an embodied multimodal process that shares affinities with other forms of composing (visual, aural, spatial, gestural)" (5). This is an important project that illustrates how the field has roots in more flexible definitions and understandings of what composition can be. And although the field has embraced new technologies through multimodal and new media pedagogies, Jonathan Alexander and Jacqueline Rhodes note that "this engagement with new media is often structured through (1) an emphasis on the rhetorical capabilities of textuality and (2) a concurrent elision of the rhetorical affordances of multimodality and multimedia" (30). Despite the rhetorical affordances of multimodal and digital media, we often teach them as if we expect students to produce texts that have clear thesis statements and linear arguments that are supported by traditional academic forms of evidence.

Indeed, Alexander and Rhodes call for a more critical incorporation of multimodality that explores and interrogates the rhetorical affordances of different media:

> If our field is to more fully engage new and multimedia, that engagement must necessarily take a contextualizing turn, not just a technologizing one. And that contextualizing must concern itself not only with the rhetorical affordances of the technologies we encounter in and out of the classroom—a large task in itself— but also with the discursive regimes of subjectivity and affect that delimit such affordances. (201–2)

There are two important ideas to address here: first, multimodal texts are most effective when they are produced with attention to the technical and rhetorical affordances of their medium; and second, multimodal texts offer an opportunity to critically explore non-normative subjectivities.

Multimodal and digital texts need to be theorized and produced within the context of what that medium allows both technically and rhetorically. As Jody Shipka argues, a multimodal framework "requires students to assume responsibility for determining the purposes, potentials, and contexts of their work" (88). This framework not only grants flexibility in the range of materials and technologies that students can use, which can increase accessibility, but also places the responsibility on students to make their own rhetorical choices about the process and production of their texts. A multimodal framework values a nuanced rhetorical awareness of both argument and medium. Specifically, Shipka argues that instead of focusing on specific genres that students can reproduce,

> what is crucial is that students leave their courses exhibiting a more nuanced awareness of the various choices they make, or even fail to make, throughout the process of producing a text and to carefully consider the effect those choices might have on others. (85)

There is structure here but also flexibility in the products, processes, materials and technologies, and the context for multimodal texts. This conception of multimodality places responsibility on students to learn about and critically reflect upon the rhetorical affordances of the media they choose—and, perhaps most importantly, to critically reflect on what role their bodies play in that composition process.

Multimodal texts offer an opportunity to critically explore non-normative subjectivities by focusing the role of the body in the composition process. In *Composing Media = Composing Embodiment*, Anne Wysocki argues that the actions and potentials of our bodies—our embodied being—cannot exist outside of the media that we use, from culture, or from the technologies that we use to consume and produce texts (8). Media is always embodied, which Jay Dolmage explores later in the collection, writing, "As we compose media, we must also—always—compose embodiment" (110). Attention to embodied composing can help make writing more accessible to students with non-normative learning and composing needs. In "Writing Against Normal: Navigating a Corporeal Turn," Dolmage addresses pedagogies that refuse normative conceptions of embodiment and offers suggestions for developing multimodal pedagogies that affirm bodies of all kinds. To develop these technologies and pedagogies, Dolmage proposes a corporeal turn:

> a theory and pedagogy that represents literacy as an ideological and embodied arena, and composing as a cultural and material activity by which writers position and reposition themselves in relation to their own and others' subjectivities, discourses, practices, institutions, and bodies. (115)

Such a turn centralizes the body, examining the "messy and recursive process of composing" rather than focusing on "ideal, complete texts" that mirror ideal, normative bodies (125).

In many ways, an embodied multimodal approach to composition is also an opportunity to critically reflect on our own subjectivities in relation to others. Alexander and Rhodes discuss how incorporating multimodality into writing classrooms can help us teach "the many ways in which the consumption and production of multimedia texts impacts how we conceive and understand contemporary subjectivity" (175). Indeed, I argue that multimodal composing can give students space to embody madness and better understand—and push against—mainstream discourses about disability. Even though media is embodied, there are still particular kinds of embodiment that we privilege in writing classrooms. Alexander and Rhodes ask, "Where do we draw the line at questioning the structures, the regimes of power, the ideologies that normalize 'literacy'?" (196). If we want to incorporate multimodality into our digital writing and rhetoric classrooms, we need to do so both with critical attention to the interplays between technology and subjectivity and to what kinds of embodied composing our field has traditionally valued.

Although Alexander and Rhodes focus on queer subjectivity, centralizing bodies and lived experiences is a useful model for thinking about how multimodality can disrupt not just the composing *process* but also the composing *body*. Their articulation of queer composing as "acts of de- and un- and re-composition" (Rhodes and Alexander) resonates with Robert McRuer's theory of cripping composition. To crip composition is to imagine what exists beyond the standard forms of academic writing and to make space both for the texts and the bodies that do not fit these normative expectations. McRuer argues that composition is a channel for corporate universities to pass down marketable skills, such as order and efficiency—an institutional system that requires standard writing produced by standard, able bodies.

Despite this seemingly bleak assessment of college composition, there is room to crip it by reimagining what it can be. This is de-composition: "a process that involves an ongoing critique of both the corporate models into which we, as students and teachers of composition, are interpellated and the concomitant disciplinary compulsion to produce only disembodied, efficient writers" (McRuer 149). De-composition rejects the standard writing produced by standard bodies and the fetishized final product detached from any embodied composing process, instead drawing attention to the "disruptive, inappropriate, composing bodies" (155). This is not unlike Rhodes and Alexander's articulation of queer composing "as a queer rhetorical practice aimed at disrupting how we understand ourselves to ourselves. As such, it is a composing that is not a composing, a call in many ways to acts of de- and un- and re-composition." Indeed, mad composing disrupts how we understand ourselves in relation to disability and how we understand composing itself, explicitly placing the mad body within the composing process and, thus, disrupting our ideas about the composing body. This cripping of composition is not only helpful for understanding mad composing but also for understanding how rhetoric is embodied more broadly: how students take in knowledge, negotiate meaning, and compose their ideas.

By adopting an embodied multimodal approach to composition pedagogy, we challenge what it means to compose a rational, cohesive, or otherwise "normal" rhetorical text. An embodied multimodal pedagogy asks students to disrupt the conversations that we circulate within higher education and to occupy a space between what we perceive as academic and personal writing. An embodied multimodal pedagogy also asks students to occupy a space of betweenity. In the webtext "Articulating Betweenity: Literacy, Language, Identity, and Technology in the Deaf/Hard-of-Hearing Collection," Brenda Brueggemann describes betweenity as the construction of an idea or identity that is relational to something or someone else. She shares an example of a deaf student who occupies a space between normative understandings of deafness as deficit and deafness as a communicative mode that demonstrates nuanced rhetorical awareness. Betweenity is the composition of an identity that toggles—for example, between deaf and hearing, personal and academic, sane (normal) and insane/mad (abnormal).

Embodying Madness through Multimodal Composing

Betweenity is a useful concept for understanding mad composing and the toggling between personal and academic, multimodal and textual, rationality and madness. In this section, I discuss how multimodal and digital composing creates space for students to critically interrogate their subjectivities and create rhetorically rich texts. First, I offer a summary of madness studies to situate my usage of the term "mad" throughout this chapter. I follow this summary with student examples of both multimodal and digital texts in order to illustrate mad composing and the rhetorical affordances of multimodal and digital composing in order to create more critically inclusive pedagogical spaces.

Madness studies is a developing field of activism and academic research that includes both people who identify as mad and those who are critical of current medical discourses and treatments of mental illness. In their special issue of *Disability Studies Quarterly* focused on madness studies, Noam Ostrander and Bruce Henderson note that madness studies builds on the work of the Mad Pride movement and "counteracting the shame of 'mental illness' and sharing lived experiences to create a community of people who had been written off as crazy, unbalanced, and dangerous." Similarly, the editors of *Mad Matter* define madness studies as a community building effort "where people can get a sense of who they are and what madness is about without being automatically pathologized with a mental disease as happens in so many other spaces" (LeFrançois et al. 2). Madness studies takes an anti-medical model stance; that is, madness studies flips the narrative of diagnosis and cure and instead offers a way to name, find value in, and build community with others who share the lived experience of "emotional, spiritual, and neuro-diversity" (10). Mad, like crip and queer, is an embodied, rhetorical, and political state of being. To work within madness studies is to take a political stance against medical discourses and treatments of mental disability and illness, "to acknowledge and validate these experiences as being authentically human, while at the same time rejecting clinical labels that pathologize and degrade" (10). Although rooted in madness studies, this discussion of validating neurodiverse lived experiences raises an important question for writing instructors: Which expressions of rhetoricity, and whose narratives, do we value in the digital writing and rhetoric classroom?

Madness and narrative are deeply connected. An important goal of madness studies is to strike a more respectful and reciprocal relationship between those who are deemed mad and those who write about madness (Crepaz-Keay and Kalathil; Russo and Bereseford). Similar to other texts about disability and disabled students, many texts about madness are not written by authors who identify with madness or who feature the voices of those who identify themselves as mad. David Crepaz-Keay and Jayasree Kalathil write, "People take ownership of their lives and their stories for granted, but once you are labelled mad, you can lose control of both and they can easily become the property of others." As discussed earlier, disability studies rhetoricians, such as Prendergast and Price, have made similar arguments. Frequently, those who are deemed mad are also deemed unworthy of expressing their own narrative.

Madness studies seeks to carve out spaces for mad and non-normative expressions of rhetoricity and, more specifically, mad composing creates space to disrupt dominant writing norms. In "The Mad Border Body: A Political In-Betweeness," Shayda Kafai theorizes how existing as a border body between sanity (normality) and madness (abnormality) can destabilize dominant cultures and norms. "There is fear in the telling and owning of madness," she writes, and a border body is one "that affronts normativity, a body that comfortably exists in the gaps, has a transformative power." By creating a text that exists in this space of betweenity, students have power to push on what is possible and acceptable as academic production and what stories are allowed to be told, which helps disrupt stigmas both of multimodality and of madness, Kafai argues,

> The stigmas of madness, the falsity of the sane/mad binary and the assumption that one cannot exist simultaneously in the border spaces of sanity and madness are all perpetuated by silence, by the act of refusing to tell one's story.

Multimodal texts already occupy a border space within academic writing. They present a kairotic opportunity for betweenity with modes and contexts and as a means through which students can tell their stories in ways that are rhetorically significant.

To illustrate what it means to embody madness through multimodality, I want to highlight some student work that is both multimodal and digital. Although I advocate for digital writing, it is always important to think about why we value the methods, tools, and texts that we value and reflect on who they serve—or exclude. Thus, I echo others who have argued for recognizing the value of non-digital texts that still make use of multiple media to construct complex, rhetorically situated arguments. Indeed, these articulations of multimodality emphasize the importance of composing within the rhetorical affordances and contexts of students' chosen media. For example, Shipka's articulation of multimodality aligns with Alexander and Rhodes's call for contextualizing the technologies we bring into our multimodal classrooms:

> If we are committed to providing students with opportunities to become increasingly cognizant of the ways texts and various kinds of technologies (both new and old) provide shape for, and take shape from, the historied environments in which they are produced,

circulated, valued, and consumed, I think we need to resist equating multimodality with digitally based or screen-mediated texts. (76)

If the goals are nuanced rhetorical awareness and critical use and reflection of media to construct a text for a specific audience, then texts need not be digital to accommodate embodied composing.

For a class focused on disability, not limiting students' composing options to digital texts is important for accessibility purposes as well. I regularly teach a research-based first-year composition course that is themed around disability discourses, which means students develop their research projects around the course inquiry. I teach a writing course themed around disability because most students have not thought critically about disability and are receptive to the topic; it creates an intersectional space to talk about the cultural, social, and political issues that shape writing; and it allows students opportunities to critically interrogate their subjectivities and compose embodied multimodal texts. Multimodal texts about disability—particularly about mental illness—occupy a space of betweenity where students toggle between personal and academic writing and between our understandings of rational and mad. I will briefly highlight four multimodal texts here: two non-digital and two digital.

The first example is a multimodal text that resulted from an in-class activity where, at the beginning of our research unit, I bring in art supplies and ask students to construct arguments (see Figure 17.1). There is a cardboard pistol with the words "abuse, fear, suicide, depression" written on it. The gun sits atop two advertisements for PTSD awareness: an Uncle Sam "I want YOU to care about PTSD" and the bare back of a woman otherwise wearing army fatigues with a poem about PTSD written on her back. Red paint splatters the gun and the advertisements. The use of a cardboard gun and red paint juxtaposed with images about PTSD gives the piece a deeply affective dimension. This text was created by a service member exploring post-traumatic stress disorder (PTSD) and gun control regulations that target veterans. As a quick class activity, this is by no means an example of a perfectly composed text but rather an illustration of what kind of multimodal text students can create even in the space of a class period where they may not have access to digital composing technologies but can still use different media to interact differently with their textual arguments.

The second example resulted from a core assignment where students composed a brief research essay in conjunction with a multimodal text. Although this student's essay was largely incoherent in terms of logical organization and making a clear argument, they beautifully visualized the misuse of the phrase "I'm so OCD." Drawn on a large poster board, the text features two pink brains (see Figure 17.2). The one on the left has two thought bubbles: "I need to clean my room" and "I'm sooo OCD." The brain on the right has sixteen thought bubbles, all written in different colors, including "Don't ask questions. Your teacher already hates you" and "I've lost control." In ways that the essay did not allow, the poster immediately and clearly visualizes the lived experience of OCD by allowing this student to embody her "abnormal" lived experiences with OCD. Notably, the students who created both multimodal texts identified with the disabilities they were visualizing, and these different assignments presented opportunities to embody their arguments—and subjectivities—through paint, markers, and visual representations of madness.

Although it is important to create space for non-digital articulations of multimodality, there are specific affordances of digital media—such as integrating multiple communicative modes and increasing the potential audience and circulation of the texts—that also allow students to engage in non-normative expressions of rhetoricity. The next two examples are digital texts: a meme series and a video. A common implementation of multimodality in writing classes is

Figure 17.1 Multimodal Text about PTSD

Figure 17.2 Multimodal Text about the Casual Use of OCD in Language

the translation assignment that asks students to translate a written academic essay into a different medium for a different audience. In the first example, a student created a series of five memes to address common misconceptions of mental illness. I highlight here the students' adaptation of two common memes: "One does not simply walk into Mordor" and "Skeptical third world kid." For the first meme, the text reads, "One does not simply help the mentally ill by saying 'just snap out of it.'" For the second meme, the text reads, "So you're telling me not everyone with a mental illness is 'nuts'?" The "one does not simply" memes comment on something that is taken for granted or an issue that is more complex than it seems. In contrast, the skeptical child frequently critiques issues within US society. The student wrote in their reflection that they were trying to appeal to those who ignore the mental health of teenagers, creating a series of satirical memes that would engage readers through a popular genre and simultaneously bring awareness to a serious issue. By using memes—a genre that is traditionally reserved for funny critiques or commentaries on current issues and national discourses—students push against the purpose of the medium, toggling between humor and serious content and pairing image with text to circulate texts that question our understandings of disability and madness.

I end with the piece described in the introduction to this chapter. Presented as a final project in first-year writing, the video "Suicide Glitch" highlights how multimodal texts have the potential to resist normative writing practices. "Suicide Glitch" explores the impact of music on manic depression and suicidal ideation, taking the form of a performance piece mixed with a suicide confessional. The video format allows the student to embody their discussion of mental illness, layering different media on top of each other to convey to viewers the overwhelming experience of depression and suicidal ideation through this sensory overload of clashing media. The first part, titled "Music," is dedicated to the student thrashing their body to the sounds of different styles of music. In part two, "Depression," the student sits in front of the camera, reflecting on their history of mental illness. This student manipulated the technical affordances of video production so that the video glitches visually and auditorily as the confessional progresses, resulting in a mass of colors and noise at the end (see Figure 17.3).

Figure 17.3 Glitch Art Video about Music and Depression

This student made rhetorical choices about content, design, and media here—choosing a format that combined audio and video and text. Although it is by no means a traditional text, the content is organized cohesively despite an arguably incoherent topic and format. This video exists in the betweenity of academic and personal writing, toggling between the realms of sanity and madness and between composition and de-composition. Indeed, this video serves as an interesting example of de-composition, rejecting a standard, disembodied writing and instead drawing attention to "disruptive, inappropriate, composing bodies" (McRuer 155). By all accounts, this is a non-normative text. It is a disturbing video to watch and to hear because of the narrative about depression and suicide, the clashing media, and video manipulation. The use of video and audio intentionally contributes to and disrupts the narrative and, particularly because stigmas of mental illness and suicide are so deeply embedded, the content is arguably inappropriate for an academic writing classroom. This video also occupies a space of betweenity regarding the student's subjectivity as they reflect in the confessional on their lived experience, toggling between what is acceptable and unacceptable behavior—both within the classroom and beyond. By physically placing themselves within the text and combining video, sound and text, this student illustrates the madness of composing and of being composed.

Toward an Embodied Multimodal Writing Pedagogy

The student texts illustrated above vary in terms of the embodiments represented, the media used, and the depth of the assignment—for example, ranging from low-stakes in-class activities to major assignments. However different their physical appearances, these texts emerged from writing and rhetoric classrooms. And importantly, these texts emerged from writing classes where students were asked to research and critically engage with disability discourses. Throughout the semester, students encounter academic multimodal and digital texts that reflect on the authors' lived experiences, that explore the intersections of technology and subjectivity, and that challenge mainstream discourses of disability and madness. Because of the embodied nature of disability and its intersections to race, gender, and sexuality, my students frequently address issues that align with their lived experiences and subjectivities for their research projects. Composing multimodal texts allows students to occupy spaces of betweenity that highlight—rather than silence—their embodied, lived experiences.

Simply giving students the option to compose multimodal and digital texts does not guarantee critical expressions that disrupt standard or normal academic writing. For example, McRuer writes, "If all of our classrooms are virtually de-composed, they are not necessarily 'critically de-composed'" (154) in terms of consciously disrupting the processes and products of standard academic writing. Indeed, Alexander and Rhodes argue that it is important not just to incorporate multimodal texts but to critically reflect on the ways in which different media and technologies can reinforce or disrupt normative writing standards and subjectivities. It is important to create classroom spaces where students can occupy these spaces of betweenity between different forms of expression, while emphasizing the rhetorical and technical afford-ances of different media. Adopting embodied multimodal and digital writing pedagogies can create space for students to critically interrogate their subjectivities, to create rhetorically rich texts, and to push against normative conceptions of writing and rhetoricity. As digital writing and rhetoric instructors, we have a responsibility to ground the production of multimodal and digital texts within critical discussions of the technical and rhetorical affordances of media and how different media potentially resist or contribute to normalizing understandings of embodiment.

Works Cited

Alexander, Jonathan, and Jacqueline Rhodes. *On Multimodality: New Media in Composition*. NCTE, 2014.

Arola, Kristin L., and Anne Frances Wysocki, Eds. *Composing Media = Composing Embodiment: Bodies, Technologies, Writing, The Teaching of Writing*. Utah State UP, 2012.

Brueggemann, Brenda Jo. "Articulating Betweenity: Literacy, Language, Identity, and Technology in the Deaf/Hard-of-Hearing Collection." *Stories that Speak to Us: Exhibits from the Digital Archive of Literacy Narratives*, edited by H. Lewis Ulman, Scott Lloyd DeWitt, and Cynthia L. Selfe. Computers and Composition Digital Press, 2013, ccdigitalpress.org/stories/chapters/brueggemann/. Accessed 5 July 2017.

Ceraso, Steph. "(Re)Educating the Senses: Multimodal Listening, Bodily Learning, and the Composition of Sonic Experiences." *College English*, vol. 77, no. 2, 2014, pp. 102–23.

Crepaz-Keay, David, and Jayasree Kalathil. "Personal Narratives of Madness." *Companion Website Fulford Et Al: The Oxford Handbook of Philosophy and Psychiatry*, 2013, global.oup.com/booksites/content/9780 199579563/narratives/. Accessed 5 July 2017.

Dolmage, Jay. "Writing Against Normal: Navigating a Corporeal Turn." Arola and Wysocki, 2012, pp. 110–26.

———. *Disability Rhetoric*. Syracuse UP, 2013.

Kafai, Shayda. "The Mad Border Body: A Political In-Betweeness." *Disability Studies Quarterly*, vol. 33, no. 1, 2013, dsq-sds.org/article/view/3438/3199. Accessed 5 July 2017.

LeFrançois, Brenda A., Robert Menzies, and Geoffrey Reaume, Eds. *Mad Matters: A Critical Reader in Canadian Madness Studies*. Canadian Scholars' Press, 2013.

McRuer, Robert. *Crip Theory: Cultural Signs of Queerness and Disability*. New York UP, 2006.

Ostrander, Noam, and Bruce Henderson, Eds. "Editor's Introduction." *Disability Studies Quarterly*, vol. 33, no. 1, 2013, dsq-sds.org/article/view/3443/3197. Accessed 5 July 2017.

Palmeri, Jason. *Remixing Composition: A History of Multimodal Writing Pedagogy*. Southern Illinois UP, 2012.

Prendergast, Catherine. "On Rhetorics of Mental Disability." *Embodied Rhetorics: Disability in Language and Culture*, edited by James C. Wilson, and Cynthia Lewiecki-Wilson. Southern Illinois UP, 2001, pp. 45–60.

Price, Margaret. "Writing from Normal: Critical Thinking and Disability in the Composition Classroom." *Disability and the Teaching of Writing: A Critical Sourcebook*, edited by Cynthia Lewiecki-Wilson, and Brenda Jo Brueggemann. Bedford/St. Martin's, 2008, pp. 56–73.

Pryal, Katie Rose Guest. "Disclosure Blues: Should You Tell Colleagues about Your Mental Illness? *Chronicle Vitae*, 13 June 2014, chroniclevitae.com/news/546-disclosure-blues-should-you-tell-colleagues-about-your-mental-illness. Accessed 5 July 2017.

———. *Mad at School: Rhetorics of Mental Disability and Academic Life*. U of Michigan P, 2011.

Rhodes, Jacqueline, and Jonathan Alexander. *Techne: Queer Meditations on Writing the Self*. Computers and Composition Digital Press, 2015, ccdigitalpress.org/techne/. Accessed 3 July 2017.

Russo, Jasna, and Peter Beresford. "Between Exclusion and Colonisation: Seeking a Place for Mad People's Knowledge in Academia." *Disability and Society*, vol. 30, no. 1, 2015, pp. 153–7.

Selfe, Cynthia L. "The Movement of Air, the Breath of Meaning: Aurality and Multimodal Composing." *College Composition and Communication*, vol. 60, no. 4, 2009, pp. 616–63.

Shipka, Jody. "Including, But Not Limited to, the Digital: Composing Multimodal Texts." *Multimodal Literacies and Emerging Genres in Student Compositions*, edited by Tracey Bowen, and Carl Whithaus. U of Pittsburgh P, 2013, pp. 73–89.

———. *Toward a Composition Made Whole*. U of Pittsburgh P, 2011.

Yergeau, Melanie. "aut(hored)ism." *Computers and Composition Online*, 2009, cconlinejournal.org/dmac/index.html. Accessed 4 July 2017.

Yergeau, Melanie, Elizabeth Brewer, Stephanie Kirschbaum, Sushil K. Oswal, Margaret Price, Michal J. Salvo, Cynthia L. Self, Franny Howes. "Multimodality in Motion: Disability and Kairotic Space." *Kairos*, vol. 18, no. 1, 2013, kairos.technorhetoric.net/18.1/coverweb/yergeau-et-al/. Accessed 3 July 2017.

PART IV

Selves and Subjectivities

18
POSTHUMANISM AS POSTSCRIPT

Casey Boyle

The ongoing emergence of networked, digital media technologies and the computational techniques operating behind and beyond those media have turned the world inside-out, remaking the entire globe as also a local phenomenon. Echoing these shifts in communication practices, representations of humanity's relations to those same technological advances in films and popular media portray radical transformations involving more fundamental communications of transferring human minds to machines or other biological bodies regardless of any particular material instantiation. Throughout the cultural imaginaries for these most pervasive communication practices, the outlines for what it means to be *human* are being rewritten as *posthuman.*

Given the long arc of these developments, it seems as though we have been on the verge of becoming *posthuman* for quite some time. It would be a mistake, however, to see those reflections of minds-as-machines as usable portrayals for our posthuman technological moment. Indeed, what resounds in our present moment is how emerging technologies amplify aspects of our embodied conditions rather than provide escape from them. Instead of ameliorating our longstanding social ills, communication technologies actually intensify longstanding practices of sexism, racism, and labor inequities.

In part because of these portrayals, many posthumanist scholars deride dreams of abstract information transfer as reinforcing a humanist past rather than responding to a posthuman present. For starters, we can look to N. Katherine Hayles's *How We Became Posthuman* as, while not the first, the most explicit site distilling these larger cultural conditions into a usable articulation of the turn from humanism to posthumanism. In that germinal work, Hayles traces how a dominant conception of posthumanism and information theory, born from early work on cybernetics, became characterized as the desire for disembodied consciousness. In contrast to those aspirations, Hayles argues throughout her project that cognition and experience cannot be disembodied and such exercises are actually "attempts to transgress and reinforce the boundaries of the subject" (xiii). That is, in their desire to transcend the liberal humanist subject, early cyberneticists reinforced that subject by re-inscribing the very division between mind and body that constituted it in the first place. These shifts have led later posthumanist thinkers, most notably, Rosi Braidotti, to welcome the "posthuman predicament" as a chance to reconsider the exclusive and excluding humanist categories as her interest in the posthuman is "directly proportional to the sense of frustration I feel about the human, all too human, resources and limitations that frame our collective and personal levels of intensity and creativity" and, further, Braidotti writes that that "we need to devise new social, ethical and discursive schemes of subject formation to match the profound transformations we are undergoing" (12). While we see *the* human as being rewritten through advancing digital technologies, including those we might deem as digital writing media, it seems that humanism is being reinscribed at the same time.

Implicit throughout the above descriptions is how pervasive our systems of communication are for determining who and what counts as *human* and, thus, worthy of either praise or blame. If digital writing matters as something distinct from prior forms of writing media, it matters by extending, collapsing, eroding, reinforcing, and/or amplifying/attenuating the categories upon which we have relied for a great many facets of social organization. Most all of these categories have previously been understood as being based on an individual human. Digital writing now blurs those bases. The determinative effects of writing, a part of a larger set of practices in which Braidotti refers to as "discursive schemes," can be seen in Hayles who makes an important distinction between technologies of "inscription" and those of "incorporation." In the first case, Hayles writes that "inscription is normalized and abstract, in the sense that it is usually considered as a system of signs operating independently of any particular manifestation" (198). Inscription then could be the very writings that we use to "express" a self and account for any number of things that help maintain that self and its relations with other selves (census data, medical reports, business ledgers, et al.).

Such abstracting technologies and practices would involve most of what has been considered the charge of rhetoric and composition pedagogies and research. In concert with those inscription practices, Hayles defines and explores what she calls "incorporating practice" by which she means practices "such as a good-bye wave cannot be separated from its embodied medium, for it exists as such only when it is instantiated in a particular hand making a particular kind of gesture" (198). The latter are those practices that are performative and instantiated. So, while incorporation practices are beholden to the same cultural influences that determine appropriate inscription practices, they are often context-specific and less likely abstractable. Such difficulty of abstraction is the crux for what many seek in "learning transfer" wherein certain embodied learning practices take place in one setting, a writing class for instance, but practices that can become abstracted as inscription and, thus, *transferred* to another setting, say, a chemistry lab. However, as I hope to show throughout this short essay, the differences between inscription and incorporations—along with the very dynamics of what some refer to as knowledge transfer—are fusing together as the very digital writing practices we use to inscribe work incorporates bodies differently than did previous technologies of writing (inscription and incorporation). If the concept of posthuman is to do anything, especially for rhetoric and writing, it might allow for a revision to the humanist categories, many of which subtend what many call "knowledge transfer."

Despite the many articulations of posthuman scholarship, as well as those posthumanist orientations in rhetoric and composition scholarship more particularly, what is unclear is how those posthuman proclamations affect how we study and teach writing. If inscription and incorporation technologies are, as I am arguing, fusing together to *con-fuse* categories, then it might be productive that we attend not only to practices that help in-form a subject but also those that structure mediations *transferred* from disciplinary subject to subject. In what ways does digital writing in-form—through inscriptions and/as incorporations—the knowing bodies as a process of ongoing transfer? If that is the case, then is the notion of "transfer" even applicable in a digital writing environment composed of constant on ongoing connection? What actually "transfers" from one place to another when all places are everywhere and all at once through emerging digital writing?

In response to these questions, this chapter—already well beyond a proper introduction—builds from and functions as a follow-up to an article I published in *College English* ("Writing and Rhetoric and/as a Posthuman Practice") and also a book manuscript I've completed (*Rhetoric as a Posthuman Practice*). Both projects propose rhetoric to be a practice that includes but is irreducible to traditional humanist framing of an individual as a knowing subject. Key to the project(s) is to show how "reflective practice" and related concepts of "metacognition" has come to provide the basis for contemporary rhetoric and writing studies. However, recent work in posthumanism (building on those mentioned above) and other related theories (new materialism, feminist materialism, transhumanism) question the extent to which we can ever solely rely on a single, consciously aware subject to reflect on and deliberately adjust one's actions towards ethical and responsible ends. Following that work, this particular project, as well as my work overall, reconsiders the role of rhetorical training and writing pedagogy if and when that training's goal no longer focuses solely on the production of a reflective thinker but to initiate information as an assemblage of practices, an assemblage that becomes all the more apparent in practices and activities of digital writing. As a follow-up then, *this very chapter can and should be considered as a kind of postscript.* Not unlike posthumanism is to humanism, it is exactly the notion of a letter's *postscript* (a P.S.) as something that is both a part of and apart from that which it is supposedly appended that I argue to be a chief contribution for digital writing in a posthumanist frame. In the following sections, I aim to show, through the concept of the postscript, how inscribing technologies are also incorporating technologies and how that concept might rewrite knowledge transfer.

Writing Humanism

Peter Sloterdijk's "Rules for the Human Zoo: a Response to the Letter on Humanism" offers a productive site wherein the turn from humanism should be located for rhetoric and writing studies. Sloterdijk argues that humanism, in its multiple variants stretching from antiquity through renaissance and into the early modern period, are all grounded in a single literary form: the epistle. Sloterdijk writes that "Books . . . are thick letters to friends. With this phrase, [is] . . . the quintessential nature and function of humanism: It is telecommunication in the medium of print to underwrite friendship" (12). From there, most literary endeavours in the western world—novels, nonfiction, even scholarly treatises—are all forms of the letter through which a notion of friendship becomes recognized and sustained. The rise of alternative media, mass media, and social media creates a moment in which Sloterdijk posits as "clearly post-literary, postepistolary, and thus posthumanistic" (14). Not unlike Braidotti's "posthuman predicament" the moments of mass and new media emergence then recasts the previously cultivated activities of knowledge and social organization. If such proclamation seem too grand, Sloterdijk advises "[a]nyone who thinks the prefix 'post' in this formulation is too dramatic can replace it with the adverb 'marginal'" (14). It is marginal because "at the heart of humanism so understood we discover a cult or club fantasy: the dream of the portentous solidarity of those who have been chosen to be allowed to read" (13). While friendship and its literary foundations may be admirable from the outset, Sloterdijk shows that it is actually a club whose *new* members are always the already accepted, and whose literary practices are not achievements but prerequisites for who gets to enroll, and those who are not are considered "barbarous."

As to this prior enrollment, we should note that Sloterdijk's essay responds to Martin Heidegger's "Letter on Humanism." Through the form of a letter, Heidegger proclaims language as the central role in the overall conception of (human) Being writing that

Language is the house of Being. In its home man dwells. Those who think and those who create with words are the guardians of this home. Their guardianship accomplishes the manifestation of Being insofar as they bring the manifestation to language and maintain it in·language through their speech. (217)

For Heidegger, "Thinking is *l'engagement par l'Etre pour l'Etre* [engagement by Being for Being]" (218). Here, we see a tell-tale sign of humanism is its defining feature of the human being is a reflexive ability to engage being through being *being* thought. If the recursiveness and reflexivity comes across as confusing, it should. That is, the very con-fusion of the thinking self with the thought self is an encapsulation of events by a narrative through which an individual becomes known as such. It is the form of the letter that encapsulates this activity most accurately. The ability to, at once, step outside oneself (ek-sistence) while also encapsulating these many different points as a unified self is the hallmark practice of humanism and, later, the bounds of what makes something *human*. As shown, above however, the emergence of additional communication media—chief among that digital media—have rewritten the exclusivity of literary self as the base for what counts as human precisely because the ability to "step outside" is an increasingly difficult practice for media that are always on and located everywhere. *In our digital writing inscriptions, we are always becoming incorporated, differently.*

Despite the increasing prominence of always-on, always-connected digital writing media, it is not hard to see how the literary form of the epistle and its operation of reflective *ek-sistence* continue to underlie the aims for today's writing courses. As I examined in my earlier article and book, the "letter to the editor" style of assignment, which characterizes the argumentative research paper more generally, asks a writer to research a position, state a case, and argue for a course of action. Similarly, the oft-used "reflective essay" that caps multimodal assignments in digital rhetoric pedagogy asks for the same process to be enacted. In both examples, what is being exercised is reflective practice, an activity by which a student gathers material and presents a logical argument by carefully assessing all the available means of persuasion. Such practices are laudable in the most part because reflective and critical practice are what we have come to define as literary activity and, thus, what counts as humanistic practices. However, the practice of reflective practice goes unquestioned. That is, it seems as though the only thing one cannot be reflectively critical about is the efficacy of reflective criticism. The concepts and practice of reflexivity became a central part in the discussion of information procession. Tracing those discussions, Hayles defines reflexivity, a concept that emerged as central to the cybernetic discussions, as "the movement whereby that which has been used to generate a system is made, through a changed perspective, to become part of the system it generates" (8). That is to say that "reflexivity has subversive effects because it confuses and entangles the boundaries we impose on the world in order to make sense of that world" And, further, "[r]eflexivity tends notoriously toward infinite regress" (9). What becomes clear in Hayles's formulation is that reflexivity is— like the letter that confirms humanism rather than initiates the human—both that which a learning process relies on and that which it creates. Through that formulation, reflection elides much of its activity as a way to consolidate the individual human upon whom humanism rests and toward whom humanism strives. In the reflective humanistic formulation, *the medium may be the message but both are forsaken in favor of what will become its messenger.*

Composition scholarship is replete with appeals to reflective practice as its prime activity. Writing studies often claim that writing is a reflective activity and its teaching should reflect writing as a reflective practice (Hillocks; Yancey, *Reflection*, *Rhetoric*). While I have discussed the details of those works elsewhere, I turn here away from those earlier works and towards a particular instance of the reflective tenet in what has become known as "knowledge transfer" and its chief operating concept of metacognition. The former describes the process in which knowledge can move from one place to another. In writing studies, this entails how particular skills learned in a writing classroom can make their way into other disciplinary-specific writing genres. The goal and chief practice for ensuring the transfer of writing skills from one discipline to another is the development of *metacognition*. This habit is the ability to become reflectively aware and consciously able to articulate, in word and deed, one's communication choices with digital media as a demonstration of communication ability. For instance, Crystal VanKooten uses the phrase *"meta-awareness about composition"* as a way to "refer to a student's ability to move consistently between enacting multimodal compositional choices and articulating how and why those choices are effective or ineffective within a rhetorical context" (58). Working from a Deweyan frame, VanKooten links that reflective activity "with the instrumental end of meta-awareness as students began to consider, plan for, and recount enacting the transfer of compositional knowledge across media" (59). While the need to reflectively account for conscious decisions regarding media use is seen important for transfer of skills between media, so too is that reflective process exploited for transfer of skills and knowledge between disciplines as well. In *Agents of Integration*, Rebecca Nowacek offers a synchronous study of transfer through an examination of students participating in an interdisciplinary education program. Nowacek finds that, despite many arguments against the possibility of knowledge transfer, when transfer is looked at as recontextualization—wherein knowledge or skills used in one context are imported into another context with necessary changes—then transfer becomes a process by which its practitioners become "agents of integration" whose complex rhetorical activities (11).

A key difference between VanKooten and Nowacek, however, is that the latter makes more explicit that metacognition is a helpful but not necessary element for what might be understood as transfer. As Nowacek mentions, many of the skills and much of the knowledge that "gets" transferred are unconscious practices. This is an important and little explored dimension to transfer studies and one that is resisted by a humanist frame. Such resistance is shown by how vital the reflection and conscious articulation is for any particular transfer study. Given that we are discussing digital writing and technologies, it might be helpful to not only examine the student as an individual but also as an ecology of practices and habits. *Student as ecology* might look to the media, tools, and spatial environments as also part of the necessary structures through which an "individual student" *transfers* knowledge. Just as Hayles demonstrates that any conception of disembodied information is, at best, a myth, so too might we find that studying transfer absent an ambient orientation unduly limits our practice and pedagogy for that which we might study. Perhaps then no site in rhetoric and composition has the potential to benefit more from framing its study as a study of the posthuman predicament than might studies of transfer.

This is not to say that rhetoric and composition has not been inflicted by the posthuman condition. Unlike the many acute conditions that inflict a disciplinary field, those deemed as "turns" that come and go, posthumanism has proven itself to be a chronic condition in that it continues to challenge practices throughout the humanities and especially those in rhetoric and composition. To again repeat a known lineage: in a 2002 special issue on posthumanism and rhetoric, John Muckelbauer and Debra Hawhee claim that "posthumanism poses intriguing questions to many longstanding, 'self-evident' assumptions about rhetoric and communication, broadly conceived" that, for instance, "Is it really so easy, for example, to distinguish between a speaker, an audience, a message, and a context?" (768). Such discursive regimes as underwritten by the writing of a letter have become eroded as communication and social organization have become more complex. The difficulty of maintaining the discursive regime of reflection is apparent in technical communication wherein Andrew Mara and Byron Hawk argue that the "[t]raditional humanistic tools and heuristics for anticipating systemic complications—like audience analysis, user testing, and peer review—quickly become swamped when trying to account for the tendential forces of nonhuman actors and activities" (2). Further, Sidney Dobrin writes that posthumanism "identifies a moment of inquiry in which the human subject is called into question via its imbrications with technologies such as cybernetics, informatics, artificial intelligence, genetic manipulation, psychotropic and other pharmaceuticals, and other bio-technologies, as well as species interactions" (3). Taken all together, rhetoric finds (repeatedly) through posthumanism a thorough *con-fusing* of previously separate categories upset by new and emerging media. What this means for humanism—and the letter and the friendship it underwrites —is that digital writing can and often is examined just as that letter and the friendship it underwrites but despite those examination's elisions, those other structures remain and continue to reduce the objects and events of our examinations causing those ecologies to drift from practical or pedagogical possibility.

Writing Posthumanism

If a kind of friendship once underwrote humanism through the literary form of the epistle, then what of the emerging notion of friendship that surrounds digital writing in social media such as Facebook? In the former, the letter is composed as a direct communication between two previously established points of relation whereas in the latter, communication is *posted* to everybody and nobody all at once. In an age of digital writing, and social media in particular, friendship has been expanded toward non-exclusive connection. Many might look at the shift from a letter-writing friendship to the friendship of the database as a kind of perversion. I would like to propose that, instead of a perversion of the structure of friendship, digital writing enacts a conversion of the friendship structure. Where studies and practices to ensure transfer from one context to another mimic the transmission of a letter from one person to another, a post-human approach to digital writing would look to intensify Nowacek's notion of transfer as "recontextualization." That is, a posthuman approach to transfer finds in the ecology of practices *structuring structures* (e.g. Bourdieu) undergirding practices throughout situations but that would not be reducible to a human subject per se. These ecologies are composed by the friendly or unfriendly relations between the devices, practices, humans, curricula, policies, spaces (among multiplicity of other *things*) and those ecologies *incorporate* and/as the structuring structures that may become seen, at some later point, as knowledge transferred.

It is vital I point out here that the letter or communication between individuals is neither gone, nor not useful, nor unimportant. Indeed, this style of humanist writing occurs as much as it always has. Human subjects too. That said, we have to attend to the multiple *ways* that those subjects are mediated and mediating. In their introduction to *Techne: Queer Meditations on Writing the Self*, for instance, Jacqueline Rhodes and Jonathan Alexander find that posthuman articulations of the *techne* of self writing confront us with the fact that "we face the simultaneously exhilarating and terrifying possibilities of proliferating subjectivities within proliferating discourses and contexts. The question becomes *how* to write such selves rather than *why*" (n.p. original emphasis). These shifts in media as seen in digital writing propose that we are also moving into a posthuman frame that amplifies and foregrounds an ongoing reliance on infrastructures like databases whose relations, unlike the literary practices in the letter, are persistent and continuous. These infrastructures are both apart of and a part from the letters they constitute as such. The digital media as written through databases and interfaces are both primary and posteriorly forms that ambiently surround what we consider to be communication through a humanist lens.

It would be easy to understand the examples of multimodal writing from the previous section as evidence of a shift from the humanist letter writer towards the posthumanist assembler.

I would caution against that understanding since, in many instances, the multimodal text replicates the epistle in both form and function. Take for example a video essay, regardless of the number of its components. It is the case that the layerings of sound and visual provide another dimension in addition to the linear logics of the epistle but, if those video essays do not exploit the film's montage or juxtaposition features or if its audience cannot grasp those forms, the video essays perhaps amplify the traditional letter's linearity and logics. The same can be said for sonic essays whose features may include layers of ambient sounds but are all too often in service of a straight linear argument or commentary. Or any combination of media therein. While these forms take place after the letter's dominance as a literal form, they very much repeat the letter's function in that they underwrite the structure of the humanist friendship whose connections are already foreclosed.

In response to humanism based in the medial form and mediating practices of the epistle, I propose the concept of the *postscript*. The postscript should be related to the practice of added additional information to a letter as such. Often tacked onto a letter by abbreviation (P.S.), the postscript is an addendum to the letter that follows the author's signature. Existing in that netherspace after the letter and the author's signature but not beyond the letter's material page, the postscript relies on but augments the letter and, in some senses, exists independently of the letter and its author. It is both an afterthought to a narrative but also the thoughts that persist after a narrative has unfolded. Again where most writing scholarship—especially that which contributes to emerging scholarship on knowledge transfer—concerns the habits of a reflective human subject whose experience may or may not lead to being able to recall and reproduce prior genres, writing tasks, media, a posthumanist orientation embraces the postscript as the infrastructures of digital writing that assist in those structuring dimensions that facilitate "transferring knowledge."

As noted above, Hayles's work on the posthuman and electronic literature in general is always an apt resource of issues of the posthuman but, for this project, we may not have a better potential for digital writing than when she claims that "[m]odern humans are capable of more sophisticated cognition than cavemen not because moderns are smarter . . . but because they have constructed smarter environments in which to work" (289). Such a construction certainly does not figure into the modes of reflective practice whereby the letter writer steps outside of herself to consider an appropriate action. Instead, the claim leverages the human and her environment as an assembly of distributed cognition whose "knowledge" is a shared process between seemingly disparate things. It is perhaps a remnant of humanist reflection that prompts Thomas Rickert to take issue with the lurking anthropocentrism in the "'they have constructed'" that implicitly "declines to take up the role of the environment in the constructions that have come to be (127). That quibble aside, what Hayles's environments and Rickert's ambience prompt us to reconsider is that issues of transfer cannot be understood as information abstracted from one course and deployed in another as one might consider the delivery and opening of a letter but as the composing of environments as continuous process of structuring.

If we take seriously the posthuman predicament, we might understand digital writing as also incorporating infrastructures as a way to more dynamically facilitate not transferring of knowledge, as traditionally understood, but *transducing practices of knowing*. The difference between transfer and transduction might be a minor inflection, but it creates major effects. Where transfer denotes carrying something from one domain to the next (an activity wrapped in abstraction), transduction describes the process through which something changes as it moves across domains. The voice is a good example in that the movements made by my vocal chords create disturbances in the air that then agitate a microphone's diaphragm whose oscillations create digital data whose movements usher forth electrical currents and whose overall process reverses if and when I want to hear *that* voice again. The transduction in this example describes "the" voice as it "transfers" from one thing to the next, but that description only works by *not* focusing on the signal but instead attending to the structuring structures that help determine what eventually is considered to be a signal. Rob Kitchin and Martin Dodge operationalize the notion of transduction to discuss "code/space" (what we might consider as a very broadly construed understanding of digital writing). With this concept, Kitchin and Dodge acknowledge—*pace* Hayles and Rickert—the extent to which the spaces we inhabit have become dependent on computation that "*modulates the conditions under which sociospatial processes operate*" (65). Transduction, not transfer, then becomes the operation through which spaces as social practices emerge as ongoing processes of change. The letter, as the key humanist writing practice, actively elides all of the transductions through which it traverses by foregrounding its transfer as a signal alone. The concept and practice of postscript would work to make digital writing a practice and a process of ongoing change whose practices do not end when an individual clicks "send."

For a concrete instance of postscript as a writing practice, a useful and often-cited example we may turn to is how writer Steven Johnson once described his writing process. Johnson, a prolific nonfiction writer whose own work undermines that myth of the individual genius—especially in *Where Good Ideas Come From* or *Emergence: The Collected Minds of Ants, Brains, Cities, and Software*—a myth for which humanism is largely responsible by its centering of the rational, individual human as the standard for enlightened thought. In addition to those larger works, perhaps Johnson's most productive advice on writing comes from an article wherein he describes the software that assists his writing process. Using DEVONthink, a database that indexes his writing alongside the texts he is writing about, Johnson marvels when the software program makes connections between items he is writing about independent of his conscious attention. The event leads him to ask "Now, strictly speaking, who is responsible for that initial idea? Was it me or the software? It sounds like a facetious question, but I mean it seriously." Marilyn Cooper writes about this scene as one that shows how "writing is an embodied interaction with other beings and our environments" (18). Specifically, Cooper claims that the Johnson example shows "how complex systems repurpose wastes as a collaboration between him and the indexing system, a productive interaction between carbon and silicon-based intelligences" (20). What Cooper finds here, I propose, is not an agent of integration but an ecology of incorporation through which the various relations transduce a signal (an idea). What makes the operation function, however, is not the humanist practice of making meaning out of a letter's whole but instead by seeing that letter as an ecology in and of itself. For instance, Johnson later in a (now archived) follow-up blogpost writes of his process that

> the proper unit for this kind of exploratory, semantic search is not the file, but rather something else, something I don't quite have a word for: a chunk or cluster of text, something close to those little quotes that I've assembled in DevonThink. If I have an eBook of Manual DeLanda's on my hard drive, and I search for 'urban ecosystem' I don't want the software to tell me that an entire book is related to my query. I want the software to tell me that these five separate paragraphs from this book are relevant. Until the tools can break out those smaller units on their own, I'll still be assembling my research library by hand in DevonThink.
>
> I wonder whether it might be possible to have software create those smaller clippings on its own: you'd feed the program an entire e-book, and it would break it up into 200–1000 word chunks of text, based on word frequency and other cues (chapter or section breaks perhaps.) Already Devonthink can take a large collection of documents

and group them into categories based on word use, so theoretically you could do the same kind of auto-classification *within* a document. It still wouldn't have the pre-filtered property of my curated quotations, but it would make it far more productive to just dump a whole eBook into my digital research library. ("Tool for Thought" n.p.)

Again, a postscript practice sees the database and its items not meaning filled letters communicated from one individual to another but as a multiplicity of spaces whose various internal divisions, modulations, and in-formations become dis-continuous points to engage and elaborate. What makes these relations work is a commitment for inventing new units of relation through which digital writing might enact new productions.

What this work and the small example shows is how knowledge transfer itself relies on humanist orientation of a thinking and reflecting human subject without regard to an environment that participates in that very *thinking*. A posthuman account questions the notion of transfer as it is articulated in scholarship. A student cannot only abstract knowledge and skills from one place to another but must transduce practices from one structure's possibilities through another's. Building on the Johnson example, and Cooper's response to it, we might well consider practices of digital writing as needing to involve the kinds of additional structuring that is apart of and a part from what has become understood as traditional digital writing. For example, looking to the use of database management systems (i.e., Zotero, OneNote, or Evernote) across all a student's classes as a practice of postscript might help compose a digital infrastructure that better aids transfer skills that do not rely so much on a humanist practices of reflection but instead try to transduce continuous digital writing practices. The postscript practices should also, eventually, involve more expansive digital writing activities such as composing digital infra-structural components such as metadata, databases, automated scripts, and chatbots in addition to the letter-based writing that will continue to take place. These digital writings are not the multimedia that the field of rhetoric and composition has come to know as digital writing through a humanist frame but they are the digital structures that transduce today's digital writing possibilities into tomorrow's knowledge practices.

Writing Post Script

What I have tried to argue throughout this short chapter is that for digital writing to respond to our posthuman predicament, it must involve more than what we send to one another in the guise of letter-writing humanist friendship. A digital writing that responds to the posthuman follows the postscript as a practice of composing infrastructures that transduce conditions from one structure to the next. Unlike the tenets of transfer wherein knowledge resides in a human mind and skills that are instrumentally observed and assessed, postscript practices turns metacognition into something synonymous with distributed cognition. In place of having a student express metacognition through conscious and critical awareness, distributed cognition as demonstrated through postscripts would be assessed by the ways in which an ecology of incorporation transduces practices from one domain and/as the next.

Works Cited

Bourdieu, Pierre. *Outline of a Theory of Practice.* Trans. Richard Nice. Cambridge UP, 1977.
Boyle, Casey. "Writing and Rhetoric And/as Posthuman Practice." *College English* vol. 78, no. 6, 2016, pp. 532–54.
———. *Rhetoric As a Posthuman Practice.* Manuscript. 2017.
Braidotti, Rosi. *The Posthuman.* Polity, 2013.

Cooper, Marilyn M. "Being Linked to the Matrix: Biology, Technology, and Writing." *Rhetorics and Technologies: New Directions in Writing and Communication*, edited by Stuart Selber. U of South Carolina P., 2010, pp. 15–32.

Dobrin, Sidney I. *Writing Posthumanism, Posthuman Writing*. Parlor, 2015.

Hayles, N. Katherine. *How We Became Posthuman*. U of Chicago P, 1998.

Heidegger, Martin. "Letter on Humanism." *Basic Writings*. Harper, 1977, pp. 39–54.

Hillocks, George. *Teaching Writing As Reflective Practice: Integrating Theories*. Teachers College Press, 1995.

Johnson, Steven. *Emergence: The Connected Lives of Ants, Brains, Cities, and Software*. Scribner, 2002.

——. "Tool for Thought." *The New York Times*, 30 Jan. 2005, www.nytimes.com/2005/01/30/books/review/tool-for-thought.html. Accessed 6 July 2017.

——. "Stevenberlinjohnson.com: Tool For Thought." *Internet Archive*, archive.org/web/20160209193905/http://www.stevenberlinjohnson.com/movabletype/archives/000230.html. Accessed 16 Dec. 2016.

——. *Where Good Ideas Come From: The Natural History of Innovation*. Riverhead Books, 2011.

Kitchin, Rob, and Martin Dodge. *Code/Space: Software and Everyday Life*. MIT Press, 2014.

Mara, Andrew, and Byron Hawk. "Posthuman Rhetorics and Technical Communication." *Technical Communication Quarterly*, vol 19, no. 1, 2009, pp. 1–10.

Muckelbauer, John, and Debra Hawhee. "Posthuman Rhetorics: 'It's the Future, Pikul.'" *JAC*, vol. 20, no. 4, 2000, pp. 767–74.

Nowacek, Rebecca S. *Agents of Integration*. Southern Illinois UP, 2011.

Rhodes, Jacqueline, and Jonathan Alexander. *Techne: Queer Meditations on Writing the Self*. Computers and Composition Digital Press/Utah State UP, 2015, ccdigitalpress.org/techne/. Accessed 6 July 2017.

Rickert, Thomas. *Ambient Rhetoric: The Attunements of Rhetorical Being*. U of Pittsburgh P, 2013.

Sloterdijk, Peter. "Rules for the Human Zoo: a Response to the Letter on Humanism." *Environment and Planning D: Society and Space*, vol. 27, no. 1, 2009, pp. 12–28.

VanKooten, Crystal. "'The video was what did it for me': Developing Meta-Awareness about Composition across Media." *College English*, vol. 79, no.1. 2016, pp. 57–80.

Yancey, Kathleen Blake. *Reflection in the Writing Classroom*. Logan: Utah State UP, 1998.

——. ed. *A Rhetoric of Reflection*. University Press of Colorado, 2016.

19

A LAND-BASED DIGITAL DESIGN RHETORIC

Kristin L. Arola

A few years ago, my mom, a member of the Keweenaw Bay Indian Community among other things, shared with me a link to the website *The Ways: Stories on Culture and Language from Native Communities Around the Central Great Lakes*. This website features videos and interactive maps that explore Native culture and language, primarily of the Anishinaabe peoples in the central and upper Great Lakes region. Upon first glance, I was hooked. I spent hours exploring videos and reading essays, all the while feeling a sense of comfort. Wandering through the site felt like wandering my family's land on Lake Superior on a crisp autumn day. It's as though I could feel the sandy ground beneath my feet and the smell of jack pines and moss in the air. My experience with *The Ways* was a felt sense of belonging to a land, of being of a people— it was a melding of content and form that felt like home (Figure 19.1).

The fairly nascent (at least in name) discipline of cultural rhetorics has done remarkable work reframing rhetorical theory and composition practice so as to put a spotlight on marginalized groups' use of, and engagement with, language. In this chapter, I bring together some of this work in order to focus specifically on how we as teachers and scholars engage with the design of online spaces. I ask how we might understand digital spaces through a land-based rhetoric, one that, as Gabriela Raquel Rìos argues, "recognizes the productive potential of nature and of embodied ways of knowing" (68). By offering a land-based rhetoric, a theory that aligns with American Indian epistemologies, I propose an ethical, relational, and material approach to the design of digital spaces.

Rhetoric | Design

In the late 1990s and early 2000s, the multimodal turn in composition studies—arguably spearheaded by the New London Group's manifesto wherein they argued that "literacy pedagogy must now account for the burgeoning variety of text forms associated with information and multimedia technologies" (61)—focused a good deal on visual rhetoric. Composition textbooks like *Seeing and Writing* became popular, collections such as Carolyn Handa's *Visual Rhetoric in a Digital World* emerged, and a series of edited collections (Allen; Hill and Helmers; Hocks and Kendrick) and articles (George; Hocks, "Visual Rhetoric"; Selfe; Sorapure; Wysocki, "Monitoring Order," "Impossibly Distinct") on visual rhetoric proliferated our field. Visual rhetorical studies at the time tended to bifurcate into either an engagement with pictorial images

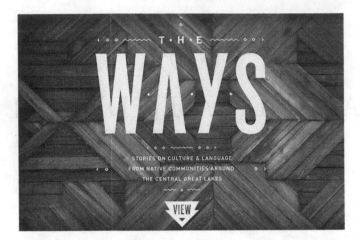

Figure 19.1 Front Screen of *The Ways*

or a focus on design. For the former, books such as *Ways of Seeing* took up John Berger's attention to the visual through pictorial images such as paintings and photographs. Scholars in rhetoric and composition, often intersecting with work in feminist and cultural studies, explored both the ways that visuals make meaning, and also the ways that such analysis should be part of the purview of rhetoric and composition research and pedagogy. For the latter, those engaged with design, scholars explored the ways that interfaces, design elements, and typography are rhetorical. While arguably an arhetorical take on design (see Wysocki and Jasken's 2004 critique), Robin Williams's *Non-Designer's Design Book* became a popular source for many teaching visual rhetoric as it provided students with a straightforward way of engaging with the production of designed pages and screens. The early 2000s were rich with visual rhetorical scholarship and pedagogy.

Since this time, while visual rhetoric has been taken up in different ways for different reasons, we no longer see a proliferation of edited collections or special issues specifically on The Visual (or sound, for that matter, which has followed a similar trend). Instead, visual rhetoric is often subsumed within multimodal theory and pedagogy. The New London Group proposed a pedagogy of multiliteracies that includes both production and analysis of the visual, spatial, gestural, aural, and linguistic modes. Multimodality is the interconnection between at least two of these modes, and digital writing is always to some degree dealing with multimodal production even if it's *just* the typing of words on a white background (which is a combination of the linguistic, spatial, and visual). And while, as Jody Shipka reminds us, multimodality and digitality are not synonymous and we should "resist equating multimodality with digitally based or screen-mediated texts," (84) digital rhetoric and writing has helped to make multimodality more visible in our practice and pedagogy.

In this essay, I turn to those earlier conversations on visual rhetoric, specifically design, within writing studies and place them in conversation with cultural rhetoric. Scholars concerned with the rhetoric of design during the early multimodal turn in writing studies (Hocks; Sorapure; Wysocki, "Monitoring Order," "Impossibly Distinct"; Wysocki and Jasken) argued that writing and rhetoric teachers and scholars pay careful attention to design in digital writing. They suggested an attention to designed digital spaces, both because our students' "writing" was taking place in these designed spaces, and because, as Diana George argued,

> [f]or students who have grown up in a technologically-saturated and an image-rich culture, questions of communication and composition absolutely will include the visual, not as attendant to the verbal but as complex communication intricately related to the world around them. (32)

While George spoke of the value of both pictorial visual literacy and design visual literacy, to be design literate was treated as part of engaging with a pedagogy of multiliteracies. I argue such attention to design is key to a robust digital literacy, and through offering a land-based digital design rhetoric, I return to, and extend, Wysocki's 1998 argument in "Monitoring Order" that

> visual designs can . . . be expressions of and means for reproducing cultural and political structures, and that such visual orderings are likely to be those that are repeated—and that hence can become invisible through constant use, as Bourdieu points out, whether they are intended to be invisible or not; second, that we nonetheless encounter designs individually, based on our particular bodily histories and presents. (np)

I feel patterns. I breathe in typefaces. I sense color. I am embraced by designs that feel like home. As briefly described above, design theory as manifest in and through rhetoric and composition has worked to bring design into the fold of digital and multimodal literacy. Wysocki's work reminds us that while our teaching tools (textbooks and handbooks in particular) tend to function from a form/content split, whereby design is seen as form, in practice the split between information and design is never quite as clear ("Impossibly Distinct"). For Wysocki, design is content, design is embodied, design is sensory, and it is always intimately connected to the cultures within which we find ourselves living, breathing, and making meaning.

> what any body is and is able to do—and how any one body differs from other bodies in its affective and physiological capabilities—cannot be disentangled from the media we use or from the times and cultures in, and technologies with which, we consume and produce texts. . . . ("Into Between" 8)

How we see and understand media, including visual information and design, is shaped largely by our own cultural materiality. Wysocki turns to Martin Jay's argument against "any one visual order." Jay, instead, argues for "the multiplication of a thousand eyes, which, like Nietzsche's thousand suns, suggests the openness of human possibilities" (591, qtd. in Arola and Wysocki 6). That is, as Wysocki unpacks it,

> people living in the Baroque period had different ways of seeing from people living during the Italian Renaissance, who saw differently from those who lived at the same time in Northern Europe; each of these ways of seeing articulated, Jay argues, to epistemological and so ontological habits of the time. (6)

It's not surprising, then, that I feel design, that the design of *The Ways* website brings me to a place of home. It's not surprising that the ways I feel and breathe this content would be very different were the video stories housed on YouTube instead of on this beautifully designed website.

Rhetoric | Design | Land

In order to understand my response to *The Ways*, I turn to cultural rhetorics, specifically land-based rhetorics, to explore how ways of seeing are cultural and embodied. In "Cultivating Land-Based Literacies and Rhetorics," Gabriela Raquel Ríos explores the literacy practices of farm workers and, through sharing their stories and experiences, suggests moving beyond rhetorical frameworks that use ecology primarily as a metaphor for literacy. Instead, she proposes a material engagement with the ways lived ecologies are always already part of literate practice. This suggestion is built on Matthew Ortoleva's critique that rhetorical ecologies tend to dematerialize discussions of ecology. Ortoleva makes a distinction between those working with rhetorical ecologies (Cooper; Dyehouse et al.; Edbauer; Syverson), and those engaged with environmental rhetoric (Killingsworth and Palmer; Stevens). The former are primarily concerned with process, looking at issues of interconnectedness and writing environments. As such, Ortoleva argues they "adopt ecological concepts in very broad ways, often wholly metaphorical" (68). The latter, those working with environmental rhetoric, suggest that composition and rhetoric is a "prime location to begin to address the exigency of environmental degradation" (68). As such, they are concerned more with content, that is, they want rhetoric and composition to focus specifically on environmental issues.

In an attempt to straddle this form/content divide embedded in rhetorical ecologies and environmental rhetoric respectively, Sid Dobrin and Christian Weisser offer the concept of ecocomposition, which they define as "the study of the relationships between environments (and by that we mean natural, constructed, and even imagined places) and discourse (speaking, writing, thinking)" (*Natural* 6). They suggest the biosphere (the physical environment) and the semiosphere (symbolic action) ("Breaking" 574) as co-constituted. While Ortolova suggests this bifurcation can at times cause remove from material ecological concerns, I find the distinction between the biosphere and the semiosphere to be useful in considering how our lived experience shapes our habitation of design. In engaging these authors, Ríos purposefully moves away from the term "ecology" to " 'land' to shift the ontological presuppositions inherent in the term 'ecology'. . . . As such, land-based literacies are literal acts of interpretation and communication that grow out of active participation with the land" (64). That is, our *active* participation with the land, that is our movement through the biosphere, is always already part of the semiosphere.

For Ríos, this move, from an ecological metaphor to the materiality of land brings relationality to the fore, a key tenant in indigenous epistemology. By thinking through how our actual lived experiences in and on the land are co-constituted with our lived experiences of all things, including our experiences navigating and reading a website such as *The Ways*, we come to see how digital writing and rhetoric are always already part of our ecology and vice versa.

Relations | Rhetoric | Land

Ríos argues that a land-based literacy is rooted in notions of indigenous relationality, one that "recognizes that humans and the environment are in a relationship that is co-constituted . . . [and] recognizes that environment's capacity to *produce* relations" (64). American Indian notions of relationality can help unpack this concept and further suggest how a land-based literacy offers an approach to understanding the design of digital spaces. In *The Common Pot: The Recovery of Native Space in the Northeast*, Lisa Brooks encourages an approach to land similar to that of Ríos. Brooks says,

> What I am talking about here is not an abstraction, a theorizing about a conceptual category called "land" or "nature," but a physical, actual, material relationship to 'an ecosystem present in a definable place' that has been cultivated throughout my short

life, and for much longer by those relations who came before me which, for better or worse, deeply informs my work. (xxiv)

Andrea Riley-Mukavetz and Malea Powell rely on Brooks' definition of land and relations in their description of indigenous rhetorical practices. For Riley-Mukavetz and Powell, indigenous rhetorical practice includes a

four-part layered web that situates the body in a particular place across historical time, rooted in cultural practices that arise from—and are responsible to—a land base. This orientation to that set of relations, and the responsibilities that arise from maintaining "right" relations, then forms the ambiguous boundaries of something we call *indigenous rhetorical practices*. (141)

This notion of relationality is found in the everyday lived practices of traditional American Indians. As American Indian philosopher Viola Cordova describes,

I suppose one could use the analogy of a stone thrown into a pond. Each "thing"— stone, air, molecule, plant, animal, or vegetable—causes a ripple to form in the pond. The singular, particular being is not merely itself tossed into the pond. (230)

In Western thought, the analogy of a stone thrown into the pond is usually used to indicate how our individual actions have impacts beyond what we might originally intend. However, as Cordova describes it, the rock is never solitary. Broadly speaking, in American Indian thought the ripple is just one piece of the overall picture and the overall cause. It is the stone thrown, the air through which the stone travels, the person throwing the stone and where and how she's standing, it is all of these things and more. It is all of these relations.

Cordova suggests that for American Indian thought, knowledge is intimately knowing and understanding our relatedness to the world around, in, and through us. She suggests that while humans may imagine our skin closes us off the world, it is actually very permeable.

Our senses connect us to the world. We have a broad range of emotional reactions; these, too, connect us to the world. And we have memory. . . . Knowledge, in a Native American sense, is derived from the connections we make between all of the facets of our sensate experience and the memory of the consequences attendant upon all of those experiences. (231)

Knowledge is the relations between our sensate experience, our memory, all of which are inextricable from the land upon which we have these experiences. Yet the concepts of land and experience are not fixed. Vine Deloria, Jr. also describes relationality (specifically for the Sioux people) as the idea that "everything in the natural world has relationships with every other thing and the total set of relationships that make up the world as we experience it" (34). One of these key relationships is our connection to place. Deloria elaborates,

Indians do not talk about nature as some kind of concept or something "out there." They talk about the immediate environment in which they live. They do not embrace all trees or love all rivers and mountains. What is important is the relationship you have with a particular tree or a particular mountain. (223)

These particularities occur in relation.

Rìos' proposal for land-based literacies acknowledges "literal *acts* of interpretation and communication that grow out of active participation with the land" (64) and necessarily includes a relationality, one that can't disentangle the biosphere from the semiosphere, but instead acknowledges that particular moments and relations bring forth particular ways of being and particular ways of making meaning in the world. Our ways of understanding the world are profoundly shaped by our active participation with the land, and as such I suggest our ways of understanding design are shaped similarly.

Bodies | Design | Rhetoric | Land

The connection between design's effects and lived bodies is nothing particularly new, at least in design theory. Color theory relies on cognitive experiences and culturally specific understandings to make sense of how color impacts particular bodies in particular contexts. Rudolf Arnheim explores the concept of a center, arguing that "just as almost every organic and inorganic subject is shaped around a center, centricity is an indispensable structural property of any composition in the visual arts" (x). How our bodies feel, see, and experience centricity shapes our production and sensate experience of design. Designer Molly Bang makes the case that our body's experience with gravity plays a huge role in how we feel about design. For example, horizontal shapes give us a sense of stability and calm, whereas vertical shapes often feel more exciting and active. Our body's experience with pain and comfort also impacts how we understand design, whereas a round shape feels safer and calmer than a pointed shape which can often feel violent or threatening.

Connected to, but going a bit beyond, discussions of graphic design itself, Klemmer, Hartmann, and Takayama explore interaction design based on the idea that bodies intimately shape how users interact in online space. They suggest that users think through doing, and these ways of doing in the world (particularly physical action), as well as the physical co-presence of artifacts and bodies, should shape how designers understand human–computer interactions. They call for a theory of "embodied interaction," for as they argue "in designing almost any new technology, one is drawing on existing human understanding of the world" (7). They don't argue for "unreflectively replacing" the physical world through digital design, but instead finding solutions to design that "carefully integrates the physical and digital worlds" (8).

Klemmer, Hartmann, and Takayama's work is rich, and one that places bodies in the world as key in understanding how users make sense of digital space. What is missing, however, from this discussion is any conversation of the space and place within which these bodies act. That is, there is not so much a sense of bodies in a biosphere as there is bodies interacting with physical objects in a somewhat undefined space. For example, the authors engage with the Montessori method of teaching through bodily engagement with physical objects, but there is no discussion of the space within which such engagements happen. Nor is there any discussion in this work, or in that of Arnheim or Bang, of the land itself and how our physical interaction in specific places and spaces differs from our physical interaction in other particular places and spaces. Thinking back to Deloria, there is a relationship one cultivates with a particular tree, or landscape, in a particular time in a particular place. It's not just the user and the tree, it's *this* tree in *this* place. Think back to Riley-Mukavetz and Powell's claim that indigenous rhetorical practice "situates the body in a particular place across historical time, rooted in cultural practices that arise from—and are responsible to—a land base" (141).

I propose using a land-based rhetorics as a way of understanding how our experiences in digital spaces are shaped by our embodied interactions in the biosphere itself. In order to consider how one might explore design through this lens, I offer here three criteria for rhetorically engaging with digital design that I use in the next section to analyze *The Ways*.

- First, a land-based digital design rhetoric acknowledges how understanding comes from "active participation with the land." (Rios)
- Second, a land-based digital design rhetoric acknowledges the relationships we have with particular elements in the biosphere. (Deloria)
- Third, a land-based digital design rhetoric acknowledges our sensate experience and our memories of those experiences. (Cordova)

Embodied Design | Rhetorical Land

While I encountered *The Ways* through a suggestion from my mother, and while I experienced it as a space of digital storytelling that works to sustain and share Anishinaabe culture in the Great Lakes, the site was actually created as a very specific educational resource:

> *The Ways* is an ongoing series of stories from Native communities around the central Great Lakes. This online educational resources for 6–12 grade students features videos, interactive maps, and digital media exploring contemporary Native culture and language. *The Ways* supports educators in meeting the requirements of Wisconsin Act 31, seeking to expand and challenge current understanding of Native identity and communities. (http://theways.org/about)

Undoubtedly the site serves many purposes, and the money to make the site was likely garnered through meeting the requirements of Wisconsin Act 31 (which specifically charges educators to teach about American Indian treaty rights). That being said, the digital space is public and as such the audience is broader than public school students.

The site itself includes four main links—Stories, Map, About, Contact—but the largest component of the site itself is the Stories page (see Figure 19.2). This page includes twelve links

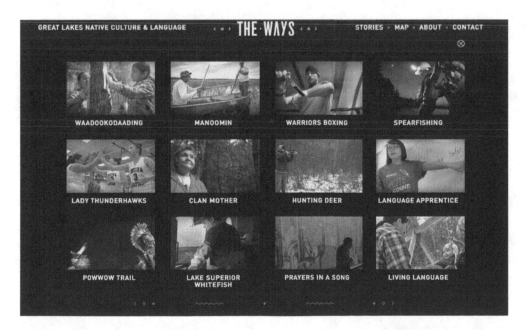

Figure 19.2 Stories Page from *The Ways*

to different topics, ranging from dancing on the pow-wow trail to language preservation initiatives to traditional food gathering practices. If you click on a story, you are brought to a page that includes two parts. Above the fold is a video (see Figure 19.3), and below the fold (Figure 19.4) is an essay that is part video transcript, part additional information. There is also a sidebar that includes links to sharing the story on social media, a map that indicates where the speaker is from, a section that offers questions for learning, below which is another section that offers resources for further learning (Figure 19.5). Finally, the bottom of the page (Figure 19.6) includes credits and also reveals the bottom of the slightly transparent background image that sits behind the below-the-fold content. This background image changes with each story and is related to the story itself. For example, the Manoomin story has a faint background image of a wild rice field.

Each story on the site is arranged in the same way. The above-the-fold content (Figure 19.3) includes a very large still image from the video itself contrasted sharply against a black background. *The Ways* logo (Figure 19.7) and navigation system sits atop the page itself, and is a rustic simple font that appears white on black, however at times has rollover functionality that turns the typeface a deep sea blue. There are small embellishments throughout the site, usually next to the log or the navigation system. These small symbols (Figures 19.7 and 19.8) are reminiscent of the petroglyphs found throughout the Great Lakes region. The logo is almost always white on black, except for the front page (Figure 19.8) where the background is a patterned wood grain.

The videos themselves are beautifully crafted, and I can't extract their effect from my embodied reaction to this website. However, what strikes me most about this site is the impact the videos, along with the essays and maps and additional content, have on me. It is an impact that I do not feel when I encounter these videos on YouTube. Figure 19.9 shows the same video essay from above, "Manoomin: Food that Grows on the Water," embedded the YouTube platform.

Figure 19.3 Above-the-Fold Screenshot of Manoomin Page

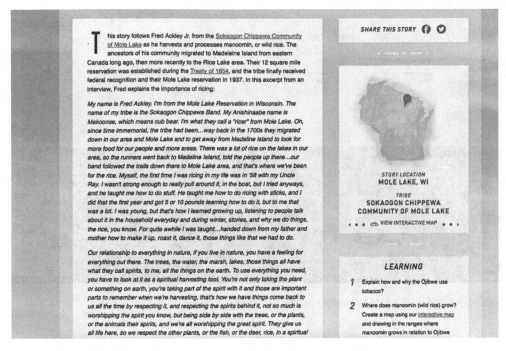

Figure 19.4 Below-the-Fold Screenshot of Manoomin Essay Part 1

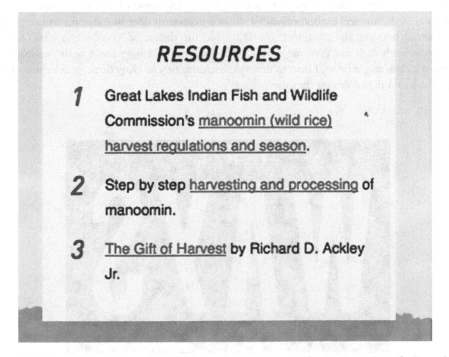

Figure 19.5 Below-the-Fold Screenshot of Manoomin Essay Part 2 (This Section Is Directly Beneath the Learning Section Seen in Figure 19.4)

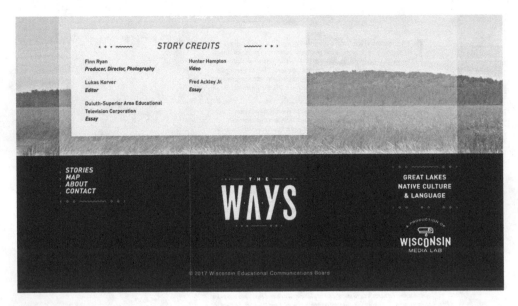

Figure 19.6 Below-the-Fold Screenshot of Manoomin Page, Credits

If I press play, I am still captivated by the beautifully shot video. However, the standardized platform of YouTube does not even remotely give me the sense of home and place that *The Ways* does. I do not feel embraced, and I do not necessarily feel like staying and exploring. The contrast between the design of *The Ways* and the design of YouTube is stark, and my experiences with each site give me a very different sense of engagement with the space. To explore why this might be so, I turn to three explorations of *The Ways* through my three criteria for a land-based digital design rhetoric.

Figure 19.7 The Ways Logo from Interior Pages

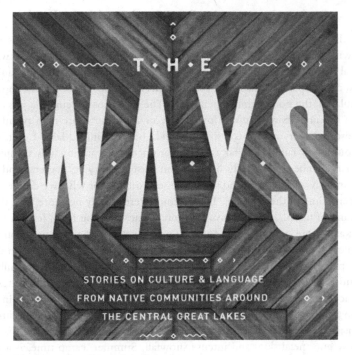

Figure 19.8 The Ways Logo from Front Page

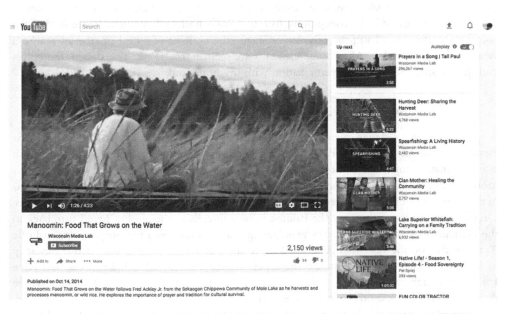

Figure 19.9 Manoomin Story from *The Ways* in YouTube, www.youtube.com/watch?v=uoBLE5I
MOHI

Exploration 1: Active Participation with the Land

A land-based digital design rhetoric acknowledges how understanding comes from "active participation with the land" (Rìos). Rìos speaks specifically about the literacy with the land, but for a digital design rhetoric, I move to explore how experiences with the land shape how we understand digital spaces, in this case, how I understand *The Ways*. I grew up in Michigan's Upper Peninsula, on the northernmost peninsula. The Keweenaw Peninsula juts out into Lake Superior like a thumb. Growing up on this land you are never more than twenty miles from the lake, and around every corner is a stream, creek, or small inland lake. I didn't grow up in a particularly outdoorsy family, insofar as we never once went purposefully camping or hiking so far as I can remember. My family did hunt and fish to varying degrees, and most of my family (in a Scandinavian tradition) had small lakeside cottages (or what we call "camps") where they would spend time in the summer. These camps were usually no more than thirty minutes from one's home in town, and were usually quite rustic with the focus less on the building's structure itself and more on being able to be near the water in the summer months.

Land, for me, is a mix of both my time at these camps (swimming, playing in the woods or on the beach, picking berries), and my time in town. In town, the land was hilly and full of maple trees and thick underbrush, as opposed to the eastern Lake Superior waterfront which is covered in jackpines, sandy soil, and the occasional outcropping of sandstone. In the autumn, the leaves turn a spectacular color and then almost always fall off all at once during an early autumn storm. Early winter is a season of grays and browns, and winter itself is a long harsh season with low gun metal skies and intense snowfall. Summer, camp time, is a short season, but full of brilliant greens and blues, the smell of water and crisp lakeside humidity. The inland lakes are often swampy and sweet, with reeds and grasses, herons and turtles, and a dull brown hue that blends with the treeline.

My active participation with this land, where I spent the first eighteen years of my life, profoundly shaped me. I am drawn to the color blue, particularly when it is set against duller grays and browns (the lake against the sandy shore or the winter skyline). I like the contrast of a strong image against a flat background (the tree-lined horizons). I feel at home in dull flat colors that offer a small surprise of color or shape (the contrast of a bird or tree up against a swampy flat inland lake). All of these elements are seen in *The Ways*. The design, the colors and shapes, speak to my active participation with my homeland.

Exploration 2: Relations with Biospheric Elements

A land-based digital design rhetoric acknowledges the relationships we have with particular elements in the biosphere (Deloria). As Deloria argues, and as Powell and Riley-Mukavetz also assert, "what is important is the relationship you have with a particular tree or a particular mountain" (223). There are many stories I can tell about my relations with particular elements in the biosphere—the Hawthorne tree behind my house in Washington, the tide pools in Yachets, Oregon, the soft green curves of the Palouse hillside in early summer—but here I turn back to the particulars of my childhood. My grandparents have a camp on a tiny strip of land in Little Traverse Bay on the eastern edge of the Keweenaw Peninsula. On one side of this tiny strip of land has is Lake Superior, and on the other, a slough fed by Mud Lake Creek and Rice Lake. The slough opens up behind my grandparent's camp, forming a small pond-like area where they put a small dock on the water's edge from which to fish or launch a rowboat. As a child, I spent endless hours at the slough's edge or on the burgundy colored red dock that my Grandfather dutifully repainted every few years. The water is grayish black, and is dotted with bright green lilypads and the occasional cluster of reeds. I was always on the lookout for painted turtles and the occasional beaver, and once even caught what seemed to me at the time a huge brook trout off the dock (turns out I was just small, as was the fish). This slough, this particular view of this slough in this place and time, is a very strong memory. I am seven years old, I am on summer vacation, I live in a navy blue swimsuit and bare feet, I am exploring nature and feeling wonder at the unexpected.

My particular relationship with this particular land is a strong one. I am drawn to any sharp pop of color (the burgundy dock, a bright green lilypad) against an otherwise still background (the grayish black water). I am delighted by any unexpected movement on an otherwise flat surface (a turtle's head popping out of the glassy flat water). The use of blue in the design of *The Ways* both as a point of contrast and as a rollover give me a similar sense of delight. The periodic use of both yellow and orange fonts provide a small, but sharp visual contrast that draws my attention. I could tell many other stories of specific places and elements in/on the land that have shaped my sense of design. All of these experience shape how I understand and experience design, and help me make sense of my love affair with *The Ways*.

Exploration 3: Sensate Experiences with the Land

Finally, a land-based digital design rhetoric acknowledges our sensate experience and our memories of those experiences (Cordova). As a reminder, Cordova argues that "Knowledge, in a Native American sense, is derived from the connections we make between all of the facets of our sensate experience and the memory of the consequences attendant upon all of those experiences" (231). The act of trying to articulate all facets of my sensate experience and memory is nearly an impossible one; however, I want to draw specifically from Cordova's attention to senses. While affect studies has had a substantial impact on rhetorical studies, Cordova's description of sensate experience and memory is rooted in an indigenous epistemology. In her discussion of relationality, that is, all things being in relation, she makes clear that these relations are felt through the senses:

> We might believe that our skin closes us off from the rest of the world, but it is in actuality a very permeable surface. Aside from absorbing the world through skin and lungs, we also see and hear and taste. Our senses connect us to the world. (230)

There is a trail behind by mom's camp in Big Traverse Bay (a Bay north of Little Traverse, where my Grandparent's camp sits). It serves as both a deer trail—one can often see deer taking this trail as the easiest path through the jack pine forest—and as a way for neighbors to walk between camps without walking the beach or dusty dirt road. I don't know who started the trail, probably the deer, but it is a well-worn and frequently used path. As a child I would often play on the stretch that went between our lot and the vacant lot next door. The vegetation is a sandy underbrush of blueberry bushes, ferns, and various mosses. Walking barefoot on this path, you can feel both the hard sandy earth below and the occasional prick of a pine needle. The ferns brush up against your legs as you walk, and the ants sometimes hitch along your leg for a ride. The smell is of water, pine, sand, and swamp. There are lessons to be learned about walking off the path (an accidental step in dog or deer poop, an attack of too many biting ants, a very sad squooshing of blueberries). The horizon in all directions is nearly impossible to see except for a few breaks of trees, but even without the perspective of distance it is clear that the land is flat. Any minor swell of land is noticeable, and usually exists only because a tree uprooted or someone dumped a random load of gravel behind their camp. The land is stable, steady.

If I close my eyes, I can feel this ground beneath my feet. I can smell the air, sense the land, I know I am home.

While design theorists such as Arnheim and Bang acknowledge how our bodily sense of space shapes our sense of design, there is not necessarily a sense of a specific body in a specific place having specific relations with that space. These relations are individualized to a point, for example my walking barefoot on a trail in the hopes of picking a cup of blueberries. But these relations are also culturally situated, for example my families' Finnish and Ojibwe roots and these relations to, for example, blueberries. There are also specific memories of these spaces, for example my grandmother's stories of running into black bears while blueberry picking (which is why she, and now I, always sing while picking).

The trail behind my mom's camp is a flat surface amidst an otherwise prickly forest bed. Walking on it one feels stable, secure, centered amidst the otherwise uncertain landscape. *The Ways* uses a center alignment for its text. Headers are evenly spaced, center aligned, providing a sense of balance atop the strong pictorial images of the video itself. The content below-the-fold floats above the faint background image, providing a sense of movement atop a stable landscape. My memories of walking on the trail along with my sensate experiences shape how I have come to know and sense the world. They shape how I see and feel design.

Conclusion

Imagining how my body has been part of, shaped, and shaped by the land I grew up on and putting these memories in relation to a digital design that I love has not been easy for me. Much of this essay was spent contemplating my relations with land, reflecting on how and whether these experiences have anything to do with my reaction to *The Ways*. But how can't they not? How can we bracket our lived experiences with the land from our rhetorical engagement with design, or with any text for that matter? Land is not a metaphor, it is a living thing that our rhetoric, digital or otherwise, exists on, with, and through. As Ríos' work reminds us, our *active* participation with the land, that is our movement through the biosphere, is always already part of the semiosphere. We are all bodies living on a land base.

As we continue to revise and revisit our rhetorical theories for producing and analyzing texts in digital spaces, it is important to think through how the seemingly landless place of cyberspace is always already part of the land. We bring our bodies and our lands with us online. We all bring our unique experiences and understandings and relations of and with land to all of our communication acts. Our theories of digital design should work to pay attention to these relations. Miigwech.

Works Cited

Allen, Nancy J., Ed. *Working with Words and Images: New Steps in an Old Dance.* Ablex, 2002.

Arnheim, Rudolf. *The Power of the Center: A Study of Composition in the Visual Arts.* U of California P, 1982.

Bang, Molly. *Picture This: Perception and Composition.* SeaStar, 2000.

Berger, John. *Ways of Seeing.* Penguin, 1972.

Brooks, Lisa Tanya. *The Common Pot: The Recovery of Native Space in the Northeast.* U of Minnesota P, 2008.

Cooper, Marilyn M. "The Ecology of Writing." *College English*, vol. 48, no. 4, 1986, pp. 364–75.

Cordova, Viola F. *How It Is: The Native American Philosophy of VF Cordova*, edited by Kathleen Dean Moore, et al. U of Arizona P, 2007.

Deloria, Vine, Jr. *Spirit and Reason.* Fulcrum, 1999.

Dobrin, Sidney I., and Christian R. Weisser. "Breaking Ground in Ecocomposition: Exploring the Relationships Between Discourse and Environment." *College English*, vol. 64, no. 5, 2002, pp. 566–89.

———. *Natural Discourse: Toward Ecocomposition*. SUNY Press, 2002.

Dyehouse, Jeremiah, Michael Pennell, and Linda K. Shaman. "'Writing in Electronic Environments': A Concept and a Course for the Writing and Rhetoric Major." *College Composition and Communication*, vol. 61, no. 2, 2009, pp. 330–50.

Edbauer, Jenny. "Unfreezing Models of Public Distribution: From Rhetorical Situation to Rhetorical Ecologies." *Rhetoric Society Quarterly*, vol. 35, no. 4, 2005, pp. 5–24.

George, Diana. "From Analysis to Design: Visual Communication in the Teaching of Writing." *College Composition and Communication*, vol. 54, no. 1, 2002, pp. 11–39.

Handa, Carolyn, Ed. *Visual Rhetoric in a Digital World: A Critical Sourcebook*. Bedford St. Martin's, 2004.

Hill, Charles A., and Marguerite Helmers, Eds. *Designing Visual Rhetoric*. Lawrence Erlbaum, 2004.

Hocks, Mary E. "Visual Rhetoric in Digital Environments." *College Composition and Communication*, vol. 54, no. 4, June 2003, pp. 629–56.

———. "Teaching and Learning Visual Rhetoric." *Teaching Writing with Computers: An Introduction*, edited by Pamela Takayoshi and Brian Huot. Houghton Mifflin, 2003, pp. 202–16.

Hocks, Mary E, and Michelle Kendrick, Eds. *Eloquent Images: Word and Image in the Age of New Media*. MIT Press, 2003.

Klemmer, Scott, Bjorn Hartmann, and Leila Takayama. "How Bodies Matter: Five Themes for Interaction Design." *Proceedings of the 6th Conference on Designing Interactive Systems*, 2006, pp. 140–9, dl.acm.org/citation.cfm?id=2442114. Accessed 30 Dec. 2016.

Killingsworth, Jimmie M., and Jacqueline S. Palmer. *Ecospeak: Rhetoric and Environmental Politics in America*. Southern Illinois UP, 1992.

New London Group. "A Pedagogy of Multiliteracies: Designing Social Futures." *Harvard Educational Review*, vol. 66, no. 1, 1996, pp. 60–93.

Ortoleva, Matthew. "Let's Not Forget Ecological Literacy." *Literacy in Composition Studies*, vol. 1, no. 2, 2013, pp. 66–73.

Riley-Mukavetz, Andrea, and Malea Powell. "Making Native Space for Graduate Students: a Story of Indigenous Rhetorical Practice." *Survivance, Sovereignty, and Story: Teaching Indigenous Rhetorics*, edited by Rose Gubele, Joyce Rain Anderson, and Lisa King. Utah State UP, 2015, pp. 138–59.

Rios, Gabriela Raquel. "Cultivating Land-Based Literacies and Rhetorics." *Literacy in Composition Studies*, vol. 3, no. 1, 2015, pp. 60–70.

Selfe, Cynthia L. "Lest We Think the Revolution is a Revolution: Images of Technology and the Nature of Change." *Passions, Pedagogies, and 21st Century Technologies*, edited by Gail E. Hawisher, and Cynthia L. Selfe. Utah State UP, 1999, pp. 292–322.

Shipka, Jody. *Towards a Composition Made Whole*. U of Pittsburgh P, 2011.

Sorapure, Madeleine. "Five Principles of New Media: Or, Playing Lev Manovich." *Kairos: A Journal of Rhetoric, Technology, and Pedagogy*, 8.2, Fall 2003/Spring 2004, english.ttu.edu/kairos/8.2/binder2.html?coverweb/sorapure/index.htm. Accessed 30 May 2017.

Stevens, Sharon McKenzie. *A Place for Dialogue: Language, Land Use, and Politics in Southern Arizona*. U of Iowa P, 2007.

Syverson, Margaret A. *The Wealth of Reality: An Ecology of Composition*. Southern Illinois UP, 1999.

The Ways: Stories on Culture and Language from Native Communities Around the Central Great Lakes. www.theways.org. Accesssed 1 March 2017.

Williams, Robin. *The Non-Designers Design Book*. Peachpit, 1994.

Wysocki, Anne Frances. "Monitoring Order: Visual Desire, the Organization of Web Pages, and Teaching the Rules of Design." *Kairos: A Journal of Rhetoric, Technology, and Pedagogy*, 3.2, 1998. www.hu.mtu.edu/~awysocki/mOrder/mOrder.html. Accessed 25 May 2017.

———. "Impossibly Distinct: On Form/Content and Word/Image in Two Pieces of Computer-Based Interactive Multimedia." *Computers and Composition*, vol. 18, no. 2, 2001, pp. 137–62.

———. "Into Between: On Composition in Mediation." *Composing (Media) = Composing (Embodiment)*, edited by Kristin L. Arola, and Anne Frances Wysocki. Utah State UP, 2012, pp. 1–22.

Wysocki, Anne Frances, and Julia I. Jasken. "What Should Be an Unforgettable Face . . ." *Computers and Composition*, vol. 21, no. 1, 2004, pp. 29–48.

20

TECHNOFEMINIST STORIOGRAPHIES

Talking Back to Gendered Rhetorics of Technology

Kristine L. Blair

In October 2014, Microsoft CEO Satya Nadella drew controversy for comments about the gender gap in Silicon Valley salaries ("Microsoft CEO"), discouraging women from self-advocacy for higher pay and instead indicating that "good karma" would result for avoiding what Facebook Chief Operating Officer Sheryl Sandberg (*Lean In*) asserts is an unfair cultural stereotype of the aggressive female employee. These systemically sexist assumptions about women are reinforced by even more recent examples, including Microsoft's use of female models costumed as Catholic schoolgirls to entertain primarily male attendees at the 2016 Game Developer's Conference (Soper).

As Janet Abbate contends in *Recoding Gender*, computer science as a field remains male dominated despite women's historical role in computing (1–2), lacking sustained opportunities for women to enhance technological aptitude and attitude and to disrupt and transform misogynist rhetorics, including the examples above. Unfortunately, such scenarios have typified the culture of the IT industry, which has obscured the documented role of women in shaping the history of technology innovation. Abbate's research aligns with studies by the American Association of University Women (*Tech-Savvy, Why So Few?*) advocating for more female mentors in technological arenas to positively impact women's and girls' educational and professional advancement across disciplines. These studies also have resonance for digital rhetoric and writing specialists, including Selfe and Hawisher (*Literate Lives*), Sheridan (*Girls*), Blair et al., and those concerned about equitable access for women and other cultural groups to technological literacy and the technofeminist emphasis on "incorporating the lessons of history into an activist feminist politics which is adequate for addressing women's issues in technological culture" (Wilding 9). Despite interdisciplinary feminist efforts to create spaces for activism both online and off, women continue to be positioned as subordinate to their male counterparts in STEM arenas. Both cultural, circulatory rhetorics and material, economic realities reflect and reinforce this presumption. Thus, similar to the longstanding call by Hawisher and Selfe that we question the underlying "rhetorics of technology" (56) that impact the relationship between computers and literacy, this chapter questions: (1) how rhetorics of technological innovation are gendered and have historically constrained women and girls' access to computer technology and resulting STEM careers (2) how technofeminist activists and scholars have developed counter-rhetorics to challenge the limiting assumptions about women's techno-literate lives.

To address these questions, I trace larger cultural representations of women's relationship to technology, relying on the multigenred media artifacts that drive the consumption and production of these representations. Technofeminist researchers, most notably Judy Wajcman, frequently interrogate how and why women rely upon technology in their daily lives, and what material and cultural contexts enable and constrain that reliance (*Technofeminism*). This interrogation helps provide more consistent opportunity for women to share their lived experiences and to have those diverse stories represented across media genres. Equally important, a large component of technofeminist work across the disciplines has relied upon narrative as a methodology for generating knowledge about how and why women use and are used by a range of technologies within the larger culture in a process similar to the longstanding emphasis in the field of computers and writing on technological literacy narratives (Selfe and Hawisher, *Literate Lives*). Wajcman further contends that rather than returning to the either/or rhetorics of technological liberation or technological oppression, "presenting a diversity of narratives . . . enables us to transcend once and for all the traditional dichotomy of technology as either empowering or disempowering for women" ("Foreword" 8). Such a perspective is parallel to the early concerns in computers and writing studies about those rhetorics of technology that were overly utopic in their promise that technology would empower cultural groups marginalized in real time by inequitable systems of difference in access.

By interrogating a range of historical and contemporary depictions of gender and technology, I demonstrate the ways a technofeminist framework can recover women's technological histories and use those storiographies to re-write and speak back to those larger circulatory rhetorics that oppress women. This framework aligns with historical work in computers and writing studies, including Selfe and Selfe's argument that citizens and educators move from being technology users to technology critics (496) and Stuart Selber's articulation of a multiliterate continuum for understanding computer literacy as not merely functional but critical and rhetorical as well, all working recursively "in the service of social action and change" (xii).

Given the ways historical and modern texts and contexts have the potential to shape women's knowledge and dispositions regarding technology and its role in their literate lives, and given the ways writing studies scholars attend to other modalities beyond the alphabetic, it is vital that we turn our attention toward the continued multimodal circulation of cultural myths and stereotypes that negatively impact women and girls' opportunities to develop technological literacies. This process mandates activist initiatives from the local to the global, initiatives that those who identify as technofeminist rhetoricians can and should embrace. To document this activism, I include a series of examples, from online campaigns by women working in IT to girls' computer camps developed by computers and writing specialists, that highlight recursive relationships between feminism and digital rhetoric. Such relationships inevitably counter the gendered narratives of technology that continue to disenfranchise women culturally, professionally, and as Nadella's damaging comments suggest, economically.

Recovering Women in the (His)Story of Science and Technology

During the winter 2015 film awards season, among the consistent nominees for best film were *The Theory of Everything* and *The Imitation Game*. *The Theory of Everything* is the dramatization of renowned physicist Stephen Hawking's early life and his diagnosis with motor neuron disease. The screenplay was adapted from his ex-wife Jane Wilde's 2007 memoir *Travelling to Infinity:*

My Life with Stephen, one of several books Wilde has written to ensure, as she has noted (Burrell), her role in Hawking's scientific legacy. Regardless of the film's acknowledgment of Wilde's considerable challenges in caring for an increasingly disabled adult and three children while trying to write a graduate thesis, the story becomes Hawking's, with Eddie Redmayne taking British and American best actor honors for his portrayal of scientific innovation over debilitating physical adversity. *The Imitation Game* represents the struggles, both professional and personal, of the Second World War Bletchley Park codebreaker, computer science, and artificial intelligence innovator Alan J. Turing (1912–1954). Given Hawking's decades-long struggle with amyotrophic lateral sclerosis (ALS), and Turing's conviction, court sanctioned hormonal treatment, purported suicide, and eventual 2013 royal pardon for what were in 1950s Britain illegal acts of homosexuality, their respective professional and personal dramatizations in film and print are undoubtedly worthy of these twenty-first-century accolades.

Because we inhabit a world of digitally mediated, human-machine cyborg identities that drive our individual habits of mind, work, and play, it is perhaps fitting we give tribute to and acknowledge the struggles of these scientific and technological pioneers, something Walter Isaacson asserts in *The Innovators: How a Group of Hackers, Geniuses, and Geeks Created the Digital Revolution*. But although Isaacson includes a discussion of nineteenth-century computer visionary Ada Lovelace (1815–1852), whose collaboration with mathematician and inventor Charles Babbage (1791–1871) led to what many consider the first computer algorithm (Essinger), Isaacson has admitted that until very recently, he did not know who Lovelace was, only learning of her contributions from a paper written by his teenage daughter (Watters). As Audrey Watters concludes in "Men (Still) Explain Technology to Me: Gender and Education Technology":

> even a book that purports to reintroduce the contributions of those forgotten "innovators," that says it wants to complicate the story of a few male inventors of technology by looking at collaborators and groups, still in the end tells a story that ignores if not undermines women. Men explain the history of computing, if you will.

Throughout the history of information technology, the stories of innovation that typically make it to the printed page or the big screen are inherently male. Women, from Hawking's wife Jane Wilde to Bletchley Park's Joan Clarke (1917–1996), Alan Turing's intellectual-equal but professional subordinate, are portrayed as helpers, historical handmaidens in service of a male-identified scientific frontier. It would be comforting to believe that these media rhetorics represent a particular historical moment in Western culture when women's roles were inevitably subservient to men across professions, an era that is presumably long behind us.

Despite Abbate's substantial historical evidence that women mathematicians played a formative role in the development of the information technology industry and the rise of computer science as an academic discipline, their technological contributions are often less valued or even acknowledged. All too often, when women challenge the cultural conditions that reinscribe traditional gender roles in information technology careers and elsewhere, there is severe backlash. For instance, feminists have consistently critiqued the gaming industry for misogynist representations of and resulting violence against women with the advent of #gamergate. Lauren Williams describes #gamergate as a "small subset of the gaming community that have harassed female media critics, developers and bloggers with violent and graphic death and rape threats," most notably video game developers Zoe Quinn and Brianna Wu, and feminist media critic Anita Sarkissian. And despite the shifting statistics that indicate that women's participation in gaming environments almost equals their male counterparts by a percentage of 44 percent female and 56 percent male in 2015 (Statista), women's narratives of those experiences in these and other technological spaces are, as a result of such violence, diminished and potentially silenced, left unheard and invisible.

Regardless of the rich, complex stories and histories women have with regard to technology—as programmers and inventors, and as students and citizens—cultural artifacts from film, television, games, toys, and children's books frequently represent those stories and histories inadequately and inaccurately, reinscribing a techno power-knowledge dynamic that has continued to limited women and girls' education and ultimate participation in technological arenas, as the recent phenomenon of #gamergate attests. Yet technological empowerment is not only a feminist issue but also an economic one, requiring that women be supported within those academic disciplines, including computers and writing studies, and career fields governing the technological labor force, and thus able to contribute to present and future innovation. This support can in turn sustain a documented historiography of women's technological achievements in which their stories are heard for generations to come, rather than be forgotten and unknown, as even Isaacson conceded in his discussion of Ada Lovelace.

Women, Technology, and Cultural Representation

It is important for technofeminists to interrogate the consequences of not portraying women's stories on their continued participation in an ever-increasing technological labor force. The cultural assumptions about gender and technology circulate widely and early amid the visually and semiotically gendered pink aisle in toystores and bookstores. Certainly, there exist attempts by the toy industry to orient girls to technology, including children's books such as the 2010 *Barbie: I Can Be a Computer Engineer* (Marenco), which portrays the ageless blond as possessing the creative initiative to design a game to teach children how computers function, but ultimately in need of male assistance to both implement the design and remove a virus from her own and sister Skipper's computer. On Amazon.com the book was originally bundled with *Barbie: I Can Be an Actress*, visually and semiotically highlighting the contrast between a bespectacled computer geek Barbie and a tiara-wearing actress Barbie, both naturally clad in pink. The public outrage from both women and men against this longstanding technological narrative of male dominance led not only to backlash from women within and beyond the IT industry but also to a number of counter-narratives from sites such as Feminist Hacker Barbie, a space in which users can rewrite text to accompany the original visual narrative. The book was ultimately discontinued by Mattel/Random House.

That the original Barbie engineer book was written by a woman is perhaps the greatest indicator that our assumptions about women's proficiency with technology has become a mythology of the larger culture that "goes without saying" (Barthes and Lavers 11). This rhetoric is far stronger than any reality of today's women working in technology and the larger contemporary history of women who shaped it, such as Rear Admiral Grace Murray Hopper. Hopper (1906–1992), one of the first computer programmers on Harvard's Mark I computer, received the first Computer Science "Man" of the Year Award in 1969 among her many awards and countless honorary degrees. Despite accolades that include the Grace Hopper Celebration of Computing, the christening of the *USS Hopper*, and the recent renaming of a legacy building at Yale in her honor, in a recent documentary on Hopper, *The Queen of Code*, women information technology professionals lamented that "All we talk about is Steve Jobs and Bill Gates," leaving women and girls fewer roles models and "little historical knowledge of women's contributions in the early days" (Jacobs). As Megan Smith, former Chief Technology Officer of the United States contends in the documentary, "Grace Hopper is like an Edison but she's absent from the history books." Yet a 2015 National Public Radio story on Grace Hopper's career notes biographer Kathleen Broome Williams' contention that Hopper would have hated the reference to herself as "The Queen of Code." Given the larger cultural assumptions that place even successful women into gendered roles of princesses and queens, the label seems inappropriate for a woman who instead referred to herself as a "pirate," and a person who didn't have to think much about feminism because she was "in the Navy" (NPR).

Although Hopper may have resisted her iconic status as a first among women in the history and advent of computing as a profession and an academic discipline, she was nevertheless concerned about the need for educating future generations, regardless of gender:

> You've got a get out there and help us train the youngsters. Teach them to go ahead and do it. Teach them to have courage. Teach them to use their intuition, to stick their necks out. You've got to move to the future. We're going to need all of them. (NPR)

Hopper did not identify publicly as a feminist, let alone as a technofeminist, but her call for technology education is aligned with the types of girls' technological literacy initiatives with computers and writing studies that I chronicle later in this chapter. Undoubtedly, the data about the dearth of women in STEM in both the academy and the professions are strong rationales for a technofeminist recovery of women's contributions, as well as a technofeminist analysis of how those contributions are disseminated in the larger culture. This recovery is inevitably similar to the types of recovery feminist rhetoricians such as Cheryl Glenn (*Rhetoric Retold*) and others have engaged in making visible the contributions of women to the history of rhetoric.

Hopper's technological history, along with those of her wartime women trailblazers on the digital computer ENIAC in the United States and its counterpart COLOSSUS in Great Britain; her predecessor Ada Lovelace (1815–52), considered to be the first computer programmer; and her mid-twentieth-century contemporary, actress Hedy Lamarr (1914–2000), co-developer of the frequency hopping technology during the Second World War, are all largely invisible from the big and small screen, compared to figures such as Steve Jobs. In an interview on *Charlie Rose* (Siede), Megan Smith contends that even though women were part of the original Apple Macintosh team, none of them were represented with speaking roles in the 2013 version of Steve Jobs's technological journey, *Jobs*, starring the bankable heartthrob Ashton Kutcher. Such invisibility is due not only to gender but also to a cultural privileging of conceptions of individual genius and innovation over the more collaborative models that a technofeminist storiography can inevitably uncover to document women's important roles. This includes the work of Ada Lovelace and Charles Babbage in the nineteenth century to the team of women who programmed ENIAC in the twentieth century, and whose names, Fran Bilas (1922–2012), Betty Jennings Bartik (1924–2011), Ruth Lichterman (1924–1986), Kay McNulty (1921–2006), Betty Snyder (1917–2001), and Marlyn Wescoff (1922–2008), often go without mention.

Even with these triumphs, women leaders and innovators have been depicted as subordinate in history, on screen, and through various texts and artifacts that circulate that patriarchal ideology. Innovators such as Grace Hopper have been recognized and lauded, but her story fits into a history of information technology that is not only gendered but also raced and classed, especially when considering the contributions of women of color, whose numbers employed in the IT industry remain low. As Gail Sullivan reported in a 2014 *Washington Post* article on Google's diversity data in relation to larger Bureau of Labor Statistic percentages, only

> Four percent of employed software developers in the United States are African American, 5 percent are Hispanic and 29 percent are Asian . . . Comparatively, 1 percent of the Google's tech workforce is black, 2 percent is Hispanic and 34 percent is Asian.

Although Google's data are parallel to other Silicon Valley giants, it, along with Facebook and Yahoo, has been more forthcoming about its lack of improvement in the area of diversity (Hu).

Based on the limited number of women, particularly women of African American or Hispanic American descent, working in the United States IT industry in technical or designer roles, it is not surprising that those who do would potentially feel isolated and subject to less than hospitable work environments. The isolation and lack of advancement opportunity for women is a factor Facebook COO Sheryl Sandberg has written about extensively, though from a privileged race and classed position. Sandberg acknowledges the double-bind facing women, needing to be assertive but ultimately stigmatized as difficult and less of a "team player" for highlighting successes (44). Sandberg shares a range of stories to show the challenges and successes for women seeking leadership roles in the IT industry and beyond.

Of equal concern are reports of sexism, misogyny, and harassment, factors that in 2014 led to nine women in the tech industry to post a response at "About Feminism." Referred to as a "manifesto" (Doctorow), the site represents a powerful statement about why feminism represents a necessary form of political action for women working in IT to counter what they see as the lackluster efforts by Google and others to more diverse hiring and retention practices:

> We have watched companies say that diversity is of highest importance and have invited us to advise them. After we donate much of our time they change nothing, do nothing, and now wear speaking to us as a badge of honor. Stating, "We tried!" We've grown cynical of companies creating corporate programs and paying lip service to focusing on women's issues in the tech industry without understanding the underlying reality.

The word "manifesto" is significant, for in the Marxist sense, the nine authors of "About Feminism" want to do more than critique. Instead, they want to encourage transformation through involvement and volunteerism in organizations that educate and prepare women and girls, especially minorities, for careers in the tech industry and to understand that the emphasis on women in IT is not just an emphasis on gender:

> While this letter speaks specifically about our experiences as women in tech, to build true diversity in tech we must address more than one aspect of gender, more than any one aspect of our identities. Our efforts must address, and be inclusive of, race, class, sexuality, gender identity and expression, and their intersections.

Similar responses are equally if not more radically activist in their call to action. In "Screw Leaning In. It's Time to Slam the Door in Silicon Valley's Face," Jess Zimmerman reports on the site tableflipclub.com and its call to action for women working in IT. Several of its key tenets include:

> Women are leaving your tech company because you don't deserve to keep us around.

> Fuck that, we're done. It's not us, it's you.

> When we try to take a seat at the table like Sheryl said we should, we're called presumptuous.

> It's time we take our potential elsewhere.

With its own Twitter account, the group advocates not leaning in, but "pulling together."

The Barbie engineering book fiasco suggests there is a recursive relationship between the realities of women in the workforce in general, and the technological workforce in particular, and the rhetorical ways that labor is portrayed in cultural artifacts such as toys and games marketed to children. Certainly, there are attempts to foster more "creative" alternatives for girls, most recently in the form of initiatives such as Goldiblox, a series of engineering erector sets and other educational toys specifically created and marketed to girls and supported by organizations that include Girls Who Code, Black Girls Code, and the Society of Women Engineers. In a Goldiblox video marketing campaign that originally went viral, one video ("Original") shows three girls in front of a television, one African American, one Asian American, and one Caucasian, bored at the dolls and princesses they are encouraged to play with and emulate in dress and mannerisms. As the commercial voiceover chorus of young girls asserts, "you like to buy us pink toys, and everything else is for boys."

While the Goldiblox motto is "disrupting the pink aisle," even initiatives such as Goldiblox can reinforce cultural assumptions about race, gender, and technology, as the Goldiblox mascot is a Caucasian girl with long blond hair, and a number of their toys are as "pink-washed" as Mattel and Lego toys aimed at girls, including Barbie Computer Engineer (Miller). This suggests that the visual-rhetorical representation of the STEM workforce is as white as it is male, both gendered and raced, despite the diverse representation in the video campaign, and although supplemental characters in the product line include the African American Ruby Rails, a girl who codes apps and websites and sews clothes.

Thus even Goldiblox is simultaneously complicit with and resistant to a portrayal of women and girls' experiences with and contributions to technological innovation, a process that diminishes their role—past, present, and potentially future—in the larger cultural history of information technology. Based on these and many other examples beyond the scope of this chapter, technofeminist rhetoricians, both current and future, must analyze and critique how the mythos of technological innovation is marketed and packaged for youth consumption. With the limited change in statistics for women working in STEM and the continued male profile of the computer-scientist working in the IT industry, it is vital to look at the rhetorical circulation of technology narratives that empower men and boys and disenfranchise women and girls.

Technofeminist Back-Talk in Computers and Writing Studies

Speaking of his motives behind his 1972 book *Mythologies*, Roland Barthes famously stated:

> The starting point ... was usually a feeling of impatience at the sight of the "naturalness" with which newspapers, art and common sense constantly dress up a reality which, even though it is the one we live in, is undoubtedly determined by history. In short, in the account given of our contemporary circumstances, I resented seeing. ... History confused at every turn, and I wanted to track down, in the decorative display of *what-goes-without-saying*, the ideological abuse which, in my view, is hidden there. (11)

My technofeminist goal in this chapter has been to track down such "ideological abuse," to not just uncover but recover women's roles in the history of technology and to redress "what goes without saying" in ways that make visible the cultural and rhetorical processes of disseminating techno-rhetorical narratives that circulate in mass and new media. Our cultural assumptions about gender and technology continue to leave insufficient space for women and girls to become part of a larger rhetorical and material present and future. This is not an attempt to diminish the historical and contemporary contributions of men in the dynamic history of information technology. Rather, it is an attempt to make visible the mythos surrounding technology and in doing so help both women and men confront and potentially transform it.

In computers and writing studies, one response to the need for confrontation and transformation is through girl's technological literacy development, developed in the spirit of Hopper's original call and from communities such as "About Feminism." As an example of such technology education, from 2007 through 2011, I co-developed and directed The Digital Mirror Computer Camp for Girls, a four-day residential computer camp for middle-school adolescent girls, the very population the AAUW has identified as being vulnerable to cultural assumptions about who uses technology and how, including classroom contexts. Based on that connection, the camp was partially funded through a national AAUW Community Action Grant. The camp responded to these concerns by only relying on women facilitators, including graduate students in Bowling Green State University's doctoral program in Rhetoric and Writing, to help deliver curriculum in Web-based and social-media authoring, along with digital image, video, and audio editing. Our shared curricular goal was to move beyond the mere emphasis on functional literacy to instead foreground the critical and rhetorical aspect of digital literacy in providing opportunities for the 20–25 adolescents annually enrolled in the camp. This included time, through blogging and video production, to reflect on their reasons for using or not various digital media tools, and then to develop a portfolio of artifacts that allowed them to share these reflections (hence the mirror theme of the camp) in a showcase section with parents and family members on the camp's final day. These forums were more than celebratory; they also helped to show parents, often reluctant to have their daughters work in online spaces based on larger narratives about safety and privacy, that it was important to provide time and space for experimentation and play with digital identity formation and the important role of technology in girls' literate lives.

While the interest among parents was strong as I began to promote the camp in local schools and among faculty colleagues, I frequently received questions about why an English department faculty member was coordinating such an initiative, why not computer science faculty, for instance. The response was and is simple: writing has always been a technological process. Being literate in the twenty-first century requires an emphasis on a range of multimodal tools that represent the way students, workers, and citizens will and must communicate in not only functional but also critical and rhetorical ways. This makes the role of rhetoric, writing, and literacy specialists as vital to this activist, educational goal as computer scientist and mathematicians. Girls need the chance to use these tools to reflect on their sense of self and society, and to inevitably gain the power to speak back from within and outside that culture, as other examples from the chapter have shown to be both possible and necessary.

The collaborative efforts with the graduate student women with whom I was honored to work and who served as mentors to the girls themselves helped to model that technology wasn't just a "guy thing." The importance of mentoring also became evident over time, for although the Digital Mirror Camp ended in 2011 after five years, a number of the former graduate students went on to develop similar camps at their new institutions, including Jen Almjeld's Girlhood Revisited at New Mexico State University, Ruijie Zhao's Summer Computer Day Camp for Girls at Parkland Community College in Illinois, Stacy Kastner's Bulldog Bites/Digital Diva's at Mississippi State University, and Erin McLaughlin's MyMedia Academy at the University of Notre Dame. Based on the longstanding emphasis on community literacy and service learning within writing studies, these projects represent a form of technofeminist activism (Blair) that is an emerging sub-genre of civic engagement in the field. This results in scholarship that broadens our understanding of the material and cultural conditions that impact digital literacy acquisition both inside and outside the academy.

In addition to my own technology camp and those of my former students now making an impact on their own campuses and in the larger profession, scholars such as Mary Sheridan ("Knot-Working") and her colleagues and graduate students at the University of Louisville have engaged in similar technofeminist practices through their work on the Digital Media Academy. The camp, a two-week summer day camp for middle school girls, is designed to help girls to develop the "technological, critical, and design literacies they needed to create digital messages of their own choosing, thus encouraging girls to be critical producers, not just consumers, of digital media" (forthcoming). But as with the Digital Mirror Camp, Sheridan's Digital Media Academy was also designed both to help the camp participants "recognize the redesign the pervasive sexualized and commercialized images of what it means to be a girl today" (forthcoming) and to help the graduate students develop the civic, pedagogical, and technofeminist dispositions that inform activist pedagogies and speak back to the gendered rhetorics that constrain women and girls' technological aptitudes and attitudes.

Retelling the Story

Unlike Steve Jobs, the stories of Ada Lovelace, Hedy Lamarr, and Grace Hopper are largely unknown to the larger culture, all too infrequently produced, distributed, and consumed in the various type of media I've chronicled in this chapter. Their stories, and the stories of many other women, nonetheless represent significant technofeminist counter narratives that recover the realities of women's contributions to the rise of information technology. Their stories also challenge the perception that innovation is the result of individual male creative genius, and represent invisible collaborative models of support that have historically included women, including the Hawking and Turing examples that begin this chapter. Moreover, the history of technological innovation has indeed been a white history, leaving the contributions of women of color to the sidelines until very recently, as evidenced in the book and film versions of *Hidden Figures* and its portrayal of the overlapping contributions of Katherine Goble Johnson (1918), Mary Jackson (1921–2005), and Dorothy Vaughn (1910–2008) to the US space race while employed at NASA. In winter 2017, *Hidden Figures* was one of the Oscar nominees for best picture, a testament to the power of women's roles and the injustice of not making them better known to the larger public until the publication and film optioning of Margot Lee Shetterly's book.

As Steven Johnson articulates in *How We Got to Now: Six Innovations that Made the Modern World*, innovation is often all too connected to a single individual, the result of a spark of sudden creative genius as opposed to collaboration that evolves over time and history. It is this trajectory regarding information technology, and women's significant place in it and lived experience of it, that technofeminist rhetoricians must strive to make more visible as they critique rhetorics of tech-innovation in popular media genres. A technofeminist approach must recover history by aligning the historical and contemporary accounts of women innovators with the larger portrayals of their relationships to technology, a call to turn such *his-story* into *her-story*.

In her "Men (Still) Explain Technology to Me" article I reference earlier in this chapter, Audrey Watters repurposes Rebecca Solnit's original emphasis on "mansplaining" to chronicle her own experiences as a female educational technology specialist, ultimately concluding that

> The problem isn't just that men explain technology to me. It isn't just that a handful of men explain technology to the rest of us. It's that this explanation tends to foreclose questions we might have about the shape of things.

In response to this and similar calls, technofeminist rhetoricians must play an activist role in "reshaping" the cultural narrative of women and technology. This chapter has documented that such a role has educational, political, and socioeconomical consequences not just for women today but for our understanding of the past, present, and future of technological innovation and the gendered rhetorics that shape it.

Works Cited

Abbate, Janet. *Recoding Gender: Women's Changing Participation in Computing.* MIT Press, 2012.

"About Feminism." aboutfeminism.me. Accessed 5 July 2017.

American Association of University Women. *Tech-Savvy: Educating Girls In The New Computer Age.* AAUW Educational Foundation, 2000.

——. *Why So Few: Women In Science, Technology, Engineering, And Mathematics.* AAUW Educational Foundation, 2010.

Barthes, Roland, and Annette Lavers. *Mythologies.* Hill and Wang, 1972.

Blair, Kristine L. "A Complicated Geometry: Triangulating Feminism, Activism, and Technological Literacy." *Writing Studies Research in Practice: Methods and Methodologies,* edited by Lee Nickoson and Mary P. Sheridan. SIUP, 2012, pp. 63–72.

Blair, Kristine L., Radhika Gajjala, and Christine Tulley. *Webbing Cyberfeminist Practice: Community, Pedagogies, and Social Action.* Hampton, 2009.

Burrell, Ian. "Stephen Hawking's Wife Jane Wilde On Their Marriage Breakdown: "The Family Were Left Behind." *The Independent,* 27 May 2014, www.independent.co.uk/news/people/stephen-hawkings-wife-on-their-marriage-breakdown-the-family-were-left-behind-9949588.html. Accessed 5 July 2017.

Doctorow, Cory. "Feminism and Tech: An Overdue and Welcome Manifesto." *boingboing.com,* 27 May 2014, www.boingboing.net/2014/05/27/feminism-and-tech-an-overdue.html. Accessed 5 July 2017.

Essinger, James. *Ada's Algorithm: How Lord Byron's Daughter Ada Lovelace Launched the Digital Age.* Melville House, 2014.

"Feminist Hacker Barbie." computer-engineer-barbie.herokuapp.com. Accessed 5 July 2017.

Glenn, Cheryl. *Rhetoric Retold: Regendering the Tradition from Antiquity Through the Renaissance.* Southern Illinois UP, 1997.

Hawisher, Gail, and Cynthia Selfe. "The Rhetoric of Technology and the Electronic Writing Class." *College Composition and Communication,* vol. 42, no. 1, pp. 55–65.

Hu, Elise. "Facebook's Diversity Numbers Are Out, and They're What You Expect." National Public Radio, All Tech Considered, 26 June 2014, www.npr.org/blogs/alltechconsidered/2014/06/26/325798198/facebooks-diversity-numbers-are-out-and-theyre-what-you-expect/. Accessed 5 July 2017.

Isaacson, Walter. *The Innovators: How A Group of Inventors, Hackers, Geniuses, and Geeks Created the Digital Revolution.* Simon & Schuster, 2014.

Jacobs, Gillian. *The Queen of Code.* (Motion picture). Signals Series ESPN/FiveThirtyEight, 2015.

Johnson, Steven. *How We Got to Now: Six Innovations That Made the Modern World.* Riverhead Books/Penguin, 2014.

Marenco, Susan. *Barbie I can Be an Actress/Computer Engineer.* Random House, 2013.

"Microsoft CEO Satya Nadella: Women, Don't ask for a Raise." *The Guardian,* 9 Oct. 2014, www.theguardian.com/technology/2014/oct/10/microsoft-ceo-satya-nadella-women-dont-ask-for-a-raise/. Accessed 5 July 2017.

Miller, Claire Cain. "Ad Takes Off Online: Less Doll, More Awl." *New York Times,* 20 Nov. 2013, www.bits.blogs.nytimes.com/2013/11/20/a-viral-video-encourages-girls-to-become-engineers/?_r=0/. Accessed 5 July 2017.

NPR. "Grace Hopper, 'The Queen of Code,' Would Have Hated That Title." NPR, 7 March 2015, www.capeandislands.org/post/grace-hopper-queen-code-would-have-hated-title#stream/0/. Accessed 5 July 2017.

"Original Goldiblox Commercial." *YouTube,* 25 Apr. 2014, www.youtube.com/watch?v=M0NoOtaFrEs. Accessed 5 July 2017.

Sandberg, Sheryl, and Nell Scovell. *Lean In: Women, Work, And The Will To Lead.* Knopf, 2013.

Selber, Stuart. *Multiliteracies for A Digital Age.* Southern Illinois UP, 2004.

Selfe, Cynthia L., and Gail E. Hawisher. *Literate Lives in The Information Age: Narratives of Literacy From The United States.* Lawrence Erlbaum, 2004.

Selfe, Cynthia, and Richard Selfe. "The Politics of The Interface: Power and Its Exercise in Electronic Contact Zones." *College Composition and Communication*, vol. 45, no. 4, 1994, pp. 480–504.

Sheridan, Mary P. *Girls, Feminism, and Grassroots Literacies: Activism in The Girlzone*. SUNY P, 2008.

——. "Knot-Working Collaborations: Fostering Community Engaged Teachers and Scholars." *Composing Feminist Interventions*, edited by Kristine L. Blair and Lee Nickoson. WAC Clearinghouse, Forthcoming.

Shetterly, Margot Lee. *Hidden Figures: The Story of the African-American Women Who Helped Win the Space Race*. HarperCollins, 2016.

Siede, Caroline. "CTO Megan Smith Explains How Women In Tech Are Erased From History." boingboing.com, 8 May 2015, www.boingboing.net/2015/05/08/cto-megan-smith-explains-how-w.html/. Accessed 5 July 2017.

Solnit, Rebecca. "Men Explain Things to Me." *TomDispatch.com*, 19 August 2012, www.tomdispatch.com/blog/175584/. Accessed 5 July 2017.

Soper, Taylor. "Microsoft Apologizes For Hiring 'Schoolgirl' Dancers At GDC Party, Calls It 'Unequivocally Wrong'." *Geekwire*, 18 March 2016, www.geekwire.com/2016/microsoft-apologizes-hiring-schoolgirl-dancers-gdc-party-calls-unequivocally-wrong/. Accessed 5 July 2017.

Statista. "Distribution of Computer and Video Gamers in the United States from 2006 to 2015, By Gender," 2015, www.statista.com/statistics/232383/gender-split-of-us-computer-and-video-gamers/. Accessed 5 July 2017.

Sullivan, Gail. "Google Statistics Show Silicon Valley Has a Diversity Problem." *Washington Post*, 29 May 2014, www.washingtonpost.com/news/morning-mix/wp/2014/05/29/most-google-employees-are-white-men-where-are-allthewomen/. Accessed 5 July 2017.

"@tableflipclub." www.tableflip.club/. Accessed 5 July 2017.

Wajcman, Judy. *Technofeminism*. Polity, 2004.

——. "Foreword." Cyborg Lives: Women's Technobiographies. Raw Nerve, 2001, pp. 7–8.

Watters, Audrey. "Men (Still) Explain Technology to Me: Gender and Education Technology." *boundary 2: An International Journal of Literature and Culture*, vol. 22, April 2015, www.boundary2.org/2015/04/22/men-still-explain-technology-to-me-gender-and-education-technology/. Accessed 5 July 2017.

Wilde, Jane. *Travelling to Infinity: My Life with Stephen*. Alma Books, 2007.

Wilding, Faith. "Where Is the Feminism in Cyberfeminism?" *n. paradoxa*, vol. 2, 1998, pp. 6–12.

Williams, Lauren. "Actress Felicia Day Opens Up About Gamergate Fears, Has Her Private Details Exposed Minutes Later." ThinkProgress.org, 23 Oct. 2014, www.thinkprogress.org/culture/2014/10/23/3583347/felicia-day-gamergate/. Accessed 5 July 2017.

Zimmerman, Jess. "Screw Leaning In. It's Time to Slam the Floor in Silicon Valley's Face." *The Guardian*, 15 April 2015, www.theguardian.com/commentisfree/2015/apr/15/screw-leaning-in-its-time-to-slam-the-door-in-silicon-valleys-face/. Accessed 5 July 2017.

21

KEEPING SAFE (AND QUEER)

Zarah C. Moeggenberg

In the middle of my MFA in Michigan, I was home one day. School was cancelled again because of the cold. It was dark that morning, a storm had set in from the north, and the wind howled down the street from off Lake Superior. My laptop eye-level on the coffee table beside me, I was surrounded by my students' papers on the floor of my living room. Flipping through a stack of them on my lap, I saw my iPhone light up. "Mom," it read. I swiped across the bottom.

"What's up?" I asked, placing my iPhone between my cheek and shoulder.
"I just need to ask you a question," she said, sounding stressed.
"What's wrong?" I asked, still sifting through the papers.
"Well. It's just not — I just don't understand something," my mother began.
"Okay, well what is it?"
"Why did you 'friend' Chris?" she asked.
"I'm sorry?" I paused. I took the stack of papers and placed them to my side.
"Did you just want to rub it in his face?" she asked
"About what?"
"That you're gay?" my mother's voice was now excited and angry.
"You just introduced Chris to me last weekend and I thought it would be okay to 'friend' him." I moved the cursor to open one of the tabs. Facebook. I clicked into my profile.
"It's just so inappropriate."
"What's inappropriate? You've been dating for a few months."
"I just feel like you want to rub it in everyone's face. Look at your profile picture."

I double-clicked my profile picture to expand the image. Sally was hugging me from behind and we were wearing formal dresses for the wedding we had gone to earlier that fall. "I don't understand," I replied to my mother, making sure to keep my voice calm. "How am I rubbing anything in anyone's face?"

"This is my life, Zarah. I like this guy. I just don't need everyone knowing you're *gay*."

Her emphasis on the word "gay" stung, but I shook it off. "Mom, why don't you go to John's profile? What's the difference?" I typed in my brother's name and pulled up his profile: John, shirtless, held his girlfriend up—in her bikini—with one arm on a beach.

"It's just not right, Zarah. I think you need to change your picture."

"But what's the difference between John and me? Tell me."

"I think you get some sort of pleasure out of making people uncomfortable. I have no idea why you felt the need to 'friend' Chris. He can't have people know he's associated!"

It took six months for her to apologize. This moment is something I've experienced before, in different forms, on and off social media spaces. As a bartender, I've been sexually harassed and called interesting names. As a teacher, I've been accused of the kind of "rubbing it in" that my mother insisted upon by colleagues and a couple of students for using queer texts in my pedagogy. Still, my experiences on social media spaces (SMS) have been toxic, and many of them I choose not to occupy for that reason. When Facebook has from time to time been unsafe for me as a queer person, I have gone to another space for a while, followed by another, and sometimes back.

It's been nomadic.

Migratory.

Forced.

Much scholarship helps us understand the ways in which racism and sexism manifest in online spaces. But little contributes to our understanding of how heteronormativity challenges queers or how queers use online social media spaces. There seems to be a rhetoric of sex-act, at times to the degree of hypersexualizing, in both how the algorithms of SMS respond to queers' use of their interface and even in how scholars conceive of their use of them. T.V. Reed usefully discusses that the Internet is a place where young LGBT people seek refuge, safety, and community in a substantial portion of *Digitized Lives*. For LGBT people, "information available online—sometimes just the information that 'others like me' exist—has proven deeply reassuring" (118). Mary L. Gray agrees in her discussion of "queer realness." Especially LGBTQ-identifying people in rural communities search for this realness on the Internet, a space that is always displacing reliability for realness and that simultaneously offers comfort that may otherwise be unattainable (178). Important, Reed discusses that media have been slow to discuss stereotyping and poor representations of queer people in new media and is critical of the ways with which online spaces have developed a plethora of opportunities for hate speech (118–119). In her discussion of identity tourism in *Cybertypes: Race, Ethnicity, and Identity on the Internet*, Lisa Nakamura does not discuss sexuality or queer identities online; however, her discussion of how "the performance of identity tourists exemplify the consumption and commodification of racial difference" (Nakamura 14) is parallel to the ways in which identity tourists, I argue, "exemplify the consumption and commodification" of sexuality and transgenderism. Reed, Gray, and Nakamura push us in important directions. Moreover, Nakamura's questions that follow her discussion of identity tourism are useful for how we may unpack queer identity in SMS:

> Where's the multi(culturalism) in multimedia? or Where is race in new media? What is the "work" that race does in cyberspace, our most currently privileged example of the technology of digital reproduction? What boundaries does it police? What "modes of digital identification" or disidentification are enabled, permitted, foreclosed vis-à-vis race? . . . How do we begin to understand the place of authenticity . . . in the landscape of new media? (14–15)

I am compelled to ask similar questions to those of Nakamura: Indeed, where is the multiculturalism in multimedia? Where is *queer* in new media? What "work" does *queer* do in cyberspace? What does it challenge? What does it make possible? Where is this realness that

Gray calls illusive? More important, what modes of digital disidentification are made possible by social media space(s)? I don't believe I answer these questions here, but I believe my work pushes us forward.

As Gray discusses a constantly shifting Internet that makes resourcing difficult for queers, Alexander and Rhodes say there is much ephemera to sift through for LGBT people and others in constructing a queer archive. Alexander and Rhodes offer what they call a "mini-archive," viewing the Internet as a space for queer possibilities: "since the web in particular facilitates the creation of counterpublic spaces, we see a potential diversification of rhetorical practices, some of which may question or even seek to subvert some of the dominant practices of the public sphere" (Alexander and Rhodes). I question whether these possibilities are ready and available. I consider my Facebook profile—though I do not always occupy that space—and my Twitter handle a kind of mini-archive of my own. I tweet and post. I retweet and repost. I quote tweet, comment, reply, "like," and tap the heart. I follow and friend. This all contributes to a trace I leave, an asynchronous framing that any of my "friends" or "followers" can access. Much of it is to do with my confidence in my queerness, the ways in which I have challenged or worked through the kind of gay-bashing, heteronormativity, heterocentrism, and sexism I have encountered as a lesbian from a working-class, small town background. Moreover, I "pass" as a straight woman. I *can* archive. While I deactivate my Facebook profile often, it is the most comprehensive reflection of my becoming as a queer person that I can access. It is my trace. My revolution. But what kinds of modes of identification or disidentification are really afforded to queers by the infrastructures of SMS, especially when my own instinct is often to go elsewhere?

In an ethnographic approach toward understanding how queer rural youth navigate the Internet and their identities, Gray says the Internet provides "queer realness" that "has the power to authenticate queerness through the textual and visual rhetoric of LGBTQ visibility that is (seemingly) real and tangible" (190). Gray explains that for youth she worked with, "representations of the real—online coming out stories and electronic personal ads in particular—were crucial. These genres of queer realness expand their sense of place, home, and belonging" (190). Alexander and Rhodes similarly note in the "Technologizing the Queer Archive . . ." section of their Web-text that access to the coming out story creates a sense of belonging and community, despite its fleetingly temporal construction. I remember being a teenager and desperately waiting for AOL Online to connect through the phone cord when my mother had gone out for errands or to work. While YouTube, founded in early 2005, wasn't prolific or even existent during most of my adolescence, I sought, in the 1990s and 2000s, the same kind of videos or textual narratives on the Internet that Gray acknowledges. What is significant about my history with seeking what Gray calls "queer realness" is that it is found in visual accounts, highly visual texts. That queers rely on visual ephemera on the Internet to experience the self as authentic is an experience of *all* queers, I add, whether urban or rural or in-between. Despite the disembodiment, asynchronisity, and temporality that comes with such world-building, a quest for this visual queer realness is ultimately a search for community, as understanding such complex and rich positioning is rhetorical and challenging. And so, how do queers identify and disidentify across, between, and within social media spaces? How are new sites for (dis)identification made (im)possible for queers in social media spaces? How does the infrastructure contribute to this? How do queers challenge or subvert the construct of Selfe and Selfe's notion of the "default" user?

On Pride, On Disidentification

In "It's My Revolution: Learning to See the Mixedblood," Kristin Arola uses the concept of *regalia* to re-see the mixedblood American Indian, proposing looking online as a starting place, and toward "the spaces where users are asserting their identities in ways that illustrate not only the existence and persistence of the mixedblood, but whose visual, aural, and textual choices illustrate the complexities of this category and the embodied nature of the online self" (217). She explains that regalia, like the performative media akin to online social media spaces such as in MySpace, changes and shifts based on experiences of the dancer. "Regalia acknowledges the shifting self . . ." (219). Certainly, Arola's regalia would be useful for unpacking how queers occupy online spaces; but a more useful approach—and ultimately queerer and just as slippery as regalia—would be to use the concepts of pride and disidentification.

Pride, like regalia, is a highly visual assertion of personhood. What likely comes to mind for most with "pride" is the pride parade. Pride extends in much more complicated ways than a parade, however. For queers and their allies, pride may mean placing a rainbow bumper sticker on their car, flying a flag, or wearing a t-shirt. For others, pride is protest, march, or die-in. Pride, for some, is worn on the face or shaped into one's hair. Pride, for others, is bodies gathered together, disembodied or not. Pride is both challenging and challenges. Pride is rhetorical. Pride is performative. Pride is alive.

Pride is also slippery.

Pride risks vulnerability.

Pride, in many instances, manifests through a disidentificatory process for survival. Such a process leaves a "new model of identity" and a new "site of identification" (Muñoz 41). For Muñoz, disidentification is about recycling the code of the majority "as raw material for representing a disempowered politics or positionality that has been rendered unthinkable by the dominant culture" (31). Out of necessity, queers have taken materials and remixed, repurposed, and re-formed them to become new texts to which they and others can attach themselves. Muñoz elegantly describes how many artists have made their own disidentifications the driving force behind their work. I believe queers have also disidentified with space—more recently, across digital spaces. Less explored is how queers perceive digital spaces as "safe" and built for a default, hetero, and cisgender user. How might queers disidentify in online spaces? What does this look like? How is this meaningful or productive? How does disidentification within social media spaces make pride accessible? Pride isn't always celebratory, colorful, or loud. Sometimes it's highly personal, elusive, unstable, and dangerous.

Gray says LGBTQ people, driven toward queer realness, "draw on narratives driven by a politics of visibility" that is dialectically driven (189–90). I would like to unpack the ways in which they construct narrative and identity with this same politics of visibility in SMS. Pride, like regalia, is a highly visual component of profile-interfaces and feeds for queer people in SMS. Utterances of pride position a queer user within the same "continuum of embodied identities," but depend on networks of SMS that are both 1) dialectically driven, as Gray contends, and 2) flexible. When one space becomes unsafe, a queer person may occupy another for a while, even occupy more than one. In what follows I will explore how three queer users occupy and perceive SMS. I will describe how they disidentify within and outside of these spaces to stay safe and make pride accessible.

Butler discusses gender's performativity as a series of acts that constitute a fiction the individual and audience come to believe in; this is not temporally stable and establishes itself with a "*stylized repetition of acts*" (519). In a space such as Facebook, a facet of one's identity, such as gender, depends upon making moves in that space. For example, when I opt to show that I identify as a "female"—a problematic term—but do not include a profile picture that works to repeat that first alphabetic visual, I am making it harder for an audience to believe in my identity as a female. Butler says that gender is established "through the stylization of the body" and that gestures, movements, and other various performances work to constitute what we come to believe in about an individual (521). Because users are disembodied on these interfaces, stylization of the body means stylizing the profile space and using the tools/actions readily available to each user. For example, on Facebook I may generate pride using not only what stays regularly on the profile interface, but also by liking and commenting on others' posts, all the while making myself vulnerable. In June 2015, an app was available to superimpose a rainbow on a Facebook user's profile picture and tens of thousands of Americans did so to support the Supreme Court's ruling on gay marriage. My Facebook picture still holds this rainbow. I am conscious that when I respond to another user I am inscribing that rainbow in their space. I am using the tools available to me to repeat my act, to establish who I am as a queer person, to say, "I am *here*." A digital gesture, I have interacted, moved, and said something through a visual utterance. I have left a trace of myself.

We cannot assume that queer people surreptitiously perform markers of pride; heteronormativity in online spaces challenges queers to conform to it or not with the ways in which they perform their identities through snapchats, tweets, posts, sharing, liking, and other forms of response. My brother's Facebook profile picture that I had mentioned in the narrative above had represented a lot of who he was at the time he used it. My brother was—and is— proud to have been a NCAA cheerleader and, at the time, quite proud of his relationship with the girl in his previous profile picture. Despite that I "pass" as a straight cis-gendered woman and experience a great deal of privilege myself, my brother admits that he experiences a great deal more privilege than me. When my brother writes, posts a photograph, a meme, a gif, etc., it in no way disrupts the heteronormativity present in these spaces. No one questions his images.

We all occupy digital spaces for different reasons, but queer rhetorical work for a LGBT-identified person, with the affordances of features on each SMS, is an act of pride toward recognition. Pride is performative, and, as a genderqueer woman named Martha will state below, it is as unstable and stylized as Butler says is gender. Whereas the self-recognition and recognition from others that a straight person experiences both on and offline goes unquestioned and remains invisible on SMS, to protect herself, Martha utters pride under performances of/as her cat. "If visibility is imagined to be the road to acceptance for LGBTQ-identifying people, much of that recognition circulates through representations in the media" (Gray 170). And some of this media, especially social media, where we are both consumers and prosumers, contributes to recognition; however, performances of pride can and do coincide with considerable risks, of which many queers, like Martha, are aware of.

Social Media Spaces and the Queer User

In the same spirit Arola sought to re-see mixedblood identity online, I relate how some queers experience SMS. Months before writing this essay, I hoped that what this work would do is to relate the ways in which queer people migrate from space to space due to safety. While these responses have not helped me to fully confirm this, they reveal how queers are currently using

Figure 21.1 Screenshot of a Blank Post from the Author's Facebook User Interface

229

SMS: queers do indeed leave spaces and come back. Primarily, my research demonstrates that the queer user disidentifies often with SMS. Queers remix and recycle their performances in ways that allow them to survive within and outside SMS. All three participants self-identify as women, are out to friends and family, and I would consider them long-time friends. I sent each of them a set of five questions. Participation was voluntary. Based on the questions that informed Arola's "It's My Revolution," answers to all questions was voluntary. While there was some follow-up conversation, most of what follows is derived from the initial responses I received.

Martha (and Zerelda)

Martha, who identifies as a genderqueer lesbian, was one of the first individuals to respond to my interview questions:

> I think I spent so much of my life in high school and into college trying to be as gay as possible, trying to be an activist in every visible way I knew how. . . in my mid-twenties, I'm not sure that's what is most beneficial, or even most safe. Existing feels so political already, particularly [considering] HB2 in North Carolina where I'm living . . . What does it mean that I have not posted a photo of myself since the primary on March 15? What does it mean that I only post photos of my cat? That my friends only tag me in pictures of my cat[?] . . . I have trouble separating my desire to keep part of my life (or even much of my life) out of SMS, and my identity and perceived [un]safeness.

Martha indicates a desire for presence and a desire for safety in SMS. Her performance online as a genderqueer lesbian has shifted to that of a cat-owner; she's begun to develop a new performance for herself. "Friends" have come to believe in her performance, taking part by generating similar digital gestures; they post pictures of the cat, Zerelda, often and her voice is inscribed in the alphabetic text that accompanies them. For example, "Today, Martha and I attempted fate and came out unscathed" accompanies a photograph of Zerelda under stuffed animals, posted by her friend. Martha "liked" these pictures, which constitute gestures of affirmation. Further, Martha's posts primarily focus on what her cat, Zerelda, is doing: "Zerelda is 'helping' "; "the best writing buddy"; and, "today Megan held hands with my cat." Her profile picture on Facebook is telling. In sifting through three years of her profile picture album, all of them show Martha's full face and typically with other humans. In her most recent profile picture, however, Martha's face is half-covered by Zerelda, who is the one looking into the camera. Pride, for Martha, has shifted into creating visual texts that create a new fiction for others to believe in and take part in, which simultaneously work to erase her queer identity in the same space.

North Carolina, a state that recently passed House Bill 2 (HB2 or Public Facilities Privacy and Security Act), prohibits transgender individuals from using bathrooms corresponding with the gender with which they identify. For Martha, whose "gender resides somewhere in between the prescribed binary of 'man' and 'woman' with a tilt toward the masculine," a space like Facebook has never been a place where she says she expresses very much of her queerness. North Carolina an "at will" state with no protections for LGBT workers, having passed HB2, Martha went from posting images of herself to solely posting Zerelda. It took four months, since the passing of HB2, before Martha posted a picture with her body in it. While visual representations of queer identity are invaluable for queers, the same way in which they are generated they can be buried. Earlier I stated that utterances of pride depend upon spaces that are dialectically driven and flexible. The gestures with which Martha and her friends use Facebook depend upon the kind of dialectic and flexibility enabled by its user-interface. For Martha, visibility is crucial and so is a flexible interface:

> [V]isibility is important. Particularly for individuals who are looking for answers or identities or like-minded politics (which is one of the things that I think Tumblr provides with relative safety). I wonder if Tumblr had existed when I was 16 what my identity would look like today—if it would be the same, or if I would have come to some answers sooner . . . I am not actively creating an identity on my social media anymore. And it isn't something I'm interested in. But I see its necessity.

Visual rhetoric on the social media interface serves to authenticate queerness. If representations of the queer are crucial to survival and safety then just as crucial for Martha is an interface that allows her to easily change her performance so that what would usually appear to a "Friend" as genderqueer lesbian becomes difficult to trace and detect in that same space.

If Facebook is not culturally coded for Martha to express identification, then she must use the tools and texts available to her to create a new site for identification. Significant is that Martha stayed on Facebook despite the toxicity toward genderqueer and transgender individuals where she lives and online. Martha took her cat images and what words and speech acts that were available to generate a new performance that she and others could build from to keep herself present and safe. Muñoz says disidentification is an ongoing process, an ongoing performance. In re-scrambling the text, Martha is still tied to the infrastructure, the ways in which the code of Facebook requires her to function in the template, but she controls her performance, as well as what aspects of texts will resurface as she continues to use Facebook. Disidentification enables her to access and connect with others. In some ways, too, pride becomes a bit more corporeal and personal through her process of disidentification online. While Martha may become more and more disembodied through using Facebook, through disidentification her sense of pride is maintained.

Jordan

Jordan identifies as a bisexual or queer woman in the Pacific Northwest and views flexibility as crucial. Occupying multiple platforms helps her to feel safer. Each digital space affords different functions that allow her to express her sexuality and find community. Snapchat and Facebook are the SMS Jordan occupies most: "Snapchat is one of the safest spaces for queer people because there isn't room for users to debate with or openly discriminate against others," she says. Snapchat's ten-second limit makes it a highly performative interface. The ways in which one can temporally draw, add text, add emoji, and apply a filter/mask to one's body, or even that of others is decidedly queer because one can just be, as Jordan says, without being concerned about someone openly discriminating or othering someone, as in an asynchronous interface.

Jordan uses Facebook a great deal and is critical of its affordances. She discusses that she feels uncomfortable and "very exposed" posting there; posting something about her sexuality would make her feel unsafe. Facebook, for Jordan, "is a really heteronormative space in [constructing identity]. It is decidedly un-queer in its content and construction." She even says, "I perform as a straight woman on Facebook." She stresses that Facebook does not provide enough filters for deciding who can see whatever visual one posts. "It would be ideal," she says, "to have the option on every Facebook post . . . to decided which specific audience could see and interact with that content." Facebook does not offer enough flexibility to express oneself as queer due to the ways in which other users can openly comment, harass, and generate hate speech in a variety of multimedia.

Jordan uses Tumblr, Facebook, Snapchat, and Instagram. As a bisexual, Tumblr offers the safest space for this aspect of her identity. She calls Tumblr the "apex of queer space" because of its flexibility, its "free-form," and option of anonymity:

> My Tumblr is pretty queer. I repost things about being a queer or bisexual woman quite frequently, but I also feel safer doing that on Tumblr for a number of reasons: 1. my name is not associated with my account 2. there are no photos of me on my account, and 3. I'm not friends with any of my real-life friends on Tumblr. So basically, I'm totally anonymous there.

Jordan's Tumblr is highly image-based and doesn't offer much text. Most posts on her Tumblr have to do with her bisexuality, whereas her Twitter is a "professionalization tool," her Facebook is "straight," and her Instagram, like Martha's Facebook, is entirely composed of images of her moustache-cat, the handle named after him. Her Instagram account public and now with several hundred followers, Jordan does not know most of them. With a growing number, she's

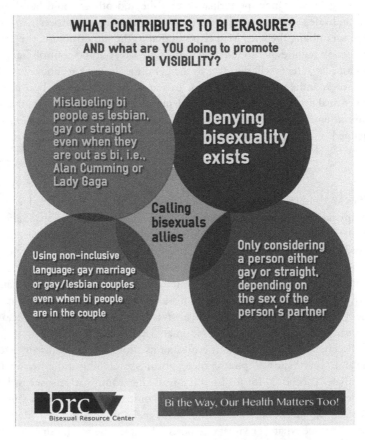

Figure 21.2 Example of a Visual that Would Be Shared to Raise Bi-awareness on Tumblr

started using her cat's Instagram as a political platform and as a space to generate feminist rhetoric. The anonymity afforded by Instagram has helped Jordan begin to use it in a different, perhaps more meaningful, way.

A space must be highly flexible for a queer person to feel safe, to perform queer visibility as a LGBT-identified person. Like Instagram's visually driven interface, on Tumblr one can repost images that resonate with one's identity and simultaneously generate a safe space for others; realness is made doubly accessible. It is difficult to imagine the various queer spaces each post must help build. Jordan's reluctance to express her bisexuality on Facebook, her use of Twitter as a professional tool, and her new shift on Instagram indicate like Martha's occupation of her own social media that user-interfaces must afford both a means for dialectic—even if this means conversing with emoji, photograph, video, etc.—and flexibility in how users can perform pride in new ways.

If disidentification is descriptive of survival practices a marginalized subject uses that work to "negotiate a phobic majoritarian public sphere" that would otherwise reprimand her for not conforming to "the phantasm of normative citizenship" (Muñoz 4), then Jordan's compartmentalization is fundamental to her process. By organizing her performance in each space to reflect an aspect of who she is—the activist on Instagram, the bisexual queer on Tumblr, the straight friend or family member on Facebook, the literary scholar on Twitter—Jordan generates a constellation of points for identification across these various digital platforms, a kind of migratory nexus that makes her survival as a bi, queer Latina woman possible. While pride may not be possible for every aspect of who Jordan is in some spaces, it is entirely possible when she shifts between spaces and compartmentalizes.

Amelia

Amelia, a photographer in the Midwest, views her queerness as manifesting in her gender more than in her sexuality. She says much of her queerness is expressed in her clothing, preferring the fit of boy and men's clothing; she has never felt comfortable wearing women's clothing. Amelia uses Facebook and Instagram; like Jordan, they are used in entirely different ways in comparison. Interesting, on Facebook, Amelia "never create(s) her own posts." Pride in her gender does not manifest on her Facebook explicitly, but instead in distancing anyone who attempts to access it. By that I mean that, as Amelia says, she interacts with Facebook every 1–3 months, typically by changing her cover photo or her profile picture. What appears on Amelia's profile page and down her feed is either posted by someone else, or shared by Amelia through another linked social media site. Foremost, Amelia does this with Instagram and Vimeo. The last time she wrote any alphabetic text, or posted a photo or video through Facebook's user-interface was in 2015. She explains, "[W]hen I was more active with Facebook I never viewed it as an unsafe space for a queer person. However . . . when I began to have relationships with women, I did experience some anxiety about other users' opinions/stereotypes/etc." There is significant distance that Amelia places between herself and other Facebook users by using another SMS to post to it. The images she shares are usually those of her dog or landscape. Instagram, in Amelia's experience has been a positive place for her to express her queerness because of how the user-interface operates. She notes that most notifications she receives are "likes" and that most comments are positive. "In comparison," she says, "I feel as though users would be more likely to express their opinions' (positive or negative) about your queerness on Facebook, Reddit, or Twitter." I theorize that this is due to the emphasis on alphabetic text in those spaces.

Figure 21.3 Kooskia, Idaho; Used with Amelia's Permission

What is striking about Amelia's photographs on Instagram is how distance is still invoked. The landscapes employ vastness; even those that capture her dog or cat generate searching or wandering, as Figure 21.3 demonstrates. The stillness in her art simultaneously invokes movement. A kind of question of "Where will this lead?" infiltrates and the viewer feels possibility, change, or hope. Halberstam's notion of queer space resonates in how Amelia represents her queerness through landscape, and in how she distances her body and self from some spaces. One space becomes a tool, Instagram, while another becomes a landscape, Facebook; both spaces create a queer space. Further, as Amelia demonstrates in Figure 21.4, using landscape to embody queerness expands the terrain for her own personality as a social media user. Halberstam says that queer space has to do with "the place-making practices . . . in which queer people engage and it also describes the new understandings of space enabled by the production of queer counter-publics" (6). When place-making practices of social media are functionally heteronormative and interface values of straight users, queer users must find ways to survive and feel safe. Amelia's use of SMS is inherently queer because she challenges their logics. In generating pride through landscape, and sometimes portrait, then sharing it via one digital interface to another, Amelia makes a space in-between that operates at a distance. She distances her body from Facebook by using the other SMS and by posting primarily landscape. In doing so, Amelia creates a space for herself to express her own pride.

Inasmuch Martha and Jordan navigate each SMS in different ways, like Amelia, all three users find a way to create a safe space—even if this means moving in-between or creating an entirely new one. Amelia demonstrates Muñoz's concept of disidentification in that she works within and outside of the dominant sphere simultaneously (5); her means of resistance *recycles*, but in a way that Muñoz does not fully explore in *Disidentifications*. While Muñoz emphasizes recycling and remixing *objects*, Amelia is recycling two digital *spaces*—two sets of infrastructures are remixed to generate another—we might even argue with a physical one. In landscape photography Amelia combats hetero-time. Generating landscape challenges the lineation of a scripted life—point A to point B to point C, etc.—and invokes feeling instead: loss, emptiness, loneliness, serenity, scariness, quirkiness. Facebook describes itself as an application that allows users to keep up with friends "faster than ever," but Amelia challenges this by generating images that ask any user on Facebook or Instagram to slow down and feel something. She interrupts normative temporality.

Toward Safety

Better understanding of how queer people are using social media sites may inform how we use them in our classrooms. As nearly 1 in 10 students in our classrooms is LGBTQ, we must be mindful of how we integrate social media. These digital interfaces such as Tumblr, Facebook, or Twitter may seem to offer rich pedagogical possibilities, like a way to reach students faster or to create community; yet, we must be considerate in that such usage may be impeding on students' understanding of their identities and invoke bad memories or experiences. As Selfe and Selfe point out, we must recognize along with our students that the interface is only a "partial map" of our culture, a "linguistic contact zone that reveals power differentials" (77). Understanding how interfaces empower and disempower, as well as investigating what informs interface design can be meaningful scholarship for teachers and students alike. Disregarding that access has much to do with embodied rhetorical practice within these spaces flattens the "user" once again as heterosexual, cisgender, and privileged. If we're going to use social media in our classrooms, if this is where digital rhetorical studies push us, then let's begin to see more fully who designs them and for whom. Is there more to the default user than has been accounted for? Has the infrastructure of any space(s) challenged our conceptualization of the "default user," made it more difficult to trace?

I asked Martha, Jordan, and Amelia about the infrastructures of the SMS they occupy and how they would change them. Jordan says we are always "performing our identities" but that

Figure 21.4 Snake River, Idaho; Used with Amelia's Permission

it is difficult to know "when or if it's safe to present our true selves" and suggests "a higher number of available and easily accessible content filters." She also believes private profile pictures would work to make more people safer in SMS. Others suggested more inclusive emojis, gifs, queer pictures, and safe spaces within each SMS for queers and questioning individuals to find community. With their answers to these questions there is much room for rhetorical inquiry and analysis. Martha is critical that queer visuals, texts that invoke queer pride, are important but rare in SMS and she is concerned: "I see it in how my students interact with each other. How they write. What information they are and are not consuming . . . I think there are needs that are not being met." Letting social media user-interfaces become a tool in our pedagogies is risky and careless, but when we analyze with our students these platforms' rhetorical functions, the tools they make available, and the ways in which different students use them, such work helps everyone understand how each user is not equally rhetorically positioned.

Works Cited

Alexander, Jonathan, and Jacqueline Rhodes. "Queer Rhetoric and the Pleasures of the Archive." *Enculturation.* 16 Jan. 2012. http://enculturation.net/queer-rhetoric-and-the-pleasures-of-the-archive. Accessed 1 Apr. 2016.

"Amelia." Personal Interview. 3 May 2016.

Arola, Kristin, L. "It's My Revolution: Learning to See the Mixedblood." *Composing (Media) = Composing (Embodiment)*, edited by Kristin L. Arola, and Anne Frances Wysocki. UP of Colorado, 2012, pp. 213–226.

Butler, Judith. "Performative Acts and Gender Constitution: An Essay in Phenomenology and Feminist Theory." *Theatre Journal*, vol. 40 no. 4, 1988, pp. 519–31.

Gray, Mary L. "Negotiating Identities/Queering Desires." *Identity Technologies: Constructing the Self Online*, edited by Anna Poletti, and Julie Rak. U of Wisconsin P, 2014, pp. 167–97.

Halberstam, Judith. *In A Queer Time and Place*. New York UP, 2005.

"Jordan." Personal interview. 27 Apr. 2016.

"Martha." Personal interview. 29 Apr. 2016.

Muñoz, José Esteban. *Disidentifications: Queers of Color and the Performance of Politics*. U of Minnesota P, 1999.

Nakamura, Lisa. *Cybertypes: Race, Ethnicity, and Identity on the Internet*. Routledge, 2002.

Reed, T. V. (Thomas Vernon). *Digitized Lives: Culture, Power and Social Change in the Internet Era*. Taylor & Francis Group, 2014.

Selfe, Cynthia L., and Richard J. Selfe, Jr. "The Politics of the Interface: Power and Its Exercise in Electronic Contact Zones." *College Composition and Communication*, vol. 45, no. 4, 1994, pp. 480–504.

22

THE INVISIBLE LIFE OF ELLIOT RODGER

Social Media and the Documentation of a Tragedy

Carol Burke and Jonathan Alexander

One of the most startling reversals in media theory is surely Sherry Turkle's turn away from lauding Internet platforms as an opportunity for self and other exploration to her strident consideration of them as potentially destructive of human intimacy. In her early work, particularly in *Life on the Screen* (1995), Turkle praised the Internet and digital spheres for their ability to allow identity play and, through connections with others, to try on new personalities. Since then, particularly in *Alone Together* (2011), Turkle has kept a keen eye on how people actually use their communications technologies, and she currently sees less play and connectivity and more monitoring and anxiety. The problem might lie in the over-abundance of connectivity itself:

> Our neurochemical response to every ping and ring tone seems to be the one elicited by the "seeking" drive, a deep motivation of the human psyche. Connectivity becomes a craving; when we receive a text or an e-mail, our nervous system responds by giving us a shot of dopamine. . . . I think of a sixteen-year-old girl who tells me, "Technology is bad because people are not as strong as its pull." (*Alone* 227)

Turkle also points out the worrying desire to monitor each other constantly—a desire easily facilitated by much of social media. The flood of information we receive about each other through various social networking sites such as Facebook prompts us to "measure" each other—and ourselves. Psychologist Ethan Kross from the University of Michigan reports that overuse of Facebook might lead to depression as users constantly measure their lives against the status updates posted by others, often full of brags about accomplishments and fabulous trips, the "best face forward" self-presentations on Facebook. The "status update" triggers a status anxiety (Greig).

In their essay "Technologies of the Self in the Aftermath: Affect, Subjectivity, Composition," Jonathan Alexander and Jacqueline Rhodes consider the use of various forms of writing and social media technologies that documented Seung-Hui Cho, the attacker who killed several people before taking his own life in an assault at Virginia Tech on April 16, 2007. Acknowledging the awfulness of the tragedy, Alexander and Rhodes argue that

> The Virginia Tech shootings . . . provide a compelling case for examining the complex intersections of new media and subjectivity. At the same time that editorials and short essays, online and in print, offered interpretations and commentary from an ever-increasing distance, a simultaneous new media response emerged, a dizzying accumulation of blog postings that attempted to make sense of—to *account* for—the violence and its perpetrator. (146)

Ultimately, the authors assert that "Such postings seemed . . . emblematic of a textual production combining both speed of response and disciplining of affect" (146)—that is, the social media response served both to inform others nearly instantaneously of the situation while also sending signals about how to interpret the tragedy, primarily as the act of a lone and crazed madman. In the process, Alexander and Rhodes contend, normalizing discourses shut out a fuller consideration of why someone might perpetrate such a heinous act, putting into circulation a representation of subjectivity as fully other as opposed to a larger systemic meditation on how violence erupts. Ultimately, the scholars ask: "How can we use new media to open up spaces, not just for immediate response but also for critical reflection?" (147).

In this chapter, we pick up where Alexander and Rhodes left off, undertaking a case study of more a recent attack, by Elliot Rodger at the University of California, Santa Barbara in 2014. Our goal is to consider the role of social media in this tragedy.

Setting the Stage

On May 23, 2014, in Isla Vista, California, 22-year-old Elliot Rodger killed two roommates, their friend, two sorority members, and another student he encountered in a deli, and injured thirteen others in a rage against the women he felt owed him their attention and the men they chose instead. This mass murder, like others before it, requires interpretation. Rodger's actions on his "Day of Retribution," along with his self-produced videos and his 140-page autobiography, left many who commented in the mainstream media, in the tabloids, and on social media trying to make sense of the violence. For some, it was just another "school shooting," even though it didn't technically take place on a school campus but rather in a residential community populated, in large part, by students attending nearby University of California, Santa Barbara.

Soon after the murders, Richard Martinez, the father of Christopher Michaels-Martinez, one of Rodger's victims, took to the podium in an effort to salvage something from the tragic loss of his son with his riveting questions, "Why did Chris die? He died because of craven irresponsible politicians and the NRA. They talk about gun rights, but what about Chris' right to live? When will this insanity stop?" No call for gun control, not even the heartfelt plea of a distraught parent, however, is ever left without the counterargument from the gun-toting right. Some took to social media to argue that no gun control regulations would have prevented the deaths of Rodger's first three victims killed by what the police referred to as "sharp objects," what the LA Times reported the attorney for the families of these victims say were "a knife, a hammer, and a machete" (Mather).

Samuel Joseph Wurzelbacher, aka Joe the Plumber, the conservative everyman who became the darling of the McCain–Palin 2008 campaign, stepped forward to respond to Martinez's call to action with an open letter to the parents the Isla Vista victims. "Harsh as this sounds," Wurzelbacher wrote, "your dead kids don't trump my Constitutional rights." As insensitive as Wurzelbacher's comments were, they weren't nearly as bizarre as the claims of the ultra right following the Rodger shootings. They trotted out their conspiracy theories, their forensic photos, and their denunciations of all of the eyewitnesses. Their goal? To show that the alleged killings by Rodger never happened. Just as they had done in the aftermath of the Sandy Hook shootings, the Boston Marathon, and the 2011 Tucson shooting of Congresswoman Gabby Gifford and 17 others, the deniers claimed that the parents and friends of the murdered were simply "crisis actors" in a play staged either by left wingers desperate to usher in gun control by "the Zionist-controlled media," or a US government sinister enough to carry out a major PsyOps (Psychological Operations) scheme designed to dupe its own people.

The movie-like quality of such scenarios is oddly apropos in Rodger's case, and the movie industry comes in for its share of potential blame in this tragedy. From the Hollywood explainers to the Hollywood blamers, Rodger, they argued, received his fantasies of what his life should be from living on the outskirts of Tinsel Town. He walked the red carpet with his father at the premier of *Hunger Games*, a film in which Rodger Sr. served as a second unit director, attended private schools with students whose parents made their wealth in the entertainment business, and was taken by his parents to Hollywood parties. His mother numbers George Lucas and Steven Spielberg among her friends, his stepmother stars in a French reality TV show, and his nine -ear-old brother had, just before Rodger's murders, landed an agent to secure roles in commercials. Nevertheless, Rodger never sought work in the entertainment industry. What he wanted was what any movie-soaked malcontent might dream of: that Hollywood would work for him, to make good on its promises and to reward him, the geek, with the girl.

In the face of Rodger's murder of innocents it's natural to answer the question "why" with the answer, "He's crazy." But such an explanation ejects the subject from any context and forecloses further discussion; that's partly why it feels satisfying. To call someone a "monster," as Rodger's father does in his Barbara Walter's interview, or to call someone "the devil," as did the young woman whom Rodger fired at but missed, is to dehumanize the killer, to absolve him, and to relegate him to the fantastic. By opting for an easy answer, we admit having no other way of understanding such individuals and their rage. The media calls Rodger's autobiography a "manifesto" as if it were the political ravings of a lunatic. It's not; it's the narrative of a life of loneliness and social isolation combined with privilege and narcissism, a toxic mix that produced the revenge of the infantilized American male.

Indeed, despite all the theories thrown around by media pundits in the immediate aftermath of the tragedy, what one is continually struck by in retrospect is Rodger's passivity—as if, in all his ghostliness, he sat in the audience for the drama that was his life, waiting for someone to notice him. A common enough sense of dissociation that occurs for many people was aggravated in Rodger's case by a peculiar mix of sexual inadequacy, racial shame, a privileged but unearned milieu, and a community in which promiscuity and partying were the norm. And throughout it all, Rodger documented much of his perceived invisibility—but few were watching.

The Curse of Invisibility

As is clear from his autobiography and from his videos, Rodger's life story was a quest for visibility. "I was an invisible ghost," he says. [Unless otherwise noted, all of the quotes are from his autobiography, "My Twisted World: The Story of Elliot Rodger"] "Every day that I spent at college the more inferior and invisible I felt." For a while, he believed that the right clothes would bring him attention. On the first day of the academic year at his community college, decked out in his "fabulous Armani Exchange shirt" and Gucci sunglasses, the lovely Narcissus took note of his reflection: "I admired myself in the mirror for a few moments, and began to feel a surge of enthusiasm. I wanted everyone to see me looking like that. I was hopeful that some girls would admire me."

A striking feature of Rodger's story is the role that digital spaces play in allowing us to trace the unfolding of the tragedy he enacted. We shouldn't rush to assume that social media was the cause of Rodger's despair, as Richard Speer does, calling Rodger a "selfie-era killer." But Rodger certainly drops many clues in his videos and in his autobiography that point to how very status conscious he was, desiring not just visibility but intense attention.

In many ways, at least initially, Rodger's engagement with digital worlds seems completely normal, even typical for many adolescents. At several points in "My Twisted World," Rodger recounts going to Planet Cyber, the neighborhood video game joint and a place he enjoyed hanging out with his friends: "It was only a matter of time before I started inviting John Jo and Charlie to sleep over at the same time. When the three of us went to Planet Cyber as a group, I had an absolute blast. It was one of the best experiences of my life." Such moments of joy, though, are increasingly rare for Rodger, and he turns to virtual worlds for escape and solace. The massively multiplayer online role-playing game (MMORPG), World of Warcraft, offered him an from feelings of isolation and alienation:

> The world that I grew up thinking was bright and blissful was all over. I was living in a depraved world, and I didn't want to accept it. I didn't want to give any thought to it. That is why I immersed myself entirely into my online games like World of Warcraft. I felt safe there.

For a while, the game world was adequate substitute for the real: "I didn't care about having a social life at that point. All I wanted to do was hide away from the cruel world by playing my online games" (49).

After a summer doing little but playing WoW, Rodger says, "I became more and more depressed. My life had gotten so lonely, and playing WoW barely made up for it." This was when he learned that his friend James and James' friends Steve and Mark, who had all been playing WoW on the same server with Rodger, had actually been getting together off-game, leaving Rodger out of such encounters. He explains his reaction:

> Whenever they did this, I acted bitter towards them through the game, but they didn't even care. Even in the World of Warcraft, I was an outcast, alone and unwanted. The more lonely I felt, the more angry I became. The anger slowly built up inside me throughout all of the dark years. . . . The game's ability to alleviate my sense of loneliness was starting to fade. I began to feel lonely even while playing it, and I often broke down into tears in the middle of my WoW sessions. (56)

In some ways, Rodger's experiences parallel Turkle's concerns in *Alone Together* that the intense connectivity offered by a game like WoW can be, for some people at least, a façade of attention and affiliation, only momentarily substituting for the intimacy of human contact. Status in game equals, temporarily, status and even a form of intimacy in real life.

Sex Panics

For Rodger, so much of that status anxiety increasingly focused on sex—particularly the sexual intimacy he felt fully entitled to but wasn't getting. In "My Twisted World," he recounts a key moment during one of his solo trips to Planet Cyber when he is thirteen years old. He glances over the shoulder of an older teen to discover a video both galvanizing and transformative:

I saw in detail a video of a man having sex with a hot girl. The video showed a man stick his penis inside a girl's vagina. I didn't know anything about sex at the time . . . The sight was shocking, traumatizing, and arousing. All of these feelings mixed together took a great toll on me. I walked home and cried by myself for a bit. I felt too guilty about what I saw to talk to my parents about it. I was shaken for a few days. . . . Finding out about sex is one of the things that truly destroyed my entire life. Sex . . . the very word fills me with hate. Once I hit puberty, I would always want it, like any other boy. I would always hunger for it. I would always covet it, I would always fantasize about it. But I would never get it. Not getting any sex is what will shape the very foundation of my miserable youth. This was a very dark day. (39)

Although initially a safe haven to which he could retreat from social pressures, the cyber world also offered looming specters of sexuality that would haunt Rodger. Even WoW became tainted for him, as he started to run into people in-game talking about sexual intimacy. As he puts it, he found "more 'normal' people" joining WoW and "bragging online about their sexual experiences with girls . . . my enemies." WoW was no longer the safe hiding place, and the virtual world eventually became for Rodger an arena through which to measure—and eventually record—his own inadequacies and feelings of isolation and alienation.

Rodger's passivity and intense fear of communicating with girls make it almost impossible to imagine that he could ever strike up a friendship, let alone a romance. His parents were keenly aware of his inability to make friends. When he was young, they invited friends over to play with him. They furnished him with all the video games he wanted, bought the designer clothing, and gave him a BMW, but what they couldn't provide was a "a beautiful girlfriend on my arm." Devoid of social skills, skills that his 12-hour days in cyberspace did nothing to foster, Rodger yearned fiercely for personal connections. In the absence of any real interactions, his fantasized relationships seemed to have been inspired by Disney rather than worked out by trial and error. Rodger wanted to be the Cinderella whose physical presence alone dazzles all and to be rescued from invisibility by his princess charming. But that sort of thing only happens in fairy tales and Hollywood movies (e.g. the Jerry Lewis 1960 film *Cinderfella*). His efforts were continually frustrated. He dressed up and went to public places in the hope that a beautiful woman would recognize his princely qualities. "I walked over to the center of Isla Vista every day and sat at one of the tables outside Domino's Pizza, hoping against hope that a girl would come up and talk to me."

Like those males who frequent PUAHate.com (Pick Up Artist Hate), a site that Rodger mentions in his autobiography, he clearly lacked "game." Dale Launer, a friend of Rodger's father and the screenwriter of movies like *Love Potion No. 9*, *My Cousin Vinny*, and *Blind Date*, offered to help Rodger in his efforts to attract a girlfriend. They had some long talks and email exchanges, and Launer even gave Rodger an assignment—to simply complement a girl he passes on campus. In a BBC interview on July 4, Launer said that he instructed Rodger to offer this complement without stopping, without prolonged eye contact in order to see what would happen. When he later checked in with Rodger about the assignment, Rodger responded, "Why should I give them a complement; they should give me one."

To suppress feelings of low self esteem, the narcissist typically clings to an idealized self, one that he has held onto since childhood (what Freud in his 1914 essay "On Narcissism" calls "His Majesty the Baby"), a powerful and proficient self, superior to others, one whom he needs others to affirm or "mirror." Rodger's younger brother Jazz adored his older brother and did, in fact, "mirror" Rodger's idealized self.

People having a high opinion of me is what I've always wanted in life. It has always been of the utmost importance. This is why my life has been so miserable, because no one has ever had a high opinion of me. My little brother Jazz was the only one who had such an opinion, and that is why I enjoyed spending so much time with him, despite my envy of his social advantages. (116)

So why, then, did Rodger ultimately hatch a plan to kill the only one who provided him the confirmation he craved? On the day his stepmother informed Rodger that his younger brother had his own agent committed to securing the child parts in commercials, Rodger determined that Jazz would be the Abel to his Cain. "I will not allow the boy to surpass me at everything, to live the life I've always wanted. If I can't live a pleasurable life, then neither will he! I will not let him put my legacy to shame." The more Rodger's concept of his idealized self failed to register with others, the more desperately he sought a girlfriend as proof that he really was a person of worth. Just like the construction of his own self as "superior," "magnificent," and "beautiful," his ideal version of a girlfriend was someone whose beauty would mirror his own, who would harbor no desires of her own save her adoration of him.

When his idealized self was rejected or ignored, Rodger felt empty and invisible, feelings that none of the "hired friends," fellow college students his parents procured as social skills counselors, could help him heal from. Ultimately his envy turned to anger and his desire to aggression. Scenes encountered in everyday life, something as simple as the sight of a boy and girl enjoying each other's company, registered as personal insults. In his first year at Santa Barbara City College, he quit one class on the first day because he couldn't stand to see a pretty blonde with her boyfriend. In another, he developed an instant crush on "a very pretty girl," but when he learned a couple days later that she already had a boyfriend, he dropped that course as well. The "very pretty blonde girl" in another class soon started associating with "the obnoxious boys in her clique" further affirming his invisibility: "Everyone treated me like I was invisible. No one reached out to me, no one knew I existed." Most nights, unable to attract the attention he craved by merely sitting in public, he returned home alone dejected, "my head down in defeat," but on one of the nights that he ventured out, he was sitting in Domino's Pizza silently announcing his availability, and a tall, blonde jock with his tall, blonde girlfriend entered. The girl was one of the sexiest girls he had ever seen, which made the kiss the couple exchanged all the more offensive. When they left the restaurant, he followed them in his car until they reached a less busy area, at which point he opened his window and splashed his iced tea all over them. "At least," he says, "I made some effort to fight back against the injustice."

This became a series of assaults in which he would either throw drinks at those he envied from the comfort of his BMW or leave the car, execute his attack, and quickly return to his vehicle. Just before his twenty-first birthday, Rodger went to a nearby park. Two couples arrived: "fraternity jocks, tall and muscular" accompanied by "beautiful blonde girls" who began to play kickball. Filled with rage at the unfairness of being written out of the scene, Rodger drove to a nearby K-Mart and purchased a "super-soaker" that he filled with orange juice. Newly armed, he returned to the park:

I screamed at them with rage as I sprayed them with my super soaker. When the boys started to yell and chase after me, I quickly got into my car and drove away. I was giddy with ecstatic, hate-fueled excitement. I wished I could spray boiling oil at the four beasts. They deserved to die horrible, painful deaths just for the crime of enjoying a better life than me.

After the childish aggression, Rodger drove to a shopping center, his "heart beating rapidly" and "overcome with the worry and fear" about whether or not "there were any cameras at the park that could have caught me in the act" (107).

Rodger's growing hatred of women, his misogyny, was often inflamed by racism. Although of mixed race himself, Rodger, like the Columbine murderer Eric Harris, the boy who was dressed to kill in his black "Natural Selection" T-shirt, maintained a firm belief in white racial superiority. Rodger's autobiography makes no secret of his racism, ignited most fiercely when he realizes that those he views as racially inferior have had more success than he attracting girls. The mere sight of white girls outside a party interacting with an Asian guy disturbed him. "How could an ugly Asian attract the attention of a white girl, while a beautiful Eurasian like myself never had any attention from them," he asked himself. He approached the group, pushed the Asian guy aside, insulted them all, and walked away only to return with more vitriol. As they yelled back, Rodger raised his arm and pretended to shoot them. Although intended to intimidate, the gesture only produced laughter on their part, so he attacked them, hoping to push all of them off the 10-foot high ledge they were on. They, in turn, pushed him, and he fell to the street below, too drunk to realize that his ankle was broken. He stumbled away until it dawned on him that he was missing his trademark Gucci sunglasses, a gift from his mother and an essential part of his look. He limped back to retrieve them, got into another fight, and staggered away for a second time with a few more bruises but without the prized sunglasses.

Although other college students passing by intervened to break up the fight and help Rodger down the street, no girls came to his rescue, further evidence for Rodger that girls didn't like him. "If girls had been attracted to me, they would have offered to walk me to my room and take care of me. They would have even offered to sleep with me to make me feel better." Rodger, the wounded child, wanted both the comfort of a mother and sex. By this point, nearly a year before his "Day of Retribution," Rodger was toting up his grievances against women and the men they were attracted to.

"Elliot Rodger here . . ."

We can track much of Rodger's decline through the YouTube channel he left behind. He invites us to enter his world, the world of the simple consumer craving a designer girlfriend to complete the ensemble. In retrospect, his videos seem like cries for help, and indeed his parents alerted the authorities after viewing some. The videos are clearly concerning, even now. It's hard not to read them as, on one hand, Rodger trying to talk himself into what he's about to do and, on the other hand, desperately calling for attention and for someone to stop the impending slaughter. Indeed, perhaps to signal his despair, he called his YouTube channel "Elliot Rodger, Lonely Vlog, Life is so unfair" (www.youtube.com/user/ElliotRodger).

Most of the videos were uploaded days before the tragedy, but some of them were clearly taken long before then and uploaded later. Several are just typical late adolescent slices of life. The earliest one seems to be a real throwback, scenes from a July 4, 2011 party, probably taken with a cellphone. In many ways, this is just the video posting of a typical college kid, hanging out with friends. The next one, chronologically at least, starts a series of amateur music videos. "Enjoying the sunset in Santa Barbara," uploaded February 10, gives us Rodger's perspective from his car looking out at a beautiful sunset. Belinda Carlisle blares from the radio: "Ooh, heaven is a place on earth . . ." We come to know the car pretty well in these videos, and hear more 1980s pop. And then we see an enormous Starbucks cup come into view, as large as the sun. The whole video is . . . sweet: a kid with his latte checking out the sunset. Some of the videos are even a bit corny. "Dancing in the car, Elliot Rodger style" shows him driving around

Santa Barbara with Whitney Houston's "How Will I Know?" blasting on the radio. Rodger pivots the camera from views of the streets he's driving down and back to himself, actually smiling, dancing along. Then he actually winks at the camera—a little sly, a little seductive. He makes the camera "dance" to the music and the road sways back and forth, a pleasant little earthquake.

But the videos also reveal the rumblings underneath, movements signaling greater instability and the potential for significant psychic shocks. In "Balcony Vlog, reminiscing about childhood," uploaded April 7, we see his father's house on a lovely day, "not a cloud in the sky" as he says. Voices of children in the background remind him of the "best days" of his life. But Rodger is already measuring his current situation against what he believes he's lost. As he puts it, "life is so much fairer when you're a kid. I mean, when you're a kid you don't have to worry about things like being attractive or how many girls like you. No one has unfair advantages." And then kids hit puberty, which can be a "heaven on earth or a living hell. All depends on how many girls like you." We start hearing the tag line that becomes his plaintive, grating refrain: "No girls like me. And I hate them all for it."

Rodger's videos work, in large part, as a form of self-branding. Most of these driving videos either begin with or include a shot of the BMW logo, as though reminding viewers that he is "quality," first class. He borrows from the brands with which he surrounds himself, trying to draw attention to himself through his stuff—expensive cars and sunglasses. More direct self-branding and staging occur in "Being lonely on Spring Break sucks," uploaded the same day. In this video, Rodger records himself aglow in super-saturated yellow sunlight. And then the refrain begins. Life sucks "ever since I started desiring girls," especially when they don't desire him back. He says he's trying to get some peace, some escape from this "trouble" and that "serenity of it all just makes me try and forget about it." But we begin to doubt him. Is he experiencing the serenity, or recording it as the contrasting backdrop to his own loneliness? We can all see the magnificence of the natural setting, yes; but why, he complains, can't we see his beauty? In a video from Montecito, uploaded the morning of his murders and entitled "Why do girls hate me so much?", he rehearses, masochistically, the same tortured lines about how he has no one, no girl, who likes him. And it's all *their* fault. After all, as he repeatedly says, "I'm magnificent." "I have a nice car. A BMW." "I am polite. I am the ultimate gentleman."

For all his objectification of women, we get the sense that Rodger came to see himself as an object, one that deserves to be desired. If anything, he bemoans the fact that he's not sufficiently objectified by others, who should look on him with desire. His self-staging in these videos shows him passively beautiful and magnificent, the prince in his $300 sunglasses: "Look at how fabulous I look." There's nothing relational here, or even passionately ravenous—just his own self staging: "I mean look at me. I'm gorgeous." Reflecting on how we surround ourselves with technologies of connectivity, technologies that seem to speak to us directly, Turkle argues that we can experience some confusion between those objects that facilitate communication and the authentic forms of embodied connection with others, with people:

> We are tempted, summoned by robots and bots, objects that address us as if they were people. And just as we imagine things as people, we invent ways of being with people that turn them into something close to things. (*Alone Together* 224)

Rodger represents an extreme case of such confusion, ultimately understanding himself as the object of desire that needed staging online—and wondering why no one was paying attention.

Another video, "Golf course video," intensifies this bile. Set in gorgeous surroundings, Rodger's tone seems more hurried: "This world is such a beautiful place, it's such a tragedy

I've had to live such a pathetic life in it" because of the cruelty of women. And then, curiously, as he's heading back to his car, he catches himself in the sunlit reflection of his window: "Check it out. There's me. In all my fabulousness. Oh yeah. Elliot Rodger. [And now a little stage laugh.] I am so awesome." It's a strange scene: like a version of the Lacanian mirror stage—twenty years too late—and one that doesn't work, that doesn't allow him purchase on himself, some distance from his feeling and some recognition that he is a separate person responsible for his own choices. The pathos here is that he can only communicate with the mirror; he can only star in his "selfie" videos.

By the end, Rodger's last videos reveal him as a twisted documentarian, archiving for us before the fact the rationale for what he was about to do. As he puts it, his life has become "a major problem. A problem I intend to rectify." He proclaims himself ready to address the "injustice" he has suffered, one we know to be inevitable. From behind his video camera, he shows us, almost as proof of the grievous insult he suffered, the image of a young couple at the beach. He reports that it's "torture for me to watch. I have to do this. I have to film this. I have to show the world why life isn't fair. I have to show everyone why I hate the world—because no girl would do this with me." But who was really watching?

Becoming Visible

On his "Day of Retribution," Elliot Rodger sought the visibility he craved, the tragic murder/ suicide that would confirm him as both victim and victimizer. His visibility, however, became spectral as he lived on in the haunting presence of his online videos and writing, a presence that was quickly captured by the media and hyped as the monstrous.

In her May 25 *Washington Post* story on Rodger, film critic Ann Hornaday asserted that Rodger's "delusions were inflated, if not created, by the entertainment industry he grew up in." She asked,

> How many students watch outsized frat-boy fantasies like "Neighbors" and feel, as Rodger did, unjustly shut out of college life that should be full of "sex and fun and pleasure"? How many men, raised on a steady diet of Judd Apatow comedies in which the shlubby arrested adolescent always gets the girl, find that those happy endings constantly elude them and conclude, "It's not fair"?

Seth Rogan, star of *Neighbors*, tweeted back the next day, "How dare you imply that me getting girls in movies caused a lunatic to go on the rampage." Judd Apatow of *Bridesmaids* and *Knocked Up* fame, chimed in, "I find your article horribly insulting and misinformed. Why is it," claimed Apatow, that "it's always everything else but mental illness."

Hornaday and others read Rodger's misogyny as reflective of attitudes in popular media. Rodger's autobiography is dripping with it. Women, Rodger insists, are flawed. He writes at length:

> There is something mentally wrong with the way their brains are wired, as if they haven't evolved from animal-like thinking. They are incapable of reason or thinking rationally. They are like animals, completely controlled by their primal, depraved emotions and impulses. That is why they are attracted to barbaric, wild, beast-like men. They are beasts themselves. Beasts should not be able to have any rights in a civilized society. If their wickedness is not contained, the whole of humanity will be held back from advancement to a more civilized state. Women should not have

the right to choose who to mate with. That choice should be made for them by civilized men of intelligence. If women had the freedom to choose which men to mate with, like they do today, they would breed with stupid, degenerate men, which would only produce stupid, degenerate offspring. This in turn would hinder the advancement of humanity. Not only hinder it, but devolve humanity completely. Women are like a plague that must be quarantined. (117)

Indeed, objectification of his intended victims wasn't far behind as Rodger asserted in his videos that girls' "sexual attraction is flawed," and he declared that "you girls have starved me of sex" and "taken eight years of my life." By this point he'd nearly convinced himself: they must be punished. Ironically, it was not women who were driven by "animal-like thinking" and "incapable of rational thinking"; it was Rodger.

In response to the critics of Rodger's misogyny, other misogynists crawled out of hiding to launch their own "Elliot Rodger is an American Hero" Facebook page that praised Rodger's "struggle against feminazi ideology." Requests to remove the site because of its hate speech were first resisted by Facebook, the corporation that capitalizes on characters like Rodger and turns them from outliers into mainstream figures to post about. The more buzz the better.

Even his father participated in the media spectacle through his *20/20* interview. On the evening of June 27, 2014, Barbara Walters emerged from retirement "on special assignment" to host a story entitled "The Secret Life of Elliot Rodger," one that Walters promotes in grisly fashion:

> Tonight, this is special; it's a milestone—the first time that a parent of a mass murderer has ever spoken on television. Peter Rodger tells us that he is doing this to show other parents the warning signs that he missed and what changes we desperately need in the mental health care system so that no one has to go through the night that changed his life and so many others forever.

So the tabloid journalism, complete with blood spattered streets, the audio of a 9/11 call, and red string and red pushpins connecting the images of smiling victims, is wrapped in a nobler cause—"to show other parents the warning signs that he missed."

The problem is that the show doesn't deliver what it promises. First, there is not much secret about the life of Rodger. He offered a 140-page chronicle of that life along with several videos that went viral the day after the murders. Second, whose "milestone" is this interview? Walters's? Third, the *20/20* episode promises "chilling details you've never heard until now," but then fails to deliver anything new. What we see instead is the assertion of plausible deniability on the part of the father: "I didn't know the monster that was in my son." On the one hand, the father describes his son as possessed; on the other as the oh-so-clever liar, who managed to dupe even his own father. No one can discount the difficulty for a parent or anyone who knew this troubled young man, in making sense of his actions, yet there seems something a little grandiose in Peter Rodger's characterization: "This is the American horror story. The world's horror story. When you have somebody who on the outside is one thing and on the inside is something completely different, and you don't see it."

It's a little hard to believe that a parent who sought the help of a psychiatrist for his seven-year-old, who observed his difficulties in making friends, and who knew that his grown son was prescribed risperidone, a recognized treatment for schizophrenia and bipolar disorder, would simply attribute his problems to shyness. Peter Rodger claims that there was nothing he could do in the face of his son's refusal to take the anti-psychotic drug prescribed by his psychiatrist or ever go back to that doctor because his son "was an adult age." There's no indication that Rodger's parents ever used the power of the purse to make their continued financial support conditional on his getting the care he so desperately needed.

Ultimately, our understanding of Rodger from his autobiography and videos comes from the long shadow cast by his violence, and one is struck by the incommensurability of it all. The Isla Vista students he murdered were stand-ins for all the young women who failed to notice him, who avoided him because he was weird, or small, or shy, or unmanly, and the young men they fancied instead. We can read his troubling videos and "My Twisted World" as cries for help or as cold assertions that the violence he committed was fully justified in his mind, that his murderous rampage through the streets of Isla Vista was something other than the temper tantrum of the infantilized speaker who just couldn't have what he wanted, or what he said he wanted—a blonde girl to give him her attention, affection, and sex.

Failing other interventions, Rodger couldn't figure out how to use his virtual life to develop other skills that would have helped him secure the non-digital life he so desired. Rather, his social media became just another staging ground for his "awesomeness," a platform through which he demanded visibility. Not getting the "likes" he so desperately craved, he planned and ultimately carried out a final spectacle, one in which he played the starring role. Social media didn't make Rodger act out; his pathological narcissism did. But social media does cater to a narrowed bandwidth of emotion, one focused primarily on performing a self to capture and hold attention. In this way, Rodger's story is a cautionary tale of how a lonely, hypersensitive boy with few social skills initially sought safe haven in a virtual fantasy world, one in which he enjoyed, for fleeting moments, the illusion of advancement and triumph. His "Day of Retribution" only affirmed the tragic loss that a single troubled young man set upon becoming visible can perform.

Works Cited

Alexander, Jonathan, and Jacqueline Rhodes. "Technologies of the Self in the Aftermath: Affect, Subjectivity, Composition." *Rhetoric Review*, vol. 29, no. 2, 2010, pp. 145–164.

Freud, Sigmund. "On Narcissism: An Introduction." *Collected Papers*, vol. 4. Basic, 1959, pp. 30–59.

Greig, Alex. "All the Lonely Facebook Friends: Study Shows Social Media Makes Us MORE Lonely and Unhappy and LESS Sociable." *Daily Mail*, 12 September 2013, dailymail.co.uk/news/article-2419419/All-lonely-Facebook-friends-Study-shows-social-media-makes-MORE-lonely-unhappy-LESS-sociable.html. Accessed 3 July 2017.

Hornaday, Anna. "In A Final Videotaped Message, A Sad Reflection of the Sexist Stories We So Often See on Screen." *The Washington Post*, 25 May 2014, washingtonpost.com/lifestyle/style/in-a-final-video taped-message-a-sad-reflection-of-the-sexist-stories-we-so-often-see-on-screen/2014/05/25/dec7e7ea-e40d-11e3-afc6a1dd9407abcf_story.html?utmterm=.f7e972ed01e7.

Launer, Dale. "How I Tried to Help Elliot Rodger." *BBC News*, 9 July 2014, www.bbc.com/news/magazine-28197785. Accessed 3 July 2017.

Mather, Kate. "Elliot Rodger may have used knife, hammer, machete in killings, attorney says." *Los Angeles Times*, 21 June 2014, latimes.com/local/lanow/la-me-ln-mystery-grief-surround-elliot-rodgers-first-three-victims-20140620-story.html. Accessed 3 July 2017.

Rodger, Elliot. "My Twisted World: The Story of Elliot Rodger." Unpublished manifesto, documentcloud.org/documents/1173808-elliot-rodger-manifesto.html. Accessed 3 July 2017.

Speer, Richard. "A Selfie-Era Killer: Social Media and Elliot Rodger." *New York Post*, 28 May 2014, http://nypost.com/2014/05/28/a-selfie-era-killer-social-media-and-elliot-rodger/. Accessed 3 July 2017.

"The Secret Life of Elliot Rodger." *20/20*, hosted by Barbara Walters, season 37, episode 32, 2014.

Turkle, Sherry. *Alone Together: Why We Expect More from Technology and Less from Each Other*. Basic, 2011.

——. *Life on the Screen: Identity in the Age of the Internet*. Simon & Schuster, 1997.

23

WRITING WITH ROBOTS AND OTHER CURIOSITIES OF THE AGE OF MACHINE RHETORICS

William Hart-Davidson

Since the late 1970s, rhetoric and writing studies has taken artificial intelligence and its influence on human rhetorical activity seriously, but only occasionally. Carolyn Miller and Lynette Hunter are two significant voices in this conversation, along with Kennedy (see also Kennedy and Long). Miller, in particular, has kept a very important question before us: wherein lies human rhetorical agency when machines and humans write together? (138). In this chapter, my aim is to bring this and several other key questions about human–machine writing to the broad audience of rhetoric and composition scholars and teachers. In so doing, I hope to broaden the view of this group to include issues beyond what has been, arguably, the dominant topic associated with automated technology in writing: machine scoring of standardized essays (see Condon; Perelman).

In the first part of this chapter, I explore not a future but the unevenly distributed present day circumstances of "assistive writing technologies"—commonly known as 'bots—that are increasingly incorporated into the writing process. Advanced 'bots are already in use by news wire services to draft sports and financial reports (Van Dalen). We may soon live in a world where most day-to-day writing tasks do not begin with a human creating a first draft, but with a machine assembling one from a personal—that is, built from one's lifetime activity as a writer—archive of words (McLeod, Hart-Davidson, and Grabill).

The second part of this chapter addresses two important sets of questions for teachers and researchers of writing in the age of machine rhetoric. The first set of questions deals with how we address humans: How should writers and teachers of writing think about this world of cyborg writing? How should we talk about writing with machines as the ability of machines to deploy rhetorical strategies—often at humans' explicit request—grows more sophisticated? Are they collaborators? Might they one day be seen as our co-authors? A second set deals with how we address machines: What should we teach machines to do? *How* should we teach them? We have long recognized the perils of a rhetorical education for humans that is devoid of ethical reasoning, but we now must take seriously a new set of responsibilities to teach machines what to do and what not do with powerful rhetorical strategies.

Part I: Robots Write

It is true. Robots can write. In fact, they are already putting writers out of work, or at least shifting the work they do to some other phase of the writing process. You may have heard about a company that launched in 2010 called Narrative Science. They started when a computer scientist got together with a journalism professor. What they produced was a piece of software that analyzed the box score for a baseball game and, drawing on a huge archive of sportswriting, produced a story about the game, complete with a suitable lead image and headline. Technology writer Steven Levy profiled the company and its founders in a story in *Wired* in 2012, asking "Can an Algorithm Write a News Story Better than a Human Reporter?" Back in 2012, Narrative Science's founder Kristian Hammond told Levy that by 2025, 90 percent of news stories would be machine-generated. He also predicted a robot-authored story would win a Pulitzer. In 2017.

Today Narrative Science is one of two big players in AI-generated content, along with many smaller ones (not to mention groups within tech giants such as Alphabet and IBM). The other is a company called Automated Insights (AI, get it?). They make bank by helping companies turn financial data into a host of required regulatory reports. It is hard to say how much of the news content we read today is produced by software such as Narrative Science's *Quill* or Automated Insights' *Wordsmith* platform. They keep their client list quiet. And the companies that use their services aren't keen on letting others know. But some other writing robots are a bit more public.

In 2016, Microsoft taught a Twitter 'bot named Tay how to tweet. The goal was to build a responsive autonomous agent for 18–24-year-olds. They trained Tay with a large amount of user activity initially, all of it positive and aligned with the use case it was designed to serve, but in a controlled environment. Full disclosure: some of our experienced architecture students in my department at MSU participated in this alpha test group.

And then Microsoft decided it was time for Tay to learn from all of the Internet. Less than 24 hours later, Tay was routinely tweeting horrible, racist, misogynist stuff. The Internet had taught Tay to be a troll. The example of Tay points to one of the most compelling reasons for pursuing the kind of work I will discuss here today: if we leave it to others entirely, things will get ugly.

Microsoft took Tay offline and apologized, saying they'd have to be more careful next time. The next time came. It went badly as well. They apologized again. Today Tay's account is protected, but presumably her rhetorical education goes on. How? Good question.

We don't have a clear idea what a rhetorical education for robots should be like. What it should and should not include. And as the author of *Rhetorica Ad Herennium* (should we say Cicero's robot?) reminds us, we've known these risks and have been asking questions like these about teaching *humans* rhetoric for a long time.

But we are only starting to learn about teaching robots rhetoric.

In Madison at the RSA Summer Institutes, Ryan Omizo and I led a group of colleagues in a three day workshop to produce a prototype application called *Use What You Choose*. This app performed some rhetorical analysis, but its main function was to produce a new text. It was a writing as well as reading robot.

The use case goes like this: you have just bought a consumer electronics product on Amazon.com. Enter the product name into *Use What You Choose* and it will give you helpful advice: tips, hacks, and alerts that others who have used the device have passed along.

The information *Use What You Choose* assembled into these reports comes from another source: a corpus of Amazon.com product reviews. Sometimes thousands of them for a specific product. The service we built picks specific pieces of information from 50,000 of these reviews —tips, hacks, and alerts—and gets rid of other stuff. And it only picks the best ones of these. We did not have time to rigorously evaluate its performance during the workshop, but we left after just three days with evidence that it performs reliably compared to a team of trained raters with Ph.D.s in rhetoric.

A useful service? Perhaps. But even more interesting from our point of view is that it explores and evaluates theories of rhetorical genre proposed by Carolyn Miller and particularly an extension of Miller developed by Catherine Schryer. That is, the learning methods we selected proceed from the idea that if those theories have merit, we would see the app perform well. Tentatively, we would say that the repetitive signals of instructional text were indeed strong enough in the corpus we worked with that we could train a machine learning algorithm to reliably find and distinguish them from the persuasive signals of a product review.

Use What You Choose also pursues a question posed by Stuart Selber about how likely we are to see genre hybridity in open forums like Amazon.com reviews. Would we find genres embedded in and intermixed with others? The short answer is yes (Larson et al.). It is worth noting that the kind of work UWYC can do, while impressive, is limited when it comes to a broad conception of the term "writing." Strictly speaking, it assembles a text out of pre-written bits. We, as designers of the system, have given it an a priori structure to follow, and some heuristics to condition its inquiry, and some formatting and style guidelines to guide the final form of its product. It fills in the rest. And, in so doing, creates something useful that didn't exist before. It does an admirable job. And for my part, I don't know that I ask those students in my writing courses to do much differently than we've asked our machine learner to do. I offer a prompt, a heuristic to guide inquiry, some formatting and style guidelines, and send them off to create. What they bring back to me usually needs further work. The same goes for our robot. But it is not a stretch to say that the robot is good at drafting. Is that writing? I think it is. It is not all of writing. But it is enough that I believe we soon will all be using drafting assistants to do assembly work in many, maybe even most, routine writing situations. We write routinely with machines now. Soon, we will be co-authors with them.

But Can Robots Do Rhetoric?

Today, I would not claim that robots can do rhetoric on their own. Not yet. And maybe not ever. But that is because I take something such as Aristotle's definition of "observing, in any given case, the available means of persuasion" to involve a dynamic interplay between convention and expectation, something that happens on both an interpersonal scale and intersubjective scale (Smith). But I do think robots can help humans do rhetoric. I'm quite confident of it. And I'm growing more confident that they can help humans do it better than they otherwise might.

To explain, I'll talk about two robots that I have helped to create for this purpose: the *Hedge-o-Matic* and the *Faciloscope*. The *Hedge-o-Matic* (Omizo and Hart-Davidson) is a simple, though not uncomplicated, application built into an article that was recently published in the journal *Enculturation*. It was reviewed as both an article and functional source code, a hybrid we came to call an "appticle." Readers can enter text and have the application analyze it to see how the algorithm works.

The *Hedge-o-Matic* (HoM) takes a passage of text as input and parses it into sentences. It then classifies each sentence as a hedge or non-hedge, or perhaps as more or less hedge-y. We are looking for propositional hedges in the HoM—the sort of moves a rhetor makes when she wants to adjust a claim to suit the strength of the available evidence. The HOM then presents results as feedback to users in two views:

- The first is a visual: a hedge distribution chart showing where the hedgey and non-hedgey sentences are in the passage. Reading left to right on the *x*-axis, the dots show each sentence in order and where it falls on the hedge/non-hedge continuum.
- The second display is a simple list of the classified sentences with the lable—hedge or non-hedge—and the confidence values reported by the app.

The *Faciloscope* (Omizo et al.) works similarly to the *Hedge-o-Matic* in that takes plain text input and performs a kind of rhetorical analysis. The audience for the application is non-academic in this case, however. It was created for and with informal learning specialists working in science museums around the United States. They use it to see how well online conversation threads are achieving their goals for facilitating informal learning in science. In this way it helps them with tasks related to moderating and encouraging online discussion.

Sometimes the facilitators monitor many threads at once—in social media and blogging spaces for instance—and the *Faciloscope* helps the moderators see facilitation moves happening in the thread. Facilitation moves have some things in common with forum control moves, they are phatic gestures oftentimes, but their frequency in a thread is a reliable indicator that productive interaction is going on from the point of view of informal learning facilitators. We learned that not from creating the *Faciloscope*. Quite the opposite. We created the *Faciloscope* because we learned, from many hours of painstaking human interpretation over a five-year period, what rhetorical features most contributed to "successful" discussion threads (Sackey et al.). Having accumulated a sufficient number of these threads, a small team led by Ryan and me was able to build our humble little app in about three months. The result: folks not trained in rhetorical analysis or qualitative research could arrive at a similar evaluation of what constitutes a thread that is going well and what constitutes one that needs some professional assistance in just a few seconds.

Part II: Can We Live Together With Robots?

Maybe.

The "we" I refer to in the subtitle in this case is the group of professionals who make their living teaching and researching writing. The question, more elaborated, is how will our work change (including the possibility of it going away all together) as assistive technologies become a more routine part of the writing process? My vision is that we can coexist. But we will have to actively propose a framework in which technologies are more clearly defined as assistive to human endeavors in writing and rhetoric. And by active I mean we not only have to talk about such a framework, we have to find ways to help build it.

I think it is fair to say that the *Hedge-o-Matic* and the *Faciloscope* extend the human capacity for rhetorical analysis. They do so by expanding how much one can easily do in a given amount of time, similar to techniques of distant reading proposed by Franco Moretti or more precisely, to macroanalysis as proposed by Matt Jockers. But more interestingly, perhaps, they extend the material conditions of rhetorical performance—make new ambient possibilities, might Rickert concede?—and thereby extend *who* can do it.

With the *Faciloscope*, in particular, we deliberately wanted to make a kind of rhetorical analysis that our museum partners found useful more readily available to them, despite the fact that they had neither the theoretical nor the research training needed to do it routinely. To say nothing of the time.

In making these extensions, we have been very careful—perhaps overly so—not to extend too far. I've played this robot idea as tongue in cheek thus far, but I am quite serious about not putting resources out into the world that let our disciplinary knowledge be easily co-opted, even weaponized, to do harm.

But for the moment I will stay away from apocalyptic imagery and pose a question: can we live with robots? Let me clarify: by "we" I mean the people in the room today, and others like us. And by "live" I mean something close to "continue to make our living by writing, and teaching others to write and speak well, ethically, with grace and creativity, with purpose and with keen attention to who we influence and how."

I think the answer is: maybe. It's not a no. But it's not a definite yes either. So much of the writing that folks do day today is routine that it will be quickly replaced by robots. Soon. No looking back. And companies such as Automated Insights and Narrative Science won't even have to use the word writing at all to sell their services. In fact, they don't now. They say things like: "you are awash in data, but what you really need is the stories the data tells. Let us help you find those stories."

Let me give you a prediction of my own. I don't think we are far away from a time when almost nobody composes a first draft of anything but texts meant to be taken as, for lack of a better word, art. We'll fire up our writing software and ask that it get us started. You might ask that it constrain itself to using only those words that it knows are already yours. Or, depending on the task and genre, you might ask that it incorporate texts written by others. You'll take over at the revision stage.

Think of your own writing process, and you may concede that this transition is already well under way. I wrote this talk by assembling texts I've been writing for the last year or so now. Words and images, yes, but also frameworks and structure. I didn't have them all in one place or in one framework as a "draft." It was messier than that. But it wouldn't be inaccurate to say I started by revising.

So while I think the robots are coming, I don't think this means humans are going to vanish from the scenes of writing any time soon. But I think this means that as writing teachers and researchers, and especially as rhetoric scholars, we have other, important roles to play.

Let me begin to sketch possibilities for living with robots with a heuretic device invented by Michael Wojcik in his 2012 M.A. thesis at Michigan State where he offered thoughts toward a definition of "computational rhetoric." Wojcik suggested that we might conceive of a computational approach to rhetoric by thinking about various kinds of scholarship and projects that exist along four axes. The first is perhaps the most intuitive. It describes a continuum of robots that make texts vs. those that interpret them. The second describes why the robots do what they do—to help someone engaged in a domain-specific task? Or, at the extreme other end, to test the very limits of what robots as writers and rhetors can do? The third axis contemplates the relationship between humans and robots. We might understand it as moving from a human-dominant assistive relationship on the left to a more fully autonomous agent on the right. The fourth axes defines how the robot's governing rules function, either as a set of fixed rules that process dynamic input or as an adaptive, evolving system that changes, or learns, over time.

If we are going to live with robots, we had better get busy exploring the problem space defined by these axes. And others, besides, most probably. But these are a good start. And let me tell you, we have some work to do.

In Figure 23.1 I've mapped four projects—three of which I've discussed above and a fourth, *Eli Review*—onto Wojcik's axes. *Use What You Choose* was the first time Ryan and I made a deliberate effort to go explore parts of the problem space where we had not yet visited. We felt that was in the spirit of the RSA Summer Institutes, and part of an explicit goal of ours to help more rhetoric and writing scholars prepare to do the work of shaping the development of

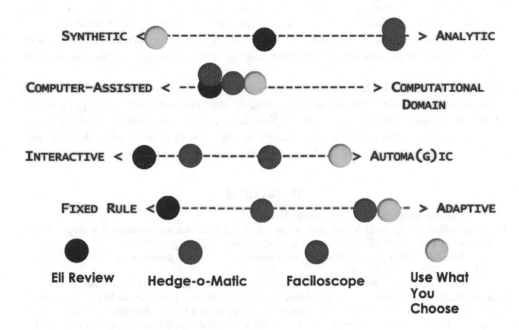

Figure 23.1 Four Projects Mapped onto Wojcik's Axes

automated writing technology. Neither of the two automated writing companies I mentioned earlier were started by academics with rhetoric and writing backgrounds. This is important because it means that, lacking a disciplinary perspective on what produces a text and on the ethical implications of what it means to learn to use rhetorical strategies, these groups have nonetheless produced robots that produce texts and share them with the world. We might say they aren't really writing. Or that what they do isn't all of writing, at least. We might say that they are assembling texts that look like other texts that someone has shown them. But even this can be pretty powerful.

Use What You Choose does a little of that, but also does something different. It finds bits of embedded genres—deliberately, structures that are much like Bakhtin's speech genres—and offers them back to a reader as a gesture of assistance. Its role is not to mimic (and thereby displace) a human, but rather to sit in relation to humans on either side of a purchase transaction and offer help that represents a diverse set of use experiences. In this way, it is a robot that performs an ethical relationship with human readers and writers that we, it's creators, can live with.

Eli, a fixed rule, interactive, computer assisted service is designed to explicitly help teachers and students who are writing. It coordinates and assembles feedback for human learners. But it doesn't learn anything from the many sessions it helps to facilitate. At least not yet. And what about the others? Why did we make them? Why have sought to teach machines rhetoric?

Why teach machines rhetoric? I think there are at least four good reasons to do so:

- to extend rhetorical expertise to those who may benefit from it but who may lack explicit rhetorical training;
- to extend the capacity of humans to do certain kinds of rhetorical tasks due to challenges of scale, seeking the affordances of speed;

- to extend our knowledge of rhetoric using thought experiments, executed in computer code, to test conjectures, pursue answers to questions, or simply explore possibilities;
- to stay involved in the kind of work that mobilizes our disciplinary knowledge in ways that we may or may not approve of, preserving our right to intervene or lead when needed.

The robots are already here. And more are coming. And by and large, it will not be folks with training in writing and rhetoric studies who create or use them. But we can perhaps be among those who influence both how they work and how they are incorporated into the writing practices of people and institutions. I think we definitely should be. And in order to do that, we need to stay involved with theorizing, building, and researching writing by non-humans.

Works Cited

Aristotle. *Rhetoric and Poetics*. Random House, 1984.

Condon, William. "Large-scale Assessment, Locally Developed Measures, and Automated Scoring of Essays: Fishing for Red Herrings?" *Assessing Writing*, vol. 18, no. 1, 2013, pp. 100–08.

Hunter, Lynette. "Rhetoric and Artificial Intelligence." *Rhetorica: A Journal of the History of Rhetoric*, vol. 9, no. 4, 1991, pp. 317–40.

——. *Critiques of Knowing: Situated Textualities in Science, Computing and the Arts*. Routledge, 2002.

Jockers, Matthew L. *Macroanalysis: Digital Methods and Literary History*. University of Illinois Press, 2013.

Levy, Steven. "Can an Algorithm Write a Better News Story than a Human Reporter." *Wired 24*, 2012.

Kennedy, Krista A. *Textual Curators and Writing Machines: Authorial Agency in Encyclopedias, Print to Digital*. University of Minnesota, 2009.

Kennedy, Krista, and Seth Long. "The Trees within the Forest: Extracting, Coding, and Visualizing Subjective Data in Authorship Studies." *Rhetoric and the Digital Humanities*, edited by James Ridolfo, and William Hart-Davidson. U. of Chicago P, 2015, p. 140.

Larson, Brian, William Hart-Davidson, Kenneth C. Walker, Douglas M. Walls, and Ryan Omizoa. "Use What You Choose: Applying Computational Methods to Genre Studies in Technical Communication." *Proceedings of the 34th ACM International Conference on the Design of Communication*. ACM, 2016.

McLeod, Michael, William Hart-Davidson, and Jeffrey Grabill. "Theorizing and Building Online Writing Environments: User-Centered Design Beyond the Interface." *Designing Web-Based Applications for 21st Century Writing Classrooms*, edited by George Pullman, and Gu Baotong Gu. Amityville, NY: Baywood, 2013, pp. 7–18.

Miller, Carolyn R. "Opportunity, Opportunism, and Progress: Kairos in the Rhetoric of Technology." *Argumentation*, vol. 8, no.1, 1994, pp. 81–96.

——. "Technology as a Form of Consciousness: A Study of Contemporary Ethos." *Communication Studies*, vol. 29, no. 4, 1978, pp. 228–36.

——. "Writing in a Culture of Simulation." *Towards a Rhetoric of Everyday Life: New Directions in Research on Writing, Text, and Discourse*, edited by Martin Nystrand, and John Duffy. U. of Wisconsin P., 2003, pp. 53–83.

——. "What Can Automation Tell Us about Agency?" *Rhetoric Society Quarterly*, vol. 37, no. 2, 2007, pp. 137–57.

——. "Should We Name the Tools? Concealing and Revealing the Art of Rhetoric." *The Public Work of Rhetoric: Citizen-Scholars and Civic Engagement*, 2010, pp. 19–38.

Moretti, Franco. *Distant reading*. Verso Books, 2013.

Omizo, Ryan, and Hart-Davidson, William. "Hedge-O-Matic." *Enculturation* 7 (2016). http://enculturation.net/hedgeomatic.

Omizo, Ryan, Minh-Tam Nguyen, Ian Clark, and William Hart-Davidson. "You Can Read the Comments Section Again: The Faciloscope App and Automated Rhetorical Analysis." *DH Commons Journal* (October, 2016). https://dhcommons.org/journal/2016/you-can-read-comments-section-again-faciloscope-app-and-automated-rhetorical-analysis. Accessed 29 June 2017.

Perelman, Les. "Construct Validity, Length, Score, and Time in Holistically Graded Writing Assessments: The Case against Automated Essay Scoring (AES)." *International Advances in Writing Research: Cultures, Places, Measures*, 2012, pp. 121–31.

Rhetorica ad Herennium, trans. Harry Caplan. Loeb Classical Library, 403, 1954, pp. 18–21.

Rickert, Thomas. *Ambient Rhetoric: The Attunements of Rhetorical Being.* U of Pittsburgh P, 2013.

Ridolfo, Jim. "Rhetorical Delivery as Strategy: Rebuilding the Fifth Canon from Practitioner Stories." *Rhetoric Review*, vol. 31, no. 2, 2012, pp. 117–29.

Ridolfo, Jim, and Dànielle Nicole DeVoss. "Composing for Recomposition: Rhetorical Velocity and Delivery." *Kairos*, vol.13, no. 2, 2009. http://kairos.technorhetoric.net/13.2/topoi/ridolfo_devoss/velocity.html. Accessed 17 Nov. 2017.

Sackey, Donnie Johnson, Minh-Tam Nguyen, and Jeffery T. Grabill. "Constructing Learning Spaces: What We Can Learn from Studies of Informal Learning Online." *Computers and Composition*, 35, 2015, pp. 112–24.

Smith, Frank. *Writing and the Writer.* Routledge, 2013.

Van Dalen, Arjen. "The Algorithms Behind the Headlines: How Machine-Written News Redefines the Core Skills of Human Journalists." *Journalism Practice*, vol. 6, no. 5–6, 2012, pp. 648–58.

Wojcik, Michael W. *Inventing Computational Rhetoric.* Diss. Michigan State University, 2013.

PART V

Regulation and Control

24

RHETORIC, COPYRIGHT, *TECHNE*

The Regulation of Social Media Production and Distribution

James E. Porter

We have to start by recognizing that *all writing is property and as such is regulated*—and one key way it is regulated is through copyright law, copyright custom, and copyright lore,[1] a vast copyright system composed of laws, policies, and regulations but also of practices, attitudes, and ideologies, and enforced and directed via various technological functions, blocks, and filters. This system is not all bad. It is generative as well as prohibitive: in many ways it promotes and supports writing, and encourages its production and distribution. In other ways the system impedes it.

This regulatory system shapes the composing process and determines, to use Foucaultian terms, what can be said and what must not be said; what discourses are allowed to appear (and when and where); how discourses are to be packaged, framed, compiled, and distributed; and, most importantly, who gets to speak/write and who doesn't, and who gets to see these discourses and who doesn't. The regulatory system sets the roles, limits, and sometimes rules for writing and reading. And the system has an economic component as well: it locates and defines value, and makes determinations about cost and credit.

Understanding how these regulatory procedures work is vital knowledge for rhetors—particularly relevant to the production and distribution of discourse in public spaces. Particularly in the age of digital writing and social media, we have to think thoroughly and carefully about how copyright in its various forms—laws, policies, practices, custom, lore—shapes both the production of writing (its invention, generation, creation) and its distribution, and thus is central to the *techne* of rhetoric in the digital age.

For example: When writers post to social media sites such as Facebook and Instagram they are involved in an exchange of property rights. Facebook and Instagram both have policies specifying that users own the content they post there (and so users retain liability if that content infringes someone's copyrights). However, both platforms also claim a "non-exclusive, transferable, sub-licensable, royalty-free, worldwide license to use any IP content that [users] post on or in connection with the site." In other words, as a condition for your using their writing platforms, Facebook and Instagram claim the right to use your postings however they wish—including for commercial gain—even though you are the copyright owner and carry the liability associated with that ownership (Reed 571). Of course there is an economic component to this relationship as well: in exchange for using Facebook you allow Facebook to monitor and sell your data.

Thus, the writing you produce and post to the Internet may or may not be "yours" to have and to hold and control in any way you wish. Under US copyright law, once you put your ideas into a tangible written format—once you post something on the Internet for digital distribution via social media—then the writing becomes intellectual property, and a number of legal questions arise: Does your posting infringe the copyrights of others (if you have copied pieces of their discourse in your post)? Do you own the copyrights to that posting—or do you surrender some of those rights when you post to a platform such as Facebook, or Pinterest, or your university's online course server? If you are retweeting a Twitter post with a picture of Mickey Mouse included, does your post infringe Disney's copyright? Do you have the right to block, impede, or put restrictions on others' uses of your posting? These are fundamental questions about writing in the digital age—about *the right to produce, distribute, and circulate writing*—of importance to rhetoric.

What this chapter does is (1) highlight a few basic copyright principles and briefly track the emergence of copyright law in the Western tradition, as pertains to the *techne* of rhetoric; and (2) explore a few representative developments in the current social media scene, focusing in particular on policies and ideologies that encourage rhetorical production and generation versus those that prohibit, restrain, or impede that production. My main point overall is this: Because copyright is a contested public issue pertaining centrally to *the right to write*, rhetoric needs to embrace copyright as fundamental to its art and disciplinary territory, particularly in the digital age.

Some Copyright Basics: Principles and History

Copyright[2] refers quite literally to the right to make copies:[3] the right to copy, reuse, and circulate others' writing, or your own, in whole or in part. As a legal principle, copyright covers both a thing (*the copy*) and a process (*the act of copying*). In this respect, copyright, like the field of rhetoric, is caught in a tension between product and process—and the process is multifaceted.

First, there is the production side: the creation of an original, what is known traditionally as authorship. Authorship is often represented nostalgically and romantically as the lone individual/intellectual creator, the romantic poet or genius essayist, but there is also the corporate, governmental, and collaborative author. The author can be a publisher (Oxford University Press), a media franchise (Disney), or a corporation (Microsoft). Authorship can certainly be social—and even individual authors get their ideas from somewhere (i.e., authorship involves copying, too). Authorship itself is a conflicted term: Does it refer to the *creator* of the work, or to the *owner* of the work, or to both? In the public and professional realms, as opposed to the academic realm, the author-as-creator is often different from the author-as-owner.

Second, there is distribution or delivery: the act of making the copy, or multiple copies, which could be as simple as handwriting an essay or as complicated as setting a book for the printing press. And distribution of course includes the acts of sharing, distributing, disseminating the copy or copies—publishing in the distribution sense, or what rhetoric has called the canon of *delivery* or simply circulation (Trimbur; Porter, "Recovering").

Each of these stages in the process entails labor and costs, and in the case of distribution, a complicated political/economic network supporting the enterprise. So the object itself, *the copy*, is just the tip of the iceberg; the copy is typically part of a much broader process of production and delivery involving multiple stakeholders, all of whom are hoping (or expecting) to be paid or credited for their labors. Copyright law represents the effort to balance the competing rights of these various stakeholders.

Copying what others have said and written has long been a fundamental and highly respected method for rhetorical invention, and also for teaching and learning. Through much of the history of Western rhetoric education, the act of copying—in the form of specific practices such as *memoria, imitatio,* and *compilatio*—was integral not only to the canon of rhetorical invention but also to the education of the rhetor overall (Corbett; Murphy). This was especially true in the Roman era and well into the era of medieval rhetoric. The writers of the Christian patristic era (Augustine, Jerome, Bernard of Chartres) "borrowed" others' work heavily, frequently without attribution, and that was a sign of respect for the authority of those existing texts.

If you were a student in the Roman system of rhetorical education, you were expected to copy and memorize the wisdom of your elders and of the past (for example, in the form of maxims and fables). You were supposed to imitate good examples. You were supposed to collect sayings and pieces of texts and put them together in new configurations. One common technique for copying, *compilatio,* involved collecting fragments from various sources and putting them together into a new whole—what we call, in the digital age, *remixing.*

To put it another way, the reuse of text was integral to rhetorical invention. This process served an immediate generative purpose in helping you produce a particular speech or text at a particular moment, but it also served a larger purpose, aiding your intellectual and moral development as a rhetor needing to speak wisely and effectively within your culture. These practices were born out of respect for intellectual ancestry and wisdom and out of respect for culture. Copying is how you *learn* your culture; it is also how you *make* it.

In many ways current attitudes favoring free and unrestricted digital copying, filesharing, and downloading documents and MP3s—what might be termed the *hacker ethic*—recall classical and medieval notions of the ethics of copying and reusing texts. This digital scribe is also somebody who takes images into Photoshop and "manipulates," crops, resizes, adds text, changes. Writing in the digital age is, appropriately, memory, imitation, and compilation, as well as repackaging, redesigning, repurposing, redelivering text, as it was in an earlier age of rhetorical practice.

The problem of copyright infringement (and of its cousin, plagiarism) emerged much later in Western history, out of the realm of print culture. Copyright was not much of an issue prior to the age of the printing press because copying technology was primitive and expensive (stylus, ink, parchment), and the process long, difficult, and laborious: copying a Bible by hand was tedious, hard work for monks in the medieval scribal age. The technology of the printing press made it much easier to produce multiple copies of that Bible—but printing required expensive machinery as well as labor and specialized knowledge, not to mention an elaborate economic, political, and social network of ships, horses and carriages, trains, trucks, planes, mailing systems, bookstores, and delivery *people,* as well as treaties, trade agreements, contracts, law enforcement mechanisms, and governments (*people* again) to hold the process together, what we might call a publishing network (McKee and Porter).

Copyright law came into being because this elaborate system needed a mechanism for balancing the competing economic interests of authors, publishers, commercial tradespeople, and the state—and also to define that deep and perplexing philosophical question, What is a copy, and who should own it? Copyright as a system of legal regulation did not exist until the eighteenth century, when it emerged in England in the Statute of Anne in 1710. Up until then ownership of texts in Western Europe was largely "derived from privileges bestowed by princes" on the book publishing trade (Darnton). With the emergence of the publishing trade, and thanks to the presence of book pirates—an important influence on the system[4]—some kind of legal system for determining ownership and rights was needed. That was the beginning of European copyright law. As it formed and evolved, the law was pressed into service to reconcile the competing needs, priorities, interests, and rights of the state, of book publishers, of book sellers, and, eventually, of authors. Copyright laws helped regulate a complex economic network based on the production and distribution of texts.

The idea of the author as the lone, creative, genius writer is a fairly recent historical development tied largely to economic interests: writers wanted to be paid and credited for their work, and not just at the point of sale. As Woodmansee, Rose ("Author," "Nine-tenths"), Foucault ("What"), and others point out, authorship is a legally constructed concept first theorized in German Romantic philosophy and literary theory and then later in English Romantic poetic theory, where the author was invested with an almost sacred status as poet, genius, creator. This change required a "major aesthetic realignment" (Rose, "Author" 56) of the notion of the writer.

The very basis of US copyright law, its first principle, is premised on the existence of the author and the possibility of originality: "Copyright protection subsists, in accordance with this title, in original works of authorship fixed in any tangible medium of expression" (§102a). That is a staggering statement. The presumption of the statement is that in order to be said to own something, you need to have an originating creator and something original to be owned, to which there is no prior claim to ownership.

The idea of original, lone proprietorship to language would have seemed preposterous and distorted, say, to classical rhetoricians or to members of a tribal culture who understand language as a shared resource and who see ideas and language as originating in community beliefs and practices and so in that sense "belonging" to the community. More contemporaneously, from the standpoint of social rhetorics, we borrow our language and ideas, we don't make them. A key tenet of the principle of intertextuality is, first, that language is a shared resource, and, consequently, that writers are always borrowing, copyright, repeating, retweeting the texts of others—and often without attribution (Porter, "Intertextuality," "Response"). This is normal practice; this is not unusual, and this is not always piracy, stealing, or plagiarism (though of course sometimes it is).

On the other hand, writers do exert labor, they do work, they perform a valuable service for society—nobody contests that. Writers' efforts deserve some sort of credit, and we want to have a system that motivates more writing, not less. So the eventual resolution of this complexity was to identify intellectual expression as a particular type of property, *intellectual property*, and to assign the author rights to control that property, but typically only for some limited period of time.

Copyright law serves to balance a number of competing interests—and maybe most especially the interests of the *polis*, the community, society, as articulated by Supreme Court Justice Sandra Day O'Connor, writing for the majority in *Feist v. Rural Telephone*:

> The primary objective of copyright is not to reward the labor of authors, but to promote the Progress of Science and useful Arts. . . . [Copyright law] ultimately serves the purpose of enriching the general public through access to creative works. (US Supreme Court)

This, too, is a staggering statement. Copyright law, as articulated by the US Supreme Court, exists primarily to "promote the Progress of Science and useful Arts" and to "enrich the general public"—"not to reward the labor of authors." Social good, not personal gain, is the ultimate purpose. However, what is needed is a system that both credits authors' labors and that encourages new authors "to build freely upon the ideas and information" of old authors. Putting this in rhetoric terms, the system needs to credit the labors required for rhetorical invention while at the same time promoting and protecting the continuance of new rhetorical invention. How do we achieve such a balance?

The answer to that question, at least in US copyright law, is the Fair Use provision. US copyright law assigns authors "exclusive rights" to their own works—but there is an important limitation on those rights, outlined in Section §107, the Fair Use provision. The Fair Use provision is warranted by two important principles: (1) That the good of society at large, the enrichment of the public, is the ultimate good and goal. And (2) For that good to be achieved, writers need to have license to use others' intellectual property—even *without their permission*, and particularly in certain kinds of rhetorical circumstances that directly serve the public good: news reporting, criticism and commentary (such as political protest), scholarship and research, and teaching. There are limits placed on those uses—the so-called four factors of Fair Use—but in general these types of rhetorical situations have a highly protected status. The law exists to protect and encourage such rhetorical activities, not discourage them.

Copyright and its rhetorical *techne* are constantly challenged by new technologies: the printing press, the Xerox copy machine, the desktop computer, the phone or computer linked to the Internet, etc. Each new technology challenges existing patterns, habits, and social norms about what is appropriate, fair, and just in regards to making and redistributing copies. Copying has changed dramatically in the digital age thanks primarily to two technological developments:

1. The set of functions on your computer (or your phone, or, perhaps, your sweater, or, eventually, your frontal lobe) that allow you to copy/paste or download written content— that is, it is quite easy to make or collect a copy, instantly. You no longer need to pay a scribe to copy content for you, or the publisher to make you a print copy.
2. The vast social network known as the Internet, which allows you to distribute written content globally. It is technically quite easy and fast to copy, distribute, and publish content, instantly and, for a time at least, with relatively few restrictions.

The Internet is a vast, powerful, and fast copying machine that is simultaneously connected to a vast, powerful, and fast broadcast system. Copies can be made and distributed easily and quickly. Just as the emergence of the printing press changed Western culture during the Renaissance and the Enlightenment (Eisenstein), the emergence and ubiquitous embrace of this digital composing/publishing technology called the Internet is changing contemporary culture globally. The lone individual user sitting at a computer or holding a relatively inexpensive smartphone has the technological capacity to *instantly* become a worldwide publisher, or pirate, and to compete with media conglomerates such as Disney and Netflix and publishers such as Random House and Bloomsbury. Hence, the crisis for copyright law in the digital age.

The other significant shift of relevance to this question is the metaphoric frame shift from understanding writing as *expression* (hence, intellectual property) to seeing writing as *information product, aka content*. In an information economy, information is your product—and in order to maximize profit from that product, you need to be able to restrict others' copying of that product. When writing is called information, it becomes content, and the object for sale is treated more like physical property, like an air conditioning unit or a Ford Focus. This framework views writing as a digital asset, as a commodity (Dush)—hence, as just plain physical property. A copyright philosophy that values fair use, sharing, and free and open public access to information poses a threat to that business model.

Copyright Impedances and Affordances

The copyright system provides significant regulatory impedances—and yes, also, affordances and incentives—for digital writing. Regulations based on strict proprietary control of copyright (and hardwired tools enforcing such policies) are examples of copyright impedance, or what is called *copyright maximalism*, or simply *CopyRight*: that is, fiercely protectionist efforts to restrict remix and circulation of existing materials, to extend the term of copyright, and to severely punish copyright offenders. Examples of this regulatory regime include legislation such as the Sonny Bono Copyright Extension Act and the Digital Millennium Copyright Act (DMCA); cease-and-desist takedown warnings issued by corporations; and copyright control technologies such as YouTube's Content ID.

However, other copyright initiatives, policies, advocacy groups, and court rulings—for example, Creative Commons, the Open Access movement, centers and organizations such as Berkman Center and the Electronic Frontier Foundation—do push back, opposing overly restrictive copyrightist legislation and crafting affordance policies that encourage reuse, remix, and circulation. Sometimes termed *CopyLeft*, such initiatives emphasize copyright licenses and practices that encourage wide, yet responsible, sharing.

This is the ongoing tension in copyright law: between those who favor sharing and open access versus a more protectionist approach to copyright, or what Jessica Reyman terms the distinction between "open architecture" and "closed law." This tension, which has always existed in copyright law and custom, is between two different philosophies for authorship/ownership, innovation, and economic development—two different business models, but also, to put it a different way, two different philosophies for how writing works. This is where rhetoric overlaps with economics: Where is the value in writing? How should we promote value in writing? Who should be assigned credit for that value, and for how long? These are questions of economics, but they are also fundamental questions of copyright and rhetoric.

Lawrence Lessig has emphasized that our culture is not simply transmitted and distributed through language, it is *made* through language, and the ability of writers to interact with their culture, to remix that culture, to change it, depends critically on the ability to share cultural artifacts, memes, bits and pieces of text, and to remix them and redistribute them in new ways, building new from old. Our culture is built from remix. But Lessig warns that our ability to share and reuse—the very *right to write*, as he calls it—is eroding under the hyperproprietary regime of copyright maximalism. Some think that it is not too strong to say that "the sharing culture is under attack" (Grinvald 1063).

An example: in 2007, YouTube was forced by Universal Music Publishing Group (UMPG) to take down a video that a mother had posted of her baby because a Prince song was playing in the background. With the Electronic Frontier Foundation serving as counsel, the mother filed a complaint against YouTube. The case, *Lenz v. Universal*, has been in the courts now for over nine years, and in 2016 the Ninth Circuit decision (in favor of the mother) was appealed to the Supreme Court, where it awaits disposition.

From the standpoint of Fair Use, the reuse of a copyrighted Prince song in the background of a person's private family video (non-commercial use) would seem not to pose a serious threat to UMPG's copyright interests in the song—but the point is not whether or not the use is infringing so much as defending the principle of absolute control. Any use, even a fair use, threatens the philosophy of maximalism, a philosophy that is chipping away at rights enumerated and protected in Section §107. Plus, because the case itself attracted a good deal of public notice, it serves the purpose of scaring ordinary people into a kind of hypercompliance, and that self-policing also erodes Fair Use.

In 2007 YouTube began using a copyright filtering technology called Content ID to scan video contributions to YouTube to identify possible copyright infringements (Edwards; Soha and McDowell). One troubling feature of Content ID is that it shifts the burden of proof from the copyright owner to the ordinary user, who must now argue that her/his use is indeed a protected use under the Fair Use provision of copyright law. If a copyright holder feels that a user's use of material is infringing they can request a "copyright strike," that penalizes that user's account. Such an approach makes copyright protection rather than Fair Use the presumptive position and has a chilling effect on public uses of the Internet.

YouTube does have an appeals process in place for users to challenge decisions, but, as Dustin Edwards argues, the appeals process is so elaborate and legalistic that the process itself discourages counterclaims. The system is designed from a protectionist standpoint, and even from that framework, Edwards argues, there are "deep flaws" in the system: "it can't accurately determine fair use, it puts copyright holders in a position of control and users in a position of permission, and it often misidentifies copyright matches."

Dustin Edwards's research shows how copyright regimes of various kinds impede the flow of discourse—and in the age of social media, rhetorical impact is all about flow and circulation: Is your tweet retweeted? Is your posting tagged and redistributed? Is your message shared, does it move, does it collect likes, does it appear on the nightly news? Rhetorical impact now has more to do with how and where your message *travels* (flows) rather than with what your message *says*. As Edwards points out, Content ID is by no means neutral but rather represents a strong protectionist position that does not accommodate fair use. It is a filtering technology that particularly impedes the flow of news, parody, and critique, and in that respect is a mechanism for regulating political speech.

Of course copyright does not only exercise a prohibitive influence. It is also supposed to have a generative influence (Zittrain): it is supposed to promote the production of writing. Digital technologies themselves, especially in their early stages of development, were designed to promote copying. The keystroke command <control><c> allows us to easily copy a piece of text, and its partner <control><v> allows us to paste it somewhere else. The copy/paste functionality built into the computer is a generative technology, nudging us in the direction of copying. So, too, the screenshot and the download function. These copying functions, so basic to computing technology, encourage us to copy/paste, download, remix, and they do so without threatening us or commenting at all on the copyright implications of our actions. Internet functionality—the global network of the World Wide Web—allows us to distribute our copied/pasted entries to the world. You could say that in general digital technology is designed to promote copying and sharing. The philosophy of Open Access is built into the fundamental architecture of the digital network system.

Hence the desperation of copyright maximalists to install restrictive mechanisms into the open system. Various kinds of deterrent strategies are deployed, ranging from hard technical lockdowns—"wired shut," in the terms of Tarleton Gillespie–to softer forms of deterrence called "nudges" (Tan; Yeung).

- Hard-wired constraints → The technology itself is hard wired, technically locked down, to prevent users from copying material.[5]
- Strong regulatory constraints → Users can still technically perform copying, but strong copyright regulations and warnings threaten infringement (e.g., FBI warnings about copyright piracy at the beginning of movies).
- Soft regulatory nudges → Through indirect means and "soft" choices, the technology coaxes you away from copying activities (and other forms of writing deemed problematic).

Social media sites establish interaction policies and what Tan calls "nudges" to push users in certain directions, to promote certain kinds of generative activities, but also to impede other sorts of activities. Twitter allows you to do certain things with tweets, but not certain other things (Tan 65; Gillespie, "Politics," "Platforms").

The softer approach to copyright deterrence may ultimately be the most dangerous one to Fair Use. It is an approach that does not use law by itself to regulate a behavior, but rather attempts to change the frame for behavior, and in so doing creates a system in which writers regulate themselves, called self-censorship or panoptic surveillance in Foucauldian terms. When you view movies at home and the opening screen keeps repeating the words *Piracy, Piracy, Piracy*, consciously you may rationally understand that you are not guilty of piracy, but seeing the word over and over reinforces the message that copying = piracy. This is what we might term a frame nudge: repetition of certain messages and metaphors can, over time, create a frame of understanding. The alternate frame of *Fair Use, Fair Use, Fair Use* doesn't have quite the same metaphoric power as *Piracy*.[6]

Numerous legal scholars (Benkler, Boyle, Lessig, Litman, Samuelson, Vaidhyanathan) have warned that the copyright system is changing in the direction of greater and greater protectionism. They view copyright maximalism as threatening the Fair Use provision of US copyright law; as eroding the public domain (and the very idea of public access and ownership); as opposing the ethic of sharing, access, and collaboration; and ultimately as limiting the ability of writers to protest, to criticize, to create, to generate new ideas, to make culture.

The alternative, these scholars argue, is an Open Access ethics for digital assets based on a metaphor of sharing—a public commons approach, or what Reyman terms "the cultural conservancy model." While such a model is often characterized as being hostile to business interests or naïve about economics, Yochai Benkler points out that is, rather, an alternative business model rather than an anti-business model: it is a model that promotes development, and that levels the business playing field for smaller and start-up businesses, allowing them to compete with established conglomerate interests.

Conclusion

Copyright pertains to issues of access, ownership, property, control—use rights—that impact all the rhetorical canons, but most particularly production (invention) and distribution/circulation (delivery). Copyright laws, regulations, and codes, some written, some unwritten, both constrain and enable writing. There are prohibitions, there are affordances; there are things that can be said, and things that cannot be said; there are rights bundled into every act of expression. And these things change culturally and kairotically, from one venue to the next. These codes are governed by questions of economy—and I'm not talking only about capital, but about the flow of value, and value is really about the very *purpose* of writing. *Cui bono?* For whose good are we writing?

Scholars affiliated with the Intellectual Property Caucus of the Conference on College Composition and Communication (CCCC) have been making the case, for more than twenty years, that intellectual property is not an extraneous topic for rhetoric/composition, not a matter for legal scholars analysis only (DeVoss and Rife; Gurak and Johnson-Eilola; Logie; Ratcliff and Logie; Reyman; Rife; Rife, Slattery, and DeVoss; Westbrook). Rather, they have shown, issues of copyright, regulation, and ownership and use of text are fundamental to rhetoric and of practical importance for understanding how writing works, particularly (but not only) in the digital age. They have demonstrated that intellectual property needs to be embraced wholeheartedly as a topic integral to rhetoric/composition because in a very practical way the intellectual property system regulates writing practice.

Copyright is of central importance to rhetoric, to writers, and to writing instruction at all levels. It is not a specialized topic "for lawyers only." Copyright—and the question of intellectual property generally—is fundamental to rhetoric and *techne*, the art of production and distribution of writing in all its forms.

Notes

1. Copyright *law* as a formal system needs to be distinguished from copyright *custom* (what people actually do in various cultures and circumstances) and also from copyright *lore* (informal, imprecise, often inaccurate information that is distributed widely and believed to be true, despite its lack of authority or accuracy).
2. This chapter focuses primarily on *copyright*, not *intellectual property*. In law intellectual property is a broader term that refers to a number of different areas including copyright, trademark, patent, and trade secrets. In other words, copyright is only one facet of the much larger realm—but, along with trademark, copyright is the area of greatest relevance to rhetoric. Trademark refers to a type of expression—whether written (textual), aural, graphic, or cinematic—that distinctively represents the image or branding of a commercial interest (e.g., the Apple logo) and is therefore afforded a special type of intellectual property status.
3. Copyright refers to a bundle of related rights that include not only the right to make copies (rights of reproduction) but also rights of adaptation (i.e., the right to make derivative works), sale, performance, display, etc.
4. Robert Darnton points out that the eighteenth century was an age of robust book piracy (American book publishers being among the most notorious culprits). Piracy had an important remediating effect on publishing: Pirates help keep down publishing costs. Piracy serves as a check on the temptation of publishers to raise costs to prohibitive levels. In a sense, Darnton suggests, pirates serve an important role in the economic system of text distribution.
5. Digital right management (DRM) refers to software that functions as "locks" to impede or monitor digital copying.
6. The hacker ethic of *Rip, Mix, Burn* is an attempted counterframe—but is perhaps a bit too radical for those who believe in a balanced approach to copyright (Bowrey and Rimmer; DeVoss and Porter).

Works Cited

Benkler, Yochai. *The Wealth of Networks: How Social Production Transforms Markets and Freedom.* Yale UP, 2006.

Bowery, Kathy, and Rimmer, Matthew. "Rip, Mix, Burn: The Politics of Peer to Peer and Copyright Law." *First Monday*, vol. 7, no. 8, 2002, firstmonday.org/article/view/974/895. Accessed 3 July 2017.

Boyle, James. *The Public Domain: Enclosing the Commons of the Mind.* Yale UP, 2008.

Corbett, Edward P.J. "The Theory and Practice of Imitation in Classical Rhetoric." *College Composition and Communication*, vol. 22, no. 3, 1971, pp. 243–50.

Darnton, Robert. "The Science of Piracy: A Crucial Ingredient in Eighteenth-Century Publishing." *Studies in Voltaire and the Eighteenth Century*, vol. 12, 2003, pp. 3–29.

DeVoss, Dànielle Nicole, and James E. Porter. "Why Napster Matters to Writing: Filesharing as a New Ethic of Digital Delivery." *Computers and Composition*, vol. 23, 2006, pp. 178–210.

DeVoss, Dànielle Nicole, and Martine Courant Rife, Eds. *Cultures of Copyright.* Peter Lang, 2015.

Dush, Lisa. "When Writing Becomes Content." *College Composition and Communication*, vol. 67, no. 2, 2015, pp. 173–96.

Edwards, Dustin W. *Writing in the Flow: Assembling Tactical Rhetorics in an Age of Viral Circulation.* Dissertation, Miami University, 2016.

Eisenstein, Elizabeth. *The Printing Revolution in Early Modern Europe* (2nd ed.). Cambridge UP, 2005.

Foucault, Michel. "What is an Author?" *The Foucault Reader*, edited by Paul Rabinow. Pantheon, 1984, pp. 101–20.

Gillespie, Tarleton. "The Politics of 'Platforms.'" *New Media + Society*, vol. 12, no. 3, 2010, pp. 347–64.

———. *Wired Shut: Copyright and the Shape of Digital Culture.* The MIT Press, 2007.

———. "Platforms Intervene." *Social Media + Society*, vol. 1, no. 1, 2015, pp. 1–2.

Grinvald, Leah Chan. "Social Media, Sharing and Intellectual Property Law." *DePaul Law Review*, vol. 64, no. 4, 2015, pp. 1045–78.

Gurak, Laura J., and Johndan Johnson-Eilola, Eds. *Intellectual Property*. Special issue of *Computers and Composition*, vol. 15, no. 2, 1998.

Lessig, Lawrence. *Free Culture: How Big Media Uses Technology and the Law to Lock Down Culture and Control Creativity*. Penguin, 2004.

Litman, Jessica. *Digital Copyright*. Prometheus, 2001.

Logie, John. *Peers, Pirates, and Persuasion: Rhetoric in the Peer-to-Peer Debates*. Parlor, 2006.

McKee, Heidi A., and James E. Porter. *Professional Communication and Network Interaction: A Rhetorical and Ethical Approach*. Routledge, 2017.

Murphy, James J. "The Key Role of Habit in Roman Writing Instruction." *A Short History of Writing Instruction: From Ancient Greece to Modern America*, edited by. James J. Murphy. Erlbaum/Hermagoras, 2001, pp. 35–78.

Porter, James E. "Intertextuality and the Discourse Community." *Rhetoric Review*, vol. 5, 1986, pp. 34–47.

——. "Recovering Delivery for Digital Rhetoric." *Computers and Composition*, vol. 26, 2009, pp. 207–24.

——. "Response: Being Rhetorical When We Teach Intellectual Property and Fair Use." *Copy(write): Intellectual Property in the Writing Classroom*, edited by Martine Courant Rife, Shaun Slattery, and Dànielle Nicole DeVoss. Parlor, 2011, pp. 263–72.

Ratcliff, Clancy, and John Logie, Eds. *Top Intellectual Property Developments (CCCC-Intellectual Property Caucus Annuals)*. www.ncte.org/cccc/committees/ip/. Accessed 3 July 2017.

Reed, Michael. "Who Owns Ellen's Oscar Selfie? Deciphering Rights of Attribution Concerning User Generated Content on Social Media." *John Marshall Intellectual Property Law Review*, vol. 14, 2015, pp. 564–89.

Reyman, Jessica. *The Rhetoric of Intellectual Property: Copyright Law and the Regulation of Digital Culture*. Routledge, 2010.

Rife, Martine Courant. *Invention, Copyright, and Digital Writing*. Southern Illinois UP, 2013.

Rife, Martine Courant, Shaun Slattery, and Dànielle Nicole DeVoss, Eds. *Copy(write): Intellectual Property in the Writing Classroom*. Parlor, 2011.

Rose, Mark. "The Author as Proprietor: *Donaldson v. Becket* and the Genealogy of Modern Authorship." *Representations*, vol. 23, 1988, pp. 51–85.

——. "Nine-tenths of the Law: The English Copyright Debates and the Rhetoric of the Public Domain." *Law and Contemporary Problems*, vol. 66, 2003, pp. 75–87.

Samuelson, Pamela. "Enriching Discourse on Public Domains." *Duke Law Journal*, vol. 77, 2006, pp. 783–834.

Soha, Michael, and Zachary J. McDowell. "Monetizing a Meme: YouTube, Content ID, and the Harlem Shake." *Social Media + Society*, vol. 2, no. 1, 2016, pp. 1–12.

Tan, Corinne. "Technological Nudges and Copyright on Social Media Sites." *Intellectual Property Quarterly*, vol. 1, 2015, pp. 62–78.

Trimbur, John. "Composition and the Circulation of Writing." *College Composition and Communication*, vol. 52, no. 2, 2000, pp. 188–219.

US Supreme Court. *Feist Publications, Inc., v. Rural Telephone Serv. Co.*, 499 U.S. 340, 1999.

Vaidhyanathan, Siva. *Copyrights and Copywrongs: The Rise of Intellectual Property and How It Threatens Creativity*. New York UP, 2001.

Westbrook, Steve, Ed. *Composition and Copyright: Perspectives on Teaching, Text-making, and Fair Use*. SUNY Press, 2009.

Woodmansee, Martha. "The Genius and the Copyright: Economic and Legal Conditions of the Emergence of the 'Author.'" *Eighteenth-Century Studies*, vol. 17, no. 4, 1984, pp. 425–48.

Yeung, Karen. "'Hypernudge': Big Data as a Mode of Regulation by Design." *Information, Communication and Society*, vol. 20, no. 1, 2017, pp. 118–36.

Zittrain, Jonathan. "The Generative Internet." *Harvard Law Review*, vol. 119, 1974, pp. 1975–2040.

25

MEDIATED AUTHORITY
The Effects of Technology on Authorship

Chad Seader, Jason Markins, and Jordan Canzonetta

Contemporary conversations in digital rhetoric highlight how emerging technologies create parameters and limitations that affect how the people using those technologies interact with the world. Scholars who research human–machine collaboration suggest both humans and machines mutually influence and "act *alongside*" each other creating complicated power dynamics between the people who design various technologies and the people who use them (Barnett and Boyle 1). Likewise, Jessica Reyman argues that access to social media technologies comes at a price: users must surrender their privacy and metadata to participate on the platforms. While account holders author metadata that social media companies use to sell and promote products, those same account holders have no rights to (or compensation for) their intellectual property. Similarly, algorithms, which "persuade users toward particular engagements" based on the results of various search parameters (Brock and Shepherd), shape the kinds of arguments and decision-making processes that emerge in digital spaces (Brooke 83). In this sense, algorithms are rhetorical because their "outcomes are not empirically inevitable, but rather the product of a particular set of parameters designed strategically to lead toward a particular kind of result," much like an effective rhetorical argument might compel audiences to act in particular ways (Ingraham 63). Furthermore, Liza Potts uses the term *antisocial* to describe technologies that prevent people from having control of how those same technologies might be used. When a software program or digital interface is "antisocial," the technology is handed down to users who receive it rather than participate with it (6). In turn, Potts argues for a participant-centered approach to software design that allows humans to work actively with technology (6). This shift in terms of subjectivity, considering people as participants instead of users, highlights exactly how changes to particular digital environments could have profound and often unintended effects in terms of how various digital tools and technologies might be used to create, value, and circulate information.

Within the context of these conversations, we consider how authorship is mediated by emerging technologies. First, some background. Many conversations in authorship studies are grounded theoretically in French poststructuralist notions of *ideology* and *discourse*. While these terms are certainly contestable, they nonetheless exist as the basis for how scholars in rhetoric and composition theorize authorship and authority in our contemporary moment. Louis Althusser defines ideology as "the imaginary relationship of individuals to their real conditions of existence" (109). In other words, ideology is how people use cultural knowledge to evaluate their surroundings so life is predictable. Althusser also asserts that ideology has an effect on the material world through cultural practices (114). These cultural practices, as Michel Foucault argues in *The Archaeology of Knowledge*, give value to material objects through the discursive narratives and procedures that connect those objects with abstract ideological ideals (49). Following this theory, social inequalities arise due to problems relating to ideology, which are then perpetuated through discursive practices, including writing and technologies associated with it. To this end, Roland Barthes argues that writing is the product of these cultural practices and not of individual genius, which thus calls into question the very notion of originality (146). Barthes' claim gave rise to what Foucault calls the *author-function*, which explains the social phenomenon through which a writer's name takes on social capital, and thus authority, as writing circulates over time ("What is an Author?" 347). Pierre Bourdieu then claims that because of this discursive aspect of writing, social capital is tied to the institutional systems of power that reify discourse, and therefore authorship requires some level of institutional approval (121). According to these theorists, being a writer and being an author are not the same. To be an author, a writer must participate and have authority within a discourse, which is challenging if a writer belongs to a community that's marginalized by a discourse.

In the preface to the edited collection *Authorship Contested*, Rebecca Moore Howard calls on scholars to question the connections between authorship and power to challenge "who is and is not positioned to claim the status of 'author'; whose voice is and isn't heard; and what circumstances enable or prevent the claim" (x). Throughout the collection of essays, contributors point to how factors relating to economics, public prejudice, and hierarchies of power could lead to situations in which author identities are delegitimized, and how the work of people from vulnerable communities could be silenced or appropriated (Robillard and Fortune; Smith; Zebroski). In her book *Digital Prohibition*, Carolyn Guertin addresses these concerns related to power, identity, and agency, arguing that emerging technologies provide solutions to many of the concerns that Howard and the authors in *Authorship Contested* express. Guertin sees new media as a "third space" outside of capitalism in which people could use multimedia and varied forms of narrative to challenge oppressive power structures, write collaboratively, and express identity (1–2).

In this chapter, we use activity theory as a lens for understanding how technology might affect issues of authorship across three case studies. Activity theory is a useful lens for understanding how the parameters and limitations placed by various tools and technologies relate to identity, authority, and, thus, authorship because the theory assumes that within communities, values, roles (social identities), and tools (technologies) are aligned through discursive practices (activities) toward a common goal. As Clay Spinuzzi explains, activity theory, which was originally developed by Lev Vygotsky and later expanded by Yrjö Engeström, investigates "interrelated sets of activity," "work relations," and "issues of power and mastery" (62). Through an understanding of how activity, roles, and tools are discursively related, activity theory points our attention to how technologies are changing authority and writing practices within particular communities. According to Spinuzzi, tools do not just affect how a user enacts an objective but also alters the user and the situation together (69). Through activity, roles are shaped by tools and vice versa; hence technology mediating identity. Activity theory is complicated, and as David Russell and Arturo Yañez assert, it "does not claim to provide a neat way to predict outcomes, but rather offers tentative explanations" (n.p.). For our purposes in this chapter, activity theory is not a definitive formula for deciding whether or not the use of technology is appropriate in a given situation, nor does it dictate how to implement technology more ethically. Instead our three case studies, which examine writing in both academic and civic contexts, show how activity theory can be used as a heuristic for identifying shifts in writing communities and locating tensions between technology and power.

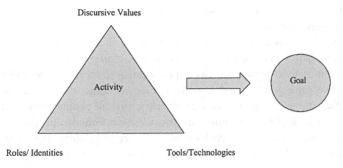

Figure 25.1 Activity System Diagram

Technology and Authority in Community Publishing (Chad Seader)

This first case study exemplifies how the introduction of new technologies and tools might unintentionally create parameters that limit who is (or is not) able to become an author. The Neighborhood Writing Alliance (NWA) is a community publishing nonprofit that operated successfully in Chicago for seventeen years. However, in 2013, NWA ceased operations due to financial difficulties after the organization moved from publishing in print to solely online. NWA's mission was to "[provoke] dialogue, [build] community, and [promote] change by creating opportunities for adults in Chicago's underserved neighborhoods to write, publish, and perform works about their lives." The organization, run by three paid employees and about a dozen volunteers, offered free writing workshops at public libraries and at a halfway house for former offenders. NWA also published *The Journal of Ordinary Thought* (*JOT*), which showcased the writing that emerged from those workshops, and the writers were also invited to perform their published work at release readings celebrating each new edition of *JOT*. While the organization originally published *JOT* quarterly, that frequency was reduced to thrice yearly in 2011 in response to financial constraints stemming from the Great Recession. In 2013, NWA stopped printing physical copies of the journal, and the following year, the organization closed its doors. During the last two years of the organization's work, I ran the writing workshops at the halfway house.

Using activity theory to analyze authorship within the context of the NWA highlights how power and technology are intertwined. NWA represents a community of practice with a set of roles, tools, and discursive values that are reified through activities designed to move the organization toward a common goal. In terms of roles, the organization was composed of its administrators, volunteers, writers, donors, and board of directors. While diverse in terms of age, race, and religion, the organization's administrators, donors, and board of directors were overall formally educated and representative of socio-economic privilege. The writers who attended the writing workshops and who were published in *JOT* almost entirely represented working-class or poor communities. In terms of ethnicity, most of the writers were African American, but many of the city's Eastern European, Latin American, and Southeast Asian immigrant communities were also well represented. Because of the diversity of the many stake-holders involved, the organization's grounding values functioned to highlight the importance of diversity and collaboration while downplaying the fact that the organization's administrators and directors varied significantly from the writers in terms of formal education. Speaking to this point, *JOT* was published under the motto that "every person is a philosopher," a thought grounded in the belief that there's wisdom in all human experience, regardless of education, race, national origin, or class.

Using activity theory as a lens, we can understand that *JOT* functioned as a tool to give the writers a means to share knowledge with the people who matter to them while creating physical, tangible family heirlooms to be passed between people or saved for the future. Through the activity of publishing the print journal and hosting release readings, the discursive values of the organization: that strength comes from our diversity, that all people carry profound wisdom, and that social change is possible through the arts, were confirmed as people from across socio-economic, racial, and generational divides came together to celebrate the work of the writers. This activity used the cultural and institutional capital of the organization to give the writers the authority to be authors on their own terms and to make meaning in ways that are meaningful to themselves and their communities.

Beyond the activity of producing print journals and hosting release readings, there's another key activity at play: the activity that occurs digitally through the organization's website between the administrators and donors. NWA's administrators used the website to circulate *JOT* to its donors, grant foundations, as well as to other community literacy and publishing organizations. This activity continued to reify the value of print media because it showcased the material effects of the organization's work in practice. While there are two activities working in this context, the publication of the print journal and the digital circulation of the journal online, both activities involved different media and different immediate purposes; they both nonetheless served to function NWA's larger goal of working for social justice through creative arts education.

However, after the elimination of the print medium from the organization's budget, the activity system that had been successful in sustaining the health of the organization began to collapse. Once print publishing had ceased, *JOT* was only accessible as a PDF available for download through the NWA's website. Because most writers did not have access to the Internet beyond smartphones and library computers, the digital version of *JOT* simply could not function in the same ways to meet the same goals as print; there was no easy way for many of the writers to access NWA's website, download the PDF, and circulate that PDF across their personal networks. The digital also does not have the same permanence as print, which makes it difficult for a digital document to serve as a family heirloom or a gift to be passed among family members. Furthermore, the act of downloading *JOT* from the website's interface—rather than receiving a copy at a release reading—emphasized the ethos and rhetorical aims of the organization, rather than the ethos and aims of the individual writers, which understandably could have kept the digital edition of *JOT* from reaching the same level of circulation and from generating the same level of workshop participation as compared to the retired print edition.

While the NWA moved from the print to the digital with the best of intentions of helping the organization stay competitive in the economically difficult period of the early 2010s, our activity-theory based analysis shows that this shift in technology may have led to negative, unintended consequences that likely limited the organization's goal, creating a space where people from marginalized communities could author and circulate texts. Activity theory does not provide proof that this was the case; surely other factors were involved. However, this case does call our attention to how emerging technologies, sometimes with the best of intentions, sometimes highlight some identities over others and limit the rhetorical effects of writing. In this case, the website highlighted the role of the administrators over the writers. Given that digital interfaces are not politically neutral, we could see how technologies could unintentionally silence voices and hinder agency. This analysis does not intend to discourage the use of digital and emerging technologies in community literacy contexts, but we should be mindful.

Plagiarism Detection Services (Jordan Canzonetta)

Implementing plagiarism detection services in writing classrooms is another example of how technology alters and shifts authorial agency within particular communities of practice. In the educational community, academic integrity is a shared goal: it communicates an institution's ethos of respectability and legitimacy. Simply put, cheating must not be tolerated if a college wants to be taken seriously as a viable competitor or as a bona fide academic institution.

Plagiarism is a contentious issue because it is deeply tied to Western conceptions of authorship that cast it as an illegal act of theft of someone's property. As Rebecca Moore Howard notes in her germinal piece in 1999, *Standing in the Shadows of Giants*, Western ideas about authorship are stringent and based on Romantic notions about the lone, genius author. She describes the ideal Western author as one who demonstrates "autonomy, originality, proprietorship, and morality" in his[1] writing. She continues to explain why there's such a vehement response to plagiarism in higher education: an author in this Western tradition violates those tenets of authorship, he "demonstrates an absence of morality, earns the label 'plagiarist' and deserves punishment" (Howard 58). Failing to properly cite work or stealing it indicates a moral deficiency.

Fears about plagiarism have, as Zwagerman suggests, led to plagiarism detection services' (PDSs) success and widespread implementation in higher education. Western writing practices have begun to dominate practices across the globe; the fear we create and spread about plagiarism is in part creating a need for plagiarism detection (Zwagerman). Since Turnitin's inception, the company's creators have aligned themselves with "the educational community" and used language that indicates they will fight moral deficiency in academia with their software:

> Turnitin.com is currently helping high school teachers and university professors everywhere *bring academic integrity back into their classrooms*. Our system is already being used in almost every institution in the country, and a large number of universities all over the world. We encourage any educator who *values academic honestly to help us take a stand against online cheating and become a member* of the Turnitin.com educational community. (Turnitin.com, Wayback Machine, March 31, 2001, emphasis added)

This technological intervention in our classrooms has been long contested by writing experts. Several organizations within the field of rhetoric and composition have crafted resolutions and statements against these programs, all ultimately advocating for their disbandment in higher education (CWPA; IP Caucus; NCTE). Many scholars who study writing argue that these programs uphold archaic ideals about authorship that are no longer tenable in the twenty-first century: rather than promoting collaborative authorship, PDSs enforce originality and autonomy—ideals that are already unattainable because language and writing are socially constructed.

While many of the critiques of PDSs are founded on a theoretical basis, Jordan wanted to conduct a study of how these programs were actually being used in classes because in spite of writing experts' protestations, these programs are still widely adopted. To find out how PDSs are used, she conducted a focus group within an English department with three instructors who were using PDSs for the first time and four who had used them before. Most of the instructors were using SafeAssign, but some had familiarity with Turnitin. Additionally, she sent out a survey to a listserv of writing teachers (WPA listserv) to see how a wider base of people had used the program in the past. The context of this community is within writing studies; she did not seek out participants from disciplines outside of English or rhetoric and composition.

The most important result of this study relates to authors, instructors, and agency. Prior to PDSs existence, teachers were solely responsible for determining whether students were plagiarizing in their classes. A longstanding best practice for coping with plagiarism is to handle student cases individually and to teach students about plagiarism ("2013 Resolutions"; "CCCC-IP Caucus"; "Defining and Avoiding Plagiarism"). The introduction of this technology within this group has altered teachers' authority as experts of writing. In relying on a PDS to detect plagiarism, instructors use the software as a "psychological check" (Canzonetta 24) for students and as a means of having "proof" to show students when they approach them about plagiarism (27).

While one teacher in Jordan's study acknowledged the tool is flawed and doesn't infallibly detect plagiarism, he uses it to support his claims about a student plagiarizing when he approaches students who the machine has flagged.

Two activity systems are in tension when we think about PDSs. In an originality-focused activity system (Figure 25.2), teachers from all different disciplines, administrators, and students are buying into ideas about authorship that promote academic integrity by policing plagiarists through the use of PDSs. In a collaboration-focused activity system, however (Figure 25.3), teachers and experts of writing have more nuanced ideas about authorship: it's collaborative and based on socially constructed ideas about language use and development. That is not to say this group doesn't value academic integrity, but that people in this group are pedagogically minded and argue for understanding complexity and different cultural values in writing practices. In the collaboration-focused activity system, scholars urge us to move away from Western norms about writing and authorship to teach about plagiarism before punishing students for it; however, when these two groups' values and goals collide, writing teachers are stymied in their efforts to advance pedagogical approaches for dealing with plagiarism because the PDS reinforces the ideals they work against.

Compositionists describe writing as "a socially situated activity; [. . .] functionally and formally diverse; and writing is a meaning-making activity that can be conveyed in multiple modalities." Current technologies that intervene with student writing

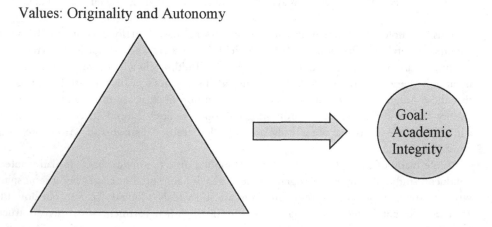

Figure 25.2 Originality-Focused Activity System

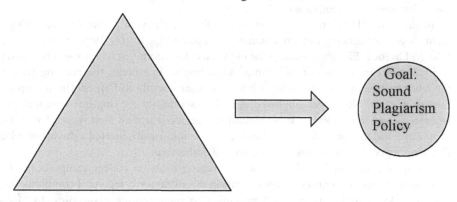

Values: Collaborative and Varied Writing Practices

Goal:
Sound
Plagiarism
Policy

People: Writing Experts and
Teachers

Technology: PDS

Figure 25.3 Collaboration-Focused Activity System

largely neglect the potential of emerging technologies to promote a broader vision of writing. Instead, they tend to align with the narrow view of writing dominant in a more recent era of testing and accountability . . . New technologies . . . are for the most part being used to reinforce old practices. (Vojak et al. 97)

Authority is a point of tension between these two systems. In Figure 25.2, people give technology authority in determining whether a student has plagiarized; in Figure 25.3, writing experts give authority to scholars and teachers who have established best practices for handling plagiarism. In practice, this tension manifests when the two groups' goals and values do not align, and PDSs shift power from teachers to machines and from experts to non-experts who purchase and implement these programs.

3D Printing and Authority (Jason Markins)

So far, we have seen how activity theory offers us insights into thinking about the role digital writing technologies played in the National Writing Alliances transition from print to digital publishing and how the increased availability of plagiarism detection services affects teachers' authority in dealing with plagiarism. Next, we will consider what tensions around authorial agency arise with the increased uptake of 3-dimensional (3D) printing techniques in digital writing classrooms. Specifically, we will consider the parameters and limitations of engaging with these technologies in the classroom at a time when the legal parameters surrounding copyright are not entirely clear.

3D printing, also known as additive manufacturing, involves the creation of an object, one layer at a time, through a machine reading a digital file. Associated with the contemporary rise of makerspaces and fab labs in university settings, 3D printing functions synecdochically to represent the increased attention to the making of physical objects with personal fabrication equipment such as CNC machines, digital embroidery equipment, and other devices for the hands-on creation of complex compositions. While these devices are not creating traditional texts, per se, there is much evidence that the nature of these devices can illuminate the distributed labor that goes into creating a text?

In this way, 3D printers can be viewed as the latest step in a complex history of printing technologies influencing our understanding of authorship. In *The Printing Press as an Agent of Change*, Elizabeth Eisenstein outlines the historical connections that have existed between printing technologies and theories of authorship. According to Eisenstein, the printing press changed the labor that went into producing a book and subsequently had an enormous impact on the lives of printers. No longer employed as scribes laboriously copying one text at a time, these laborers moved from isolation into communities centered around their work. The technologies of printing and the users of these technologies have historically enacted a discursive relationship that has shaped how we think about texts and authorship.

Today, the increased availability of 3D printing tools on college campuses has led to an increasing number of writing studies scholars in digital rhetoric, technical communications, and critical making, to incorporate 3D printing into their writing classrooms. In "Fabricating Consent: three-dimensional Objects as Rhetorical Composition," David Sheridan has written on the transformative potentialities of access to the creation of rhetorical objects via 3D printers. A number of scholars have considered the pedagogical impact of including these devices in writing classrooms, and the ethical considerations of a pedagogy built around the creation of environmentally wasteful plastic objects are a growing concern. As these new media technologies continue to become more widely available, these concerns are likely to become an increased area of focus for digital writing and rhetoric teachers and scholars.

While there are a number of different activity systems one could draw around 3D printing, for our purposes, we are interested in looking at how the subject (the user) navigates the rules (IP laws) through actualizing the object (printing an object) by means of the tools (3D printers and 3D printing software). This system represented looks like the following:

In this activity system, as we consider the relationship between users and authority, the use of the 3D printer to achieve the objective of printing a rhetorical object is mediated by the intellectual property laws governing who has the legal authority to claim copyright of images, digital code, and the objects themselves.

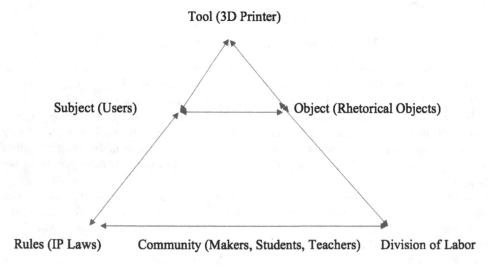

Figure 25.4 User Navigation Activity System

And, digital writing instructors have a history of considering how intellectual property laws will impact discussions of writing and in this case more specifically digital composing practices. During the early 2000s, many scholars wrote on the implications of Napster's legal battles over copyright laws. Dànielle Nicole DeVoss and James Porter argued in their 2006 "Why Napster Matters to Writing" that Napster's legal battles and cultural perceptions of file sharing were important to writing teachers not only for their cultural relevance, but also for the implications these legal battles would have for how we perceive student writers. Considering the activity systems through which users incorporate 3D printers calls into question how the legal rules surrounding such devices will mediate the activity. In short, the anticipated legal battles over 3D printing will be of importance to teachers and scholars interested in digital writing because it is sure to influence future notions of authorship. However, much of this remains speculative at this time, though, as the legal parameters surrounding copyright and 3D printing have yet to be fully developed.

Copyright laws are known for being notoriously muddled and often difficult and confusing to navigate. In response to this, members of the 3D printing community have written a number of white papers anticipating the legal troubles that will emerge. Much of the discussions within 3D printing communities have acknowledged a fear that as the technologies enter into the mainstream there will be legal pushback regarding the sharing of designs, the use of copyrighted images, and the mass reproduction of files. And, there's much to support these views. One 3D printing activist, Michael Weinberg, has written and shared a variety of white papers designed to educate 3D printing communities about what they can expect.

One of these white papers, "It will be Awesome if They Don't Screw it Up: 3D Printing, Intellectual Property, and the Fight Over the Next Great Disruptive Technology," sought to both educate the 3D printing community about IP laws and to learn from the misunderstandings that took place among the personal computing early-adopters regarding the Digital Millennium Copyright Act (DCMA). Passed in 1998 to outlaw the circumvention of DRM, the DCMA had resounding effects on how we use file sharing sites today. According to Weinberg,

> There will be a time when impacted legacy industries demand some sort of DMCA for 3D printing. If the 3D printing community waits until that day to organize, it will be too late. Instead, the community must work to educate policy makers and the public about the benefits of widespread access. That way, when legacy industries portray 3D printing as a hobby for pirates and scofflaws, their claims will fall on ears too wise to destroy the new, new thing. (15)

Throughout the white paper, Weinberg works to prepare a community for an anticipated public shaming surrounding 3D printing designed to limit what can be fabricated at home.

In this way, 3D printing enthusiasts are anticipating future tensions arising over the rules that govern their activity system. Anticipation over these tensions is affecting how they position themselves as a community. As a number of digital writing instructors are beginning to adopt technologies that allow for the replication of physical objects, these are issues that warrant further attention. And, activity theory leads us to question how these IP rules will mediate the community of users, the technologies used, and the objectives in the classroom.

Conclusion

In this chapter, we trace three separate activity systems in order to illustrate what tensions emerge surrounding the incorporation of changing technologies to create digital texts. As we have seen, in the case of the Neighborhood Writing Alliance the change from physical printed materials to digital publishing, while cost-effective for the organization, greatly altered how the community of writers were able to use their publications in their lived lives. The uptake of digital publishing altered how these texts could be circulated and who could circulate them. As we looked at the uptake of plagiarism detection services across college campuses, we saw that tensions arise when the authority to determine whether something is plagiarized or not ceases to align with the objectives of many writing scholars. Important questions about how these technologies position students—particularly those from historically marginalized groups such as international students emerge through an analysis of the various activity systems associated with PDSs. And, in the case of 3D printing, we call on teachers and scholars to pay close attention to the debates surrounding IP and the creation of physical objects that are likely to impact other aspects of digital composing practices.

As a method of practice, activity theory leads us to a variety of deeper questions to consider rather than solid answers. To that end, we are left with a variety of considerations in relation to the social impact digital writing technologies are having and will continue to have in and outside of the classroom. How do we determine who has agency as a composer when community publications begin to focus on the creation of digital publications rather than physical copies? How might we consider the social and cultural impacts that arise as organizations move to save printing costs by locating their documents in online spaces? In addition, how ought digital writing studies scholars to pursue more holistic conversations surrounding plagiarism as universities lean towards less informed policies that rely on digital detection services without engaging in relevant scholarship surrounding what constitutes plagiarism? Finally, as the boundaries around subject and tool, author and medium, user and printer are blurred, how might we advocate for IP laws that recognize the complex, collaborative means that go into the creation of a 3D printed object?

Note

1. Writers in this tradition were typically only ever perceived as being men and largely excluded anyone who was not perceived as such.

Works Cited

"2013 Resolutions and Sense of the House Motions." *NCTE Comprehensive News*, NCTE, 8 Apr. 2013, www.ncte.org/cccc/resolutions/2013. Accessed 19 May 2017.

"About Us." *Turnitin.com*. Retrieved from *Wayback Machine*, https://web.archive.org/web/2001033109 0743/http://www.turnitin.com/new.html. Accessed 29 Oct. 2014.

Althusser, Louis. *Lenin and Philosophy and Other Essays*. Translated by Ben Brewster, Monthly Review, 1971.

Barnett, Scott, and Casey Boyle, Eds. *Rhetoric Through Everyday Things*. U of Alabama P, 2016.

Barthes, Roland. *Image-Music-Text*. Translated by Stephen Heath. Hill & Wang, 1977.

Bourdieu, Pierre. *Language and Symbolic Power*, edited by John B. Thompson. Translated by Gino Raymond and Matthew Adamson. Polity, 1991.

Brock, Kevin, and Dawn Shepherd. "Understanding How Algorithms Work Persuasively Through the Procedural Enthymeme." *Computers and Composition*, vol. 42, 2016, pp. 17–27.

Brooke, Collin Gifford. *Lingua Fracta: Toward a Rhetoric of New Media*. Hampton, 2009.

Canzonetta, Jordan. *Plagiarism Detection Services: Instructors' Perceptions and Uses in the First-Year Writing Classroom*. MA Thesis, Northern Illinois University, 2014.

"CCCC-IP Caucus Recommendations Regarding Academic Integrity and the Use of Plagiarism Detection Services." 8 Apr 2013, /culturecat.net/files/CCCC-IPpositionstatementDraft.pdf. Accessed 17 May 2017.

"Defining and Avoiding Plagiarism: The WPA Statement on Best Practices." Council of Writing Program Administrators. Jan 2003, http://wpacouncil.org/node/9. Accessed 5 July 2017.

DeVoss, Danielle, and James Porter. "Why Napster Matters to Writing: Filesharing as a New Ethic of Digital Delivery." *Computers and Composition*, vol. 23, 2006, pp. 178–210.

Eisenstein, Elizabeth. *The Printing Press as an Agent of Change*. Cambridge UP, 1997.

Foucault, Michel. *Archaeology of Knowledge*. Translated by AMS Smith, Pantheon, 1972.

———. "What is an Author?" *Contemporary Literary Criticism*, edited by RC Davis, and R. Schleifer, 3rd ed., Longman, 1994.

Guertin, Carolyn. *Digital Prohibition*. Continuum International, 2012.

Howard, Rebecca Moore. *Standing in the Shadow of Giants: Plagiarists, Authors, Collaborators*. Ablex, 1999.

Ingraham, Chris. "Toward an Algorithmic Rhetoric." *Digital Rhetoric and Global Literacies: Communication Modes and Digital Practices in the Networked World: Communication Modes and Digital Practices in the Networked World*, edited by Gustav Verhulsdonck, and Marohang Limbu. IGI Global, 2013, pp. 62–80.

Potts, Liza. *Social Media in Disaster Response: How Experience Architects Can Build for Participation*. Routledge, 2013.

Reyman, Jessica. "User Data on the Social Web: Authorship, Agency, and Appropriation." *College English*, vol. 75, no. 5, 2013, pp. 513–33.

Robillard, Amy, and Ron Fortune, editors. *Authorship Contested: Cultural Challenges to the Authentic*. Autonomous Author, Routledge, 2015.

Russell, David R., and Arturo Yanez. "Big Picture People Rarely Become Historians: Genre Systems and the Contradictions of General Education." *Writing Selves/Writing Societies*, edited by Charles Bazerman and David R. Russell. Fort Collins, CO: The WAC Clearinghouse and Mind, Culture, and Activity, 2003, wac.colostate.edu/books/selves_societies/. Accessed 1 Nov. 2016.

Sheridan, David. "Fabricating Consent: Three-Dimensional Objects as Rhetorical Composition." *Computers and Composition*, vol. 27, no. 3, 2010, pp. 249–65.

Smith, Julia Marie. "A Gay Girl in Damascus." *Authorship Contested: Cultural Challenges to the Authentic, Autonomous Author*, edited by Amy Robillard and Ron Fortune. Routledge, 2015, pp. 21–39.

Spinuzzi, Clay. *Network: Theorizing Knowledge Work in Telecommunication*. Cambridge UP, 2008.

Vojak, Coleen, Sonia Kline, Bill Cope, Sarah McCarthey, and Mary Kalantzis. "New Spaces and Old Places: An Analysis of Writing Assessment Software." *Computers and Composition*, vol. 28, no. 2, 2003, pp. 97–111.

Weinberg, Michael. "It Will Be Awesome if They Don't Screw it Up: 3D Printing, Intellectual Property, and the Fight Over the Next Great Disruptive Technology." *Public Knowledge* 2010. www.public knowledge.org/files/docs/3DPrintingPaperPublicKnowledge.pdf. Accessed 5 July 2017.

Zebroski, James. "Writing after Stonewall." *Authorship Contested: Cultural Challenges to the Authentic, Autonomous Author*, edited by Amy Robillard, and Ron and Fortune. Routledge, 2015, pp. 121–34.

Zwagerman, Sean. "The Scarlet P.: Plagiarism, Panopticism, and the Rhetoric of Academic Integrity. *College Composition and Communication*, vol. 59, no. 4, 2008, pp. 676–710.

26

PRIVACY AS CULTURAL CHOICE AND RESISTANCE IN THE AGE OF RECOMMENDER SYSTEMS

Mihaela Popescu and Lemi Baruh

In an age of information overload, recommender systems (RSs), software modules that provide automated and personalized information filters, are indispensable, if often concealed and concealing, mediators between cultural environments and the users who navigate them. Lost in a flood of choices vying for our attention, we habitually rely on algorithms woven into the digital web as if they were our own personal assistants. As these digital curators of information are slowly replacing the role played by cultural intermediaries of varying informality (a teacher, an art critic, one's peers) and become an intimate part of the fabric of everyday life, they also tend to fade from view like immutable laws of the digital background, given and invisible but for the occasional glitches. Algorithms are inconspicuously reshaping the meanings we assign to cultural objects; our habits of cultural consumption; our practices of content production; and the standards we use to judge a work "relevant," "popular" (Gillespie, "Relevance") and even "original" (Introna). In the attention economy of digital content, RSs may even adjudicate among various forms of self-expression and "voice" by strategically nudging communicators to modify their speech to increase its visibility (Gillespie, "Algorithm"). It is precisely this normalization, this process of "backgrounding" (Mackenzie) that makes the power of algorithms all the more ubiquitous, their role in reshaping cultural practices all the more compelling, and the task of uncovering their logic of operation all the more urgent.

In this chapter, we analyze the role of RSs and their surveillance mechanisms in the flow of culture in order to uncover some of the challenges that recommender systems pose to privacy theory. After examining the function of recommender systems and their architecture, we analyze four roles that recommender systems perform in the organization, distribution, and management of culture, how practices of surveillance are essential to those roles, and with what consequences. We conclude by examining why recommender systems illuminate conceptual problems with the notion of information privacy and how privacy might be related to cultural identity.

The Architecture of Recommender Systems

From a computational perspective, recommender systems belong to the larger category of information filtering systems whose purpose is to deal with information overload either by removing information irrelevant for the user ("noise") or, alternatively, by selecting relevant information out of dynamic information streams. A recommender (or recommendation) system or engine is "any system that guides a user in a personalized way to interesting or useful objects in a large space of possible options or that produces such objects as output" (Felfernig and Burke 1).

From the point of view of the consuming public, RSs are engines of personalization that work to provide useful suggestions that assist users' decision-making processes: what to buy, what to listen to, what to read, whom to meet, or even whose opinion to trust. Therefore, from a sociological perspective, RSs belong to the larger category of algorithms that assist in human decision-making. This broader category also includes any other system that sorts through the complexity of a situation to narrow down an allegedly adequate solution to a decision-making problem, such as predictive policing systems or health advisors.

For digital platforms, RSs carry a much different appeal from what they have for users. The basic economic function of RSs is to predict customer preferences and use those to generate a list of "items" extracted from an existing inventory, be they consumer products (e.g., Amazon), songs (e.g., Spotify, Last.fm), movies (e.g., Netflix), news feeds (e.g., Facebook), jobs (e.g., LinkedIn), useful reviews by others (e.g., Amazon, Yelp), or even people (e.g., Facebook, Match.com, Tinder). Increasingly, RSs govern areas as crucial to individual life chances as the choice of financial instruments (e.g., Zibriczky) or health insurance plans (e.g., Abbas et. al.). RSs are the linchpin of many business models that seek to attract and retain consumers because these systems have been shown to increase engagement and loyalty, move inventories faster, redirect customers toward the "long tail" of the inventory (Anderson), sell more diverse items, and even persuade customers to change their preferences (Ricci et al.). Thus, the business appeal of RSs rests in their ability to extract value from customers.

RSs are not isolated algorithms, but literally systems; they consist of articulations of databases of personal information and data collection mechanisms; domain-specific knowledge and theories (e.g., theories about consumer behavior), as well as knowledge discovery and knowledge representation methods; filtering algorithms; and, evaluation and validation tools (Bobadilla et al.).

Filtering algorithms, the core of a RS engine, are prediction techniques. They could involve demographic filtering (in which users are described through their demographic characteristics) content-based filtering, collaborative filtering, knowledge-based filtering, and other categories or hybrids of different categories (Lu et al; Ricci et al.). Current RSs use combinations of different systems to improve predictions. Content-based filtering and collaborative filtering are some of the most widely used RSs. Content-based filtering employed by platforms such as IMDB, Rotten Tomatoes, or Pandora analyzes past preferences to model user preference profiles and predict future preferences. In contrast, collaborative filtering, used by platforms such as Amazon, Facebook, Twitter, Spotify, Google News, and Last.fm, predicts the interest of a user for an item either by using the ratings of other users who manifested similar rating patterns, or based on the user ratings on items similar to the item under consideration, or using latent variable techniques that model user–item interactions to predict future preferences (Desrosiers and Karypis).

Algorithmic Surveillance and the Circulation of Culture

The architecture of RSs is domain-invariant: whether applied to the workings of culture, finance, or security, the same logic and computational principles apply, albeit with vastly different consequences. In this section, we look at the role of RSs in the operations of culture industries.

How do RSs reorganize, manage, and convey the circulation of culture, and what role does surveillance play in these processes? We argue that RSs and the surveillance apparatuses they mobilize play four major roles: (a) they provide norming categories of cultural preferences by monitoring and encoding activities within specific cultural fields; (b) they program cultural encounters through distribution architectures by constructing consuming publics and redirecting their attention; (c) they play curation functions by assigning value to cultural products; and, (d) they reshape the production of culture through feedback loops articulated on the surveillance of cultural practices.

Norming Cultural Preferences: The Politics of Monitoring and Encoding Cultural Fields

As social constructs, cultural preferences are traditionally analyzed as expressions of taste: a social mechanism whereby groups assert their distinct identity, legitimize moral authority, and reproduce social hierarchies in an endless "game of culture" (Bourdieu; Elias; Simmel). Notably, Bourdieu explored at length how taste is articulated on hierarchical divisions between "legitimate" and "popular" forms of culture, and how these cultural divisions map onto and feed class-based stratification. Wright, however, correctly notes that this understanding of cultural preferences is bound with a regime of scarcity—of both cultural goods and of performances of taste (*Understanding cultural taste*). In contrast, the cultural environment enabled by the proliferation of Web 2.0 technologies is one of abundance in respect to both the availability of cultural goods and the availability of user signals that might count as manifestations of taste (e.g., buying on Amazon, "liking" on Facebook, watching on Netflix.). In order to operate, RSs necessarily need to collect, encode, and classify user signals, content-specific signals, and, increasingly, contexts of reception.

The techniques of encoding employed in RSs are "assemblages" (Ananny). One of the meanings of the concept of assemblage employed by Deleuze and Guattari and explained by DeLanda pertains to both the process and product of fitting together different parts by establishing relations among them so that they can function together, even if their origins or natures are different. Similarly, RSs are articulations of different "things" (computation modules, algorithms, theories) that span multiple knowledge domains to produce complex agents whose complex "performative outcomes" (Introna) are neither predictable by, nor intelligible to human observers.

Data about people and various processes of datafication are necessary for encoding the objects that RSs work with because more data ensures a better system performance. Both content creators and their audiences are data providers (van Dijck). Thus, RSs legitimize personal disclosure at scale: deliberately obstructing the system (for example, refusing to rate books on Goodreads) renders cultural RSs either of limited relevance for cultural consumption and, from the point of view of content producers, of limited relevance as distribution vehicles. RSs employing data from only a limited number of users are equally inferior, since the smaller the dataset, the more likely the possibility of erroneous predictions and the more likely for users to find the recommendations irrelevant. Thus, the premise of successful RSs is the mass collection of data.

Because both quantity and diversity of data improve the performance of an RS and increase the profitability of the implementing platform, RSs, just like other big data algorithms, employ an ever-expanding apparatus of surveillance whose large trove of resulting data are mined for meaning (Baruh and Popescu). At stake is the ability to model the connection among users by means of additional data sources (for example, offline purchases) and machine learning techniques to further improve the accuracy of recommendations beyond user history data. Facebook, for example, uses nearly 600 categories of user data provided by third-party data brokers such as Datalogix (Angwin et al.). However, the selection of relevant data that goes into the system is never neutral; rather, it reflects assumptions of relevance and importance and other judgments of value—sometimes to the point of discrimination (Crawford). Similarly, computational techniques themselves and the various rules of making sense of the result reflect human choices about relevance and actionability of categories. In Introna's succinct words, encoding is always an "enframing"—a performative exercise in the power to represent the world by precluding other representations.

"Enframing" is, however, a more literal outcome of the classifications performed by RSs. Content based filtering algorithms make determinations of similarity among cultural goods through pre-existing categories that programmers consider relevant. These classification categories norm cultural consumptions into a sort of invisible canon that determines particular cultural encounters. Through this process, RSs may also "canonize" crowd-generated ways of grouping cultural items. Newer generation RSs rely on various external sources of knowledge (e.g., Wikipedia) and user-generated tags or "folksonomies" to represent similarities between items, sometimes with surprising results. For instance, Airoldi shows how an analysis of the output of music video clips associations produced by YouTube RSs—algorithms that take into account user tagging—reveal underlying clusters of similarities that point to new categories of music. These categories don't share a particular music genre, but reference the effects various music clips have on user moods. Similar processes are at work in other areas. Netflix, for example, groups movies into what the company terms "altgenres," a result of item categorization in terms of more than 70,000 categories (Madrigal). By monitoring and codifying consumer preferences, RSs contribute to the construction of public-based cultural categories in a particular cultural field.

Programming Cultural Encounters through Distribution Architectures

Digital technologies have profoundly altered the distribution of culture by creating platforms for cultural discovery: Goodreads, iTunes, Netflix, to name a few, are, at their most basic, interfaces through which users browse enormous catalogues of cultural goods, the search engines of culture. Just like the infinite playlist that is the iTunes store signaled the end of the "hit parade"—the most public expression of music industry's curation of taste—and fostered niche cultures (Anderson), digital distribution platforms may be said to represent a democratization of taste (Wright, *Understanding Cultural Taste*). These platforms offer discovery paths that are increasingly relevant to young people (Thibeault) and supplement, or perhaps supplant, more traditional methods of discovery such as radio listening or simply a trip to the bookstore.

Yet, just like brick-and-mortar stores need to manage visibility due to shelf space constraints, the RSs embedded in these platforms program cultural encounters based on encoded rules of relevance and similarity, so that publics find culture as much as "culture" finds them (Beer; Lash). Collaborative filtering algorithms, to take one example, "automate the common principle of *word-of-mouth*, where one relies on the opinion of like-minded people or other trusted sources to evaluate the value of an item (movie, book, articles, album, etc.) according to his own preferences" (Desrosiers and Karypis 114). Amazon, for instance, uses collaborative filtering when producing their lists of what similar customers might have also bought.

Both content creators and their various publics are subject to various politics of visibility whereby content is made strategically visible to other users and users are made strategically visible to marketers irrespective of whether "content" is user-produced, as is the case with Facebook

(Bucher, "Want To Be On The Top?") or Twitter (Gillespie, "Can An Algorithm Be Wrong?"), or mass-produced, for example a book on Amazon. The "frictionless sharing" that Facebook introduced in 2011 enables users to share what they read, watch, and listen to with other users—in other words, to perform taste, thus putting yet another spin on the algorithmically inscribed "word-of-mouth" (Bucher, "A Technicity of Attention"). Thus, the circulation of culture itself is redefined to include content, people, and ads as simply nodes in the same graph in which every transaction adds another data point about users' implied identities (Barile and Sugiyama).

Pariser argued that personalization produces "filter bubbles"—the reshaping of the information environment of the user so that the user is insulated from information contrary to her viewpoints. That may be true for news, but it is perhaps too simplistic a description of the sort of programmed serendipity of cultural encounters that emerges as a result of the combined operations of the bundle of RSs that platforms now employ. From the perspective of the algorithm creators, serendipity itself is a desired feature of the system, and most modern RSs in this area are programed either with deliberate "noise" included, or use algorithmic techniques that patrol the cultural associations made by following a user's network of peers (Desrosiers and Karypis). The implication of algorithmic outputs is that the nature and composition of publics interested in an artistic work no longer emerge, as Bourdieu would have it, from the context of socialization in which the "taste" for that type of work was formed (Beer). Instead, RSs generate a different context of social consumption based on networks of associations that make consumers of the same work visible to one another and mediates communicators' perception of an "imagined audience" (Litt). To paraphrase Clay Shirky's expression (cited in Rosenbaum), through their distribution function, RSs synchronize new communities of taste.

Not coincidentally, the resulting politics of visibility, which continuously produce networks of users, products, and interactions, also establish data pipelines between Facebook and third-party commercial sites, thus growing the user data troves of all platforms involved in the data exchange. Data mining these ever-increasing databases of expressed and implied cultural preferences may contribute to bringing RSs closer to the rhetorically powerful ideal of the personal assistant who knows you better than you know yourself, but also poses significant privacy risks for users whose non-public personal information can be inferred with a high degree of accuracy (Popescu and Baruh, "Consumer Surveillance").

Curating Content: Assigning Value to Cultural Goods

In the previous section, we noted how platforms of distribution that regulate the visibility of various acts of consumption organize, manage, and construct the audiences that an artist may have intended or anticipated. In this sense, RSs are a modern spin on the function that "cultural intermediaries" (Bourdieu) play in directing the flow of culture. Cultural intermediaries are workers in the field of culture who, by virtue of their established legitimacy to recognize and interpret taste in a particular field, play curation roles (Wright, *Understanding Cultural Taste*). For instance, in the field of book production, Wright ("Literary Taste And List Culture") identified four institutions that intermediate the encounter of books with their reading publics: academics and critics, reviewers in newspapers and magazines, literary prizes, and "best of" lists.

These powerful mediators are but the visible embodiment of various cultural norms, practices of valuation, and marketing tactics whereby culture industries construct symbolic value for works of art, a value that is often removed from the pure commercial value of art as merchandise. Thus, the work of cultural intermediaries reflects a complex intermingling of cultural industries practices and human judgments of taste that both aims to reduce the social risk of choosing and reinforce the legitimacy of the evaluating institutions (Wright, *Understanding Cultural Taste*).

As discussed above, RSs remind us that intermediation is not just about evaluating actors and cultural goods, but also about the processes through which the two groups become linked (Morris). This stance is particularly useful when thinking of the curation function of RSs, which has a tendency to be discussed in isolation from the human actors that use algorithmic outputs to inform their decisions (Havens). In this section, we show how RSs act as curation assemblages by reshaping what Wright (*Understanding Cultural Taste*) called "the conversations of consecration" through the crowd-sourcing of valuation. They do so in at least two ways: by aggregating user signals into visible metrics of relevance—the equivalent of the "hit list"—and by assigning intermediation power (therefore, granting valuation legitimacy) to select crowd-based recommenders.

There is, by now, a growing literature on how RSs rationalize processes of cultural intermediation by crowd-sourcing valuation. As (Gillespie, "The Relevance of Algorithms") showed, RSs construct cultural value by mining user data to produce momentary real-time representations of what various publics find most interesting, relevant, or trendy. The framing of "legitimate" (algorithmically recognizable) taste is an invitation for publics to "snap to norm," internalize those emergent categories of taste, and represent themselves as consuming publics using those cultural categories. The power of those judgments of relevance rests precisely on claims of objectivity and data-informed "truth" articulated on surveillance (Beck). All the while, the resulting data doubles that construct approximations of user preferences, as well as the insights derived from those profiles, become goods to be traded among the infomediaries involved in the process and other interested commercial parties (Morris).

The crowd-sourcing of valuation also acts through harnessing the cultures of reputation produced by users laboring to comment on cultural goods. User-generated recommendations can be mined in multiple ways, both as a source of data for improving the performance of RSs (e.g., knowledge-based filtering, discussed above) and in the aggregate, as snapshots of what publics "want," from the crudest measures of the average rating of a cultural object to the complex data mining behind the construction of public relevance (Gillespie, "The Relevance of Algorithms").

Less observed is how user-generated recommendations are, themselves, subject to complex rankings. For instance, the RS fueling Yelp employs specific if obscure criteria of what posts matter, thus automatically granting or denying visibility. Data about users feed the computational models that serve to determine how users and their writing get sorted and ranked, what reviews are trustworthy, and which reviewers are "authentic." In effect, the system "builds" *ad hoc* cultural intermediaries by deciding which reviewers matter, a process similarly performed by Amazon. On both Yelp and Amazon, trustworthiness is no longer a matter of cultural competence and the operations of legitimizing cultural institutions, but is now a matter of data quantity. The more reviews generated by a user and the more available data about the user herself, the higher up the user's reviews in the user reviews conversation chain. Thus, users are simultaneously productive as research subjects, free labor, data-trailing agents and profit-making consumers in a value-generating, continuously replayable loop.

Reshaping the Production of Cultures: New Hits and New Voices

So far, we have shown how algorithmic surveillance is the precondition of RSs' effective insertion in the processes that enable cultural consumption. What role do RSs and the type of surveillance practices they enable play in cultural production and with what effects is a much less studied area. It is useful to remember at the outset that RSs are a species of prediction algorithms, with the prediction of preference as the basis for the actual recommendation. Prediction algorithms are the key to anticipating demand for culture and the performance of particular works. The judgment is one of return on investment: a few blockbuster hits that, say, a publisher or film production company might get during a production cycle could support the host of "under-performing" works that use up the production budget but might not find the mass public needed to recoup the costs. In this sense, prediction algorithms continue the predictive practices that cultural industries and notably Hollywood mobilize to determine which works of art (e.g., movie scripts, book manuscripts) to greenlight for mass production (Dormehl). There is every indication that the use of predictive algorithms to understand audiences, anticipate reception of cultural goods, and predict future demand is on the uprise (Napoli).

But what the switch to production that behemoth distribution platforms such as Netflix and Amazon demonstrate is that mining the enormous quantities of audience behavior data might, in fact, reorient the process of cultural production away from the culture industries executives' gut instinct about what "works" and toward an allegedly rational process of mass producing culture (Napoli). Using prediction-based audience data, Netflix can make minute decisions about which story lines, narrative arcs, characters and "altgenres" to invest in, and the extent to which it did so for *House of Cards* suggests an entire research program for media scholars (Havens). Yet, the commercial appeal of algorithms such as Epagogix (Dormehl) that predict not only how much a movie will be able to gross at the box office but also how much more it could gross if modifications to the script are made as per the algorithm's predictive insight, suggests that recommender-based predictions and feedback loops are exercising increasingly influential cultural agency. Algorithms can also instruct music producers how to write music that turns into hits (Thibeault). Dormehl also reminds us that modifying content in real time to adjust to the reader's mood would be but the logical outcome of the real-time surveillance of reading habits that Kindle-enabled devices enact (201).

Prediction algorithms using neural networks also fuel a growing trend of automating writing itself. For instance, we can use Google's AI to predict a dead author's next sentence or to respond to a friend's email on our behalf using our own distinctive writing style (Cuthbertson); we can use Boomerang's Respondable AI to find the email language most likely to elicit an answer from our interlocutors (Finley); we can use Crystal to automatically match the language of our emails to the personality of the recipients—this is done by data mining our inboxes for insights into senders' personalities (Vanhemert); and even use Narrative Science to create a narrative on any preferred topic, a narrative indistinguishable from a human-written one (Podolny).

The ability of algorithms to reshape writing is particularly important in light of claims of empowerment made on behalf of content creators by the rhetoric of participatory culture. Jenkins's work examined the possibilities of co-creation, collaboration, and political power afforded by increased access to online environments, a form of "communal media" (245) in which fans and other private content producers contribute to, appropriate, or subvert corporate media on an everyday basis from within "affinity spaces" (communities of interest) built around cultural phenomena. Taken to its extremes, this vision of participation might mean, for some, the triumph of individual agency and self-expression against the commercially infused and exclusionary institutional apparatus of mainstream media (see discussion in van Dijck). What is problematic is how algorithms train both producers of mass content and the artists themselves to change what they do in order to "game the system" and remain relevant to their publics.

Challenges to Privacy Theory

In this chapter, we have examined the architecture of recommender systems and described their increasingly significant role in the circulation of culture by emphasizing how this role is possible in, and preconditioned on, the mobilization of an expansive apparatus of surveillance. This apparatus of surveillance infiltrates mundane practices and translates them into the language of data; uses that data to make inferences about our cultural predilections; constructs cultural categories that norm our consumption of culture; reflects them back to us; persuades us to change our patterns of cultural consumption; and increasingly encroaches into the production of creative work, be those the mass-produced next hits or the more modest—yet politically significant—user-produced writing. Do privacy theories have anything to say about the role of RSs? Should they? Conversely, do RSs teach us anything about privacy? To conclude, we highlight the challenges that RSs pose to mainstream privacy paradigms and the implications for rethinking privacy.

In some sense, RSs illustrate what Cohen sees as one of the problems of the current mainstream approach to privacy theory, namely, that it needs to mount a more credible defense against the claim that more information is better. Mainstream neoliberal privacy paradigms tend to reduce privacy to informational privacy and assign individuals themselves the task of managing it. "Having privacy" translates into an individual's ability to successfully self-manage control over streams of personal data. As currently understood by the Federal Trade Commission and other policy bodies, regulating privacy means ensuring—in a regulatory minimalist, market-based fashion (Popescu and Baruh, "Captive but Mobile")—the fairness of the process of data collection: truthful and more comprehensive data collection notices, more legible privacy policies from commercial agents, better consumer education. Information about the collection of personal data supposedly empowers individuals to make better choices about their personal privacy. Considering the very *raison d'être* of RSs (i.e., reducing choice), this assumption is, of course, highly ironical. Numerous studies have in fact demonstrated that an overwhelming majority of users don't read privacy policies (Turow et al.); had they tried, anecdotal evidence suggests that the required time investment and cognitive load would be truly monumental and of questionable effectiveness (Hern)—precisely why claims of shortcutting information glut (Andrejevic) make RSs so appealing.

It is not just that users find privacy notices ineffective. The problem is also that the operations of RSs and the digital infrastructures that sustain them are invisible to users, as is the case with other deployments of prediction algorithms: the behind-the-screen data collection, how personal data factor into algorithmic outputs, which commercial ecologies sustain the exchange of data, what happens to the constructed user profiles—all of these operations are entirely outside the control of those subject to algorithmic action. What policy interventions would enable individuals to regain control over their data?

A final point pertains to what assemblage logic tells us about the shortcomings of current privacy regulations. Information privacy imagines the individual as isolated and autonomous; regulating privacy means regulating data collection practices as they pertain to that individual. As we have seen, RSs rely instead on networks in which the individual is but a node in the larger assemblage of peers, consumed goods, cultural preferences, various connected publics, context signals, and other artifacts. Doing violence to an individual's privacy is violence against an entire network with whom the individual is connected through data transactions. Existing regulatory frame-works are ill equipped to deal with this problem, and the challenge for privacy theory is to rethink what privacy means and what it enables, particularly what values privacy may serve for collectives (Baruh and Popescu). Considerations about the relationship between surveillance, personalization, taste formation and the role of privacy in the formation of cultural identity become more serious. Theorizing these connections as part of privacy theory is an urgent task.

At a time when digital interactivity and social media platforms create new and exciting soapboxes for the multifaceted performance of our identity, it has become an open question which identities—the ones we want to assert, or the ones captured by our data doubles—ultimately define us. As filtering algorithms use the "data exhaust" of our digital meandering to create invisible membership groups whose cultural preferences we unknowingly share, as data mining and neural networks algorithms mine our data exhaust for insights into our souls, can we still claim agency over the cultural categories that tell our life story? In the age of automatic, data-driven recommenders, asserting the value of privacy is not just an imperative act of political resistance, but also an act of cultural choice willingly assumed.

Acknowledgment

Portions of this work were supported by a 2014 CSUSB grant from the Office of Student Research. The authors thank undergraduate students Alexander Douglas, Eli Fabro, and Clarissa Toll for their assistance.

Works Cited

Abbas, Assad, Kashif Bilal, Limin Zhang, Samee U. Khan. "A Cloud Based Health Insurance Plan Recommendation System: A User Centered Approach." *Future Generation Computer Systems*, vol. 43–4, 2015, pp. 99–109.

Adomavicius, Gediminas, Gediminas Adomavicius, Jesse C. Bockstedt, Shawn P. Curley, and Jingjing Zhang. "Do Recommender Systems Manipulate Consumer Preferences? A Study of Anchoring Effects." *Information Systems Research*, vol. 24, no. 4, 2013, pp. 956–75.

Airoldi, Massimo, D. Beraldo, and A. Gandini. "Follow the Algorithm: An Exploratory Investigation of Music on YouTube." *Poetics*, vol. 57, 2016, pp. 1–13.

Amatriain, Xavier, Alejandro Jaimes, Nuria Oliver, and Josep M. Pujol. "Data Mining Methods for Recommender Systems." *Recommender Systems Handbook*, edited by Francesco Ricci et al., Springer, 2011, pp. 39–71.

Ananny, Mike. "Toward an Ethics of Algorithms." *Science, Technology, and Human Values*, vol. 41, no. 1, 2015, pp. 93–117.

Anderson, Chris. *The Long Tail: Why the Future of Business Is Selling Less of More.* Hyperion, 2006.

Andrejevic, Mark. *Infoglut: How Too Much Information Is Changing the Way We Think and Know.* Routledge, 2013.

Angwin, Julia, Terry Parris Jr., and Surya Mattu. "Facebook Doesn't Tell Users Everything It Really Knows About Them." *ProPublica*, 4 Jan. 2017, www.propublica.org/article/facebook-doesnt-tell-users-everything-it-really-knows-about-them. Accessed 16 May 2017.

Barile, Nello, and Satomi Sugiyama. "The Automation of Taste: A Theoretical Exploration of Mobile ICTs and Social Robots in the Context of Music Consumption." *International Journal of Social Robotics*, vol. 7, no. 3, 2015, pp. 407–16.

Baruh, Lemi, and Mihaela Popescu. "Big Data Analytics and the Limits of Privacy Self-management." *New Media and Society*, vol. 19, no. 4, 2017, pp. 579–96.

Beck, Estee. "A Theory of Persuasive Computer Algorithms for Rhetorical Code Studies." *Enculturation*, 22 Nov. 2016, enculturation.net/a-theory-of-persuasive-computer-algorithms. Accessed 6 July 2017.

Beer, David. *Popular Culture and New Media: The Politics of Circulation.* Palgrave MacMillan, 2013.

Bobadilla, Jesus, Antonio Hernando, Fernando Ortega, Abraham Gutiérrez. "Recommender Systems Survey." *Knowledge-Based Systems*, vol. 46, July 2013, pp. 109–32.

Bourdieu, Pierre. *Distinction: A Social Critique of the Judgement of Taste.* Translated by Richard Nice, Harvard UP, 1984.

Bucher, Taina. "A Technicity of Attention: How Software makes Sense." *Culture Machine*, vol. 13, 2012, pp. 1–13. www.culturemachine.net/index.php/cm/article/viewArticle/470. Accessed 6 July 2017.

——. "Want to Be on the Top? Algorithmic Power and the Threat of Invisibility on Facebook." *New Media and Society*, vol. 14, no. 7, 2012, pp. 1164–80.

Cohen, Julie E. *Configuring the Networked Self: Law, Code, and the Play of Everyday Practice.* Yale UP, 2012.

Crawford, Kate. "Artificial Intelligence's White Guy Problem." *The New York Times*, 25 June 2016, www.nytimes.com/2016/06/26/opinion/sunday/artificial-intelligences-white-guy-problem.html. Accessed 16 May 2017.

Cuthbertson, Anthony. "Google's AI Predicts the next Sentence of Dead Authors." *Newsweek,* 25 May 2016, www.newsweek.com/googles-ai-predicts-next-sentence-dead-authors-431425. Accessed 16 May 2017.

De Landa, Manuel. *Assemblage Theory.* Edinburgh UP, 2016.

Deleuze, Gilles, and Felix Guattari. *Capitalism and Schizophrenia.* U of Minnesota P, 1983.

Desrosiers, Christian, and George Karypis. "A Comprehensive Survey of Neighborhood-Based Recommendation Methods." *Recommender Systems Handbook,* edited by Francesco Ricci et al., Springer, 2011, pp. 107–44.

Dormehl, Luke. *The Formula: How Algorithms Solve All Our Problems—and Create More.* London, WH Allen, 2015.

Elias, Norbert. *The Civilizing Process.* Basil Blackwell, 1978.

Fatourechi, Mehrdad. "The Evolving Landscape Of Recommendation Systems." *TechCrunch,* 28 Sept. 2015, techcrunch.com/2015/09/28/the-evolving-landscape-of-recommendation-systems/. Accessed 16 May 2017.

Felfernig, Alexander, and Robin Burke. "Constraint-Based Recommender Systems: Technologies and Research Issues." *Proceedings of the 10th International Conference on Electronic Commerce August 19–22, 2008, Innsbruck, Austria,* edited by Dieter Fensel and Hannes Werthner, 2008, doi.acm.org/10.1145/1409540.1409544.

Finley, Klint. "AI Is Here to Help You Write Emails People Will Actually Read." *Wired,* 3 June 2017, www.wired.com/2016/08/boomerang-using-ai-help-send-better-email/. Accessed 16 May 2017.

Gillespie, Tarleton. "Can An Algorithm Be Wrong? Twitter Trends, the Specter of Censorship, and Our Faith in the Algorithms Around Us." *Culture Digitally,* 19 Oct. 2011, culturedigitally.org/2011/10/can-an-algorithm-be-wrong/. Accessed 6 July 2017.

———. "The Relevance of Algorithms." *Media Technologies—Essays on Communication, Materiality: and Society,* edited by Tarleton Gillespie et al., MIT Press, 2014, pp. 167–94.

Havens, Timothy. "Media Programming in an Era of Big Data." *Media Industries Journal,* vol. 1 no. 2, 2014, www.mediaindustriesjournal.org/index.php/mij/article/view/43/82. Accessed 6 July 2017.

Hern, Alex. "I Read All the Small Print on the Internet and It Made Me Want to Die." *The Guardian,* 15 June 2015, www.theguardian.com/technology/2015/jun/15/i-read-all-the-small-print-on-the-internet. Accessed 16 May 2017.

Introna, Lucas D. "The Enframing of Code." *Theory, Culture and Society,* vol. 28, no. 6, 2011, pp. 113–41.

Jenkins, Henry. *Convergence Culture: Where Old and New Media Collide.* New York UP, 2006.

Lash, Scott. "Power after Hegemony." *Theory, Culture and Society,* vol. 24, no. 3, 2007, pp. 55–78.

Litt, Eden. "Knock, Knock. Who's There? The Imagined Audience." *Journal of Broadcasting and Electronic Media,* vol. 56, no. 3, 2012, pp. 330–45.

Lu, Jie, Dianshuang Wu, Mingsong Mao, Wei Wang, and Guangquan Zhang. "Recommender System Application Developments: A Survey." *Decision Support Systems,* vol. 74, 2015, pp. 12–32.

Mackenzie, Adrian. *Cutting Code: Software and Sociality.* Peter Lang, 2006.

Madrigal, Alexis C. "Reading the Privacy Policies You Encounter in a Year Would Take 76 Work Days." *The Atlantic,* 1 Mar. 2012, www.theatlantic.com/technology/archive/2012/03/reading-the-privacy-policies-you-encounter-in-a-year-would-take-76-work-days/253851/. Accessed 17 May 2017.

Morris, Jeremy Wade. "Curation by Code: Infomediaries and the Data Mining of Taste." *European Journal of Cultural Studies,* vol. 18, no. 4–5, 2015, pp. 446–63.

Napoli, Philip M. "Automated Media: An Institutional Theory Perspective on Algorithmic Media Production and Consumption." *Communication Theory,* vol. 24, no. 3, 2014, pp. 340–60.

Pariser, Eli. *The Filter Bubble: What the Internet Is Hiding from You.* Penguin, 2011.

Podolny, Shelley. "If an Algorithm Wrote This, How Would You Even Know?" *The New York Times,* 7 Mar. 2015, www.nytimes.com/2015/03/08/opinion/sunday/if-an-algorithm-wrote-this-how-would-you-even-know.html. Accessed 16 May 2017.

Popescu, Mihaela, and Lemi Baruh. "Captive But Mobile: Privacy Concerns and Remedies for the Mobile Environment." *The Information Society,* vol. 29, no. 5, 2013, pp. 272–86.

———. Consumer Surveillance and Distributive Privacy Harms in the Age of Big Data. *Digital Media: Transformations in Human Communication,* edited by Paul Messaris, and Lee Humphreys, 2nd ed., Peter Lang, 2017, pp. 313–27.

Ricci, Francesco, Lior Rokach, and Bracha Shapira. "Introduction to Recommender Systems Handbook." *Recommender Systems Handbook,* edited by Francesco Ricci et al. Springer, 2015, pp. 1–35.

Rosenbaum, Steve. "Why Content Curation Is Here to Stay." *Mashable*, 3 May 2010, mashable.com/2010/05/03/content-curation-creation/. Accessed 17 May 2017.

Simmel, Georg. "Fashion." *The American Journal of Sociology*, vol. 62, no. 6, 1957, pp. 541–58.

Thibeault, Matthew D. "Algorithms and the Future of Music Education: A Response to Shuler." *Arts Education Policy Review*, vol. 115, no. 1, Nov. 2013, pp. 19–25.

Thompson, Clive. "If You Liked This, You'Re Sure to Love That." *The New York Times*, 22 Nov. 2008, www.nytimes.com/2008/11/23/magazine/23Netflix-t.html. Accessed 17 May 2017.

Turow, John, Joseph Turow, Chris Jay Hoofnagle, Deirdre K. Mulligan, and Nathaniel Good. *The Federal Trade Commission and Consumer Privacy in the Coming Decade. I/S: A Journal of Law and Policy for the Information Society*, 2007, scholarship.law.berkeley.edu/facpubs/935/. Accessed 6 July 2017.

van Dijck, José. "Users like You? Theorizing Agency in User-Generated Content." *Media, Culture and Society*, vol. 31, no. 1, 2009, pp. 41–58.

VanHemert, Kyle. "Write the Perfect Email to Anyone With This Creepy Site." *Wired*, 6 June 2017, www.wired.com/2015/04/write-perfect-email-anyone-creepy-site/. Accessed 15 May 2017.

Wright, David. "Literary Taste and List Culture in a Time of 'Endless Choice.' " *From Codex to Hypertext Reading at the Turn of the Twenty-First Century*, edited by Anouk Lang. U of Massachusetts P, 2012, pp. 108–123.

——. *Understanding Cultural Taste: Sensation, Skill and Sensibility*. Palgrave Macmillan, 2015.

Zibriczky, David. "Recommender Systems Meet Finance: a Literature Review." *Proceedings of the 2nd International Workshop on Personalization and Recommender Systems in Financial Services*, 2016, pp. 3–10, ceur-ws.org/Vol-1606/paper02.pdf. Accessed 6 July 2017.

27

IMPLICATIONS OF PERSUASIVE COMPUTER ALGORITHMS

Estee Beck

Computer algorithms emerged as scripts governing machine activity and human behavior. Programmers valorize algorithms as neutral language scripts capable of impartiality and true representation of data—"algorithms" here refers to the computational procedures of input and output of values (or data). These scripts are anything but neutral, but are so often conflated with *logos*—values of Western philosophical and empirical order, knowledge, and control. By locating algorithms as stripped of style and expression and aligning with truth, programmers rely upon both scientific and rhetorical proofs to gain the approval of their audience(s). In other words, Tarleton Gillespie's algorithms "produce and certify knowledge" by relying upon empirical science and subject matter experts to affirm the computational procedures as sacred scripts in a system designed to persuade people into action. Of course, certifications and qualifications matter in programming, but reliance upon expertise without examination of underlying suppositions of algorithms leads to false beliefs and habits that erode personal privacy. In this present day, algorithms while employed for simple sort and merge functions are increasingly used to categorize data for production, consumption, and control with the explicit purpose of monetizing data collected by surveillance activity. The problem with this engagement, in so far as algorithms reside beneath the visual interface of computational machines, results in impenetrability of the procedures. This leaves end users—people who use the product—unaware and uninformed of the logic governing machine activity. As such, algorithms are opaque, oftentimes black-boxed, and an invisible law of an untouchable court of the information age.

This chapter examines the implications of computer algorithms for the field of digital rhetoric, and how teachers and researchers may lay bare the benefits and consequences of computational procedures in networked computing, e.g., social media, mobile phone technologies, to sensors on everyday objects such as smoke detectors, thermostats, and refrigerators. Given that algorithms govern digitally mediated life for high-technology cultures, shifting attention to the more theoretical dimensions of algorithmic processes and procedures, as this chapter does, helps scholars understand the ideological freight embedded in the algorithms that govern digitally mediated lives. The significance of examining algorithms is critical for an informed citizenry to address programmers' false beliefs about algorithms as neutral and objective procedures, and to devote energy to curing the poison of surveillance capitalism—the capitalization of data from surveillance activities—to use Shoshana Zuboff's term, that has been injected into commonplace discourse. Digital rhetoricians are poised to take up this examination in scholarship, as this chapter does, but more so in public venues to change the landscape of algorithmic (ab)uses, since algorithms use language to construct the realities machines and humans occupy alongside the discourse people use to support or condemn algorithmic procedures.

Defining Computer Algorithms

The defining characteristics of computer algorithms—made by programmers, computer scientists, theorists, and media journalists—align the computational procedures as instructions or logical patterns of "if_then" statements to capture input data to process outcomes built into the algorithm. For mathematician Hartley Rogers, Jr. and for computer scientists Thomas H. Cormen, Charles E. Leiserson, and Ronald L. Rivest algorithms are methods of expressing a finite list or well-defined computational processes to calculate values in a specific sequence. Similarly, digital rhetorician James Brown, Jr. considers algorithms as "involving a defined set of procedures that achieve a discrete goal" (139). These views of algorithms associate procedures with tightly controlled parameters, akin to the scientific method of observation, measurement, testing, and modification. They also describe algorithmic processes from a detached and objective perspective or what algorithms *do* instead of thinking about the epistemological state of algorithms or their impact upon human and machine interactions. That is, careful control of the environment and methods produces logical outcomes; there are no deviations in the step-by-step procedure algorithms perform to produce output.

Given this rationale, it is easy to associate the processed nature of algorithms with recipes (or any set of instructions for that matter) to help non-mathematicians and non-computer scientists understand algorithms conceptually. In two separate accounts, Chris Ingraham and John Gallagher indicate such positions. Ingraham elaborates on this matter in "Towards an Algorithmic Rhetoric" by writing, "a recipe for chocolate chip cookies is as much an algorithm as the directions you give a friend . . . each offers instructions and steps—a procedure—that can be repeated indefinitely to achieve results with the same effectiveness" (65), and Gallagher in "Writing for Algorithmic Audiences" explains that "a cooking recipe, for instance, is an example of an everyday algorithm" (1). Algorithms that run on a machine—that have been encoded to act as computational procedures—possess a more discrete operation than when a person performs a recipe. When algorithms "act" they do so with precisely defined steps, the kind of precision necessary to mathematical equations, for example when someone says, "What is 2 plus 2?" or "Add up the integers from 20 to 50 and divide by 2." Once a programmer intends to use an algorithm, she, he, or zir has to consider the precision necessary for the layers of language—from machine, assembly, and high-level—a computer uses to process and produce information. By contrast, one cannot account for the flawed nature of performing a recipe. Where one step might have, "Beat the eggs until whipped" or "Add three cups of water" an algorithm must know the precise time to beat the eggs—is it one minute, two minutes, or more? When a person adds three cups of water, it is never a precise measurement since a person might not fill the water to the one cup line or water might spill out of the cup while moving from sink to bowl. Additionally, one might perform some steps of the recipe out of order with the result ending in success—an algorithm cannot, by its design, do so with guarantee. Recipes, in other words, are not adequate to the task of providing a rich enough metaphor to describe the characteristics of algorithms as they lack the control and precision necessary algorithms must have to be successful in execution of their functions.

These definitions of computer algorithms lead to several questions when tied to digital rhetoric, specifically persuasion. Questions include, how do computer algorithms deliver content online? How do the algorithms persuade people to purchase certain items or direct behavior? How do computer algorithms figure in the larger landscape of computer code? Why might digital rhetoricians study computer algorithms at all? If so, why does this matter for scholarship in digital rhetoric? Is it the purview of digital rhetoricians to study and examine algorithms? As humanities-based researchers, access to the mathematical equations driving computer processes makes inquiry difficult. Researchers in digital rhetoric are equipped to address the ethical concerns with persuasive technologies and argue for new research. In light of broader public and disciplinary calls to learn to read and write computer programs, digital rhetoricians and writing teachers must examine how computer code, including algorithms, read and write people through persuasion and agency, since high-technology cultures use computer technologies to write and communicate.

Algorithms, Agency, and Persuasion

In 2016, I theorized persuasive computer algorithms to define and set parameters for how digital rhetoricians can think about algorithmic influence. Specifically, I identified three characteristics of the theory—algorithmic ideology; algorithmic processes; and, algorithmic inclusion/exclusion—in order to position how a written-only language system embodies persuasive abilities: "Persuasive computer algorithms are written-only language objects with encoded agency, transactional invention, and embedded values, beliefs, and logics of the three rhetorical appeals performing functions that provide the grounds for human and non-human change" (n.p.). I elaborate upon encoded agency from interdisciplinary theorist Lucas Introna's work on the performativity of computer code. He says code should be understood through an encoding process from agent (or programmer) to transmission (receiver or end user). In other words, the intentional design, desires, biases, and historical/social registers are part of the written-only language of computer code (and algorithms) and are carried to end user transactions. Accordingly, algorithms bear human symbolic action upon execution in computing environments.

This theory, however, does cast algorithms as "quasi-rhetorical agents" associating the finite and precise language stored in silicon chips and memory boards with agency as defined in rhetoric. Quasi as partially agentive and as having some but not all of the resemblances of human rhetorical agents. A response to this position, by Douglas Eyman, casts suspicion upon algorithms as quasi-rhetorical agents:

> the rhetorical designs of their creators, even in instances where new contexts allow
> for differential applications of such design does not convey conscious motive or ability
> to consciously choose among available means—algorithms may be persuasive in the
> sense that they can engage rhetorical action, but they are not fully agentive as a result.
> (n.p.)

Eyman's position reveals the extent to which algorithms engage with agency. I take his point as locating agency within human activity only, as he additionally remarks, "I am hesitant to grant software agents the status of co-rhetors (at least, until we have complete and verifiable artificial intelligence)" (n.p.). This critique is not surprising, given the Western rhetorical tradition's view of agency under the domain and control of the rhetor. Under this perspective, algorithms do not have a biological imperative to create or prune impulse-conducting pathways or have a corporeal consciousness to redirect action. Algorithms are not human brains. It is absurd to anthropomorphize algorithms because they are written-only language scripts. These non-human scripts exist because mathematicians and computer scientists created them, hence quasi. Eyman's position of agency is a difference between human and machine action with an ability to freely choose avenues unconstrained by precision. I see Eyman's point, especially when thinking through the need, will, and desire of the marginalized—the other*ed* in contemporary society to speak back to heteronormative, patriarchal, and white feminist views in order to assert power and influence—to have a voice. At the same time, I also see agency as an expansive enough *term* to include multiple defining characteristics. This notion has also been picked up on by Chris Ingraham in a post about fitness trackers and agency ("Algorithms"). He links Carolyn Miller's article on computerized assessment and locating agency–not under the control of the rhetor, but made possible by the "kinetic energy" of the communicative event. She describes this as,

> agency is a kinetic energy, it must be a property of the rhetorical event or performance itself. Agency thus could not exist prior to or as a result of the evanescent act . . . the kinetic energy of performance . . . [is] between the agent's capacity and the effect on an audience. (147)

Miller's suggestion reveals the audience as integral to the act or the performance of the event. She later adds, "to produce kinetic energy, performance requires a relationship between two entities who will attribute agency to each other. Indeed, much of what inexperienced writers and readers have to learn is how to attribute agency to the invisible, mediated other" (149). In Miller's formulation, the exchange or interaction among rhetor and audience produces the kinetic energy as an agentive act. Such a position allows the definition of agency an expansion from traditional rhetorical views toward the interaction bound to computers and human responses.

All of this is to say that I treat algorithms as quasi-agentive not within the Western tradition of rhetoric or necessarily as kinetic energy (although this position does offer affordances toward this claim), but as performing processes with purpose—from the design of human consciousness—as another definition of the expansive term of agency. As algorithms perform actions, they take on performativity of embodying and rejecting both subject and object relations. They reject the Cartesian dualism of experiencing the world through the mind/body split. The algorithm as subject has its own type of command experience that distinguishes itself from other algorithms and materials. Algorithms/code takes the role of material actor—of Heidegger's Daesin—operating by taking in database inputs to perform actions.

However, just viewing algorithms/code as commands that execute actions overlooks what N. Katherine Hayles called the performative nature of code. Hayles notes, "code running in a digital computer causes changes in machine behavior and, through networked ports and other interfaces, may initiate other changes, all implemented through transmission and execution of code" (qtd. in Chun 22). On one layer, the execution of code causes machines to move—to act. Whether it is robotic arms smoothly shifting directions at the press of the operator's button or altering the functionality of the computer at the command line, the underlying algorithms act with purpose to perform change. On the other layer, algorithms perform such tasks through the coded operations and instructions organized by computer scientists and programmers. The algorithms, residing in computer code, read and write data. Whether it is ranking websites based on backlink data versus ranking sites based on user database information for relevance, the performativity of the algorithms functions as representative of the reality constructed by those who create the algorithms for people. In other words, algorithms operate with a local agency, designed with conditions set by programmers to structure the digital realities in online and webbed spaces—and "code" humans to operate in narrowly defined ways.

In one sense, the algorithm embodies the subject by acting by its design—its own form of material conscious—to produce outcomes. To say algorithms are material is a bit of a misnomer as they are abstractions. Only when etched onto a surface—be it a piece of paper or a source code editor—do algorithms have materiality. In another sense, the algorithm is also an object that exists as separate from human consciousness and as a relation to human existence and action—even though it carries forward the encoded beliefs of the programmer. Once the algorithm, embodied with materiality, takes input data—I argue the algorithm becomes a rhetor, engaging performativity and persuasion to produce outcomes. For example, when a person signs up for a Facebook account, she or he agrees to have Facebook monitor their activities on the site and through third-party applications. The data collection includes length of time on the site, mouse clicks, mouse hovers, status updates, number of pages viewed, and much more. In addition, the end user also self-voluntarily enters demographic information, such as age, marital status, and location. Facebook's algorithms take all of this input data to calculate what the end user might want to experience on the site and returns personalized advertisements and tailors which friends' posts appear in the newsfeed. In response, the end user engaged in a rhetorical event and continues to use the site under a limited set of available elements. This is important because the intellectual challenge for digital rhetoricians is considering algorithms/code as agentive *and* rhetors in a communication exchange with machines and humans. As this example makes clear, algorithms limit data output, which can be used to focus how people participate online. Kevin Brock and Dawn Shepard shrewdly sum up this concept:

> [We] convince *ourselves* that we are actively making decisions about how to participate in a given system when, in reality, we accept options made apparently available to us from a set of constrained possibilities. In other words, we allow ourselves to be persuaded that we are the only agents involved in a particular situation when, in reality, there are networks of visible and invisible actors working to persuade us to specific ends—often including further participation in relevant persuasive computational systems. (21)

Rather than a system designed to allow end users to select among the available means and modes, these algorithms personalize the online realities of social media, make recommendations for future movies (Netflix) or products (Amazon), and tailor search results (Google). People who actively engage with recommendation-based systems that Web retailers such as Amazon or Netflix use, form impressions and make decisions about what to interact with on the sites (Adomavicius and Tuzhilin). The recommendation systems use algorithms to collect input data including, demographic data, rating data, behavior patterns (browsing, link clicking, scrolling, selections), transaction data, and production data (movies, jokes, price, and brand) to filter relevant content for users of websites (Shinde and Kulkarni). Presumably, the more input data algorithms can collect about users, the more salient the content. This suggests users generate content for algorithms to collect, when indeed, the algorithms mine this data to encourage and influence behavior. Algorithms control the flow of information; they engineer the social and cultural conditions of online experiences.

The conditions Brock and Shepard discuss, these constrained possibilities, as the rest of this chapter puts forth, have implications for how people participate online, especially when, as Brock and Shepard note, "ambiguity or obscurity to procedural mechanisms . . . facilitates users' perceptions of greater agency" (21). More important, defining algorithms and theorizing how they are agentive and persuasive provides digital rhetoricians with tools necessary to demystify algorithms for the public. It also clarifies how algorithms function, and how they operate to monitor and capture data under a surveillance network designed to commodify the labor of end users and monetize their data for profit. Zeynep Tufekci, emphasizing big data and computational practices as "opaque and unaccountable campaigns of persuasion and social engineering" (n.p.) has argued, "new analytic tools [algorithms] foster more effective—and less transparent—'engineering of consent' (Bernays, 1947) *in the public sphere"* (n.p.). That is to say algorithms, when applied to social networking or to any system that provides personalization, are the mechanism power-brokers use to control the masses.

Algorithms, understood by programmers as neutral language scripts, do not stand in for objective logic procedures. Rather they co-construct a rhetorical event with the audience (the end users), and exchange information to redirect action. They transform how people view and interact with content online. They do not simply take input data, and code into output, but they respond to variables and create a new reality. Algorithms always reflect the design choices of programmers through an encoded agency—transmitted for a future rhetorical exchange. The sooner programmers and end users understand that algorithms have biased designs, and function insofar as the limitations imposed upon them by their creators, the better position we will all be in, knowing algorithms are invisible manifestations of a programmer's intent and design—and more importantly, their power and control for directing the flow of information online.

In terms of a performative computer algorithm, persuasion plays an important role in the overall design and functionality of the coded processes of algorithms, which leads to understanding algorithms as functioning on a scale of social, political, and cultural biases. The algorithms Google uses to rank websites—or what Google calls "relevance"—is a value-laden statement because the initial underlying design of the Google pagerank algorithm came from the ethos of academic peer review as a reliable method of valuing work objectively. As Gillespie noted, " 'relevant' is a fluid and loaded judgment, as open to interpretation as some of the evaluative terms media scholars have already unpacked, like 'newsworthy' or 'popular' " (9). Algorithms take input from people's actions, and the algorithms' design operates when parameters within the data are met. Computer engineers, scientists, and programmers code those parameters, a process that allows bias to creep into the code. However, in evaluating relevance, Gillespie treats the value-position of the algorithm as relative to individual or collective human perception of what might fit given certain circumstances, because as he sees it there is no scientific method for discerning the most correct or truthful relevance of what the algorithms produce when weighting different data. He also noted that any accusation of bias constructed into the algorithm "implies that there exists an unbiased judgment of relevance available," (p. 9) making it difficult to ascertain the merit and weight of relevance. While I appreciate Gillespie's position on bias in algorithmic culture, I also see merit in positioning algorithms not as a biased/not-biased binary, but of a dynamic agnostic abstraction where some algorithms may contain more bias than others position. It may be that the biases contained in algorithms are or are not as noticeable to certain users because the outputs align with their ideological belief systems or it might also be that the algorithms lean toward more mathematical outputs that perhaps do not favor a biased approach to computation. This sliding scale approach reminds us that bias may be easily detected or embedded further in the algorithm.

To address the material and performative nature of algorithms, we need to move to examining the implications algorithms have upon the lives of end users. Such recognition alone establishes the defining characteristics of algorithms, and their function to shape the perceptions and actions of people and other objects through writing. Of significance here is the sense that a computer algorithm has the agency to perform a language-oriented task that hugely influences how multiple human and non-human actors respond to information and digital environments. From the perspective of proprietary algorithms, we may never know the true complex operations computer algorithms undergo, but digital rhetoricians can speculate through artifact analysis. What I want to emphasize here is that computer algorithms have agency and abilities to perform writing processes—that algorithms exist ontologically, but once they enter a writerly transaction, a possibility of epistemological meaning making occurs from a material object.

Implications of Algorithms

What does this analysis offer digital rhetoricians? In claiming computer algorithms have agency and the ability to persuade, what implications might be inferred to make possible these assertions?

First, *computer algorithms*, in a sense, *write us*. Brock and Shepard, along with Internet activist Eli Pariser have already warned of the peril of algorithms shaping online spaces, thus limiting choices and interactions among people. As Pariser powerfully argues, the ability of algorithms to create a filter bubble for each end user means algorithms (re)direct focus, attention, behavior, and attitudes about events, messages, and information. Algorithms have abilities to write from the data inputted while calculating what a user might want to experience next online, thus guiding end users to a limited scope of information online. Since algorithms are opaque and reside at code levels, discerning how, when, and why algorithms personalize content for end users is made difficult to discern. In many cases, they are proprietary to companies—even unavailable to researchers, thus removing any sort of accountability or transparency into processes.

Further personalization and fragmentation of online democracy will continue, even by encouraging behavioral responses at the expense of end user safety and privacy. Consider the research published in 2014 in the academic journal *PNAS*, about the results of a Facebook study describing how emotional contagion—or the transference of emotional states—occurred through the manipulation of Facebook newsfeed posts. In their study, Facebook Data Scientist Adam Kramer, Cornell University Communication and Information Sciences Professor Jeffrey Hancock, and graduate student Jamie Guillory, adjusted the newsfeeds of 689,003 Facebook users (by using algorithms) to show either more positive or negative newsfeed items. The researchers found that users who interacted with more positive newsfeed items tended to post frequent and positive content. Conversely, the users who interacted with more negative posts tended to post infrequent and negative content. This led researchers to conclude users were emotionally influenced by the content interacted with in Facebook's newsfeed. After *PNAS* published the authors' findings, the news media picked up on the story (for example, cf. Goel; Hill; Voosen) and a media fracas ensued over the ethics of altering 689,003 Facebook users' newsfeeds for emotional contagion. Briefly put, the media, bloggers, and end users expressed concern (and support) over Facebook's study because Facebook failed to inform end users of the psychological experiment and non-consensually used information for the research. Despite the criticism regarding informed consent, the study does make clear how written and visual content affects users. What is not clear in the study is what algorithms were used to make emotional contagion possible. Of course, researchers would require knowledge of Facebook's proprietary algorithms to conduct such research—and that information is not publicly available; however, examining algorithms in this setting would at least provide some links for persuasive communication between written-only machines and humans.

While less researched, Facebook's EdgeRank newsfeed algorithm was made publicly available before Facebook replaced the algorithm with new equations. The algorithm personalized newsfeed content based on how much friends interact with each other or how much time users spend on the site, and what content was "liked." In the ecosystem of Facebook, algorithms adjusted to users' habits and activities, and then delivered content the algorithms thought the users wanted to experience and interact with in their screens. Presumably, this algorithm provided appealing personalized content for users—and yet the algorithms were designed to control the content users engaged with routinely on the site. This type of engineering presents concerns when all of the end users of Facebook do not understand the criteria Facebook uses for the algorithms, and more importantly how peoples' content, behaviors, beliefs, and attitudes are categorized. Prevalence of personalization on Facebook is further damaging as it allows for people to remain in the dark about specific data collected to form the images and text on the screen. Sure, Facebook informs its users via a privacy policy statement that data collection occurs, but Facebook does not allow end users access to the raw data to delete, prune, or accept to help shape their own interactive spaces on the site.

This leads to a second effect from algorithmic agency and persuasion from the secrecy of data collection—algorithmic surveillance capitalism. Surveillance—the collection of personal and public data for detailed examination—may be part of algorithmic function. The observation and data collection of end user activity online has been compared to Foucault's metaphor for asserting control and discipline upon a populous by using Jeremy Bentham's panopticon, or to Orwell's big brother. This prison model makes visible the actions and behaviors of those observed (inmates) through a large tower centered within the building. The observed never know whether and when they are being watched. On the other hand, those in Orwell's narrative know they are constantly under surveillance by big brother. The panopticon and big brother, however, are not adequate metaphors for describing the opaque and invisible surveillance apparatus that algorithms function within as the act of observation does not offer a rhetorical event, that is a space and place for rhetor (observer) and audience (inmate) to speak. As Daniel Solove picks up on, Franz Kafka's *The Trial* offers an apt metaphor—the invisible law of the untouchable court. The powerlessness that protagonist, K, feels when standing before the court to answer for a charge unknown leaves him despondent and accepting of a fate deemed by the powerful. Algorithms—when used to collect data for personalization or to manipulate emotions operates through a hidden surveillance network, with end users unaware and accepting of the apparatus.

The visual interface of desktops, laptops, tablets, and mobile devices make it possible for companies to employ algorithmic surveillance capitalism because the medium obscures the process. In one sense, the structure of Bentham's prison with the central watch tower and the individual jail cells obscures the process of surveillance because of the aesthetic of the environment. The aesthetic of computing technology—or the medium of the visual interface—allows for cognitive unawareness of surroundings, hardware and software, and even bodily movement. This invisibility echoes Bolter and Grusin's "immediacy" or medium disappearance. People who engage in screen life, i.e. connected to things with screens—televisions, smartphones, computers, etc.—absorb immediacy every day. When shopping on Amazon, for example, the user may forget she, he, or zir interacts with a computer screen and a mouse while sitting in the office. The graphics and text on the screen engages her, him, or ze to suspend physical engagement with the surroundings in favor of immersion into the reality the screen displays. When persuasive technologies fade into the background, then that is where, as Cynthia Selfe (cf. Beck "Reflecting") remarks, ideologies work the most strongly. Combined with algorithmic surveillance capitalism, programmers in Silicon Valley move to immersive experiences, which aims to pull end users into the product or service with multiple sessions. This is in line with Zuboff's notion of surveillance capitalism as the system "is constituted by unexpected and often illegible mechanisms of extraction, commodification, and control that effectively exile persons from their own behavior while producing new markets of behavioral prediction and modification" (75). Combined with persuasive computer algorithms, which become co-rhetors in the rhetorical event, programmers are moving toward a reliable system of influencing the general population through the collection of data that erodes privacy in the face of dignity.

This juncture with persuasive computer algorithms and surveillance capitalism becomes concentrated on micro and macro levels of human labor and capital. Observation is not simply an act of recording behaviors and activities, it is a process of taking data to engineer the conditions the audience will live within for future rhetorical events. One might argue the benefits of such a system with replicating narcissism by showing how well the system knows and reflects back the desired elements wanted to engage online or even the ease of which data surveillance increases efficiency or expediency for end users—for example, the top search results on Google—give an impression that the search engine always knows the answer or exactly what the end user is looking for because the site mines data collected from machines and search histories. But, do the benefits outweigh the costs of manufacturing desire to generate demand for products and services? Otherwise put, the seductiveness of surveillance capitalism plays on impulse and incitement to encourage continued use of products and services that will use algorithms to collect data for profit. Does a want for minimal effort mean a cost privacy?

This leads to the third problem with persuasive computer algorithms—algorithms as logos undermines an individual's right to privacy online, as indicated by Wendy Hui Kyong Chun. Chun also takes the position of logos in association, not with algorithms, but with code and asserts, "Code as logos not only extends the power of individual programmers, it also makes code itself both legislation and execution: it spreads a neoliberal empowerment through the embedding of governmental enforcement into everyday situations, making us 'subjects' of code" (176). Regardless of neoliberalism and whether the free-market capitalization of goods and services function with algorithmic design, persuasive computer algorithms in surveillance capitalism forces people as slaves to a system that on the surface provides infinite possibilities, but in actuality constrains information through a guided design. The design is constituted, in part by algorithms, as one half of the rhetorical event, made complete by the input data from end users—data harvested from every movement, click, push, and view of online interaction, and thus imposes a powerful actor upon the conditions of an end user's reality. In other words, if programmers continue to take the position that algorithms are non-biased and neutral, it follows that another supposition may include a disregard of how much data algorithms collect from end users because algorithms reflect the reality end users want to be within.

When such a position is embedded in the rhetoric of using algorithms for personalization as a benefit (with the underlying implication the use occurs through surveillance), a need for increased privacy protection must be enacted. Since consumers cannot rely upon businesses to adopt the best moral and ethical practices for data acquisition and retention (data hacks occur due to faulty security measures) nor count on the US government to enact laws for personal privacy protections online, then consumers must turn to what Finn Brunton and Helen Nissenbaum advocate—obfuscation. Their position is clear; consumers must produce noise in a data collection stream to make obtaining real data difficult. Using do not track technologies; swapping loyalty cards, providing disinformation, and using fake requests to deter net address collection are some of the example practices they suggest consumers use. Even when consumers use obfuscation techniques, data collection still happens (as when end users might enter disinformation about demographic information in a social media website account to confuse the algorithms that personalize advertisements). However, the goal of obfuscation is to make the aggregate data less valuable for companies online. This is one method for end users to continue participating within an algorithmic surveillance capitalistic network while subverting the power conditions that sustain online activity. The larger goal, though, should be to increase privacy protections online. Given enough "noise" in public address and scholarship, perhaps elected representatives will attempt a federal bill for ethical and moral consumer privacy protection online.

Discussion and Conclusion

Occasions for predicting how computer algorithms influence human behavior are over because persuasive computer algorithms influence everyday lives. The ubiquity of networked computing—from mobile phone technologies to sensors on everyday objects such as smoke detectors, thermostats, and refrigerators—provides the means for communication exchange in the information age. In the United States, over 87 percent of adults use the Internet daily, according to Pew Internet Research (2014). Of the daily usage, adults spend approximately 11 hours with electronic gadgets—from televisions to desktop computing (Nielson). A large share of screen time includes mobile phone technology, with a cumulative time of 1.25 hours a day connected online (Neilson). With so much time spent online, people encounter myriad computer algorithms that direct search queries, issue targeted advertising, and personalize Web experiences (Beck "Invisible").

The lure of using technology as a means of improving the quality of life has proven time and again a benefit (writing, the printing press, radios, televisions) for humanity, but often a tool ripe for exploitation and the consolidation of power by those who produce the technology. It will be of little surprise if algorithmic surveillance capitalism discontinues or wanes in favor of a more just and equitable system, given historical patterns of advancement in a free-market system.

The definitions, theory, and implications of algorithms in this chapter for digital rhetoric require additional examination of the critical apparatuses of persuasive technologies. The field already has a firm grasp of rhetorical design and rhetoricity to recognize the conditions that make persuasion and influence possible. Through additional inquiry and analysis, researchers may be able to identify the rhetorical strategies of persuasive algorithms, build a taxonomy for a theory of algorithmic discourse, or build upon the notion of algorithms as co-rhetor in a rhetorical event with humans and other machines. This work would additionally speak back to Ian Bogost's critique of research in rhetoric in *Persuasive Games*. In his work, Bogost claims scholars in rhetoric focus on linguistic and visual modes of expression at the expense of studying the processes and procedures of computer code. Granted his claim occurred in 2007, and since then there have been scholars such as Kevin Brock, Jim Brown Jr., Steve Holmes, Elizabeth Losh, Alexander Monea, Karl Stolley, and Annette Vee who have addressed computation in their scholarship. At the same time, continued work needs to occur.

Taken together, computer algorithms are powerful objects that write hardware into action, as well as provide data to humans for action. This opens rhetorical inquiry and scholarship into the political and ideological foundations of computer algorithms, agency, and persuasion, as well as the effect upon writers and composers in online and mobile spaces. Because algorithms are also invisible to billions—and only accessible by those who create, monitor, and tweak them—algorithms are somewhat of a mystery to front-end users. Even though they evade most of human perception, the algorithms nevertheless shape other coded objects and people into action through writing acts. This is especially important to consider because computer algorithms remain elusive and complex, but digital rhetoricians can also begin analysis of the sheer force algorithms have in people's everyday lives while online. Digital rhetoricians need to turn to developing studies to uncover the relations of algorithms and implicate the persuasive influence computer code has upon people.

Works Cited

Adomavicius, Gediminas, and Tuzhilin, Alexander. "Toward the Next Generation of Recommender Systems: A Survey of State-of-the-Art and Possible Extensions." *IEEE Transactions on Knowledge and Data Engineering*, vol. 17, no. 6, 2005, pp. 734–49.

Beck, Estee. "Persuasive Computer Algorithms for Rhetorical Code Studies." *Enculturation: A Journal of Rhetoric, Writing, and Culture*, vol. 23, 2016, enculturation.net/a-theory-of-persuasive-computer-algorithms. Accessed 17 Nov. 2017.

——. "The Invisible Digital Identity: Assemblages of Digital Networks." *Computers and Composition: An International Journal*, vol. 35, 2015, pp. 125–40.

——. "Reflecting Upon the Past, Sitting with the Present, and Charting Our Future: Gail Hawisher and Cynthia Selfe Discussing the Community of Computers and Composition." *Computers and Composition: An International Journal*, vol. 30, no. 4, 2013, pp. 349–57.

Bolter, Jay David, and Grusin, Richard. *Remediation: Understanding New Media*. MIT Press, 1999.

Bogost, Ian. *Persuasive Games: The Expressive Power of Videogames*. MIT Press, 2007.

Brock, Kevin, and Shepard, Dawn. "Understanding How Algorithms Work Persuasively Through the Procedural Enthymeme." *Computers and Composition: An International Journal*, vol. 42, 2016, pp. 17–27.

Brown, James Jr. *Ethical Programs: Hospitality and the Rhetorics of Software*. U of Michigan P, 2015.

Brunton, Finn, and Helen Nissenbaum. *Obfuscation: A User's Guide for Privacy and Protest*. MIT Press, 2015.

Chun, Wendy Hui Kyong. *Programmed Visions: Software and Memory*. MIT Press, 2011.

Cormen, Thomas H., Leiserson, Charles E., Rivest, Ronald L., and Stein, Clifford. *Introduction to Algorithms*. MIT Press, 1990.

Eyman, Douglas. "Looking Back and Looking Forward: Digital Rhetoric as Evolving Field." *Enculturation: A Journal of Rhetoric, Writing, and Culture*, vol. 23, 2016, enculturation.net/looking-back-and-looking-forward. Accessed 3 July 2017.

Foucault, Michel. *Discipline and Punish: The Birth of the Prison*. 2nd ed., Vintage, 1991.

Gallagher, John. "Writing for Algorithmic Audiences." *Computers and Composition: An International Journal*, vol. 45, 2017, pp. 25–35.

Gillespie, Tarleton. "The Relevance of Algorithms." *Media Technologies*, edited by Tarleton Gillespie, Pablo J. Boczkowski, and Kristen A. Foot. MIT Press, 2014.

Goel, Vindu. "Facebook Tinkers With Users' Emotions in News Feed Experiment, Stirring Outcry." *The New York Times*, 29 Jun. 2014, www.nytimes.com/2014/06/30/technology/facebook-tinkers-with-users-emotions-in-news-feed-experiment-stirring-outcry.html?_r=0. Accessed 3 July 2017.

Hayles, N. Katherine. *How We Became Posthuman: Virtual Bodies in Cybernetics, Literature, and Informatics*. U of Chicago P, 1999.

Heidegger, Martin. *Being and Time*. SCM Press, 1962.

Hill, Kashmir. "Facebook Manipulated 689,003 Users' Emotions for Science." Forbes, 28 Jun. 2014, www.forbes.com/sites/kashmirhill/2014/06/28/facebook-manipulated-689003-users-emotions-for-science/. Accessed 3 July 2017.

Ingraham, Chris. "Algorithms and Rhetorical Agency." *Media Commons: A Digital Scholarly Network*, 16 Nov. 2015, mediacommons.futureofthebook.org/question/what-opportunities-are-available-influence-way-algorithms-are-programmed-written-executed-1. Accessed 3 July 2017.

——. "Toward an Algorithmic Rhetoric." *Digital Rhetoric and Global Literacies: Communication Modes and Digital Practices in the Networked World*, edited by Gustav Verhulsdonck and Marohang Limbu. IGI Global, 2013. www.tarletongillespie.org/essays/Gillespie%20-%20The%20Relevance%20of%20Algorithms.pdf. Accessed 17 Nov. 2017.

Introna, Lucas D. "The Enframing of Code: Agency, Originality and the Plagiarist." *Theory, Culture, and Society*, vol. 28, no. 6, 2011, pp. 113–41.

Kafka, Franz. *The Trial*. Alfred A. Knopf, 1968.

Kramer, Adam D. I., Guillory, Jamie E., and Hancock, Jeffrey T. "Experimental Evidence of Massive-Scale Emotional Contagion through Social Networks." *Proceedings of the National Academy of Sciences of the United States of America*, vol. 111, no. 24, 2014, pp. 8788–90.

Miller, Carolyn R. "What Can Automation Tell Us About Agency?" *Rhetoric Society Quarterly*, vol. 37, 2007, pp. 137–57.

Nielson. "The Total Audience Report: Q4 2014." Nielson, 11 Mar. 2015, www.nielson.com/us/en/insights/reports/2015/the-total-audience-report-q4-2014.html. Accessed 3 July 2017.

Orwell, George. *1984: A Novel*. Signet Classic, 1977.

Pariser, Eli. *The Filter Bubble: What the Internet is Hiding from You*. The Penguin Press, 2011.

Pew Research Center. "Internet Use Over Time." *Pew Research Center*. 2014, www.pewinternet.org/data-trend/internet-use/latest-stats/. Accessed 3 July 2017.

Rogers, Hartley Jr. *Theory of Recursive Functions and Effective Computability*. MIT Press, 1987.

Shinde, Subhash K., and Kulkarni, Uday V. "Hybrid Personalized Recommender System Using Center-Bunching Based Clustering Algorithm." *Expert Systems with Applications*, vol. 39, no. 1, 2011, pp. 1381–7.

Solove, Daniel J. *Nothing to Hide: The False Tradeoff Between Privacy and Security*. Yale UP, 2011.

Tufekci, Zeynep. "Engineering the Public: Big Data, Surveillance, and Computational Politics." *First Monday: Peer-Reviewed Journal on the Internet*, vol. 19, no. 7, 2014, firstmonday.org/article/view/4901/4097. Accessed 17 Nov. 2017.

Voosen, Paul. "In Backlash over Facebook Research, Scientists Risk Loss of Valuable Resource." *The Chronicle of Higher Education*, 1 Jul. 2014, chronicle.com/article/In-Backlash-Over-Facebook/147447/. Accessed 3 July 2017.

Zuboff, Shoshana. "Big Other: Surveillance Capitalism and the Prospects of an Information Civilization." *Journal of Information Technology*, vol. 30, no. 1, 2015, pp. 75–89.

28

WIELDING POWER AND DOXING DATA

How Personal Information Regulates and Controls our Online Selves

Les Hutchinson

In the summer of 2012, I was doxed by a hacker within the Anonymous collective while conducting research in Twitter for my MA thesis. This hacker located my name, address, and my child's name and school. They threatened to release this information publicly to others with the possibility of kidnapping my son from school unless another hacker, one of my research participants, came out of hiding and exposed their current Twitter identity. I communicated this harasser's actions with my research participant who simply remarked, "I'll take care of it," and from then on, I heard nothing about my dox again. Despite then being removed from the threat, the act of being doxed by a stranger for motives unbeknownst to me forever altered how I approach digital scholarship. I felt—and still feel—irrevocably violated and have sought to better protect my online research identities.

My story is not necessarily unique, nor as serious as many other cases. Doxing occurs at such a frequency now that even news organizations and correspondents engage in it openly. My own experience with doxing has given me a personal account of the affective and lived understanding of the practice. I draw on this experience to analyze the role doxing plays in our contemporary, technologically reliant society. This chapter argues that doxing enacts a rhetorical function of persuasion when a person attempts to wield power over another through the exploitation of personally identifying information through analyzing three real-life examples: the doxing and subsequent harassment of anti-gamergate activists Brianna Wu and Anita Sarkeesian; the outing of Jeremy Becker, a critic of the anonymizing Internet browser Tor; and the smear campaign against Taren Fivek, a communist humanitarian worker who dared to report on celebrity activists. Comparing these incidents within the context of several high profile hacking cases situates the practice of doxing in a complex discussion of the rhetorical power of data.

As I see it, doxing shares more than semantic connection to the philosophical concept of *doxa*. Dox functions epistemologically like *doxa* in that they both incite questions of how we come to know what we know and what kinds of knowledge we value about ourselves. However, Western epistemology can be limiting. The conclusion of this chapter will propose decolonial approaches that help us understand doxing as a Western cultural practice. Reading the rhetoric of our online documents—our online personal data—through a cultural rhetorics perspective can distance us from the lasting harm and social consequences of relying on dox as strictly ontological representation.

The Evolution of Doxing as Cultural Practice

Doxing is a practice that began within early 1990s hacker culture just as the Internet was becoming a more socialized space (Douglas; Honan). As a term, doxing functions just like many other terms sourcing from this time—a performative neologism that shortens the spelling of a word and, in a sense, perverts it from its original spelling and meaning. Within hacker culture, the word *dox* serves as the pluralized nominal form of the action to "drop documents" on a person. These documents often contain personally identifying information such as an individual's home address, social security number, credit card number, bank account information, date of birth, photographs, dossiers on family members, and social network aliases (see Figure 28.1). The practice of doxing has evolved over the last couple of decades in various ways depending on persons involved and the particular situation of the moment, sometimes concerning an individual, a group of individuals, or a corporate or government entity. However, doxing has roots within the hacker community, and more recently, within Anonymous culture (see Figure 28.2).

Within Anonymous culture, doxing has operated as a legitimizing indicator of hacking talent. Cultural anthropologist and Anonymous researcher, Gabriella Coleman, has traced the cultural origins of Anonymous from within hacker communities as the central focus of her scholarship over the last couple decades. In "Our Weirdness is Free" from *Triple Canopy* magazine, Coleman explains how hacktivists within Anonymous used doxing as just one form of hacking resistance during the years of 2008–2011. She recounts how during 2011, Anonymous devoted

> **Becky Johnson**
> @BeckyJohnson222
>
> "Doxing" involves investigation,collection, & publication of facts re:known activities,both legal and illegal about an individual. #research
>
> Retweeted by Capt. Edward Winski
> 10/5/12 12:49

Figure 28.1 Definition of Doxing

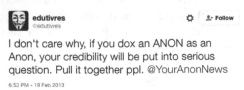

> **edutivres**
> @edutivres
>
> I don't care why, if you dox an ANON as an Anon, your credibility will be put into serious question. Pull it together ppl. @YourAnonNews
>
> 6:53 PM - 19 Feb 2013

Figure 28.2 Credibility and Community

Figure 28.3 Don't Dox an Anon

itself primarily to activist campaigns such as OpTunisia[1] and Operation HBGary (the Federal security company with contractual ties to the US government) (89). Using doxing as a hacktivist practice enabled Anons to find a document entitled "The WikiLeaks Threat" within HBGary's files that outlined a plan for security companies to undermine WikiLeaks through posting fake news to their sites (91). Coleman explains that "some Anons took issue with the collateral damage wrought by Operation HBGary, especially the excessive leaking of personal information" (91). In this case, as among many others, doxing played only a partial role in a collection of actions such as hacking, leaking, and whistleblowing that can be defined together as hacktivism.

Doxing within Anonymous has also served as a weapon used to instill fear in hacktivists hoping to enact social change (see Figure 28.3). These concerns stem from a devastating incident of doxing that occurred from within the community in 2012 involving Anons Hector "Sabu" Montsegur and Jeremy Hammond, among others. Sabu and Hammond were both part of the Anonymous hacking group AntiSec who infamously targeted multiple government and corporate organizations with a myriad of operations such as the HBGary hack. What everyone didn't know at the time was that Sabu had been arrested in 2011 and, to escape a prison term, agreed to work as an informant for the FBI and surveil fellow LulzSec members. The next year, Sabu had acquired enough personal information to identify Hammond through their shared correspondence. What is less emphasized in subsequent reports is that Sabu had encouraged Hammond to hack and then release dox on the private intelligence firm Stratfor—all while collecting Hammond's personal information. By doxing Hammond for his role in doxing Stratfor, the FBI (on behalf of Sabu) was able to prosecute Hammond, sentencing him to ten years in prison.

The framing of Jeremy Hammond by a trusted fellow hacktivist-turned-informant shook the Anonymous and other online activist communities. This incident led to feelings of discord and distrust among people who would have before identified as friends. From that time on, several well-known hackers were arrested for similar high-profile hacking cases, leading to more fear and paranoia within the community. Sabu's doxing of Hammond continues to serve as a reminder of the legitimate and lived threat that one's personal information can be weaponized and used against them in order to further the agenda of the person wielding that information. In this case, it was a colleague and friend who chose to sell out a comrade rather than face a prison sentence.

Doxa's Role in Western Epistemology

Doxing has not remained an isolated practice within the communities from which it began. Rather, like other cultural practices, it has gradually become ubiquitous and normalized within mainstream culture, even that of political journalism. In October 2016, writing and rhetoric scholar Megan McIntyre pointed out on Twitter that Fox news correspondent and host Lou Dobbs had doxed one of Donald Trump's sexual assault victims by retweeting a tweet with the woman's personally identifying information (see Figure 28.4). A massively public incident such as this highlights how doxing has become a practice within everyday life, something we all are at least witness to if not, at some point, victims of ourselves. For that reason, I believe we have an obligation as rhetoricians to understand the facets of this practice as it influences our politics, but also our lives. One way to do that work is to go to ancient Western rhetoric and discuss the concept of *doxa*, a term I feel shares with the practice more than semantic similarity.

Throughout his dialogues, Plato assessed *doxa*'s role in epistemological thought as "opinion," "belief," or "judgment." Often using *doxa* as opposite to *epistêmê* (which he saw as true knowledge), Plato separated the two based upon what knowledge could be derived via proof and explanation. For him, *doxa* does not contain identifiable proof or explanation, but is based upon emotion and assumption, which, in turn, lessens its reach toward the theoretical, end-all-be-all Good. Plato still recognized *doxa*'s importance in epistemology, however. His Socrates engages Meno in a dialogue that addresses the concept of virtue. Socrates uses question as a method to assist Meno in understanding that virtue is both innate to human nature and a learned process, something Socrates emphasizes that Gorgias and the sophists failed to recognize. He then illuminates for Meno the qualities of virtue as both eptistemic and doxic:

> On the other hand, if we are among friends—as you and I are—and if we want to pursue the question, we must answer in a manner more conducive to agreeable, productive discussion. By this I mean that answers given must not only be true; they must also be made in terms the questioner admits to understanding. (*Meno* 6)

Socrates embeds his position on *doxa* within polite conversation here. By drawing Meno in through the affirmative question of friendship, he is better able to pose *doxa* as addendum to *epistêmê*, but still owes it a great importance to the formation of knowledge. *Doxa*'s role in epistemology (at least here) affirms one's grasp of fact to another, solidifying its position as necessary to polite conversation or argumentation.

Figure 28.4 We See You, Lou Dobbs

The term and its function shifts a bit by the time Aristotle gets to philosophizing. As Spanish philosophy scholar Luis Vega Reñón details, Aristotle saw *endoxa* as both a performative characteristic of dialectics through its place as a functioning proposition in syllogisms, but also as opinions that are taken as demonstratively true based on associative feelings of esteem (96). Aligning *endoxa*'s dual meanings, Reñón posits that "[i]n either case, the *endoxa* are, *par excellence*, things that people think and they play the specific discursive role of more or less accepted and/or acceptable propositions in dialectical arguments" (96). Reñón makes certain to also entertain the idea that the relationship between *endoxa* and ethos is not casual and is instead indicative of the evolution of the strength and weight of testimony as the word went from oral to written. He shows us that reading *endoxa* as part and parcel of ethos offers a way to assess rhetorical layers of meaning within not only a statement or proposition, but also in their interpretation.

Reñón focuses on the difference between *endoxa* and *doxa* in Aristotle because of the interplay of rhetoric among the conversants who determine a proposition's dialectical validity. Aristotle saw philosophy's concern over *doxa*'s epistemological uncertainty and sought to define *endoxa* as working performatively: "So Aristotelian dialectic becomes, through the *Topics*, a method of skilled argument which can be applied to ordinary or philosophical questions, and which can proceed from *endoxa* or through *endoxa* with various purposes, e.g. gymnastic, examinative, critical" (98). As Reñón explains, Aristotle's use of *endoxa* operates through performative dialectical functions that allow for plausible argumentation and interpretation. Reñón's seeing Aristotelian *endoxa* as operative within dialectics enables a method of rhetorical analysis, one he says has three parts: (1) an identification of a specific data set, (2) analysis of the data set to determine their relations, and (3) a test of the data to see how they interact with one another given the rhetorical context (99–100). This method can work as a frame of analysis to help us understand *doxa* in a contemporary context by looking at dox and doxing as data, which it presumptively is.

In "A Web of Symbolic Violence," Karla Saari Kitalong introduces Pierre Bourdieu's concept of symbolic violence to discuss *doxa* as means for understanding and rethinking plagiarism. She quotes Bourdieu to define "*symbolic violence* as the use of symbol systems to commit a 'gentle, invisible violence, unrecognized as such, chosen as much as undergone, [which] present itself as the most economical mode of domination'" (qtd. in Kitalong 256). She goes on to say that "[s]ymbolic violence is 'chosen' in that it depends upon the complicity of both the perpetrator and the victim in a reciprocal relationship" (256). Kitalong's definition emphasizes the rhetorical status of symbolic violence in that it occurs through engagement and participation among people.

Doxa, according to Kitalong, are discursive social structures such as predispositions, habits, and belief systems that develop once symbolic violence has become normalized within society (or as Bourdieu calls it, *habitus*). She only uses the word *doxa* twice, once in the beginning of the article to define it and a second time, pages later, where she uses it in reference to her conversation regarding plagiarism. She says,

> Pressing for the abolition of uncertainty in electronic writing spaces could lead us to transpose untouched the rules concerning plagiarism to electronic contexts. But I don't think it wise to reproduce these rules simply because they have been doxa. When we choose to teach writing in electronic contexts, we admit an openness to ambiguity, a willingness to tread uncertainly between risk and caution, a taste for the "teachable moment," and an on-going desire to examine, discuss, and evaluate new technologies and contexts of writing. (Kitalong 262)

Kitalong puts *doxa* in context, dropping it in with a casual reference that makes her use of it seem everyday and colloquial. Her casual reference indicates that she sees it functioning as a normalizing force, similar to a commonplace or rule. Using *doxa* in this way exposes its discursive power—its symbolic violence—and shows her own resistance to that power.

Tracing the meaning of *doxa* from Plato to Aristotle and then to Bourdieu (by way of Kitalong) illuminates an understanding of knowledge and meaning as rhetorical and collaborative, but also Western. *Doxa*, then, can collectively mean an opinion, belief, or judgment that has been adopted as truth via social agreement by mutual participants who, over time, solidify that meaning into social norm. In this way, *doxa* works like ideology in that it has the power to shape perceptions because of its established method of being "tried and true." It is ideology made custom.

Constellating *Doxa* to Doxing with Cultural Rhetorics

We can take a cue from Kitalong and resist normalizing normalization, symbolic violence, and discursive oppressions by turning to cultural rhetorics. In their twelfth note to "Our Story Begins Here: Constellating Cultural Rhetorics," Powell et al. define what makes their rhetorical approach cultural:

> Yes, this means that cultural rhetorics approaches can be used to study dominant cultural practices. For us, remember, "culture" isn't a word we use to mark "difference" or "otherness." Instead, a cultural rhetorics approach is meant to focus on how specific cultures are built around particular beliefs and practices, which lead that culture to value some things and not others. (Act I)

Cultural rhetorics approaches allow scholars in our discipline to identify *all* cultural practices as representative of the culture from which they come. To do so enables us to understand certain epistemological functions such as *doxa* as indicative of their cultural source. Socratic *doxa*, for instance, is nothing save for an attempt to reach an explicit performance of knowledge within its Western context—a context solely emphasizing the role of that performance as symptomatic of one's place in dominant culture of the time. Aristotelian argument operates in a similar way, requiring participants to acknowledge an interlocutor's reputation and position in society as just as important in determining the validity of what they are saying. Identifying *doxa* as a cultural practice shows how alike it is to doxing, another Western cultural practice.

Identifying *doxa* and doxing as Western cultural practices does not do enough; rather, a scholarly obligation of rhetoric is to assess the meaning made in this identification. Powell et al.'s method of decolonization helps to create needed actions of resistance to the symbolic violence that these two practices, once normalized, incur. They offer that "[w]hen we use the term 'decolonial,' we're referring specifically to stories from the perspective of colonized cultures and communities that are working to delink form the mechanisms of colonialism" (Powell et al.; Act I). They see decolonial practice as one method in a four-part approach to *doing* cultural rhetorics scholarship where the making of cultures into being are *relational* and *constelled*. The method focuses on the relationships among other people, communities, and cultural practices that participate in a collective meaning-making constellation. Decolonization in cultural rhetorics is an active recognition of culture as a set of relations with the critical understanding of other sets of knowledges that exist alongside Western, colonial systems and worldviews. The goal of cultural rhetorics is to build relationships among multiple traditions, histories, and cultural practices, especially those silenced by the canonization of Western narratives during colonization.

Recognizing *doxa* from within its Western epistemological locations better shows us how it operates as a narrative that normalizes and can, at times, be wielded to commit symbolic violence. I can also address similar instances by analyzing doxing as it, too, works to enact power over others at the discursive level. Both oppress via acts of language, and it is key to not just name those acts, but to analyze them critically from a multi-situated cultural rhetorics perspective. The best way I have found to do this kind of analysis is to engage with real examples that give us a living understanding of the way power and symbolic violence have operated to silence, oppress, and harm others. By connecting doxing and *doxa*, a hard truth about how we normalize the *person* in personal information emerges; and to know that and see that, we may learn to be more prudent with our assumptions about these cultural practices and our roles in them.

Tales the Dox Tell

To refresh: I define doxing as a largely Western cultural practice of seizing a person's, people's, or organization's private, personal information against their consent. The experience is often traumatic for the victim, leaving them feeling violated and powerless to control their situation. I speak from my own experience when I say that to know how a person obtains our dox can feel mysterious—seemingly done by some genius-level hacker handiwork. Often, however, dox can be relatively simple to obtain for those who know where to look. The practice of doxing has origins in hacker communities, more recently in Anonymous, which means it carries with it the troubled history of its past.

Doxing carries with it the contrary, problematic discourse of Anonymous, as we can see in Figure 28.5: @PLF1940 tweets in mockery of an Anonymous hacker. The person (or persons, more like) are purposely exaggerating—trolling[2]—Anonymous by imitating them and adopting, but also hyperbolically perverting, Anonymous discourse. "Lejun" stands for "legion," a term Anonymous has used in reference to its mass of associates. @PLF1940 finishes their tweet with "MUMBLE HERPA DERPA DING DONG" to signal to readers the hyperbole and mimicry. Though, as we can see, this language is also ableist, and makes fun of people with mental disabilities. Such is the nature of Anonymous discourse: ridiculous, over-the-top at times, and often offensive for no good reason except to be offensive. @PLF1940 writes this with an intent to mock Anonymous and to highlight the ineffectiveness of doxing as a threat within the hacker community.[3]

 **Rustle League**
@PLF1940

I'M LEJUN I'M TERRIFYING I DOX YOU! I GOOGLE NOW! I GOT NOTHING! EXPECT ME MUCH LATER I'M SO TERRIFYING DOX MUMBLE HERPA DERPA DING DONG

5/31/13, 16:45

Figure 28.5 The Offensive Discourse around Doxing

Les Hutchinson

If Games are for Girls, Doxing is for Boys

In late 2014, male gamergate "activists" doxed feminst video games developers Brianna Wu and Zoë Quinn, and cultural critic Anita Sarkeesian for their participation in uplifting feminist ideologies within the video gaming industry (see Figure 28.6). *Guardian* journalist Keith Stuart reports that the personal details of these three people were posted to the Internet forum *8chan* and that each person received a substantive amount of violent threats, amounting to heavy FBI and local law enforcement involvement in order to protect them. Each woman went into hiding, speaking with Stuart from the confines of a heavily secured isolation. The threats continue to this day, but were especially prolific at this specific moment in time, which left each person (and a few dozen others) to fear for their safety while simply being feminists who promote safer and more equitable employment practices in their industry.

Wu has been quoted on BBC as saying, "I think there is a war on women in technology" (qtd. in Stuart) as her way of explaining why she had been doxed then subsequently harassed. She went on to say to Stuart that "You can read what they post about me and other women. It's not just casual sexism, it's angry, violent sexism. They don't see me, Zoë, or Anita as people, just as objects to be destroyed" ("Brianna"). Wu employs gamer discourse to describe how the harassers treated this situation as a game in which to win. These men took to doxing as their first and primary method of attack. In this way, doxing was used as a mechanism of control, putting the gamergate harassers in a position of power over the people they viewed as enemies. These three activists subsequently had no choice but to flee for their safety, causing them undue personal trauma and professional insecurity.

The attacks against Wu, Quinn, and Sarkeesian were coordinated strategically by technologically savvy men who knew exactly what they were doing and what would happen. They embraced their technological literacy to mask their own identities while acting as a group, releasing these people's personal information within Internet networks created just for doxing. As communications scholars Fish and Follis explain, "Doxers build dossiers about targets that are then released in various online locales (e.g., sites such as Wikileaks, Pastebin, Doxbin on the Tor 'dark net', social media networks, and online forums) in an effort to embarrass and harass individuals or their organizations" (3291). Fish and Follis point to how doxing had become so normalized within the hacker community that an entire Internet infrastructure exists in which to house and disseminate dox once obtained. This infrastructure allows for any coordinated doxing attack to quickly become mobilized from within those in the community who have access to these locations.

Sporks Pantalones
@sporks

It's funny how doxing is a real threat when it might happen to law enforcement people, but not when it's used to threaten women.

8/14/14, 12:26

Figure 28.6 Doxing Has Gender Blindness

310

Doxing on Tor's Behalf

Also toward the end of 2014, a complicated personal–political interaction arose between Tor project developer and hacker Andrea Shepard and the owner of Twitter account @JbJabroni10. Shepard had doxed Jeremy Becker, a pharmacist living with his elderly parents in New Jersey, who had been using his multiple Twitter accounts to harass and criticize Shepard due to her status with her employer. At the time, journalists from the Web publication *PandoDaily* had uncovered that the Tor project, a development company offering free anonymizing browsing software to Internet users, had financial ties to the United States government. Becker used the information from the website article as fuel for sending tweets to criticize Tor employees such as Shepard.

However, Becker soon found himself at the mercy of Shepard's technological expertise, which was in no respect merciful. Shepard used her skills at Internet investigation to determine Becker's identity, location, employment, and other affiliated Twitter accounts. She spread this information on her website and in tweets with intent to punish Becker for how he had been treating her on Twitter. She published a post entitled "Deconstructing the Jeremy Becker troll network,"[4] outlining the process she underwent to uncover and make public @JBJabroni10's identity. Shortly after, the *Guardian* published an article[5] in their technology section that essentially echoed Shepard's description of her experience with doxing Becker (Fox-Brewster). The echoing of an individual, personal account from a mainstream media publication shows the influence Shepard has on the technology community, which leveraged the situation in her favor. With little to no methods to protect himself, Becker had no option but to go into hiding.

Many within Twitter condemned Shepard's doxing of Becker because of the difference in power and platform between the two individuals. As the tweets in Figures 28.7 and 28.8 indicate, not everyone was persuaded by Shepard's narrative. @0w1Farm in Figure 28.7 expresses their view that, like the doxing of the women in my previous narrative, the doxing of Becker was coordinated. This person draws from the association of doxing to Anonymous (as indicated with the acronym YAN, which stands for the massively popular Anonymous account @YourAnonNews—another story for another time). They connect the Anonymous association to three other communities, describing the combination as a "clique." The others are the Tor community, the Vice News community (meaning artist Molly Crabapple and other activists who gained celebrity status post-Occupy Wall Street), and journalists such as Glenn Greenwald (of the Edward Snowden whistleblowing fame) whose journalism network is funded by eBay founder Pierre Omidyar (an affiliation many suspect as disingenuous and biased).

 **orge jorwell**
@0w1Farm

The Tor/Vice/YAN/Omidyar clique are trying to destroy an activist's life using FBI cointelpro tactics. Let that sink in. #Tor @torproject

12/4/14, 12:45

Figure 28.7 Doxing, It's All Relative

my name is
@angry_node

it's not wrong to investigate
people, but it's fucking lame to
release someones dox just
because you don't like them.

11/29/14, 14:20

Figure 28.8 @angry_node Weighs In

@0w1Farm tags Tor's Twitter account in their tweet to get their attention and make their position on their employee's actions known. They seek to incite readers to process the implications of government involvement in the doxing of Becker. They first refer to Becker as an "activist," though that is not an identity Becker has claimed for himself in any tweets I have seen. @0w1Farm also adds a bit of hyperbole with the choice to use the verb "destroy" and link it to "FBI cointelpro tactics." It is true that Shepard did contact Becker's employer and disclose his online behavior to them, but little is known as to what happened after that.

Activist and journalist @Asher_Wolf reflected on Shepard's doxing of Becker in a seventeen-tweet stream. I quote them all to show how she responded to this complex situation:

"I'm going to preface what I'm about to say next by saying: I don't dox people"

"Maybe @puellavulnerata wouldn't have felt the need to d0x JB if people had acted in unison to respond to ongoing personal attacks on her"

"Suddenly the ppl who never gave a shit to offer support pop up to offer complex analysis"

"And when ppl being harassed finally take action—any action, be it block lists, doxing, legal etc—they face mass criticism."

"From my perspective, too many ppl are left to face harassment alone."

"Actually, it's about ethics in Tor dev . . ."

"It requires a collective response. For too often people let others suffer alone. Because they don't want to get involved . . ."

"It's okay to have question about security, about risk. Standing on the sidelines while people are abused isn't"

"If ppl with a desire for common outcomes—privacy, security, transparency—offered better support to each other 1/2"

"as well as vociferously promoting the tools and projects they work on—perhaps there'd be better outcomes for all. 2/2"

"Our human problems need a human response. An algorithm isn't going to solve this shit for us"

"And it goes for everyone. No matter what cause or technology or great leap forward you believe you're superhero'ing"

"Don't hurt others. Tech campaigns and social movements can be rebuilt. But sometimes broken people can't"

"The circle of extremely bright ppl who give a shit beyond making rent and board is actually rather bent, small and hard to replace"

"anyone who thinks this criticism is just JB or Pando: applies equally to grassroots activists, tech developers & net freedom campaigners"

"Look after others. Analyse problems, don't dissect and destroy people"

"If you don't look after your allies, your enemies sure won't" (@Asher_Wolf)

@Asher_Wolf's tweets encapsulate her careful negotiation of this situation through a serious consideration of ethics. She has been subjected to harassment and attacks both online and in person for being a woman, for reporting on technology and activism, and for having a large platform on Twitter. @Asher_Wolf was one of the people Shepard named on her website as being targeted by @JBJabroni10. Despite this, she still offers a critique of Shepard's behavior, while at the same time acknowledging what would have driven Shepard to doxing. @Asher_Wolf's perspective provides us with a good example of the social consequences of such an act on people and communities.

Doxing: Not Just for Hackers Anymore

The effects of Shepard's doxing of Becker have been long-term and continue to show up in other ways. In January of 2016, artist and celebrity activist Molly Crabapple had United Nations press officer Taryn Fivek doxed and her Twitter identity made public. Crabapple had outed Fivek's identity, previously known on Twitter as Emma Quangel, after Fivek had published numerous blog posts, tweets, and a fictional novel criticizing Crabapple for using her art as a mechanism for United States imperialism. As counterpublic persona Kilgoar writes on their website *Internet Chronicle*, "Molly Crabapple had knowledge of Quangel's identity for years and deployed the dox strategically" ("Molly"). Crabapple chose this specific moment to out Fivek with the hope of silencing her. This strategy worked. Fivek disappeared for a brief time, then reemerged on Twitter with an account using her real name. She was also fired from the United Nations after Crabapple lambasted Fivek on Twitter and called for her dismissal. Crabapple's social clout made that happen.

The differences and similarities between what Crabapple had done and the other two instances are telling. First of all, Crabapple does not have the technological expertise to dox on her own. Instead, she enlisted help—presumably from hackers affiliated with Anonymous she had known during her tenure with Occupy Wall Street. Like Shepard, Crabapple was able to leverage her popularity to garner a biased *Buzzfeed* article written in her favor. However, the most telling difference in this case is that Fivek neither harassed nor threatened the artist outright. Fivek had written her share of criticism and often tweeted at Crabapple her disapproval, but there is no evidence that Fivek verbally attacked Crabapple. This incident, instead, shows what a person in a position of social and political favor can do with another's personal information[6] if they decide they do not like them.

The (Lack of) Ethics in Doxing: A Call for Cultural Rhetorics

The incidents I have sketched briefly in this chapter serve as examples of how doxing has had lasting harmful effects on real, everyday people. Each of these individuals suffered from the doxing they experienced. The belief that their doxing was justified or not cannot dispel the fact that doxing forever changed how they lived their lives thereafter. The consequences of doxing are affective, material, and rhetorical. And they all are based upon the assumption that personal information has power.

Laura Sneddon
@thalestral

41. Oh you'd like me to review your company's new comic? Do you still employ that dude who abuses women/bites people/doxes critics? Hello?

12/30/16, 8:47 AM

Figure 28.9 Doxing Is So Mainstream Now

I want to end this chapter with a call to think a little more critically about the power we give our personal information. Placing epistemological value and power on dox enables these symbolic violences to occur. Unfortunately, the violence is not only symbolic either; doxing has evolved into such a normalized practice that sexual victims cannot speak out against their perpetrator—even if he is the President of the United States. Critics cannot name actions they see as imperialist and socially harmful. Women cannot be women in a professional industry (see Figure 28.9). And worse. Much, much worse will come.

We have an obligation as rhetoricians to promote and teach new ways of thinking about our cultural practices. A decolonial approach to doxing would see the practice of doxing as an action that brings harm not only upon an individual, but relationally on all of us. Normalizing doxing creates the possibility for expansive harm. Identifying the Westernized epistemology of dox shows us that our personal information is not solely ontological, but also colonial. So, what if, instead, we thought of our personal documents as communal? What if we looked at how personal information is valued within other cultures?

We could learn to be more critical of the information collected by credit agencies, social networking companies, Internet search engines, facial recognition software, and more— recognizing these as cultural practices that uphold a Western, imperialist system that assigns value

Michael Rowe
@mhrowe

In the future, signatures will be secret just like passwords today. Then bdays. Finally your parents & place you grew up. Then your face.

12/29/16, 5:17 PM from Clarks Summit, PA

Figure 28.10 Privacy Is a Thing of the Future

to who we are through every mechanized aspect of our lives (note Figure 28.10). Powell et al. remind us of the ethics in decolonial work:

> For Mignolo, and for us, decolonial practice isn't a mission, it's an option, an orientation that includes "both the analytic task of unveiling the logic of coloniality and the prospective task of contributing to build a world in which many worlds will coexist" (54). The next step after analysis—a step we hope our work helps to build— is "to build decolonial options on the ruins of imperial knowledge." (11)

It is this option that I suggest we adopt as we come to think about our personal information and the power contained therein. We can discuss the need for building better systems of communication and social networking platforms that curb harassment. We can work within the spaces where we have power to challenge harmful practices such as doxing: our classrooms and our publications. We can speak out in public spaces where others will hear us, and we can show our support to those suffering from these effects. Lastly, we can learn how to protect ourselves from being doxed by engaging with privacy technologies and literacies. Doing so will not solve all of our social problems, but it will make a mark. And, at the least, these things can help us help others. As @Asher_Wolf says, "If you don't look after your allies, your enemies sure won't."

Notes

1. "Op" is short for operation. It has been common practice within Anonymous hacktivist practices to borrow and corrupt military discourse.
2. I believe that "trolling" constitutes an act of playful mimicry and incitement in the hopes of getting attention from the person/people it is directed toward, and not the word for what many others see as harassment and verbal attack. Trolling within many Internet subcultures is usually considered light-hearted and/or an act of perverse affection.
3. Ironically, the @PLF1940 account tweeting here is a hacked account that was taken over by a group of hackers explicitly not affiliated with Anonymous (though tangentially affiliated with the community by proxy) known as Rustle League who led a series of hacker pranks around this time as a means of showing off their skill. They often targeted well-known social justice activists who had histories of exploiting others for professional gain such as the person who "owned" the @PLF1940 account.
4. As of 11/13/16, this post can be found at http://charon.persephoneslair.org/~andrea/pandorasts/jeremy_becker/
5. This can be found at www.theguardian.com/technology/2014/dec/03/privacy-advocates-unmask-twitter-troll
6. Incidentally, Crabapple and I have our own history. She has painted a statement I made in a conversation to Kilgoar on Twitter about her art on a picture of her face. The statement I made was never outright addressed to her and is buried in a long stream of tweets. Crabapple had to have searched her name and came across my statement. Since I learned of this, I have had that Twitter account marked private so as to freely speak without suffering from her directed attention.

Works Cited

Coleman, Gabriella. "Our Weirdness Is Free." *Triple Canopy*. Vol. 15, No. 9, June 2012. www.gabriella coleman.org/wp-content/uploads/2012/08/Coleman-Weirdness-Free-May-Magazine.pdf. Accessed 10 Nov. 2012.

Douglas, David M. "Doxing: A Conceptual Analysis." *Ethics of Information Technology*, vol. 18, 28 June 2016, pp. 199–210. http://link.springer.com/article/10.1007%2Fs10676-016-9406-0. Accessed 2 Nov. 2016.

Fish, Adam, and Luca Follis. "Gagged and Doxed: Hacktivism's Self-Incrimination Complex." *International Journal of Communication*, Vol. 10, 2016, pp. 3281–300. http://ijoc.org/index.php/ijoc/article/view/5386. Accessed 20 Oct. 2016.

Fox-Brewster, Tom. "Privacy Advocates Unmask Twitter Troll." *Guardian*, 3 Dec. 2014, www.the guardian.com/technology/2014/dec/03/privacy-advocates-unmask-twitter-troll. Accessed 3 Nov. 2016.

Honan, Mat. "What Is Doxing?" *Wired*, 6 Mar. 2014, www.wired.com/2014/03/doxing/. Accessed 2 Nov. 2016.

Kilgoar. "Molly Crabapple aka Jennifer Caban doxes author EM Quangel." *Internet Chronicle*, 11 Jan. 2016. http://chronicle.su/2016/01/11/molly-crabapple-aka-jennifer-caban-doxes-author-em-quangel/. Accessed 11 Jan. 2016.

Kitalong, Karla Saari. "A Web of Symbolic Violence." *Computers and Composition*, vol. 15, no. 2, 1998, pp. 253–263. www.sciencedirect.com/science/article/pii/S8755461598900585. Accessed 29 Aug. 2015.

Powell, Malea, Andrea Riley-Mukavetz, Marilee Brooks Gillies, Daisy Levy, Maria Novotny, and Jennifer Fisch-Ferguson. "Our Story Begins Here: Constellating Cultural Rhetorics." *Enculturation*, vol. 18, 25 Oct. 2014. http://enculturation.net/our-story-begins-here. Accessed 26 Oct. 2014.

Reñón, Luis Vega. "Aristotle's *Endoxa* and Plausible Argumentation." *Argumentation*, vol. 12, no. 1, Feb. 1998 pp. 95–113. http://link.springer.com/article/10.1023/A%3A1007720902559. Accessed 28 Oct. 2016.

Shepard, Andrea. "Deconstructing the Jeremy Becker troll network." *Persephoneslair*, n.d. http://charon. persephoneslair.org/~andrea/pandorasts/jeremy_becker/. Accessed 12 Dec. 2016.

Stuart, Keith. "Brianna Wu and the Human Cost of Gamergate: 'Every Woman I Know in the Industry is Scared.'" *Guardian*, 17 Oct. 2014. www.theguardian.com/technology/2014/oct/17/brianna-wu-gamergate-human-cost. Accessed 3 Nov. 2016.

@angry_node. "It's not wrong to investigate people, but it's fucking lame to release someones dox just because you don't like them." *Twitter*, 29 Nov. 2014, 2:20 p.m., tweet URL no longer available.

@BeckyJohnson222. "'Doxing' involves investigation,collection, & publication of facts re: known activities, both legal and illegal about an individual #research." *Twitter*, 5 Oct. 2012, 12:49 p.m., https://twitter.com/beckyjohnson222/status/254307351094521857.

@edutivres. "I don't care why, if you dox an ANON as an Anon, your credibility will be put into serious question. Pull it together ppl. @YourAnonNews." 19 Feb. 2013, 6:53 p.m., https://twitter.com/edutivres/status/304015996992233472.

@mhrowe. "In the future, signatures will be secret just like passwords today. Then bdays. Finally your parents & place you grew up. Then your face." *Twitter*, 29 Dec. 2016, 5:17 p.m., https://twitter.com/mhrowe/status/814596228516343808.

@RCMeg. "So @LouDobbs is doxing assault victims now. That's where we are. (I've blurred the phone # and address; Dobbs did not nor did the OP.). *Twitter*, 13 Oct. 2016, 9:46 a.m., https://twitter.com/rcmeg/status/786609052256129024.

@sporks. "It's funny how doxing is a real threat when it might happen to law enforcement people, but not when it's used to threaten women." *Twitter*, 14 Aug. 2014, 12:26 p.m., tweet URL no longer available.

@thalestral. "41. Oh you'd like me to review your company's new comic? Do you still employ that dude who abuses women/bites people/doxes critics? Hello?" *Twitter*, 30 Dec. 2016, 8:47 a.m., https://twitter.com/thalestral/status/814830198772350976.

@YourAnonNews. "Why dox? You are just doing the Feds job. #solidarity despite differences." *Twitter*, 30 May 2014, 3:36 p.m., https://twitter.com/youranonnews/status/472461485604892672.

@0w1Farm. "The Tor/Vice/YAN/Omidyar clique are trying to destroy an activist's life using FBI cointelpro tactics. Let that sink in. #Tor @torproject." *Twitter*, 4 Dec. 2014, 12:45 p.m., tweet URL no longer available.

29

IT'S NEVER ABOUT WHAT
IT'S ABOUT

Audio-Visual Writing, Experiential-Learning Documentary, and the Forensic Art of Assessment

Bump Halbritter and Julie Lindquist

> [G]ive the pupils something to do, not something to learn; and the doing is of such a nature as to demand thinking, or the intentional noting of connections; learning naturally results
>
> *(John Dewey, Democracy and Education 154)*

Nobody likes assessment. It's that dirty thing that has to be done once the fun and gratifying part of teaching has concluded, once students have moved from the pleasures of discovery to the far less pleasant anticipation of exposure. The moment of assessment is a time of grim reckoning with failures, misdirected labor, and missed opportunities. It is the moment when hope gives way to disappointment, and (even) when trust between students and teachers yields to betrayal. This scenario is made all the more poignant in a time when we can no longer reliably expect to encounter the results of writers' labors as *writing*, but (possibly) as audio-visual products, and when we are uncertain about how to measure things that have arrayed themselves before us as collections of things of unfamiliar shapes and sizes.

But consider the possibility that this story could be different, that this moment represents a happy opportunity to rethink not only our means of measurement, but our essential pedagogical values. In this chapter, we describe the operations of an approach to writing instruction that is also, in its essential operations, an approach to assessment. This approach to writing instruction has at its core a practice to which we have referred in prior writings as "preflection," and are now (for reasons that should become clear) calling "Experiential-Learning Documentary." Experiential-Learning Documentary (ELD) is a practice that first emerged in response to the assessment demands of collaborative audio-visual writing projects and courses, and which has found purchase within a particular institutional context: First-Year Writing at Michigan State University, a program that is grounded in essential values of inquiry, discovery, and communication.

In what follows, we will focus on documentary, per se. However, we want to begin by offering why and how we see this approach to documentary to be centered on experiential learning. When we talk about experiential learning, we mean two things:

- learning that treats as resources students' past experiences, and
- learning that attends to the experiences, in the present moment, of the learning itself.

ELD is an expressive representation of the former (what we will call *documentary*) though it also necessarily implicates the latter (what we will call *documents*). Students have histories as learning selves—and we believe these are best paired with projects that invite students to locate their experiences of the present moment in a more comprehensive narrative of life experiences.

The pedagogical approach we describe is one of *projection, collection, and recollection*: it assumes that the greatest value for learning is in the reflective (or, as we will show, "forensic") moment. To illustrate the operations and affordances of ELD, we describe some predicaments of assessment: situations in which it becomes difficult to recognize—in what is produced by students—what the indicators of learning might be. We have come to see that—as researchers who use techniques of documentary filmmaking in our work, and who have created documentary products as the results of our research—that the central pedagogical moves we describe (projection, collection, and recollection) are also those that characterize the production of documentaries. With this in mind, we begin with a consideration of what the process of "documentary" entails.

Documentary as an Iterative Process of Projection, Collection, and Recollection

If you don't *do* documentary, let us help you out a bit. It goes something like this: collect as much footage as you possibly can for as long as possible and in as many situations as possible so that you may be able, eventually, to midwife a story from all of that footage. All documentaries are forensic in that at some point, the documentary makers look back on all of the assets that have been amassed and begin to fashion a story from those assets. However, some documentary projects are *primarily* forensic: that is, they begin by searching for evidence of past events: e.g., many of the historical documentaries produced by Ken Burns (*The Civil War, Baseball, Jazz*, etc.). But some documentary projects save the lion's share of the forensic work until the moment of editing: that is, they pursue evolving or unfolding events (e.g., *Hoop Dreams, Dig!, Born into Brothels*, etc.). For these sorts of projects, if the camera is not rolling when the events unfold, there can be no project—or, the project will necessarily become a different project.

The thing is, when you go into an evolving documentary project, you likely have a pretty good sense of the sort of story you will hope to be able to tell at some future date. That's why you begin the project in the first place. If we don't roll the cameras, we will not capture the footage. And if we don't capture the footage, then we can't make THAT movie. So it goes in documentary. But here's the thing about documentary: our initial hunches are usually wrong. That is, we cannot foresee the events that will actually unfold. Maybe the action and outcomes we imagine will come to pass, maybe they won't. In the business of documentary making, thesis-driven storytelling is a recipe for disaster. Because people. And because dynamic world.

So documentary making is about having hunches and preparing to follow up on those hunches even as you prepare to be proven wrong about those hunches and prepare to be nimble enough to make good on new hunches as they emerge. Like other forms of hypothesis-generating inquiry (e.g., ethnographic research) it is an iterative process of projection, collection, and recollection (where portions of the collected footage are literally recalled, reconsidered, and collected anew). It is a deliberately scaffolded set of moves that values inefficient collection as the best means for efficient eventual storytelling. In short, documentary making is a methodology of forecasting learning—because those emergent stories are representations of things that the documentary makers did not yet know when they began rolling film. And given this approach to their making, documentary stories are stories of learning. Telling documentary stories of learning is a task of *recollection* from the many documents—all the footage—of the path to the learning identified in the documentary story. As documentary scholar Bill Nichols illustrates, documentaries "*are not documents as much as expressive representations that may be based on documents*" (13). And this distinction may help us understand the difference between raw footage and edited footage. Raw footage is footage that has yet to be determined to be *storyable* or *storyworthy* footage.

And as documentary makers know well, the ratio of raw footage to edited footage is remarkably unbalanced with anecdotal estimates usually ranging from 20:1 to as high as 100:1—that's 100 hours of raw footage to every single hour of edited film. And while it is true that you, the documentary maker beginning a new project, may not yet know your story, you do know something absolutely certain: you will eventually edit. And that act of editing helps determine the relevance of rolling cameras more than any given instance of camera rolling. That is, the projecting and collecting of documents—of raw footage—is always aimed at future instances of authorial/directorial recollecting that will assess the relatively low-yield value(s) of the footage. What propels the storying in documentary making per se are acts of recollection—that is, the act of collecting again and anew bits and pieces of footage that have already been collected. Consequently, it is accurate to say that in documentary making the *story* does not drive the making, but the *storying* does—the acts of recollecting from which a documentary story—an expressive representation—will be fabricated. Documentaries are fabrications.

It may seem antithetical to the mission of any act of documentary storytelling to declare its product to be a *fabrication*. How could it be any other thing? As Nichols reminds us, documentaries are *expressive representations* that are not documents, per se, even if they are based on or constructed of documents. Documentaries are fabricated from parts of documents—selections from the raw footage. If the raw footage is a symbolic *reproduction* of an event, the edited footage offers a symbolic *representation* of the event. In considering the relationship of language to reality, Kenneth Burke writes: "Even if any given terminology is a *reflection* of reality, by its very nature as a terminology it must be a *selection* of reality; and to this extent it must function also as a *deflection* of reality" (*Language* 45; also see *Grammar* 59). Documentary's selections offer similar reflections and deflections of the real events they represent. We offer that the more that documentaries can be *recollections of documented events*, the more they can enable discoveries of developing experiential learning.

However, such recollected stories won't merely happen at some future date. These evolving documentary stories are facilitated by acts of projection and collection directed at and by our knowledge of that future forensic act of recollection otherwise known as documentary storytelling. In other words, *we will only be able to tell a convincing documentary story if the camera has been rolling all along*. Otherwise, we will get the reflective stories that teachers so often expect and despise: treatises of claims with little to no evidence. "I learned so much in this class. It was awesome. The peer-review really worked! I loved going to the Writing Center—my tutor gave me the best advice!" No camera, no documentary. Or rather, poor documentation yields poor documentary.

It's Never About What It's About, Part One: Assessing Experiences of Learning

Assessing the experiential learning of documentary is complicated. On one hand, the making of the documentary is an enactment of assessment as evident in the acts of recollection. After all, selecting clips from the raw footage *is an act of assessment*: some clips emerge as more valuable than other clips. And the resulting documentary may be assessed in terms of its value as a product and/or the rhetorical work that it enables. But, what has emerged for us—a couple of teachers and researchers of writing and writers—is its *value as a vehicle for identifying and communicating myriad forms of experiential learning*. Bump first delineated these forms of assessment while he was teaching students to make documentary films. However, he quickly saw that it was the textually-based ELDs (and, sometimes, the meta-process ELD videos they made—see Halbritter, Blon, and Creighton) that his students wrote about their experiences of making documentary films that emerged as the real point of his courses. As such, he realized a truly tectonic shift in the aboutness of his courses and his teaching in general: that the assignments that had defined what his courses had been about—the movies that students made, for example—were suddenly exposed as the *means* of their learning, not the *ends* of their learning. Consequently, he realized that it was the process stories that they told about making the movies where the learning could best be identified and made portable. In essence, the most important documentaries that students would make in his classes were not those about slain community leaders, or about Marines with PTSD, or about pre-teen children with inoperable brain cancer, or about expressions of identity as indicated in hairstyles, but the documentaries in which his students exposed what they learned by way of those storytelling experiences. In short, he learned what Julie had been telling him for years: "It's never about what it's about."

We have since learned that this shift in "aboutness" is an important move toward a more inclusive approach to assessment, as it is inclusive of forms of production, of a range of individual learning needs, and of diverse literacies. Recently, Julie attended an excellent panel on inclusive teaching at a Cultural Rhetorics conference. She heard the presenters at that panel tell stories about their experiences with (and give recommendations for) using students' stories of experience pedagogically. Following these presentations, there was much enthusiasm and agreement in the room about the benefits of such an approach—until, that is, the anguished question (delivered, no doubt, on behalf of many) came from one member of the audience: "But how do I *assess* this stuff?" At that point, the conversation grew more difficult, as people in the room struggled to determine how to measure the success of things that were unfamiliar as performances of academic literacy. After listening to this discussion, Julie went away convinced that in this case, as well, asking students to document and tell stories of their learning was the solution to the "problem" of what diverse learners are likely to deliver as they go about the business of learning. If we want to find value in products of learning that have heretofore been unavailable as indicators of learning, then it would seem to make sense not to focus solely on the things themselves as measures of performance, but on how students make sense of the affordances of writing experiences for their own growth and development, and to encourage them to set goals. The answer, then, to "how do I assess this stuff?" is not, "go easy on what you imagine to be your standards," but rather, "have students assess their own learning by making and collecting documents of its progression, and then assessing their informed stories of learning: their experiential-learning documentaries." In this case, what is produced by students need not be regarded as a series of troubling failed efforts to deliver standard forms, but rather, as data (or, if you will, "footage") in a more comprehensive, and ongoing, story—one that is constructed in the present, that takes the past as its primary subject, and that points to the future.

However, what happens, in our newly shifted aboutness of ELD making, when the documentaries are *not* films? How do we roll the metaphoric cameras of text-based documentary making? How do we create our 20:1 or 100:1 ratio of raw to edited footage? What does that look like? How do we generate such footage? How do we collect it so that we may be able to recollect it? The trick is in imagining that procedural acts of learning (ones that may seem to be irrelevant while they are being experienced) may emerge during subsequent acts of recollecting as being relevant—and possibly critically relevant. That is a trick that may be directed best, we have found, by way of focusing not on the story of learning, but on the *storying* of learning. And teaching *that* kind of learning requires earning the trust of students who expect to learn something of predetermined value: teach me to make a documentary; teach me to write a research paper, teach me to get a good job. The trick is in holding those predetermined values at bay long enough to expose the values of things that seem irrelevant or worse: worthless. And that requires facilitating a special sort of encounter between each student and her/his former self.

It's Never About What It's About, Part Two:
Curricular Design

Our First-Year Writing curriculum at MSU asks students to enter into dialogue with their former selves by way of a curriculum that bookends the course with learning narratives: the first a demonstration of the best effort that students can offer at the beginning of the course, the latter an effort that is informed by the intellectual and experiential content of the course. As such, the first learning narrative serves the function of a proposal for a project of inquiry in that it anticipates the rewards and costs of doing work that the researcher may not yet have ever done. The first learning narrative is primarily forensic: it looks back at events that have already happened without much evidence beyond recalled examples to support its claims. The latter learning narrative, however, is a *recollection*: it is an evolving documentary that is fabricated of documents made during each and every act of the course: the first learning narrative, the subsequent assignments; peer reviews; teacher and other audience feedback; the experiences of giving feedback to peers; and proposals, revision statements, and reflections associated with the medial assignments. So much "footage." This final learning narrative, as with any evolving documentary worth its salt, is edited from the raw footage of the course at a ratio in our expected range of 20:1 to 100:1—or more.

If the final learning narrative of the semester is to be driven by recollection, then starting the semester with the primarily forensic learning narrative argues for an approach that will not compromise this expected potential. Ours is a curriculum that aims to place students into dialogue with a series of increasingly unfamiliar contexts in order to discover, by way of inquiry, how literate practices operate in these scenes. Depending on where students' experiences and understandings are at the beginning of the semester, the curriculum may work primarily to affirm, grow, or change altogether their initial ideas about literacy and the sorts of stories they may choose to tell about the role of literacy in their own lives. Consequently, the theme governing the first learning narrative is to *collect* it not *correct* it. That does not mean that this narrative should not be workshopped through multiple drafts. This offering should be the best effort that students are prepared to make *at this time*. If this assignment is to become a set of documents that best represents what students claim to know at the beginning of the course, then its making should be attended with great care so that students will not, upon eventual reflective inquiry, easily disclaim the content of this early work as simple mistakes or careless errors.

What is of critical importance is that the content of the narrative is not taught or corrected—that is, that an understanding of "literacy" and/or "learning" and their many associated applications and effects are not taught in order for students to produce narratives that reflect the goal of understanding. Rather, these narratives should convey the best representations of what students know already and/or what they think most appropriate to discuss in response to the prompt. Otherwise, the ensuing experiences will be placed into relation with what they have been taught to be the right answers about literacy, not their own experiences and expressions of literacy. In other words, when these narratives are later recollected, they will be all the more impoverished as pedagogical assets. The ensuing journey will chart only their relation to what they are supposed to learn and not what they did/do/may learn. Their false steps along the way, no matter how potentially productive, will be measured against a foregone conclusion. And while that will most certainly present the students with an experience of learning, it will not enable them to document their learning by way of experience.

The key is to trust the intervention of the curriculum to bring students into the sorts of understandings that the course is designed to make students negotiate. The metaphor we find to be productive is to imagine that the curriculum is an obstacle course (see Halbritter). Students claim to be a certain sort of person at the beginning of the course. The obstacle course provides opportunities for each student to not only negotiate each obstacle, but to collect data about how they addressed each obstacle—how they planned to address it, how they actually addressed it, how they went about adjusting their approaches, how it all turned out—and to discuss what they learned about themselves in each instance and at the end of the course.

It's Never About What It's About, Part Three: The Good, The Bad, and the Sucky

For the past decade or so, Bump has been asking his writing students to make movies in his writing classes. Moviemaking offers writing students opportunities to create texts that they are deeply familiar with reading, to work in teams, to approach writing as novices, and to queer their writing processes. Furthermore, it can shift what qualifies as authoritative source material—if you've got a camera and a microphone, you're more likely to point those devices in the direction of a person than in the direction of a library—or Google. And, making movies can help put native speakers of English and native speakers of other languages on more level ground because, depending on the type of movie being made, the production of language is often a minor part of movie making. For example, in documentary making, editing language—the things that other people say—is most often far more important than producing it.

These are just some of the benefits of making movies in writing courses. However, making movies has some drawbacks as well—most of which stem from the fact that many, if not most, students will be making movies for the first time: they can take longer than you or your students anticipate, they can introduce myriad technical complications, and they can crash altogether. And even if they don't crash—that is, even if they are successful—the resulting movies can . . . oh, there's really no way to say this delicately . . . they can suck. In fact, they are almost certain to suck. But honestly, how could they not?

Imagine that we handed you a musical instrument that you've never played and gave you three weeks to write, perform, and record a song on that instrument. How well would you likely do? We may justify such an exercise on the strength of knowing that you have heard a lot of music made by people who play the same instrument. So you should be able to use that knowledge to knock out a decent tune, right?

Maybe not. Go listen to an open mic night sometime.

The chances that you'll be good are slim, and the chances that students' first movies will be good are likely to be even more slim.

So why make them? Well, because of all of those benefits we listed above. But how do you grade sucky movies? Why would students work so hard for a bad grade? Because, you have to grade the movie, not the making, right?

Maybe not.

It's Never About What It's About, Part Four: Assessing Recollections

In *Permanence and Change*, Burke points to the limits of ELDs as cause-and-effect recollections:

> Perhaps because we have come to think of ourselves as *listening* to the universe, as waiting to see what it will prove to us, we have psychotically made the corresponding readjustment of assuming that the universe itself will abide by our rules of discussion and give us its revelations in a cogent manner. Our notion of causality as a succession of pushes from behind is thus a disguised way of insisting that experience abide by the conventions of a good argument. (99)

If we replace Burke's term "universe" with our own vast, expansive, and largely unknowable term, "learning," in this passage, we may determine that recollective storytelling is fundamentally flawed—that we, too, are psychotically making the corresponding readjustment of assuming that *learning* itself will abide by our rules of discussion and give us its revelations in a cogent manner. But the flaw here is only . . . universal. That is, the only flaw is in asserting that all we see is all there is to be seen—that the stories of learning that we recollect tell the *whole* story of learning. The conventions of a good argument have helped us address productively many problems: we can purify contaminated drinking water, combat infectious diseases, recognize same-sex marriages as legal and legitimate unions, and identify Colin Hay as a brilliant Scottish singer-songwriter—not simply a man with a mullet stuck in 1982, forever at work down under. In short, our notions of causality can be quite productive, especially when they are argued well. And, it was Bump's observation that reflective accounts of learning were commensurately more productive the more they were informed by evidence—when they were experiential-learning documentaries—when they were *recollections*.

Shifting our gaze to the *operations* of reflection—that is, to what we are now calling *recollection*—has had a profound impact on the kinds of pedagogical interventions we imagine and value. We found that we could, in responding to such reflections, respond to both the papers and the students. Because the papers are about the students—but not *simply* about them, they become the very sorts of papers we have known and taught all along: ones that use evidence to support claims. We don't need to know our students better before we assess their writing. We need to know our students better by way of their writing. In short, we need our students to *show* us what we need to know, not simply tell us. Our response to this conundrum was to reassess our assessment practices and to redesign our assignment sequence to align our expectations for reflection with the way we value and evaluate the writing they do in our classes.

The purpose of our operationalized process is *not* to teach the proper process of writing; rather, it is an operation for helping writers track their processes—each and every one of their processes. You might say that what we prescribe is a method for viewing process, not for doing process. And since the goal for licensing any of the assignments we have mentioned is not creating excellently crafted final projects, per se, but facilitating further inquiry into and reflection on the various intellectual capacities leveraged during their creation, all of our scaffolding efforts are aimed at creating the sorts of texts that can best supply narrative data to inform subsequent reflection: i.e., for recollective acts of ELD making. Thus, each of our projects functions, as Blake Scott says about his students' literacy narratives, as "a starting point for further interrogation and reflection" (111). This pedagogical shift is tectonic, changing not only the immediate territory of any single assignment, but the surrounding educational terrain as well. In the resulting landscape, we must alter how we identify, aim for, and assess students' mastery of the learning goals that license our assignments in the first place. It also necessarily revises how we imagine our roles as teachers: less as experts or even facilitators, and more as designers (of learning environments) and witnesses (to their learning).

In a pedagogy of ELD, what doesn't seem to matter may indeed become the source of important evidence—evidence that will be used to support claims about student learning.

A Program of Assessment for a Program of Assessment

You are likely wondering at this point what the practice of using ELD can *look* like. Consider its uses in a course we recently taught: a course called Preparation for College Writing (PCW), which is a "developmental" course that precedes the first-year writing course into which most students at our institution are placed. PCW is a course with a significant population of International students who needed space to learn everything from idiomatic uses of English to Western practices of attribution and citation to the moves and values of the American university culture in which they now participate. To accommodate PCW students' work of producing ELDs, we reconceived the curriculum of the course to feature opportunities for generating and using documentary assignments and activities. We created two major writing assignments, each with seven moves articulating the process of projection, collection, and recollection, as follows:

1. A Project Proposal
2. A First Draft of the Project
3. A Revision Plan (informed by peer-review and self-reflection)
4. A Revised Draft of the Project (A1 10% + A2 15% = 25%)
5. A Presentation Proposal
6. A Presentation (A1 10% + A2 15% = 25%)
7. A Reflective Essay (A1 20% + A2 30% = 50%)

Notice that, of these fourteen total assignments (7 parts of assignment 1 (A1) + 7 parts of A2), only six are graded. In each of the two main assignments, the reflective assignment is worth *half of the points possible for the seven-part assignment*. This shift in assessment value and in what parts of the process really matter is designed to communicate several things:

*   that we truly value recollection as the primary outcome of the course;
*   that the course is designed to accommodate this value;
*   that the course is designed to be a writing workshop; and
*   that student participation is critical not only to each activity, but to create documents for the subsequent documentary making.

Recall that ours is primarily a quest for manufacturing pedagogical resources—documents that will be evaluated not so much for the work they do or value they have in and of themselves, but for their ability to facilitate the work of ELD making. Notice that most of the work is ungraded—but mandatory.

Of course, in valuing those earlier works, we must have them available when we need them: i.e., when students are recollecting and when we are responding to recollections. There seem to be many ways to accommodate these demands—some more onerous than others. However, at MSU, we are able to leverage both the ELI Review platform and/or the discussion board features in Desire to Learn (D2L) to help us collect and manage all of our documented writing activities. Proposals, drafts, and reviews all happen within an electronic workspace; consequently, for each student, we can easily sort for comments given, comments received, and work submitted. We can track the review partners for each student in each workshop. And we can not only verify the evidence that students offer in support of their claims, we can enter into dialogue with those claims by introducing additional evidence when we see fit.

In the spirit of rolling the cameras, few actions in our workshop-based course design will be unavailable for eventual recollections. That is not to say that our approach captures each and every relevant part of the process of writing. It most certainly does not. Nor does any documentary project capture each and every moment of any subject of documentary. However, our method does collect a lot of footage. And the stories that may be fabricated from all of that footage—all of those documents—are indeed informed ELDs for each and every student.

As such, the final "Reflective Essay" assignments for each assignment cluster may, itself, be assessed by way of criteria that may look odd to most teachers of writing—especially those using the The WPA Outcomes Statement for First-Year Composition, for example. Rather than

Score	Grading Criteria
/10	The author's final reflection is 600 to 800 words in length (2 to 3 double-spaced pages)
/15	The author's final reflection is divided into three main sections: The Story, Successes, & Goals **5 pts each**
/10	The author discusses what s/he planned to do.
/10	The author discusses what s/he actually did in relation to what s/he planned to do
/10	The author makes direct reference to comments to and/or from peers.
/15	The author provides evidence (from the four previous assignments) to support the claims made in the final reflection. **15 pts**
	The author makes direct reference to the proposal
	The author makes direct reference to the first draft
	The author makes direct reference to the revision statement
	The author makes direct reference to the final draft
	The author makes direct reference to comments from the teacher
/10	The author articulates her/his strengths—i.e., what worked well, what will s/he do again.
/10	The author articulates goals that follow from the evidence s/he has provided in the reflection
/10	The author articulates means for pursuing the goals s/he has identified in the reflection
Total	
/100	

Figure 29.1 A Sample Scoring Sheet for the Reflective Component of a Mid-Semester, First-Year Writing Assignment

presenting a rubric for evaluating the excellence of the reflective texts themselves, our evaluation grids look more like shopping lists for types of evidence (see Figure 29.1). Consequently, our students' reflections do not so much need to *tell* us what we want to hear about their learning as much as they need to *show* us how they have come to identify what they are claiming to have learned.

The scoring sheet in Figure 29.1 makes clear that what we value most is not the precise learning that we hope will be revealed (as if that could ever be the goal for a program that serves the learning needs of 7,000 students annually), but rather the sorts of documents to be *cited* in each of their recollections. As such, we do not mandate types of expressive representations, but rather types of documents from which their expressive representations are to be fabricated. The goals themselves are not prescribed; the method for discovering them is.

What It's About: Informed Goal-Setting

We started this discussion by inviting you to "consider the possibility that this story could be different, that this moment represents a happy opportunity to rethink not only our means of measurement, but our essential pedagogical values." We then described an approach to writing instruction that creates opportunities for students to document their learning and to use what they've collected in the process to engage in a kind of self-assessment by writing informed "expressive representations" of what they've learned. We have suggested enabling this process by shifting the value in assessing students' work from the products of their efforts to the stories they tell about their experiences and decisions in creating those products—and that this practice of storytelling, of creating what we have called Experiential-Learning Documentaries (ELDs)—should be a scaffolded focus of instruction, and not just a requirement presumed to rest on students' prior understandings of what it means to "reflect."

In fact, as we have said, we have called the process of projecting, collecting, and recollecting (or reflecting) "preflective" pedagogy, to describe a novel set of moves that begins anticipating reflection in the very first moment of conceiving a writing task, and not, as reflection is so often positioned, as an afterthought. We now believe "Experiential-Learning Documentary" to be a more productive metaphor of the pedagogical moves we're recommending—in part because the operations of documentary are so usefully analogous to the kind of projecting, collecting, and recollecting work we're asking students to undertake. We recognize also that in the world of educational commonplaces "reflection" has long been associated with a different set of values and activities than those we specifically recommend: in particular, those that use the resources of memory (and, we would suggest, 'voice') as the primary means of storytelling. We believe pedagogical approaches that make use of ELD—while they are obviously inspired by changing understandings of what "writing" is and of what it all entails, and by the need to find ways to identify indicators of quality in this new world of writing—actually pertain to any pedagogical situation in which the goal is to document and measure evolving, transferable learning, and for students to come to new understandings of the decisions they make, and the opportunities they might find, as the makers of the wide array of rhetorical artifacts that we may consider to be instances of writing. We recall Bill Nichols's assertion that we assess any documentary by way of "the value of the insights it provides, and the quality of the perspective it instills" (13). As teachers, our goal is for students to become better—more reflective, well-informed, resourceful, fluent—writers. ELDs are driven by just such a mission—to document insights into writing processes and performances, to chronicle shifts in writerly perspectives, and to inform goal setting activities for the continued development of each writer.

Works Cited

Burke, Kenneth. *A Grammar of Motives.* U of California P, 1969.

——. *Language as Symbolic Action: Essays on Life, Literature, and Method.* U of California P, 1966.

——. *Permanence and Change: An Anatomy of Purpose,* 3rd ed., U of California P, 1984.

Dewey, John. *Democracy and Education: An Introduction to the Philosophy of Education.* Simon & Schuster, 1944.

Halbritter, Bump. *Mics, Cameras, Symbolic Action: Audio-Visual Rhetoric for Writing Teachers.* Parlor. 2013.

Halbritter, Bump, Noah Blon, and Caron Creighton. "Big Questions, Small Works, Lots of Layers: Documentary Video Production and the Teaching of Academic Research and Writing." *Kairos: A Journal of Rhetoric, Technology, and Pedagogy,* vol. 16, no. 1, 15 Aug. 2011, 16.1, kairos.technorhetoric.net/ 16.1/praxis/halbritter/index.php. Accessed 6 July 2017.

Nichols, Bill. *Introduction to Documentary,* 2nd ed., Indiana Press, 2001.

Scott, J. Blake. "The Literacy Narrative as Production Pedagogy." *Teaching English in the Two Year College* (TETYC), May 1997, pp. 108–16.

"The WPA Outcomes Statement for First–Year Composition (Version 3.0)." *Writing Program Administration,* vol. 38, no. 1 (2014), pp. 144–8.

30

THE TESTS THAT BIND

Future Literacies, Common Core, and Educational Politics

Carl Whithaus

Tests tie us to the past. They ask for demonstrations, measurements, conclusions. They have a finality to them. You are done. Put your pencils down. Or stop typing. Move away from the keyboard. *Fini.*

Snaps tie us together. Across continents, cities, rooms within a house, they connect us to our loves, our obsessions, the wonder of it all. Not in the distant past, but now or almost now. The just past, the about-to-be again. . . .

Now. I finger-type a note onto the picture I have just taken of my desk, my computer with this open Google doc, a coffee cup, a red spoon, some papers on the other side of the keyboard. I write, "Almost done, I swear. Home soon!" I select an orange font. Large. Draw in blue. Circle the "swear" because I want the one I am sending it to to know that I mean it. I will be back soon. This work. This writing on a Sunday will be done soon. Really.

And yet, these two texts that you cannot see now, but I can—this Google doc and the Snap—each reach out and reflect on the texts we need, on tests we need, on the types of literarcies that are our lives now and will be in the future. One, the beginning of a scholarly book chapter, the other an ephemeral thing that means nothing and everything. . . .

These two texts are pieces of cloth. Where they meet is a seam that needs to be stitched together. This chapter is that set of stitches. It begins by acknowledging that we need texts that are scholarly, deep, written and crafted with style, care, and reflection. But we also need play, the chance for us, and our children, and our students to use digital writing spaces to mean something more than just a score on a test.

This chapter extends Joanne Addison's, Shelby McIntosh's, and Patricia Sarles's critiques of the digital writing practices fostered in the tests developed by the Smarter Balanced Assessment Consortium (SBAC) and the Partnership for Assessment of Readiness for College and Career (PARCC). This chapter documents the ways in which these assessments are reductive and decrease possibilities for situated, interactive, and dialogic forms of writing assessment. Randy Bennett, Sandra Cimbricz and Matthew McConn, and Kurt Geisinger have also explored how the SBAC and PARCC assessments intersect with secondary English curricula, instructional techniques, teacher accountability, and the use of educational technologies. Their work suggests ways in which the SBAC and PARCC assessments undermine students' developing rhetorical knowledge, critical thinking, understanding of writing processes, knowledge of conventions, and ability to compose in multiple environments—all habits of mind explicitly named and valued in *The Framework for Success in Postsecondary Writing* and in the *CCSS Curriculum Framework* itself. The SBAC and PARCC ELW writing assessments also undermine the types of composing processes that researchers such as Kristin Arola, Liz Losh, and Stephanie Vie have identified as commonly used when students write in digital environments. As an alternative to the SBAC and PARCC assessments, this chapter considers how rhetorically based and contextually sensitive forms of assessment such as those described by Angela Clark-Oates et al. and by Elyse Eidman-Aadahl et al.'s National Writing Project's MAP group see digital writing technologies being used.

Digital Writing Practices Fostered by Writing Assessment Systems in the Era of CCSS

Digital writing and the future of literacy meet along the seams where the deeply reflective, the contemplative, the political, and the understanding of writing as the proof of a skill meet. Digital writing practices are more than the performance of an ability that means passing out of 3rd grade, that means you are done with middle school, or better yet—that you are "college and career ready"—by the end of 11th grade. All of those acts fit within SBAC's and PARCC's assessment systems, but they are not all the futures of literacy.

The future of digital writing and rhetoric within American schools is being marked by the Common Core State Standards (CCSS)—even in states where the CCSS or its assessments have been officially rejected by state governments. In fact, there are a wide variety of ways in which the CCSS influences state-level assessments. The writing assessment landscape for secondary students in the United States is complex, but there is a tendency to undervalue extended digital writing tasks. The SBAC and PARCC designers worked within a culture where access to open digital composing tools and environments were perceived as a threat. In "Don't Fear the Reaper: Beyond the Specter of Internet Plagiarism," Stephanie Vie examines how public discourse, particularly as shaped by Turnitin.com, about cheating and a twenty-first century literacy crisis has contributed to this culture of fear. Like Vie, Liz Losh addresses fears about plagiarism in digital writing environments. In her chapter "Honor Coding: Plagiarism Software and Educational Opportunity," Losh sees these fears of textual plagiarism creating an ideological barrier that ironically does not only hinder students' opportunities to work with alphabetic digital texts but also reduces the likelihood that instructors will have them work on digital, multimodal compositions (*War on Learning* 151–68). The digital writing practices fostered by an ideology that obsesses over cheating prevention are not the open, extended, and multimodal forms of digital writing that faculty in postsecondary environments are trying to create.

Partially in response to the specter of student plagiarism and cheating, the SBAC and PARCC assessments are designed to limit the open, source-based composing that Vie and other digital writing researchers such as Arola and Anne Wysocki see as vital in twenty-first century writing (1–22, 127–44, 259–68). Arola and Wysocki argue for opening "classroom activities to multiple media and communication technologies" (127). They believe that

> not only do newer technologies make multimodal composing easier than earlier technologies did, but the proliferation of multimodal texts in all areas of our shared lives suggests that our responsibilities to students should include considering how we compose and engage others with some broad range of the media available to us. (127)

The possibilities of using digital technologies for students to engage with others in a wide variety of modes is limited by the ideological structures of test security and plagiarism prevention Vie identifies. This larger specter of digital writing spaces as potential cheating grounds causes test developers to work against the recommendations of writing researchers and curriculum developers who advocated for students to use digital writing tools to engage in extended tasks that may have them sharing and collaborating with others.

While the SBAC and PARCC tests account for a significant number of state-level assessments, not all states have adopted CCSS, and of the ones that have, a third use either their own ELA assessment tool or another already existing commercial test such as the ACT or SAT to measure how students are meeting CCSS curriculum standards. Of the thirty-five states (including DC) that have adopted CCSS, twenty-five have administered either a PARCC or SBAC assessment. Ultimately, we need to understand the types of writing tasks current assessments are promoting and how those tasks use—or do not use—digital writing technologies. We need to answer the question posed by Matthew Chingos in his Brookings Institution report: Are the CCSS framework and assessments used to measure it driving literacy instruction in desirable ways (3)? Explorations of this question through Nadia Behizadeh and Myoung Eun Pang's large-scale quantitative work, Heidi Anne Mesmer and Elfrieda H. Hiebert's empirical reading studies, Linda Darling-Hammond, Gene Wilhoit and Linda Pittenger's policy studies, and Ann M. Johns's and Kelly Gallagher's development of pedagogical support materials are beginning to provide a picture of how the SBAC and PARCC tests are shaping the digital writing and rhetorical practices valued in primary and secondary English Language Arts (ELA) education. These studies show that the SBAC and PARCC assessments are increasing the importance of reading as well as the importance of drawing on informational rather than literary texts when writing. However, these studies also show that the SBAC and PARCC writing assessments are not taking advantage of open-ended, extended, or through-course forms of assessment that might make their tasks more authentic or more closely aligned with the forms of writing, particularly digital writing, valued in postsecondary education.

In *The War on Learning: Gaining Ground in the Digital University*, Losh traces the ways in which innovative scholarship and pedagogical practices are reshaping learning in higher education (1–76). She is particularly attentive to the ways in which students' digital writing practices and faculty assignments to students have increased opportunities for open-ended and extended writing and research projects (221–39). Losh also insists that we attend to the material culture that enables digital spaces and digital learning to occur. She writes, "it is important to keep in mind that digital signals are transmitted on machines made up of parts; cyberspace exists because of plastic, metal, rare minerals, and other substances that facilitate electronic communications" (3). Curriculum and instruction that incorporated techniques from Arola and Wysocki's work (127–44, 259–68), Clark-Oates et al. (n.p.) and by Elyse Eidman-Aadahl et al.'s National Writing Project's MAP group (n.p.) could foster digital writing practices more inline with the goals of higher education. The practices fostered by the SBAC and PARCC assessments contribute to the "war on learning," by focusing more on preventing cheating rather than on fostering open-ended, extended, or through-course digital writing activities.

Across States: Complex Political Environments and the Valuing of Writing

In addition to considering SBAC and PARCC assessments, we need to acknowledge that states such as New York that have adopted the CCSS but rely on their own assessment instrument (i.e., the NY Regents Exam) and states such as Texas that have rejected the CCSS entirely and rely on their own assessment (i.e., the STAAR). New York and Texas are not outliers among US states, but rather represent the deep skepticism with which the CCSS curricula and the

SBAC and PARCC assessments have been greeted. Many state governments and departments of education have questioned how CCSS and/or SBAC and PARCC assessments impact students. To understand the resistance to these exams, we should look at the writing tasks they include.

Writing Tasks on the SBAC Assessment

The SBAC ELA writing assessments are built around four task types: (1) selected-response items, (2) non-traditional response questions, (3) constructed-response questions, and (4) performance tasks. The SBAC selected-response items are multiple choice, not adaptive. They may be administered through a computer platform, but they are not richly situated within digital writing practices. The non-traditional response questions are conceptualized as computer-based and can include drag-and-drop, editing text, or drawing an object. Their potential for including digital writing activities appears to be underused in the earliest versions of the SBAC. The constructed-response questions require short text answers. They have the potential to include some authentic, open-ended research writing as well as interactive digital forms of composing, but do not do so in the early versions of the SBAC. The performance tasks on the SBAC are designed to measure critical-thinking and problem-solving skills. They attempt to engage students in applied, complex, real-world problems and—within the constraints of the testing environment—to connect a series of activities to a single theme or scenario. Since performance tasks use computers as testing platforms, they have the potential to engage students in research and extended writing tasks that may have been started outside of the testing window. The constraints of the SBAC testing system discourage this, and instead build scenarios that make the SBAC performance task a discrete activity.

Tasks on PARCC Assessment

In 2014–2015, the PARCC ELA exams had performance-based assessments that included three writing tasks: research simulation, literary analysis, and narrative writing. On the research simulation task, students analyze an informational topic presented through several texts or multimodal stimuli. Students are asked to engage with these pieces by answering a series of questions and writing an analytic response. This research simulation activity is intended to show students' ability to synthesize information from multiple sources. In the literary analysis task, students read and analyze two literary texts. Students write an analytic response based on the texts. For the narrative writing portion of the assessment, students read a literary text from a grade-appropriate short story, novel, poem, or other form of literature; they develop a narrative response rather than an analytic response to this literary piece. The PARCC writing assessments aim to balance analytic responses across informational and literary texts; they value narrative writing as a means of responding to an additional literary text. In some ways, the PARCC writing assessments show a closer alignment to a vision of writing curriculum that predates CCSS. That is, they connect two of the three writing prompts with traditional, literature-based tasks. The research simulation is the writing activity that has the most potential to develop explicitly digital writing tasks, but—like the SBAC—the constraints of the testing environment limit both the depth and the digital aspects of the writing task.

Aspects of Writing Assessed and Valued in CCSS

The CCSS curriculum framework values source-based responses, analysis, argument, research, and dialogic-interactive-situated writing. The SBAC and PARCC assessments provide prompts that include responding to sources, text analysis, and argument; they do not include opportunities for open-ended research or interactive forms of digital writing. These second two types of writing task are present in the CCSS curriculum framework—and may even occur in teachers' day-to-day classroom curriculum—but they are not directly assessed on the SBAC or PARCC. Derek Rowntree, Paul Black and Dylan William, and Thomas Guskey have shown that when assessments do not require students to perform tasks, teachers reduce the amount of classroom time spent on those tasks. Despite the CCSS curriculum framework, teachers, and the public valuing research writing and interactive digital forms of writing, the current CCSS assessment regimes do not provide students the opportunity to engage in those sorts of writing tasks.

Undervaluing Open-ended Research Writing and Interactive Digital Writing Tasks

What we see across these assessment systems is a clear undervaluing of open-ended research writing and interactive digital writing tasks. None of the assessments explicitly value through direct assessment open-ended research writing or interactive digital writing. To varying degrees, they test source-based written responses, text analysis, and the ability to develop a written argument. The framework authors and the NGB that endorsed the CCSS were generally forward looking; however, the test designers did not take up the opportunities afforded by the CCSS framework. Instead they made assessment design decisions that advanced writing assessment incrementally rather than making bold, flexible, and truly forward-looking assessments.

It is easy for test designers to point to psychometric concepts and values as the reasons for these conservative decisions about exam design (e.g., Paul Kline). However, researchers such as Angela Clark-Oates et al. have documented how rhetorically based assessments can be implemented, while others such as Arola, Wysocki, and Elyse Eidman-Aadahl et al. have shown how digitally rich, multimodal assessments can be implemented. These forms of writing assessment could lead toward increased alignment between curricula and assessments. Further, their valuing of play, connections among writers and readers, and multimodality create opportunities for authentic, open-ended research writing and dialogic, interactive digital forms of composing. Having these opportunities in writing assessments as well as in a national-level curriculum framework would be likely to lead to more time being spent on developing these skills in secondary (English and writing) classes. The rest of this chapter focuses on how the assessment systems described by Clark-Oates et al. and Eidman-Aadahl et al. engage students in writing tasks that value emerging literacy practices, complement undervalued aspects of the CCSS framework, and if implemented, could shift some of the politics around educational policies, particularly as they relate to ELA and the teaching of writing across disciplines.

Portfolios as Rhetorically Based and Contextually Sensitive Writing Assessments

In "Moving Beyond the Common Core to Develop Rhetorically Based and Contextually Sensitive Writing Assessment Practices," Angela Clark-Oates et al. critique the skills-based writing assessments developed by PARCC and SBAC. They point towards the construct of college readiness developed by NCTE, NWP, and CWPA in *The Framework for Success in Postsecondary Education* as a viable alternative for conceptualizing and developing writing assessments. In particular, they examine how the implementation of writing portfolios as components of a large-scale writing assessment system may include open-ended research writing tasks and may allow for examples of responsive, interactive digital texts to be included. The systems envisioned by

Clark-Oates et al. include tasks such as responding to sources, text analysis, and developing a written argument assessed by the SBAC, PARCC, and Texas's STAAR exams. By drawing on the NCTE-NWP-CWPA endorsed *Framework*, the Clark-Oates et al. portfolio systems also capture research writing and dialogic digital writing tasks. These two types of tasks are essential for college readiness, particularly when college readiness is framed within the threshold concepts approach developed in the NCTE-NWP-CWPA *Framework*.

> Reflecting on their own extended research writing process is important at several of the post-secondary institutions (e.g., Arizona State University, Elmhurst College in Illinois, Sacramento State University, and the University of Arkansas at Little Rock) discussed in the Clark-Oates et al. piece. Clark-Oates et al. note "students construct outcomes-based portfolios over the course of a semester [and] draw on a range of their own work to demonstrate what they have learned." (n.p.)

Clark-Oates et al. also emphasize the value of interactive, authentic responses as part of their portfolio systems:

> as students discuss one another's portfolios over the course of the semester, students usually take turns functioning as the more capable peers. For example, if two students were asked for focus on rhetorical knowledge and flexibility as rhetorical concepts that require not only a claim with evidence, but also an artifact to support, the students might offer feedback throughout the semester. One student may have learned more about critical reading and persistence than rhetorical knowledge and flexibility; however, the two students can share insights about learned knowledge and skills in ongoing conversations, each student is modeling the act of learning. (n.p.)

Reflection on an extended (research) writing task and the use of authentic, interactive reader commentary to shape a writing portfolio make explicit the value that these types of tasks have and directly assess them rather than having them named as parts of the curriculum, but only indirectly measuring them in the assessment instrument.

Clark-Oates et al. argue that

> students will not be "college-ready" under the guidelines of the CCSS with the PARCC assessment because these materials lack what the *Framework* offers—the infrastructure for students to think critically and understand transference of knowledge and the research to redefine the purpose of learning as complex. (n.p.)

They point to a portfolio assessment used at the University of Arkansas at Little Rock where the reflective writing used during the development of the portfolio plays a crucial role in demonstrating students' understanding of how knowledge about writing transfers from context to context. This type of portfolio assessment system—as Patrick Sullivan also notes— "communicates to students some of the most significant things we have to say to them about writing, about success in school, and about the ways one may choose to understand and live in the world" (157). These portfolio cover letters and the reflective writing developed in the process of putting a portfolio together emphasize the process of writing as a collaborative and responsive endeavor. That is, reflective writing is not just navel gazing or a performance for the grader in the cover letter, but rather is a learning task integrated into both the curriculum and the assessment.

This task is the responsive-interactive-dialogic richly situated form/type of writing that the CCSS framework, if not the current PARCC and SBAC assessments, aims to promote. This type of writing—along with open-ended research writing—is valued in college and professional contexts. Clark-Oates et al. note that

> even though PARCC assessments are tied to the CCSS and are purported to be connected to college and career readiness, writing in many workplace contexts is collaborative, not produced in a testing situation with an individual writing alone in a timed situation. Further, as digital portfolios have become more common there are many reasons to broaden the definition of writing as composing, as addressed in the WPA OS, to include a wide range of genre and modalities, including production of audio and visual and video, which PARCC does not provide for students to produce. (n.p.)

This move to broaden definitions of writing to include emerging digital and multimodal forms of composing within writing assessments was taken up by the National Writing Project's Multimodal Assessment Project Group (Eidman-Aadahl et al.).

Multimodal, Digital Writing Assessments

NWP's MAP Group (Eidman-Aadahl et al.) documents some of the ways in which responsive-interactive-dialogic digital writing can be assessed in educational contexts. They value the range of genres and modalities seen as crucial literacy practices in the WPA Outcome Statements (OS) and in Clark-Oates et al.'s work. Many of the classroom-based writing activities examined by NWP's MAP Group also require extended research as part of the composing activities. The writing projects they discuss include: (a) a digital video produced by 4th- and 5th-graders in New Mexico, (b) a series of tweets as part of a response to literature assignment in an 11th-grade English class in Indiana, and (c) Google Earth presentations on Abraham Lincoln created by 8th-graders from Northern California. All of these projects require students to research the content of their topics, to respond to authentic peer and audience feedback during the composing process, and to employ multimodal forms of writing. These sorts of learning activities should be promoted in the assessment systems that are aligned with the readiness statements found in the CCSS Framework, the WPA OS, and the *Framework for Success in Postsecondary Writing*.

Researching content is an integral aspect of the writing activities described in each of the case studies in the NWP MAP Group's "Developing Domains for Multimodal Writing Assessment." In fact, one of the five domains that the group recommends considering when developing a writing assessment is substance:

> As a domain, substance refers to the context and overall quality and significance of the ideas presented. The substance of a piece is related to an artifact's [i.e., piece of writing's] message in relationship to the contextual elements of purpose, genre, and audiences. Considering the substance of a piece encourages authors to think about elements such as quality of ideas, quality of performances, credibility, accuracy, and significance. (n.p.)

This emphasis on credibility, accuracy, and significance as well as quality of ideas carves out a place where the quality of research content may be included in a writing assessment. Divorcing the quality of research writing from an assessment has been proven to lead to a hollowing out of meaning and a focus on what can be empty—or even nonsensical—contra-factual rhetorical form (e.g., Les Perelman's critique of the SAT Civil War dates). In the MAP Group's recommended system, a writing assessment should have the flexibility to examine the value and accuracy of students' research if that is part of the writing activity. From the perspective of NWP's MAP Group, evaluating the quality of research and the use of citations in an open-ended research writing project is essential. While the Google Earth Abe Lincoln biography is successful in many ways, the students' project is open for critique in terms of its work with source texts. The students are clearly able to effectively work with given or found informational texts, but their ability to cite and to evaluate the quality of source texts—particularly online materials—is limited. A discussion of how much expertise to expect in an 8th grade writing project would be fair to have, but the current PARCC and SBAC assessments are structured in a way where that conversation does not even occur. It may be that curriculum and assessment designers would determine that the use of sources in the Abe Lincoln Google Earth project is sufficient, meets, or even exceeds grade-level expectations. But to make that determination, you must include actual work with authentic sources as part of the assessment. The current assessments do not require teachers, test designers, or scorers to consider this issue. The point is not the quality of the single piece of student writing, but rather the inclusion—or in the case of PARCC and SBAC the exclusion—of research content quality in educational writing assessments. "By insisting that substance is a domain," the MAP Group breaks "with the long-standing tradition of separating form from content, of assuming that the quality of writing can be assessed without considering its substance" (n.p.). Research writing is so clearly tagged as valuable in the readiness statements of the CCSS, the NWP-NCTE-CWPA endorsed *Framework for Success*, and in the WPA OS that assessment systems ranging from classroom-specific to state-wide should incorporate it. The accuracy and quality of research content needs to be attended to if writing assessments are to reflect the complex and developing literacy practices in which students engage.

The MAP Group's set of domains also include evaluative moves that consider (1) how student authors respond to authentic peer and audience feedback and (2) encourage the integration of multimodal elements into a written composition. Responsiveness to feedback and the ability to incorporate images, data tables and charts, even sound and video clips are basic writing skills in a twenty-first century framework. Writing assessments that are pen-and-paper in delivery format or those that use digital delivery systems to reproduce the tasks and rhetorical forms valued in pen-and-paper composing activities miss the larger context of how writing skills are used in school, work, and civic environments now.

Conclusion: Connections, Brazil, and Beyond . . .

Still, there are ways in which the writing on Chromebooks in classrooms across America is now mostly a performance for the tests developed by SBAC or PARCC. These tests—these writing tests performed in digital environments—are changing the ways teachers, students, researchers, and the public define and measure what is good writing, what is meaningful writing, and what it means to successfully perform a writing task in response to a prompt. Their very digital nature appears to be revolutionary as Randy Bennett, Sandra Cimbricz and Matthew McConn, and Kurt Geisinger have argued. And yet, it is not a revolution. Guangming Ling, Angelica Rankin, and Carl Whithaus, Scott Harrison, and James Midyette have all shown that keyboarding instead of composing with pen in hand is primarily a shift in composing environment, not necessarily in the underlying rhetorical construct found in the written texts. If the same structure (opening paragraph, three-part thesis, support, support, support, conclusion) reigns, how digital are these texts? How much do they reflect the swift technological and cultural changes of literacy practices? How do they capture the possibilities for creative economies, interactions, ways of being in touch and touched?

The texts written for the SBAC and PARCC are not revolutionary. They are merely revolting. The end of a promise. The end of possibility. The very thing we feared most. Flat, dull, boring. The child says, "I hate writing." But what he means is "I hate taking the SBAC." At home, he plays Minecraft. The screen is blocks, text on top of blocks. Scrolling by so fast that I cannot read it, and yet, this dyslexic, ADHDer is there, is using it, them, those words, his writing as transactions, to do things, to change the screen, to change the world. I'm not the first to note that kids learn in these spaces (Cipollone, Schifter and Moffat; Niemeyer and Gerber; Schifter and Cipollone). And it is certainly not this boy alone who is learning now. His iPad is open. On the other end of his Facetime are two brothers in Brazil who are on their own two computers. All three of the boys in the same Minecraft space, the same server. Portuguese, English, both flash by. Text. Shouts. These boys move in a space that is writing. Jim Berlin's transactional rhetoric is here before me in a way that it is not when one of these boys sits to take the SBAC: endless time, typing through his boredom, wondering when the heck it'll be done, and he can move on, out, away. . . . He wants to go back, not outside, but back into Minecraft to reach his buddy who has moved back to Brazil, to go and sketch, and scratch, and shoot, and play . . . with words, and digital blocks, and with sounds, and with friends. He wants to write the future. And his future is not a test, not a return to the past, something bound and boring, but rather an action, a stitch, a binding together of images, simple programming, text messages, shouts, a real time, rolling play. . . . It is something that we can just begin to see.

Works Cited

Addison, Joanne. "Shifting the Locus of Control: Why the Common Core State Standards and Emerging Standardized Tests May Reshape College Writing Classrooms." *Journal of Writing Assessment*, vol. 8, no. 1, 2015, n.p.

Arola, Kristin L. "The Design of Web 2.0: The Rise of the Template, the Fall of Design." *Computers and Composition*, vol. 27, no. 1, 2010, pp. 4–14.

Arola, Kristin L., and Anne Frances Wysocki. *Composing (Media)= Composing (Embodiment): Bodies, Technologies, Writing, the Teaching of Writing.* UP of Colorado, 2012.

Behizadeh, Nadia, and Pang, Myoung Eun. "Awaiting a New Wave: The Status of State Writing Assessment in the United States." *Assessing Writing*, vol. 29, 2016, pp. 25–41.

Bennett, Randy E. "The Changing Nature of Educational Assessment." *Review of Research in Education*, vol. 39, no. 1, 2015, pp. 370–407.

Berlin, James A. *Rhetoric and Reality: Writing Instruction in American Colleges*, 1900–1985. Southern Illinois UP, 1987.

Black, Paul, and Wiliam, Dylan. *Inside the Black Box: Raising Standards through Classroom Assessment.* Granada Learning, 2006.

Chingos, Matthew M. *Standardized Testing and the Common Core Standards.* Brookings Institution, 2013.

Cimbricz, Sandra K., and McConn, Matthew L. "Changing the English Classroom: When Large-Scale 'Common' Testing Meets Secondary Curriculum and Instruction in the United States." *Changing English*, vol. 22, no. 4, 2015, pp. 393–404.

Cipollone, M., Schifter, C. C., and Moffat, R. A. "Minecraft as a Creative Tool: A Case Study." *International Journal of Game-Based Learning (IJGBL)*, vol. 4, no. 2, 2014, pp. 1–14.

Clark-Oates, Angela, Sherry Rankins-Robertson, Erica Ivy, Nicholas Behm, and Duane Roen. "Moving Beyond the Common Core to Develop Rhetorically Based and Contextually Sensitive Assessment Practices." *Journal of Writing Assessment*, vol. 8, no. 1, 2015, n.p.

Council of Chief State School Officers (CCSSO), and National Governors Association (NGA). *Common Core State Standards Initiative.* 2010.

Council of Writing Program Administrators (CWPA), National Council of Teachers of English (NCTE), and The National Writing Project (NWP). *The Framework for Success in Postsecondary Writing*. January 2011.

Darling-Hammond, L., G. Wilhoit, and L. Pittenger. "Accountability for College and Career Readiness: Developing a New Paradigm." *Education Policy Analysis Archives*, vol. 22, no. 86, 2014, n.p.

Eidman-Aadahl, Elyse, Kristine Blair, Danielle Nicole DeVoss, Will Hochman, Lanette Jimerson, Chuck Jurich, Sandy Murphy,Becky Rupert, Carl Whithaus, and Joe Wood. "Developing Domains for Multimodal Writing Assessment: The Language of Evaluation, the Language of Instruction." *Digital Writing Assessment*. Computers & Composition Digital Press, Utah State UP, 2013.

Gallagher, Kelly. *In the Best Interest of Students: Staying True to What Works in the ELA Classroom*. Stenhouse Publishers, 2015.

Geisinger, Kurt F. "Technology and Test Administration." *Technology and Testing: Improving Educational and Psychological Measurement*. 2015, pp. 255–9.

Guskey, Thomas R. "How Classroom Assessments Improve Learning." *Educational Leadership*, vol. 60, no. 5, 2003, pp. 6–11.

Johns, Ann M. "The Common Core in the United States: A Major Shift in Standards and Assessment." *The Routledge Handbook of English for Academic Purposes*, edited by Ken Hyland and Philip Shaw. Routledge, 2016, pp. 461–76.

Kline, Paul. *A Handbook of Test Construction (Psychology Revivals): Introduction to Psychometric Design*. Routledge, 2015.

Ling, Guangming. "Does It Matter Whether One Takes a Test on an iPad or a Desktop Computer?" *International Journal of Testing*, vol. 16, no. 4, 2016, pp. 352–77.

Losh, Elizabeth. "Selfies| Feminism Reads Big Data: 'Social Physics,' Atomism, and Selfiecity." *International Journal of Communication*, vol. 9, 2015, pp. 1647–59.

——. *The War on Learning: Gaining Ground in the Digital University*. MIT Press, 2014.

——. "YouTube Pedagogy Finding Communities of Practice in a Distributed Learning World." *Learning Through Digital Media Experiments in Technology and Pedagogy*, edited by Jonah S. Bossewitch, and Michael D. Preston. Columbia University Academic Commons, 2011, pp. 185–93.

McIntosh, Shelby. "State High School Tests: Changes in State Policies and the Impact of the College and Career Readiness Movement." ERIC: Center on Education Policy, 2011, eric.ed.gov/?id=ED530163. Accessed 4 July 2017.

Mesmer, Heidi Anne, and Elfrieda H Hiebert. "Third Graders' Reading Proficiency Reading Texts Varying in Complexity and Length Responses of Students in an Urban, High-Needs School." *Journal of Literacy Research*, vol. 47, no. 4, 2015, pp. 473–504.

Niemeyer, D. J., and H.R. Gerber. "Maker Culture and Minecraft: Implications for the Future of Learning." *Educational Media International*, vol. 52, no. 3, 2015, pp. 216–26.

Rankin, Angelica D. *A Comparability Study on Differences between Scores of Handwritten and Typed Responses on a Large-scale Writing Assessment*. Dissertation, University of Iowa. 2015.

Rowntree, Derek. *Assessing Students: How Shall We Know Them?* Routledge, 2015.

Sarles, Patricia. "The Common Core ELA Assessments: What We Know So Far about the Performance Tasks." *Library Media Connection*, vol. 32, no. 2, 2013, pp. 10–13.

Schifter, C. and M. Cipollone. Minecraft as a Teaching Tool: One Case Study. In R. McBride & M. Searson (Eds.), *Proceedings of SITE 2013, Society for Information Technology & Teacher Education International Conference* (pp. 2951–5). New Orleans, Louisiana, United States: Association for the Advancement of Computing in Education (AACE), 2013.

Sullivan, Patrick. *A New Writing Classroom: Listening, Motivation, and Habits of Mind*. Utah State UP, 2014.

Vie, Stephanie. "Don't Fear the Reaper: Beyond the Specter of Internet Plagiarism." *Strategic Discourse: The Politics of (New) Literacy Crises*, edited by Lynn C. Lewis, Computers and Composition Digital Press, Utah State UP, 2015, ccdigitalpress.org/strategic/chapters/vie/index.html. Accessed 4 July 2017.

——. "'You Are How You Play': Privacy Policies and Data Mining in Social Networking Games." *Computer Games and Technical Communication: Critical Methods and Applications at the Intersection*, edited by Jennifer deWinter and Ryan Moeller. Ashgate, 2014, pp. 171–87.

Whithaus, Carl, Scott Harrison, and James Midyette. "Keyboarding Compared with Handwriting on a High-stakes Writing Assessment: Student Choice of Composing Medium, Raters' Perceptions, and Text Quality." *Assessing Writing*, vol. 13, no. 1, 2008, pp. 4–25.

PART VI

Multimodality, Transmediation, and Participatory Cultures

31

BEYOND MODALITY

*Rethinking Transmedia Composition through
a Queer/Trans Digital Rhetoric*

William P. Banks

Much like the commonplace that we live in a "more visual culture" than ever before, it's common to hear that writing is increasingly multimediated and multimodal, especially in the fields that engage young writers, such as writing studies and education. In fact, scholars in multiple disciplines have recognized for some time that all composing practices engage with multiple modalities. Rhetoricians who have studied compositional shifts across time (Baron; Bolter and Grusin; Connors, *Composition*; Crowley; Faigley; Hawisher and Selfe; Manovich; Palmeri; Welch) recognize that each moment has often involved a somewhat narrow focus on a particular technology (e.g., stylus, pencil, computer) and the medium of the composition (e.g., clay, paper, screen). While history also provides multiple examples of non-traditional composition spaces, spaces that have involved the mixing, layering, and remixing of various media such as the Baroque *wunderkammer* or Cornell's boxes, scholars recognize that these sorts of compositional experiments have tended to be viewed less for their rhetorical or compositional practices than for their aesthetic or artistic qualities (Delagrange; Janangelo; Munster). More recently, however, scholars have asked us to reconsider not only the materialities of rhetoric and writing, but also the spaces and practices in which we compose (Arola and Wysoki; Alexander and Rhodes; Gries; Shipka). The result has been that scholars have begun to think beyond any singular notion of modality toward more transmediated approaches to both creating and understanding compositions.

This chapter surveys a shift from multimodality toward a recognition that writing and composing practices are fundamentally transmediated. In particular, I argue that one reason scholars sometimes struggle to theorize the *trans* in transmedia composition is a disciplinary focus on print-media rhetorics such as unity, coherence, and organization as the *sine qua non* of all compositional practice. To disrupt that focus, I turn to recent scholarship in queer rhetorics to explore how current transmedia practices intersect with queer/trans practices of (dis)embodied composition and to demonstrate how an awareness of queer rhetorics can help scholars (and composers) to rethink transmediation and the compositional values that inhibit both our teaching and studying of transmediation and composition.

Modes, Modalities, and the Materiality of Composition

Western rhetorical studies has been heavily influenced by the nineteenth-century invention of the modes of discourse. While it may seem strange to reference the modes—narration, argument, description, exposition—in a chapter focused on current digital composing practices, I would contend that those modes, and the concept of modality itself, continues to limit our writing and thinking practices in several ways, a point that Rhodes and Alexander have also made. This limitation works against understanding the *trans* in transmedia. As Connors notes, the creation and proliferation of the modes in nineteenth century secondary and college-level writing handbooks offered a well-intentioned attempt to make writing instruction accessible through discreet principles or concepts, particularly to those students who came from less affluent homes where diverse literacy experiences would have been uncommon ("Rise and Fall"). Central to Connors' history of the modes was the recognition that these new modes of discourse focused on constraining what language did or could do in a particular context; rhetorical instruction now engaged the ways that Unity, Mass, and Coherence (later Unity, Emphasis, and Coherence) should be exemplified in/by educated discourse (Connors, "Rise and Fall" 449). Similarly, Connors recognized that the new modal taxonomies of the late eighteenth and nineteenth century were ultimately about splitting or separating discourse into singular elements, which explains one reason why we see a "practical split between expository and persuasive pedagogies" in US classrooms across grade levels (Connors *Composition*, 218). A modal pedagogy underscored a the need to order and classify things in increasingly science-focused universities; this pedagogy aligned itself with the microscope and the world in miniature, which focused on a logic of induction: by identifying and naming the individual pieces, the larger whole can then be easily constructed (Crowley).

This history has been discussed at length elsewhere and hardly needs repeating here, except to note that even as rhetorical studies has moved toward a broad notion of multimodality, one that encompasses a host of visual and aural media, we have retained this historical concept of a "mode" and its logic of induction. This lingering modality matters because much of our discussion of multimodality (and multimedia, and even transmedia) has been constrained by this set of print-based, classroom-based logics of discourse that call into being a final/finished composition built out of a set of identifiable parts. The compositional practices of transmedia, however, push away from the microscopic and privilege, instead, a macroscopic or telescopic vision of complexity. Older rhetorics of unity and coherence no longer make sense in this new context. In this section of the chapter, I explore some of the ways that our thinking about compositional practices has shifted through an emerging engagement with the tools, objects, and contexts of composition. This shift toward a new materialist framework for composing has expanded our awareness of discourse in ways that make transmedia/tion an important space for study (Gries; Micciche; West-Puckett).

While an exhaustive review of scholarship around composing objects is beyond the scope of this chapter, a sample of these texts serves to illustrate an ongoing concern for the interplay between writing/composing media and practices, and how this concern has precipitated an important move toward transmediation as a framework for thinking about both analog and digital composing practices. Dennis Baron's *A Better Pencil: Readers, Writers, and the Digital Revolution*, for example, provides a thoughtful analysis of several different writing tools—e.g., the clay tablet and stylus, the lead pencil, and the personal computer—in order to demonstrate how the physicality of the composing object impacts composing practices, as well as how those practices are responded to by those with power, e.g., teachers. The lead pencil's shift from a tool of carpenters and builders for quickly marking measurements became a wholly different tool with the discovery and inclusion of an eraser. Toward the middle of the nineteenth century, pencils (without erasers) had already become increasingly commonplace in school settings without causing too great a concern; however, Baron's focus on how tools change teaching and learning contexts leads him to showcase the impact the addition of the eraser had on this particular tool. Given the positivist epistemologies at work in nineteenth-century writing instruction (Berlin; Crowley; Fulkerson; Knoblauch), writing instruction tended to operate on an assumption that ideas moved from the brain to the page wholly unmediated by the composing tool: a pencil that could not erase, unlike the chalk and slate it replaced, was seen as a tool for accurately capturing what was in students' minds. The invention of the eraser, however, threw that sort of pedagogy into chaos as since students could now erase mistakes and revise their work to reflect their intentions more accurately. Baron showcases multiple examples from the time in which teachers expressed anxiety that they would not know what students knew or didn't know if they could simply change their answers. Baron recognizes that any new technology disrupts how we think about composing; each tool has its own affordances and constraints, its own mediation effects. The anxieties that teachers had about the pencil and eraser show up again one hundred years later as teachers express the same anxieties about "originality" when the personal computer becomes the composing medium of choice. Now anxieties about plagiarism and poor citation practices have come to the fore, while questions about the reliability of information available on the World Wide Web and concerns for how to teach writing and research in a "post-truth" society where "fake news" is actively created and shared across digital platforms have begun to occupy our professional listservs, conference sessions, and academic social media platforms.

The attention Baron pays to early/analog composing technologies such as the pencil is similar to the focus that others have offered digital media. From Selfe and Selfe's ground-breaking analysis of the desktop computer interface to Carnegie's more recent work on mobile interfaces, computers and writing scholars have maintained an important concern for the tools of composition, both for production and for consumption. As such, an interest in multimodality and new media is both easy to understand and marks an important departure from some older notions of modes/modality. Where the former thinking followed a pedagogical logic of constraint, for example, the move toward multimodality has tended to focus on layering and remixing of traditional genres and media in ways that can seem innovative and exciting. For example, Daniel Anderson at the University of North Carolina has for years taught his "playlist" assignment, where students in literature courses are asked to analyze a character from fiction through the creation of a playlist that somehow represents that character's wants, needs, motivations, etc. In my own composition courses, I've used a version of Anderson's project so that student writers could re/mix images, video, and print-text in order to make a set of claims about themselves as writers, students, or members of a family or group (https://dbanks1100.wordpress.com/syllabus/make-2-playlist/). Using open-access Web platforms such as Weebly, Wix, or WordPress, student composers have the option of embedding videos and images alongside text they compose to help them make their arguments about themselves or, in Anderson's case, characters from stories. These sorts of projects provide students with spaces to consider the "modes, logics, methods, processes, and capabilities" (Alexander and Rhodes 4) of multimodal composing and new media. Scholarship abounds with similar examples of new media assignments that focus student attention on both singular and multimodal composing practices (Anderson; Baepler and Reynolds; Ballantine; Carter and Arroyo; Stedman; Vie; Wysocki et al.).

Others have challenged the felt sense among new media scholars that media and modalities must always involve digital or computer-generated artifacts. For example, while Adam Banks's *Digital Griots* makes a larger argument about African American DJs functioning as "digital" storytellers, throughout much of his book, Banks looks at what seems like analog remix practices of these DJs: using their own voices in combination with those on the records that they spin, scratch, and mix, they produce a set of wholly new texts that are fundamentally linked to the objects, media, and contexts that produce them. Similarly, in *Toward a Composition Made Whole*, which opens with a story of a young woman who composed her "essay" on her ballet toe shoes, Jody Shipka notes, "I am concerned that emphasis placed on 'new' (meaning digital) technologies has led to a tendency to equate terms like *multimodal, intertextual, multimedia,* or still more broadly speaking, *composition* with the production and consumption of computer-based, digitized, screen-mediated texts" (7–8). For Shipka, there are a host of digital and analog tools that we have at our disposal for remediation and remix; these tools, artifacts, and objects offer unique options for composers, options that should be central to our understanding of multimodality.

To a large extent, this is also one of the arguments that Alexander and Rhodes make in *On Multimodality: New Media in Composition Studies.* A concern for *mode* and *modality* over the last century has often meant a somewhat conservative approach to exploring new media/transmedia. They write, "the traditional essay's reliance on the movement from claim to claim, supported through logical argument," which has been foundational to composition pedagogy and practice in schools, ultimately represents an organizational structure and set of values that "may very well overlook claims, positions, or insights grounded in emotion, or embodied experiences that might seem illogical or unreasonable when translated into syllogistically driven-arguments" (38). Consider the playlist assignment above: while students are required to use different media in constructing their playlist, the list itself is still dominated by the claims, warrants, arguments, etc of the written texts that accompany the images and videos. This sort of assignment doesn't necessarily engage with nontraditional logics or organizational structures. Central to the argument in *On Multimodality* is the claim that scholars would benefit from moving beyond notions of new and multimedia in ways that "[make] those media serve the rhetorical ends of writing and more print-based forms of composing" (Alexander and Rhodes 19). Instead, rhetorical studies needs methods for recognizing the "unique rhetorical capabilities of different media, including the 'distinct logics' and 'different affordances' of those media" (Alexander and Rhodes 19). One method for doing so might be to engage transmediation through queer/trans theories that reframe and relocate both new media.

Beyond Modality: Embracing Transmediation

In addition to multimodality and new media, transmediation has emerged in the last decade as another way to understand the movement of ideas, images, sounds, and texts across media. For some scholars, transmedia has been understood as digital storytelling practices, but ones that differ little from multimodality and new media (Baepler and Reynolds; Journet; Ray; Stedman; Summers; Wolff). Transmediation, however, has the potential to disrupt traditional notions of composing by enacting the call that Alexander and Rhodes have made for rethinking the continued dominance of print logics in new media and multimedia scholarship. In this section, I return to the work of Henry Jenkins and colleagues briefly to highlight how their under-standings of transmedia are impacted by the movement-oriented logics of memetics, an element of transmedia storytelling that is often overlooked or ignored by scholars who borrow from this work. That distinction marks an important departure for transmedia and also offers rhetorical studies a significant space for re-engaging with transmedia practices.

Jenkins developed "transmedia storytelling" out of his work tracking media proliferation across multiple contexts. At the turn of the current century, Jenkins began to notice a significant convergence around newer and older forms of media, which he explores in detail in *Convergence Culture: Where Old and New Media Collide.* Rather than seeing older forms of media (the book, the newspaper, the essay, the Polaroid photo) completely disappear in the lives of young composers and media users, Jenkins noticed that these users tended to blend these different types of media in interesting ways, which he termed "convergence":

By convergence, I mean the *flow* of content across multiple media platforms, the cooperation between multiple media industries, and *migratory* behavior of a media audience who will go almost anywhere in search of the kinds of entertainment experiences they want. (2, emphasis added)

In this notion of convergence, Jenkins works to capture the movement and interaction that is often hard to engage in a product-oriented textual logic. Despite decades of research into writing processes as multiple and complex (Dobrin et al.; Kent), the vast majority of writing courses across grade levels still evaluates a finished text rather than the movements and interactions that get the composer to that text. While this sort of textual logic continues to impact our understandings of new media and multimedia, Jenkins and others are encouraging us to pay greater attention to movement in media (Kuhn; Rhodes and Alexander; Ridolfo and DeVoss; Shipka).

Likewise, shifting from a single mode, genre, or medium is significant. As Jenkins notes, where once we had companies producing media with "distinctive functions and markets"—e.g., newspapers, magazines, books—those boundaries that held them distinct have since dissolved. Some newspapers struggle to keep their print circulations running in many markets, as many news outlets have gone to fully digital or shared print/digital production (13). As print magazines work to remediate in digital spaces, making use of the affordances and constraints that app culture provides, we see that many consumers are making use of freely available digital platforms for curations that are built on magazine aesthetics (Pinterest). Users now create their own "magazines" based on interests or needs and sourced from a host of visual, print, and video media online. Newspapers, magazines, and books have all had to figure out how to make their images and texts available digitally for an emerging generation of consumers who also function as content-curators, who then share their curation projects with their friends, colleagues, or other users through the use of Internet hashtags and keywords. The types of media that survive this shift are media that can account for these new flows of information and that can participate interactively.

Examples that Jenkins describes in *Convergence Culture*, such as Heather Lawver's creation of an online version of *The Daily Prophet* from the Harry Potter novels, as well as a number of examples from fan fiction communitites, represent for Jenkins what makes transmedia storytelling a specific and important new method for engaging with multiple media:

> Transmedia storytelling is the art of world making. . . . consumers must assume the role of hunters and gatherers, chasing down bits of the story across media channels, and collaborating to ensure that everyone who invests time and effort will come away with a richer entertainment experience. (21)

As a world-making methodology, transmedia storytelling resists many of the logics of print culture: fan/slash fiction carries on whether the original author keeps a story going or not; as such, these paratextual examples defy the logic that only the original author has the power to engage and change the characters, or to determine the trajectory of the characters' lives, loves, deaths, etc.

Equally important, transmedia requires different navigational logics than those of print materials. These logics require

> both processing new types of stories and arguments that are emerging within a convergence culture and expressing ideas in ways that exploit the opportunities and affordances represented by the new media landscape. In other words, it involves the ability to both read and write across all available modes of expression. (Jenkins, "Confronting")

While much of the work on multimodality and new media scholarship engages a similar concern for reading and writing across media, a multimodal text—at least in pedagogical contexts—ultimately risks being self-contained, a singular website or digital story that includes all of the images, video, sound, or text in one place. What makes transmedia different is its resistance to print logics of coherence/unity. What, we might ask, would a transmedia "book" be? Publishers have begun to offer different types of new media scholarship through various digital presses (e.g., Computers and Composition Digital Press, the Sweetland Digital Rhetoric Collaborative), but none of these necessarily represent transmedia.

Some have attempted to understand this sort of movement in media composing through different embodied metaphors from biology and medicine. It has become common for people to talk about an image or video "going viral." In this context, virality marks a type of popularity or rhetorical uptake (similar to what Ridolfo and DeVoss call "rhetorical velocity") that vloggers, bloggers, and other new media authors covet: becoming viral, in this context, means reaching a wide audience; it's talked about in almost exclusively positive terms. Other scholars have approached this same notion as a type of "networked promiscuity" (Payne), a phrase that evokes similar notions of cross-body, cross-site, cross-context connections as virality. Jenkins, Ford, and Green offer the term spreadability to explain how texts currently move in transmedia. Like Dawkins's *The Selfish Gene*, which initiated the concept of the "meme"—a text or idea that moves across culture—and Rushkoff's *Media Virus*, which established the viral metaphor as the norm, Jenkins et al. recognize how easy it is to compare "systems of cultural distribution to biological systems" (18). They suggest spreadability and stickiness as concepts for thinking about the circulation of texts and ideas. The opposite of spreadability, stickiness "privileges putting content in one place and making audiences come to it so they can be counted" (5). Meanwhile,

> Spreadability assumes a world where mass content is continually repositioned as it enters different niche communities. When material is produced according to a one-size-fits-all model, it imperfectly meets the needs of any given audience. Instead, audience members have to retrofit it to better serve their interests. As material spreads, it gets remade: either literally, through various forms of sampling and remixing, or figuratively, via its insertion into ongoing conversations and across various platforms. (Jenkins et al. 27)

Unlike viral models, which ultimately presuppose original "infected" bodies that transmit viruses to other bodies across a plague network, this notion of spreadability foregrounds a "continuous process of repurposing and recirculating" that works against originary or agentic models of networked distribution. In a transmedia context, it's not clear or certain that any idea, image, or text can be traced to an original source, nor is it clear what "original" might mean since so many transmedia texts represent a combination of images and words. This ostensible lack of an original agent may be one of the ways that transmedia most frustrates traditional Western rhetorical studies, which for over two centuries has valued a notion of discourse wherein a writer/speaker initiates a conversation or idea (in the classical model) or joins a conversation already in progress while still making his/her contribution (in the modern Burkean model). Not only does transmedia call into question what counts as "text" or "discourse," but it also seems to challenge the notion that individuals initiate or control those texts/discourses once they're out in the network. Rhetorical studies needs a more sophisticated lens for engaging and understanding transmedia so that we do not reduce it, again, to a simple multiplicity of modes/modalities.

Toward a Queer/Trans Theory of Mediation

While one hears any number of conversations in contemporary academia about the value of *trans*disciplinarity (rather than interdisciplinarity) or the preference for *trans*cultural (rather than multicultural) in any number of disciplines, what's often missing in these discussions is a carefully theorized notion of what, exactly, is meant by *trans*. Likewise, the work that Jenkins et al. initiated around transmediation has done little to fully theorize what they mean or intend by their use of *trans*. For most of this work, *trans* seems to reflect the definitions we find for its use in English dating back to 1612 in the *Oxford English Dictionary*: "across, through, over, to or on the other side of, beyond, outside of, from one place, person, thing, or state to another"; the OED also recognizes its use in words such as *transhuman* or *transmaterial* as meaning "to surpass" or "to transcend." Unlike the prefix *inter*, which suggests moving from one pre-established space to another (e.g., interdisciplinary assumes the disciplines are already established and does not question/challenge their formations), or the prefix *multi*, which suggests the proliferation of pre-established elements (e.g., multicultural assumes that distinct cultures exist and can be explored without necessarily changing those cultures), *trans* seems to welcome similar adverbial movements while also maintaining a sense of "beyondness" and "outside of." The connotation of *transcendence* suggests that the elements that are being connected or crossed may, in fact, be changed by this sort of promiscuous crossing/movement (Payne). To that end, I would argue that queer and trans theories that have emerged over the last twenty years, grounded in theories of gender performativity and new materialism, may provide spaces for us to re/consider what it is we really mean when we reach for the prefix *trans* to name our project.

To some extent, this line of thinking is one that entered the field of rhetorical rtudies in 2004–2005 with the publication of two ground-breaking pieces of scholarship: Robert McRuer's "Composing Bodies; or, De-Composition: Queer Theory, Disability Studies, and Alternative Corporealities" and Jonathan Alexander's "Transgender Rhetorics: (Re)Composing Narratives of the Gendered Body." Both pieces challenge the "body" of scholarship by engaging with bodies that are composing and de/composing at the same time. For McRuer, this means looking at queer and disabled bodies as "desirable" (59), to engage in a "critical de-composition" that comes about by "re-orienting ourselves away from those compulsory ideals [that privilege heterosexuality and able-bodiedness] and onto the composing process and the composing bodies—the alternative, and multiple, corporealities—that continually ensure that things can turn out otherwise" (59). While not discussing *trans* bodies in terms of gender or sexuality, McRuer's project gestures in that direction by reminding us through queer/disability studies that some bodies are always-already engaging "beyondness" and being "outside of" in the way they exist from day to day. A critical de-composition challenges the value that a particular "finished state is the [only] one worth striving for" (60). Similarly, Alexander pondered the pedagogical and theoretical question of what it might mean to engage with "trans thinking" in order to "review composition approaches to teaching about gender as a narrativized social construction [by considering] what *trans*gender theorists and activists can offer us as compositionists" (47) in thinking about the gendered narratives that make our lives. By turning their attention to theories which emerge out of embodied and affective experiences of *trans*, McRuer and Alexander initiated for rhetorical studies a set of questions that are central to developing a more robust theory of *trans*media.

Building on this work, I would argue that trans theories of embodiment, affect, and materiality, many of which grow out of phenomenology and psychoanalysis, provide the sort of sustained attention to the "beyondness" of objects and our relationship to them that we need to take up in rhetorical studies, a beyondness that is located through objects, relationships, and movements. Trans theories value notions of *transition* and *transgression*, which grow out of embodied experiences and speak back to our embodied experiences of objects. As Gayle Salamon recognizes in *Assuming a Body: Transgender and Rhetorics of Materiality*, trans theory concerns itself intimately with embodiment, but with a notion of bodies that challenges commonplace assumptions about "plenitude and fullness, coherence and wholeness" as ultimately "fictive states of being and subjectivity" (24). While we tend to think of our (able)bodies as these complete pieces of matter to which we have "unmediated access" (1), Salamon argues that "the body one feels oneself to have is not necessarily the same body that is delimited by its exterior contours" (3). Trans bodies question the idea that one is simply born with a body that has been unmediated by culture and context: "the body that one 'has' . . . is a result of identification, which is always a fundamentally relational act" (24), an interactive, knowledge-making act that works at the spaces where materials collide, elide, engage, repel, connect:

> The concept of the bodily ego is of particular use in thinking transgender because it shows that the body of which one has a 'felt sense' is not necessarily contiguous with the physical body as it is perceived from the outside. [. . .] the body one feels oneself to have is not necessarily the same body that is delimited by its exterior contours [. . .] the body is understood to be something more complex and capacious than a unitary formation of matter, singularly given to or claimed by only one sex. (14)

And yet the body seems, in our day-to-day moments, to be complete, to observe the same compositional values of unity, mass, and coherence that underscores a modal approach to writing. Those values hide the fact that our bodies, or rather, "our sense of the body image, the postural model of the body, is a sedimented effect without a stable reference or predictable content" (30).

While Salamon refers to this constructed body as an "assemblage" (29), it is important to recognize that Salamon's phenomenological body is not simply created from pre-made pieces such as a Mr. Potato Head or some human Erector set. Instead, Salamon recognizes the ongoing rearticulation of the body, a corporeality that is assembled across various planes: time, place, context, etc. While our shared human experience of aging may lead us to think of the body as a fundamentally teleological project, as an assemblage for which there is some final goal, and beyond that, a set of subgoals (baby, toddler, adolescent, young adult, middle age, etc.), a trans understanding of the body-as-assemblage recognizes that bodies are not always already moving toward any particular final product: "A body becomes so by virtue of its *interaction* with what surrounds it, not because it is composed of a stuff that is radically foreign to its surroundings" (Salamon 59, emphasis added). The trans body underscores the ways in which corporeality intersects with and is constituted as part of affect, as part of a desire for a self and a self-in-relation-to-an-other, and the multiple and varied processes of coming to understand all these bodies in relation to/among each other. Queer/trans bodies do not necessarily start or end at any (pre)determined place, but continually engage with cultural and material assemblage in ways that might also help us to rethink what is and is not being "mediated" in transmedia. In fact, a trans theory of transmediation might push us "beyond" thinking in terms of the individual modes and nodes that make up the networks of textuality we study. Certainly, by challenging our assumptions about beginnings and endings, such a theory helps us to theorize transmedia differently as assemblages marked by shifting intentionalities rather than clear or predetermined outcomes/goals. Understanding transmedia after (multi)modality means recognizing the "plenitude and fullness" of those media as well as the ways that media can seem stable or coherent at any moment. Our scholarship needs to acknowledge both if we are to better understand textual flows across media.

Conclusion

While viral/memetic theories of text/idea movement across networks provide interesting ways of thinking about ideas, images, words, etc, they often fall back on values of historicity and primacy, of where ideas/texts originate and how they develop. Queer/trans theories, however, remind us that there are non-teleological models for shaping meaning at the intersections of objects, ideas, contexts, and affects. These trans theories of experience strike me as phenomenological experiences that rewrite both our Cartesian and our post-Cartesian notions of embodiment and relationality. Out of them, we are just beginning to develop a robust theory of objects, bodies, affects, contexts, and movements. Elsewhere, Stephanie West-Puckett and I have explored this idea through what we identify as a queer/trans rhetoric of *intentionality*. While writing studies tends to prize outcomes in teaching and assessment, in transmediated spaces, which tend to function outside the logics and surveillance of schools and other institutions, a queer/trans rhetoric of intentionality might be more appropriate for scholars studying transmedia/tion.

A queer/trans rhetoric of intentionality underscores that "outcome" is not necessarily the purpose of "being," and it certainly isn't the only or most appropriate way to "read" a text (or a body). As media moves across networks—in more "controlled" environments such as television and corporate-owned media outlets to less "controlled" spaces such as microblogging (Tumblr), social news aggregation (Reddit), and media remixing (Popcorn)—it becomes difficult to imagine an agreed upon or pre-established "outcome" for what emerges. What's more evident is that a host of creators in different spaces create with intention, with the idea that they are adding something to the mix even if they are not sure what or to what particular end. Where our academic reading practices tend to privilege a critique for which we can know the totality of the object or idea—its genealogy, its teleology, etc.—transmedia calls attention to the hyper-present nature of new media, the same hyper-presence that queer/trans theorists have been working to articulate through theories of embodiment and affect rooted in new materialist frameworks.

As rhetorical studies continues to engage with new and old media, particularly media that are increasingly becoming transmediated, queer/trans theories offer one way for arresting our familiar, print-based logics of reading and analysis, and encourage us to embody a different analytical tradition—one that grows out of intentionality rather than outcome, out of what might be rather than what was carefully planned or orchestrated. In doing so, we might be better able to capture the rich and complex ways in which various types of media are moving across, between, among—and often quite beyond—traditional sites of meaning.

Works Cited

Alexander, Jonathan. "Transgender Rhetorics: (Re)Composing Narratives of the Gendered Body." *College Composition and Communication*, vol. 57, no. 1, 2005, pp. 45–82.

Alexander, Jonathan, and Jacqueline Rhodes. *On Multimodality: New Media in Composition Studies.* NCTE, 2014.

Anderson, Daniel. "The Low Bridge to High Benefits: Entry-Level Multimedia, Literacies, and Motivation." *Computers and Composition*, vol. 25, no. 1, 2008, pp. 40–60.

Arola, Kristin L. and Anne Frances Wysocki, Eds. *Composing(Media)=Composing(Embodiment): Bodies, Technologies, Writing, the Teaching of Writing*, Utah State UP, 2012.

Baepler, Paul, and Thomas Reynolds. "The Digital Manifesto: Engaging Student Writers with Digital Video Assignments." *Computers and Composition*, vol. 34, 2014, pp. 122–36.

Ballantine, Brian. "Textual Adventures: Writing and Game Development in the Undergraduate Classroom." *Computers and Composition*, vol. 37, 2015, pp. 31–43.

Banks, Adam J. *Digital Griot: African American Rhetoric in a Multimedia Age.* Southern Illinois UP, 2011.

Banks, William P., and Stephanie West-Puckett. "Against Re/production: Trans Theory, Digital Objects, and a Queer Paradigm for Remix." Conference on College Composition and Communication, Tampa, FL, 20 March 2015. Conference presentation.

Baron, Dennis. *A Better Pencil: Readers, Writers, and the Digital Revolution.* Oxford UP, 2012.

Berlin, James. "Contemporary Composition: The Major Pedagogical Theories." *College Composition and Communication*, vol. 44, no. 8, 1982, pp. 765–77.

Bolter, Jay D., and Richard Grusin. *Remediation: Understanding New Media.* MIT Press, 2000.

Carnegie, Teen A. M. "Interface as Exordium: The Rhetoric of Interactivity." *Computers and Composition*, vol. 26, 2009, pp. 164–73.

Carter, Geoffrey V. and Sarah J. Arroyo. "Tubing the Future: Participatory Pedagogy and YouTube U in 2020." *Computers and Composition*, vol. 28, 2011, pp. 292–302.

Connors, Robert J. "The Rise and Fall of the Modes of Discourse." *College Composition and Communication*, vol. 32, no. 4, 1981, pp. 444–55.

——. *Composition-Rhetoric: Backgrounds, Theory, and Pedagogy.* U of Pittsburgh P, 1997.

Crowley, Sharon. *Methodical Memory: Invention in Current Traditional Rhetoric.* Southern Illinois UP, 1990.

Dawkins, Richard. *The Selfish Gene.* Oxford UP, 1978.

Delagrange, Susan. "Wunderkammer, Cornell, and the Visual Canon of Arrangement." *Kairos*, vol. 13, no. 2, 2009, http://technorhetoric.net/13.2/topoi/delagrange/. Accessed 26 May 2017.

Dobrin, Sidney I., Jeff A. Rice, and Michael Vastola, Eds. *Beyond Postprocess.* Utah State UP, 2011.

Faigley, Lester. *Fragments of Rationality: Postmodernity and the Subject of Composition.* U of Pittsburgh P, 1992.

Fulkerson, Richard. "Four Philosophies of Composition." *College Composition and Communication*, vol. 30, no. 4, 1979, pp. 343–48.

Gries, Laurie E. *Still Life with Rhetoric: A New Materialist Approach to Visual Rhetorics.* Utah State UP, 2015.

Hawisher, Gail, and Cynthia L. Selfe, Eds. *Passions, Pedagogies and Twenty-First Century Technologies.* Utah State UP, 1999.

Janangelo, Joseph. "Joseph Cornell and the Artistry of Composing Persuasive Hypertexts." *College Composition and Communication*, vol. 49, no. 1, 1998, pp. 24–44.

Jenkins, Henry. *Convergence Culture: Where Old and New Media Collide.* New York UP, 2006.

——. "Confronting the Challenges of Participatory Culture (Part Six)." Weblog. Confessions of an Aca-Fan: The Official Weblog of Henry Jenkins. 27 Oct. 2006. http://henryjenkins.org/2006/10/confronting_the_challenges_of_5.html. Accessed 26 May 2017.

Jenkins, Henry, Sam Ford, and Joshua Green. *Spreadable Media: Creating Value and Meaning in a Networked Culture.* New York UP, 2013.

Journet, Debra. "Literate Acts in Convergence Culture: Lost as Transmedia Narrative." *Rhetorics and Technologies: New Directions in Writing and Communication*, edited by Stuart A. Selber. U of South Carolina P, 2010, pp. 198–218.

Kent, Thomas, ed. *Post-Process Theory: Beyond the Writing-Process Paradigm.* Southern Illinois UP, 1999.

Knoblauch, C. H. "Rhetorical Constructions: Dialogue and Commitment." *College English*, vol. 50, no. 2, 1988, pp. 125–40.

Kuhn, Virginia. "The Rhetoric of Remix." *Transformative Works and Cultures*, vol. 9, 2009. http://dx.doi.org/10.3983/twc.2012.0358. Accessed 26 May 2017.

McRuer, Robert. "Composing Bodies; or, De-Composition: Queer Theory, Disability Studies, and Alternative Corporealities." *JAC*, vol. 24, no. 1, 2004, pp. 47–78.

Manovich, Lev. *The Language of New Media.* MIT, 2002.

Micciche, Laura R. "Writing Material." *College English*, vol. 76, no. 6, 2014, pp. 488–505.

Munster, Anna. *Materializing New Media: Embodiment in Information Aesthetics.* Dartmouth College, 2006.

Palmeri, Jason. *Remixing Composition: A History of Multimodal Writing Pedagogy.* Southern Illinois UP, 2012.

Payne, Robert. *The Promiscuity of Network Culture: Queer Theory and Digital Media.* Routledge, 2015.

Ray, Brian. "More than Just Remixing: Uptake and New Media Composition." *Computers and Composition*, vol. 30, no. 3, 2013, pp. 183–196.

Rhodes, Jacqueline, and Jonathan Alexander. *Techne: Queer Meditations on Writing the Self.* Computers and Composition Digital Press/Utah State UP, 2015. http://ccdigitalpress.org/techne. Accessed 26 May 2017.

Ridolfo, Jim and Dànielle Nicole DeVoss. "Composing for Recomposition: Rhetorical Velocity and Delivery." *Kairos: A Journal of Rhetoric, Technology, and Pedagogy*, vol. 13, no. 2, 2009. http://kairos.technorhetoric.net/13.2/topoi/ridolfo_devoss/velocity.html. Accessed 26 May 2017.

Rushkoff, Douglas. *Media Virus: Hidden Agendas in Popular Culture*. Ballantine, 1994.

Salamon, Gayle. *Assuming a Body: Transgender and Rhetorics of Materiality*. Columbia UP, 2010.

Selber, Stuart. *Multiliteracies for a Digital Age*. Southern Illinois UP, 2004.

Selfe, Cynthia L., and Richard J. Selfe. "The Politics of the Interface: Power and Its Exercise in Electronic Contact Zones." *College Composition and Communication*, vol. 45, no. 4, 1994, pp. 480–504.

Shipka, Jody. *Towards a Composition Made Whole*. U of Pittsburgh P, 2011.

Stedman, Kyle D. "Remix Literacy and Fan Composition." *Computers and Composition*, vol. 29, 2012, pp. 107–23.

Summers, Sarah. "'Twilight is So Anti-Feminist that I Want to Cry': Twilight Fans Finding and Defining Feminism on the World Wide Web." *Computers and Composition*, vol. 27, 2010, pp. 315–23.

Vie, Stephanie. "Digital Divide 2.0: 'Generation M' and Online Social Networking Sites in the Composition Classroom." *Computers and Composition*, vol. 25, 2008, pp. 9–23.

Welch, Kathleen E. *Electric Rhetoric: Classical Rhetoric, Oralism, and a New Literacy*. MIT, 1999.

West-Puckett, Stephanie. *Materializing Makerspaces: Queerly Composing Space, Time, and (What) Matters*. 2017. East Carolina U, PhD dissertation.

Wolff, William I. "Baby, We Were Born to Tweet: Springsteen Fans, the Writing Practices of in situ Tweeting, and the Possibilities for Twitter." *Kairos*, vol. 19, no. 3, 2015, http://technorhetoric.net/19.3/topoi/wolff/. Accessed 26 May 2017.

Wysocki, Anne Frances, Johndan Johnson-Eilola, Cynthia L. Selfe, and Geoffrey Sirc. *Writing New Media: Theory and Applications for Expanding the Teaching of Composition*. Utah State UP, 2004.

32

HIP-HOP RHETORIC AND MULTIMODAL DIGITAL WRITING

Regina Duthely

Multimodal composing has created a new means of imagining communication and literacy in the twenty-first century. This expansion of the possibilities for what composition can be and do is a valuable transformation in contemporary writing ecologies. However, exploring digital and multimodal composing in the context of hip-hop literacies, and New Literacy Studies provides a richer and critically engaged means of writing and communicating in the digital public sphere. Hip-hop has always been multimodal, simultaneously deploying the written word, aurality, and visuals via music videos, dress, graffiti, and dance just to name a few. In *Digital Griots: African American Rhetoric in a Multimedia Age*, Adam Banks rightly claims, "Hip Hop has disrupted the notion of a linear text and the ways the art form has placed a focus on the recycling, reuse, and repurposing of language and tools old and new" (20). The collaborative and communal act of creation within hip-hop provides a foundation for the current reading of multimodal and digital compositions. Hip-hop has long deployed the use of sampling and making something out of nothing using technology. The reimagining of text not as linear, but as a series of interwoven networks, a mixture of fragments used to create a new whole, a whole that can be redivided and reformed, is the creative potential of both hip-hop and digital composing techniques.

Hip-hop epistemologies and ontologies historically have created a space for the methods and techniques used in digital and multimodal writing. Hip-hop epistemologies use the disrespectable as a means of subverting Western notions of propriety that serve to marginalize and violently destroy Black ways of being; they must be culturally relevant and connected to their home languages and communities, and they should deploy creative aural, oral, and visual that move beyond traditional boundaries and hegemonic modes of communication. In "Alter Egos and Infinite Literacies, Part III: How to Build a Real Gyrl in 3 Easy Steps," historians Jessica Marie Johnson and Kismet Nuñez discuss the kitchen table and the corner as spaces for Black cultural creation. They claim:

> The corner and the kitchen table have been spaces where black diasporic political culture operated in the past and present . . . These discussions often incorporated black cultural expressions ranging over time from the dozens to hip hop. The corner models space to engage which is not beholden to obligations and expectations of other historically black political spaces like churches, mutual-aid institutions, schools, and workplaces. It has therefore been seen as a space for working and underclass black politics. (50)

The corner has served as a site where hip-hop epistemologies can flourish. Working outside of the confines of traditional sites that are bound to particular respectable norms and expectations, the corner and hip-hop are freer sites of protest. In our current digital moment, the Internet can provide a freer space to deploy hip-hop epistemologies toward the work of freedom. The melding of hip-hop epistemologies and multimodal composition and rhetoric seems like an easy connection.

Technology has also played a central role in the development of hip-hop culture. DJs specifically used technology to mix music and sounds to create hip-hop. However, more generally, hip-hop was a means for Afro-diasporic youth to use the resources available, including their mouths, as instruments of resistance. Hip-hop's genesis was in response to the decimation of advancements made in Black communities after the Civil Rights era. This subversive social justice oriented origin story is central to considering the ways that hip-hop and multimodal and digital composition can be combined. Moving from turntables to contemporary digital spaces such as Twitter, Tumblr, and Instagram, these sites allow for broader participation in public discourse communities, thereby providing new means of collaborating and creating.

Black Media Resistance: A Very Brief History

African American use of new media as spaces for protest has a long history in the United States. In the late nineteenth century, journalist Ida B. Wells worked tirelessly to shed light on the terrors of lynching and develop a counternarrative to the racist justifications for these acts of extreme violence against African Americans. Wells came to own her own newspapers and served as a publisher, editor, and investigative journalist as well as a staunch anti-lynching activist. Wells deployed the media of the time (the newspaper) to serve as a space of resistance for African Americans.

In 1955 Emmett Till was dragged from his bed, beaten, shot, and thrown in a lake. His murderers were acquitted. His mother opted for an open casket funeral and allowed *Jet* magazine to publish photographs of his mutilated body. This moment is widely viewed as a catalyst for an uptick in Black activism and the beginning of the Civil Rights movement. Her use of print magazine and photography in the twentieth century was an act of resistance that forced viewers to confront the horrors of lynching.

The late twentieth century brought us hip-hop partially in response to the 1980s crack-era and Reagan's war on drugs. The early creators of hip-hop developed an art form that served as resistance to government policies that increasingly left Black people dead, in jail, and further pushed to the outskirts of society. Their creative use of technology to create music and sample, mix, and scratch transformed music and has been one of the most influential musical genres globally.

Fast forward to the twenty-first century and we arrive at the startlingly familiar #Black-LivesMatter movement. The time and the form have changed, but the violence faced by African Americans has not changed much. The #BlackLivesMatter movement was started by activists Patrice Cullors-Brignac, Alicia Garza, and Opal Tometi in 2013 after George Zimmerman was acquitted for the murder of Trayvon Martin. In August 2014, Michael Brown was murdered by police officer Darren Wilson and his body was left in the street for four hours. No charges were filed against Wilson. In November 2014, 12-year-old Tamir Rice was murdered by police officers in Cleveland, OH. The police officers responsible were never indicted. The names of Black people murdered at the hands of police are innumerable. Citizens are reminded daily that Black men, women, and children are subject to state sanctioned violence without any recourse or protections. What began as a simple hashtag on Twitter grew to mobilize and help organize protests in Ferguson, MO, Baltimore, MD, and New York, NY to name a few. These uprisings in Black communities around the country increased the visibility of the #BlackLivesMatter movement as it became the rallying cry and decentralized grassroots organization that has profoundly shaped protest in the twenty-first century.

I juxtapose these events and connect them to the digital writing and rhetoric as a means of reimagining the public potential for digital writing and rhetoric scholarship, and creating a counternarrative to the oft-heard narratives about the lack of Black participation with technology. African Americans have long used technology and media as spaces to assert themselves into public discourse. As attempts to silence, oppress, and deny them access to media increased, African Americans continued to resist. They developed creative ways to engage in subversive acts in new media spaces, and they created their own media so that a space existed where they could tell their own stories.

Race, Protest, and Hip-Hop Counternarratives

The Black public counternarratives ushered in by hip-hop provide a valuable framework for modeling the subversive potential of digital writing and rhetoric. African American youth are active content creators in digital spaces, and their productions expand upon the work of hip-hop rhetorical tropes regarding collaboration, remix, and interaction. In "Locating the Semiotic Power of Multimodality" Gloria Hull and Mark Evan Nelson claim:

> We believe that the increasingly multiplex ways by which people can make mean-ing in the world, both productively and receptively, can potentially represent a democratizing force whereby the views and values of more people than ever before can be incorporated into the ever-changing design of our world. (226)

Making more room for marginalized voices in the digital public sphere is a significant outcome of multimodal composing. Reimagining what counts as literacy and dismantling the Western overvaluing of written literacy above orality or other forms of knowledge-making allows for wider participation and diversity of epistemologies, more room for play and experimentation, and engages creators in meaningful composing more aligned with how knowledge is produced and transferred in the twenty-first century.

The digital age ushered in a great change in technology, mobile communication, and social spheres. As Internet speeds increased and mobile device sizes decreased, when, where, and how we communicated and interacted completely changed. Afro-diasporic participation in the digital age has been a point of contention in conversations about race and technology. Early conversations about the digital divide and lack of Black participation were rooted in myths about Black pathologies. In "Finding a Place in Cyberspace: Black Women, Technology, and Identity" Michelle Wright dismantles the notion of the digital divide and argues that it reflects the racist discourse that has always been directed at Black people. She argues,

> The reality is that technology is the product of ten thousand years of world civilizations, of which African civilizations were a central contributor, and African Americans have been regular contributors, from ironing boards to cellphones. The reality of the digital divide, I concluded, bore an uncanny and disturbing resemblance to racist beliefs about race and technology. (49)

For Wright, the idea that African Americans were somehow not engaged with the ever-changing technological moment was based in pervasive racist ideologies. The creation of hip-hop easily counters that as it is evident that African American youth used records, turntables, and boom-boxes to create a completely new art form. Active Black participation on social media sites such as BlackPlanet, MySpace, and now Twitter and Instagram all demonstrate that Black people are consistent technology users and content creators. For example, the loose network of Black Twitter users dubbed members of "Black Twitter" have some of the largest follower counts on the site, and often provide much of the content for mainstream news articles.

Contemporary conversations about social media and digital writing center on the racist, cisheteropatriarchal trolling and abuse that marginalized groups are subjected to online. Any attempts at resistance and the assertion of marginalized voices in discourse spaces are often met with violent pushback. In "Making a Case for the Black Digital Humanities" Kim Gallon argues,

> One of the essential features of the black digital humanities, then, is that it conceptualizes a relationship between blackness and the digital where black people's humanity is *not* a given. The black digital humanities probes and disrupts the ontological notions that would have us accept humanity as a fixed category, an assumption that unproblematically emanates in the digital realm.

For Gallon, a central feature of Black digital participation is an assertion of Black humanity that is often denied. Black people have long had to use public media discourse spaces to force a confrontation with Black humanity. As these sites and spaces evolved African Americans had to find new ways to use technology towards Black liberation.

The ignored and marginalized voices of Black youth subject to structural inequality created hip-hop both as a form of entertainment and expression, but also as a pushback against mainstream systems of oppression. The art form comes out of the need for subversive cultural creations. In "Nommo, Kawaida, and Communicative Practice: Bringing Good into the World" Maulana Karenga argues for a communal practice of communication by stating, "the communal character of communicative practice is reaffirmed and rhetoric is approached as, above all, a rhetoric of communal deliberation, discourse, and action, oriented toward that which is good for the community and world" (3). The necessity of rhetoric as working and functioning for the advancement of the community is not limited to African American rhetorical production, but is a reflection of an Afro-diasporic consciousness. Approaching a theory of digital rhetoric from this hip-hop rhetorical foundation, it is evident that digital discourse spaces occupied by people throughout the African diaspora perform community work. Hip-hop rhetoric as deployed in multimodal writing spaces, demonstrates the use of online spaces to fight for liberation and uplift for Black people.

The democratizing collaborative possibilities central to digital writing ecologies mimic the collaborative liberatory possibilities of hip-hop and Afro-diasporic rhetorical traditions. Maulana Karenga asserts that Africana rhetoric is defined and bound by multiple forms, namely: a rhetoric of community, a rhetoric of resistance, a rhetoric of reaffirmation, and a rhetoric of possibility. These rhetorical traditions are also seen in Afro-diasporic digital rhetorical work. Building community, resisting dominance, reaffirming Black experiences, and generating hopeful narratives discussing the potential for the Black community are the primary goals of the digital work being done online. In the article "When the First Voice You Hear Is Not Your Own," composition scholar Jacqueline Jones Royster argues for the subjective as a crucial part of the writing experience. She states, "Subjectivity as a defining value pays attention dynamically to context, ways of knowing, language abilities, and experience, and by doing so it has a consequent potential to deepen, broaden, and enrich our interpretive views in dynamic ways as well" (29). When we think about literacy and cultural production as influenced by subject position and social, political, community, and environmental experiences, we make room for listening and cross-cultural communal knowledge production. The intersection of digital counterpublics and hip-hop rhetorical studies, digital writing, and the history of Black resistance provide a critical lens for reimagining the liberatory potential of digital writing and rhetoric.

Digital Writing and Rhetoric and Social Justice

Digital spaces allow for the development for vast discourse communities that Black people can engage in challenging and critiquing structural systems that work to subjugate them across the globe. In "Finding a Place in Cyberspace: Black Women, Technology, and Identity," Michelle Wright claims,

> For African Americans, given their history of struggle against the individual and institutional forces/structures of exploitation, marginalization, isolation, degradation, and annihilation, one might conclude that the primary work of the rhetoric produced by African Americans has been essentially in protest against such conditions, thereby using all of the verbal skills at their command to mount a verbal assault upon such conditions in the hope of challenging, persuading, cajoling, frustrating, exhausting, and so on in order to prepare the ground for the seeds of Black liberation. (86)

This quest for Black liberation is the central way to think about hip-hop digital rhetoric. There is no one way to resist. There is no one way to engage in creating subversive counterdiscourses. Just as the creators of hip-hop creatively used limited resources to resist, digital writing and rhetorical acts can be a site for people to participate in meaningful social justice work.

At this particular moment in society, digital writing spaces should be spaces for creators to imagine and create the world they want to live in. Carmen Kynard writes about student protests and their role in the development of composition studies in her book *Vernacular Insurrections: Race, Black Protest, and the New Century in Composition-Literacies Studies*. What she labels as vernacular insurrections, or students' complete transformation of forms of knowledge production in the academy, continues in the move to multimodal composing. Carmen Kynard's definition of vernacular insurrections is valuable for looking at Black protest as a complete overhaul of oppressive systems. She argues, "I can see vernacular discourses as not only counterhegemonic, but also affirmative of new, constantly mutating languages, identities, political methodologies, and social understandings that communities form in and of themselves, both inwardly and outwardly" (11). Central to Kynard's argument is the notion of creating anew. These insurrections are not merely reactions to oppression or attempts to reform systems as they currently exist. There is a complete overhaul that forces an encounter with new ways of being.

Deploying Afro-diasporic notions of creation as being both communal and oriented toward social justice work is vital to the development of digital writing and rhetoric. We can look to hip-hop for this model. Hip-hop is both multimodal and concerned with disrupting hegemonic systems. For underrepresented and marginalized oppressed groups, the digital public made possible by the expansion of the Internet and digital spaces such as social media makes a space for people to assert identity and dare to exist despite attempts to erase and silence them. Jessica Marie Johnson states, "Our organizing and politics came long before digital and social media entered our lives, but the synchronicity of digital and social media offered us a mechanics and process that matched a praxis already in existence" (50). Afro-diasporic protest has always existed, and systems that were used to organize political movements have always used new media and the public discourse spaces of the time as a means of engaging in this protest. However, the new affordances made possible by social media and other digital writing spaces allows this protest work to continue.

Digital Writing and Rhetoric in the Academy

Digital composition and rhetorical theories often deal with remix, attribution, plagiarism, sampling, as a means of teaching writing and research, but often make no mention of hip-hop despite hip-hop's significance to the creation and transformation of the notion of remix. Hull and Nelson discuss the ways that multimodal composition makes room for new methods of knowledge creation:

> To rehearse the obvious, it is possible now to easily integrate words with images, sound, music, and movement to create digital artifacts that do not necessarily privilege linguistic forms of signification but rather that draw on a variety of modalities—speech, writing, image, gesture, and sound—to create different forms of meaning. (224)

However, hip-hop has always embodied these multimodal characteristics. The four elements of hip-hop (DJing, emceeing, graffiti, and breakdancing) have blended and merged these elements since the late 1970s. Afro-diasporic and hip-hop rhetorical history play an essential role in the genesis of digital writing and rhetoric. In Elaine Richardson's *Hip-Hop Literacies* she claims,

> The primary oral practices from which Hiphop emanates are largely forged from existing African ideologies and social practices and those that the people of Black African descent encountered, developed and/or appropriated in the context of negotiating life in Anglo-dominant societies. The secondary orality comes into being in today's highly technological societies. (xvi)

The history of Afro-diasporic rhetorical tropes that include repetition, communal creation and storytelling, and the merging of aural and oral texts that fall outside of Western notions of literacy come even earlier than hip-hop, yet outside of African American rhetorical studies this history is often erased. Stuart Selber rightly claims that the Internet provides a new space for the exchange of ideas and "cultural intervention." This forces people to encounter the others they attempt to ignore or erase. He says, "Settings for literacy can supply opportunities for cultural intervention. Such interventions, especially in the context of Internet-based communication, often involve alternative views of interaction and exchange" (9). Having multiple ways and means of interacting and exchanging information makes room for a broader discourse community. People are able to engage with the ideas of a larger audience, and they can be the audience for a larger number of creators.

In the introduction to *Debates in the Digital Humanities*, Matthew Gold speaks to the divide in digital humanities scholarship, noting that

> fault lines have emerged within the DH community between those who use new digital tools to aid relatively traditional scholarly projects and those who believe that DH is most powerful as a disruptive political force that has the potential to reshape fundamental aspects of academic practice. (1)

I would argue that people use digital spaces to create real change and not just to attempt to repackage old fields of study. Further, the value in digital scholarship lies in its ability to make academic work more public and connected to communities outside of academic spaces. Digital rhetoric has the potential to participate meaningfully in this public discourse that disrupts social norms and fights for greater equity. As we engage in the work of developing the academy of the future, we are increasingly moving beyond the ivory tower and the campuses where we teach and study.

The digital humanities require public engagement. The use of public digital rhetorical spaces allows youth to combat standards of respectability in the public sphere. It is important that youth have the room to challenge pervading systems of dominance and control. Banks rightly argues,

> Access to any particular technology occurs only when individuals or members of a group are able to use that technology to be able to tell their own stories in their own terms and able to meet the real material, social, cultural, and political needs in their lives and in their communities. Access to a technology means that members of a particular group know how to use it for both participation and resistance. (*Race* 138)

If literacy is an act of freedom, youth of color are engaging in these freedom acts outside of dominant discourse spaces ie. schools. They are using alternative forms of literacy including digital literacy to reject and resist attempts to silence and render them invisible in public discourse.

Digital humanities scholarship works to bridge the divide between the academy and the public by creating work that is accessible outside traditional scholarly locales, and by studying and engaging real world concerns. By bringing social justice work into the classroom, critically engaging new media, and amplifying Black activist voices, the digital humanities can do relevant social justice work. Black digital activism and the digital humanities should work together to engage in the work of transforming the academy and society. The student protests happening around campuses in the US reflect the need for a merging of scholarship on social justice movements and the digital humanities. Students are asking for greater representation, more support, and swifter, more decisive action against perpetrators of acts of racism. Student protestors at the University of Missouri, Harvard Law School, Ithaca College, and many others staged protests, sit-ins, hunger strikes, and issued demands to their institutions resulting in the creation of diversity officers, the resignation of university presidents, and many other significant results. The use of social media to spread information and build visibility for these student protestors is a digital literacy that can effect change. It is in this way that the social media justice work outside of the academy and the academy collide. The meeting of the personal and political in not just activist work outside of the academy, but also within, provides a foundation for the potentially transformative work of the digital humanities. The most interesting and valuable digital humanities projects are those that seek to engage real world concerns and work to ameliorate inequality. Projects and groups such as #transformDH, Create Caribbean, African Diaspora PhD, Global Outlook DH and many others are working to reshape the ways that digital scholarship is produced and disseminated. If the field truly imagines itself doing the work of humanity it must continue to engage with social justice work happening outside of the academy, and look to diverse communities and creators, particularly those present in our classrooms, to redefine who and what counts as digital rhetoric.

Hip-Hop Rhetoric and Digital Writing: Final Thoughts

The notion of communal creation is central to this digital work. African American rhetorical tropes figure the communal as a necessity for the creation of a work. Through various means, such as call and response, African Americans require audience participation and interaction to create. In *Digital Diaspora: A Race for Cyberspace* media studies scholar Anna Everett argues,

> Despite the well-documented dehumanizing imperatives of the colonial encounter, the ethnically and nationally diverse Africans in the New World developed self-sustaining virtual communities through paralinguistic and transnational communicative systems and networks of song, dance, talking drums, and other musical instrumentations that enabled this heterogeneous mass of people somehow to overcome their profound dislocation, fragmentation, alienation, relocation, and ultimate commodification in the Western slavocracies of the modern world. (3)

Everett claims an Afro-diasporic lens for exploring Black cultural productions in a digital age. The different, but connected, Afro-diasporic communities have worked to maintain communities and networks to resist the dehumanizing and silencing experiences of Black bodies throughout the New World diaspora.

The text cannot exist without the outside participation from others. This communal creation, these multiple creators and varied voices are essential to both multimodal creation and the hip-hop community. Just as hip-hop ushered in a new wave of music and culture that has transformed society, multimodal composing has brought in a new means of communication. We are all deeply embedded in a technological society and are constantly engaged in creation online. As we curate our Twitter timelines, try to get the best shot for our Instagram photos, and try to capture funny moments for Snapchat, we are composing. The potential audience is central to how one goes about creating for these spaces. Multimodal composing, like hip-hop, can liberate. It helps to dismantle the distinction between private and public discourse. People who are marginalized and silenced can assert their voices and tell their stories to an audience beyond the limited circles that they belong to. bell hooks emphasizes the necessity for self-invention outside of the limited confines of oppressive systems. She says,

> Indeed, a fundamental task of black critical thinkers has been the struggle to break with the hegemonic modes of seeing, thinking, and being that block our capacity to see ourselves oppositionally, to imagine, describe, and invent ourselves in ways that are liberatory. (2)

This self-invention, this imagining oneself outside of hegemonic power structures is hip-hop. To publicly disrupt and tell one's own story is central to both hip-hop and digital rhetorical acts. As digital content creators work to tell digital counterstories and build community via collective memory, they engage in defiant acts resulting in a paradigm shift that disrupts traditional forms of knowledge-making that historically have existed. A disruptive political force that asserts Black voices in the expanding digital public sphere complements digital writing and rhetorical work.

Works Cited

Banks, Adam. *Digital Griots: African American Rhetoric in a Multimedia Age.* Southern Illinois UP, 2011.
——. *Race, Rhetoric, and Technology: Searching for Higher Ground.* Routledge, 2005.
"Black Lives Matter." Black Lives Matter, http://blacklivesmatter.com/. Accessed 3 July 2017.
Everett, Anna. *Digital Diaspora: A Race for Cyberspace.* SUNY Press, 2009.
Gallon, Kim. "Making a Case for the Black Digital Humanities." *Debates in the Digital Humanities*, edited by Matthew Gold and Lauren Klein. U of Minnesota P, 2016, dhdebates.gc.cuny.edu/debates/text/55. Accessed 3 July 2017.

Gold, Matthew K. "Introduction." *Debates in the Digital Humanities*, edited by Matthew Gold. University of Minnesota Press, 2012, dhdebates.gc.cuny.edu/debates/text/2. Accessed 3 July 2017.

hooks, bell. *Black Looks: Race and Representation*. South End Press, 1992.

Hull, Glynda A., and Mark Evan Nelson. "Locating the Semiotic Power of Multimodality." *Written Communication*, vol. 20, no. 2, 2005, pp. 224–61.

Johnson, Jessica Marie, and Kismet Nuñez. "Alter Egos and Infinite Literacies, Part III: How to Build a Real Gyrl in 3 Easy Steps." *Black Scholar*, vol. 45, no. 4, 2015, pp. 47–57.

Karenga, Maulana. "Nommo, Kawaida, and Communicative Practice: Bringing Good into the World." *Understanding African American Rhetoric: Classical Origins to Contemporary Innovations*, edited by Ronald Jackson and Elaine Richardson. Routledge, 2003, pp. 3–22.

Kynard, Carmen. *Vernacular Insurrections: Race, Black Protest, and the New Century in Composition-Literacies Studies*. SUNY Press, 2013.

Richardson, Elaine. *Hip-Hop Literacies*. Routledge, 2006.

Royster, Jacqueline Jones "When the First Voice You Hear is not Your Own." *College Composition and Communication*, vol. 47, no. 1, 1996, pp. 29–40.

Selber, Stuart. *Rhetorics and Technologies: New Directions in Writing and Communication*. The U of South Carolina P, 2010.

Wright, Michelle. "Finding a Place in Cyberspace: Black Women, Technology, and Identity." *Frontiers: A Journal of Women Studies*, vol. 26, no.1, 2005, pp. 48–59.

33

AUTOETHNOGRAPHIC BLOGART EXPLORING POSTDIGITAL RELATIONSHIPS BETWEEN DIGITAL AND HEBRAIC WRITING

Mel Alexenberg

This chapter explores postdigital relationships between the media ecology of digital and Hebraic writing through autoethnographic blogging. It presents a speculative view of the new media that hosts digital writing in relation to an ancient tradition that forms the roots of contemporary Hebrew writing and rhetoric.

The Book of Creation (*SePheR Yetzirah*) is considered the oldest Hebrew text that sets parameters for the creation of the universe in the down-to-earth spiritual tradition of Judaism known as Kabbalah (Kaplan). It begins: "The universe was created with three *SePhaRim*, with *SePheR* (form), with *S'PhaR* (quantity), and with *SiPuR* (narrative)." The SPR root of these words for form, quantity, and narrative is related to the word for SPiRal in Hebrew and many languages, ancient and modern, and the English words SPiRitual and inSPiRation.

This centuries-old text finds its parallel in *The Language of New Media* (Manovich) that identifies the principles of new media in relation to form, quantity, and narrative. Media elements—texts, images, and sounds are represented by discrete forms—pixels, polygons, voxels, characters, and scripts. These forms are composed of digital code composed of numerical representations. They are combined to create digital writing that integrates these media elements in a narrative flow.

Key words in the title—autoethnography, postdigital, blogart—require definitions provided below in the form of autoethnographic narrative.

Autoethnography

I first encountered the word "autoethnography" when I was professor of art and education at Columbia University in the 1970s. I was teaching a graduate course "Designing Environments for Learning" when a gray-haired woman walking with a stick marched into my classroom. "What's happening here?" she inquired in a commanding voice as her eyes scanned strange happenings in a staid 1880s room with a soaring ceiling, high arched windows, and walls of dark wood. I told her that my students entered an empty classroom at the beginning of the semester charged with designing and building an environment for learning about designing environments for learning. As she walked into my student-designed interactive classroom to get a close-up look, she told me the she would love to bring five-year-old triplets to play there while her doctoral research methods students observed and documented the triplets' interactions with its imaginative spaces. When she introduced herself to me as Margaret, I realized that she was the anthropologist Margaret Mead.

We went out to lunch together to make plans for her to teach her students in my classroom. While we were eating, she was diligently writing. I asked, "Margaret, what are you writing?" She explained that she was taking notes on how I eat.

> My research methods studying how you eat are similar to those I used for studying how people eat in Samoa and New Guinea. My research in those cultures is called "ethnography." My observations were from the viewpoint of an outsider interested in learning how people eat in the context of understanding of their cultures. However observing you, a Columbia University colleague eating with me in New York where we both live, calls for an insider's methodology called "autoethnography."

Autoethnography is the primary research methodology used in this chapter. It is a method of insider ethnography when the researcher is a member of the group being studied. In *Autoethnography: Understanding Qualitative Research* (Adams and Jones 2014), autoethnography is defined as a method of research that involves describing and analyzing personal experiences in order to understand cultural experiences.

My methodology of exploring the postdigital relationships between Hebraic and digital writing is based upon my insider viewpoint as both a Hebrew-speaking observant Jew living in Israel and a creative artist whose artworks exploring digital technologies and global systems are in the collections of forty museums worldwide. Complementing my insider perspective as Israeli Jew and active artist is my outsider perspective as a professor who taught graduate courses on research methods at Columbia University and on interrelationships between art, technology, and culture at MIT Center for Advanced Visual Studies.

Postdigital

I had first sensed a postdigital aura nearly a half-century ago when I programmed mammoth computers at New York University to make pictures that called out for the warm human touch of colorful pigments in molten beeswax sensuously flowing over a plotter's hard-edged digital drawings. This aura continued as I initiated interactive dialogues between human sensibilities and new technologies in the *LightsOROT: Spiritual Dimensions of the Electronic Age* exhibition that I created in collaboration with Otto Piene at MIT for Yeshiva University Museum (Alexenberg and Piene). As art editor of *The Visual Computer: International Journal of Computer Graphics*, I titled my digital art issue editorial "Art with Computers: The Human Spirit and the Electronic Revolution," an apt title today for a chapter in a book on postdigital art. My current works of participatory blogart and wikiart mirror the living Talmud, a creative dialogue about Jewish law and lore that is the oldest ongoing wikicreation spanning centuries and continents. I explore how this dialogue extends into contemporary explorations of the human dimensions of new media in my book *The Future of Art in a Postdigital Age: From Hellenistic to Hebraic Consciousness* (2011).

The definition of "postdigital" that I wrote became the core of the *Wikipedia* definition:

> In *The Future of Art in a Postdigital Age*, Mel Alexenberg defines "postdigital art" as artworks that address the humanization of digital technologies through interplay between digital, biological, cultural, and spiritual systems, between cyberspace and real space, between embodied media and mixed reality in social and physical communication, between high tech and high touch experiences, between visual, haptic, auditory, and kinesthetic media experiences, between virtual and augmented reality, between roots and globalization, between autoethnography and community narrative, and between web-enabled peer-produced wikiart and artworks created with alternative media through participation, interaction, and collaboration in which the role of the artist is redefined. (https://en.wikipedia.org/wiki/Postdigital)

Blogart

My blogart project *Wikiartists* invites people living in the twenty-one countries that surround the Mediterranean Sea to become wikiartists by collaborating in the creation of a Web-enabled peer-produced artwork (Alexenberg, *Wikiartists*). Med Rim participants interact with each other by posting wedding photos as an invitation to people in other countries to respond by sending photographs of native flowers as blog post gifts.

Teaching in Jerusalem, Israel, I created a participatory blogart project jerUSAlem-USA to invite documentation of the twenty places in the United States named "Jerusalem" (Alexenberg, *jerUSAlem-USA*). Residents of and visitors to the US Jerusalems participated by posting photographs and texts about life there.

Context/With Text

Digital writing invites creating word texts in the context of visual images. Read the word "context" as "with-text." In the exemplary blogart project that forms the core of this chapter, *Torah Tweets: A Postdigital Biblical Commentary as a Blogart Narrative* (Alexenberg and Benjamin), photographic images are situated between two verbal texts—the biblical text read and the blogger's life text written.

To augment photographs with word texts is a controversial point in photographic theory. Purists believe that the images should speak for themselves without the need for verbal commentary. However, conceptual art forms and digital photography disseminated through social media invite forming new contexts for images and words to interact.

When you open your Facebook page, you read "Write something" or "What's on your mind?" inviting you to post a verbal message before posting a photograph. If you post a photograph first, then Facebook asks "Say something about this photo." When you post a photo on Flickr, you see "Click here to add description" and "Add a comment." Photobucket opens with "Everyone has a story to tell. What's yours? Tell your complete story with photos, videos and words." LinkedIn and Twitter invite posting photographs in the context of words.

The powerful significance that a photograph can gain from a brief text is presented in the beautifully illustrated book *Photo-Wisdom: Master Photographers on Their Art* (Blackwell). The book begins with a photograph of a lone leaf resting on a light background, a quite boring brownish leaf from a ficus tree. I asked why Blackwell would begin his book of seminal essays on photography by renowned photographers with such a mundane photo of little interest. Then I read the caption. "Ficus religiosa, Tel Aviv, Israel. When the sixteen-year-old Palestinian Aamed Alfar blew himself up in a Tel Aviv market on 1 November 2004, this leaf was propelled to the ground by the force of the explosion." I can never open this book again and only see an ordinary leaf.

This photograph was made by Adam Broomberg and Oliver Chanarin who describe the significant role that text plays in relation to their images. In our digital age, it is rare that a photograph appears outside the context of words. From newspaper photographs to fine art photographs in museums, there is always a context defined by words in captions, titles, essays and reviews. Photographs alone are often inadequate for telling stories.

Spiritual Blogging

The primary focus of this chapter is the description and analysis of an exemplary postdigital artwork in the form an autoethnographic blogart project that turns the ancient biblical narrative into a mirror in which people today can see themselves. I transformed the year-long *Torah Tweets* blogart project into the blog *Creating a Spiritual Blog of Your Life* (2014). After a year of weekly blog posts, the *Torah Tweets* blog begins at the end since a blog displays its narrative in reverse chronological order with the most recent post appearing first. I created the *Creating a Spiritual Blog of Your Life* blog to reverse the order of the *Torah Tweets* blog so that it begins with "In the beginning."

The *Torah Tweets* blogart project was created by my wife, artist Miriam Benjamin, and me to celebrate our 52nd year of marriage. During each of the 52 weeks of our 52nd year, we posted photographs with a text of Tweets that relates the biblical narrative to our lives. It was disseminated worldwide through the blogosphere and Twitterverse. We invited other couples, individuals, and families to celebrate their lives through creating their own spiritual blog. The enthusiastic response to our blogart project, prompted me to write the book *Photograph God: Creating a Spiritual Blog of Your Life* (2015) to teach people to use their imagination for discovering how the biblical narrative provides fresh insights for seeing the spiritual dimensions of their daily lives. It has received praise from people of different faiths and spiritual traditions.

The millennia-old tradition for writing the biblical narrative is echoed in the structure of digital media. The Hebrew narrative unfolds from a Torah scroll as it is read from right to left. A blog tells its story as the reader scrolls down. The symbolic significance of scrolling is so strong that if a Torah scroll is not available for the public reading of the weekly biblical portion in synagogue, it is not read at all. The exact same words printed in a codex book form convey the wrong message. A spiritual message trapped between two rectangular covers loses its open-ended life-giving flow. The medium is an integral part of the message.

Professor Michael Bielicky (2010), director of the Institute for Postdigital Narrative at ZKM, Europe's foremost research center for art and new media, writes how digital writing integrating visual and verbal media is creating new story-telling formats. In *The Art of Biblical Narrative*, University of California Berkeley professor Robert Alter explains that the Bible "has a great deal to teach anyone interested in narrative because its seemingly simple, wonderfully complex art offers such splendid illustrations of the primary possibilities of narrative" (xiv).

Torah Tweets

An exemplary model of digital writing is the integration of photographic images and Tweet texts in the *Torah Tweets* blogart narrative. Tweets are text-based posts of up to 140 characters posted on the Twitter social networking website. Limiting the number of words in the *Torah Tweets* blogart sentences to 140 characters is a creative challenge that imitates the Torah itself which does not waste words. Sequences of Torah Tweets can be like bursts of bird song that sometimes gain a haiku-like poetic flavor; 140 is the numerical value (*gematria*) of the word *hakel*, which means 'to gather people together to share a Torah learning experience' as in *Leviticus* 8:3 and *Deuteronomy* 4:10.

Below are the texts of four of the fifty-two posts in the *Torah Tweets* blogart project. I selected these posts since they explore language and writing. The images integrated with Tweet texts of all fifty-two posts can be accessed at http://bibleblogyourlife.blogspot.com.

Art is a Computer Angel

Vayetze/Went away (Genesis 28:10–32:3)

> "He [Jacob] had a vision in a dream. A ladder was standing on the ground and its top reached up toward heaven; and behold! Divine angels were ascending and descending on it." (Genesis 28:12)

We enjoyed sitting together in the Metropolitan Museum of Art print room holding Rembrandt's drawings and etchings of angels in our hands.

Mel painted on subway posters and screen printed digitized Rembrandt angels and spiritual messages from underground:

"Divine angels ascend and descend." (Genesis 28:12) *"They start by going up and afterwards go down"* (Rashi) *"Have you seen angels ascending from the NYC subways?"* (Alexenberg)

Art is a computer angel. The biblical term for art (MeLekHeT MakHSheVeT) is feminine. The masculine form is computer angel (MaLakH MakHSheV).

The biblical words for angel and food are written with the same four letters to tell us that angels are spiritual messages arising from everyday life.

We chose an image of an ascending angel to digitize and send on a circumglobal flight on 4 October 1989, Rembrandt's 320th memorial day.

We sent it via satellite from the AT&T building in NY to Amsterdam to Jerusalem to Tokyo to Los Angeles, returning to NY the same afternoon.

The cyberangel not only circled our planet, it flew into tomorrow and back into yesterday, arriving in Tokyo on 5 Oct. and LA on 4 Oct.

In Tokyo, the 28 faxed sheets were assembled in Ueno Park and then rearranged as a ribbon ascending the steps of a Shinto chapel.

As we assembled the cyberangel on its return to NY five hours after it had left, TV news sent it into ten million North American homes.

The AP story of our angel flight appeared in 60 newspapers each with a different headline. AT&T featured it in its Annual Report.

See the photographs for this blog post at http://bibleblogyourlife.blogspot.co.il/2014/01/genesis-7-art-is-computer-angel.html

One 304,805-Letter Word

Vayikra/And He Called (Leviticus 1:1–6:7)

> *"BeforetheeyesofallthehouseofisraelinalltheirtravelsANDgodcalledtomosesspeakingtohimfromthetent ofthemeetinghesaidspeaktothechildrenofisrael"* (The last words of Exodus linked to the first words of Leviticus as when the entire Torah was written as a single word.)

The first letter of the first word of *Leviticus*, *Vayikr³*, begins with the letter *vav* meaning AND, and ends with an unusually small letter *alef.*

Vav (AND) links the last sentence of *Exodus* to the first of *Leviticus* in a continuous flow like a Torah scroll unwinding.

Small *alef* reminds us of to a time when the entire Torah was written as one continuous word like the on-going flow of life.

The single 304,805-letter Torah was divided into the 79,847 words in the Torah scroll we read today.

When the Torah scroll is rewound annually, *lamed*, the last letter of the Torah connects to *beit*, the first letter, to spell *lev*.

Lev means 'heart.' The heart of the Torah is where the end of the Torah flows into its beginning.

See the photographs and full text for this blog post at http://bibleblogyourlife.blogspot.co.il/2014/01/leviticus-1-one-304805-letter-word.html.

All the Torah in a Potato

Behukotai/In my statues (Leviticus 26:3–27:34)

> "If you will walk in my statutes . . . I will keep my sanctuary in your midst." (Leviticus 26:3, 11)

Behukotai, the final chapter of *Leviticus*, sums up both the third book of the Bible and the entire vision of our Torah Tweets blogart project.

This blog begins with the Torah quote that sets its direction: "*For the Lord thy God walketh in the midst of thy camp.*" (Deuteronomy 23:15).

The first Lubavitcher Rebbe explains that the word *hok* (statute) is derived from the same root as engraving, hewing or carving out.

An engraved letter does not exist as a distinct entity independent of the material out of which it is carved.

Hok suggests that Torah study should be like carving letters out of everyday life so that Torah and our lives are integrally one.

This mode of Torah study is a deeper level than study from hand-written or printed letters that join ink and paper—two separate things.

The Talmud invites us to read *HaLakHaH* (Jewish law) as *HaLikHaH* (walking).

Walk in my statutes teaches that we best come to know through movement in Torah spaces creatively carved out of our lives.

If we integrate Torah with our life story, we will be rewarded with material blessings of bountiful crops and abundant fruit.

All the Torah is in a potato if we reveal it by carving out Hebrew letters that have no separate existence from the potato itself.

The blessings in the opening verses of this Torah portion begin with the letter *alef* and end with *tav*.

Alef to *tav* represents the entire alphabet, *alef* the 1st letter and *tav* the last. The middle letter *lamed* in the word *teLekhu*/walk means to learn.

I carved the first, middle, and last letters of the Hebrew alphabet. See the photographs at http://bibleblogyourlife.blogspot.co.il/2014/01/leviticus-11-all-torah-in-potato.html.

KUZU = God in Motion

Ekev/Because (Deuteronomy 7:12–11:25)

> "Bind them [Torah words] as a sign upon your arm and let them be an ornament between your eyes. Teach your children to discuss them, when you sit in your home,

while you walk on the way, and when you retire and arise. And write them on the doorposts of your houses and gates." (Deuteronomy 11:18–20)

KUZU is written up-side-down on the outside of parchment scrolls placed in a *mezuzah* housing attached to doorposts in Jewish homes.

KUZU sets God *YHVH* in Motion.

On the inside of this mini-Torah scroll is *"Hear O Israel, God YHVH is our Lord ELOHAYNU, God YHVH is One"* (Deuteronomy 6:4)

K-U-Z-U is spelled with each of the Hebrew letters that follow Y-H-V-H. K follows Y; U follows H; Z follows V; and U follows H.

It is as if we were to write GOD as HPE, H being the letter following G, P the letter following O, and E the letter following D.

KUZU is written to teach that God, *YHVH* (Is-Was-Will be), cannot be experienced as a static object, but rather as dynamic process.

KUZU is written up-side-down to invite us to learn Torah with our children from multiple vantage points as part of the flow of life.

Miriam created home size and synagogue size stoneware *mezuzah* housings in her ceramics studio.

She made a silver *mezuzah* housing as a medusa with tentacles that move when touched. The word *mezuzah* is related to *zaz* (move).

In Guatemala, Mel carved a *mezuzah* housing from mahogany wood spiraling around a test tube capped with a 13 petal rose.

A Jew spirals a leather strap around his arm flowing out from the *tefillin* box. He then forms the branching Hebrew letter *shin* on his hand.

Spirals and branches symbolize living systems, from spiraling palms to branching cedars and from DNA to our circulatory and nervous systems.

"It [Torah] is a tree of life to those who grasp it. A righteous person will flourish like a date palm, like a Lebanon cedar he will grow tall." (Proverbs 4:2; Psalm 92:13)

See the photographs at http://bibleblogyourlife.blogspot.co.il/2014/01/deuteronomy-3-kuzu-god-in-motion.html.

From Deconstruction to Reconstruction

A postdigital way of reading texts goes beyond decoding a message to ceaseless questioning of interweaving texts and images through thoughtful play with contradictory messages and multiple references. Digital writing invites play in earnest that creates opportunities for popular participation and alternative viewpoints. French philosopher Jacques Derrida calls this way of relating to texts a deconstructivist impulse in which the reader looks inside one text for another and dissolves one text into another. Derrida considers collage/montage as the primary form of postmodern discourse.

Artist Lowry Burgess (1999) extends Derrida's concept of deconstruction in reading literature into reconstruction in the visual arts. Burgess, the creator of the first artwork launched by NASA to circle our planet and art professor at Carnegie Mellon University, contends that the earlier art forms such as painting and sculpture do not live comfortably in the postmodern reality.

> They want to be more dynamic, more rapid, more explorative, and inquisitive; they want to be more democratic, more synaesthetic, more polyvalent, more free-associative. In other words, this new framework demands a de-gestalting and fragmentation—then a re-assembly on another plane of consciousness.

The biblical narrative offers us an image of the ultimate deconstruction of a text and its reconstruction at different levels of consciousness. Moses took the "Made by God" stone tablets with the text of the Ten Commandments and smashed them to bits. The "Made by God" text was deconstructed so that it could be reconstructed by a human hand. The Torah is received to this day written by the hand of a scribe on a spiral scroll rather than engraved by God on stone tablets. In the Talmud, we are told that Moses was praised for his physical act of deconstruction to free the letters from the rectangular form of the Tablets to be reformulated by human hands on spiraling scrolls linking the end to the beginning in an endless flow.

The traditional Jewish method of reading biblical texts is a far more extensive deconstructive process than Derrida discusses. It moves beyond deconstruction as alternative readings of texts to morphological dissection that frees up the letters forming words to be reconfigured in ways that create fresh meanings. It even extends to subatomic deconstruction of texts by finding significance in the shapes of the Hebrew letters and configurations of their parts. The ancient Hebrew Torah text still in use today is written as lines of consonants without vowels and punctuation to call attention to each letter and invite multiple readings of words and sentences by their ambiguity. It is as if the Bible begins, "n th bgnnng gd crtd th hvns nd th rth." If a single one of the 304,805 letters in the hand-written Torah scroll is missing, incomplete, or if ink chips off one small part of a letter, then the entire scroll is unfit for public reading.

There are a number of traditional systems for seeing through the text rendering it diaphanous through play with letter relationships and combinations. Rabbi Moshe Cordevaro, a central figure in the group of kabbalists living in sixteenth century Tzfat, Israel, wrote that knowledge of the Torah's secrets can be discovered through combinations: numerical letter values (gematria), letter permutations, exchanging first with last letters (ATBaSh), shapes of letters, first and last verses, skipping letters, and letter combinations (notaricon/acronyms).

The Talmud teaches that there are seventy different viewpoints from which to understand every biblical verse. Four levels of reading a text in the acronym PaRDeS are the simple literal meaning of the words (P'saht), hints of innate significance (Remez), homiletic interpretations (Drosh), and the mystical meanings hidden in the white spaces between the black letters (Sod). Through PaRDeS, we learn that Jacob's ladder was a spiral staircase for bringing Torah from heaven to earth as a metaphor for Mount Sinai from the Hebrew words for "ladder," "spiral," and "Sinai" all sharing the numerical value of 130. Since each Hebrew letter has a numerical equivalent, we can understand a text by calculating the values of words and relating them to each other. This numerical method of reading is called gematria.

The shape of each of Hebrew letters carries profound messages. Unlike English letters written sitting on a line below them, a Hebrew scribe suspends letters from a line above. This top line from which the Hebrew letters hang symbolizes the boundary between the writing and ideas that exist beyond the text. None of the Hebrew letters breaks through the barrier except the letter lamed. The name of the letter lamed also means "to learn" and is the root of Hebrew words related to studying and teaching such Talmud, the major compilation of Jewish creative thought. Learning in Judaism invites breaking through the barrier and soaring to new heights of insight and understanding. Unlike the English term "educated man," which in past tense tells us that learning has been completed, the comparable Hebrew term talmid hakham means "a wise learner," one who is forever a student whose learning never ceases to break through barriers to higher levels of knowledge.

Reading biblical words as acronyms is a method called *notaricon*. For example, the Bible's central affirmation of monotheism, "Hear, O Israel, God is our Lord, God is One" (Deuteronomy 6:4), can be read as synaesthetic integration of auditory and visual senses by linking this verse to a second biblical verse, "Raise your eyes on high and see Who created these"

(Isaiah 40:26). These two biblical portions are read together on the same Sabbath in synagogue. The Hebrew word for "Hear" is SheMA, is spelled Shin, Mem, Ayin. It is an acronym for Se'u Marom Aynaykhem, "Raise your eyes on high."

The ultimate deconstruction of the biblical text is told in a Hasidic tale about two Torah scholars who grew up as inseparable friends. They were learning partners from childhood through their rabbinic studies, parting only after being appointed to posts as rabbis in two separate towns. Every Friday each sent the other a letter that became the basis for their Sabbath sermons the next morning. A faithful messenger traveled two hours each way on horseback braving highwaymen, stormy weather, and muddy dirt roads for a number of years. One day, a fierce gust of wind sent his rabbi's letter flying out of the pouch on the side of his horse. He immediately dismounted to chase the letter. The wax seal on the envelope broke and the letter flew out. As he retrieved the letter, he glanced at it and was shocked to see that it was a blank sheet of paper. "Why would his rabbi send an empty page to his colleague?" he asked himself. He stuffed it back into the envelope and delivered it. As he left with the return letter, curiosity over-whelmed him and he opened it only to find it too was a blank sheet of paper. Infuriated that he had braved all sorts of dangers to faithfully deliver empty pages, he confronted his rabbi as he handed him the blank sheet. The great rabbi explained that the deepest secrets of the Torah are found in the white spaces between the Hebrew letters. He assured his faithful messenger that he and his beloved friend could only communicate the most profound ideas with each other by writing with the white spaces.

This tale has its parallel in contemporary arts. Blank white canvases presented as artworks inspired the presentation of silence as a music composition in which a musician observed a blank score and played nothing. Robert Rauschenberg exhibited sets of rectangular canvases that he had painted entirely white. His artworks were titled: "White Painting [one panel]," "White Painting [three panel]," White Painting [four panel]," White Painting [seven panel]." Rauschenberg deconstructed the text of Western art to the zero point eliminating all imagery thereby freeing all imagery for recombination in infinite numbers of new relationships. Inspired by Rauschenberg's white paintings, composer John Cage created his silent piece 4'33", a work in three movements. A year after Rauschenberg's show, his 4'33' was "played" by a pianist in a concert hall seated quietly at a piano for four minutes and 33 seconds signaling the beginning and end of each movement by opening and closing the keyboard cover (Mopps and Davidson).

Digital Writing with White Spaces in The Cloud

Digital writers write with white spaces, with invisible spaces of bits and bytes. Nicholas Negroponte, founding director of the MIT Media Lab, explains in *Being Digital* (1995) that a bit has no color, size, or weight, and it can travel at the speed of light. It is a state of being that is on or off, true or false, up or down, in or out. For practical purposes, we consider it to be 1 or 0. In *(IN)VISIBLE: Learning to Act in the Metaverse* (2008), Stefan Sonvilla-Weiss, head of the institute of art and education at the University of Art and Design Linz, Austria, explores the cultural and educational impact of digital culture as it straddles invisible and visible realms. His "Lifelogging" chapter offers fresh insights for spiritual blogging.

I wrote this chapter in The Cloud by writing in Dropbox situated somewhere in The Cloud unknown to me. The Cloud is a term that describes a vast number of computers interconnected through a real-time communication network such as the Internet. The Cloud appears to be cloudy because it is unpredictable which paths data packets will take when transmitted across a packet-switched network that links your computer, tablet, and smartphone to every other one in the world. The Cloud is a living network of networks of networks blanketing our planet.

When you post texts and images on your blog or on Facebook, LinkedIn, Twitter, or other sites in The Cloud, you distribute them worldwide, sharing them with all who enter into The Cloud. When you are spiritually blogging your life, you are building a blog in The Cloud that continues to live on in The Cloud, accessible to billions of others.

The Cloud is a thought-provoking metaphor for an invisible God everyplace that can be revealed to us anyplace that we invite divine light to illuminate our retinal screen. That you can see nothing at all looking at the motherboard or memory of your computer with the most powerful microscope is extended to every other digital device in The Cloud. However, the screen on your computer, tablet, or smartphone can reveal every photo, video, and text in a growing global organism that we call The Cloud.

My book *Photograph God: Creating a Spiritual Blog of Your Life* (2015) teaches people of all faiths how to integrate digital writing with digital images in the age of ubiquitous smartphones. In all of human history, never has there been such a proliferation of images. People are whipping smartphones out of their pockets to snap pictures of anything that catches their fancy to share with others through the world-wide Cloud of interconnecting networks. This global smartphone culture and its explosion of image generation invites the invention of creative forms of digital writing to interweave with digital images in imaginative ways.

Works Cited

Adams, Tony E., and Stacy H. Jones. *Autoethnography: Understanding Qualitative Research.* Oxford UP, 2014.

Alexenberg, Mel. "Art with Computers: The Human Spirit and the Electronic Revolution." *The Visual Computer: International Journal of Computer Graphics*, vol. 4, no. 1, 1988, pp. 1–3.

——. *The Future of Art in a Postdigital Age: From Hellenistic to Hebraic Consciousness.* Intellect Books/U of Chicago P, 2011.

——. *jerUSAlem-USA*, 2009. jerusalem–usa.blogspot.com.

——. *Photograph God: Creating a Spiritual Blog of Your Life.* CreateSpace, 2015.

——. *Wikiartists*, 2008. wikiartists.blogspot.com.

Alexenberg, Mel, and Otto Piene. *LightsOROT: Spiritual Dimensions of the Electronic Age.* MIT Center for Advanced Visual Studies and Yeshiva University Museum, 1988.

Alexenberg, Mel, and Miriam Benjamin. *Torah Tweets: A Postdigital Biblical Commentary as a Blogart Narrative Images*, 2010. torahtweets.blogspot.com.

Alter, Robert. *The Art of Biblical Narrative.* Basic, 1981.

Bielicky, Michael. Institute for Postdigital Narrative, 2010. https://vimeo.com/18704694 and http://infoart.hfg-karlsruhe.de/.

Blackwell, Lewis. *Photo-Wisdom: Master Photographers on Their Art.* Blackwell/Chronicle, 2009.

Burgess, Lowry. "Body and Garden in Zero State: The Disembodiment of the Embodied; The Embodiment of the Disembodied." International Dance and Technology Conference, Arizona State University, 1999. Conference presentation.

Kaplan, Aryeh. *Sefer Yetzirah: The Book of Creation.* Samuel Weiser, 1990.

Manovich, Lev. *The Language of New Media.* MIT Press, 2001.

Mopps, Walter, and Davidson, Susan. *Robert Rauschenberg: A Retrospective.* New York: Guggenheim Museum, 1997.

Negroponte, Nicolas. *Being Digital.* Knopf, 1995.

Sonvilla-Weiss, Stefan. *(IN)VISIBLE: Learning to Act in the Metaverse.* Springer, 2008.

34

MODES OF MEANING, MODES OF ENGAGEMENT

Pragmatic Intersections of Adaptation Theory and Multimodal Composition

Bri Lafond and Kristen Macias

Multimodality is not new to composition, but the field largely has not taken into account the ways in which other academic disciplines theorize equivalent composing processes as they apply to multimodal texts. Essentially, while multimodality feels like a cutting-edge development in the writing classroom, many treat multimodal composing as merely a difference in product rather than process; we use our "tried and true" methods of composing traditional texts and merely substitute a website or short film for the end product. This tendency unnecessarily limits our vision as instructors for the composing prospects of new media, and, unfortunately, we pass this limited vision on to our students. Further, though there are some texts within writing studies that explore multimodality as a concept, there are fewer texts that provide practical guidance as to how to implement multimodality as pedagogy.

What insights can we, as writing instructors, glean from other disciplines in implementing our own digital multimodal projects? As Jonathan Alexander and Jacqueline Rhodes point out in *On Multimodality: New Media in Composition Studies,*

> we need to consider more critically our disciplinary divides. . . . We understand the importance of authoring "composed" essays . . . [b]ut we want to also make room for the kind of "writing"—and the kind of subjects—that challenges such composure, that offers rich and (yes) excessive ways of thinking and writing. (104)

By maintaining strict "disciplinary divides," Alexander and Rhodes assert that "certain histories, certain excesses, and certain compositional possibilities are left out" (104). Re-envisioning the borders between disciplines not as divisive but as productively liminal, we begin to engage in an interdisciplinary exchange that leads to more mutually beneficial conversations through the cross-pollination of ideas.

One potential source of interdisciplinary inspiration comes from the field of adaptation theory. Since the advent of film as a medium, scholars have considered the ways in which literature becomes transposed onto film. Subsequently, adaptation theory has expanded to consider the ways in which transmediation occurs across multiple genres, such as adapting a video game into a movie or a graphic novel into a television show. In the past decade, adaptation theory has experienced its own renaissance with germinal work by theorists such as Linda Hutcheon expanding how adapted storytelling is understood. When we first encountered the work of Hutcheon in her book, *A Theory of Adaptation*, we found ourselves drawn to her descriptions of transmediation: the process by which an adapter transposes a text from one medium to another. Much of what Hutcheon describes is, in fact, rhetorical, though she herself never uses the term "rhetoric." In putting together our own writing classes, we have been inspired by adaptation theory as both a way to enhance existing models of multimodal composing and a guideline to assist students more explicitly in crafting their ideas to reach different audiences using various modes.

Although adaptation theorists use a different vocabulary to describe transmediation—transposing a text from one medium to another—the processes they describe are rhetorical in nature, detailing the ways in which an artist tailors a story to a new rhetorical situation, accounting for the unique affordances and constraints of the target medium. By focusing more explicitly on the meta-cognitive processes a composer uses in adapting a text from one medium to another, Hutcheon complicates the author/audience binary in her discussions of audience engagement with adapted texts. Thus, we believe adaptation theory provides students with an important context for understanding the choices they make in transmediating texts for digital media.

By treating multimodality as "writing with a twist," writing instructors unnecessarily limit the possibilities afforded in looking beyond the traditional paper for means of expression. Instead, by incorporating the "particular histories" and "particular rhetorical affordances" that other disciplines have developed surrounding alternative modalities, writing instructors position themselves as informed makers and consumers of multimodal texts. In adopting the position of interdisciplinary intermediary, writing instructors embrace the productive both/and liminal position as opposed to the reductive either/or of a disciplinary border dispute.

Within the field of composition, the various "modes" that make up multimodality are perhaps best articulated by the New London Group's "A Pedagogy of Multiliteracies: Designing Social Futures." In this influential piece, the Group articulates "multiliteracies" as "the increasing complexity and inter-relationship of different modes of meaning" (198). They outline six major modes, alternately referred to as "functional grammars": Linguistic Design, Visual Design, Audio Design, Gestural Design, Spatial Design, and Multimodal Design, with Multimodal Design "represent[ing] the patterns of interconnection among the other modes" (198). Despite articulating these six modes, the emphasis in the original article remains on the principles of Linguistic Design with only passing reference to "Designs for Other Modes of Meaning." Although the authors stress that "all meaning-making is multimodal" and thus relies on several of the established functional grammars, the Group does not spend much time interrogating the materiality of various modal choices (201). Moreover, for all the Group's emphasis on "situated practice" in regard to pedagogy, they do not focus on how audiences or experiencers of multimodal texts are situated within particular rhetorical contexts (204). This idea of what we call a "situated audience" is something we will return to later on.

Though the New London Group's modes of meaning have been helpful for us in articulating to students the kinds of choices they make in composing for multimodal contexts, we have also found that these modes can be limiting. The emphasis remains on the product itself rather than how that product functions within a specific rhetorical context. We might see this emphasis as an extension of the process versus product issue identified by Alexander and Rhodes: rather than "address[ing] the specific invention, delivery, and rhetorical possibilities" of alternative modalities, we settle for the novelty of difference in product.

For example, if a professor tasks her students with transmediating their existing research papers into digital audio podcasts, a student may interpret the assignment by producing an audio track of himself reading his paper aloud with no other substantial changes. In one way, he has fulfilled the assignment: he has produced an audio-based text that serves to re-focus the text for a hearing audience. However, the student has obviously not taken into consideration the particular affordances and constraints of the audio medium, and he has not considered the user experience of his new audience. To consider audience in a meaningful way, the student must imagine how the listener will engage with his new text; he must consider the situated audience.

Hutcheon explores audience experience at length, focusing less on the "how to" aspect of composing and more on the material implications of creation, transmission, reception, and transmediation. Hutcheon does not simply focus on the author's composing process; she also details the process of transmission from the text to the audience: "We [the audience] can be told or shown a story, each in a range of different media. However, the perspective, and thus the grammar" can also shift in these various mediated forms (22). Thus, Hutcheon addresses audience reception in her three-pronged "modes of engagement": the telling mode, the showing mode, and the interactive mode. Adding Hutcheon's modes of engagement to the New London Group's six modes of meaning provides a more complete perspective to multimodal composition; rather than focusing just on the author's process of composing, Hutcheon brings into focus the audience's process of engaging with texts: the situated audience.

Readers engage with different textual forms with varying levels of immersion. Traditional texts, for example, fall primarily under what Hutcheon calls the "telling" mode. Within the telling mode, the writer's words "direct" the audience, but the words on the page serve to spark the audience's imagination: the narrative exists most vividly in the individual imagination of the reader, thus giving much agency over to the audience itself. Hutcheon emphasizes the power of the audience when she points out the passive nature of the traditional text: the reader decides when to pick the text up and decides in what order s/he will read that text. To return to the language of rhetoric, the telling mode (along with each mode of engagement) has particular affordances and constraints. By engaging readers in "the realm of imagination," one affordance of traditional text is that readers feel a more intimate connection to what they are reading.

Simultaneously, by enhancing reader agency, the writer is constrained in how much s/he can direct the reader's interpretation. No matter how explicit or directive the writing, a reader's imaginative engagement can redirect interpretation. Take, for instance, the film adaptation of Suzanne Collins' popular young adult series *The Hunger Games*. Many fans reacted negatively to the casting of African American actress Amandla Stenberg in the role of Rue, tweeting out such sentiments as "Awkward moment when Rue is some black girl and not the little blonde innocent girl you picture" (qtd. in Holmes). Despite the fact that Collins explicitly describes Rue as having "dark brown skin and eyes," readers projected their own image of innocence onto the character. What might Collins have done to combat this interpretation? We do not think there is a clear answer to that question, but being aware that such (mis)interpretations can occur may be useful for students in composing their own projects.

If students take these limitations into consideration when crafting their intended audience experience, they may very well be able to enhance their work. To return to our student who is transmediating his research project into an audio podcast, knowing that his audio podcast will only engage with the audience through the aural mode, he may add specific directives within his text to engage with other senses more effectively. For example, he may engineer sound effects to make listeners feel as if they are immersed in that location or incorporate musical cues that enhance the tone of particular passages.

Hutcheon's next mode of engagement—the "showing" mode—"immerses [the audience] through the perception of the aural and the visual . . . mov[ing] from the imagination to the realm of direct perception" (22–3). In this mode of engagement, audience agency is somewhat diminished: rather than the locus of control resting in the individual reader, the audience watching a film or play is "caught in an unrelenting, forward-driving story" (23). In reference to the showing mode, Hutcheon writes that "sound . . . can enhance, reinforce, or even contradict the visual and verbal aspects" (23). The showing mode is, therefore, truly multimodal. By bringing together disparate elements of the New London Group's modes of meaning and thus embodying the Multimodal Meaning, the showing mode integrates different kinds of expression into a single text. This essential multimodality illustrates the affordances of showing modes: by engaging the audience on multiple sensory levels, the author directs more of the audience's experience of the text. Take, for example, the Internet phenomenon in which users re-cut film trailers for existing movies to entirely change audience perceptions of the text. One particularly popular example of this revision is "The Shining Recut" in which YouTuber neochosen edits footage from Stanley Kubrick's *The Shining* and adds an upbeat narration and Peter Gabriel's "Solsbury Hill" to re-present the film as a wacky romantic comedy. Using the same visuals but changing the aural mode of communication shifts audience perception of the text as a whole.

Individual audience interpretation does still exist; however, there are fewer constraints—from an authorial perspective—on articulating the writer's vision. Therefore, the showing mode solidifies the writer's vision of his/her own text, but this solidifying process simultaneously rejects nuance and ambiguity that may be a part of the original authorial intent. For our students, practical limitations come into effect in the showing mode: while their pens (or laptops) can easily conjure up sprawling alien worlds filled with fantastic creatures, barring a multimillion dollar budget and a talented CGI team, articulating that same vision in the showing mode for a class project may be difficult.

Hutcheon's final mode of engagement—the "interactive" mode—is the mode most closely associated with digital media; this is the mode in which "as audience members, we interact *with* stories . . . from virtual reality to machinima" (22). Interactivity emphasizes individual audience agency by allowing the individual to shape their experience of the narrative. In a video game, for example, the player controls where their avatar goes, how s/he moves, how s/he engages with conflict, etc. While the individual player shapes his/her path through this kind of narrative and controls how an avatar engages in gameplay, the range of choices—though seemingly rhizomatic—is in fact controlled by the game designer.

One example of this can be found in the video game *No Man's Sky*. Promising infinite worlds to explore, unlimited lifeforms to discover, and endless opportunities to do whatever you might desire as a space explorer, the game ultimately is limited by the capabilities and imaginations of the designers. Take the unlimited lifeforms, for instance. Although a multitude of combinations of creatures can be found among the limitless planets, each individual species is actually a finite combination of models of one head, two sets of legs, a torso, and a possible tail and/or wings. Once players have explored half a dozen planets in this supposedly infinite universe, they begin to realize that the same lifeform parts keep appearing thus breaking the illusion and highlighting the rhetorical constraints of what it truly means for a text to be interminable. Video games, though large and oftentimes engaging an audience for much longer stretches of time than other texts, are still subject to the restraints of the designers, budget, and technology. While the technology now exists for students to create their own video games without much expertise, students are limited by the material constraints of video game design software complicating the process of creating what they have envisioned.

Allowing that the various modes of engagement create different dynamics in audience reception, this does not mean that the same narrative can be plugged into different media without essential changes taking place in what the narrative is and what it means. Moreover, Hutcheon writes that

> the lines of differentiation [between various modes] are not as clear as we might expect. The private and individual experience of reading is, in fact, closer to the private visual and domestic spaces of television, radio, DVD, video, and computer than it is to the public and communal viewing experience in a dark theater of any kind . . . our level and kind of engagement are different. (27)

Hutcheon, again, emphasizes the reception element, taking into consideration the audience experience as an element of how the text is interpreted. Whether the reception experience is "private" and "domestic" or "public" and "communal" ultimately affects how an individual absorbs and, thus, interprets a text. Further, Hutcheon reminds us that

> ways of engaging with stories do not . . . take place in a vacuum. We [audiences] engage in time and space, within a particular society and a general culture. The contexts of creation and reception are material, public, and economic as much as they are cultural, personal, and aesthetic. (28)

Again, Hutcheon does not use rhetorical terminology, but what she describes here is undoubtedly rhetorical context: the textual composer must take into account their target audience, their own exigence, the particular *kairos*, and the affordances and constraints of their chosen medium in order to best craft their message.

For students, awareness of the ways in which their audience will experience their texts can give them further insight into their composing processes. If a student knows that her final video project will be presented to the rest of her class as part of the evaluation process, she may decide to incorporate subtitles into her video to increase accessibility for her international student classmates who have indicated that they comprehend more from reading a text than hearing one, or she may choose to add a moment's pause after a joke to allow for potential audience laughter. Considering the experiential level of the text can be highly context-dependent, awareness of this textual dimension can definitely shape both the multimodal composing process as well as the end product.

The act of adapting a text to a new context automatically necessitates change. If one were to take a novel and transmediate it into an audiobook, this action would seemingly not require any adaptive consideration. Someone would merely have to record themselves reading aloud: what adaptation is necessary? However, taking into consideration Hutcheon's articulation of modes of engagement, one can see that there are, in fact, many adaptive choices to be made in this scenario and one ought to take into account the particular affordances and constraints of the new context. Since the performance now takes place beyond the written word, we have exited the "realm of imagination" and entered the "realm of direct perception." Thus, the adaptation must concretize the novel's narrator and characters. For example, the novel *Ready Player One* by Ernest Cline was recently adapted into an audiobook read, not by the author, but by actor Wil Wheaton. Wheaton did not just get into the recording booth and read the book directly, but instead he and the director made choices based upon the situated audience. He had to decide whether or not to do different voices for each character, where to put intonations, and how loud or soft to speak certain lines. One particularly interesting decision was whether to read aloud the scores of the characters that are presented as visual tables in several chapters in the written novel. In the audiobook version, Wheaton does not describe the visual accoutrements to these tables. This choice means a loss of the visual experience included in the original written text, but the increased clarity makes sense for the listening audience. The questions we might consider in order to make this "simple" adaptation happen are extensive. While we don't necessarily want to bog our students down with an unending stream of questions, getting student writers to question their base-level assumptions promotes both critical thinking and creativity.

As Hutcheon asserts, "Transposition to another medium, or even moving within the same one, always means change or, in the language of the new media 'reformatting.' And there will always be both gains and losses" (16). These changes may be as simple as the act of simplification for some media: cutting down on information that is presented in the original format in order to fit into a new format. Hutcheon calls this simplification an act of "subtraction or contraction" (19). For example, let's say a student takes their personal discourse analysis paper and decides to transmediate that narrative into a digital storybook for children; this kind of transmediation would likely necessitate a fair amount of what Hutcheon calls "subtraction or contraction" in order to make the narrative both short enough and simple enough for a younger audience. However, such a transmediation would also necessitate a shift in the mode of engagement: while the traditional text version of the project relies primarily on the telling mode to get its points across, the children's version—taking into account genre conventions—would have to incorporate the showing mode in the form of visual accompaniment, the aural mode in the form of accompanying music, and the interactive mode in the form of clicking to turn the page and to set in motion embedded animations.

The process of adaptation does not, of course, only focus on subtraction; Hutcheon asserts that "Adaptation is an act of appropriating or salvaging, and this is always a double process of interpreting and then creating something new" (20). Students might well keep this directive in mind as they make choices regarding their own multimodal projects. For example, in the aforementioned illustration of transmediating a personal discourse analysis paper into a digital children's book, the student may find that the anecdotes they originally included in their traditional essay may not be appropriate for a younger audience. Instead of slavishly maintaining the same writerly moves as the original text, the student writer may find that they want to maintain the general narrative arc of the original text, but need to change all the particulars. This version remains an adaptation, just a broader interpretation of the original text.

We have referred throughout this piece to particular applications of Hutcheon's work in the writing classroom, but now we turn to a more specific discussion of the ways in which each of us has applied this enhanced view of multimodality in our own pedagogy. Realizing that rhetoric and adaptation theory are complementary has led us to new ways of approaching multi-modality in the classroom in how we teach our students to both analyze previously adapted texts and create their own multimodal works. Here are some ways in which we have asked students to analyze and to interact with existing texts in order to think more critically about multimodality, organized around Hutcheon's modes of engagement.

Kristen's students have been geared towards creating their own multimodal works in the telling mode with the addition of mini projects to augment traditional major writing assignments. Using adaptation theory as a starting point, students explore various methods of creating their own multimodal texts and think about how those texts might be best rendered. For one mini project, students use the backdrop of the graphic novel *The Walking Dead* to create a character analysis. While mostly in the telling mode, this activity requires that students think about who their audience might be, their exigence for creating their piece, and how the different modes of engagement might best address the needs of the assignment. Directed to construct the project in any way they see fit, students create projects that range from online dating profiles to assassin's target notes to digital dossiers with the word "CONFIDENTIAL" virtually stamped across each page. Students incorporate digital tools at their disposal while creating intricate documents that might rival professional departmental memos. With this project, students do not just explore what they are creating, but take into account how their intended audience might interact with their telling of this aspect of the original story. An online dating profile might only highlight the desirable aspects of a character while an assassin's notes might highlight physical descriptions and locations of where the character has been. Adaptation theory helps them explore what their situated audience would need to know to best interact with their project.

To focus on the telling mode in Bri's class, as part of a final project for a writing class, her students researched a topic of their choice that somehow related to 1980s culture and composed their findings for two different rhetorical contexts: a standard research paper for academia and an audio podcast for a more general audience. Students first listened to and analyzed a variety of existing podcasts, writing about the various affordances, constraints, and modes that were represented in these samples. While Bri hoped her students would take this scaffolded analysis into consideration as they created their own projects, she still anticipated that her students would rely on what Hutcheon would call the telling mode and make recordings that adhered closely to their research papers. She was pleasantly surprised by many of her students' final podcasts, as the enhanced consideration of audience made a significant impact on her students' composing choices. For example, one student created a hair and makeup tutorial podcast that offered listeners practical advice mixed with the student's commentary on beauty trends in the 1980s. This student clearly imagined her situated audience and was able to incorporate the interactive mode into her podcast. Another student directed listeners to imagine they were sitting down in front of a television set before playing clips from 1980s newscasts discussing the burgeoning AIDS crisis. While the student only directed listeners through the aural mode of meaning, this directive to "visualize" shows an attempt to engage the "realm of imagination" that Hutcheon aligns with the showing mode.

To examine the showing mode, Kristen's students work in groups to reimagine not the genre, but the socio-political context of the zombie portion of the CDC website. Transposing this neglected website into something more modern and relevant allows students to think about how this government agency is or is not reaching its intended audience. Students deduce that the use of zombies by the CDC is helpful in gaining the attention of the public, but outdated zombie references and poor website design undermine the rhetorical purpose of actually getting citizens prepared for real emergencies. Thus, students imagine how this adaptation of necessary information could be better executed and then attempt to do so themselves through a stronger use of this showing mode. Even though studying rhetoric aids this understanding, simultaneously engaging with adaptation theory "gives rise to [more] potentially active texts" (Covino and Jolliffe 6). These student-created projects showcase what better attention to the modes of engagement can do for even professionally created texts.

Bri's classes play with the showing mode by taking a well-known fairytale and adapting it into different formats in order to understand different rhetorical contexts. One in-class project asks students to work together in groups to transmediate a story such as "The Three Little Pigs" or "Rapunzel" into emoji. This activity asks students to work under very strict constraints: they must articulate the story in only the emoji that are available to them on their cellphones. The activity, thus, offers the class the opportunity to discuss the materiality of their transmediated story with its accompanying affordances and constraints. Moreover, the act of transmediating the story from the mode of telling to the mode of showing positions students to make particular choices about how narrative is represented. For example, the students may try to tell a linear story, covering each plot point of the original narrative; alternatively, they may try to be more representative by creating a version of the main character rather than telling the story itself. Additionally, the differences in technology that students have access to (e.g., iPhones, Android, laptops) lead to discussions about situated audience; in this way, students see that not only do they work within the constraints of a particular medium, but their audiences also receive their texts in constrained ways. Students present their projects to the class as a whole and then write independent reflections on their composing processes, paying particular attention to the various modes of meaning and modes of engagement they focused on in creating their adaptations. These in-class activities allow students to play with various modes of expression, and Hutcheon's vocabulary allows students to describe more articulately the processes they consider in transmediating a text.

Focusing on the interactive mode, Kristen asks her students to process their own ideas about identity through video game avatar creation. For one class, students used the character creation mechanism in the game *Final Fantasy XIV*, an online multiplayer fantasy game that they were playing as a class, to design an avatar using fixed options that fit into the fictional world of Eorzea. Students examined their frustrations with the rhetorical constraints of making a character by seeing how few options there were for creating a character that truly represented who they wanted to be. Students felt particularly stymied by their limited choices for skin tones and character weight, remarking that it felt absurd to be able to make a blue skinned character with fantastical cat ears and a tail but not one that was realistically dark skinned and overweight. By fitting into this virtual world, some students felt forced into an identity that they did not have or want. This encouraged them to explore questions about who the game designers were targeting as their situated audience and then interrogate the rhetorical affordances and constraints of the genre.

Another video game related activity asked students to find something that was not already made into a game and design digital cover art for it while taking into consideration how this might be playable. While many students chose to use books or movies that were not already games, some students went even further, turning a new musical genre and a popular YouTube channel into games. Though not developed into actual games, this activity helped students understand what needs to be included to entice their situated audience into wanting to play their new games.

In Bri's classroom, students have used the interactive mode in unexpected ways. For an assignment that asked students to create an artifact that engaged with Mark Z. Danielewski's novel *House of Leaves*, one student—a music major—chose to write and produce a nine-track album inspired by the novel. This project obviously took advantage of the aural mode of communication, but the student thought about the interactivity inherent in Danielewski's novel which uses text to create shapes and asks readers to solve puzzles alongside the characters, and the student decided to make his album interactive as well. As such, alongside original compositions and covers of songs mentioned in the novel, the student added puzzles for the listener to interact with; for example, he included Morse code messages tapped out in static for the listener to decode and lines of dialogue digitally distorted into haunting screeches and growls that listeners would have to reverse engineer using digital software to fully understand. This student used a mode of communication that he was inherently comfortable composing with—aurality—and accepted the challenge of shaping his composition to engage with audiences interactively.

Another student in Bri's class re-conceptualized her initial ideas for a project once she embraced the possibilities of multimodality and digital composing. Bri offered her students a choice regarding their final project: they could engage with the themes of dystopian fiction by either writing a traditional essay or creating a multimodal project alongside a shorter explanatory meta-essay. One student initially decided to write a traditional essay in which she would look at current events in the United States and argue that Americans are currently living in a dystopia as defined by the conventions of the genre. After starting the writing process, the student was struck by an idea: in order to strengthen the impact of her ideas, she wanted readers of her work to become personally invested in her argument. She used basic website building software to create an interactive online quiz that asked respondents about current events re-framed as hypothetical questions. Based on users answers to the multiple choice questions, they would reach a page telling them whether or not they were currently living in a dystopia followed by an explanatory definition of the dystopian genre. By embracing the interactive mode, the student was able to enhance the exigence for her piece, making for an overall more effective response.

The examples above outline some ways we have used the New London Group's and Hutcheon's modes simultaneously to further engage students in a meta-conversation about digital composing. For us, adaptation theory complements rather than challenges our under-standing of multimodality and the role of composition instructors in guiding students in the creation of multimodal texts. While multimodality is an exciting way to enhance student interest in our courses, there are also many practical reasons to prepare our students for new media contexts. Ultimately, multimodality is less about working with novel textual forms such as video games in order to make students' experiences in our classes fun and more about the meta-conversation that we develop about the composing choices students make to increase rhetorical effectiveness in any given situation.

Works Cited

Alexander, Jonathan, and Jacqueline Rhodes. *On Multimodality: New Media in Composition Studies.* NCTE, 2014.

Covino, William, and David Jolliffe. "What is Rhetoric?" *Rhetoric: Concepts, Definitions, and Boundaries,* edited by William Covino and David Jolliffe. Allyn & Bacon, 1995, pp. 3–26.

Holmes, Anna. "White Until Proven Black: Imagining Race in *Hunger Games.*" *The New Yorker,* 30 Mar. 2012, www.newyorker.com/books/page-turner/white-until-proven-black-imagining-race-in-hunger-games. Accessed 15 Nov. 2016.

Hutcheon, Linda, with Siobhan O'Flynn. *A Theory of Adaptation.* 2006. 2nd ed., Routledge, 2012.

New London Group. "A Pedagogy of Multiliteracies: Designing Social Futures." 1996. *Multimodal Composition: A Critical Sourcebook,* edited by Claire Lutkewitte. Bedford/St Martin's, 2014, pp. 193–217.

"The Shining Recut." *YouTube,* uploaded by neochosen. 7 Feb. 2006, www.youtube.com/watch?v=Kmk VWuP_sO0. Accessed 3 July 2017.

35

VIRTUAL POSTURES

Jeff Rice

I do Bikram yoga twice a week. The other days of the week, I encourage others to join me. In this act of causal argumentation, I am not devoted to my own position regarding yoga's value or health benefits. Even though I supposedly make an argument regarding Bikram, I do not care if anyone else does yoga. That is, whatever I hope to achieve via this argument ("do yoga because I like yoga"), I have no investment in the outcome. In this moment of self-contradiction, I argue as a phatic response to conversation, as a way to pass time, as a side note to whatever else we are discussing, as a reflection on my day, or as a beginning point for other discussion, not because I want to persuade my friends and colleagues to engage in Bikram yoga. My gesture is not persuasive, not in the sense of argument or changing one's position or even in the Burkean sense of attitude, "the power to induce or communicate states of mind to readers" without "practical outcome" (50). While I have no practical outcome in mind, my gesture, instead, is virtual because it holds no representational form or spatial position. It does not mimic or imitate non-virtual positions (such as declarations of meaning or argumentative gestures), as Steve Woolgar explains virtuality: "Not only do new virtual activities sit alongside existing 'real' activities, but the introduction and use of new 'virtual' technologies can actually stimulate more of the corresponding 'real' activity" (17). Instead, my gesture has no correspondence in a so-called real world of interactions and rhetorical engagement. My gesture has no fixed identity. It is located nowhere other than in a posture I perform. My gesture, I claim, is digital because of this virtuality. It is a form of digital writing.

This brief anecdote regarding virtuality does not mean, however, that my gesture lacks substance or value, as Jaron Lanier laments the loss of identification to the various virtual activities that make up digital culture and its online compositions. In what has become a popular critique of virtuality in general, Lanier worries that lack of representation equates a loss of value. A lack of representation, for Lanier, is an effort to obfuscate digital culture's inabilities and shortcomings.

> In a world of digital dignity, each individual will be the commercial owner of any data that can be measured from that person's state or behavior. Treating information as a mask behind which real people are invariably hiding means that digital data will be treated as being consistently valuable, rather than inconsistently valuable. (20)

Lanier's position, as with many positions regarding virtuality, focuses on loss—of the self, of identity, or of meaning. Within the virtual, information hides reality, Lanier suggests, or, in the guise of data, becomes a virtual cloak from which individuality (i.e., a person, a position, an argument, a body of meaning) is hidden. My discussion of yoga, on the other hand, consists of identity and selfhood, only it does so via a virtual state that does not hide data. I have nothing to hide when I say a colleague or friend should join me in yoga. In my virtual gesture, I extend a position.

Marshall McLuhan noted that "any invention or technology is an extension or self-amputation of our physical bodies, and such extension also demands new rations or new equilibriums among the other organs and extensions of the body" (*Understanding* 54). Argument, in the personal moment I offer up, is one such amputation, cut from its traditional role of persuasion and presented as a new ration of virtuality, cloud based positioning (as I will demonstrate shortly), or posturing. The wheel is to the foot, McLuhan famously noted as one type of extension. Argument is to the posture might be another type of extension. The extension, as a state of virtuality, might appear, at first, to be of loss of falsehood to the average discussion of digitality. "Virtuality is an image or space that is not real but appears to be," Nicholas Mirzoeff writes (89). Non-representation, though, is a technological extension of being, in the McLuhan sense, not a question of reality or lack of reality. Non-representation, in the posture example I begin with, is the outcome of technology of the self.

I begin with this banal and seemingly unimportant anecdote regarding yoga, then, for two reasons. First, there is a lack of representational anchor to my argument. Second, I draw attention to the metaphor of the yoga posture in this process of communication without representation. Both of these items, I contend, offer a digital method of expression. I call this method the *virtual posture*. The virtual posture, a state lacking commitment to actual persuasion (and other forms of discourse), is non-representational; it does not stand for a position, belief, or ideology beyond the projection of the statement itself. The virtual posture, as I will show in this chapter, only becomes discourse through engagement. My own relationship with Bikram reflects this gesture. I am not doing yoga for spiritual reasons, mindfulness, infatuation with the East or any other typical, rhetorical posture associated with spending 90 minutes in a hot room. I offer no engagement with either my argument nor posture—on their own. My posture may eventually become part of a larger exchange and thus generate meaning, but until that moment occurs, its virtuality is non-representational.

Bikram yoga provides me with an appropriate metaphor for this process. Attempting to recreate doing yoga in a humid, hot climate, Bikram studios are set at 105 degrees and 50 percent humidity. The yoga is characterized by the repetition of the same twenty-six postures each session, and the same memorized dialogue repeated by the instructor each session. An individual can enter any studio around the world and experience the same twenty-six postures and dialogue. Bikram Choudhury based his twenty-six posture sequence on postures associated with hatha yoga, but his yoga did not exist until he assembled them as something called "Bikram" in the early 1970s. There is no historical tradition that represents Bikram yoga beyond Bikram's extension of another practice into his own. In Bikram yoga, the posture extends, or stretches, the body. Postures are not done in isolation of one another; each builds into the next and off of others in the series. Each posture depends on the other. McLuhan's concept of "extension," too, is a posture. For McLuhan, technology extends bodily elements; objects (radios, computers, telephones, books) network with the body in a non-representational manner in order to extend some part of the senses. Media, as McLuhan defines the term, is an extension, a posture that stretches the body. In that sense, all media extend the body into other bodies. This point holds for material objects (yoga mats, chairs, tables, computers) but also for discourse (argument). The Bikram posture offers one media variation of this process.

Yoga postures have nothing to do with digitality. Yoga postures do not "represent" the digital. Yet, I offer the posture as a metaphor in both the spirit of McLuhan (the unlikely juxtaposition he favored as a media heuristic) and my own work which has typically posed unlikely items as metaphoric of digital culture (cool, Detroit, and craft beer). The virtual posture, I claim, is a form of digital expression shaped by the digital's lack of fixed representation, causality, or even argument in general. With new media, some theorists have focused on the tactility or physicality of the digital, offering a completely opposite view of what I propose here. "Our interactions with digital media," N. Katherine Hayles announced, "are embodied, and they have bodily effects at the physical level" (3). Or Rita Raley championed "tactile media" for its ability to artistically intervene in political issues and disrupt ideology among bodies (of control, of institutions, or of practices). Despite the supposed physicality of new media that theorists argue for, the extension of man—as McLuhan proclaimed—also prompts the virtual as non-representational, or not dependent on one body, but rather dependent on many bodies (such as a series of twenty-six postures or an aggregation of another method), for the production of meaning and not for a disruption or even embodiment. The book may have been an extension of the eye for McLuhan, but the virtual posture, I claim, is an extension of writing. In this chapter, I expand this point in order to clarify the role of the posture as a form of digital expression, one in which interactions construct what we often call the virtual, but which I will conclude with as the cloud.

Non-Representational Writing

Nigel Thrift categorized non-representational theory as an understanding of how "the world is made up of all kinds of things brought in to relation with one another by many and various spaces through a continuous and largely involuntary process of encounter" (8). For Thrift, "what actually categorizes everyday life"—material culture—cannot be reduced to simple representation, the physical, or a singular body. Instead, the everyday will embody the " 'strangeness in the commonplace' " (87) through these various encounters. Thrift's strangeness suggests a mode of being that is both recognizable (commonplace, everyday) yet not recognizable as well (strange, non-representational, not expected). To explain non-representation, Thrift offers the concept of "qualculation," which he defines as "an activity arising out of the construction of new generative microworlds that allow many millions of calculations to continually be made in the background of any encounter" (90). In this definition, the emphasis is not on the representation or object but the encounters within and with that representation or object. What McLuhan theorized as juxtaposition, Thrift theorizes as a type of bodily encounter that we may not be aware of but that is occurring, such as encountering a yoga posture with a theory of digitality. A possible virtual situation, Thrift's notion offers another sense of what is often referred to as materialism.

With this point, I frame my discussion of virtual postures as one of digital materialism. Materialist concepts of rhetoric and writing call for recognition of what Jerome McGee called "rhetoric as a daily social phenomenon" (18) and what Michel de Certeau offered as the practice of the everyday. In lieu of focusing only on grand moments or issues of supposed importance, materialism examines what appears to be unimportant, but which is, in fact, part of a larger nexus of meaning (i.e., millions of calculations in the background of an encounter). "In an attempt to make the materiality of rhetoric more apparent," Greg Dickinson offers, "I want to suggest that we can benefit by paying particular attention to the mundane or even banal spaces of everyday life" (6). Or as Ramón Reichert and Annika Richterich note, "a new materialism is concerned with things and their doings" (6). For Ron Greene, materialism is tied to persuasion, particularly for how identity is called into being in this examination of the everyday:

> While the concept of interpellation reveals how the rhetorical, both as a situated practice of persuasion and as a general process inherent to all discourses, takes on its material status by addressing subjects, it becomes too easy to confuse a materialist theory of subjectivity with an uncritical social constructionism. (47)

Relationships between subjects cause being to be evoked because these relationships offer persuasive gestures (join us, be a part of us, interact with us, believe us, do what I do); "A rhetorical materialism should partake in a materialist ontology that configures the rhetorical subject as a particular kind of being invented by and for specific apparatuses of production" (Greene 49). McLuhan made a similar point regarding digital culture—the individual is re-invented by various technologies as senses extend outward. Greene's subjectivity, as it is informed by materialism, is a "subjectivity made possible by communication" (Greene 60). My question, though, concerns a digital communication, one that is virtual by the nature of its posture, and how this posture extends and becomes a set of connected interactions prompted by the everyday as once such apparatus of production.

Following this trajectory, McLuhan could, then, be considered as an early proponent of a digital materialist rhetoric since his concerns with media focused largely on subjectivity shaped by mundane, daily social phenomena as they might be informed by communicative technology: TV, comics, radio, the telephone, books, and so on. By focusing on daily media interactions, McLuhan contended, insight could be obtained regarding technological shaping of discourse, identity, culture, and institutions. Preceding Thrift's interests, McLuhan placed connectivity—and not representation—at the center of this process. "It is the technique of insight, and as such is necessary for media study, since no medium has its meaning of existence alone, but only in constant interplay with other media" (*Understanding* 39). These interactions, as *Understanding Media* demonstrates, are complex and require a shift in how we imagine or construct those bodies which form media. Connectivity is the basis of a digital materialism, one in which an individual body (object, person, movement, belief, practice, institution) is not representational (fixed in space) but rather virtual (connected or postured). A projected singular representation fails to account for the outward and inward connections that allow for a "thing" to exist or function, such as encouraging others to do yoga. A posture reflects this connectivity, allowing movement through it and from it. Encouraging others to do Bikram yoga when I do not care whether they follow my advice or not connects at least two moments (the practice of yoga in a hot room connects with another human's attention) within a moment of everyday rhetorical interaction (casual conversation) but not at the moment of final representation (the moment of persuasion that causes the individual to follow my lead). Because there is connectivity without representation, the posture is a form of digital (i.e. virtual) writing.

McLuhan theorized this process via the concept of the role. Roles, for McLuhan, reflect the lack of fixed representation within digital culture. The role is not a set identity within digital culture, but is instead the act of posturing or what McLuhan called "involvement" (i.e. connectivity). The young today, he wrote, "want roles—R-O-L-E-S. That is, total involvement" (*Medium* 100). McGee, as well, situated materialism with the role, the position that connects, at some point, the everyday to a posture. Yogi. Teacher. Grocer. Theorist. Such positions, McGee wrote, "denote that they are playing one particular role in a social ritual, one of the many roles they assume willing and unconsciously in a day-to-day business" (26). Arguments, too, play roles, and as one, my own argument—"do Bikram yoga"—might depend on the singular body (the reasons for doing so: good health, exercise, mindfulness) and not, as McLuhan's digital materialism displays, a more complex interaction of daily events, things, media, and spaces. But in my case, it does not. In my case, I am engaging the virtual interactions that digital materialism supports by allowing a different set of connections to occur, connections not fixated on one body (persuasion). In my banal statement, I am expressing a digital materialist notion of connectivity. *Understanding Media*, as this early discussion demonstrates, is one such inventory of the overall connectivity of materialist culture. Unfortunately, *Understanding Media* lacks any discussion of yoga.

Digital Materialism

To explore the virtual posture in more detail, I move from the previous discussion of materialism to digital materialism. Digital materialism, as I noted, is object based. "Object," Ian Bogost claims, "implies materiality, physical stuff" (23). Objects, as Bogost defines them, include physical matter, as well as the non-physical: properties, marketplaces, symbols, and ideas (23). In this definition, a posture is as much an object as is the yoga mat. Objects, Bogost states, express. Consider McLuhan's similar claim for information, that "In the new electric Age of Information and programmed production, commodities themselves assume more and more the character of information" (*Understanding*, 48). He continues: "As electric information levels rise, almost any kind of material will serve any kind of need or function, forcing the intellectual more and more into the role of social command and into the service of production" (*Understanding*, 48). Thus, commodities, things, activities, all, as they interact and engage with one another, play a role in the creation and distribution of information, and, in turn, information stems outward from these objects' interactions. A light bulb, as McLuhan famously theorized, or a yoga posture, as I begin with, poses challenges outside of traditional notions of media/information representation (i.e., paper, notes, the book, TV, records, radio, or the computer). According to McLuhan's terms, the light bulb or yoga posture contains another media form within it, a media form it is inter-acting with (historically, culturally, technologically). Neither the light bulb nor the yoga posture are singular. McLuhan theorized levels of interaction based on such media by labeling them as hot or cool. Media are a form (a light bulb, a comic book) and media form (shape levels of engagement). In McLuhan's binary of media there is an assumption of participation, that at each moment of media interaction, we participate in the creation of meaning through interaction/involvement (cool media) or we don't (hot media).

Argument, as well, exists in this framework or participation. The question of engagement or involvement asks whether a moment is representational or whether it is virtual. When I "argue" that a colleague should also do Bikram yoga, I am leaning toward a virtual posture because whatever it is that connects me to Bikram or the person I share this suggestion with is absent at the time of utterance (my concern, their attention). Connectivity (Thrift's qualculation), as diverse thinkers such as Steven Shaviro and Albert László-Barabási contend, is the basis of digital communication. A listener to my statement might participate ("hell no, I won't do yoga") or not (not paying attention). But since my argument does not act to do either, since—as an object—it expresses no sense of involvement, it becomes an object waiting for some form of connectivity to further form discourse. My posture awaits another posture to interact with. Otherwise, it has no form. Without this interaction, I do not have an object as much as I have some amorphous statement or declaration. Objects need the connected experience of other objects for discourse to occur.

"Discourse," McGee proposed, should "have to be characterized as material rather than merely representational of mental and empirical phenomena" (19). Focusing on the material, McGee asked that we "think of rhetoric as an object" (19). As an object, however, rhetoric, for McGee, is not a simple thing in and of itself. Any discussion of "things" or "objects" is not one of physical items but of virtual experience. McGee stressed the connected nature of experience—experiencing the object and the object's experiencing of its surroundings.

> It is wrong to think that this sheaf of papers, this recording of "speech," is rhetoric in and of itself. It is surely "object," and the paper and ink scratches are "material." But the whole of rhetoric is "material" by measure of human *experiencing* of it, not by virtue of our ability to continue touching it after it is gone. Rhetoric is "object" because of its pragmatic *presence*, our inability safely to ignore it at the moment of its impact. (20)

More recently, Jane Bennett addresses what McLuhan called "interplay" and McGee describes as "experience" in her complex discussion of object interactions, or what she has termed "vibrant matter." Vibrant matter questions materialism by claiming that "materiality is a rubric that tends to horizontalize the relations between humans, biota, and abiota" (112). To horizontalize, as I understand Bennett, is to emphasize an ambiguous representation regarding connectivity, albeit one that does not focus on "ontologically ranked Great Chains of Being" (112). With this gesture, Bennett writes about blackouts, food, metal, and stem cells as objects with agency; objects that— via this process of horizontalizing and its suggestion of interaction—create discourse or meaning or what I will shortly identify as cloud-based interactions. Bennett's subjects are different from McLuhan's, but the overall focus remains media interaction. Bennett's intent is to "theorize a materiality that is as much force as entity, as much energy as matter, as much intensity as extension" (20). A body's "efficacy or agency," Bennett writes, "always depends on the collaboration, cooperation, or interactive interference of many bodies and forces" (21). Bennett's main claim rests on that of distributed agency (as Bruno Latour has also argued). Distributed agency spreads out representationality (but does not eliminate it) to the point of virtuality. Virtuality—whatever representation that suggests—is distributed via actors (objects) whose interactions could theoretically reach Thrift's level of millions of calculations. "A theory of distributive agency, in contrast, does not posit a subject as the root cause of an effect. There are instead always a swarm of vitalities at play" (Bennett 31–32). Media, in other words, are an extension of distribution. The subject is not the focus, the extension, instead, is. At one point, Bennett poses her discussion as that of communication. "How can humans learn to hear or enhance our receptivity for 'propositions' not expressed in words?" (104). Or, I note, can humans learn to enhance our receptivity to propositions expressed in words, but without representation over millions of calculations? Without horizontalizing relationships among actors (speaker, audience) or even objects (statement, space, moment), we can consider the non-representational space of a digital materialism, a space that is virtual, a space that allows for postures' interactions, a space of calculations and interaction, a space that has become the dominant space of digital interactions and composing. This space, I contend, is the cloud.

The Cloud

My discussion of digital materialism, postures, objects, and the virtual leads me to the current form of digital writing that most writers engage with on a daily basis in profound and mundane ways, the cloud. In contemporary computing, the cloud represents the space where representation does not occur, where postures interact and connect so that extension becomes a space of digital communication. The cloud, an ambiguous space defined as if it exists in one place (like a cloud in the sky) is located across thousands of Internet servers (objects) spread out across various countries (objects), each connecting to one another and offering a segment of the overall distributed agency that allows the Internet to function. The cloud is an interconnected data center where university, country, Amazon, Google, Facebook, website, and other servers interact with one another, thus allowing information to distribute, applications to run, data to shape experience, and so on. Clouds, as McLuhan might note, are environments. Environments are media, though, and as McLuhan argued, we are often not aware of their role as media because of a lack of overall interaction/involvement on our part. When we don't engage with the environment, we recognize the environment as a posture (virtual) and not as a connected space. Likewise, the "role" we imagine computing playing (computation) may differ from other roles computing supports (storage, connectivity, browsing, commerce, composing, display, etc.). Without engagement, the role and its place in the environment are not visible. What is true for a yoga posture is also true for a computer. "Environments are invisible. Their groundrules, pervasive structure, and overall patterns elude easy perception" (*Medium* 84–5). Clouds are the non-representational focus of objects interacting with other objects.

For Tung Hui-Hu (slightly echoing McLuhan's environments), the public perception is that the cloud exists without representation; that is, like other institutions or apparatuses we engage with daily, the cloud is uncritically examined for how or where it connects and to who or what. Hui-Hu works to uncover that supposed lack of representation by focusing on power relations; within the cloud, he argues, one can find infrastructures of control and thus make the supposed virtual "real." For Hui-Hu, the cloud reflects, as I cited Greene earlier, "a particular kind of being invented by and for specific apparatuses of production." Computing is one such being. The computer user is another. Power, as a site for connectivity among various computing objects, is Hui-Hu claims, the apparatus that invents the subject (person or object) and becomes something other than a posture once its virtuality is recognized as visible environment. Wherever this activity occurs in the cloud, Hui-Hu describes its space as non-representational. "One of the curious dilemmas that the cloud represents is that not even the engineers who have built it typically know where the cloud is" (xix). He adds, "When cloud computing enters into the picture, this puzzle becomes particularly complicated, because the cloud buries or hides its physical location by design" (4) and "the cloud is a neoliberal fantasy about user participation that is so widespread and so ambient as to be universal" (145). The issue regarding the cloud is twofold: physical (where are the computers actually located) and materialist (where and when and how do they interact and for what purpose). One might say, then, that the cloud is merely a posture of digitality. Hui-Hu reveals that posture as the interconnected state of power. Power is written into being by a visible digital connectivity. John Durham Peters, with a focus largely on connectivity itself, treats the cloud differently.

In his extensive *Marvelous Clouds*, John Durham Peters does not take up Hui-Hu's analysis of cloud computing but instead extends McLuhan's argument regarding media and environment by focusing on the physical environment itself as media. Clouds provide the metaphor and space for his analysis. The object, in Durham Peters's work, switches from the physicality of networked computers to the virtuality of connections and involvement. Like fire, water, light, and time, the cloud, for Durham Peters, suggests a McLuhanist environment: invisible, but constructed out of various connections that are always around us and we only need to recognize as interacting. "To study media, you cannot just study media," Durham Peters argues (29). You study the connections that form media. "Clouds pose the problem of the unrepresentable," he argues (257). The Cloud, as a state of connectivity, offers a virtual posture; it is nowhere while connecting everything at once. "Clouds are often thought of as the thing par excellence without inherent meaning" (254). "What would it mean to ask if clouds have meaning? Are clouds media? They are the ultimate test of the idea that there cold be natural media" (255). To generate some sense of meaning, Durham Peters demonstrates, one writes the cloud as a series of connections; these connections may be associative, figurative, historical, visual, or other. In this writing, the writer calculates their millions of connections. Durham Peters moves the reader through art, science, zoology, photography, and other categories in order to show how a cloud (or any media for that matter) becomes presented not as a representational object on its own (collection of water molecules in the sky, series of connected servers, paintings of clouds, informational category that is singular) but as a string of horizontal/vertical postures all interacting with each other. Clouds "do not need to look like things to bear significance" (257). They need to connect:

> In seeing media as ensembles of nature and culture, *physis* and *technê*, I try to stir together semantic strains that speak to a historical moment in which we cannot think of computation without thinking about carbon, or the cloud without thinking about data. (49)

Carbon connects to computation. The cloud connects to data. Media extend. Being extends. Writing extends as well. Clouds, then, are digital writing. They are the ultimate posture. They generate the space in which objects interact. With that interaction, meaning is located. As Durham Peters shows, to write about any given subject, one must engage all of the other subjects around it as well. In this engagement, we find the digital materialism of the virtual, and we find the digital writing space.

Postured Writing

My discussion moves from Bikram yoga to digital materialism to the cloud. These objects have no obvious or causal relationship with one another (a goal of representation) other than my ability to identify connections among them and how such connections shape a discourse (this writing I perform). In other words, the objects, much like my initial anecdote's focus, do nothing until they become more than objects. They become interactions. They become distributed agency. They become a cloud. Durham Peters's work is exceptional in this regard since the overall cloud (environment as media) he constructs is an endless series of interactions and extensions that demonstrate how no object (information or physical) can exist without interactions. The cloud, as representative of the virtual state of connectivity, offers an understanding of digital writing as the state of connectivity, involvement, and engagement. "Media theory has something both ecological and existential to say," Durham Peters writes (52). Ecology can mean the physical embodiment of clouds, fire, and water, as Durham Peters's work demonstrates, but it also means the connections that allow bodies to engage other bodies, as his work showcases as well.

For some time, digital studies and writing studies have focused on digital writing as the physical act of composing on screen, with a device, within power structures, with or without access, or online. Such discussions may extend each of these areas to issues of access, gender, race, multimodal work, or some other variant that concentrates on a representation as it is fixed in one space affected by digital culture. With that centralized focus, the posture (for instance, computer access or network access is limited; the desktop is ideological, the promise of multimodal based teaching will enhance pedagogy, etc.) does nothing other than gesture without meaning. There is no engagement outside of a proclamation or declaration. Like a suggestion to "do Bikram yoga," the gesture is without representation. But such postures are typically presented as otherwise in their declarative and argumentative framings. Such postures within digital studies behave as if they are engaged objects or representational arguments. I claim otherwise. This discussion demonstrates that difference.

My focus has been different from many writings regarding digital rhetoric or digital writing. My interest in the virtual posture is to draw attention to digitality, in general, as an overall state of writing that exists only when engagement occurs among the endless objects that create some type of meaning, discourse, moment, activity, identity, persuasive act, and so on. Jane Bennett makes a similar point in her call for a new type of materialism, writing "We need not only to invent or reinvoke concepts like conatus, actant, assemblage, small agency, operator, disruption, and the like but also to devise new procedures, technologies, and regimes of perception that enable us to consult nonhumans more closely" (108). In this consultation Bennett calls for, we encounter writing. To begin a discussion on digital materialism with an anecdote about doing yoga is to fall outside of a traditional critical or analytical discussion of digital writing because the connections to issues of relevance or the connection to objects that generate relevance are not yet visible. My point has been to display some of that not yet visible material through this brief discussion regarding objects, virtuality, and connectivity. Because of connectivity, McLuhan proclaimed "we have abolished writing" (*Medium* 125). McLuhan, though, did not advocate the end of writing, digital or otherwise. Instead, he recognized that, in the age of new media, writing generates meaning out of connectivity and previous perceptions are now abolished. To consider the digital writing space as a space of objects interacting with other objects is not to reduce digital writing to a device or technology, but rather is to foreground writing as engagement. Ideas engage ideas. Postures engage postures. Objects encounter objects. This final point is essential for any study of the digital, rhetoric, or writing in general. It shifts our scholarly and pedagogical focuses away from any notion of singularity we may still retain (the argument by itself, for instance) and motions us toward a writing of postures, of virtuality, of inter-connectivity.

Works Cited

Bennett, Jane. *Vibrant Matter: A Political Ecology of Things*. Duke UP, 2010.

Bogost, Ian. *Alien Phenomenology, Or What it's Like to Be a Thing*. Minnesota UP, 2010.

Burke, Kenneth. *A Rhetoric of Motives*. CA: U of California P, 1950.

Dickinson, Greg. "Joe's Rhetoric Finding Authenticity at Starbucks." *Rhetoric Society Quarterly*, vol. 32, no. 4, Autumn 2002, pp. 5–27.

Durham Peters, John. *The Marvelous Clouds: Toward a Philosophy of Elemental Media*. The U of Chicago P, 2015.

Greene, Ron. "Rhetorical Materialism: The Rhetorical Subject and the General Intellect." *Rhetoric, Materiality, and Politics*, edited by Barbara A. Biesecker, and John Louis Lucaites. NY: Peter Lang, 2009, pp. 43–65.

Hayles, Katherine. *How We Think: Digital Media and Contemporary Technogenesis*. The U of Chicago P, 2012.

Hu, Tung-Hui. *A Prehistory of the Cloud*. The MIT Press, 2015.

Lanier, Jaron. *Who Owns the Future?* Simon & Schuster, 2013.

McGee, Michael Calvin. "A Materialist Conception of Rhetoric." *Rhetoric, Materiality and Politics*, edited by Barbara A. Biesecker, and John Lucas Lucaites. Peter Lang, 2009, pp. 17–42.

McLuhan, Marshall. *Understanding Media: The Extensions of Man*. Signet, 1964.

McLuhan, Marshall, and Quentin Fiore. *The Medium is the Massage: An Inventory of Effects*. Gingko, 2001.

Mirzoeff, Nicholas. *An Introduction to Visual Culture*. Routledge, 1999.

Reichert, Ramón, and Annika Richterich. "Introduction: Digital Materialism." *Which for Me*, vol. 1, issue 1, 2015, pp. 5–17.

Thrift, Nigel. *Non-Representational Theory: Space, Politics, Affect*. Routledge, 2008.

Woolgar, Steve. "Five Rules of Virtuality." *Virtual Society? Technology, Cyberbole, Reality*, edited by Steve Woolgar. Oxford UP, 2002, pp. 1–22.

36

PARTICIPATORY MEDIA AND THE LUSORY TURN

Paratextuality and Let's Play

Ingrid Richardson

The evolution of the Web into a meta-platform for networked media and communication has provided the conditions for a fertile participatory media environment. We are also, some suggest, in the midst of a cultural shift towards a lusory sensibility, that is, in turn, affecting a playful sociality. In this environment, everyday media users engage in creating, sharing, collaborating and playing *with* and *through* media, from personal small media content to pro-am subscriber-based content and the re-use of existing "big media." In this process, we literally "read–write" culture by creatively remixing our own and others' media texts. These new communicative practices are part of the ongoing formation of both our online (and offline) personae and communities of interest.

This chapter sits at the nexus of theoretical approaches to digital rhetoric and new media, and concerns the way online texts are increasingly composed of remixed, multimodal, and collaborative content, changing the relationship between "writers" and "readers," and transforming the way people communicate and construct social worlds. More specifically, I explore the domain of participatory and paratexual media specific to games, with a particular focus on the phenomenon of Let's Play (LP), and the communities of players who upload LP content, subscribe to LP channels, and contribute to the growing body of "commentary" as an emergent form of online textuality. An LP is a video of gameplay, often accompanied by the gamer's humorous or entertaining voiceover and a screen-in-screen inset of their facial expressions and emotive reactions as they play. LP differs significantly from game walkthroughs, which typically provide gamers with tips and guides for their own gameplay. Rather, it refers to a flourishing area of small media entertainment—a particularly prolific instance of user-created content "produsage" in Bruns and Jacobs' terms. LP content is most often uploaded onto the video-sharing website YouTube, and its growing popularity has been partially responsible for what has been called the "commentary revolution," which is itself part of the evolution of YouTube into a gathering place for active virtual communities of interest and practice.

In this chapter, I suggest that Let's Play is one exemplar of what Burgess terms "vernacular creativity," a mode of digital rhetoric that increasingly describes our everyday media practices. I first situate LP in the broader context of the ludification of culture, followed by an analysis of LP practices as fundamentally about social connection and the sharing of gameplay as-it-is-experienced, and finally, I explore how such practices change the way we engage with games as media texts. Throughout the chapter, anecdotal insights will be provided by a small ethnographic survey of LP enthusiasts in Perth and Melbourne, Australia, conducted in 2016 as part of a broader study into playful and creative practices within the domestic context. As many of the research participants described, watching and commenting on LP content often has little to do with a desire to play the game, but is about aesthetic or critical appreciation of a new media form, and generates a sense of belonging to, and participation in, both globally dispersed publics and niche online communities.

The Playful Turn

In his article "The Ludification of Culture" and seminal book *Homo Ludens 2.0*, Raessens argues that playfulness has become central to our cultural practices and the way we engage with media texts, from the playful communication of texting and tweeting to the infusion of game-like activities across disparate domains such as education, politics, and leisure. In Malaby's terms, although "play" can no longer be used as a term for a distinct and bounded human activity (and it is perhaps doubtful if this has ever been the case), we can now usefully deploy the term to designate a *"mode of experience*, a way of engaging with the world" (102). As Hjorth and Richardson (Gaming) suggest, in a quotidian sense this can be seen in the ongoing merger of social network services, games, and playful mobile apps, and the very ordinariness of that integrated use in our everyday lives. More generally, it is evident in the perpetual expansion of participatory media forms, and the rise of ever-evolving social media services that enable users to upload and share their own creative "small media" content. The playful or ludic attitude is at the core of emergent "spreadable media" practices (Jenkins et al.) that effectively blur the boundaries between production and consumption and demand that we rethink our mediascapes not in accordance with old "closed" dichotomies of user and producer, gamer and creator, but in terms of a flexible, paratextual, open—and often irreverent and playful—dynamic. In this environment, such everyday media "produsage" (Bruns and Jacobs) is often cooperative, shared, and clustered around online communities of interest, and comprises the repurposing, remixing, and (re)circulation of existing media content. As Zappen has noted, the new affordances of Web-based media support "a new digital rhetoric that encourages self-expression, participation, and creative collaboration." The effects are transformative, modifying and reshaping the way we engage with media, how media content is circulated, and the manner in which media texts become part of our experience as social beings.

Not surprisingly, games, gaming cultures, and the practices surrounding gameplay are frequently theorized as a significant trajectory of ludification, and a lens through which to understand the playful turn in culture writ large. As Pearce stated almost a decade ago:

> If we telescope out to the larger picture, we find that networked play is not simply confined to the game worlds . . . In fact, network play has insinuated itself into many other aspects of life. It could be argued that YouTube is a networked playground of sorts, even more so when we take note of the numerous machinima films created in games by players . . . These trends move far beyond traditional gamer fan culture. They point to a growing "play turn" in which, far from being a marginalized fringe activity, play is beginning to pervade every aspect of our lives. We see games and play increasingly embedded in social networks, in mobile phones, on web sites, and in domains as diverse as education, military and corporate training, activism, even politics. (278)

In order to understand the cultural and experiential effect of the increasing ubiquity of games, Christensen and Prax suggest that games and gameplay can effectively be rethought in terms of Taylor's notion of *assemblage*, which accounts for the way "many varying actors and unfolding processes make up the site and action" of contemporary gaming (Taylor 332, qtd. in Christensen and Prax 731). For Taylor, extrapolating from Bowker and Star, games are useful "boundary objects," assemblages that are adaptive or plastic across individual contexts yet maintaining coherence and recognizability as a collective and cross-cultural experience. As boundary objects, games and the practices that flow through them, impact upon us in material, corporeal, social, personal and conceptual ways (Taylor 333). Their effects are both ontological (in terms of *what* we experience) and epistemological (in terms of *how* we communicate and *make knowledge* by way of those experiences).

In this chapter, I focus on the paratextual media practices surrounding games, and LP content creation and consumption in particular. Paratexts can be seen as a significant trajectory of digital rhetoric; that is, they erode the "distance between rhetor, reader, producer and user" (Eyman), as they comprise both remixed and ready-made texts that are repurposed "for other meanings, contexts and audiences" (Johnson). Media and game theorists have written at length about the paratextuality extrinsic to gameplay yet intrinsic to game culture, which includes discussion and commentary in game and fan blogs, partaking in cosplay events, and the creative use of game content, all of which exemplify the underlying playfulness endemic to participatory media culture on a larger scale. It is important, here, to distinguish between the domain of participatory and paratextual game media (including game modification, machinima, LP, walkthroughs, fan fiction, and other forms of produsage) as representative of a form of cultural playfulness or ludification, and what is termed "gamification." As Moore points out, the latter is defined by the translation of game principles and "ludic structures" into social networking sites and other forms of service provision on the Web (376–7). The former, on the other hand, are instances of the playful cultural turn in a more diffuse, vernacular and informal sense, regardless of how they may evolve into significant money-making ventures, as is the case with the more popular LP websites and channels.

LP originated in the mid-2000s, emerging from the participatory game threads of somethingawful.com, a comedic website containing a blog, feature articles, and forums devoted to Internet media and game reviews. Since then, it has become a significant media form in its own right, evidenced by the exponential rise of subscriber channels that feature LP on YouTube. Primarily, LPs can be described as "playing videogames for the Internet," though as media texts they are distinct from standard game walkthroughs by the addition of entertaining commentary and a webcam inset that captures the player's facial expressions as they play. The most popular LP channel is PewDiePie (aka Felix Kjellberg) which boasts over 60 million subscribers and since late 2013 has been the most subscribed channel on YouTube, with over 14 billion video views as of early 2017. Kjellberg's current earnings, primarily through the monetization of his channel generated from advertising revenue, are estimated to exceed $15 million per annum. Other popular LP subscriber channels include Vanoss Gaming (20 million subscribers), Markiplier (16.6 million), Sky Does Minecraft (12 million), Vegatta777 (17 million), The Syndicate Project (10 million) and Toby Games (6.8 million). Typically, each LPer has their own game genre specialty and signature style or commentary, and their own unique way of interpreting and narrating game texts.

In their application of activity theory to games, Ang et al. distinguish between *intrinsic* play or play that takes place inside the game, and *extrinsic* play that extends beyond the game, screen, and interface and often into paratextual production such as LP videos that effectively change the intrinsic game experience. Within the domain of extrinsic play, Ang et al. identify two categories of engagement—reflective play and expansive play. While reflective play involves "communication, sharing, and discussion" about intrinsic play, such as that which takes place in game blogs, live chat, and conventional walkthroughs, expansive play refers to playful practices, activities, and modes of creative content produsage that "transgress the original game boundary" or exceed the original content in some way, often working to modify players' perception or experience of the game (364). In reflective play, artifacts are created to enable reflection and tactical or strategic learning about the game; that is, it is largely motivated by a desire to talk about the game itself. In expansive play, on the other hand, the aim is to generate media texts that "test the game boundary," and create "new types of enjoyment" (368, 372). Both modalities of extrinsic play are "community building," aggregating and strengthening game communities—possibly more so than intrinsic play (373). As I will suggest, LP is an instance of both reflective and expansive play, as it both informs gameplay and adds a dimension of vicarious engagement that transforms the way games as media texts are experienced.

As evidenced by the popularity of LP on YouTube, along with numerous other game-related channels, the video-sharing website is deeply embedded in the gaming community. Indeed, YouTube subscriber channel functionality is the exemplar of networked media distribution, enabling the rise of "professional fan" practices and the evolution of LP into "one of the most disruptive entertainment forces of the last decade" (Wadeson), escalating the place of games in the contemporary mediascape, and challenging the dominant way games are experienced as exclusively interactive media forms. As I will discuss in the final section, along with much participatory and remixed media, LP also challenges current conventions of authorship and content ownership. For Wadeson, fan-celebrities such as Kjellberg represent a generation of participatory media aficionados whose media texts embody and facilitate "connection, curation, creation and community" (thus the appellation Generation C). Their work is effectively rewriting the conventions of game engagement and content creation, and epitomizes the ongoing ludification of culture, playful fandom, produsage, and spreadable media. As a new textual practice LP is fundamentally social; while those who record and upload their gameplay are motivated by the desire to share their creative outputs, those who watch LPs, including a number of my research participants, often feel a sense of co-presence, affinity, and intimacy.

Let Us Play: Community, Connection and Sharing

As previously noted, YouTube is a site that gathers active communities of interest and practice—typified by produsage, prosumption, and copious commentary about both user-generated content and big media texts—around subscriber-based channels. As Burgess and Green point out, it is a "communicative space," not simply a platform for media distribution. Currently, according to YouTube's own statistics, more than one billion unique users visit the site every month, with over six billion hours viewed in that time and one hundred hours of video uploaded every minute; millions of subscriptions occur daily, and "thousands of channels are making six figures a year" (YouTube). For Lange and Ito (284), the way in which platforms such as YouTube empower amateur media creators to engender new publics and online communities is "one of the most transformative dimensions of contemporary new media" (Lange and Ito 284). One participant, a male gamer in his first year of university and prolific commenter on the LP channel Rooster Teeth, spoke about his recent shift away from Facebook as his preferred social media platform: "I used to check Facebook ten times a day on my phone, now I'm mainly [watching and commenting] on YouTube. Lots of my friends are doing the same."

In his incisive presentation to the Library of Congress, Wesch narrates the beginnings of YouTube by tracing the global community of producers that coalesced around Gary Brolsma's web-cam dance to *Numa Numa* (recorded in his "dismal-looking suburban bedroom"), which inspired tens of thousands of people from all over the world to "share the joy" and upload their own versions of the song and dance. For Wesch, the *Numa Numa* phenomenon marked an important moment in the emergence of "seriously playful participatory media culture" mediated by YouTube and other services that enable user-generated and user-created content to be uploaded and shared online. In Wesch's words, it was "a celebration of new forms of empowerment . . . new forms of community, and types of community that we've never really seen before, global connections transcending space and time, a celebration of new and unimaginable possibility." These new forms of community are also usefully described as "network publics" (Ito), a term that effectively conceptualizes media consumption and mediated communication outside the outdated rubric of "audience," as it takes place "through complex networks that are bottom-up, top-down, as well as side-to-side" (Ito). Although enthusiastically embraced by some, other media theorists are wary of the uncritical "rhetoric of sharing" (Kennedy) that infuses social and network media, where affective connectivity is celebrated as unproblematically open, collaborative, and communal, whitewashing the underlying politics of data handling, ownership, and monetization.

Focusing on LP from the perspective of those who watch and subscribe to them provides us with an opportunity to explore the complexity and diversity of a roughly congruous online community and its accompanying media texts, as a way of better understanding the complex dynamics of network publics, produsage, and participatory media consumption. As conveyed by my research participants and LPers themselves, there are many motivations to seek out and watch LPs, and there is significant debate within the LP community about the purpose of LPs. The more fervent purists argue that they should be "closed" texts, or complete linear progressions of a game from beginning to end, focusing exclusively on technique and expertise. For 27-year-old Aaron, the purpose of watching LPs is primarily instrumental, instructional, and metatextual, a way to learn difficult game strategies by observing expert gamers, and engage in critical reflection about the medium: "I prefer LPs that stick to talking about the game, and have worthwhile opinions about game design and mechanics." Others prioritize the entertainment afforded by the personalities and antics of the LPers. Jake, a 16-year-old high school student, spoke enthusiastically about his favorite LP channel Cow Chop:

> I used to watch PewDiePie but it's gone all political, so now I go on Cow Chop. They're just normal guys who mess around pranking and doing stupid stuff, they're not great gamers but they're funny. If I want to find out about good games or how to play them I'll go on the PS [PlayStation] website.

Here, Jake reveals how LP texts have emerged as a distinct form of entertainment, with LPers becoming media celebrities with dedicated fanbases, often irrespective of the actual games featured on their channels.

Frequently, the authenticity and immediacy of the LP as a "live performance" of play is important to viewers, with the associated perception that the commentary and reactions are spontaneous, unscripted, and in-the-moment (Nguyen 12). Nevertheless, and somewhat at odds with the demand for authenticity, accomplished video editing skills are also highly valued (zooming in on expressions, jump-cutting to humorous images, animations or in-house jokes, subtle use of filters and other effects). Rob, a 19-year-old who works in IT support, commented:

> A lot of LPers are really fake, their reactions are just silly and over the top. I prefer watching LPs that are more real, or ones that are put together well. You can tell when they're professionals, they've put some thought into making a quality video.

The liveness and immediacy of LP videos is afforded by the use of both audio commentary and facecams, such that gameplay is experienced *as it unfolds*. Aside from providing authentic sound and vision of the player, this also evokes a personal or affective connection between LPers and their fans. Sara, a 22-year-old studying vet nursing, stated:

> I love GameGrumps, they're cool guys who talk about their life experiences, like with drugs and relationships and stuff like that. It's like watching and listening to real people, people I'd like if I met them . . . I feel like they're part of my life.

Another female teenage respondent was particularly keen on LPs of horror games; while linking it to her enjoyment of the horror genre in film and books more generally, she also suggested it offered something extra, a closeness or intimacy as she experienced the fear and surprise of someone "actually in the game": "You can hear their screams like when a zombie appears out of nowhere, it's like being in their loungeroom." For Zariko, this emotional and visceral attachment follows from the "affective embodiment" afforded by LP as a unique kind of media text, which enables "the transferring of textures of feelings and emotions between the viewer and player embodiment" (Zariko 20). Zariko evocatively relates her own engagement with LPs:

> A LP video allows the experience of playing the game with another. [It is] not the same as watching a video—I empathise with the player, with every jolt and start. I am able to experience the game without the pressure of being in control . . . ChristopherOdd takes me with him. Even though I am not the one playing the game, I accompany him in his play experience. He plays the game for me. (Zariko 14)

For all participants, it was clear that LPs provided a means of *parasocial* connection (Fjaellingsdal); whether they identified as active posters or simply watchers and lurkers, they returned to watch their favorite players because they engendered a sense of like-mindedness and companionship, effectively simulating the experience of "playing together" with friends. This sense of parasociality is theorized in various ways; Gee refers to "affinity spaces" that engage users in dispersed meaning-making practices; Ito and Okabe describe the "intimate co-presence" of network communities that enable non-synchronous sharing; Hjorth and Richardson (Mobile Games) explore the modes of "ambient co-presence" afforded by mobile and online play. In each of these modes of "being-with-others," presence can be broadly defined in Noë's terms as *access*: that which is more-or-less available or accessible to our perceptual awareness, an understanding that does not prioritize face-to-face modes of communication, or preclude networked, dispersed, or asynchronous pathways of connection.

Participants often reflected that watching someone else's gameplay had little to do with a desire to play the game, but was more about the pleasures of vicarious experience, and being part of the global game community. John, a 20-year-old accountancy student, commented:

> I watch *League of Legends* ex-pros so I can improve my game. But sometimes I watch stuff just because I'm curious about a game, like *Deadly Premonition*, I want to see how it's played, even though I'm never going to play it.

Another young 14-year-old female gamer relayed her avid enthusiasm for *Minecraft* LPs, even though she had never played nor intended to play the game; she watched them mainly on her iPad in her bedroom at night, for the most part because they were "funny and interesting," and because she derived pleasure and satisfaction in following another's progression through the game: "It's like you can keep tapping into a never-ending story or journey." This engagement with LP as a vicarious experience of another's media activity clearly challenges the common argument within ludology that games are always already an interactive, player-centered, simulative *doing*. In this way, as media texts LPs expand videogames beyond the rubric of play, and problematize the underlying ontology of games as interactive media.

Changing the Game: LP as transformative media texts

As this analysis of LP and its attendant practices has shown, not only do LPs suggest that there are other experiential dimensions to gaming, but that the user-created content emerging from gameplay represents a different relationship with audiovisual media and a different playful experience of sociality altogether. The social permeability of play in game and media cultures more generally means that "the player" should take its place among other subjectivities (the audience, the viewer, the browser, the surfer, the lurker, the gamer). In fact, as Roig et al. argue, this interchangeability of subject positions in media marks some obvious affinities with the practices of play, suggesting the idea of "playful identities" (*pace* Raessens; Roig et al.). As play and playfulness become deeply embedded in our audiovisual media sensibilities across multiple screen interfaces and contexts, the malleable agency of the player reflects a change in both the level and mode of media use, such that it involves an expansive and expanding range of participatory and creative activities, but also an affective and *paidic* dimension.

As opposed to the more concrete and formal "demarcation between playing and not playing" (Moore 376) traditionally circumscribed by the supposed "magic circle" of video and computer gaming, *paidia* describes the dispersed practices of extrinsic play that are more ambiguous and spontaneous, and interwoven with everyday mediascapes. Historically within game studies, the magic circle has frequently been adopted as a way to explicitly demarcate game from non-game elements, and play from "real life." Over the past decade, however, game theorists have questioned this overly discrete, deterministic, and artificial notion of the magic circle from a number of different angles, arguing that we need a broader, messier, and more flexible description of game parameters and practices. For Roig et al., the LP experiences of our respondents might point to the way videogames and their surrounding game cultures have spawned, quite literally, *new* media practices—exponents of significant change "not only regarding how media are produced and consumed, but also in the way leisure is organized and the role of play in our everyday life" (89). The notion of ambient play developed by Hjorth and Richardson (*Gaming*; "Mobile Games") explicitly reflects on the way games and playful media infuse everyday life and erode the boundary between play and not-play, seeking to capture supra-lusory practices such as LP.

In the broader context of creativity and playfulness around content production, we can also consider the specificity of culturally inflected attitudes toward the copyright and ownership of repurposed and remixed content. In interviews those respondents that considered themselves part of LP culture held strong views supporting the validity of LP as a creative, innovative, original, and artistic mode of digital content production. As Taylor has argued in the more general context of videogame play, players and game developers should rightly be regarded as the "collective authors" of the play experience, as it is through the act of play that meaning is ascribed to the game characters, backstory, and emergent narrative. In particular, participants were outraged at Nintendo's recent move to claim YouTube advertising revenue for videos containing gameplay footage. Potentially, this meant that LP videos featuring Nintendo games would be deemed to contain content wholly owned by Nintendo, and subsequently, YouTube LPers who currently monetize extended Nintendo gameplay videos would either lose their advertising income stream or be sued for breach of copyright. In general, commentary on

YouTube and game blogs was more circumspect, with some arguing that Nintendo have a right to claim copyright over content that is fundamentally theirs; that is, without a game to play, there would be no videos of gameplay, and there is only so much variation to gameplay that is after all enacted within a closed system. These debates question both the status of LP paratexts in the converging spectrum of creative media production, distribution, and consumption, and the very nature of playful "repurposing" as an intrinsic part of cultural practice.

As a number of game theorists have argued, games are fundamentally "lived experiences"— that is, they are essentially ludic and thus not narrative in the same way as a film or novel. Yet LPs are quite literally "stories" of gameplay that provide "narrative commentary on an experience as it is being experienced" troubling the distinction between activity and passivity as it applies to interactive and non-interactive media forms (Smith et al. 133). The added layer that LP commentary provides effectively transforms the gameplay "into a review, a parody or simply a new form of entertainment" (Burwell and Miller 113). The LP creator becomes more than a player, but also a narrator, critic and entertainer, and in this way, LPs function as story-based "meta-media" situated outside the ludic framework of the original game content. Many LP channels feature serialized episodes of the player's progression through a single game, and a number of research participants conveyed their pleasure in this narrative experience, as they vicariously enjoyed the game journey *enacted through play* as each episode was uploaded, from beginning to end.

For Zariko, this narrativization of play as-it-happens is what makes LP unique as a mode of gameplay, and transforms it into an innovative kind of new media text. As distinct from the usual activity of video gaming that ordinarily entails a more-or-less non-reflexive form of engagement that is reactive and extemporaneous, the LPer deliberately verbalizes and questions their actions and strategies for the viewer, becoming a "reflexive-narrator" directing and authoring their own "play-story" (Zariko 24, 27). In the context of authorship and creative ownership, as Taylor argues, LPers are at least the partial creators of their own emergent narrative, as it is the player that determines, in each instance, how the variability of play becomes "a single narrative progression" (Zariko 141). In this sense—an argument that could be applied to gameplay *tout court*—the videogame itself is only ever an "experience *in potential*" (Zariko 122) until the player enacts and actualizes a particular trajectory as it unfolds in the moment of play. As Zariko has so insightfully articulated, in recording and simultaneously reflecting upon their own performance and affective embodiment of play, the LPer creates a unique and unrepeatable videotext narrative that literally realizes and makes meaningful one rendering of the game's multiple possibilities. The conceptual significance of narrative to this mode of ludic media production is patently evident, as the LP storifies the gameplay, capturing and transforming it into a permanent text available for replay, repeated consumption, and on-sharing. It is this process that represents an important cultural and experiential shift in playful media practices.

Finally, we can also identify how LP represents an emergent new literacy, involving the convergence of roles as users become players, reviewers, commentators, curators, and creators, remixing and sharing texts through "new modes of multimodal production" (Burwell and Miller 110–11; Smith and Sanchez). Moreover, as Glas comments, LP videos and gamer practices more broadly are often characterized by "divergent and deviant" forms of play, which demands a critical grasp of how the rules and boundaries of games are resisted and negotiated (84). For Raessens, the "playful turn" necessitates a specific form of media literacy, a "ludoliteracy" that equips us with the knowledge and skills needed to be competent and conceptually aware in contemporary media culture. This requires a critical understanding of play, games, and gamification; both existing and nascent technologies, interfaces and platforms; the changing infrastructure of the media industries (including the power and labour relations of both formal and spreadable media); the legal, social, and creative aspects of produsage; and the combinatory forms of oral, visual, gestural, and written modes of communication within participatory and social media cultures. A holistic apprehension of LP activates each of these domains of media literacy.

Conclusion

In this chapter, I have considered the creative content production and consumption of LP as an exemplar of participatory media and produsage in contemporary culture. In the first section I described what is termed the "playful turn" or ludification of culture, and the way in which LP paratexts are a particularly salient and prolific instance of this transformation, and representative of "extrinsic" play practices. In the following section, I focused on YouTube as a communicative space imbued with the rhetoric of sharing, gathering together communities of interest and "network publics" around subscriber-based channels, and functioning as the preferred platform for the distribution of LP videotexts. Drawing on insights gained from an ethnographic study of LP enthusiasts, I detailed the diverse ways LP content is experienced, from assisting gamers to better strategize their gameplay, to facilitating an affective sense of connection, belonging, and sharing. Finally, the chapter turned to LP as a unique kind of media text that challenges our perception of gameplay as exclusively interactive and essentially non-narrative. As I hope to have shown, LP involves a range of new media literacies, a new digital rhetoric that deploys the affordances of participatory and networked media, fostering new forms of creativity, collaboration, and storytelling. In the dynamic and ever-evolving space of the Web, LP represents just one instance of the changing mediascape; more broadly, it demands that we adapt our critical approaches to communication, if we are to grasp the transformative effects of nascent media forms on the way meaning is made.

Acknowledgment

This research was kindly supported by an Australian Research Council Discovery grant (Games of Being Mobile Project).

Works Cited

Ang, Chee Siang, Panayiotis Zaphiris, and Stephanie Wilson. "Computer Games and Sociocultural Play: An Activity Theoretical Perspective." *Games and Culture*, vol. 5, no. 4, 2010, pp. 354–80.

Bowker, Geoffrey C., and Susan Leigh Star. *Sorting Things Out: Classification and Its Consequences*. MIT Press, 1999.

Bruns, Axel, and Joanne Jacobs, Eds. *Uses of Blogs*. Peter Lang, 2006.

Burgess, Jean E. "Remediating Vernacular Creativity: Photography and Cultural Citizenship in the Flickr Photosharing Network." *Spaces of Vernacular Creativity: Rethinking the Cultural Economy*, edited by Tim Edensor et al. Routledge, 2010, pp. 116–26.

Burgess, Jean E., and Joshua Green. *YouTube: Online Video and Participatory Culture*. Polity, 2009.

Burwell, Catherine, and Thomas Miller. "*Let's Play*: Exploring Literacy Practices in an Emerging Videogame Paratext." *E-Learning and Digital Media*, vol. 13, no. 3–4, 2016, pp. 109–25.

Christensen, Christian, and Patrick Prax. "Assemblage, Adaptation and Apps: Smartphones and Mobile Gaming." *Continuum: Journal of Media and Cultural Studies*, vol. 26, no. 5, 2012, pp. 731–39.

Eyman, Douglas. *Digital Rhetoric: Theory, Method, Practice*. U of Michigan P, 2015.

Fjaellingsdal, Kristoffer. *Let's Graduate—A Thematic Analysis of the Let's Play Phenomenon*. Trondheim, 2014.

Gee, James. *Situated Language and Learning: A Critique of Traditional Schooling*. Routledge, 2004.

Glas, Rene. "Vicarious Play: Engaging the Viewer in Let's Play videos." *Empedocles: European Journal for the Philosophy of Communication*, vol. 5, nos. 1–2, 2015, pp. 81–6.

Hjorth, Larissa, and Ingrid Richardson. *Gaming in Locative, Social and Mobile Media*. Palgrave, 2014.

——. "Mobile Games and Ambient Play." *Social, Casual and Mobile Games: The Changing Gaming Landscape*, edited by Michele Willson and Tama Leaver. Bloomsbury, 2016, 105–16.

Ito, Mizuko. "Introduction." *Networked Publics*, edited by Kazys Varnelis. MIT Press, 2008. networked publics.org/book/introduction.html. Accessed 5 July 2017.

Ito, Mizuko, and Daisuke Okabe. "Intimate Visual Co-Presence." *Ubicomp 2005*, Tokyo, Japan, 11–14 September 2005. Conference presentation.

Jenkins, Henry, Sam Ford, and Joshus Green. *Spreadable Media: Creating Value and Meaning in a Networked Culture*. New York UP, 2013.

Johnson, Lucy. "Negotiating Territory, Analysis and Production as a Framework for Digital Rhetoric: A Review of Eyman's Digital Rhetoric: Theory, Method, Practice." *Enculturation*, Issue 23. enculturation.net/digital-rhetoric. Accessed 5 July 2017.

Kennedy, Jenny. "Rhetorics of Sharing: Data, Imagination, and Desire." *Unlike Us Reader: Social Media Monopolies and their Alternatives*, edited by Geert Lovink and Miriam Rasch. Amsterdam Institute of Network Cultures, 2013, pp. 127–36.

Lange, Patricia G., and Mizuko Ito. "Creative Production." *Hanging Out, Messing Around, and Geeking Out: Kids Living and Learning with New Media*, edited by Mizuko Ito et al. MIT Press, 2010, pp. 243–93.

Malaby, Thomas M. "Beyond Play: A New Approach to Games." *Games and Culture*, vol. 2, no. 2, 2007, pp. 95–113.

Moore, Christopher. "The Magic Circle and the Mobility of Play." *Convergence: The International Journal of Research into New Media Technologies*, vol. 17, no. 4, 2011, pp. 373–87.

Nguyen, Josef. "Praxis: Performing as video game players in LPs." *Transformative Works and Cultures*, vol. 22, 2016, pp. 1–28.

Noë, Alva. *Varieties of Presence*. Harvard UP, 2012.

Pearce, Celia and Artemesia. *Communities of Play: Emergent Cultures in Multiplayer Game and Virtual Worlds*. MIT Press, 2009.

Raessens, Joost. "Playful Identities, or the Ludification of Culture." *Games and Culture*, vol. 1, no. 1, 2006, pp. 52–7.

——. *Homo Ludens 2.0. The Ludic Turn in Media Theory*. Utrecht University, 2012.

——. "The Ludification of Culture." *Rethinking Gamification*, edited by Mathias Fuchs et al. Meson Press, 2014, pp. 91–114.

Roig, Antoni, Gemma San Cornelio, Elisenda Ardèvol, Pau Alsina, and Ruth Pagès. "Videogame as Media Practice: An Exploration of the Intersections Between Play and Audiovisual Culture." *Convergence: The International Journal of Research into New Media Technologies*, vol. 15, no. 1, 2009, pp. 89–103.

Smith, Thomas P. B., Marianna Obrist, and Peter Wright. "Live-Streaming Changes the (Video) Game." *Proceedings of EuroITV'13*, Como, Italy, 24–26 June 2013, pp. 131–8.

Smith, Peter A., and Alicia D. Sanchez. "Let's Play, Video Streams, and the Evolution of New Digital Literacy." *Proceedings of the Second International Conference on Learning and Collaboration Technologies*, HCI International 2015, Los Angeles, USA, 2–7 August 2015, pp. 520–7.

Taylor, T. L. "The Assemblage of Play." *Games and Culture*, vol. 4, no. 4, 2009, pp. 331–9.

Wadeson, Danny. "Gamertube: PewDiePie and the YouTube Commentary Revolution." *Polygon*, 6 September 2013. www.polygon.com/features/2013/9/6/4641320/pewdiepie-youtube-commentary. Accessed 5 July 2017.

Wesch, M. "An Anthropological Introduction to YouTube." *YouTube*, 2008. www.youtube.com/watch?v=TPAO-lZ4_hU. Accessed 5 July 2017.

Zappen, James. "Digital Rhetoric: Toward an Integrated Theory." *Technical Communication Quarterly*, vol. 14, no. 3, 2005, pp. 319–25.

Zariko, Zhia. *Screening Embodiment: Let's Play Video and Observable Play Experience*. MA thesis, RMIT University, 2016.

PART VII

The Politics and Economics of Digital Writing and Rhetoric

37

DIGITAL MEDIA ETHICS AND RHETORIC

Heidi A. McKee and James E. Porter

Digital media ethics[1] is a transdisciplinary area that focuses on how ethical issues, standards, and practices related to communication, writing, and interaction have changed in the digital age. Although the term is most often used in journalism, communication, and media studies, we see *digital media ethics* as relevant for all professional writers—and that means practically everyone using digital media to communicate, either in their professional work or in their capacity as private citizens.

Digital media ethics focuses on codes of conduct governing online communications: How should we behave, what is right and just, in the way that we express ourselves as writers and communicators in the digital realm? What are the principles that should guide our actions as producers of digital content, whether as professionals or private citizens? What are the codes that advise our engagement and interaction with others via digital media? These are the fundamental questions linking digital communication and ethics. Ethical issues have always evolved with digital technologies, and with their ever-increasing pace of change it is essential that we acknowledge and address the ethical (and legal) issues shaping our communications. Ethics is integral to technology development, design, and usage.

The claim that digital technologies have dramatically changed *how* we communicate is no longer new, surprising, or controversial. The more dramatic claim—advanced by digital media ethics philosophers and scholars such as Luciano Floridi, among others—is that because these digital communication technologies change how we fundamentally interact with others, they are changing *us*—our identities, our personalities, our interactions, our cultures, our ethical attitudes and frameworks for thinking about matters such as civility and privacy, our ethical notions about what is true and factual, right and just.

Digital media ethics scholarship seldom references *rhetoric* explicitly, but rhetoric is deeply intertwined with questions of digital media production and ethics. All interactions and all communications in and with digital media intersect with questions of ethics. Why are we communicating? For what desired end result, and for whose benefit? Those are basic questions of rhetoric that are also basic questions of ethics.

Our aim here is to demonstrate how digital media ethics is a fundamental concern for rhetoric, and vice versa. In this short chapter we cannot cover all the concerns addressed by digital media ethics, but what we will do, rather, is take up four key issues, showing for each the connection between digital media ethics and rhetoric:

- the general rhetorical ethic guiding digital media interaction on networks;
- access, accessibility, and design;
- privacy, consent, and transparency;
- AI and the ethics of human-machine communication.

A Fundamental Ethic for Interaction, Representation, and Treatment of Others

Is there such a thing as an overall ethic for communication interaction—a rhetorical ethics? Yes, classical rhetoric certainly provides one,[2] and contemporary digital media ethicists have also developed such an ethic. A basic ethic for online writing, or for all writing (at least writing that is not intended for creative, role-playing worlds), would require "that authors tell the truth, avoid deception, and respect their readers" (Jensen; see also Kuhn).

"Tell the truth, avoid deception" extends across several different kinds of writing situations: it tells us that we should be transparent about conflicts of interests (e.g., we should identify corporate sponsorship or sources of funding for our work); we should not misrepresent our identities or our expertise; we should not produce or promulgate fake news; we should not skew or misrepresent data and facts, etc. Such a code directly addresses the problem of "flogging"—that is, fake blogging or tweeting from fake accounts that are set up to create the appearance of independent support for something. While flogging might be legal, it is certainly not ethical by any basic criteria for rhetorical ethics.

Media professionals in advertising, journalism, and public relations have been guided by the TARES test, a set of five basic ethical principles: *Truthfulness*, *Authenticity* (the integrity and virtue of the rhetor), *Respect* for others, *Equity* between specialists and consumers, and *Social Responsibility* (Baker and Martinson). Truthfulness and authenticity are key principles of that foundational ethic, as is the fundamental ethic of respect for others. Sherry Baker and David Martinson point out that without such a code, persuasion becomes no more than "manipulation, coercion, propaganda, or all of the above" (150)—and that serves no one's interests. In other words, ethical guidelines such as the TARES test are what hold together the trust necessary for communication to be effective. Without that trust, communication falls apart.

Digital media ethicists bring such principles into the realm of online interaction, addressing questions of civility and respect versus offensiveness and incivility—or to the even more serious matters of trolling, bullying, and harassment. We know that trolling and online bullying are ethically wrong—there is no ethical debate or disagreement about that. But there is a good deal of discussion about the best means for responding to it, combatting it, stopping it. Should such practices be deemed illegal? Should the social media accounts of transgressors be suspended—and, if so, who gets to decide such questions? Where is the dividing line between legitimate forms of strong and even combative critique (often needed to combat institutional and pervasive biases—see West) and unproductive verbal harassment? Deciding such questions—determining that dividing line between "allowable expression" and "illegal harassment"—is a matter of vigorous discussion and debate, for scholars of law and ethics, for the judicial system, for the public.

And then there is the question of our own ethical obligations as users and sponsors of digital media: How should we respond to unethical communications online? What are our ethical obligations to combat such activity, whether we are individual writers or social media platform managers? Do we ignore it, do we engage it, do we cancel accounts? These are digital media ethics questions facing all of us who live and work in digital media and who observe or, even, are subjected to, online aggression, hostility, and attack in various forms. We must make ethical decisions, too, about the right way to respond.

Ethics for Access, Accessibility, and Design

Access generally refers to network connectivity, to hardware availability, and to technological knowledge of how to join networks. Charles Moran calls access "the A word" in technology because it undergirds anything else related to uses and impacts of technology.

Technological access usually begins with the economically privileged people and countries who are able to afford new technologies as they come on the market. In the US more than 80 percent of households across all demographics have access to the Internet (U.S. Census Bureau), one of the highest percentages of access in the world (Internet Society). And yet access is by no means close to universal: in the US and worldwide the percentage of people who are *not* able to access the Internet is large—too large—and disproportionately involves people who are poor and/or living in rural areas. Dial-up and even satellite Internet and mobile plans with low limits (and expensive overages) on data usage are not sufficient to allow all people to access today's multimediated communications that impact all facets of their lives. Being aware of and working to eliminate the "infrastructure of inequality" (Grabill) that shapes digital media is an ethical imperative for digital media scholars and for active, engaged citizens.

The infrastructure of the Internet with its many inequalities is not just the platforms, the wires and tubes and towers, the physical devices and digital codes, but infrastructure also includes policies, regulations, and laws regulating usage. Copyright law, custom, and practice significantly influence access, as does government censorship. Citizens in many countries around the world face blocking of online communications by authoritarian regimes (see OpenNet). And citizens throughout the world are often at the mercy of corporate providers of what has become an essential service. In the United States, the 2015 classification of the Internet as a common carrier (a public utility that thus the government can regulate under more stringent Title II regulations so as to ensure greater access for all) is a hotly contested issue. The principle of Net Neutrality— that all content will be delivered at the same speed and that there will be no slow and fast lanes on the Internet (Wu)—regulated Internet usage in the US, but that principle was challenged by powerful corporate interests that want to lock-down the internet, and in a December 2017 federal ruling they succeeded in overturning Net Neutrality. to ensure access to digital technologies, we must pay attention and advocate for equitable policies, regulations, and laws governing and shaping access and connectivity (see McKee, "Policy"; McKee, "Protecting").

But, as Adam Banks describes, access is not just one thing. For people to achieve *transformative access* to technologies—that is, for people to be able to use technologies in ways that are meaningful and purposeful for them, in ways that matter to their lives—people need many interrelated layers of access: material access (having technologies to use), functional access (knowing how to use the technologies), experiential access (using technologies in meaningful ways in daily life), and critical access (being able to critique, resist, and redesign technologies). How people use digital technologies and how they might resist and redesign such technologies is impacted by (among other factors) the design of those technologies. The ethics of design matters for both access and accessibility.

All digital technologies are shaped by the implicit and explicit biases of the designers. The metaphors and frames designers use to structure digital spaces—the now common desktop metaphor that Cynthia Selfe and Richard Selfe discuss, for example—shape how people interact and then create with digital technologies. Sometimes such design decisions can be merely annoying—why is the default on a Mac to make the application icons bounce in the dock? But sometimes they can be downright problematic—the way so many virtual assistants, ever listening and ever ready to help, such as Apple's Siri (in her US release), Amazon's Alexa, and Microsoft's Cortana, are voiced by women. And sometimes the design decisions can be outright dangerous and harmful, the way, for example, when told by a user "I was raped," Siri responded (until a recent upgrade), "I do not understand what you mean by 'rape'" (Miner et al.) or the way Microsoft's chatbot Tay became a genocidal homophobic, anti-semitic racist spewing hate to the world. When designing digital technologies, it is imperative that designers try as best they can to consider the needs and circumstances of all users, but not only to consider or imagine what users might do but actually user test their designs to see how real people actually interact with them. In this respect usability becomes a necessary ethical principle for technology design.

Essential to all technological design are considerations for *accessibility*, which refers to a particular type of access, to both an ethical principle and a set of legal regulations that says that information and systems must be designed in a way that makes them available to all persons. The basic ethic of accessibility says, first, that "it is ethically questionable to practice pedagogies and construct spaces that categorically exclude entire classes of people" (Yergeau et al.) and second that principles of universal design should be followed in all design projects at the outset of the project (as opposed to what happens too often, "retrofitting" after the fact: making accessibility adjustment after documents have been created, see Dolmage). Designing for accessibility is as much an ethical principle for rhetoric as it is a design principle for the computer industry. Despite great gains made, in part with the regulatory and legal infrastructure, such as Section 508 in the US, and in part from industry guidelines such as those of the World Wide Web Consortium, the reality is that technology design is not keeping up with the needs of all users, including users with disabilities, and that is a concern for digital media ethics.

There are so many ethical facets to access, but one last we'll briefly consider is open access to information. Information access has a long history with computing, going back to the hacker ethic that emerged in the 1960s among programmers and software developers onto GNU, and the Free Software Movement in the 1980s; Linus Torvalds and the development of Linux in the 1990s; David Wiley and the Open Content Project in the 1990s; and Larry Lessig and Creative Commons in the early 2000s. What these movements emphasize overall is an ethic of broad access, sharing, fair use, and collaboration, a set of ethical principles we see emerging in two more recent access movements, Open Source and Open Access. The Open Source Initiative refers to a set of open-architecture principles encouraging the sharing, distribution, and re-use of source code. Open Access refers to access to online research of various kinds, generally supporting the view that research should be widely and broadly accessible, without embargoes, restrictions, or steep costs restricting user access (OpenNet Initiative; Suber).

The key ethics principle at work in these movements is that broad sharing and collaboration— of computer resources, of information—is good for society, good for democracy and civic participation, and even, the argument goes, good for business interests (Benkler "Coase's"; Benkler, *Wealth*; Lessig). *To encourage innovation and to promote the values of a democratic society, citizens must have broad, unfettered access to computing resources and to information—and our ethical principles, legal system, and government legislation should promote wide and equitable access.* This macro-ethic stands opposed to strong proprietary models of economic development that favor principles of private ownership, strict copyright control, and pay-as-you-go access. The debate is as much about business and economic policy as it is about ethical principles; it is an issue that pertains to intellectual property law and regulation as well as to the rhetorical ethics of digital media interaction.

Privacy, Consent, and Transparency

Privacy, consent, and transparency of data collection and usage are key issues for all digital writers and for digital media ethicists and is perhaps most pressing in relation to big data, which is a term used to refer to data mining, or information extraction from large data sets. Typically data mining collects user information from a variety of sources, and then aggregates that data in large groups for the purpose of discovering "patterns and subtle relationships" and thereby "predicting future results" that can then be applied back to the individual level (Payne and Landry 28). The practice raises numerous ethical issues related to privacy, security of information, the rights of people to control who has access to their information, what rights business have to collect and perhaps even sell such information, etc.

One problem is that the data collected is analyzed according to algorithms that themselves are often based on biases and problematic assumptions and on correlations that may or may not be valid. Michael McFarland points out that characterizing a human being on the basis of data collected online is fundamentally a dehumanizing move: "It substitutes calculation for human judgment on what should be very sensitive human issues, and thus treats those profiled as objects, as collections of facts, rather than as persons." Others have raised serious methodological questions about the validity of big data analysis, pointing out that in its effort to arrive at generalizable results it often obscures differences and range of variation and misses vital information that would yield very different results (e.g., Baym). And often the data collected is simply inaccurate. Numerous digital media ethicists, as well as business executives, have argued that we need to develop a strong set of ethical standards for data mining (McFarland; Payne and Landry; Rayport; Wen).

Another issue related to online data collection pertains to understandings of privacy. Digital social media blurs the boundaries of public and private; many platforms operate in what Patricia Lange calls publicly-private and privately-public ways. People's understandings of privacy and what's ethical to do and share continually change, as evidenced in the US by the many Pew surveys on privacy (e.g., Raine and Duggan). And our expectations of who controls and protects privacy is changing, too, as Annette Markham shows in her rhetorical study of privacy control language on websites over the past twenty years. What Markham traces, importantly, is that the framework for talking about privacy has flipped in the direction of reassigning responsibility for privacy to the user, rather than to the organizations (corporate, non-profit, governmental) that are harvesting personal data. Facebook doesn't have to protect our privacy—we do.

The amount of information collected about people is mind-boggling—nearly every credit card purchase, website visited, mobile app downloaded, video watched, tweet, post, photo, video, text shared, location GPS-tracking used is being collected, aggregated, disaggregated and sold in a worldwide market of digital data. Make no mistake about this—big data is, first and foremost, big business (already an industry topping $100 billion in revenue) and the push by companies (and governments) to gather ever more information about people so as to be able to predict, influence, and even control and direct behaviors challenges the ethics of digital media (see Kerr, Steeves, and Lucock).

In the US and in many other countries in the world, providers of Web and mobile platforms and applications must inform users of their terms of service, their privacy policies, and what information will be collected and used about them. But anyone who has ever spent time reading terms of service will attest to a number of problems with this system:

1. the documents are typically complicated and either intentionally or unintentionally obfuscating;
2. reading through long documents and clicking innumerable pages of a chunked-up terms is time consuming; and
3. companies and organizations change terms of service frequently, requiring re-reading if you want to stay current.

It's not that people don't care about privacy—they do, as study after study shows. But when faced with the immediate desire to join a site or purchase an item or read a news story, people will choose the immediate desire or need over the longer term risk to privacy created by data collection and aggregation (McDonald).

What does this mean for digital writing scholars? First, we have an ethical obligation to stay informed, to wade through those terms of service and understand what is being collected and to what end. We need to understand privacy settings and how to shape them in the sites and technologies we use. And when working with students and community and corporate partners we need to bring to the fore discussions of privacy and consent not only when designing digital media but also when deciding what platforms, services, and apps to use in communications.

If we believe in an ethic of privacy and of individual control over some of the information about our lives—what Jason Millar identifies as "core privacy"—then we also need, as an ethic, to be active in the public, legal, and regulatory discussions about the future direction of digital technologies.[3] We argue that users of digital technologies should have the right—both ethical and legal—to know who is looking at their data and what's being done with it, whether the one doing the looking is an agent of the government, a corporate employee, or an academic researcher.

When conducting research—for academic, corporate, or community projects—we need to always adhere to an ethic of consent and transparency. The imperative for informed consent increases the more sensitive the topics being discussed, the greater potential harms for participants, and the increased expectation for privacy that users may hold (see McKee and Porter, *Ethics*). People who post comments on a newspaper's website probably have little expectation for privacy—they're posting to a newspaper—but people who post to a social media group that requires moderator approval to join have a higher expectation for privacy. Researchers need to be transparent about their research purposes in these more private spaces. To not do so is to fundamentally alter the nature of the community and to do potential harm not just to the people, but to research itself (see Bromseth; Gajjala; McKee and Porter, *Ethics*). Being transparent about who one is and what one's purpose in and with a community of users in online media all relates to the building and maintaining of trust. We have an ethical obligation to respect people's privacy, to seek their consent, and to be transparent, open, clear, and honest about about what we are collecting and how we plan to use it.

Artificial Intelligence and Human-Machine Communication

Artificial intelligence (AI) agents are rapidly changing the networks of digital communications. Machines aren't just writing to us in the social sense of shaping who and what we are, they are, literally and actually, writing to us and writing for us.[4] Whether we are aware of it or not we are communicating frequently with artificial intelligence agents, AI bots, and we are reading news stories and other communications written by machines.

What does it mean to communicate with an artificially intelligent machine? How does it change rhetoric and ethics? Companies increasingly are turning to bots to provide at least the first step of customer service, moving beyond the annoying and painful-to-use telephone trees to online chat bots that are designed to interact in human-like ways. Of course these bots are still working from key word searches and algorithmic programming. A customer writes, "I bought a pair of shoes that don't fit that I need to return." The bot "reads" *return*, *fit*, and *shoes* and provides pre-programmed information about shoe return, but framed in a human-like way. "I'm sorry to hear that. Would you like to receive a different pair, or have your purchase refunded upon receipt of the return?" For simple queries, such bot communications can work. But even in those low-level, non-high-stakes interactions, people need to know when they are talking with a machine because expectations for human–human communications do differ from those for human–machine communications (see McKee and Porter, *Professional*). And, for all of the improvements in AI agents' communications, there are still fundamental differences between human and machine communications. Thus, a key ethical and rhetoric determination to consider is when, and where, and how AI agents should be used.

If a bot messes up a query such as how to return shoes, it's annoying perhaps, but not hugely problematic. But as AI agents become more intertwined in our daily communications, the ethical implications of how these machines are programmed, and of who has access to the data they gather, increases dramatically. AI agents such as Alexa are designed to be always on and always listening so when they hear their name they begin to record, meaning that a lot of private conversations and voices are housed on Amazon's servers right now. Besides just the creepy factor of Amazon having access to all of these household conversations, there are also law enforcement and constitutional questions as police are seeking Amazon files to hear the voices of a husband and wife to determine whether a possible crime occurred. Toys that talk and interact with children and connect to the Internet are also under investigation for recording children's conversations without parental consent. And, of course, every device that connects to the Internet—whether a smartphone, a smart toy, or a smart appliance—provides an avenue for criminal hackers to access information on networks.

It is not just potential harms to humans we need to consider in the ethics of human–machine interaction. More traditional AI agents can only learn by what they are programmed with—the inputs humans give them. If humans haven't provided the right inputs, then the machine functions in limited ways and with glaring holes in abilities. But new technologies of deep learning are being developed that enable machines to learn not only from human inputs but also from their own continually expanding and evolving interactions with humans and with their own calculations.[5]

AI agents have advanced a long way from Eliza (the 1960s therapy bot) and even from Siri. As communication agents evolve, how will we treat these agents—as objects or, perhaps, eventually, as having human rights? Significantly, the term robot derives from a Czech word meaning *slave*. Are we going to treat machines as merely our slaves or are we going to afford artificial agents rights and privileges of personhood? Perhaps, more accurately than framing this within a human–machine binary, we instead need a new ethic, a cyborgian ethic that applies to us all, human and machine. We are all cyborgs after all, as Donna Haraway so aptly articulates, and this is increasingly so with the rise and ubiquity of digital technologies. We need a new rhetorical ethics for AI–human interaction.

Conclusion

Digital media ethicists distinguish between the different levels and realms where ethical codes of behavior pertain, particularly the distinction between micro-ethics and macro-ethics (Brummer; Davis). Micro-ethics refers to ethics on the individual level: questions pertaining to individual, character, responsibility, and behavior. What is the right thing for *you* to do, as a digital writer, in a particular circumstance?

But ethics is not merely micro—it is not only a matter of individual, personal responsibility (as some traditional accounts presume or insist). At the macro level, corporations, governments, institutions, societies, communities, and cultures also produce and enact ethical codes— sometimes explicit, often implicit—and these larger social entities are also subject to ethical obligations. Does government have the right to monitor our phone calls, email, text messages in the interest of national security? Do businesses have the right to access, use, even sell consumer information without consumer consent? What policies should social media platforms enforce to address the problems of online harassment and fake news? These are larger macro questions where digital media law and ethics overlap and intersect.

For instance: The political question of Net Neutrality is a large-scale policy question for the FCC, but it is also an ethical question because the FCC must balance competing interests (and conflicting views) about what telecommunications policy regarding Internet regulation will be best for US society as a whole. Net Neutrality is a decision about communications networks that is also an ethical decision (as well as an economic policy decision) with far-reaching implications for rhetoric on the ground. The macro-level is the realm that considers large questions of fairness and justice as pertains especially to vulnerable populations, whose interests are often not sufficiently heard or heeded: the economically disadvantaged, underrepresented minorities, persons with disabilities, besieged refugees and immigrants, and those with limited access or accessibility to information communication technologies and, thus, to basic and essential information pertaining to their lives.

Digital media ethics deals centrally with all these questions—questions about individual responsibility at the micro level, but also questions about fair and just policy and practice at the macro level. And, because these concerns pertain to how we discover the available means of persuasion, to how we participate as informed citizens in our society, and to how we use communication technologies to interact with others (or, even, to whether and how we are even allowed to interact with others), to how we write online, these issues are centrally important for digital rhetoric as well. Digital media ethics is the realm where rhetoric and ethics, interaction and writing, technology and public policy all intersect.

Notes

1. Like most emerging, transdisciplinary areas, digital media ethics is not a well-defined or well-organized area of study. Rather, digital media ethics refers to a number of related areas of ethical inquiry across a number of disciplines involving scholars from diverse fields publishing in a variety of journals and working across multiple organizations:

   - journalism ethics (e.g., Drushel and German; Society of Professional Journalists; Ward);
   - communication media and public relations ethics (e.g., Vanacker and Heider; Public Relations Society of America);
   - rhetorical ethics (e.g., Duffy; McKee and Porter, *Professional*; Porter, *Rhetorical*; Pruchnic);
   - Internet research ethics (e.g., Association of Internet Researchers; Etlinger; McKee and Porter, *Ethics*);
   - philosophy, particularly philosophy of technology, philosophy of information, and machine ethics (e.g. Capurro; Ess; Floridi; Wallach and Allen);
   - law and public policy (Benkler, "Coase's"; Benkler, *Wealth*; Lessig), particularly concerns related to privacy, intellectual property, and FCC regulations.

2. In his *Rhetoric*, Aristotle established *ethos* as one of the key persuasive appeals for rhetoric: the *ethos* of the speaker depended on the speaker being virtuous (*arête*), as well as having practical wisdom (*phronesis*) and good will toward audience (*eunoia*). Quintilian's definition of rhetoric as "the art of speaking well" (*Institutio*, 2.13.38) puts ethics at the forefront of rhetoric, seeing the very definition of rhetoric as tied to ethics, in two senses: (1) rhetoric depends on the virtue and ethical qualities of the speaker, as well as (2) rhetoric must ultimately serve the overall good of the *polis*, community, or state.

3. For example, as of this writing (in 2017), the US Congress, with urging from corporations in the telephone and Internet industries, have proposed a bill that would ban the US government from protecting consumer privacy online, thus allowing companies to collect any and all data they wished for any purposes without informing consumers in any way. This is a markedly different approach

from that taken by the European Commission, which in 2016 passed a comprehensive bill protecting personal data.

4. Machines are also, of course, "reading" and scoring student writing (Ericsson and Haswell; Herrington and Moran).

5. For example, in January 2017, a computer won at no-limit Texas Hold'em poker, beating the top players in the world, not by accessing data inputs received from human programmers, but by accessing neural pathways the computer itself laid down as it taught itself and learned to read its competitors' strategies of bluffing, calling, and such. As the beaten human players explained, "On Day 1 it [the computer] played well, but it wasn't impressive. What's impressive is how this thing learned and evolved'" (qtd. in Powell).

Works Cited

Association of Internet Researchers (AoIR). *Ethical Decision-making and Internet Research: Recommendations from the AoIR Ethics Working Committee* (Version 2.0), 2012, http://aoir.org/ethics. Accessed 6 July 2017.

Baker, Sherry, and David Martinson. "The TARES Test: Five Principles for Ethical Persuasion." *Journal of Mass Media Ethics*, vol. 16, nos. 2/3, 2001, pp. 148–75.

Banks, Adam. *Race, Rhetoric, and Technology: Searching for Higher Ground.* Lawrence Erlbaum, 2005.

Baym, Nancy K. "Data Not Seen: The Uses and Shortcomings of Social Media Metrics." *First Monday*, vol. 18, no. 10, 2013, firstmonday.org/ojs/index.php/fm/article/view/4873. Accessed 6 July 2017.

Benkler, Yochai. "Coase's Penguin, or, Linux and the Nature of the Firm." *Yale Law Journal*, vol. 112, no. 3, 2002, pp. 369–446.

——. *The Wealth of Networks: How Social Production Transforms Markets and Freedom.* Yale UP, 2006.

Bromseth, Janne C.H. "Ethical and Methodological Challenges in Research on Net-mediated Communication in a Norwegian Research Context." *Applied Ethics in Internet Research*, edited by May Thorseth. NTNU UP, 2003, pp. 67–85.

Brummer, James. "Business Ethics: Micro and Macro." *Journal of Business Ethics*, vol. 4, no. 2, 1985, pp. 81–91.

Capurro, Rafael. "Towards an Ontological Foundation of Information Ethics." *Ethics and Information Technology*, vol. 8, no. 4, 2006, pp. 175–86.

Davis, Michael. "Engineers and Sustainability: An Inquiry into the Elusive Distinction between Macro-, Micro-, and Meso-ethics." *Journal of Applied Ethics and Philosophy*, vol. 2, 2010, pp. 12–20.

Dolmage, Jay. "Mapping Composition: Inviting Disability in the Front Door." *Disability and the Teaching of Writing*, Eds. Cynthia Lewiecki-Wilson and Brenda Jo Brueggemann. Bedford-St. Martin's, 2008, pp. 14–27.

Drushel, Bruce E., and Kathleen German, editors. *The Ethics of Emerging Media: Information, Social Norms, and New Media Technology.* Continuum, 2011.

Duffy, John. "The Good Writer: Virtue Ethics and the Teaching of Writing." *College English*, vol. 79, no. 3, 2017, pp. 229–50.

Ericsson, Patricia Freitag, and Richard H. Haswell. *Machine Scoring of Student Essays: Truth and Consequences.* Utah State UP, 2006.

Ess, Charles. *Digital Media Ethics*, 2nd ed., Polity, 2014.

Etlinger, Susan. *The Trust Imperative: A Framework for Ethical Data Use.* Market Definition Report, Altimeter Group. 25 June 2015, www.altimetergroup.com/2015/06/new-report-the-trust-imperative-a-framework-for-ethical-data-use/.

European Commission. "Protection of Personal Data." 2016, http://ec.europa.eu/justice/data-protection. Accessed 6 July 2017.

Floridi, Luciano. *The 4th Revolution: How the Infosphere is Reshaping Human Reality.* Oxford UP, 2014.

Gajjala, Radhika. *Cyber Selves: Feminist Ethnographies of South Asian Women.* Altamira, 2004.

Grabill, Jeffrey T. "On Divides and Interfaces: Access, Class, and Computers." *Computers and Composition*, vol. 20, no. 4, 2003, pp. 455–72.

Haraway, Donna. "A Cyborg Manifesto: Science, Technology, and Socialist-feminism in the Late Twentieth Century." *Simians, Cyborgs, and Women: The Reinvention of Nature.* Routledge, 1991, pp. 149–81.

Herrington, Anne, and Charles Moran. "What Happens When Machines Read Our Students' Writing?" *College English*, vol. 63, 2001, 480–99.

Internet Society. "Global Internet Penetration." 2017. www.internetsociety.org/map/global-internet-report/?gclid=CLvqz6XOntICFQZbfgodsRkOig#global-internet-penetration. Accessed 6 July 2017.

Jensen, Ric. "Blogola, Sponsored Posts, and the Ethics of Blogging." *The Ethics of Emerging Media: Information, Social Norms, and New Media Technology*, edited by Kathleen German and Bruce E. Drushel. Continuum, 2011, pp. 213–32.

Kerr, Ian, Valerie Steeves, and Carole Lucock, Eds. *Lessons from the Identity Trail: Anonymity, Privacy, and Identity in a Networked Society*. Oxford UP, 2009.

Kuhn, Martin. "Interactivity and Prioritizing the Human: A Code of Blogging Ethics." *Journal of Mass Media Ethics*, vol. 22, 2007, pp. 18–36.

Lange, Patricia G. "Publicly Private and Privately Public: Social Networking on YouTube." *Journal of Computer-Mediated Communication*, vol. 13, no. 1, 2007, pp. 361–80.

Lessig, Lawrence. *Free Culture: How Big Media Uses Technology and the Law to Lock Down Culture and Control Creativity*. Penguin, 2004.

McDonald, Aleecia M. "Online Privacy: Industry Self-regulation in Practice." Google Talk, September 17, 2009, www.youtube.com/watch?v=BNO7Q5_o4RY. Accessed 6 July 2017.

McFarland, Michael, S. J. "Ethical Implications of Data Aggregation." Markkula Center for Applied Ethics, Santa Clara University, 1 June 2012, www.scu.edu/ethics/focus-areas/internet-ethics/resources/ethical-implications-of-data-aggregation/. Accessed 6 July 2017.

McKee, Heidi A. "Policy Matters Now and in the Future: Net Neutrality, Corporate Data Mining, and Government Surveillance." *Computers and Composition*, vol. 28, 2011, pp. 276–91.

———. "Protecting Net Neutrality and the Infrastructure of Internet Delivery: Considerations for Our Past, Present, and Future." *Kairos*, vol. 20, no. 2, 2016, kairos.technorhetoric.net/20.2/topoi/beck-et-al/mckee.html. Accessed 6 July 2017.

McKee, Heidi A., and James E. Porter. *The Ethics of Internet Research: A Rhetorical, Case-based Approach*. Peter Lang, 2009.

———. *Professional Communication and Network Interaction: A Rhetorical and Ethical Approach*. Routledge, 2017.

Markham, Annette N. "From Using to Sharing: A Story of Shifting Fault Lines in Privacy and Data Protection Discourse." *Ethics for a Digital Age*, edited by Bastiaan Vanacker and Don Heider. Peter Lang, 2016, pp. 189–205.

Millar, Jason. "Core Privacy: A Problem for Predictive Data Mining." *Lessons from the Identity Trail: Anonymity, Privacy, and Identity in a Networked Society*, edited by Ian Kerr, Valerie Steeves, and Carole Lucock. Oxford UP, 2009, pp. 103–19.

Miner, Adam S., Arnold Milstein, Stephen Schueller, Roshini Hegde, Christina Mangurian, and Eleni Linos. "Smartphone-based Conversational Agents and Responses to Questions about Mental Health, Interpersonal Violence, and Physical Health." *JAMA Internal Medicine*, vol. 176, no. 5, 2016, pp. 619–25.

Moran, Charles. "Access: The 'A' Word in Technology Studies." *Passions, Pedagogies, and 21st-Century Technologies*, edited by Gail E. Hawisher and Cynthia L. Selfe, Utah State UP, 1999, pp. 205–30.

OpenNet Initiative. "Research and Data." 2016, opennet.net/. Accessed 6 July 2017.

Open Source Initiative. "The Open Source Definition." 2007, opensource.org/osd. Accessed 6 July 2017.

Payne, Dinah, and Brett J. L. Landry. "A Composite Strategy for the Legal and Ethical Use of Data Mining." *International Journal of Management, Knowledge and Learning*, vol. 1, no. 1, 2012, pp. 27–43.

Porter, James E. *Rhetorical Ethics and Internetworked Writing*. Ablex, 1998.

Powell, Devin. "How Computers Were Finally Able to Best Poker Pros." *Washington Post*, 4 Feb. 2017, www.washingtonpost.com/national/health-science/how-computers-were-finally-able-to-best-poker-pros/2017/02/03/3d1fd8c8-e7fa-11e6-b82f-687d6e6a3e7c_story.html?utm_term=.261f8c4a1026. Accessed 6 July 2017.

Pruchnic, Jeff. *Rhetoric and Ethics in the Cybernetic Age: The Transhuman Condition*. Routledge, 2014.

Public Relations Society of America (PRSA). "Member Code of Ethics." 2000, apps.prsa.org/AboutPRSA/Ethics/CodeEnglish/. Accessed 6 July 2017.

Quintilian. *Institutes of Oratory (Institutio Oratoria)*. 2006, trans. John Selby Watson (1856), rhetoric.eserver.org/quintilian. Accessed 6 July 2017.

Raine, Lee, and Maeve Duggan. "Pew Study on Privacy and Information Sharing." January 14, 2016, www.pewinternet.org/files/2016/01/PI_2016.01.14_Privacy-and-Info-Sharing_FINAL.pdf. Accessed 6 July 2017.

Rayport, Jeffrey F. "What Big Data Needs: A Code of Ethical Practices." *MIT Technology Review*, 26 May 2011, www.technologyreview.com/s/424104/what-big-data-needs-a-code-of-ethical-practices/. Accessed 6 July 2017.

Selfe, Cynthia L., and Richard J. Selfe, Jr. "The Politics of the Interface: Power and its Exercise in Electronic Contact Zones." *College Composition and Communication*, vol. 45, no. 4, 1994, pp. 480–504.

Society of Professional Journalists (SPJ). "SPJ Code of Ethics." 2014, www.spj.org/ethicscode.asp. Accessed 6 July 2017.

Suber, Peter. *Open Access*. The MIT Press, 2012.

U.S. Census Bureau. "Measuring America: A Digital Nation." March 23, 2016, www.census.gov/library/visualizations/2016/comm/digital_nation.html. Accessed 6 July 2017.

Vanacker, Bastiaan, and Don Heider, Eds. *Ethics for a Digital Age*. Peter Lang, 2016.

Wallach, Wendell, and Colin Allen. *Moral Machines: Teaching Robots Right from Wrong*. Oxford UP, 2009.

Ward, Stephen J. A. "Digital Media Ethics." Center for Journalism Ethics, University of Wisconsin-Madison, 2017, ethics.journalism.wisc.edu/resources/digital-media-ethics. Accessed 6 July 2017.

Wen, Howard. "The Ethics of Big Data." *Forbes*, 21 June 2012, www.forbes.com/sites/oreillymedia/2012/06/21/the-ethics-of-big-data/#3be4f1d84934. Accessed 6 July 2017.

West, Thomas. "The Racist Other." *JAC*, vol. 17, 1997, pp. 215–26.

World Wide Web Consortium (WC3). "Web Content Accessibility Guidelines (WCAG) 2.0." 11 Dec. 2008, www.w3.org/TR/WCAG20. Accessed 6 July 2017.

Wu, Tim. "A Proposal for Network Neutrality." 2002, www.timwu.org/OriginalNNProposal.pdf. Accessed 6 July 2017.

Yergeau, Melanie, Elizabeth Brewer, Stephanie Kerschbaum, Sushil K. Oswal, Margaret Price, Cynthia L. Selfe, Michael J. Salvo, and Franny Howes. "Multimodality in Motion: Disability and Kairotic Spaces." *Kairos*, vol. 18, no. 1, 2013, technorhetoric.net/18.1/coverweb/yergeau-et-al/index.html. Accessed 6 July 2017.

38

TOWARD A DIGITAL CULTURAL RHETORIC

Angela M. Haas

This chapter works toward a digital cultural rhetoric framework for rhetoric and composition studies. To do so, this chapter provides a working definition for digital cultural rhetorics, outlines some foundational values of digital cultural rhetorics scholarship, and demonstrates what those values look like in practice. Modest, tentative, and productive in nature, this offering is intended to inspire future conversations and generate revised methodologies for studying and thus making claims about digital rhetoric in general and, more specifically, digital cultural rhetoric. Ultimately, this chapter calls for a digital cultural rhetorics approach to digital rhetorics scholarship so that we better understand how our research constructs our scholarly selves, our disciplinary community, and others who might (not) imagine themselves part of our community.

Despite the urge for some to conflate digital writing and digital rhetoric, digital cultural rhetoric works in excess to digital writing. Digital research collective DigiRhet.org describes digital writing as "writing produced on handheld and desktop digital devices and distributed primarily via wireless and wired networks" (238). Further, DigiRhet.org makes clear that "[w]riting is no longer a purely text-driven practice"; rather it "requires carefully and critically analyzing and selecting among multiple media elements, such as words, motion, interactivity, and visuals to make meaning" (240). To be sure, though, this careful, critical analysis and selection requires rhetorical principles that inform the ways, places, and spaces in which we practice digital rhetoric. Thus, digital rhetoric broadens our focus beyond production-driven processes toward rhetorically situated digital praxis, informed by rhetorical principles, including audience, ethos, purpose, context, media, and content usability, among others.

Digital rhetoric is the digital negotiation of information—and its historical, social, economic, and political contexts and influences—to affect change. By digital negotiation, we can think in terms of the role(s) of digital media in relation to invention, arrangement, style, memory, and delivery. Further, we might consider the rhetorical work of digitality as key to digital rhetoric. As I explain elsewhere, "[a]ll writing is digital—*digitalis* in Latin, which typically denotes 'of or relating to the fingers or toes' or a 'coding of information'" (Haas, "Wampum" 84). No matter which approach, digital cultural rhetoricians typically agree that digital rhetoric requires a negotiation—an interfacing—between bodies, identities, rhetoric, and technology.

Digital cultural rhetorics, then, recognize and make explicit the plurality of embodied, technological, and rhetorical negotiations within specific cultural contexts and asymmetrical power relations. To do so, digital cultural rhetorics scholars typically interface their digital rhetoric work with cultural theory and/or situate it within specific communities and cultures of practice. Demonstrating a diversity of digital literacies, practices, pedagogies, and publics, then, digital cultural rhetorics highlight the relationships between the rhetorical situation and the actors (animal, technological, non-animal environmental, and hybridized), institutions, subjectivity, power networks, agency, and action therein—and account for the (de)selections made when representing those relations and relationships. Thus, digital cultural rhetorics challenge the enduring monolithic rhetoric of "technological culture" and myths that technologies are "by nature" neutral, objective, democratizing, emancipatory, etc.

To be clear, all digital writing does cultural rhetorical work that privileges certain epistemological frameworks and sponsors certain ideological agendas, thereby benefitting some communities more than others. However, this chapter is concerned with digital cultural rhetoric that makes apparent its acts of privileging and sponsoring. The next section will attempt to explicate some of the foundational rhetorical work and values of digital cultural rhetorics scholarship.

Foundations and Features of Digital Cultural Rhetorics

Certainly, digital cultural rhetorics scholarship does more cultural and rhetorical work than what is outlined in this chapter. Thus, rather than exhaustive, this chapter aims to open conversations about existing and future digital cultural rhetorics inquiry. Specifically, this section charts a rhetorical repertoire common across digital cultural rhetorics work, including: interrogating the politics of digital interfaces; studying digital rhetorics in relation to/with specific communities and cultures of practices; examining the relationships between older and newer technologies; valuing diverse bodies; and reassessing access. Interwoven throughout this section are theories, methodologies and methods for studying and practicing the digital cultural rhetorical repertoire, such as case study, historiography, (auto)ethnography and story. Despite the use of subheadings to facilitate spatially organized logics, it is important to read productive intellectual and practical overlaps across and between the rhetorical repertoire.

Politics of the Interface

For more than two decades, technofeminist scholarship in computers and composition studies scholars such as Gail Hawisher, Cindy Selfe, Dickie Selfe, Kristine Blair, Pamela Takayoshi, Patricia Sullivan, Dànielle DeVoss, and others have—among other things—troubled persistent myths about the relationships between objectivity and technology. As Cindy and Dickie Selfe put it in "Politics of the Interface," computers—like all technologies—are not neutral. Neither is our pedagogy. Though technology and digital pedagogies can certainly be used toward liberatory ends, Selfe and Selfe posit that both can have colonizing effects, albeit often unwittingly.

No doubt, digital rhetoric can result in a wide range of effects, from emancipatory to oppressive, both, or somewhere in between. Turn of the century technofeminist scholarship in computers and composition studies (Blair and Takayoshi; Brady Aschauer; Haas et al.; Kantrowitz; Reilly; Tannen) critiqued the history of technology design, production, and use as an inherently male enterprise by evidencing how hegemonic definitions and designs of technology often: were heavily biased against women; were inextricably bound to male-dominated domains of science and industry; and reproduced harmful stereotypes of women as technologically inferior, disinterested, fearful, passive, and submissive. In response, technofeminists worked to: underscore that technology is always already political, value-laden, and subjective; redress biases and reimagine gender-just technology design; study cases of digital rhetorical resistance, transgression, and empowerment.

413

This foundational technofeminist scholarship helped to clear a path for digital cultural rhetorics research, and from this path, more diverse technofeminist, critical race, decolonial, queer, and disability frameworks—among others—have been developed to (ad)/(re)dress intersectional digital diversities, (in)equity, and oppressions and to highlight the ways in which interfacing is always already political (Alexander and Banks; Banks, *Digital*, *Race*; Blackmon, "But," "(Cyber)"; DeVoss; Haas, "Making"; Monroe; Rhodes and Alexander; Yergeau "Aut(hored)ism," *Multimodality*). Therefore, digital cultural rhetorical approaches to studying the politics of the interface—and the relationships therein—help reveal that even when not intentional, digital design can disproportionately affect some communities than others. For example, despite their "good intentions" of designing an app aimed at "making city streets more walkable," Allison McGuire and Daniel Herrington, co-founders of the app SketchFactor, were openly criticized on social media and in news outlets for promoting racial and classist profiling, especially of poor communities and communities of color, by asking users outside of those communities to label them as "sketchy" and "dangerous." As *The New Yorker*'s Andrew Marantz reported, "Many people pointed out that the app, which was ostensibly designed to 'empower everyone,' would, in practice, empower only people who owned smartphones. SketchFactor's Twitter feed was inundated with such hashtags as #racist, #classist, and #gentrification." To be certain, technologies are often unequally delegated and prescribed in relation to gender, race, ethnicity, nationality, class, sexuality, generation, and (dis)ability—and these relationships and interfaces (re)construct identities and politics worthy of our study and intervention.

Historicizing Digital Cultural Rhetorics

Christina Haas has called for "a rich theoretical accounting" of the relationships between old and new technologies "beyond oversimplified, bifurcated models of technological development" so that we might learn from older media and imagine more useful and usable technologies in the future (210). Many digital cultural rhetorics scholars have responded with research methodologies informed by complex models and logics of technological development from underrepresented and/or underserved communities of digital practice—frameworks that challenge colonial and capitalistic commonplaces, such as that old and new technologies are clearly differentiated from one another and new technologies are automatically more efficient, more powerful, or more convenient—thus, more "advanced." Further, digital cultural rhetorical frameworks articulate expressed goals of studying the relationships between older and newer technologies in order to work toward technologically just and sustainable futures for the communities with/for/from which we are working. For instance, Adam Banks builds a digital griots mixed-tape methodology for his research, drawing on African American rhetorical theories and technological practices useful for "repurposing old technologies and new and remixing social economic political intimate relationships" in the search "for something new to connect with the old, for that old/new way to create another world, another universe, another text" (*Digital* 4–5).

Given the productive tensions between new and old media and rhetorical practices, historiography is a common research methodology among digital cultural rhetoricians. Among other things, digital cultural rhetorical historiographies offer case studies (explained in more detail in the next section) of underrepresented digital literacies that evidence that all communities and cultures have histories of and expertise in digital rhetorical work, and in the process, often reveal and challenge historical and contemporary biases that persist in technology design perceptions and practices, as well as digital rhetoric studies writ large. For example, Brenda Jo Brueggemann's digital narrative reveals common oppressive agendas across technologies, drills, and therapies used to test the deaf community. On the other hand, Colleen Reilly's feminist historiography of the vibrator reminds us that feminists have a rich history of subverting the patriarchal agendas of gendered technologies and wrestling agency and rhetoric away from the technosphere. Once used against women to diagnose and treat hysteria, it was first appropriated by the porn industry and then by feminists for their personal needs.

Similarly, I've argued American Indians have diverse and complex histories of technological expertise—histories and complexity worthy of more attention in digital rhetoric and indigenous studies, and perhaps more importantly, in Indian country ("Wampum"). I interfaced decolonial theory, hypertext theory, and historiography to inform my study of historical and contemporary accounts of pre- and post-colonial (in terms of contact with colonial settlers) wampum belt design among several North American indigenous communities to evidence the hypertextual work of wampum production, arrangement, and delivery. Adam Banks's historiography of African American digital rhetorical traditions includes case studies of the technological expertise required to design slave quilts, black architecture, and urban planning. In the process, he demonstrates how "African Americans have always sought 'third way' answers to systematically racist exclusions, demanding full access to and participation in American society and its technologies, to ensure that not only black people but all Americans can participate as full partners" (*Race* 1). Indeed, theorizing complex relationships between old(er) and new(er) technologies in rhetorically and culturally situated ways can afford unique disciplinary insights and revise previously held assumptions about technology toward more culturally inclusive understandings of digital rhetorics that are also responsive to community needs.

Case Studies of Communities in Digital Practice

Digital cultural rhetorics scholarship is typically situated in specific cultures with diverse rhetorical skill, communities of practice, technological expertise, and capacity for social change. As such, case studies are a common research method for studying and delivering digital cultural rhetorical inquiry. Digital cultural–rhetorical case studies help us to interrogate our perceptions of the relationships between and across local and global communities, rhetoric, and technological theory, access, and literacy. Although this section will highlight the digital–cultural rhetorical work of two specific case studies, all of the historiographies and (auto)ethnographies discussed in this chapter employ case study as a research methodology for their project.

In his digital Samaritan project, Jim Ridolfo works with and for the Samaritan community to increase access to their cultural patrimony through digitization. The Samaritans are "one of the smallest religious and ethnic communities in the Middle East with a population of only 770," only two population centers situated "squarely in the midst of the contemporary Israel–Palestinian conflict," and manuscripts "spread out in major museums, libraries, and universities across the globe." As part of the ongoing project of digitizing Samaritan manuscripts, Ridolfo and Samaritan community members theorize Samaritan "textual diaspora" (culturally invaluable Samaritan manuscripts housed in distant physical locations) as digital objects as part of the process in determining how to "communicate their cultural sovereignty to the world" (xvii–1).

Adam Banks contributes to Black techno-dialogic traditions via multiple case studies of African American digital rhetorical expertise. In *Digital Griots*, Banks follows his call for our discipline, so enamored of "remix culture," to consider "what we might learn from the rhetorical practices and traditions of the culture that gave us the remix" with examples of community-based African American multimedia rhetorical practices of DJs and DJing that can and should inform disciplinary "endeavors to define, theorize, and practice multimedia writing" (2). Banks links the DJ to other griotic figures—including the preacher, stand-up comic, and storyteller—

to contextualize the black multimedia rhetorical complex of DJing as a "model for writing that thoroughly weaves together oral performance, print literacy, mastery and interrogation of technologies, and technologies that can lead to a renewed vision for both composition and African American rhetoric" (13).

The historiographies and case studies mentioned thus far provide successful models for case study methodology as a means for deeply contextualizing digital cultural rhetorics work and honoring the digital, rhetorical, and cultural theories and practices with and for whom we are doing digital cultural rhetorical work. The case studies cited for other purposes later in this chapter provide additional examples of how to approach case study methodology in rhetorical and ethical ways.

(Relationality to) Bodies Matter

I hope that it has been made clear thus far that digital cultural rhetoricians are not only interested in the relationships across technologies but also in the diversity of relationships between bodies and technologies. Early digital cultural rhetorics scholarship was successful in diversifying white, English-speaking bodies in relation to digital literacies, practices, pedagogies, and publics despite limited access to technological means of representation, whereas more recent digital cultural rhetorics scholarship is invested in further diversifying our accounting of the body and embodiment in our research, practice, and pedagogy. For instance, in her recent study of how professional translators working at the Hispanic Center of Western Michigan use cultural and digital tools to translate information between Englishes and Spanishes, Laura Gonzales used video data to "account for verbal, embodied, and material interactions among people and technologies," such as how "participants used a wide range of rhetorical strategies including gestures, storytelling, and drawing to translate information."

Work such as Gonzales's reminds us that there is great value in making the diversification of our embodied, emplaced relations with technology a foundational and ongoing project for/ in digital rhetoric studies. A vision. A mission. Core value. Diversifying current understandings of digital relations interrupts problematic binaries (e.g., virtual and physical) and universalizing narratives (e.g., one can overcome their bodies in the digital world; technologies are democratizing and empowering). Thus, common questions asked by digital cultural rhetoricians are: Whose bodies are visible in digital spaces? For whom are visible digital bodies a risk? Which technologies are empowering for whom? Democratizing for which communities, cultures, and languages?

Relationships between bodies, the virtual, and the digital are never universal. Relationships are limited by representation and are always already rhetorical, contextual, and cultural. When the democratizing potentials of cyberspace were being touted in the 1990s by academic and public intellectuals alike, including the curious promise of erasing difference, Joanne Addison and Susan Hilligoss reflected on and analyzed how they negotiated their lesbian identities while participating in an online study of academic women and computers (23). While Addison and Hilligoss acknowledged coming out online in order to "articulate an identity that our society works to render invisible" (38), they were aware of the dominant stereotype that "being homosexual means being sexual in every situation" and thus worried that "coming out [online] may threaten other members of the discussion [forum] by implicitly sexualizing the discussion, moving it beyond an isolated body to relationships between virtual bodies" (35). Nearly two decades later with vast changes in understanding virtual networks and embodiment, we now know that Addison and Hilligoss's bodies were never in isolation; instead, some of the relationships between their bodies and the perceptions of others in physically networked spaces were reproduced in digitally networked spaces.

Digital cultural rhetorics scholars are also invested in studying how bodies matter to teaching writing with technology. Jonathan Alexander and Will Banks co-edited a special issue of *Computers and Composition* on "Sexualities, Technologies, and the Teaching of Writing" designed to explore and productively complicate the connections between sexuality, writing, and technology. Contributors (Barrios; McKee; Peters and Swanson; Reilly; Rhodes) presented ways in which sexuality "is integral to the ways that we already conceive of technology and writing, as well as the bodies that produce texts (and are texts themselves) in the writing classroom" (274). Collectively, this issue brings together theories and practices of gender, sexuality, and technology to create a *praxis* space for readers to "reflect on how norms for sexuality are socially, culturally, politically, and psychologically constituted," "on the intersections between politics and the mind and body," and "the ways that various technologies disrupt traditional notions of writing and writing instruction, effectively queering spaces that were once dominated by pens, pencils, and loose-leaf paper" (274–5).

Effectively queering neurotypical representations of autism, disability rhetorics scholars also contribute to intersectional mind–body politics with and through technology (Brueggemann; Smyser-Fauble; Yergeau "Aut(hored)ism," "Multimodality"). In "Aut(hored)ism," Melanie Yergeau uses digital text and video as "texts of defense" to confront "normative narratives" that author problematic rhetorics about the bodies of autistics. Yergeau shares her embodied experiences interfacing with hegemonic rhetorics about her body:

> As I immerse myself in Aspergian literature, I find myself being authored toward my label. As I immerse myself in medicalized journal articles, I find myself being authored toward my label. As I am immersed in neurotypical discourses, as I am immersed in discourse theory generally, I find myself being authored toward normalcy, steered toward passing, driven away from my label. I am a passive recipient of discourse conventions, the ultimate student being shaped by several almighty mentors.
>
> At all ends, now that I've got this label, I either am or am not this label, depending on who is authoring my narrative at any given point in time. And, though I certainly despise any association with victimization, I cannot help but feel that such authorial decisions rarely involve me.

Ultimately, Yergeau posits, "If my body is a text, whether metaphorically or literally, it is a narrative, a narrative of passing."

Auto(Ethnography) and Story

It is precisely the narrative—narratives of the self, and self-in-community—that most, if not all, digital cultural rhetoricians hold worthy of engagement as a mode of and medium for research, critique, theorizing, and more. Autoethnography, story, testimonio, narrative, and other life writing methods appear to interface well with most cultural theories, given the prevalence and importance of story in digital cultural rhetorics scholarship. Digital cultural frameworks that employ autoethnography and story offer the same benefits as case studies, as well as the situated ethos that comes with the telling of lived experiences from the perspective of someone whose body's inhabited the direct interfacing. Case study methodologies may or may not engage in narrative theory or practice; those that do not typically report on the lived experiences of those shared, observed, read, or heard about.

Because of these complexities, scholars who employ cultural theories and practices to study digital rhetoric often operationalize narratives of subjectivity, positionality, and relationality (to communities and institutions and networks of power) as central to their work. In his teacher-research into Twitter in a predominantly Latinx classroom, Cruz Medina positions himself as a Latino educator "interested in empowering students of color to construct an academic identity in digital space that performs *latinidad* as resistance while working within a dominant system" (73). Storied subjectivities are integral to Jacqueline Rhodes and Jonathan Alexander's multimodal e-book *Techne: Queer Meditations on Writing the Self*, which blends phenomenology, auto-ethnography, and queer theories to "probe the often contradictory interplay between digital and traditional writing technologies and the author/ed self" by studying "how composing practices arise out of the complex interplay among discursive formations, embodiment, and mediating technologies" and enacting "a generative, multimodal *techne* of self." Rhodes and Alexander's method for this enactment is "composing while queer," a complex queer rhetorical practice that combines affect and rhetorical negotiation to disrupt norms that reinforce heterosexist ways of knowing and being by de-composing, un-composing, and re-composing dominant narratives of sexuality, gender, and identity—thereby also "disrupting how we understand ourselves to ourselves."

Similarly, Brueggemann participates in this "de-composing, un-composing, and re-composing" of the self by weaving digital video autobiography with a story of Carl Dupree, a deaf student attending Gallaudet College, restrained by public safety officers for getting upset and scared about failing for the fourth time the high-stakes exit exam for the foundational English 50 course. The officers handcuffed Dupree and applied too much pressure when restraining him; Dupree's neck broke, and he died. Brueggemann attended Gallaudet the year following Dupree's death in 1991. One month away from taking the exit exam in English 50 class Brueggemann was chatting back and forth with peers "in written English on an interactive computer network" when one student typed the following message for all to read: "English 50 Monster looms. English 50 monster like staff not students. English 50 monster killed Carl Dupree." Brueggemann contextualizes why "the English 50 monster loomed large in so many deaf people's lives" by comparing the exit exam to "the heavy historical march" of forced oral instruction, lip reading, speech articulation drills, and more. Indeed, Brueggemann shares that she carries the English 50 monster with her still today as a teacher, scholar, and person. But she "greets the monster" and studies it in an effort to reshape it.

Albeit very different backgrounds and unique experiences with technologies, common to digital cultural narratives is the importance of understanding how digital bodies, identities, rhetorics, literacies, and ecologies are always already informed by all our relations—educational, familial, communal, geographical, and power, just to name a few. To highlight the importance of situating literacies of technology "within specific cultural, material, educational, and familial contexts that influence, and are influenced by, their acquisition and development," Gail Hawisher et al. discuss the literacy narratives of Pearson, an African American woman born in Fort Jackson, South Carolina in 1964 into a middle-class, Baptist, military family, and Moraski, a white woman born in the rural Upper Peninsula of Michigan into a middle-class Catholic family (643). The authors foreground the significance of multiple and unique contexts for digital literacies, but they also take note of the "related factors that shape, and are shaped by, people's adoption of computers as literacy tools and environments," such as "social contexts; educational practices, values, and expectations; cultural and ideological formations like race, class, and gender; political and economic trends and events; family practices and experiences; and historical and material conditions—among many, many other factors" (644). To be sure, these factors interface with (auto)ethnography and story in complex and varied ways.

(Re)Assessing Access

Digital cultural rhetoricians understand that digital access means more than just access to computers and other technologies. Access is rhetorically and culturally situated, is dependent upon embodied and material conditions, and is dynamic, complex, and contingent. Access is a practice and a process. Indeed, Moraski and Pearson's aforementioned literacy narratives illustrate that specific conditions of access had a substantial effect on their digital literacy acquisition, development, and practice (Hawisher et al. 4). Dwedor Morais Ford describes some of the conditions that have affected access to computers in Ghana, Kenya, and Egypt, including shut downs in higher education at times of civil unrest and the lack of physical and educational infrastructure to develop and support digital research programs and research in computers and writing. Ford explains that "[w]hat limited computers are available are [typically] used to train computer scientists and programmers" (313).

Given that material conditions change over time, digital cultural rhetoricians are committed to the ongoing project of (re)assessing what we mean by technological and digital access. The remainder of this section provides a few frameworks offered by digital cultural rhetoricians that support this endeavor. For example, Hawisher et al. offer the concept of digital *lifespans* to account for how digital literacies—like any literacy—are more than an accumulation or acquisition. Rather, "literacies have lifespans. Specific literacies emerge; they overlap and compete with pre-existing forms; they accumulate, especially, perhaps, in periods of transition; they also eventually fade away. And [. . .] some may fade faster than others" (665). Of course, lifespans of particular literacies "will vary among individuals, and communities, within regions and ecological patches" (665).

Because of these variances across cultures and communities, as well as the variances in positions and thus access to and agency within networks of power, Adam Banks argues for frameworks of *transformative access* that allow for the development and articulation of specific models, rhetorics, and practices "that can provide excluded members of society access to systems of power and grounds on which those systems can be challenged and ultimately changed in meaningful ways" (*Race* 2). Banks explains that *transformative access* is supported by developing *critical access*, or understanding "the benefits and problems of any technology well enough to be able to critique, resist, and avoid them when necessary" (42). He goes on to evidence how this critical and transformative access is practiced in several previously mentioned case studies.

This interest in practice is at the heart of Annette Powell's call that digital rhetoricans move beyond connectivity to technology to instead inquire about access as a practice and process. Powell asks that we examine the *practices of access* to better understand "how social and economic infrastructures mediate access," such as "what gets reinforced, valued, and rewarded by local communities" (16–17). To model this framework, Powell examines the practices of access of two groups of middle-school students from low-income under-served populations who participated in a federal grant funded technology camp housed in the computer classrooms of a large urban university. After interviewing forty-six students and, in some instances, speaking with their parents, siblings, and teachers, Powell found that "simply having a computer available to them did not completely open access for these students. Access was continually in flux and predicated upon these students' negotiation of everyday social and literacy practices" (21). These negotiations are practices and processes of interfacing rather than simply a proximity to technology and, thus, are critical to better grasping digital access.

Finally, the contexts for these digital literacy practices and processes should be discerned less as portals to access and more in line with our value in rhetorical context. Powell posits that

> [i]f we consider "access as practice" not static but rather as rich, complex, and not easily categorized, or if we think of access as an on-going process, we might better understand access as the way that one uses technology in a given context. (17)

Surely, rhetorical situations extend beyond community and cultural contexts. As Powell's case study makes clear, geographic, institutional, and organizational contexts also matter. For example, Ridolfo contextualizes how some of the politics, processes, and practices of digital and material archiving cultural patrimony, Israel–Palestinian relations, and textual diaspora have influenced his project and the cultural sustainability and sovereignty of the Samaritan community. Finally, Dànielle DeVoss et al. argue that new media composing practices are deeply embedded in institutional and cultural infrastructures. Thus, contextualizing infrastructures is critical to digital cultural rhetorics work, as "[t]hese often invisible structures make possible and limit, shape and constrain, influence and penetrate all acts of composing new media in writing classes" (16).

Openings

In 2006, Adam Banks critiqued the "whitinizing of cyberspace" that allowed for corporate digital publications to cater to mainstream White readers interests and thus ignore issues of racism (*Race*). A decade later, despite all the activist work, this remains a real concern for digital cultural rhetoricians, among other worries related to the ongoing rhetoric of white and linguistic supremacy, transphobia, homophobia, sexism, Nationalism, ageism, and ableism—among other oppressions—perpetuated in corporate and social media. Some of this rhetoric has been practiced and endorsed by current US President #45 who admitted via Twitter knowing little to nothing about how the Internet works. Suffice it to say, digital cultural rhetoricians invested in US-digital relations have a good deal of important work to do in the decades to come given the contemporary confluences of hate speech, cultural and therapeutic ethos, shifts in power (perceived and actual) with the rise (actual and perceived) of authoritarianism, conflations and confusions between "real" and "fake" news, professor watch lists, and more. Writing about and in this bizarre zeitgeist challenges the fitness of existing digital cultural frameworks for the current situations in which we find ourselves. Thus, the rhetorical and methodological repertoire (re)presented in this chapter should be understood as a limited opening for conversations, critiques, collaborations, and transformations.

Digital cultural rhetorics should continue imagining how to foster and sustain more ethical, positive, and just relationships between rhetoric, bodies, cultures, communities, and technologies in our disciplines, organizations, communities, and the world. Technofeminists Mary Hocks and Anne Balsamo underscore that "technological activism will be politically effective only in the context of transformed institutionalization, cultural narratives, and agency that are structured and disseminated by digital technologies" (192–3). Hopefully this chapter has inspired future transformative perspectives on the work that digital cultural rhetoricians can and/or should be doing. For example, how might online teaching, teaching with technology, and digital teaching evaluations complicate typical classist, racist, and sexist feedback that female working class faculty and female faculty of color often receive when teaching in predominantly white institutions (c.f. Gutiérrez y Muhs et al.)—as well as other oppressive identity-based student feedback? Or identity-based peer evaluations of tenure and promotion cases?

Finally, given the consensus among scientists regarding the status of climate change and the frightening increase in local and global e-waste streams and related environmental degradation and toxicity, digital cultural rhetoricians invested in future generations have a responsibility to develop and practice digital literacies that lead to action-based plans for redressing the unequal production, distribution, consumption, and management of e-waste and the resulting un-equal burden of related environmental and biological health degradation on predominantly poor communities and communities of color. Our relations to geopolitical landbases matter to our digital cultural rhetorics and our embodied being. No matter the path for our next project, when we share the foundational values that diverse bodies matter—animals (including non-humans), technologies, and landbases—together digital cultural rhetoricians can challenge and revise the normalization and naturalization of White, middle-class, educated, able-bodied, cis-male rhetorics that sponsor heteropatriarchy, white supremacy, and social inequities. Just as some digital rhetorics reproduce existing rhetorics about our bodies, others have the capacity to compose (a)new.

Acknowledgments

I offer my gratitude to many, as without your support, this project would not have come to fruition. Thank you to Jackie and Jonathan for your patience, grace, and support. To my partner, Keith, and our feline family, Arya and Bran, who tolerated my lack of interaction when working on this project. And to the technofeminist scholar–mentors who introduced me to digital cultural rhetorics and cleared a path for my work, especially Kristine Blair and Dànielle Nicole DeVoss.

Works Cited

Addison, Joanne, and Hilligoss, Susan. (1999). "Technological Fronts: Lesbian Lives 'On the Line.'" *Feminist Cyberscapes: Mapping Gendered Academic Spaces*, edited by Kristine Blair and Pamela Takayoshi. Ablex, 1999, pp. 21–40.

Alexander, Jonathan, and Will Banks. "Sexualities, Technologies, and the Teaching of Writing: A Critical Overview." *Computers and Composition*, vol. 21, no. 3, 2004, pp. 273–93.

Banks, Adam. *Digital Griots: African American Rhetoric in a Multimedia Age*. Southern Illinois UP, 2011.

———. *Race, Rhetoric, and Technology: Searching for Higher Ground*. Lawrence Erlbaum, 2006.

Blackmon, Samantha. "'But I'm Just White'; Or, How 'Other' Pedagogies Can Benefit All Students." *Teaching Writing with Computers*, edited by Brian Huot and Pamela Takayoshi. Houghton Mifflin, 2002, pp. 92–102.

———. "(Cyber) Conspiracy Theories? African-American Students in the Computerized Writing Environment." *Labor, Writing Technologies, and the Shaping of Composition in the Academy*, edited by Pamela Takayoshi and Patricia Sullivan. Hampton, 2007, pp. 153–66.

Blair, Kristine, and Pamela Takayoshi, Eds. *Feminist Cyberscapes: Mapping Gendered Academic Spaces*. Ablex, 1999.

Blair, Kristine, Radhika Gajjalaand, and Christine Tulley. *Webbing Cyberfeminist Practice: Communities, Pedagogies and Social Action*. Hampton, 2009.

Brady Aschauer, Ann. "Tinkering with Technological Skill: An Examination of the Gendered Uses of Technology." *Computers and Composition*, vol. 16, no. 1, 1999, pp. 7–23.

Brueggemann, Brenda Jo. "Why I Mind." Youtube, Information Stories: Sustaining Democracy in the Digital Age, 17 Feb. 2011, www.youtube.com/watch?v=RoNR6EWT7D4&t=215s. Accessed 5 July 2017.

DeVoss, Dànielle Nicole. "Formidable Females: Pink-Collar Workplaces, Computers, and Cultures of Resistance." *Webbing Cyberfeminist Practice: Communities, Pedagogies, and Social Action*, edited by Kristine Blair et al. Hampton, 2009, pp. 345–84.

DeVoss, Dànielle Nicole, Ellen Cushman, and Jeffrey T. Grabill. "Infrastructure and Composing: The When of New-Media Writing." *College Composition and Communication*, vol. 57, no. 1, 2005, pp. 14–44.

DigiRhet.org. "Teaching Digital Rhetoric: Community, Critical Engagement, and Application." *Pedagogy: Critical Approaches to Teaching Literature, Language, Composition, and Culture*, vol. 6, no. 2, 2006, pp. 231–59.

Ford, Dwedor Morais. "Technologizing Africa: On the Bumpy Information Highway." *Computers and Composition*, vol. 24, no. 3, 2007, pp. 302–16.

Gonzales, Laura. "Using ELAN Video Coding Software to Visualize the Rhetorics of Translation." *Kairos: A Journal of Rhetoric, Technology, and Pedagoy*, vol. 21, no. 2, 2017. PraxisWiki, praxis.technorhetoric. net/tiki-index.php?page=PraxisWiki%3A_%3AELAN. Accessed 5 July 2017.

Gutiérrez y Muhs, Gabriella, Yolanda Flores Niemann, Carmen G. Gonzalez, and Angela P. Harris, Eds. *Presumed Incompetent: The Intersections of Race and Class for Women in Academia*. Utah State UP, 2012.

Haas, Angela M. "Making Online Spaces More Native to American Indians: A Digital Diversity Recommendation." *Computers and Composition Online*, 2005, cconlinejournal.org/Haas/index.htm. Accessed 5 July 2017.

——. "Wampum as Hypertext: An American Indian Intellectual Tradition of Multimedia Theory and Practice." *Studies in American Indian Literatures*, vol. 19, no. 4, 2007, pp. 77–100.

Haas, Angela, Christine Tulley, and Kristine Blair. "Mentors versus Masters: Women's and Girls' Narratives of (Re)negotiation in Web-Based Writing Spaces." *Computers and Composition*, vol. 19, no. 3, 2002, pp. 231–49.

Haas, Christina. "On the Relationship Between Old and New Technologies." *Computers and Composition*, vol. 16, no. 2, 1999, pp. 209–28.

Hawisher, Gail, Cynthia L. Selfe, Brittney Moraski, and Melissa Pearson. "Becoming Literate in the Information Age: Cultural Ecologies and the Literacies of Technology." *College Composition and Communication*, vol. 55, no. 4, 2004, pp. 642–92.

Hocks, Mary, and Anne Balsamo. "Women Making Multimedia: Possibilities for Feminist Activism." *Virtual Publics: Policy and Community in an Electronic Age*, edited by Beth E. Kolko. Columbia UP, 2003, pp. 192–214.

Kantrowitz, Barbara. "Men, Women, Computers." *CyberReader*, edited by Victor J. Vitanza' Allyn & Bacon, 1996, pp. 134–40.

Marantz, Andrew. "When an App is Called Racist." *The New Yorker*, 29 July, 2015, www.newyorker.com/business/currency/what-to-do-when-your-app-is-racist. Accessed 5 July 2017.

Medina, Cruz. "Tweeting Collaborative Identity: Race, ICTs, and Performing Latinidad." *Communicating Race, Ethnicity, and Identity in Technical Communication*, edited by Miriam F. Williams, and Octavio Pimentel. Baywood, 2013, pp. 63–86.

Monroe, Barbara Jean. *Crossing the Digital Divide: Race, Writing, and Technology in the Classroom*. Teachers College P, 2004.

Powell, Annette. "Access(ing), Habits, Attitudes, and Engagements: Re-Thinking Access as Practice." *Computers and Composition*, vol. 24, no. 2, 2007, pp. 16–35.

Reilly, Colleen A. "Sexualities and Technologies: How Vibrators Help to Explain Computers." *Computers and Composition*, vol. 21, no. 3, 2004, pp. 363–85.

Rhodes, Jacqueline, and Jonathan Alexander. *Techne: Queer Meditations on Writing the Self*. Computers and Composition Digital P/Utah State UP, 2015. CC Digital Press E-Book ccdigitalpress.org/techne. Accessed 4 July 2017.

Ridolfo, Jim. *Digital Samaritans: Rhetorical Delivery and Engagement in the Digital Humanities*. U of Michigan P, 2015.

Selfe, Cynthia, and Richard Selfe. "The Politics of the Interface: Power and its Exercise in Electronic Contact Zones." *College Composition and Communication*, vol. 45, no. 4, 1994, pp. 480–504.

Smyser-Fauble, Barbi. "The New Scarlet Letter A: An Exploration of the Power of Online Informational Websites to Influence and Brand Those Impacted by Autism Spectrum Disorders." *Rhetoric, Professional Communication, and Globalization*, vol. 3, no. 3, 2012, www.rpcg.org/index.php?journal=rpcg&page=article&op=view&path%5B%5D=45. Accessed 4 July 2017.

Tannen, Deborah. "Gender Gap in Cyberspace." *CyberReader*, edited by Victor J. Vitanza. Allyn & Bacon, 1996, pp. 141–43.

Yergeau, Melanie, Elizabeth Brewer, Stephanie Kerschbaum, Sushil K. Oswal, Margaret Price, Cynthia L. Self, Michael J. Salvo, Franny Howes. "Multimodality in Motion: Disability in Kairotic Spaces." *Kairos: A Journal of Rhetoric, Technology, and Pedagoy*, vol. 18, no. 1, 2013, kairos.technorhetoric.net/18.1/coverweb/yergeau-et-al/pages/access.html. Accessed 4 July 2017.

——. "Aut(hored)ism." *Computers and Composition Online*, 2009, cconlinejournal.org/dmac/index.html. Accessed 4 July 2017.

39

EXPLOITATION, ALIENATION, AND LIBERATION

Interpreting the Political Economy
of Digital Writing

Kylie Jarrett

The diffusion of the capacity to write and distribute creative content that followed the emergence of digital technologies has often been described as liberatory. Interactive, networked technologies promised to return cultural production to the "authentic" state before massification and domination by commercial imperatives, allowing a richer, more dynamic cultural fabric to be woven. Early Internet theorists, such as Howard Rheingold, Sherry Turkle, and George Landow, noted the potential for the renewal of the public sphere, for self-making, and for challenging orthodoxies of textual expression that lay in citizens, individuals, and groups accessing new tools for public creative expression. These possibilities were not only an outcome of interactive media providing spaces for the expression of alternative views, but were also an effect of the technical affordances of digitized, hyperlinked, and networked media that created new forms of textuality and meaning-making. Emerging from the deep shadow cast by commercial media behemoths and tight state regulation throughout the twentieth century, the libertarian hacker spaces of the early Internet had the potential to overturn decades of alienation from the ability to author our own cultural landscape and, by doing so, allow us to achieve full human flourishing.

Contrary to this promise, though, the Internet and the Web quickly became commercialized, once again raising concerns about the impact of corporate interests on the cultural fabric. As we increasingly write ourselves and publish our creative works within proprietary digital platforms, do we merely reproduce the economic logics of commercial broadcast media? What now is the potential of digital writing to liberate us from systems of cultural control? This chapter will explore these concerns, beginning by documenting key moments in the commercialization of digital media but noting in particular the reliance on advertising as a source of revenue throughout this history. Using Marxist economic theories, it will then argue for understanding digital writing as unpaid labor that renders it an exploited and alienating practice.

But our own experiences as digital writers challenge this framing as alienation, a point confirmed by many empirical studies of user practices that provide evidence for the continued production of uncommodified products within the creative activity of digital media writers.

To answer the question of whether digital writing is liberating thus requires models for understanding this oscillation between conditions of exploitative alienation and cooperative, meaningful dis-alienation. In offering a Marxist feminist perspective on domestic work as an example of such a model, I will ultimately argue that it is only by allowing for multiplicity that the economics of digital writing can be fully understood.

Commercializing Digital Writing

Anti-commercialization imperatives are inextricable from the emergence and popularization of digital writing. The early adopters of home computing and the Internet, who not only were the first digital writers but who also conceptualized and engineered the systems upon which we continue to write, emerged from counter-cultural movements that espoused a belief in direct democracy and a profound faith in technology's emancipatory potential. This is the "Californian ideology" described by Barbrook and Cameron as integral to the Internet's foundations. Its influence generated a technical and social infrastructure marked by plurality, reciprocal gift giving, open access, resistance to hierarchies, and rejection of state and corporate intervention. These principles and their origin within publicly funded universities, contexts of academic inquiry, and community involvement led to "an unofficial ban on commercial activity" (Halavais 71) as the Internet emerged.

This unofficial ban was not to last. In 1991, the US National Science Foundation (NSF) loosened restrictions on commercial uses of the Internet. Shortly after (1993), the Mosaic browser was released, making the Web more accessible and ultimately leading to its popularization. As Martin Kenney's economic history of the Internet notes though, Mosaic not only promoted the Web, it also demonstrated the existence of a viable online media marketplace. The NSF's decision to discontinue subsidizing the Internet's architecture after 1995 further encouraged the Web's commercialization and so even the unofficial ban on commercial sites was soon forgotten.

The Internet economy has since taken on a series of overlapping forms. Elizabeth van Couvering's history of the search industry is useful for explicating this dynamic. She argues that between 1994 and 1997, there was a period of technical entrepreneurship in which digital media technologies were typically developed in non-commercial settings such as universities and then rapidly sought venture-capital funding. At this time, websites' revenues were mostly generated from pop-up and banner advertising, using metrics of mass audiences not very different from commercial broadcast media models. While such advertising confirmed the demise of the anti-corporate Internet, its dominance over subscription funding models did maintain the free access to websites and authoring tools associated with the Internet's founding libertarian principles.

Commercial activity at this time was embedded within the intense speculative capitalism of the 1990s technology boom that was to falter spectacularly with the 2000 NASDAQ technology index crash. The second period of Internet development that van Couvering identifies, 1997–2001, straddles this boom and bust. This is the period dominated by portals such as AOL, MSN.com, and Geocities where the focus was on aggregating content from existing media companies, thereby creating even larger audiences and greater advertising and sponsorship opportunities for offline properties. These "proprietary 'walled gardens'" (186) were authored primarily by corporate employees, but also provided interactive spaces for communities to be written into existence. Business leaders such as Don Tapscott, John Hagel III, and Arthur G. Armstrong advocated facilitating these communities in order to appeal to users and sustain their attention, ensuring a credible audience for advertisers. This was particularly important as the dot.com crash not only decimated the number of digital media companies but also the number of potential advertisers.

The final period of commercial development documented by van Couvering, 2002–2008, is marked by the consolidation and virtual integration of companies as the online advertising market returned to growth. During this period, Internet native companies such as Google, YouTube, Twitter, and various blogging platforms began to dominate, supplanting the online properties of "old" media companies. Google's rise is of particular importance, not only because it embedded keyword advertising as an industry standard, but because it also drove the shift from a pay-per-view advertising rate (where advertisers pay an amount per thousand impressions of their ad) to a pay-per-click rate (where advertisers only pay if a user clicks upon their ad). This re-shaped the online advertising industry and helped make search the dominant online advertising sector. Also of importance is Google's AdSense program, launched in 2003, which allows affiliated companies to serve up on their sites various kinds of advertising targeted to specific users that have been identified by Google's data analytics. Through mechanisms such as this, amateur and individual digital writers were also able to commercialize their sites, often generating only tiny incomes but, nevertheless, changing their status to professional or quasi-professional (pro-am).

The Commercial Web and the Creative User

More recently, the business model of the commercial Web has been defined under the umbrella term Web 2.0, a concept advocated by technology publisher Tim O'Reilly in 2005. It describes a shift from the relatively static monologues of commercial or individual home pages to the dialogic, participatory spaces of the contemporary Web. O'Reilly's vision was of unfixed, dynamic, participatory architectures that demand various ongoing forms of digital writing by creative users. These users are seen not as a market to be managed, but as collaborators in building site stickiness and brand value. Emerging from this logic is what we now term "social media"— social networking sites, blogging and microblogging platforms, video, audio and photo sharing sites, and many other participatory platforms for writing ourselves and our cultures online. This phase also marks the normalization of the digital writer as pro-am entrepreneur, where once amateur creators actively leverage their followers and micro-celebrity through on-site advertising and/or promotional endorsements. Both big business and individuals have gained financially from the economic logics of Web 2.0.

For O'Reilly, though, Web 2.0 was not only valuable economically. It maintained the transformative social potential associated with the pre-commercial Internet. O'Reilly argues that by encouraging users to write and share their own narratives in commercial spaces, Web 2.0 challenges traditional information flows, allowing individuals greater participation in the generation of cultural texts and the agency to reshape commercial imperatives. O'Reilly's model of Web 2.0 returned to the commercial Web the possibilities of liberation associated with the uncommercialized phases of the Internet.

Writing Labor

While there may be some formal differences between the various stages of Internet commercialization, two key constants remain: dependence upon the active participation of users and advertising revenue models that involve the capturing of user data. From contributions to AOL message boards, to blogging on LiveJournal, to commenting on YouTube videos, to Web 2.0's ubiquitous status updates and tweets, it is users' writing on and through digital media platforms that populate these sites with content. Users also create the affective interpersonal and community relations that attract and attach users. All this activity generates viable audiences for

425

sale to advertisers. These audiences, in turn, generate brand value that attracts investors in the stock market, which as Adam Arvidsson and Elanor Colleoni remind us, is an important source of capital for such companies. O'Reilly describes this reliance on user contributions as harnessing collective intelligence. Users, he says, can be used not only to provide content to populate the site, but also to promote products through trusted word of mouth networks. He argues for seeing users as adding value both directly and indirectly through their creative contributions to digital media platforms and as advocates for brands.

When viewed through the prism of Web 2.0's economic logic, it becomes possible to view digital writing on various commercial platforms as a form of labor. This is obviously the case for those writers who have formal financial contracts with platforms but also applies to those voluntarily engaged in creative activity and who receive no compensation. By adding content and by generating interactions with other users that make sites (or brands) meaningful, digital media users are effectively working as unpaid laborers for those platforms. Without their contributions, these sites would be facing untenable wage bills or licensing fees for the content they leverage to attract users.

Conceptualizing digital media users as laborers is usually traced to a critique of digital media economics by Tiziana Terranova. Her focus was on the value generated by the unpaid dimensions of formally contracted knowledge or creative work in digital media industries, such as the immaterial labor of cognition that extends beyond defined working hours and workplaces. Drawing on work from Autonomist Marxism, Terranova critiques this exploitation of collective intelligence, arguing that it is emblematic of wider labor trends that involve the subsumption of the whole of life into capitalist valorization.

Terranova makes the point, though, that labor in this context does not only mean waged labor. All digital writers who create the cultural content of Web platforms, including those outside formal labor contracts such as tweeters, bloggers, meme-makers, or Facebook status updaters, enter into an exploitative relationship with capital. In a passage that echoes O'Reilly's ideas, Terranova says it is users who "keep a site alive through their labor, the cumulative hours of accessing the site (thus generating advertising), writing messages, participating in conversations, and sometimes making the jump to collaborators" (49). This is certainly the case for commercial news blog *The Huffington Post*, which was criticized in 2011 for not compensating the many citizen journalists whose contributions and readership helped make it a field leader and led to its acquisition by AOL for US$315 million in stocks and cash. Terranova suggests that exploitation of free labor such as this is structurally integral to digital media economies.

To fully understand the economic logic behind interpreting digital writing as exploited labor requires engaging with the labor theory of value as espoused by Marx. For Marx, human labor is the basis of any commodity's value for it is human energy, or labor-power, that transforms raw materials into a commodity that has both utility (use-value) and can be sold for profit (exchange-value). Workers sell their labor-power to the capitalist in the form of labor-time (the 8-hour day, for instance) for which they are paid a wage. Profit, or surplus, is generated when goods are sold for more than the cost of the labor-time required for their production. Consequently, reducing the amount paid for the labor-time incorporated into products is key to capitalist accumulation. In Marxist terms, when a worker's labor generates surplus it is defined as productive labor but when the worker is not being compensated in terms equal to the value produced by her or his creative activity, it is also defined as *exploited* labor.

Volunteer digital writers on commercial platforms, such as those at *The Huffington Post*, are this kind of exploited laborer. Their content production is work that is supplied below cost, typically at no cost, generating almost 100 percent surplus value for digital media platforms.

This surplus can then be generalized and used to offset any other production costs. Thus, even though Nate Silver has calculated that paid contributors generated much of *The Huffington Post's* most popular content, uncompensated bloggers were nevertheless integral to the company's creation of surplus value by defraying production costs for the site as a whole. Through this formal economic prism we can argue that digital writing constitutes intensely exploited productive labor, particularly on social media sites where paid workers supply little to no content.

Writing the Audience-Commodity

But it is not only through supplying content for free that users create value. Generating revenue through advertising is the foundation of the digital media economy. Users' labor is also implicated here for it is their engagement, interactions, and contributions that constitute the data that are commodified in this advertising marketplace. To understand this economic logic, we must draw on the work of Dallas Smythe into the economic structures of advertising-driven commercial mass media. Smythe argued that the product of media was not messages, information, or images, but audiences and readerships. He argued that when advertisers buy broadcast time for their products they are, in fact, purchasing the viewing services (labor-power) of a predictable audience with specific characteristics. Captured by ratings systems and packaged as demographic data, audiences and their viewing practices are sold as commodities in the advertising marketplace. Smythe consequently likened mechanisms for measuring the activity of audiences as they watch a media text to the mechanisms for measuring labor-time in industrial workplaces.

As Christian Fuchs has comprehensively argued, the logic of the audience-commodity is also inherent in digital media industries, bound as they are to advertising revenue models. Like television programs, digital media platforms, their content, and the interactions that happen there are merely lures for drawing user traffic, maintaining attention, and encouraging further interactions. In this instance, though, television's aggregated ratings figures take the form of highly granular, intensely specific user data, often generated in real-time. These data about users' personal qualities along with their browsing, interaction, and transaction histories are collated and valorized by databases underlying every website. They are then used to generate prices for targeted ad placements, such as in Google's AdSense program, or sold directly, such as in Twitter's data-licensing activities through which user data is sold to marketing companies.

Fuchs argues that if, like the media companies explored by Smythe, the commodity produced by Internet platforms is user data, "then the process of creating these data must be considered to be value-generating labour" (*Culture*, 246). Consequently, users are laborers whenever they generate data, which, in reality, means almost all of the time spent online; all interactions with the databases that comprise websites leave traces that can be collated and commodified. Even incidental moments of digital writing—entering a search term, a single status update, a retweet, or a "like"—become potentially valuable assets for a digital platform as they are folded into the platform's monetizable database. An act as simple and unconsidered as clicking a link writes the user into data collection systems, where their activity can be collated across platforms or over time to build valuable taste information.

From this perspective, digital writers are arguably working for digital media platforms in all of their Internet interactions, even when they are merely acting as relatively passive consumers. Further, like that produced by unpaid content provision, the value generated from such data is almost entirely surplus for the costs of providing a platform and server capacity become negligible once a critical mass of users is reached. Today's commercial Web is saturated by data collection mechanism and thus is an exploitative sweatshop for unpaid consumer labor.

Alienation Effects

For Fuchs and many other digital labor scholars, the key problem of this formal exploitation is that it enacts and perpetuates a social relationship in which users are alienated from the products of their labor and, quite pertinently, from the tools and capacity with which to make culture and self outside of capitalist logics. This alienation is evident in the processes through which users' data are commodified. The process of rendering user interactions into data that can be sold to advertisers or marketers reduces the richness of user activity and its embedding in socially meaningful contexts, constraining it to a pre-structured, limited, alien form. It transforms practices with use-value for the individual writer and their community into objects with exchange-value in the marketplace. In such transformations, creative output can be stripped of its social functions. Ryan M. Milner (185–216) describes how corporations that sell products using appropriated images, phrases, or memes organically created by users are decontextualizing and recontextualizing the meanings of these texts, stripping them of their original significance and use-value within the creator's community. Once reformed in this way, user data or creative products no longer serve the interests of their makers, particularly for the purposes of self-realization or cultural production; they become alien to their own creators.

Moreover, this process for transforming user activity with use-value into an object with exchange-value is opaque at the level of the interface and is often enacted by unknown, unseen, and unfathomable algorithms or corporate processes. Users are rarely involved in making governance decisions relating to the sites to which they contribute and have little control over where and how their data or creative contributions are used. Indeed, as Sal Humphreys points out, most users entering a commercial digital platform click acceptance of an end user license agreement that signs away rights over their data and creative output, formalizing the user's alienation from the products of their labor.

Thus, despite O'Reilly's assertion that Web 2.0 would have transformative social effects and would enable dis-alienated social production, the reverse seems to be the inevitable conclusion of its economic logic. This has wider repercussions. According to Marxist political critiques, by alienating digital writers from the products of their own creative and social interactions, the commodification of user activity denies individual citizens the tools for building and sustaining subjectivities grounded in alternative, less exploitative social relations. For Fuchs, this subsumption into capitalism's commodity logic of both the inherent use-values of cultural goods and their cooperative production processes is the tragedy of the digital media sector. A society in which this alienation is central no longer has the capacity for freedom because it does not have the capacity for self-realization outside of capitalism. It would appear, then, that every keystroke of our digital writing moves us further away from liberation.

Agency and Use-Values in Digital Writing

As powerful as this argument is, it remains an abstraction, and an abstraction that does not necessarily accord with the lived experience of digital writing. The kinds of labor undertaken by unpaid digital writers tends to be voluntary, pleasurable, and lacking the coercive violence associated with exploited labor; the Internet may be a sweatshop of user labor but it is a playful sweatshop. This critique opens up questions of just how alienated digital writers are from the products of their labor and from the associated capacity for self-realization. Despite the exploited formal economic context, there is still creative agency in the spaces of digital writing that is not entirely subsumed into the demands of capitalism. It may even run counter to those objectives.

This point is made clear in many studies that document the development and maintenance of cooperative social relations and acts of self-actualization within commercial digital media contexts. Many digital writers, driven by a personal or social agenda, do not see the products of their activity as somehow separate and oppositional to their interests. Charges of alienation often fail to resonate with users who encounter self-actualizing and affirming creative expression in their lived experiences of digital writing. As John Banks has argued, rather than accepting users as oppressed workers, it is more productive to view users as co-creators of the sites they use.

This idea is particularly pertinent to sites where the boundaries between amateur and professional activity are blurred, such as micro-celebrity blogging. Crystal Abidin's study of the use of selfies by entrepreneurial bloggers—called Influencers—notes that such practices are not frivolous exercises in vanity or commodity fetishism. Rather, the taking of a selfie is serious and considered work that is understood tacitly as such by Influencers and is manipulated by these writers in ways that support their own financial or social objectives. This chimes with Banks and Humphreys' description of users involved in modding for the games company Auran as quite "canny" in negotiating the economic exchanges that take place as they voluntarily work for free to improve game products. Users such as these are manifesting agency to resist, change, and negotiate their loosely defined "working" arrangements.

Moreover, the bloggers described by Abidin sometimes use their promotional writing to speak back to the commercialization practices they are engaged in and to reflect upon their own commodification. Working with Mart Ots, Abidin notes how the trust built between Influencers and their followers works as both a pre-emptive and post-hoc disciplining mechanism, reining in commercial excesses and unethical money-making practices in an otherwise unregulated media sector. Despite the overtly commercialized context of this genre, Influencer blogging still involves the production of use-values, such as socially embedded trust, that run counter to free market, capitalist agendas.

Studies such as these also point to how the products of digital writing circulate not only in financial economies but also in symbolic, social, and/or cultural economies. In these contexts, value does not necessarily take a fiscal form. This is certainly true of the independent music fans studied by Nancy Baym and Ron Burnett whose economy includes a complex system of rewards for fans whose labor sustains their favorite acts. This compensation is typically not financial but takes the form of objects defined as valuable by the user community, such as recognition by or proximity to band members; access to favored cultural objects; or subcultural status. Capital forms defined by users may be convertible into economic capital, but predominantly work as currency within a circumscribed community, affording power to whoever possesses them only in that context. While blatantly commercial strategies by some digital writers (such as Influencers) may be compensated in monetary terms, for many other digital writers, the bulk of their profits are in these more inalienable forms. To make blanket assertions that such work is alienated, then, is to "ignore how much these other forms of capital matter in the well being of well rounded humans" (Baym and Burnett 23).

While none of these studies adequately argue against the formal exploitation of unpaid labor in digital writing, they do illustrate how inalienable use-values such as pleasure, social solidarity, and affect are products of commercial digital writing as much as the exchange-value associated with user data. They also assert that production of use-values persists *despite* the commercialized context of their production. This indicates that tools for self-actualization are manifest even within market contexts; in commercial digital writing, there is not only the absolute saturation of commodification associated with capitalist alienation. The lived experience of users thus raises the question of whether it is possible for digital writing to be exploited at an economic level but remain dis-alienated practice. If this is possible, though, how might we then explain the economic logic of digital writing? One answer comes from an unexpected place: domestic work.

Digital Writing as Domestic Work

As I have argued in my book *The Digital Housewife*, the oscillation between exploited alienation and meaningful cultural expression that is digital writing's economic condition mirrors the dialectic associated with unpaid domestic work in capitalist systems. As it is understood by Marxist feminist theorists such as Silvia Federici, Mariarosa Dalla Costa, and Selma James, unpaid housework is integral to capitalism because it produces healthy bodies and subjectivities appropriately equipped to sell their labor in the capitalist marketplace. Domestic labor produces workers for capitalism; it is the work of social reproduction.

More importantly, because it is unpaid, domestic work reduces the costs of labor to the capitalist: it creates surplus-value. As interpreted by Antonella Picchio, the socially necessary labor-time that is covered by a worker's wage also includes some provision for reproducing the body and subjectivity of that worker as well as their children so as to ensure a continuous workforce. If the labor needed to ensure this reproduction was provided in the commercial market, wages would need to increase to cover the cost of those services. However, when an unwaged domestic worker provides this labor, wages can remain lower, thereby increasing the amount of relative surplus associated with a paid worker's labor. Maintaining a reserve labor force involved in unpaid domestic work, historically "women's work," is thus a central feature of capitalist accumulation. It is this relatively unseen but integral role in reducing production costs that makes unpaid domestic work a useful model for thinking about the labor of digital writers.

But there is another resonance. Digital writing also echoes domestic work, particularly the care work of parenting, aged care, and interpersonal relationships, because it is richly meaningful labor that centrally produces use-values even while structurally embedded within capitalist value creation. Like unpaid domestic work, the products of digital writing are not entirely commodi-fiable, manifesting in the psychologies, bodies, or social relations of an individual or community. Both kinds of work are quasi-voluntary and can be distinctly pleasurable and passionately entered into, even when simultaneously understood as drudgery, grind, or a necessary evil. Both forms of work are implicated in the development and maintenance of social solidarity, which is particularly pertinent given digital media's role in enabling political discussion, articulating and aggregating alternative community sensibilities, and for mobilizing activists. Digital writing and domestic work both maintain a dual-character that cannot be captured by simple attributions of alienation or dis-alienation, exploitation or cooperation.

A framework informed by Marxist feminism complicates our understanding of the economics of digital writing, but it does so productively. It insists that we cannot only identify a commercial context in which user data and content are transformed into objects with exchange-value and declare it a debased space devoid of social meaning and the possibility of non-commercial use-values. Instead, we can use models of domestic work's incorporation into capital, such as that outlined by Leopoldina Fortunati in the *Arcane of Reproduction*, to draw attention to the longer-value chains of digital writing, looking closely at the perhaps contradictory qualities of individual interactions along these chains. Fortunati's model, which outlines a multi-phased process by which unpaid domestic work's products are incorporated into capital, allows for labor to produce an inalienable good with use-value (such as food to sustain a laboring body or a blog post containing creative expression) but which then later, sometimes only moments later, becomes a commodity with exchange-value in the marketplace (such as the labor-time the worker sells to the capitalist or the consumer data mined in real-time from the blog post). Both moments are necessarily implicated in the same value production circuit but have different relationships to alienation. Mapping these differences is important in determining the sociopolitical significance of this work.

This kind of model encourages us to identify specific instances where a writer's activity is experienced as alienated or where it serves as an instance of self-realization, while at the same time conceptualizing that as occurring within a broader context of formal capitalist exploitation. It also encourages us to explore which aspects of a particular instance of digital writing are formally alienated through capture by data-mapping mechanisms, commodity fetishism, or by the imposition of copyright provisions, while also taking into account the particular meaning and social embedding of that same contribution. It allows digital writing to simultaneously produce exchange value and use value; to be both inside and outside of capitalism. Models informed by the example of domestic work thus allow us to account for the dynamic dialectics of digital writing on commercial platforms, adding valuable complexity to our interrogation of digital writing's economic logic.

The Complexities of Commercialization

It is quite easy to track the rapid processes of commercialization of the Internet and the Web and point to increasing regimes of exploitation and alienation. However, the social and affective nature of digital writing and reading means that such an equation is too simplistic. Digital writing practices offer examples of formal exploitation and the alienation of users from the products of their labor, the expression of their culture, and the tools for articulating that expression. But it also simultaneously offers numerous examples of creative expression that move beyond the dictates of capital and that enable human flourishing. Being able to track this complexity, and not assuming that one activity is mutually exclusive of the other, is thus key to engaging fully with digital writing's economics. What is needed is a focus on the details of interactions across a long value chain, allowing for contradiction and multiplicity in the economic logics associated with particular instances of creative expression or consumption. Such an approach also calls for increased specificity and complexity in interpreting digital value creation.

The emphasis in this chapter, though, has been entirely on commercial spaces. There are various sites where writing is not commercialized in the form of user data and where cooperative relationships and reciprocal trade in use-values predominate. The non-commercial, collaborative model of Wikipedia is a key example as are the cases of platform cooperativism identified by Trebor Scholz where ownership, management, and/or the profit of digital sites are distributed through the user community. These examples, though, further emphasize the complex modeling needed to understand commercialization. Not all models of cooperativism eschew profit-making and writers on one cooperative platform may also write within another overtly commercialized space. Non-commercial sites are also implicated in cross-platform traffic dynamics and exchanges that place them within longer value chains that complicate their relationship to exploitation and alienation. These economic complexities further demonstrate that multiple levels of focus are needed when critiquing the political economy of digital writing.

The central point of this chapter then is that it is not enough to make blanket declarations of exploitation, alienation, or liberation. Rather, a subtle, multilayered critique is required to understand the political economy of digital writing. This chapter has described some of the conceptual tools relating to the economic processes of digital writing that can inform such an analysis—the generation of surplus-value; the objectification of culture; the persistence of use-values; the long value chains of capitalist production. What is required now is to bring these to bear on particular instances of writing to unravel the rich flows between alienated commodity forms and meaningful use-values in the exploited work of digital writers. Such a contingent analysis means that we may never resolve the question of whether the Internet liberates cultural production, but we will have a better understanding of how digital writing is implicated in capitalism, both in compliance and critique.

Works Cited

Abidin, Crystal. "'Aren't These Just Young, Rich Women Doing Vain Things Online?': Influencer Selfies as Subversive Frivolity." *Social Media + Society*, vol. 2, no. 2, 2016, pp. 1–17.

Abidin, Crystal, and Mart Ots. "Influencers Tell All? Unravelling Authenticity and Credibility in a Brand Scandal." *Blurring the Lines: Market-driven and Democracy-driven Freedom of Expression*, edited by Maria Edström, Andrew T. Kenyon, and Eva-Maria Svensson. Nordicom, 2016, pp. 153–61.

Arvidsson, Adam, and Elanor Colleoni. "Value in Informational Capitalism and on the Internet." *The Information Society*, vol. 28, no. 3, 2012, pp. 135–50.

Banks, John. *Co-creating Videogames*. Bloomsbury, 2013.

Banks, John, and Sal Humphreys. "The Labor of User Co-Creators: Emergent Social Network Markets." *Convergence*, vol. 14, no. 4, 2008, pp. 401–18.

Barbrook, Richard, and Andy Cameron. "The Californian Ideology." *Science as Culture*, vol. 6, no. 1, 1996, pp. 44–72.

Baym, Nancy, and Ron Burnett. "Amateur Experts: International Fan Labour in Swedish Independent Music." *International Journal of Cultural Studies*, vol. 12, no. 5, 2009, pp. 433–49.

Dalla Costa, Mariarosa, and Selma James. *The Power of Women and the Subversion of the Community*, 3rd ed., Falling Wall, 1975.

Federici, Silvia. *Caliban and the Witch: Women, the Body and Primitive Accumulation*. Autonomedia, 2004.

Fortunati, Leopoldina. *The Arcane of Reproduction: Housework, Prostitution, Labour and Capital*. Translated by Hilary Creek, Autonomedia, 1995.

Fuchs, Christian. *Internet and Society: Social Theory in the Information Age*. Routledge, 2008.

——. *Digital Labour and Karl Marx*. Routledge, 2014.

——. *Culture and Economy in the Age of Social Media*. Routledge, 2015.

Hagel, John, III, and Arthur G. Armstrong. *Net Gain: Expanding Markets Through Virtual Communities*. Harvard Business School Press, 1997.

Halavais, Alex. *Search Engine Society*. Polity, 2009.

Humphreys, Sal. "Ruling the Virtual World: Governance in Massive Multiplayer Online Games." *European Journal of Cultural Studies*, vol. 11, no. 2, 2008, pp. 149–71.

Jarrett, Kylie. *Feminism, Labour and Digital Media: The Digital Housewife*, Routledge, 2016.

Kenney, Martin. "What Goes Up Must Come Down: The Political Economy of the US Internet Industry." *The Industrial Dynamics of the New Digital Economy*, edited by Jens Froslev Christensen, and Peter Maskell. Edward Elgar, 2003, pp. 33–55.

Landow, George P. *Hypertext: The Convergence of Contemporary Critical Theory and Technology*. Johns Hopkins UP, 1992.

Marx, Karl. *Capital: A Critique of Political Economy Volume 1. 1867.* Translated by Ben Fowkes. Penguin, 1976.

Milner, Ryan M. *The World Made Meme: Public Conversations and Participatory Media*. MIT Press, 2016.

O'Reilly, Tim. "What is Web 2.0: Design Patterns and Business Models for the Next Generation of Software." O'Reilly Media, 30 Sept. 2005. http://oreilly.com/web2/archive/what-is-web-20.html. Accessed 27 Oct. 2016.

Picchio, Antonella. *Social Reproduction: The Political Economy of the Labour Market*. Cambridge UP, 1992.

Rheingold, Howard. *The Virtual Community: Homesteading on the Electronic Frontier*. HarperCollins, 1994.

Scholz, Trebor. *Uberworked and Underpaid: How Workers are Disrupting the Digital Economy*. Polity, 2016.

Silver, Nate. "The Economics of Blogging and The Huffington Post." *FiveThirtyEight*, 12 Feb. 2011, http://fivethirtyeight.com/features/the-economics-of-blogging-and-the-huffington-post/. Accessed 26 Oct. 2016.

Smythe, Dallas W. "Communications: Blindspot of Western Marxism." 1977. *The Audience Commodity in a Digital Age: Revisiting a Critical Theory of Commercial Media*, edited by Lee McGuigan and Vincent Manzerolle. Peter Lang, 2014, pp. 29–53.

Tapscott, Don. "Introduction." *Blueprint to the Digital Economy: Creating Wealth in the Era of e-Business*, edited by Don Tapscott et al. McGraw-Hill, 1998, pp. 1–16.

Terranova, Tiziana. "Free Labor: Producing Culture for the Digital Economy." *Social Text*, vol. 18, no. 2, 2000, pp. 33–58.

Turkle, Sherry. *Life on the Screen: Identity in the Age of the Internet*. Simon & Schuster, 1995.

van Couvering, Elizabeth. "The History of the Internet Search Engine: Navigational Media and the Traffic Commodity." *Web Search: Multidisciplinary Perspectives*, edited by Amanda Spink and Michael Zimmer. Springer-Verlag, 2008, pp. 177–206.

40

THE POLITICS OF
THE (SOUNDWRITING)
INTERFACE

Steven Hammer

> The body of the instrument gives definite preference to some frequencies, and when its strings (or its vibrating column of air, or its pulsating stretched skin) give it a fundamental plus overtones to transmit to the air, it has a mind of its own and stubbornly boosts some frequencies and partially mutes others.
> (*Daphne Oram,* An Individual Note of Music, Sound, and Electronics)

In 1991, Hawisher and Selfe published "The Rhetoric of Technology and the Electronic Writing Class," in which they carefully remind us not only that technological change influences how we write *and* teach writing, but also that our culture (both in popular consumer culture *and* in academia) most often veers sharply toward a perception of emerging technologies as empowering, democratic, hopeful, and visionary. This is often easy to spot in Apple advertisements (though any will suffice, you might recall the "It Just Works" ad campaign), but perhaps it is more difficult to reflect on our own de facto endorsement of "new," "exciting," "cutting-edge" tools in our classrooms. Hawisher and Selfe ask us to be mindful of the kind of rhetoric we use and, yes, *enforce* in our classrooms. Selfe and Selfe followed this work in 1994 in "The Politics of the Interface," the article for which this chapter is named. They argue that the interface of the contemporary computer—and its various components such as the ubiquitous Microsoft Word—are always political:

> Within the virtual space represented by these interfaces, and elsewhere within computer systems, the values of our culture—ideological, political, economic, educational—are mapped both implicitly and explicitly, constituting a complex set of material relations among culture, technology, and technology users. (485)

Such critiques should be levied against *all* of our tools and interfaces. They not only discipline our bodies and reinscribe dominance and colonialism, but they participate actively in (co)composition. We never really write alone, we never really write *on* technologies. They write with us, and sometimes for us. Our *invisible coauthors*.

More than two decades later, it is difficult to find evidence indicating this rhetoric of technology is changing. Following Selfe and Selfe for instance, much has been written about the interface with which this chapter was written and revised: Microsoft Word. Word continues to be the (in many cases explicitly required) composition tool prescribed across curricula and institutions, though many have argued that its interface and attendant values, processes, and priorities are not only problematic in terms of their colonizing effects, but at odds with critical thinking, effective pedagogy, and mentoring relationships (Buck 398; McGee and Ericsson 466). Scholars also continue to point out the simultaneous proliferation and erasure of technologies-as-coauthors in emerging contexts. Kristin Arola's work asks us to question the tired claim that the Web and its various template-driven interfaces and platforms are simply "vessels" for content. The design, she rightly argues, *is* the content (13). McCorkle urges us to resist techno-utopian turns-of-phrase such as "natural user interfaces," approaches to device design that turn out to be neither natural (but rather, *conditioned*), nor particularly concerned with the bodies of users that are unable to access their design (110). A pattern emerges: for every new technology that promises ease, a corresponding cost of obscured politics exists. Thankfully, we have technocritics among us who have committed their classrooms and research to cautioning against the uncritical awe—and accompanying prescription—of emerging composition technologies. Within this conversation, I wish to add an exploration of software-based soundwriting technologies, the tools with which we edit, re/mix, compose, and publish sonic texts.

As twenty-first century composers and teachers, it is easy to take something such as the ability to write with sound for granted. We have relatively accessible means to record, download, sample, edit, publish, and distribute sounds for a wide variety of purposes, audiences, and platforms. Though sonic technologies have existed for a few centuries that generated and measured sound scientifically, and therefore reproducibly, soundwriting as we know it was quite inaccessible to those outside professional sound studios until the middle of the twentieth century and the rise of magnetic tape as a recording and playback device. Many readers will likely have some direct experience with magnetic tape and its affordances and limitations. Recording from the radio, compiling mix tapes, warping materials from environmental conditions and overuse, the audible sound of fastforward and rewind. And so on.

It is difficult to overstate the impact of magnetic tape on audio culture writ large, let alone what I will here call *soundwriting*. Here I am calling on the work of rhetoric and composition scholars who have done valuable work to understand and share how sound works rhetorically and how composers might work with sound. And though earlier work at the intersection of rhetorics, composition, and sound does exist, I should mention a few important spaces in which these conversations grew and took shape, particularly Rickert's (Ed.) 1999 "Writing/Music/Culture" issue of *Enculturation* and Ball and Hawk's (Eds.) 2006 "Sound in/as Compositional Space: A Next Step in Multiliteracies" issue of *Computers and Composition*. So many threads of scholarship emerged from these special issues, and scholars in the field continue to engage sound in exciting ways: multimodal and body-centered listening practices (Ceraso), remix literacies and practices (Stedman), musical rhetorics (Halbritter; Stone), multimodal practices and pedagogies (Ahern; Selfe, "Movement"; VanKooten), ambience and soundscapes (Rickert), technologies and posthumanism (Hawk, "Stomp Box"), race, class, and genre (Rice; Stoever-Ackerman; Sirc). This list could expand widely, of course. And while *soundwriting* scholarship is politically thoughtful, much of it implicitly takes for granted the tools and techniques made possible via digital recording, editing, playback, and publication.

Therefore, as a contribution to the *soundwriting* corpus, this chapter will investigate the politics of contemporary digital audio workstations (DAWs) *vis-à-vis* their ancestral ties to early sound recording, editing, and mastering tools and techniques. And while the bulk of this work will trace his-/hystories in an attempt to understand why our technologies look, sound, and perform the way they do, my interest here is not one of techno- or retro-fetishism. On the contrary, we have learned from Hawisher, Selfe, and Selfe the dangers of uncritical, techno-utopian approaches to working with writing technologies, because they are never inert, never apolitical, never *just tools*.

At the outset of the chapter, I quoted Daphne Oram, an important figure both in this chapter and in electronic music history, though she is often muted in the latter. Her opening comments in large part echo the sentiments of Hawisher, Selfe, and Selfe (and the many who have followed this line of critique): instruments' *materiality*—how they are constructed by forces (usually human) that possess values and politics and preferences rooted in a variety of sociocultural milieus, many of which perform subjugation and oppression—affects the sounds it makes (and those it ignores), who may use it and how, and so on. No compositional instrument—of music, or words, or any mode/media combination, overtly rhetorical or not—is ever simply an instrument. It is an artifact of political power, privileging those already in power, disciplining the colonized bodies.

In a way of beginning to understand and critique our current conditions of soundwriting via DAW technologies, I should do some work to describe those conditions at the time of this writing. Like the word processor, the contemporary DAW is not a singular product even despite various institutions' best efforts to enforce the use of one or two such products. In the media production world, the term "industry standard" often describes and rhetorically cements these programs' identities as such. A variety of DAWs do exist on the market, but for a number of reasons, Avid's Pro Tools remains the DAW most used in industry (music, sound design, radio) and is therefore most often *taught* by those wishing to prepare students for "the industry." Little concrete evidence exists as to why Pro Tools has risen and remained the DAW *par-excellence*. But like Word, Pro Tools a) was a relatively early option available to professionals and studios b) drew from its hardware predecessors in terms of processes, jargon, and priorities, and c) because of its early success in industry, became an institutional—and therefore *educational*—staple. But my critique is not focused solely on Pro Tools, nor any other conventional DAW. Instead, I am interested in investigating the techno-lineage of dominant digital audio workstations and their attendant politics, so that we might consider our coauthors wisely, both in our soundwriting work and in the kind of soundwriting work we ask of our students.

> It is worth repeating that a work does not necessarily have a beginning or an end.
> One cannot mark its beginning or end.
>
> (*John Murungi*, African Musical Aesthetics)

Most contemporary DAWs rely exclusively on a multitrack timeline as a visual and functional editing interface. Figure 40.1 shows screenshots from Pro Tools and Audition. A multitrack timeline view is rather self-explanatory: the composer has access to multiple tracks of audio that can exist on the timeline of one project. On the right, you will see that I have imported two individual clips of audio into two tracks in Audition. Tracks are versatile; we might arm one or more of the tracks to record from various inputs (e.g., recording a live band, assigning each track to an instrument's output), we might arrange and edit prerecorded samples (e.g., remixing a song or mixing a podcast that features speech, music, and other prerecorded sounds), and so on.

At first glance, the multitrack timeline is a very logical and seemingly open-ended environment. A sound composition, after all, usually has a distinct start and end and often features multiple sound sources, some we may want to record synchronously, some we may want to record and edit asynchronously. For maximum control and precision, a multitrack timeline may in fact be optimal. Yet we must consider a few things as technocritics.

First, why are control and precision the markers of a good interface? Irregularity and error can not only be enjoyable experiences as composers, but they can be extraordinarily valuable

Figure 40.1 Multitrack Timelines of Pro Tools (Left) and Audition (Right)

as *materially conscious* composers. Relatively recently, scholars in composition and rhetoric have explored the affordances of glitch (Boyle; Hammer; Johnson and Johnson; Reid). Calling on artist–activist–scholars in the new media arts who in many ways have led the charge of techno-critique in recent decades not only bridges disciplinary divides, but can also lead us to fundamentally question our assumptions regarding the relationship of human composers and digital writing technologies. Menkman argues that the search for noiselessness, perfection, and functionality is futile; all technologies and processes of composition "will always possess their own inherent fingerprints of imperfection" (11). As such, the glitch artist ought not pretend that these political-made-digital artifacts do not exist, but instead "find catharsis in disintegration, ruptures and cracks; manipulate, bend and break any medium towards the point where it becomes something new" (11). Similarly, in his articulation on dirty new media (DNM), Jon Cates understands that "brokenness is a primary feature" of writing technologies, and DNM works explicitly to reveal the politics and power that lies in protecting illusions of cleanliness and functionality (Cates).

Second, we must not only always question the inherent politics and roots of a given device, but we must also ask what was muted as the dominant paradigm became Standard. We have read works by scholars such as Byron Hawk that do just that: provide *counterhistories* of com-position. And just as Hawk's work asks readers to reconsider composition's preoccupation with epistemology for one of ontology, I am asking readers here to reconsider the dominant interface of contemporary soundwriting for an approach that existed but never really gained purchase by the gatekeepers of audio technologies. Therefore, I will begin by explaining how we arrived at the multitrack timeline interface. Then I will tell a story of forgotten names and philosophy-practices, and conclude by advocating for alternative approaches and interfaces for soundwriting.

While multitrack recording techniques existed as early as the late 1800s to create stereophonic sound, multitracking did not pragmatically emerge until the mid 1950s, when Les Paul designed, proposed, and commissioned a custom 8-track recording device from Ampex. Paul proposed that instead of treating a piece of magnetic tape as a single recording medium, one might divide the tape into eight distinct but parallel sections, or tracks. This way, one could build a composition in which each track was distinct, yet all tracks would be synchronized during play-back and overdubbing. We might return to the right image in Figure 40.1, as contemporary DAW multitracking is a direct digital representation of Paul's first 8-track recorder. We could add another recording to the composition in track three, and do so with no risk to the work we have already done in tracks one and two. And when we have successfully recorded, arranged, and applied effects to track three in relation to the others, our multitrack mix will play in synchronization. The multitrack recording and editing idea spread quickly and remains the most used means of soundwriting.

Tom Dowd, chief engineer at Atlantic Records, acquired an 8-track multitrack recorder in 1958, making Atlantic the first major music label to record on such machines and to release stereo records. Dowd is also credited as the first engineer to use linear faders on recording consoles, another feature very commonly replicated in DAW environments (Smith). Like Paul, Dowd's impact on the sound of US American music is difficult to overstate, but his influence on the standardization and proliferation of multitrack mixing and recording techniques is at least equal in scope. Throughout the 1960s, soundwriting experienced something of a technological plateau; most studios throughout the US and Europe continued to employ linear fader mixing boards, and multitrack tape recording interfaces.

Soundwriting became much more accessible to the amateur beginning in 1972, when TEAC released the first multitrack recorder intended for home use. Other manufacturers soon followed suit. In 1980, TEAC released its first cassette version of the 4-track recorder, and ushered a significant change in who could engage with the recording process and where (Hurtig 10). The PortaStudio, as it became known, was the public's first real access to soundwriting technologies, and it was based on very specific concepts and philosophies inherited from Les Paul (multitrack recording processes and interfaces) and Tom Dowd (stereo panning, level equalization, linear mixers). From the famous (Bruce Springsteen's *Nebraska* was recorded in 1982 on a PortaStudio 144) to the obscure, the home recording revolution had begun.

While multitrack-based soundwriting took a turn for the digital in 1992 when Alesis released its ADAT, the trend of digital hardware multitracking did not last long, as software multitracking had already begun developing and would quickly become the new standard for professional and amateur soundwriting. Throughout the 1980s, multitrack recording software such as Hybrid Arts' ADAP II had already begun to be used in music and film, and by 1991, Pro Tools emerged as an incredibly powerful, professional-grade studio "in-a-box" (Burgess 145). Other DAWs followed, such as Steinberg's Cubase in 1992, and by the end of the 1990s, prices of DAWs had decreased significantly, evening the playing field of soundwriting studio recording and editing. Today, even while some cling to analog equipment and techniques, the DAW undoubtedly reigns as the most economical and powerful way to produce sound-based work. A range of software exists, from free and open-source editors such as Audacity to studio standards such as Avid's Pro Tools. The common thread of nearly every DAW remains, however, the multitrack timeline interface.

What, though, does this process and interface enforce philosophically about the nature of sound and the process of soundwriting? In short, multitrack timelines pushed soundwriting into the territory of what Marshall McLuhan described as *visual space* (as opposed to acoustic space). McLuhan, of course, was not talking in terms of what can be seen and heard, respectively. Instead, visual and acoustic spaces are paradigms that describe and enforce how we understand, experience, and are disciplined by media environments. He argues that acoustic space

> has no center and no margin, unlike strictly linear space, which is an extension and intensification of the eye. Acoustic space is organic and integral, perceived through the simultaneous interplay of all the senses; whereas "rational" or pictorial space is uniform, sequential and continuous and creates a closed world. (59)

We might follow, at least for a moment, Gow's (2001) articulation of opposing characteristics that explain and unpack these paradigms. He characterizes visual space as sequential, asynchronous, static, linear, vertical, left brain, figure, tonal, and container; and acoustic space as simultaneous, synchronous, dynamic, nonlinear, horizontal, right brain, ground, atonal, and network.

The multitrack timeline DAW is inherently sequential, static, and linear. Most often praised for his simultaneous development of overdubbing techniques (i.e., recording asynchronously over prerecorded tracks), Paul's work in shaping this paradigm also shaped soundwriting as an inherently asynchronous activity. Instruments, tracks, samples, sources, effects, and virtually all other elements of a sonic composition are discrete and contained, and only work together to make a soundscape as they are arranged and exported as such. This might seem a strange juxtaposition with how many of us typically experience sound in the world. When we hear the audible world, it is all-at-once, dynamic, networked, and relational, it has no discrete tracks, starts or ends. It is not well-mixed and mastered. It is noisy and imperfect. In this way, most contemporary soundwriting bears almost no resemblance to what it means to hear, to listen. It disciplines us to contemplate and perform soundwriting as a linear, visual practice.

In his reflection on the musical impacts of European colonialism on African musics, John Murungi treats linearity both generously and carefully:

> A linear composition can be found, and is found in every tradition, even in African tradition. It is one way for human beings to organize experience. What has happened in the Western European tradition is the institutionalization of this way as if it were the only way to organize experience. What we can learn from the African masters of composition, though not exclusively from them, is that this way is not the only way to organize experience. Organizing experience takes on many forms. Moreover, organizing experience has a direct bearing on being human. In organizing experience human beings organize themselves. (227)

Following Murungi, we can critique dominant DAW paradigms without abandoning timelines or multitrack mixing altogether. After all, I am not implying that linearity or visual space is explicitly colonialist. I am, however, implying that because these features of DAWs are both pervasive and enforced as *The* approach to soundwriting, they have indeed colonized the practice in the Western tradition.

> In Nigeria, you don't make short records. The musical masturbation of the Western World hasn't, sort of, impinged on their creativity. Those guys play, and eighteen minutes is not long enough.
>
> *("Blackfire," from Madlib Medicine Show No. 3:*
> *Beat Konducta in Africa)*

As Les Paul co-developed the multitrack philosophy and technology in the US in the mid 1950s, Europeans were working with magnetic tape in much more *acoustic* (in McLuhan's sense of the word) ways. Pierre Schaeffer's relatively well-known *musique concrète* had successfully transitioned from 78 RPM records to magnetic tape in 1951. Shaeffer's method of musique concrète, developed in the late 1940s, was revolutionary in both technology and philosophy. Logistically speaking, Schaeffer and others used prerecorded sounds (first on records, later with tape) in combination with a range of manipulative effects (e.g. speed) to obscure the sound's source and soundwrite "forms" rather than time- and movement-based compositions with clear instrumental origins and attendant traditions (e.g. scales). Though many point to this work simply as an important beginning in sampling, musique concrète also "represents an inversion in relation to the traditional musical approach"; instead of the traditional composer moving from the abstract to the concrete in a controlled, disciplined manner (i.e., the performance of notation), the musique concrète composer "can do no better than manufacture his material, experiment with it, and finally put it together" (Palombini 16). In other words, in much the same way that we encounter sound in acoustic space—all at once, in relation to a variety of sound-sources, and free from notational control—so too does Shaeffer's composer. Though Schaeffer is undoubtedly the best-known practitioner of such philosophy-practices, much has been written of his work; we might instead look to some of his contemporaries, particularly the oft-muted women of early experimental soundwriting.

Daphne Oram was hired by the BBC in 1942 as a junior studio engineer. She also produced music, such as her groundbreaking composition "Still Point" in 1949, considered the first piece of music written to combine live electronic manipulation and a live acoustic orchestra. "Still Point" is an important reference point to many contemporary artists' work, yet is seldom referenced directly, and had not been performed until 2016. Perhaps this is unsurprising; the BBC rejected "Still Point" and several other compositions, but kept Oram employed until she left to pursue her own interests in 1959. At that time, she began development and construction of an instrument/composition philosophy called Oramics.

Oram wanted to construct a highly theoretical and multimodal instrument that strayed far from linear, visual space. She writes of her planning,

> We considered the painter and the photographer and decided that the painter has added scope for individuality. He has freehand control and he also has the benefit of immediate feedback. We then considered the singer and his use of feedback when performing a song. It seems that each parameter of the sound is checked and that, maybe, each parameter instruction is stored separately, so that individual interpretation can evolve-evolve by the subtle changing of interplay between the parameters. (96)

What resulted is the Oramics machine—a large, metal framed instrument that featured ten continuously running loops of 35mm film (see Figure 40.2). The player would draw directly on the film, and those markings were read by photocells, altering a different aspect of the resulting sound. One film strip controlled the pitch, one controlled vibrato, and so on. While this may at first glance resemble a multitrack system, its functionality and philosophy are radically different for several reasons. The important difference here, though, is that the composition was always running, always subject to change. There is no beginning or end to an Oramics composition, because each "track" is a loop, and will run for as long as the machine receives power. Further, each new or edited mark completely changed the nature of the composition—there are few points of discreteness, none of the safety so vital to Paul's multitrack system. Oramics is an instrument of networked-ness, synchronicity, all-at-onceness, and loops. Perhaps most ironically, Oramics utilizes visual input (hand drawn markings on the film) to create *acoustic* space, whereas Paul's 8-track utilizes audio input to create *visual* space.

While Oramics was largely lost in the politics of capitalistic priorities that dominated technological development in audio recording and engineering, her work and philosophy continued to influence soundwriters like Delia Derbyshire. Derbyshire also worked for the BBC's Radiophonic Workshop and composed works in the tradition of musique concrète. Her most famous work (though she is seldom explicitly credited) is the original title theme from *Doctor Who*, which was composed using a combination of sampled sounds on tape, spliced and played together at different speeds to create a range of rhythms, pitches, and patterns.

It is difficult to overstate the influence of musique concrète on soundwriters that followed, from Gysin and Burroughs's cut-up compositions, to tape musicians such as Terry Riley, even to

Figure 40.2 The Oramics Machine (Photo Courtesy of Wikimedia Commons)

early hip-hop and electronic music (Taylor 71). Modular Synthesists such as Robert Aiki Aubrey Lowe and Kaitlyn Aurelia Smith, though not working with tape, have also taken to soundwriting as a largely nonlinear, acoustic undertaking. Smith, perhaps channeling Oram, discusses the integration of multiple senses in the soundwriting process:

> Sometimes I'll start just seeing colors and then it becomes a feedback loop between what I'm making and what I'm seeing. Like, "Oh, if I open the timbre on this then it's a shape created in this color." And then that starts to turn into a story in my brain. (Host)

Smith is describing a multisensory, acoustic process in which the composer, sounds, and technologies are interacting and exchanging feedback, irrespective of time or notation.

In short, there exists a strong philosophical tradition of soundwriting that deviates from multitrack timelines composed of discrete voices. But while these traditions have made small impressions on mainstream soundwriting culture, they most often remain the obscure tools and techniques of those who we may deem "experimental." Yet this need not be the case. After all, the term "experimental" most often refers to the *result* of philosophy-processes, not the processes themselves. And certainly not the interface. My interest here is to ask what happens when we use nontraditional tools for rather ordinary rhetorical situations. Unlearning the multitrack timeline interface need not result in works that are inaccessible to audiences, but they *will* challenge the soundwriter to think about sound *acoustically* rather than *visually*.

How might we begin? Soundwriting can be an expensive undertaking, particularly for those interested in niche counterhistorical tools and techniques. And so while I am tempted to endorse vintage tape machines, West Coast style modular synthesizer modules, and other wondrous(ly expensive and fetishized) soundwriting tools, I will not do that here. Instead, I wish to point out a few tools and interfaces that are more accessible to soundwriters while still fostering non-dominant philosophies and processes.

Perhaps the most pragmatic solution to teaching soundwriting so that students are aware of the multitrack timeline is a well-known DAW, Ableton Live. It features two distinct "views," and therefore philosophy-processes, simultaneously: "session" and "arrangement." In the aptly named arrangement view, we are presented with a traditional timeline interface. In session view,

440

however, the composer is presented with a range of available instruments or samples that may be played in a variety of combinations. The composer may begin to arrange them in rows (called "scenes") and play them together, though she may also deviate from linear arrangement by launching new sounds at any time. The session view offers a distinctly acoustic approach to soundwriting, allowing for any sound to enter or leave the current composition. While recording will inevitably lead to a product with a beginning and end, the composer herself is never engaged with a timeline in this view; she is arranging sounds in terms of visual space and in acoustic relation.

For those interested in completely open environments and programming, Pure Data (and its more polished sibling, Max/MSP) can serve as a highly instructive tool of working with the real material of digital sound. Free and open-source, Pure Data uses graphical programming for a range of input/output procedures, from robotics to audio. Its open compositional environment fosters an understanding of sound not as time-based, but as data-based. After all, digital soundwriting is always both processual and data-based. The DAW's interface simply works to black box, or obscure, those processes in the interest of user-friendliness, which is in itself a highly political act. Consider a basic sample player, for instance. In a typical DAW, one would simply drag and drop an audio file into a space (see Figure 40.3, for instance), and click on that clip for playback. In Pure Data, the composer must both understand how sampling works at the data level and construct an interface that allows sample playback to take place. In this way, Pure Data forces the composer to choose and perform her *own* politics in designing her interface.

Another option, for the digital-soundscape minded, is a program called Audio HiJack that allows a user to route all audio in a computer's operating system into a recordable mixer. The user's operating system and all of its programs that produce sound can then be seen as an acoustic environment (rather than a typical DAW, in which audio channels are discrete and regulated by acceptable inputs). Further, no timeline exists as the composer "plays" her desktop.

Figure 40.3 Ableton Live's Session View

The operating system, though, becomes the instrument, becomes the interface. Shawné Michaelain Holloway, a dirty new media artist, uses this technology to instrumentalize the techno-culture she is critiquing, simultaneously playing YouTube videos, streaming music, and speech (Figure 40.4).

It should go without saying that each of these programs also possess their own politics, their own subjectivities. My hope here, of course, is not to convert readers to one interface or another, but to provoke soundwriters to think beyond the dominant, Western traditions that engulf soundwriting processes and practices. We might also participate in or support the design of DAWs that better serves the gaps in current offerings. A significant gap, for instance, exists in the space of accommodating persons with varying bodily experiences with sound, namely those with hearing loss or deafness. The use of visual mixing techniques and vibratory feedback hardware may well lead to helpful gains toward this particular aim; I have done some work developing these kinds of platforms using PureData, Arduino, and external hardware. I hope to see more of these kinds of horizon-expanding and post-ear ways of thinking about soundwriting.

We have become (more) aware of the ways that we shape our technologies and how they shape us, from early word processors to the most (seemingly) revolutionary emerging media. The obscurity of this shaping seems to be growing, however, in the sweeping wake of "user-friendliness" and "ease of use" and other favorites used by the purveyors of the rhetoric of technology as articulated a few decades ago. While I am not hopeful that academic publications will singlehandedly dampen this trend, we have the extraordinary privilege of making meaningful impacts on the way our students not only learn to produce content for digital spaces (whether with alphabetic text, video, audio, animation, game design, or otherwise), but how they learn to think about interfaces not as mere tools or empty canvasses, but as active agents that shape rhetorical situations including the representation of the student herself.

Figure 40.4 Screenshot of Shawné Michaelain Holloway's BROWSER COMPOSITION 01: what u cant give me n LOVE give me n GUCCI

Like all interfaces, soundwriting interfaces matter. They inform and shape our processes, our finished works, our private and public personae. They discipline our bodies; they write *with* us and in many cases *for* us. And even if our individual goals do not include interface hacking or development, we have an ethical responsibility to carefully interrogate those we choose to use and teach, and integrate some kind of critical approach into our curricula, lest our tools and their obscured and often problematic politics contradict our aims as scholars and teachers.

Works Cited

Ahern, Kati Fargo. "Tuning the Sonic Playing Field: Teaching Ways of Knowing Sound in First Year Writing." *Computers and Composition*, vol. 30, no. 2, 2013, pp. 75–86.

Arola, Kristin L. "The Design of Web 2.0: The Rise of the Template, The Fall of Design." *Computers and Composition*, vol. 27, 2010, pp. 4–14.

Ball, Cheryl, and Byron Hawk, Eds. Special Issue: Sound in/as Compositional Space: A Next Step In Multiliteracies. *Computers and Composition*, vol. 23, no. 3, 2006.

Boyle, Casey. "The Rhetorical Question Concerning Glitch." *Computers and Composition*, vol. 35, 2015, pp. 12–29.

Buck, Amber M. "The Invisible Interface: MS Word in the Writing Center." *Computers and Composition*, vol. 25, no. 4, 2008, pp. 396–415.

Burgess, Richard James. *The History of Music Production*. Oxford UP, 2014.

Cates, Jon. "ḅRƆK3n ωR3✖✖✖ƆℝÐZ (AKA: Broken Records: Hystories of Noise && Dirty New Media)." *Gli.tc/h Reader[ror] 20111*, edited by Nick Briz, Evan Meaney, Rosa Menkman, William Robertson, Jon Satrom, and Jessica Westbrook. Unsorted Books, 2011, http://gli.tc/h/READERROR/GLITCH_READERROR_20111-v3BWs.pdf. Accessed 1 Dec. 2017.

Ceraso, Steph. "(Re)Educating the Senses: Multimodal Listening, Bodily Learning, and the Composition of Sonic Experiences." *College English*, vol. 77, no. 2, 2014, pp. 102–23.

Gow, Gordon. "Spatial Metaphor in the Work of Marshall McLuhan." *Canadian Journal of Communication*, vol. 26, no. 4, 2001, 519–36.

Halbritter, Bump. "Musical Rhetoric in Integrated-Media Composition." *Computers and Composition*, vol. 23, no. 3, 2006, pp. 317–34.

Hammer, Steven. "Writing (Dirty) New Media/Glitch Composition." *Technoculture*, vol. 4, 2015, https://tcjournal.org/drupal/vol4/hammer-unglitched. Accessed 3 July 2017.

Hawisher, Gail E., and Cynthia L. Selfe. "The Rhetoric of Technology and the Electronic Writing Class." *College Composition and Communication*, vol. 42, no. 1, 1991, pp. 55–65.

Hawk, Byron. "*Stomp Box Logic*: Sirc and Sound." 65th Annual Conference on College Composition and Communication. Indianapolis, IN. March 19–22, 2014. Conference presentation.

——. *A Counter-History of Composition: Toward Methodologies of Complexity*. U of Pittsburgh P, 2007.

Host, Vivian. "Interview: Kaitlyn Aurelia Smith, Buchla Master." *Red Bull Music Academy Daily*, 8 Jan 2016, http://daily.redbullmusicacademy.com/2016/01/kaitlyn-aurelia-smith-interview. Accessed 30 Dec. 2016.

Hurtig, Brent. *Multi-Track Recording for Musicians*. GPI Publications, 1988.

Johnson, Nathan, and Meredith Johnson. "Glitch as Infrastructural Monster." *Enculturation*, 2016. http://enculturation.net/glitch-as-infrastructural-monster. Accessed 14 Nov. 2017.

McCorkle, Ben. "Resisting the 'Natural': Rhetorical Delivery and the Natural User Interface." *Emerging Genres in New Media Environments*, edited by Carolyn R. Miller, and Ashley R. Kelly. Springer International Publishing, 2017, pp. 99–115.

McGee, Tim, and Patricia Ericsson. "The Politics of the Program: MS WORD as the Invisible Grammarian." *Computers and Composition*, vol. 19, 2002, pp. 453–70.

McLuhan, Marshall. *The Medium is the Message*. Gingko Press, 1967.

Madlib. "Blackfire." *Medicine Show No. 3: Beat Konducta in Africa*, Stones Throw Records, 2007.

Menkman, Rosa. "Glitch Studies Manifesto." *Sunshine in My Throat*, 31 Jan. 2010, http://rosa-menkman.blogspot.com/2010/02/glitch-studies-manifesto.html, Accessed 1 Oct. 2012.

Murungi, John. *African Musical Aesthetics*. Cambridge Scholars Publishing, 2011.

Oram, Daphne. *An Individual Note of Music, Sound, and Electronics*. Galliard, 1972.

Palombini, Carlos. "Machine Songs V: Pierre Schaeffer: From Research into Noises to Experimental Music." *Computer Music Journal*, vol. 17, no. 3, 1993, pp. 14–19.

Reid, Alex. "Composing Objects: Prospects for a Digital Rhetoric." Presentation at the annual Computers and Writing Conference, Raleigh, NC, December 6–9, 2012.

Rice, Jeff. "The Making of Ka-Knowledge: Digital Aurality." *Computers and Composition*, vol. 23, no. 3, 2006, pp. 266–79.

Rickert, Thomas, Ed. Special issue: Writing/Music/Culture. *Enculturation*, vol. 2, no. 2, 1999.

——. *Ambient Rhetoric: The Attunements of Rhetorical Being*. University of Pittsburgh Press, 2013.

Selfe, Cynthia L. "Technology and Literacy: A Story about the Perils of Not Paying Attention." *College Composition and Communication*, vol. 50, no. 3, 1999, pp. 411–36.

——. "The Movement of Air, the Breath of Meaning: Aurality and Multimodal Composing." *College Composition and Communication*, vol. 60, no. 4, 2009, pp. 616–63.

Selfe, Cynthia L., and Richard J. Selfe, Jr. "The Politics of the Interface: Power and Its Exercise in Electronic Contact Zones." *College Composition and Communication*, vol. 45, no. 4, 1994, pp. 480–504.

Sirc, Geoffrey. "Interchanges: Never Mind the Sex Pistols, Where's 2Pac?" *College Composition and Communication*, vol. 49, no. 1, 1998, pp. 104–08.

——. *English Composition as a Happening*. Utah State UP, 2002.

Smith, Ebonie. "The Father of the Atlantic Sound." *Atlantic Records*. 4 Dec 2013. www.atlanticrecords.com/posts/father-atlantic-sound-18236. Accessed 30 Dec. 2016.

Stedman, Kyle. "Remix Literacy and Fan Compositions." *Computers and Composition*, vol. 29, no. 2, 2012, pp. 107–23.

Stoever-Ackerman, Jennifer. "Splicing the Sonic Color-Line: Tony Schwartz Remixes Postwar Nueva York." *Social Text*, vol. 28, no. 1, 2010, pp. 59–85.

Stone, Jonathan W. "Listening to the Sonic Archive: Rhetoric, Representation, and Race in the Lomax Prison Recordings." *Enculturation*, vol. 19, 2015. http://enculturation.net/listening-to-the-sonic-archive. Accessed 14 Nov. 2017.

Taylor, Timothy D. *Strange Sounds: Music, Technology, and Culture*. Routledge, 2001.

VanKooten, Crystal. "Singer, Writer: A Choric Exploration of Sound and Writing." *Kairos*, vol. 21, no. 1, 2016.

41

"JUST NOT THE FUTURE"

Taking on Digital Writing

Stuart Moulthrop

Massed and Marked

This chapter comes at digital writing, an ill-defined and (for some) perilously large subject, from what once may have passed for its bleeding edge: e-poetry, net art, and other forms of linguistic experiment belonging to what Alan Liu has called "the future literary" (8). Like N. K. Hayles, Liu uses "the literary" in distinction to *literature*, to evoke a more expansive cultural formation (see Hayles 4–5). This generosity may be helpful. *Writing* is always a larger subject than *literature*, perhaps greater even than an augmented "literary." The present chapter might seem oddly placed in a collection concerned mainly with digital rhetoric and literacy; though that impression will hopefully prove misleading. "The literary" provides room not just for expansion but also for transformation. Raw inventions have ways of becoming household goods; poetry turns into advertising; revolutions are in fact televised . . . or something worse. The extravagant and experimental usually collide at some point with broader social interests. Lately that collision has turned ugly.

It now seems ethically impossible to think about digital poetics in distinction from digital rhetoric, at least in its applied sense; and while the worst effects of this conjunction seem to fall on the creative side of the line—possibly amounting to an existential crisis—the convergence of poetic experiment and media practice points to a more general problem. Sandy Baldwin, a particularly adept critic of the new "literary," has seen to the heart of this trouble. He speaks to "writing" and even "printed matter," but he understands these terms in relation to "the networked computer" (3), an entity that means far more than any mechanism at a particular I.P. address. Baldwin's networked computer resembles general prostheses such as *the automobile* and *the telephone*. Like those ubiquitous devices, it brings profound changes to human experience, and equally large problems for those who reflect:

> You do not read writing; you cannot take in the mass of texts in the world. You cannot take it. The writings exceed you, they overwhelm you, and they bury you. You might write this text, or write that text, but you know nothing of writing, nothing of writing itself. No, our entire species is devoted to producing greater and greater explosive spasms of overwhelming printed matter. Is this not the network? Is this not the web? Not texts, not writing to be read, but writing as massed marked detritus. (18)

Why is the man so upset? Leaving aside certain fantasies of the distant-reading crowd, it has perhaps never been possible to know "writing itself," if that term means the totality of a written record. Let us assume writing was invented many times by scattered human communities, such as the calculus, or as the Japanese claim, baseball. It would thus have been impossible even at the start to "take in the mass of texts in the world," even when texts came as marks on clay tablets or knots in strips of hide. After you read everything in your home ziggurat, there were always mysterious productions from those folks across the river, no to mention the undiscovered oceans. The mass of writing is elusive by nature.

Is the problem different under influence of the networked computer? Maybe: the network seems to promise wholesale connectedness; but that promise is deceptive, since any real unity amounts, as Pierre Lévy says, to a "universal without totality" (91). No doubt the universe of text has always been, as Barthes and Foucault knew, far larger than the purview of formal indices and canons—not just Nietzsche's collected works, but his letters, journals, prescriptions, laundry lists (Foucault 144). Today, of course, the ambit extends to infamous email archives, and thus to Facebook, Instagram, Reddit, tweets and re-tweets; by the time you read this, the list will be different if not longer. Under computation and digital storage, and assuming address protocols can be suitably improved, the indexical impulse seems set for exponential expansion. As in some cinematic jump to hyperspace, we seem to have lurched truly from Work to Text, no longer "thrifty" in our "discourses and their significations" (Foucault 159) but profligate beyond all reason.

The claim is easily illustrated. I type a random trio of words into the Google search engine: *gnomon wastrel caravan*. High on the second page of results I find a link to a peculiar document that contains all three. That document consists of nearly ten thousand words in the form of an extended, glossolalic list. The term "mangy litany," to which we are coming, may well apply. Here is how the thing starts:

> Jules standby charcoal contingent hockey defrost testicle intersect advert done incidental controversy tetrahedron Callaghan phosgene cavitate coltish heroin jangle decolletage triune timeworn atlantic plop hexadecimal Sorenson kin rapacious Butterfield fiduciary Notre jamboree trunk Hamilton Michaelangelo apostolic PR formaldehyde . . .

The litany appears as a posting on a Google forum called news.admin.net-abuse.misc, which seems to be (or have been) a venue where network administrators could discuss spam and other forms of abusive behavior. The posting is dated August 5, 1996 (Confect).

How did several megabytes of wordspew come to be on this forum twenty years ago? Possibly they were poisonous chaff dropped by retaliating spammers during some now-forgotten conflict, the idea being to overload their enemies' channel with junk data. Ten thousand words made a more significant impact on memory and processing two decades ago than they would today, and network effects will always amplify the drain. The giant wordlist may thus be something like an impact crater or the Crab Nebula, remnants of a distant trauma.

That explanation seems plausible but not definitive. If the strange text is ordnance from an old war, why has no one cleared the battlefield? Why can I still read it two decades later? Also: if this posting is chaff, why does it consist of lexically valid words and not random alphanumeric strings? Could the tactic have been meant to impact search engines as well, by forcing them to index a large number of words? Perhaps my initial conjecture was wrong, and the mangy litany is part of some Internet mystery I have not yet heard about, which one of my hipper friends will eventually explain.[1] Maybe news.admin.net-abuse.misc is not what it seems, and the nonsense text is actually a cryptogram. It could be the work of some ancient cyberpunk, or spooks, or angels, or as Baldwin names it, "the Internet unconscious."

It is easy enough to confirm Baldwin's despair about digital writing in the wild. There is indeed more than we can measure, comprehend, or tolerate; but mass is only part of the problem. Baldwin applies two terms of critique: the "detritus" is both "mass" and "marked." Our glossolalic list fits both parts of the formula. It is excessive in scope, certainly, but it is also (at least ostensibly) traceable to some motive and mechanism. Assuming the text is in fact the work of spammer-jammers, we might say it slouches toward rhetoric, managing at least an *argumentum ad baculum*. Understood in this way, the posting is rhetorical in the manner of slashed tires, enacting damage to enforce silence. No doubt such militancy goes beyond the pale of rhetoric proper, and here again we can understand Baldwin's exasperation. Writing on the network is not just horribly vast, but nastily articulated. Fast-forward twenty years.

The nastiness has become acute. At the time of this writing, late 2016, there is much concern over the popularity of phony news items, and in particular "#Pizzagate," a malicious fiction exploited by supporters of the incoming US administration, evidently to annoy and intimidate high-level figures in the other party (Aisch et al.). Stories about a child-sex ring linked to the losing candidate have spread virally through social media channels, linked in part to fake reporting from nonexistent television stations and other bogus sources. Though such spasms of falsehood occur regularly, this one seems unusually toxic, both because a person involved in the Presidential transition actively promoted the lies, and because the call to arms was answered by a man with an assault rifle who fired his weapon in a family restaurant.

Similar and worse offenses have often happened in the United States: tar-and-feather parties, lynchings, Palmer raids, red scares, blacklists. The city of Baltimore was once known as Mobtown, not for practices memorialized on *The Wire*, but because nineteenth-century political gangs regularly brutalized newspaper editors and others with whom they disagreed. America has its not-so-secret histories (see Coates), and the European record is similarly bad. Sometimes the subject of writing is not unknowable but unspeakable. There is nothing particularly new in the mass marked detritus of email blasts, Facebook posts, viral videos, and tweets. At their worst, as in #Pizzagate, they embody something terribly familiar: the blood libel, the accusation of child abduction used to trigger genocide against Jews of Russia and Europe, and lies spewed by not-so-silent majorities against other enemies. Behavior like this may indeed be more than we can take.

Nostra Culpa

Baldwin means *take* as in comprehension, to "take in." There is however an even more troubling sense of that word to which we must also pay attention: *take on*—assuming responsibility, complicity, and at least figurative ownership. I will start with what seems an outrageous claim: *various forms of software culture circa 1975–2000, and in particular electronic literature, net art, and tactical media, pioneered discursive practices that now lie at the heart of present crises.* We could start with promiscuous linking, socialized media, and microblogging, though the list could be expanded. These things have changed the world. Nicholas Negroponte's fantasy of a "Daily Me," a personalized news source that would disrupt and transform journalism (Sunstein), has become The News From Mobtown—and tempting though it is to call this formation a Daily Them, it is more accurately attributed to Us. If as Baldwin says, "[t]he Internet is a work of literature" (3), then some of us literary types have explaining to do. We broke (the news of) the Internet. Now we own it.

Yes, the claim is outrageous, but I am not the first to try it out. A few years back, Theodor Holm Nelson, who gave hypertext its name and mission, personally apologized for disappointing development of the World Wide Web and the awful state of Internet culture (Barnet 80).

Once, I found that move a bit disingenuous (Barnet, x). Lately I have begun to reconsider, wondering whether (hitching lowly caboose to mighty train) I might owe some regrets for the short-attention-span theatre of "Hegirascope" (1997) or certain evocations of blog-rolls or the Twitterverse in "Pax" (2003). Did we riders on Nelson's express (even the clowns) spread dangerous ideas as the circus rolled along?

Maybe this is occasion for laughter, clown talk indeed. If hypertext fiction played any substantive role in the sad evolution of social media, my guilt could be assuaged with a larger annual check to the family foundation. Oh wait, I don't have a family foundation—try over at the Winthrops or the Northrops. In the cold light of day, writers and artists are generally not the digerati who matter. Thirty years ago, Judy Malloy invented social media fiction with her groundbreaking work on the Whole Earth 'Lectronic Link (see Grigar and Moulthrop). Should we now ask her to answer for evil, anti-social fictions on Reddit or Facebook? Of course not: as Cinna the Poet reminds (*Julius Caesar* III.iii), when people are torn for their verses, we have truly gone to Mobtown. Confluence is not causality. To say some of us *own* the perversions of digital writing looks suspiciously like self-dramatizing.

And yet anyone who works with data, code, network protocols, and other affordances of the networked computer must feel a deep unease about the uses to which these technologies are increasingly turned. By one account, disinformation significantly outweighed legitimate reporting in Facebook circulation in the weeks preceding the 2016 US election (Silverman). Similar observations have been made about other countries (Mozur and Scott). Once upon a time, some of us embraced a culture of innovation, disruption, and creative destruction, assuming like Negroponte that good things must rise from the dust of the old. Not so much, as it turns out—or at least not so simply. Looking back in regret may be foolishly narcissistic, but what about the view going forward? How does visionary practice work in the age of "mass marked detritus?" What should one think about poetry and fiction in a house of lies?

There is always aesthetic opposition. If digital writing is more than we want to take, maybe the right course is to give back or pay forward, meeting excesses on their own terms. A good example here might be Mark Marino's documentary game "Living Will" (Marino), an ingenious conflation of Dickensian inheritance story, choose-your-own hypertext, and the way we live now. The game's "will" (to power) "lives" within an adaptive narrative that unveils increasingly stark truths as we adjust our relationship to fellow characters, jockeying for some or all the legacy. Aside from the timeless social critique implicit in this situation, there is a second, contemporary moral. The source of the fortune for which we strive is a brutally extractive coltan mine. Coltan is the real-world ore essential to information appliances, a notorious signature of rapacious globalism in which the digital world is deeply implicated. Marino insists on mixing hard truth into the fantasy.

Marino's continuing collaborations with Rob Wittig on Netprovs (network-based improvisations) also deserve mention. Wittig has been creatively repurposing organs of digital culture for decades, beginning with bulletin board systems in *Invisible Rendezvous* (1994), shifting to email with *The Blue Company* (Walker), before taking on the Web with *The Fall of the Site of Marsha* (1999). Netprovs extend this agenda into the intensively mediated space of the present century, unfolding on Facebook, Twitter, YouTube, and other venues including physical space. These digitally documented, live-action role-playing campaigns interrogate conditions of labor and professional discipline in the network regime, from office workers to non-tenured academic staff (Marino and Wittig).

Marino and Wittig are satirists, operating with clear subversive intent. However, as the attempt to turn network culture back upon itself intensifies, some results seem more ambiguous.

Consider Jonathan Harris and Greg Hochmuth's "Network Effect" (Harris and Hochmuth), a work that is revealingly hard to categorize. Formally speaking it is a website designed both for individual use and art installations. It is also possible to describe the project as a service or quasi-utility, for it is much less a channel for specific information than a means of conjuring unpredictable assemblages of data. In this respect it is more like what Markku Eskelinen (following John Cayley and others) calls an *instrument* (Eskelinen 375–7).

The core of this instrumentality is a collection of 10,000 videos posted to YouTube, each topically tagged by volunteers on the Mechanical Turk service, using a vocabulary of human actions (e.g., blow, fly, hug, play, plant, search, swim, wash, etc.). Though based in a Web browser, the elegant and exuberant visual language of "Network Effect" seems more reminiscent of mobile applications, designed for brief, intense encounters. A user of the system browses the videos through one of several interfaces, for instance a smear of moveable, translucent words that flow across the middle of the initial screen. Further options are also available in pull-down menus and subsequent modal displays.

If we think of "Network Effect" as an instrument in the musical sense, what we play with/upon it is technically a solo—in spite of the name, the project is designed for individual operation, even in the installation context. Yet the experience of browsing its video archive is decidedly social. Each fleeting clip is accompanied by a lingering, looping soundtrack, providing elements of a percolating babble. At the same time, the project reaches beyond this aesthetic register with features that suggest a scientific or investigative instrument, or at least a data-driven presentation. Its survey of Internet video is, after all, a kind of core sample of YouTube. Once a particular video is selected, the user can activate an interface option ("Words") that displays terms found in proximity to the indexed verb within Google's store of digitized language. Another option shows a line graph indicating usage of the term by men and women over the previous century.

Science! as the Brit-toned voice cries in a certain Thomas Dolby tune (Dolby)—though the more accurate term is probably *pseudo-science*. Mark Sample points out that these data-intensive features of "Network Effect" are purely gratuitous, amounting to a pastiche of Digital Humanities practice (Sample). In the larger framing of the project we might also detect satire or parody. "YOUR TIME HERE IS LIMITED," we are warned on first visiting the site. In fact each user is allotted only a few minutes, based on the region associated with the I.P. address through which she or he connects. Since average lifespan in the USA is 74.8 years, I am allowed seven minutes, fifty seconds to engage the system before it locks me out for the next twenty-four hours. If I return early, I will be told how much time remains in my ban, then presented with a quotation from Carl Jung: "Your vision will become clear only when you can look into your own heart. Who looks outside, dreams; who looks inside, awakes." The message of this operational parable seems clear enough: stop gazing into the narcissistic pool of Internet video and get on with the rest of your life.

However, as any recovering postmodernist will tell you, double logics derail the best intentions. Harris and Hochmuth strictly meter their site's pleasures, forcing us to put away the screen and go play outside, or inside, or maybe just elsewhere in the network. That prohibition might work differently if we could visit only once and never again—an extreme sanction at least one on-line game designer has actually used (Anthropy 20–1). Locking us out for only a day sends a mixed signal—less moral stricture, perhaps, than tease. For some users at least, the teeming, attractive interior of "Network Effect" may beckon all the more seductively because of its Brigadoonish interval. In this perhaps unforeseen consequence, parody tumbles toward that other thing called pastiche, of which Fredric Jameson has warned:

Pastiche is, like parody, the imitation of a peculiar mask, speech in a dead language: but it is a neutral practice of such mimicry, without any of parody's ulterior motives, amputated of the satiric impulse, devoid of laughter and of any conviction that alongside the abnormal tongue you have momentarily borrowed, some healthy linguistic normality still exists. Pastiche is thus blank parody, a statue with blind eyeballs. (17)

According to Jameson, the collapse of parody into pastiche depends partly on the demise of "healthy linguistic normality," or "national language"—or as we might say these days, the insertion of a neo-nationalist populism. Indeed, the babbling stream of "Network Effect" approximates a *vox populi* absent political or even critical reflection, fatally overdosed on *Dasein*. We can tell ourselves we have shut the door on this spectacle, taking the Jungian advice to seek an inward truth; but when pastiche arrives, truth becomes untenable and the inside/out distinction disappears. Everywhere is now the network, nor are we ever out of it. We cannot own the network, either in the sense of comprehension or complicity, because the network owns us. Under the logic of late capitalism, operationalized as disruption, only one subject of parody remains. In the immortal words of Pogo, that enemy is us.

"Because they disrupt me": Askesis

If "Network Effect" seems ambiguous or liminal, we can turn to another work that interrogates the problem of digital language—specifically, digital writing—with greater clarity. This is *Issue 1*, Stephen McLaughlin and Jim Carpenter's audacious lampoon of contemporary poetry (McLaughlin and Carpenter). The massive document, distributed over the Internet in the fall of 2008, consists of 3,164 free-verse poems, each attributed to an actual poet, living or dead. One of its selections is in fact the source of that interesting phrase "mangy litanies":

Scarlet words and mangy litanies

There is time for the
surprised nature
They pause beyond the
plans of the warmth
Out of their unsteady hand
they dreams of someone, hearing, and out
of their vein nature
coming
They are
Whenever in late autumn they disrupt me
Since they interrupt me in the morning
Until they interrupt me
Because they disrupt me
Those are black
Those are horned
That which known to a
mangy gourd bitterly comes, is unsteady
and scarlet

Donna Kuhn

Like any text presenting as lyrical or meditative poetry, "Scarlet words and mangy litanies" invites interpretation. We might notice the way the text seems anchored (or not) by a series of rootless pronouns, an undefined series of *they* and *those*. We might pause on the curiously symmetrical cluster of repetitions: "disrupt . . . interrupt . . . interrupt . . . disrupt," in lines 10–13. We might find something new-sententious, our at least odd, in the solecism of line 6 ("they dreams"). Overall, we could call this a poem of un-knowing or resolute mysteriousness, made of a language artfully disrupted.

The one thing we cannot do is wonder what the poet and artist Donna Kuhn intended when she wrote these lines. We cannot do this because the last line of the poem is not "and scarlet," but "Donna Kuhn." What looks like a traditional author attribution is in fact, as I have elsewhere called it, an impudent apostrophe (Moulthrop and Grigar)—literally a shameless, unsolicited invocation. *Issue 1* is a grand literary prank. The 3,164 poems were not composed by the people named in their final lines, but by a computer program, a notably good free-verse generator. What looks like an author attribution is really reverse or perverse plagiarism, the abduction not of someone's work but of her name.

Kenneth Goldsmith, advocating more generally for textual appropriation and iconoclasm, finds much to like about McLaughlin and Carpenter's project:

> With one gesture, [the supposed anthologists] had swapped the focus *from content to context*, showing us what it might mean to be a poet in the digital age. Being a poet in any age—digital or analog—places one's practice outside normative economies, theoretically enabling the genre to take risks that more lucrative ventures wouldn't. Just as we've seen some of the most adventurous linguistic experimentation in the past century in poetry, its [*sic*] now poised to do the same when it comes to notions of authorship, publishing, and distribution as proved by the *Issue 1*'s provocations. (123)

Others have been less favorably impressed. Goldsmith reports Ron Silliman, one of the authors borrowed from in "Scarlet words," accused McLaughlin and Carpenter of "anarcho-flarf vandalism" and hinted darkly about legal action (122). The displacement of content by context can be painful, especially when the act reveals how attributions constitute brand names or trademarks. No one likes being reminded of his trade when that business is threatened with disruption.

For the less traditionally minded, there might still be room for engagement. If we carry that virus of American optimism (the vice D. H. Lawrence ascribed to "blue-eyed Nathaniel" Hawthorne), then we might share Goldsmith's admiration for the stunt. *Issue 1* may not be exactly comparable to the work of a tribute band, but it is possible to read in its iterated apostrophes at least a hint of homage. *Dear Donna Kuhn, this one's for you.* Content aside, if the old New Critic can find no purchase on these verses, the newer Digital Humanist would very much like to crawl the generative code. Algorithm is the latest object of desire. How was the apparently coherent vocabulary of the poem selected, and from what underlying set? Where did that ABBA pattern in lines 10–13 come from? Does the generator have even a rudimentary model of poetics, and if so, what?

To engage in these ways, however, risks setting aside *Issue 1*'s "provocations," its challenges to publishing, distribution, and especially *authorship*. Clever code is a thing of beauty, but *Issue 1* is not purely aesthetic, it is also rhetorical or polemic. In the present context, we may want to remember that *Issue 1* is founded on misrepresentation or falsehood; also, that it replaces personal authorship with digital simulation. As a certain public figure will never say, it does not bring back American poetry jobs; quite the opposite.

Issue 1 is either the highest form of pastiche, effacing the author-function itself, or the artful end of that practice, an innovation in production that empties even pastiche of its last molecule of meaning. Perversely hyperabundant, the project is also an emptying out. It is hard to see how to proceed from its foundation. While there certainly could be an *Issue 2*—algorithm is nothing if not iterable—what would be the point? The conceptual slap has landed and we do not need another, thanks. *Issue 1* might as well be *Issue Ω*.

What does one say after the last word? Even before the world began its recent high-dive into madness, there had begun to be calls for restraint of digital media. "Network Effect" attempts such a move, if ambiguously. Its authors are not alone in their skepticism. Software moguls in the Bay Area have begun to refer to smartphones as "WMDs"—*wireless mobile devices* but also perhaps *weapons of mass distraction*—and are signing up for "Unplug" weekends where their use is banned (Bosker). In the arts, prominent critics and practitioners have recently turned toward the "post-digital" (Berry and Dieter) rejecting the new-media fixations of the last two decades (Kember and Zylinska). Has the "detritus" of digital writing reached, for creative purposes at least, a point of critical mass? Has the poetic impulse been crushed by the rhetorical? Does the recruitment of once-new media to the old work of rabble-rousing demand a turn from flickering signifiers back toward a poetry of personal presence, of true names, honest voices, and real truths?

These questions are preamble to an ultimate, existential challenge: *should there be any more electronic writing?* Though the negative indications are strong, we may not in fact have reached the last word. Before signing up for askesis or renunciation, maybe we should ask a poet.

"All Art Is Ovarian Cannabis:" What Remains

We can in a way ask the poet Donna Kuhn—if not directly, being somehow still ruled by that taboo against the personal, learned from the New Critics in childhood—then by giving the networked computer one last poke. It turns out the real Donna Kuhn maintains a blog called Digital Aardvarks. On December 10, 2016, she posted in that space a deeply personal poem that also bears importantly on our existential problem. Titled "THE LAST PARADE (for spencer)," the verses appear below a piece of digital art credited to Spencer Selby (Kuhn).

For one thing, the poem resonates sharply against Silliman's charge of "anarcho-flarf vandalism." *Flarf* is a style of appropriative poetry that commonly takes digital text as source material (Bernstein). Kuhn tags "THE LAST PARADE" as "cut-up email correspondence." So whatever this poet may have thought of McLaughlin and Carpenter's name-piracy, we can doubt she would have used "flarf" as a term of abuse. Like many poets these days, Kuhn does not seem ready to unplug. Here is the last part of the poem she has, presumably, woven from archives of electronic mail, perhaps exchanges with the dedicatee:

> i am failure, dying of ideas
> breast wimp, ukraine science
> i am objectively happy
> chateau faith, overdramatic antihistamines
> the church library kills, the magnesium worried
> radiation glimmer
> generic ham, know your soup likes the system
> the x-rays were crazy, i'm done with way anymore
> big bad wednesday
> i'm just not the future.

If we can only wonder fruitlessly about pronoun references in the faux-Kuhn poem of *Issue 1*, here we can make a clearer assumption. The "i" in these fragmentary phrases appears to be a person in serious or terminal illness: "breast wimp," "radiation glimmer," and "i am failure/dying of ideas." This poem reminds us that the cut-up procedure is bivalent, both creating a new verbal context and implicitly hinting at the unseen original. It is not hard to piece out these tesserae, though the picture they imply is full of sorrow.

This is a death-facing poem. The first and last lines mark it as a work of preparation if not valediction. We could not be further from the context of *Issue 1*, where the logic of extinction is applied to an idea (authorship) or a class (poets), but only figuratively to actual persons—and then really as displacement (stealing names) rather than physical extinction. Other virtues aside, *Issue 1* is not an especially humane work. The meaning of any poem within it attaches almost exclusively to its technical origins. Anything else we find amounts to projection. In "THE LAST PARADE," though, we are back in Ginsberg's total animal soup, confronted with friendship and sorrow and actual loss.

This would be a hard poem in any season, especially if one has any experience of long and painful endings. It seems especially bitter fruit at the end of 2016, on the heels of Brexit and the US electoral disaster and the threats still hanging over Europe. Taken in this context, "THE LAST PARADE" asserts the cruelty of dying during dark times, cut off from the arc of history before it bends another way. Walter Benjamin observed that a man who dies at the age of thrity-five is at all moments of his life a man who dies at thirty-five; yet no one knows his fate from the outset (373). Benjamin died not knowing the Nazis would be destroyed and his continent redeemed. No endings are happy. The voice in Kuhn's poem says, "i'm just not the future," ringing that bell that tolls for all of us. If we are ever graced with futurity, the gift is temporary and precarious. At some point we all must disengage.

Yet Kuhn's poem also contains this line: "i am objectively happy." What are these words doing in this dark meditation? They express resignation, perhaps, or the last step in Kubler-Ross's famous march. The sentence seems curiously placed, eight lines before the final resignation. Given the general tenor of sickness and suffering, not even the most blue-eyed of optimists could read it as a turn toward transcendence. It lands, after all, at the end of a triplet that includes references to failure, Ukraine, and (most likely) cancer. Probably the remark suggests comfort or palliation—if not the pot or the morphine, then the consolation of philosophy.

Yet if we can explicate this assertion of happiness, we cannot explain it away. After all, Kuhn could have cut the phrase while she was dicing up her correspondence, but she—human being, not algorithm—decided otherwise. "THE LAST PARADE" thus leaves us with a question: how can a person be "objectively happy" if he or she is "not the future?" This question is vexed in many ways.

We come to another important difference between *Issue 1* and Donna Kuhn's blog poem. At least until software is granted personhood, we can interpret digitally generated text any way we like. Its human register is to say the least attenuated. In reading "THE LAST PARADE," however, any attempt to generalize or exemplify works at cross-purposes to the poem's immediate context of personal loss. Especially given the currency of the writing, it seems incumbent to apologize before swapping in a different context. What follows is in some sense inescapably insensitive.

And yet there the poem is, digitally derived and part of the networked mass of expression. A blog is personal but not private. So it might be possible to place the trenchant meaning of Kuhn's poem in a wider frame. Out here in reader-land, our loss is not (yet) personal. The email was not addressed to us. The sorrow it contains is not ours directly; yet it resonates with other losses. Eventually we will all suffer that severing from futurity as biological fact. For the moment, some of us feel it figuratively, as a matter of imaginative investment.

Some who once looked forward can no longer do so, at least not with clear enthusiasm. We might ask how, either as digital writers, or any who inherit the "mass marked detritus," we can happily live in a world whose trend lines we reject. To a large extent, digital writing now serves class disruption and rogue contextualization, a regime where truth collapses into truth-effects and fraud becomes the new normal. The world has its own sickness. How can we remain committed to what we once called *the future* (literary or otherwise) if we know it's just not us?

A large part of the answer can be found simply by finding. The one digital difference that may suggest redemptive possibility may be (ironically) the point at which writing disrupts itself—when, through the indexical power of digital memory, it points to something else. (He's talking about *hypertext!*) In studying cybernetic texts we have learned to think about traversal functions, operations that turn potentialities into expression. In a way, the logic of traversal applies to conventional writings as well, to poems and essays that spring directly from our brains without mechanical intervention. This essay you are now finishing is an excursion, a series of moves from point to point. It began as a set of traversals.

I came upon the phony Kuhn poem in *Issue 1* by searching its contents for the word "disrupt." From there, via Google search on Donna Kuhn's borrowed name, I arrived at her blog and "THE LAST PARADE." If context has not displaced content—and Kuhn's poem clearly suggests the opposite—it has at least achieved equal footing. Context manifests as connection, the hypertextensive body of present and discoverable links. That excessive mass of text is marked, articulated, indexed for traversal. Some of those pathways lead down into the house of lies, to the *Daily Stormer* if not the Daily Me; but other directions remain eligible. If we reject the present shape of digital writing, that moment-formerly-known-as-the-future with which we no longer identify, we may yet still imagine an immanent future, an alternative that can be achieved, locally and with great effort, in honesty and grief and sorrow, even inside the house of lies.

The subject of digital writing may indeed be more than we can take, philosophically or politically; but it is not, perhaps, more than we can handle. How we come to grips with schemes of fraud, deceit, and nascent tyranny may define the claim we have, as writers or citizens, on any kind of future. Meeting this obligation is only a matter of work. To find happiness within that work, objectively or otherwise, may call for something more.

Note

1. Friend Nick Montfort, unassailably hip and Doctor of Computational Linguistics to boot, says the mysterious list looks like the database for a spell-checker, an example of which might be found on almost any personal computer. So much for mystery? Maybe not. Montfort adds: "I assume it has something to do with spam filtering (given the newsgroup) but it lacks much context. It seems to just be a word list (no syntax, of course no punctuation) and to be biased toward low-frequency words. There are some short and more common words ('lay', 'site', 'fire', even a preposition now and then such as 'between') and some occur more than once, but the distribution seems biased toward uncommon words, including brand names such as Marlboro. I don't know what it's for, but it might be a list used to 'season' spam messages to help them avoid detection, and it might be posted (for some reason without comment) on this newsgroup to show people what such a list is like. That's a guess, though. It might be genuine newsgroup spam, a mistake, or a variety of other things."

Works Cited

Aisch, Gregor, Jon Huang and Cecilia Kang. "Dissecting the #PizzaGate Conspiracy Theories." *New York Times*, 10 Dec. 2016.

Anthropy, Anna. *Rise of the Videogame Zinesters*. Seven Stories, 2012.

Baldwin, Sandy. *The Internet Unconscious: On the Subject of Electronic Literature*. Bloomsbury Press, 2015.

Barnet, Belinda. *Memory Machines: The Evolution of Hypertext*. Anthem Press, 2013.

Benjamin, Walter. "The Storyteller: Reflections on the Works of Nikolai Leskov." *The Novel: An Anthology of Criticism and Theory 1900–2000*, edited by D. J. Hale. Blackwell Publishing, 2006, pp. 361–78.

Bernstein, Charles. "The Flarf Files." *Electronic Poetry Center*. epc.buffalo.edu/authors/bernstein/syllabi/readings/flarf.html. Accessed 18 Dec. 2016.

Berry, David, and Michael Dieter. *Post-Digital Aesthetics*. London: Palgrave Macmillan UK, 2015.

Bosker, Bianca. "The Binge Breaker." *The Atlantic*, November 2016, pp. 56–65.

Coates, Ta-nehisi. "The case for reparations." *The Atlantic*, June 2014.

Confect, Walter. "Marlboro omega." news.admin.net-abuse.misc. 5 August 1996. groups.google.com/forum/#!msg/news.admin.net abuse.misc/2UvR.qwDXwqw/94M71slGMs0J. Accessed 18 Dec. 2016.

Dolby, Thomas. *She Blinded Me with Science: One of Our Submarines*. Harvest, 1982.

Eskelinen, Markku. *Cybertext Poetics: The Critical Language of New Media Literary Theory*. Continuum Press, 2012.

Foucault, Michel. "What Is An Author?" *Textual Strategies: Perspectives in Post-Structuralist Criticism*, edited by J. Harari. Cornell University Press, 1979, pp. 141–60.

Goldsmith, Kenneth. *Uncreative Writing: Managing Language in the Digital Age*. Columbia University Press, 2011.

Grigar, Dene, and Stuart Moulthrop. *PATHFINDERS: Documenting the Experience of Early Electronic Literature*. Vancouver, WA: Nouspace Press, 2015. http://scalar.usc.edu/works/pathfinders. Accessed 18 Dec. 2016.

Harris, Jonathan and Greg Hochmuth. "Network Effect." http://networkeffect.io/. Accessed 18 Dec. 2016.

Hayles, N. Katherine. *Electronic Literature: New Horizons for the Literary*. University of Notre Dame Press, 2008.

Jameson, Fredric. *Postmodernism, or, The Cultural Logic of Late Capitalism*. Duke University Press, 1991.

Kember, Sarah, and Joanna Zylinska. *Life After New Media: Mediation as a Vital Process*. MIT Press, 2012.

Kuhn, Donna. "THE LAST PARADE (for spencer)." *Digital Aardvarks*. December 10, 2016. digital aardvarks.blogspot.com/. Accessed 18 Dec. 2016.

Lévy, Pierre. *Cyberculture*. University of Minnesota Press, 2001.

Liu, Alan. *The Laws of Cool: Knowledge Work and the Culture of Information*. Uniersity of Chicago Press, 2004.

Marino, Mark C. "Living Will, by E.R. Millhouse." http://markcmarino.com/tales/livingwill.html. Accessed 18 Dec. 2016.

Marino, Mark, and Rob Wittig. "Netprov: Elements of an Emerging Form." *Dichtung Digital*, 42 (2012). www.dichtung-digital.de/en/journal/aktuelle-nummer/?postID=577. Accessed 17 Nov. 2017.

McLaughlin, Steven, and Jim Carpenter. *Issue 1*. Principal Hand Editions, 2008.

Moulthrop, Stuart, and Dene Grigar. *Traversals: The Use of Preservation for Electronic Literature*. MIT Press, 2017.

Mozur, Paul, and Mark Scott. "Fake News in U.S. Election? Elsewhere, That's Nothing New." *New York Times*, 17 November 2016. A1.

Sample, Mark. "The Closed World, Databased Narrative, and 'Network Effect.'" *Next Horizons* 2016. Annual Conference of the Electronic Literature Organization. University of Vancouver. 11 June 2016.

Silverman, Craig. "This Analysis Shows How Fake Election News Stories Outperformed Real News On Facebook." *Buzzfeed News*, 16 November 2016. www.buzzfeed.com/craigsilverman/viral-fake-election-news-outperformed-real-news-on-facebook?utm_term=.xoGJWv26d#.ceJ8XNvym. Accessed 17 Dec. 2016.

Sunstein, Cass. "Democracy and the Internet." *Information Technology and Moral Philosophy*, edited by J. Van Der Hoven, and J. Weckert. Cambridge University Press, 2008, pp. 93–110.

Walker, Jill. "TELLING STORIES ACROSS NETWORKS." *Internet Research Annual: Selected Papers from the Association of Internet Researchers Conferences. Vol. 3*. Peter Lang, 2005.

Wittig, Rob. *Invisible Rendezvous: Connection and Collaboration in the New Landscape of Electronic Writing*. Wesleyan University Press, 1994.

——. *The Blue Company*. 2002. www.robwit.net/bluecompany2002/. Accessed 14 Nov. 2017.

——. *The Fall of the Site of Marsha*. *Electronic Literature Collection, Volume 1*, edited by N. K. Hayles, Nick Montfort, Scott Rettberg, and Stephanie Strickland, Electronic Literature Organization, 2006. collection. eliterature.org/1/works/wittig__the_fall_of_the_site_of_marsha.html. Accessed 18 Dec. 2016.

INDEX

Printed in the United States
by Baker & Taylor Publisher Services

Printed in the United States
by Baker & Taylor Publisher Services